CRIMEA

By the same author

We'll Support You Ever More: The Impertinent Saga of Scottish
Fitba (ed., with Ian Archer)
Jock Tamson's Bairns: Essays on a Scots Childhood (ed.)
Precipitous City: The Story of Literary Edinburgh
A Diary of Edinburgh (with Richard Demarco)
Edinburgh
Death Before Dishonour: The True Story of Fighting Mac
The Macmillan Companion to Scottish Literature
James and Jim: The Biography of James Kennaway
The Kitchener Enigma
The Best Years of Their Lives: The National Service Experience,
1945–1963
War Report: The War Correspondent's View of Battle from the
Crimea to the Falklands
The Last Days of the Raj
A Dictionary of Military Quotations
Anatomy of a Regiment: Ceremony and Soldiering in the Welsh
Guards
In Flanders Fields: Scottish Poetry and Prose of the First World
War (ed.)
Glubb Pasha: The Life and Times of Sir John Bagot Glubb,
Commander of the Arab Legion
The Mainstream Companion to Scottish Literature
Orde Wingate: Irregular Soldier
Winds of Change: The End of Empire in Africa
Scottish War Stories (ed.)

CRIMEA

THE GREAT CRIMEAN WAR
1854–1856

TREVOR ROYLE

ST. MARTIN'S PRESS
NEW YORK

CRIMEA

ISBN 0-312-23079-6

Library of Congress Cataloging-in-Publication Data
is available from the Library of Congress.

First published in Great Britain
by Little, Brown and Company.

First St. Martin's edition: April 2000.

10 9 8 7 6 5 4 3 2 1

Contents

Note on Spelling

Since the time of the Crimean War there have been changes in the spelling of Russian names and place names. Where these have been used in extracts from contemporary papers the mid–nineteenth usage has been kept, otherwise a modern spelling has been preferred. This refers in particular to Sevastopol (Sebastopol), Balaklava (Balaclava), Kronstadt (Cronstadt), Malakov (Malakoff), Orlov (Orloff), Gorchakov (Gorchakoff) and Kornilov (Korniloff).

Preface

The Crimean War is either one of history's bad jokes or one of the compulsive subjects of historical writing. Of the two extremes I prefer Correlli Barnett's description to that penned by Philip Guedalla in his study of the great French marshals: the Crimean War does provide grounds for obsession. It encompassed maladministration on a grand scale and human suffering, if not without parallel then at least minutely recorded by the watching war correspondents. Disaster marched hand in hand with heroism, the people of Britain and France stood appalled by the suffering of the men fighting in their name and, for the first time, showed that they cared. In fact it would be easy to write the story of the conflict as if it were simply a catalogue of blunders redeemed by basic human courage and a refusal to surrender to overwhelming odds.

There was, of course, much more to the war than that. The diplomatic initiatives which preceded it and ended it were confused and subject to unnecessary compromise; and like other wars it introduced technical changes which affected the future course of warfare. For all of the participants the war destroyed the long peace of 1815 and set in train the succession of European wars and power-struggles which dominated the second half of the nineteenth century. Also, by failing to solve the Eastern Question, in particular the assertion of Balkan nationalism, the war paved the way for the greater conflagration of 1914 which shaped the course of twentieth-century history. On that score alone the Crimean War is worth revisiting.

In recent years historians have argued that the conflict should be known more correctly as the war against Russia because it included naval campaigns in the Baltic and the Pacific. Although there is much to commend the idea, it is too late in the day to change such a well

known title. In popular usage it is the Crimean War and it would
only have become a global conflict if the United States had entered
the war. As I hope I have shown, there is sufficient contemporary
evidence to prove that this was not an impossibility.

Because the war has been discussed and documented so fully
it would be invidious of me not to acknowledge the labours of
previous historians. Of particular benefit to me has been the work
of the following writers whose books are listed in the bibliography:
Winfried Baumgart, C.L. Bazancourt, J.B. Conacher, J.S. Curtiss,
R.L.V. ffrench-Blake, David M. Goldfrank, Brison D. Gooch, Alain
Goutmann, Basil Greenhill and Ann Giffard, Christopher Hibbert,
A.W. Kinglake, Andrew Lambert, Alan Palmer, Norman Rich, Ann
Pottinger Saab, Paul Schroeder, Albert Seaton, John Sweetman, A.V.
Tarle, Harold Temperley and Cecil Woodham-Smith.

For help with locating Russian documents I am grateful to the
valuable suggestions made by Hugh Vinter. In Washington my good
friend Jamie Dettmer provided excellent strategic support and I would
like to thank Jennie Inman for all her sterling work in translating
French documents and dealing with uncertain transcriptions. The
staffs of the National Army Museum, the National Library of Scotland
and the Public Record Office at Kew provided their usual professional
assistance and advice and I am also grateful for similar help from the
National Archives in Washington.

Friends and relations provided me with useful information about
family archives relating to the campaign in the Crimea or made
extensive loans of personal papers or letter books. In particular I wish
to thank General Sir Michael Gow (whose regiment, the Scots Guards,
served as the Scots Fusilier Guards in the Crimea), Major-General
Jonathan Hall (whose regiment, the Royal Scots Dragoon Guards
served as the Royal Scots Greys in the Crimea), my mother-in-law
Angela Rathbone, and Gabriel and Lois Ronay.

Part of the book was written while I was a visiting fellow at the
Institute for Advanced Studies in the Humanities at the University of
Edinburgh. No writer could wish for a more stimulating or hospitable
environment and I am grateful to the institute's director, Professor
Peter Jones, for his ready support and good cheer. I also want to
thank his assistants Anthea Taylor and Charis Stewart for making my
stay such an enjoyable experience.

Once completed, the manuscript was read by Alan Palmer, the
doyen of historians of the period, who offered many useful suggestions

and some much needed corrections. I am grateful to him for his help and encouragement although it goes without saying that I alone am responsible for the published text. On that score, too, I could not have hoped for a wiser editor than the admirable John Bright-Holmes, without whose ministrations this would be a lesser book.

Trevor Royle
Autumn 1999

Prologue

1851

It was such a time of pleasure, of pride, of satisfaction & of deep thankfulness, it is the triumph of peace & goodwill towards all, – of art, of commerce, – of my beloved Husband – & of triumph for my country.

Queen Victoria, Journal, *18 July 1851*

The structure was the wonder of its age, a great cathedral of iron and glass which dominated the open ground on the south side of Hyde Park between Queen's Drive and Rotten Row. Seen from afar its glittering glass panels reflected the high summer sun while the right angles of its light-blue wrought-iron framework provided a sense of solidity, even permanence. Puffs of smoke from the discreet chimneys of its boiler-room hinted at its industrial purpose but the overall impression provided by the shimmering panes was one of pride and reverence. London had never seen anything like it before and not even the Gothic extravaganza of the Palace of Westminster, nearing completion on the Thames, could rival this strange confection.

Punch hailed it as the Crystal Palace; officially it was known as the 'Great Exhibition of the Works of Industry of all Nations', but to the people of Britain in the summer of 1851 it was quite simply a living expression of their country's ever-growing majesty. Surely no other people could have constructed such a marvel, such a monument to art and technology which seemed to master the elements and make light of industrial science? As Queen Victoria noted when it was opened to the public gaze on 1 May, it was 'the most beautiful and imposing and touching spectacle ever seen'.

The Crystal Palace was indeed a miracle of modern engineering technology. Four thousand tons of iron and 400 tons of glass had been used in its construction; the 293,655 panes alone covered 900,000 square feet. It was almost two thousand feet long – three times the length of St Paul's Cathedral – and 400 hundred feet wide. An army of over two thousand workmen had been enlisted to build it and a huge vaulted wooden roof had been thrown over the central crossing to save three ancient elms from the woodman's axe. Best of all, for a people who were becoming increasingly conscious of the benefits of free trade, the entire structure had been built for £80,000, fifty per cent less than an earlier design for a mundane brick-built edifice. Not only had the gentlemen of the Exhibition Committee been responsible for creating a strange masterpiece but they had done so through careful husbandry of their financial resources. What better advertisement could there be for the free division of labour and absence of government interference which underpinned Victorian economic theory?

That it should have sprung into being owed everything to the brilliance of a former greenhouse architect, Joseph Paxton, and the foresight and enthusiasm of Queen Victoria's consort, Prince Albert of Saxe-Coburg-Gotha. The former made use of his experience of building the extravagant lily house at Chatsworth in Derbyshire, the home of the Duke of Devonshire; the latter fell back on his belief that the world was on the verge of industrial enlightenment, that Britain itself was to be the engine of technological change. Inventiveness and business acumen were thus brought together at the same point in history and the result was an awesome structure which gave British people a sense of pride in their own capabilities. Visiting the exhibition three weeks after it opened, a rising young Conservative politician, Benjamin Disraeli, was moved to declare that it was 'an enchanted pile, which the sagacious taste and prescient philanthropy of an enlightened Prince have raised for the glory and the instruction of two hemispheres.'[1]

Not everyone approved. When the plans were first made public croakers complained that it would either fall down in the high winds or expand and explode in the summer heat. The Treasury refused to be impressed by the supposed benefits and scaremongering members of parliament warned that the proposal was little more than a monument to hubris which would cost the country dear. Furthermore it would attract huge crowds of the wrong sort of the people and the ensuing disorder would lead to the kind of revolution – or even 'famine and pestilence' – which had swept through Europe in 1848 but which thankfully had avoided Britain. Worse, many of those visitors to the capital would be foreigners, come to gawp at a dangerous monstrosity.

Despite those warnings Prince Albert and his committee persevered. The necessary funds were raised – the refreshment contract was sold to Messrs Schweppe for £5,500 – and, though they were not cheap, the ticket sales were phenomenal. Season tickets cost three guineas for gentlemen, two for ladies; the second day's entrance cost £1, the fourth five shillings, and thereafter there were special 'shilling days' which allowed everyone, from Cockney clerks to besmocked farmers up for the day from Kent or Sussex, to ponder their nation's achievements. (Remaining true to the prevailing trading ethos, these 'economy' days had their own frugalities – the exhibition's great Sommerophone organ was silent, much to the dismay of Disraeli who claimed that its pulsating brass tones 'might have a humanising effect on the dogstealers, cabmen and coalheavers' enjoying a day out.) However much they had paid, though, they all helped to swell the crowd of 6,063,986 people who had arrived in London from all over the world to trek through the glittering galleries during those momentous five months of the Great Exhibition of 1851.

What then had they come to see, that huge, variegated army of visiting dignitaries and ordinary folk? It was not just the sense of occasion and the splendour of the Crystal Palace itself: its contents, too, were a source of inspiration and curiosity. Beneath the archways of iron and glass were halls chockful of wonders. Here were steam engines working, pistons and connecting-rods pulsating with energy; in all its grandeur stood the Great Western locomotive *Lord of the Isles*, a monster with eight-foot driving wheels capable of running at over seventy miles per hour; a reconstruction of a medieval court was a reminder of past glories, and curios from distant lands extolled the wonders of Britain's growing world empire. A profusion of sculptures paid homage to the arts, while working mechanical models and hissing gas lamps pointed the way to a scarcely imaginable future.

All this was progress and, better still, most of it was British and therefore satisfyingly solid and dependable. That much had been made clear even before the exhibition opened its doors to the public when squads of soldiers had stamped up and down its wooden floors and fired blank round shot overhead. Nothing faltered. The great building had remained unmoved before the might of an army unbeaten in the field since the great days of Waterloo nearly forty years earlier. The symbolism was not lost on those who watched: the country was fast reaching the apogee of its greatness; arrogance and resolution were respected as virtues and the rest of the world was there to be dominated.

In no other contemporary publication is the brave new world of trade, profit and overweening superiority so clearly caught as in *Dombey and Son* by Charles Dickens. The novelist was a frequent and delighted visitor to the Crystal Palace and even though his novel had been published three years earlier its mood reflects the optimism of the times – at least, as it was experienced in Britain:

> The earth was made for Dombey and Son to trade in, the sun and the moon were made to give them light. Rivers and seas were formed to float their ships; rainbows to give them the promise of fair weather; winds blew for or against their enterprises; stars and planets circled in their orbits, to preserve inviolate a system of which they were centre.

Elsewhere the harmonies were less self-evident. On the other side of the English Channel in the summer of 1851 France had emerged unscathed from one of its periodic bouts of constitutional instability and political fractiousness, but the country was still gripped by a general loss of confidence. Its industrial development lagged years behind Britain's, it was still essentially an agricultural society whose manufacturing workforce consisted mainly of peasants working as artisans in factories and what amounted to its heavy industrial base was concentrated in the Paris basin. By 1850 there were fewer than three thousand miles of railway lines and French bankers had shown themselves to be wary of investing in the railway boom that had shaken the rest of Europe. Even those who did have employment in the new industries were scandalously poor and, compared to their British equivalents, badly treated. As early as 1835 the novelist Honoré de Balzac, was remarking in the introduction to *La Fille aux yeux d'or* that one of the most terrible spectacles of contemporary life in France was the aspect of the Parisian proletariat, a new and down-trodden class: 'men whose distorted, eager faces distil through every pore the thoughts, the desires, the poison that is seething in their brains'. This is very different from the easy self-confidence expressed by his contemporary Charles Dickens.

Not that there was no hope. Following the fall of the monarchy in 1848 and a euphoric, though brief, period of democratic experiment, Prince Louis Napoleon had come to power as president of the new Second Republic. The nephew of Napoleon Bonaparte, he was an inveterate romantic revolutionary who had spent several years in exile following a sequence of misguided attempts to overthrow the royal house of Bourbon. The name alone was enough to give him his position and his prestige but years of imprisonment and orphanage from France had helped to sharpen his political mind and, although he lacked his famous uncle's pride and cynicism, he made it clear at an early stage that he wanted to restore France's fortunes through a policy of modernisation at home and bold statesmanship abroad. In the summer of 1851 French ambitions were stirring again and they were to be centred on the name which had provided them with their own days of greatness and pride: Napoleon.

The bloodless revolution which had swept through France in 1848 had left a legacy of political turmoil. Revolutionary nationalism had also stirred in Austria, Italy and Germany but in France the triumphant republicans had no clear plans about how to restore social order or to bridge the gulf between rich and poor. Radicals demanded a universal suffrage, the middle classes feared that rapid change would erode their position, and conservatives and royalists looked back wistfully to the old certainties of firm rule. By the beginning of 1851 there was a definite feeling abroad that a new *jacquerie*, or revolt of the masses, was imminent, that France was about to be plunged into social disorder and chaos, and that only an absolute ruler, backed by the army, could save the nation.

And so it happened that, while the people of Britain were luxuriating in the feeling that their country was marching towards an even more shining future, France was caught between the fear of socialist revolution and a restoration of the monarchy through the Orleanist Prince de Joinville. Louis Napoleon believed that he could command the public support to seize power, bring back universal suffrage and force the Assembly to accept the will of the people, but would the army support him? Several senior officers had political aspirations of their own and the most powerful of these, the head of the army General Nicholas Changarnier, was fond of comparing Louis Napoleon to Thomas Diafoirus, the mountebank quack doctor in Molière's play,

Le Malade Imaginaire. Clearly Louis Napoleon had to look elsewhere and in April 1851 he found his man in Brigadier-General Leroy de Saint-Arnaud who had learned his soldiering during the French military occupation of Algeria in the 1830s.

Although respected within the army as a dependable professional soldier – outside the army he was scarcely known – Saint-Arnaud was a political animal who was much concerned by what he saw as France's degeneration. To him the radicals in the Assembly were 'instruments of disorder; journalists, poets, Masons, teachers, painters and escaped convicts' and he was prepared to follow any leader who would save France from 'the social republic and Communism'. By the end of the summer this relatively obscure commander was back in France as head of the army and installed near Paris as one of the plotters prepared to back Louis Napoleon's plans for a coup d'état. Soon the cry of '*Vive l'Empereur!*' was heard whenever Louis Napoleon inspected his troops in an army which burned to avenge the humiliation of Waterloo. By November Saint-Arnaud was Minister for War and the Bonapartist tradition ensured Louis Napoleon his praetorian guard.

The pretext for the coup d'état was the Assembly's refusal to allow the revision of the constitution which would give Louis Napoleon a second term in office as President but, backed by the army, he was in a perfect position to seize power. On 2 December the coup took place; the Assembly was dismissed and royalists and republicans arrested. A fortnight later, on 18 December, a plebiscite was held and the people of France voted overwhelmingly to support the new constitution. Within a year Louis Napoleon had been created emperor for ten years as Napoleon III and Saint-Arnaud was installed as France's most powerful military figure. Paradoxically, the revolution of 1848, which had promised universal suffrage and new freedoms, ended with an *appel au peuple* which ushered in the Second Empire and rule by what amounted to military dictatorship.

In Britain the coup was greeted with considerable disquiet. France was still the traditional enemy and a Catholic one at that. *The Times* spoke for many Protestants when its leader of 27 December claimed that 'black flocks of Jesuits and priests of every shade' were swarming over France singing 'their insolent song of triumph' and it published lurid descriptions of the violence which had accompanied the take-over. At an official level Britain's ambassador in Paris, Lord Normanby, condemned Louis Napoleon as did the Tory grandees Lord Aberdeen and Lord Derby. However, there was a surprising measure of support for the new order from the admittedly pro-French foreign secretary, Lord Palmerston, but when he overstepped his mark by congratulating the French ambassador, Count Walewski, he was sacked by the prime minister, Lord John Russell.

The year 1851 ended with relations between the traditional enemies being as bad as they had ever been. The following year began no better. When, in January and in an attempt to improve Franco-British relations, Louis Napoleon invited a number of British politicians to dine with him at the Elysée Palace, *The Times* thundered that it was a disgrace that they had deigned to sit at the same table as 'a perjurer, traitor, butcher and robber'. However, such was the volatility of their relationships that, within a few months, both countries would find it necessary to combine their strategic interests. The reason for this entente was Russia.

Not many people in western Europe were aware of what happened inside the huge Russian empire and what they did know they did not much like. Constitutional or representative government was non-existent and the period between 1848 and 1855 has been described by Isaiah Berlin, the historian and philosopher, as 'the darkest hour in the night of Russian obscurantism in the nineteenth century'. Its autocratic ruler, Tsar Nicholas I, used a highly efficient secret police, the dreaded Third Section, to maintain order, serfdom still survived and industrial development was negligible. Roads, where they existed, were primitive; railways were in their infancy – the only line of any importance, between Moscow and St Petersburg, did not open until 1851 – and steam navigation depended on the increasingly obsolete paddle-wheel. It was the only country of any note unable to send its exhibits for display at Britain's Great Exhibition. In short, Russia was a country with a primitive economic and financial system yet it was still feared on account of its imperial ambitions and its military potential, both of which lay at the heart of tsarist power.

Small wonder that Russia was viewed with such distaste by most forward-looking people in the west. Here was an obscurantist, slave-owning autocracy which ruled by dint of secret policemen and Cossack troopers, the oppressor of the Poles and the enemy of all the hopes engendered by the year of revolutions. Nicholas himself lived up to the caricature by claiming to be a humble sentry, 'Europe's gendarme', the last bulwark against new-fangled liberal ideas. He told the world that his enemies were constitutionalism, nationalism and socialism and to protect holy Russia he would extirpate them

wherever they were found. In pursuit of that aim he had sent
Russian forces into Hungary in the summer of 1849 to put down
the fledgling republic founded by Lajos Kossuth and to restore the
country to Austrian rule. Moreover, he made no secret of his desire
to impose his will – and Russian interests – on the rest of Europe.
With the absolute monarchies of Austria and Prussia he had signed
understandings to guard against the threat of further revolution and to
forestall the creation of a united Germany; but by 1851 what interested
him most was the crumbling Ottoman Empire. More than anything
else, his concern to protect Russian interests in the Balkans, the Black
Sea and Constantinople put him on a collision course with Britain and
France – both of whom had strategic concerns in the same region.

   Nicholas was not worried by the prospect for the simple reason
that he believed the threat of war would prevent its outbreak. The
first problem with Nicholas was that he considered himself to be
as much a soldier as an emperor and that diplomacy was simply a
question of combining forcefulness with personal charm. The second
difficulty was that he did not recognise the dangers in his sense of
infallibility. At home, in gloomy backward Russia, the manifestations
of his supposed omnipotence could be alarming but at least they
were confined to domestic matters. His subjects he regarded as
unruly recruits and he was not above stopping them in the street
to correct some infringement of Russia's myriad laws. Opponents
were declared insane, courtiers lived in constant fear of his capricious
moods and all Guards officers were forced to grow moustaches – and
if they happened to be blond the whiskers had to be dyed black. The
result was chaos. Civil servants were only prepared to work within
the country's Byzantine code of rules and even the most innocent
application could take weeks to process. As a result bribery was
an everyday fact of life and, coupled with the country's industrial
backwardness, Russia was in a state of advanced social and economic
paralysis. 'Alone of all the peoples in the world we have not given
anything to the world, and we have not learned anything from the
world,' wrote the philosopher Peter Chaadev in 1836. 'We have not
added a single idea to the pool of human ideas.'[2]

   None of this criticism prevented Tsar Nicholas from pursuing a
rigorous foreign policy (for his pains Chaadev was declared insane)
and fawning courtiers were more than happy to ingratiate themselves by encouraging wilder expansionist dreams. As the Grand
Duke of Muscovy the tsar still laid claim to Constantinople and

the strategically important Straits which provided maritime access to the Mediterranean. Throughout his reign Nicholas claimed that he 'did not want an inch of Turkish soil' but, paradoxically, his denials only fuelled British and French fears that he did in fact have territorial claims on Constantinople and its empire. Together with hegemony over the Balkans this would give him the window into Europe which his predecessors had long coveted. And that was not all: as his sycophants told him, Russia could then expand to embrace the whole world:

> Seven inland seas and seven mighty rivers
> From the Nile to the Neva
> From Elba to China
> From the Volga to the Euphrates
> From the Ganges to the Danube
> Such is our Empire to be.

As a romantic poet and a courtier Fyodor Tyutchev had a vested interest in penning those lines, but even though his fellow diplomats might have distanced themselves from the hyperbole of his poem 'Russian Geography', there was an accepted belief at court that Russia's destiny lay in expanding its empire. How this was to be accomplished was less easy to comprehend. Like most other things in Russia the armed forces were all veneer and little substance. In spite of, or perhaps because of, Nicholas's fascination with things military the army was strong on ceremonial and weak on battle tactics. There were few staff officers, the chain of command was rudimentary and weapons and field training were old-fashioned; in both instances there had been little progress since the Napoleonic Wars. Even the Black Sea fleet was a motley collection of wooden-hulled warships powered mainly by sail. The soldiers and sailors were brave and physically tough but these qualities were no substitute for ability and preparedness.

True, there had been successful campaigns against the Persians in 1826 and against the Turks in the Balkans two years later, but more recently the might of the Russian army had been humbled by the rebellious mountain peoples of Georgia led by the notorious warlord, Shamyl. While attending a Royal review of Russia's forces in 1851, the tsar's son-in-law Prince Alexander of Hesse could not help but compare the elegance and apparent power of the cavalry with the army's ineffectual efforts against the poorly equipped rebels in the mountains around Tiflis. The young man knew what he was talking about: he had served as a staff officer in that same Caucasian campaign and personally witnessed the feebleness of the Russian army.

Unlike its European neighbours Turkey had not been affected by the year of revolutions but in 1851 it was not a country in the rudest of health. Once upon a time its Ottoman Empire had been all-powerful, controlling lands in the Balkans, Hungary, the Caucasus and the Middle East: by the beginning of the nineteenth century it was in recession and its outer limits had either gained independence or had come under the control of neighbouring predatory powers. Egypt and Greece enjoyed autonomy, Hungary had been freed by Austria, and Russia had moved into the territories around the Black Sea and the Danube delta. The recession of the Ottoman Empire was also accompanied by an assertion of various Balkan nationalisms, especially amongst the Slav peoples who regarded Russia as their liberator and natural ally, and this led to continuing friction between the governments in Constantinople and St Petersburg. Known collectively as the Eastern Question, this strategic realignment was destined to tease the great European powers right up to the outbreak of the First World War in 1914. It was also to provide the main reason why Britain, France, Russia and Turkey should suddenly find themselves embroiled in a war within three years of the Great Exhibition closing its doors to the public.

In Nicholas's famous phrase Turkey was a 'sick man', a country in decline whose demise would have repercussions throughout Europe. What was needed, he argued, was a plan to prop up the Sultan's empire and then to divide its legacy after death. To this end he attempted to draw Britain into his confidence. In the late spring of 1844 he arrived incognito in London to draw up a memorandum of understanding on the dissolution of the Ottoman Empire, and nine years later he rarely missed an opportunity of bombarding the British minister in St Petersburg, Sir George Hamilton Seymour, with his ideas for a division of the spoils. Not unnaturally perhaps, the patient – the Sultan Abd-el-Mejid – was not consulted but this did not mean that he was left to his own devices. In addition to Russia's traditional interest in Turkish affairs – which often amounted to coercion – both Britain and France maintained powerful diplomatic missions at Constantinople and both were concerned to prevent Russian intimidation diminishing their own strategic interests. Turkey might be a sick man but Britain and France were not prepared to leave him on the sickbed, a prey to Russian avarice.

Sadly, Turkey's sickness was not hypochondria. Centuries of bureaucratic incompetence had weakened the once all-powerful Ottoman Empire and in the Balkans its authority was crumbling. Nationalist agitation amongst non-Muslims encouraged demands for independence from Constantinople rule and these were heard with considerable sympathy in St Petersburg. In his increasingly eccentric old age Nicholas came to believe that it was his duty to act as their protector and saviour and he was prepared to seize Constantinople in pursuit of those aims. Then, in concert with the other great Christian powers, Russia should take the lead in liberating the Christians languishing under Ottoman rule in nations as diverse as the Danubian principalities of Moldavia and Wallachia; Serbia, Bulgaria and Greece. Each should be declared independent and the Turks sent packing, bag and baggage, out of Europe.

As 1851 drew to a close London still basked in the memory of the Great Exhibition and the splendour of the Crystal Palace. In Paris parliamentary democracy had been suspended and Napoleon was installed as a virtual dictator who dreamed of restoring *la Gloire*. In Tsarskoe Seloe, his palace outside St Petersburg, Nicholas fretted about the sick man on his deathbed in Constantinople and continued to tell himself that he was the rightful guardian of Turkey's ten million orthodox Christians. To the British government Nicholas's ideas were alarming but they were merely plans for an uncertain future. As such they were little more than diplomatic guesswork and Britain had kept a cool distance from the proposals made by the tsar in 1844. True, Britain's traditional distrust of France meant that relations between London and Paris would never be entirely smooth. And equally true, Russia was regarded with suspicion, not just because it was a backward despotism but because the tsar's strategic interests seemed to threaten India. As for Turkey its decaying structures had to be propped up, not because Britain approved of them in any way but because they were preferable to seeing Russia encamped in southern central Europe.

At that stage war was mentioned by no one; manoeuvre, intrigue and negotiation underpinned the language of diplomacy in the despatches between the capitals. Although none of the participants could have foreseen it at the time, 1851 was destined to be the last lull before the great storm.

PART I

1

A Churchwardens' Quarrel

We should deeply regret any dispute that might lead to conflict between two of the great Powers of Europe; but when we reflect that the quarrel is for exclusive privileges in a spot near which the heavenly host proclaimed peace on earth and good-will towards men — when we see rival churches contending for mastery in the very place where Christ died for mankind — the thought of such a spectacle is melancholy indeed!

Lord Malmesbury, Britain's Foreign Secretary, 1852

The spark to the tinderbox was the key to the main door of the Church of the Nativity in Bethlehem. By tradition, history, and a common usage which had been built up over the centuries, the great key was in the possession of the monks of the eastern, or Greek Orthodox, branch of the Christian church; they were the guardians of the grotto in which lay the sacred manger where Christ himself was thought to have been born. That state of affairs was contested with equal fervour by their great rivals, the monks of the Roman Catholic, or Latin, church who had been palmed off with the keys to the lesser inner doors to the narthex (the vestibule between the porch and the nave). There was also the question of whether or not a silver star adorned with the arms of France should be permitted to stand in the Sanctuary of the Nativity, but in the spring of 1852 the rivals' paramount thoughts were concentrated on the possession of the great key to the church's main west door.

'Is it true,' asked the antiquarian Alexander William Kinglake, who wrote the first history of the Crimean war, 'that for this cause armies were gathering, and that for the sake of the key and

the silver star, the peace of the nations was brought into danger?'[1]

The short answer was, yes. There were of course other more
pressing strategic reasons caused mainly by the impending demise
of the Ottoman Empire, and the differing attitudes of the main
European powers towards the problem; but they might have been
settled diplomatically had it not been for the confrontation between
France and Russia over the guardianship of Palestine's Holy Places.

It was an argument which had its origins in the history of the early
Christian church. For centuries the sacred places of the Holy Land had
been objects of intense Christian devotion. Nazareth, Bethlehem and
Jerusalem were magnets for pilgrims from all over Europe anxious to
seek pardon for sins or simply to add a further spiritual dimension to
their lives. To them these names were not just places of veneration
but living reminders of an age when Jesus Christ walked amongst
mankind. To visit Jerusalem was to see the bible come alive. In the
Old City stood the Holy Sepulchre, the Via Dolorosa and the house
of Caiaphas where Jesus was brought after his arrest. Outside the walls
could be found the path to Bethany over the Mount of Olives where
the crowd strewed olive branches and shouted 'Hosanna!' There were
also equally sonorous memorials to the faiths of Judaism and Islam,
reminders that Jerusalem and Palestine are home to several religions.
Indeed, bloody wars had been fought by the Christian powers to
protect their holy places from the influence of Islam and to restore
them to Christian rule.

During the period of the crusades great battles were waged between
Christians and 'infidels' and by the end of the eleventh century the
Holy Land had become a kind of European Christian province.
Unfortunately the piety and grace which fuelled those clashes could
not keep the Christians from quarrelling amongst themselves. Ever
since the long decline of the Roman empire in the fourth and fifth
centuries the church had split into two rival communions. The
Emperor Constantine's decision to move the seat of his power to
Byzantium in AD330 had created two patriarchs, one in the east
and the other in Rome in the west. They soon became rivals, but
in 1054 the split became much wider when the Bishop of Rome
excommunicated his counterpart in the east, thereby creating an
eastern or Greek communion under the Patriarch of Constantinople
and a western or Latin church which looked to the leadership of
the Pope.

It was not just a spiritual divide: following the loss of Jerusalem in 1204 the crusaders turned their wrath on the eastern church and sacked Constantinople. Within a hundred years the Holy Land had been lost and the enmity between the two churches increased. In 1453 the schism was made complete when Byzantium, or Constantinople, fell to the Islamic Turks to give their Ottoman Empire a gateway to Europe. However, to begin with, the new regime tolerated the Eastern Church which not only prospered but grew in faith and set about converting the inhabitants of the great Russian land mass to the north.

Soon Russia was to emerge as the strongest of the Orthodox communions; successive tsars considered themselves to be the rightful protectors of the holy places of Palestine and they took a dim view of the Latins' pretensions which had the backing of France. (In 1520 Francis I had accepted that responsibility following his meeting with King Henry VIII at the Field of the Cloth of Gold.) Not only had Russian money maintained the shrines for many centuries while they were under the control of the Ottoman Empire but countless thousands of Russians had been Palestine's most devout pilgrims. Kinglake wrote:

> When the Emperor of Russia sought to gain or to keep for his Church the holy shrines of Palestine, he spoke on behalf of fifty millions of brave, pious, devoted subjects, of whom thousands for the sake of the cause would joyfully risk their lives. From the serf in his hut, even up to the great Tsar himself, the faith professed was the faith really glowing in his heart, and violently swaying the will.[2]

Kinglake had a good understanding of the problem. He had visited the Holy Land in 1834 and as a result had written *Eothen*, a lively and disinterested account of his travels and the people he met. To him the Russians were intensely pious pilgrims who had made the long and dangerous journey from their homelands over the Caucasus mountains and on through the wastes of Kurdistan and Syria into Palestine. This holy enterprise was the culmination of a life well spent – whatever the cost in material terms, for many did not return and others used up their life savings simply to tell their neighbours that they had worshipped at the spot were Christ was born or at the stone on which his crucified body was washed and anointed in preparation for burial in the tomb.

On the other hand, and in stark contrast, the standard French pilgrim seemed to be a johnny-come-lately, 'a mere [French] tourist, with a journal and a theory, and a plan of writing a book'. During the years of the Bourbons the kings of France had taken a great interest in the Holy Land and had been pleased to count themselves as the protectors of the Latin monks. The last intervention had come in 1740 when King Louis XV had obtained from the Sultan of Turkey an agreement whose capitulations confirmed the rights of the Latin church in Palestine. One hundred years later, though, the effects of the French Revolution and the early nineteenth-century Enlightenment had encouraged a more secular attitude to religious affairs and French (and other western European) visitors to the holy places did not always behave with the decorum expected of evangelists. Amongst their number was Richard Curzon, a British member of Parliament and notorious plunderer of Byzantine religious remains, who had witnessed the annual Good Friday celebration in the Church of the Holy Sepulchre in 1834 when the Christian miracle of light from heaven was re-enacted:

> The behaviour of the pilgrims was riotous in the extreme; the crowd was so great that many persons actually crawled over the heads of others, and some made pyramids of men by standing on each other's shoulders, as I have seen them do at Astley's . . . At one time, before the church was so full, they made a racecourse round the sepulchre; and some, almost in a state of nudity, danced about with frantic gestures, yelling and screaming as if they were possessed.
>
> Altogether it was a scene of disorder and profanation, which it is impossible to describe.[3]

In this case, though, the pilgrims' 'screams and tumult' quickly developed into a riot in which several hundred worshippers died or were killed by panicking Turkish soldiers. While the catastrophe was 'a fearful visitation' at a time when Christ's resurrection was being celebrated, Curzon also noted that the so-called miracle was an 'evident absurdity' perpetrated by the monks who 'for the purposes of worldly gain, had deluded their ignorant followers with the performance of a trick in relighting the candles, which had been extinguished on Good Friday, with fire which they affirmed had been sent down from heaven in answer to their prayers'.

In addition to the religious impetuosity witnessed by Curzon, the monks themselves often had skirmishes, fighting not just with fists but also with candlesticks and other solemn artefacts. If the wrangling had been left to the occasional brawl all might have been well but unfortunately both the tsar and the new emperor of France took a keen interest in the dispute and were determined to solve it to the satisfaction of their co-religionists. The eastern and the western churches might have been separated by a thousand miles but in 1852 they found their point of conflict within the confined space of the Church of the Nativity in Bethlehem.

Nicholas I had both temporal and spiritual reasons for wanting to extend his protection of the eastern church within the Ottoman Empire. Napoleon III's were rather different. Having dismissed the French parliament he needed all the support he could get, most especially from the Roman Catholics, before he could declare himself emperor. It suited him therefore to have France play a greater role in Palestine and 'to put an end to these deplorable and too-frequent quarrels about the possession of the Holy Places'. To that end the Marquis de Lavalette, his ambassador to the Porte – or the Sublime Porte, the court or government of the Ottoman Empire – insisted that the Turks honour the agreement made in 1740 which confirmed that France had 'sovereign authority' in the Holy Land. Otherwise, hinted de Lavalette, force might have to be used.

On 9 February 1852 the Porte agreed the validity of the Latin claims but no sooner had the concession been made than the Turks were forced to bow once more, this time to Russian counter-claims. Basing his argument on an agreement, or firman, of 1757 which restored Greek rights in Palestine and on the Treaty of Kutchuk-Kainarji (1774) which gave Russia protection of the Christian religion within the Ottoman Empire, Nicholas's ambassador succeeded in getting a new firman ratifying the privileges of the Greek Church. This revoked the agreement made to the French who responded by backing up their demands with a show of force.

Later that summer, much to Nicholas's fury and to Britain's irritation, Napoleon III ordered the 90-gun steam-powered battleship *Charlemagne* to sail through the Dardanelles. This was a clear violation of the London Convention of 1841 which kept the Straits closed to naval vessels, but it also provided a telling demonstration of French sea power. It was nothing less than gunboat diplomacy and it seemed to work. Impressed by the speed and strength of the French warship, and persuaded by French diplomacy and money, Sultan Abd-el-Medjid listened ever more intently to the French demands. At the beginning of December he gave orders that the keys to the Church of the Nativity were to be surrendered to the Latins and that the French-backed church was to have supreme authority over the Holy Places. On 22 December a new silver star was brought from Jaffa and as Kinglake wrote, in great state 'the keys of the great door of the church, together with the keys of the sacred manger, were handed over to the Latins'.

Napoleon III had scored a considerable diplomatic victory. His subjects were much gratified, but in so doing he had also prepared the ground for a much greater and more dangerous confrontation. Given the strength of Russian religious convictions Tsar Nicholas was unwilling to accept the Sultan's decision – which he regarded as an affront not just to him but to the millions of Orthodox Christians under his protection – and he was determined to have it reversed, if need be by using force himself.

Russia and Turkey were no strangers to discord: there had been numerous armed confrontations between the two countries since they first clashed over possession of Astrakhan in 1569. Under the rule of Peter the Great there had been a long-running war over the steppe lands of the Ukraine and access to the Black Sea, and the early years of the nineteenth century had seen Russia attempting to take advantage of Ottoman decline by expanding her own imperial holdings. In 1828 Russia supported the Greeks in their war of independence and used it as a pretext for further military operations in the Balkans and the Caucasus. Although the Turkish army was no pushover, major defeats at Akhalzoc and Kulrucha forced them to sue for peace and, at the resultant Treaty of Adrianople in 1829, Russia was granted Ottoman territory in the Caucasus and at the mouth of the Danube in Bessarabia.

Having used the mailed fist in the past, Russia could see no reason for not using it again in 1853. The Russian 4th and 5th Army Corps were mobilised on the border with the Danubian principalities of Moldavia and Wallachia and the veteran Russian chancellor and head of the foreign ministry, Count Nesselrode, issued a warning that his country could not 'swallow the insult which she has received from the Porte . . . *vis pacem, para bellum!*' ('If you wish for peace, prepare for war.')[4] At the same time he laid plans to outwit France on the diplomatic front, first by weakening her influence at the Porte and, second, by courting the support of Britain, at that time Turkey's principal European ally.

With his lengthy experience of European diplomacy – he had served in the Paris embassy before 1812 and had been first secretary of state at the foreign ministry since 1816 and chancellor since 1845 – Nesselrode was well aware of the influence exerted by the French ambassador at the Porte, the Marquis de Lavalette, whom he suspected of bribing the Sultan's Grand Vizier, Mehemet Ali, and the Turkish foreign minister, Fuad Effendi (later Pasha). This supposition was not ill-founded. France enjoyed healthy trading links with the Ottoman Empire and had, therefore, a vested interest in retaining their diplomatic primacy at the Porte; but as Nesselrode told Seymour, the British ambassador at St Petersburg, this did not mean that Russia could meekly accept the situation. As Seymour reported, quoting Nesselrode verbatim:

> [The row over the Holy Places] had assumed a new character – that the acts of injustice towards the Greek church which it had been desired to prevent had been perpetrated and consequently that now the object must be to find a remedy for these wrongs. That the success of French negotiations at Constantinople was to be ascribed solely to intrigue and violence – violence which had been supposed to be the *ultima ratio* of kings, being, it had been seen, the means which the present Ruler of France was in the habit of employing in the first instance.[5]

Under those circumstances Nesselrode also warned that Nicholas would use whatever means at his disposal to reverse the decision, and that the armies had been mobilised to reinforce Russian diplomacy. Even at that early stage the Russian chancellor believed that, unless France backed down, war was inevitable. In a remarkably prescient letter written to Brunnov, his ambassador in London, on 2 January 1853, he forecast that France was forcing a confrontation and that in the conflict Russia would 'face the whole world alone and without allies, because Prussia will be of no account and indifferent to the question, and Austria will be more or less neutral, if not favourable to the Porte'. Moreover, Britain would side with France to exert its superior naval strength, 'the theatre being distant, other than soldiers to be employed as a landing force, it will require mainly ships to open to us the Straits of Constantinople [the passage from the Black Sea to the Mediterranean through the Bosplate and the Dardanelles], and the

united naval forces of Turkey, England and France will make quick
work of the Russian fleet.'[6]

Some of these fears Nesselrode attempted to pass on to Seymour
but the British ambassador decided not to take the warnings at face
value. As he explained in a despatch on 9 January, 'His Majesty's
violence of language does not always portend violence in action'.[7]

Born in 1797, the eldest son of the Earl of Hertford, Seymour
had been destined for a career in the Royal Navy but his precocious
intelligence took him first to Eton and then to Merton College,
Oxford. Following a short period at court as a gentleman usher he
entered the Foreign Office and was posted to The Hague in 1817.
His career also included postings to Berlin, Constantinople and Lisbon.
Before taking up the post of ambassador in St Petersburg in April the
crowning achievement of his career had been the negotiation of the
treaty which secured Belgium's independence in 1839 but it was in
the Russian capital that he was to achieve a lasting place in history.

At the time St Petersburg had attracted some of Europe's most
capable diplomatists. France was represented by General de Castelbajac, a cautious aristocrat who had Napoleon III's ear and who was
generally liked by his colleagues. (Seymour called him 'a kind-hearted
and conciliatory man, but troubled occasionally with that susceptibility
which not uncommonly renders a Frenchman more intent upon
trifles than upon matters of serious import'.) Prussia also had a
heavyweight ambassador in General de Roekow who enjoyed a
particularly close relationship with the tsar; indeed, Seymour thought
he was 'much more of a Russian Cabinet minister than a diplomat'.
About the Austrian ambassador, though, Seymour was less kind: Baron
Lebzeltern he reported to be 'a thoroughly incompetent Levant[ine],
quite unsuited to be at the head of a great Mission'.[8]

And at the centre of the diplomatic community stood the elfin
figure of Karl Robert Nesselrode, the man who had directed Russia's
foreign policy since the end of the wars against Napoleon. Born in
1796 in Lisbon, where his father acted as Russian ambassador, he was
one of the many Germans in Russian service, a fact which made
him an enemy of the rival Slav faction, and like Seymour he had
been destined for a career in the navy. However, an inability to
overcome sea-sickness had ruined his chances and he turned instead
to a diplomatic career. His father thought it a bad choice – 'He
does not have the devil in him, and without the devil a diplomat
can go nowhere' – but he quickly proved himself to be a cool and

reliable minister. On the Eastern Question he favoured a policy of rapprochement with Britain in order to curb French influence at the Porte but his main concern had always been European stability. With Metternich, he had been one of the architects of the Holy Alliance which came into being in 1816 to bind together the absolute monarchies of Russia, Austria and Prussia.

However, it was not with Austria and Prussia that Nicholas was concerned during the quarrel over the Holy Places. Both countries were in stalemate over the question of German unification and Nicholas and Nesselrode had played a major role in keeping them apart in 1850 when war had seemed inevitable. In any case, with regard to the Holy Alliance, Nicholas considered himself to be the senior partner. That left Britain and France. Unfortunately Nicholas could make little sense of either country, despite the fact that he had excellent ambassadors in Paris and London in Kisselev and Brunnov. France he disliked because it seemed to him to be a centre of revolutionary thought, and he had no time for Napoleon III whom he considered an impostor. Alone among Europe's monarchs he refused to address him as '*mon frère*' ('my brother'), or to use the numeral III, and could not understand why Queen Victoria had agreed to either form of address. 'Because it is a precedent,' explained Seymour. To which the tsar replied 'that he thought it was unfortunate that the precedent should have been followed'.[9]

The matter of Nicholas's salutation was to put a strain on relations between St Petersburg and Paris in 1852 and 1853. Even Nesselrode refused to use any other form of address than 'the Ruler of France' when discussing Napoleon III with Seymour and General de Roekow, the Prussian ambassador, and Nicholas never relented on the question. Napoleon III could be '*mon cher ami*' or nothing.

Britain was a different matter. Nicholas admired Queen Victoria and was convinced that his personal charm had created an 'understanding' during his visit in 1844. To a certain extent this was true. Victoria called him 'the mighty potentate' but her tendency to stand in awe of powerful men was not enough to cement relations. Nicholas had to deal with politicians and here, despite Nesselrode's promptings, he was at a loss. Being an autocrat he could not understand that Britain's politicians were answerable to parliament and were unable to deal with him unilaterally. However, that failing did not prevent him from courting their interest.

Of George Hamilton Gordon, the 4th Earl of Aberdeen, he

had particularly high hopes. Then aged sixty-eight, he had just, in 1852, come to power as prime minister of a Peelite-Whig coalition government with a formidable Cabinet 'of all the talents' including Lord John Russell as foreign secretary and Lord Palmerston as home secretary. However, Nicholas was not interested in the minutiae of British domestic politics: what concerned him most was the direction of Aberdeen's foreign policy. The two men had met during the tsar's visit to London in 1844 when Nicholas had warned about the strategic implications of Turkey's impending demise. Although the then prime minister Sir Robert Peel and his foreign secretary Aberdeen remained cautious they signed a memorandum, 'the spirit and scope of which was to support Russia in her legitimate protectorship of the Greek religion and the Holy Shrines, and to do so without consulting France.'

Almost ten years later Nicholas hoped that the same pro-Russian and anti-French mood would inform British foreign policy and he placed considerable faith in Aberdeen's commitment to the 1844 memorandum. He had good reason to hope that it would for Aberdeen was suspicious of France and shortly before becoming prime minister had confided to Brunnov, the Russian ambassador, that he feared a French invasion as part of Napoleon III's ambitions to retrieve his country's influence in Europe. Moreover, Aberdeen had made little secret of his dislike of Ottoman rule and was not keen to support them against Russia when the lives of Christians were at stake. 'I despise the Turks,' he told friends, 'for I consider their government the most evil and most oppressive in all the world.'[10]

From Brunnov Nicholas also heard that Aberdeen, as a former ambassador and foreign secretary, would direct foreign policy: Lord John Russell resigned after eight weeks and was succeeded in February 1853 by the affable, though frequently indecisive Lord Clarendon. Given the British prime minister's fears about French motives and his suspicions about Ottoman rule Nicholas clearly believed that an opportunity existed to drive a wedge between London and Paris and to isolate France.

With that in mind he set about winning Seymour's ear. Shortly after arriving in St Petersburg the new British ambassador had complained that it was well-nigh impossible to gain an audience with the tsar whereas 'the Prussian Envoy sees the Emperor as often in the course of each day as the English Minister does in the course of the year.'[11] All that was to change in the second week of January 1853. The occasion was a concert given in the Mikhailovsky Palace to celebrate the forty-sixth birthday of the Grand Duchess Elena Pavlona, the tsar's sister-in-law, and amongst the guests were Seymour and his wife. In a 'secret and confidential' despatch written on 11 January Seymour reported to Russell that 'the Emperor came up to me in the most gracious manner' to congratulate Aberdeen on his appointment and that he 'trusted the Ministry would be of long duration'. Then he turned to his first theme:

> You know my feelings, the Emperor said, with regard to England . . . it was intended that the two countries should be upon terms of close amity, and I feel sure that this will continue to be the case. You have now been a certain time here and, as you have seen, there have been very few points upon which we have disagreed, our interests in fact are upon almost all questions the same.[12]

Choosing his words carefully Seymour replied that that was indeed the case, the only exception being the question of Napoleon III's nomenclature. The emperor replied that the 'No. III . . . would involve a long explanation': for the time being he was more concerned to repeat 'that it is very essential that the two Governments, that is, *that the English Government and I, and I and the English Government* should be upon the best terms and the necessity was never greater than at present'. In particular Turkey required considerable discussion and he hoped that Seymour would call upon him soon. At that he shook Seymour's hand to conclude the interview but, sensing that the conversation was unfinished, the British ambassador asked the tsar to 'add a few words which may tend to calm the anxiety with regard to the affairs of Turkey which passing events are so calculated to excite on the part of Her Majesty's Government.'

Nicholas smiled and nodded but it was obvious to Seymour that he was not prepared to comment on the reasons for the military deployments in the south. Instead, speaking in French which was the language of the Court and of diplomacy, he made his famous comment that 'the Affairs of Turkey are in a very disorganised condition, the Country itself seems to be falling to pieces (*menace ruine*), the fall will be a great misfortune and it is very important that England and Russia should come to a perfectly good understanding upon these affairs, and that neither should take any decisive step of which the other is not apprised.'

'*Tenez*,' the Emperor said as if proceeding with his remark. '*Tenez — nous avons sur les bras un homme malade — un homme gravement malade — ce sera, je vous le dis franchement, un grand malheur si un de ces jours il devait nous échapper surtout avant que toutes les dispositions nécessaires fussent prises — mais enfin ce n'est point le moment de vous parler de cela.*'★

It was clear that the Emperor did not intend to prolong the conversation, but I determined upon having the last word. I therefore said — '*Votre Majesté est si gracieux qu'il me permettra de lui faire encore une observation. Votre Majesté dit que l'homme est malade — c'est bien vrai, mais Votre Majesté daignera m'excuser si je lui fais observer, que c'est à l'homme généreux et fort de ménager l'homme malade et faible.*'†13

It was not the first time that Turkey had been described as 'a sick man' (*un homme malade*) — Nicholas had used the expression as long ago as 1844 — but it was the first time that the tsar had outlined so clearly his intentions and Seymour ended his despatch with the firm recommendation that 'if Her Majesty's Government do not come to an understanding with Russia as to what is to happen in the event of the sudden downfall of Turkey they will have the less reason for complaining if results displeasing to England should be prepared':

The sum is probably this, that England has to desire a close concert with Russia with a view to preventing the downfall of Turkey — while Russia would be well pleased that the concert should apply to the events by which this down downfall [*sic*] is to be followed.14

It was the beginning of a curious episode in Seymour's career. After months of having been ignored by the tsar he became his confidant and was rightly suspicious about the unexpected turn-around. Certainly,

---

★ 'Look here, we have a sick man on our hands — a seriously sick man. It would, to be frank with you, be a great tragedy if one of these days he should leave us, especially before any of the necessary arrangements have been made — but anyway, now is not the time to speak to you about this'.
† Your Majesty is so gracious that he will no doubt permit me to make one more observation. Your Majesty states that the man is sick — this is clearly true, but if Your Majesty will be so good as to excuse me, may I put the point to him that it is up to the strong and generous man to treat with consideration anyone who is ill and weak.

his lengthy despatches to Russell in January and February 1853 betray both his curiosity and a healthy scepticism. Nicholas, he told Russell, 'occasionally takes a precipitate step; but as reflection arrives, reason and Count Nesselrode make themselves heard'. And in a confidential despatch of 22 January he explained that his sudden elevation had been made possible not just through the tsar's desire to court Britain but also through Nicholas's displeasure with France, on account of the row over the Holy Places, and with Austria and Prussia because their rulers had agreed to address Napoleon III as '*mon frère*'.

Five days after the first meeting, on 14 January, Seymour was once more in the tsar's company, this time at his palace outside St Petersburg at Tsarskoe Seloe. Once again Nicholas showed that he was 'desirous to speak to him upon Eastern Affairs' and he began with a preamble stating that he no longer shared Catherine the Great's dreams of creating a vast empire which would embrace Ottoman territories because Russia was already 'so vast, so happily circumstanced in every way'. However, he did owe an historic obligation to the Christian communities of the Ottoman Empire 'whose interests I am called upon to watch over (*surveiller*) while the right of doing so is secured to me by Treaty [Kutchuk-Kainarji].' For that reason Turkey's decline was a matter of considerable interest and he was anxious to prepare contingency plans 'in concert' with Britain. Seymour replied that, although Turkey's condition was 'deplorable', it was better to shore it up than to prepare for an event which might or might not happen in the near future:

> With regard to contingent arrangements, Her Majesty's government, as Your Majesty is well aware, objects as a general rule to taking engagements upon possible eventualities, and would, perhaps, be particularly disinclined to doing so in this instance. If I may be allowed to say so, a great disinclination (*répugnance*) might be expected in England to disposing by anticipation (*d'escompter*) of the succession of an old friend and ally.[15]

It was on this point that Nicholas was to make a serious diplomatic error. In speaking to Seymour he assured him that he was addressing him as 'a friend and gentleman' who would pass on his thoughts about the 'sick man' to the British Cabinet with the recommendation that the two countries reach an understanding. To a certain extent

Seymour was sufficiently flattered to do this – he ended his despatch
of 22 January with the thought that 'a noble triumph would be
obtained by the civilisation of the 19th century if the void left by
the extinction of Mohammedan Rule in Europe could be filled up
without an interruption of the general Peace in consequence of the
Precautions adopted by the two principal Governments the most
interested in the destinies of Turkey.' But this general statement of
hopes for peace was not the same as agreeing a common policy for
the dismemberment of the Ottoman empire as outlined by the tsar.
Worse, Nicholas thought that it was, even though Nesselrode warned
him that 'the fundamental condition of her [Britain's] policy has always
been never to make commitments for a more or less uncertain future,
but to wait for the event in order to decide what course to adopt'.

Even when Russell replied warning that 'no man and no engagement could guarantee the future' and that Britain would not commit
itself to the Russian proposals, Nicholas refused to be deterred. Shortly
after the second meeting he instructed Nesselrode to tell Seymour
that he regarded the dissolution of Turkey with 'dread . . . sincere
dread' and that he expected a degree of understanding with Britain.
If not, Russia might have to occupy Constantinople as a temporary
expediency 'if everything were left to chance'. Bluster of this kind
did not deter Seymour but he was concerned that the tsar seemed
to be deliberately misreading the British position. As January passed
into February the tone of his despatches became more worried as he
attempted to impart to Russell the strength of Nicholas's belief that
Aberdeen's government would support Russia in any move against
Turkey.

So, what was Britain's policy? It went against the grain to make
preparations for the dismemberment of the Ottoman Empire and
successive governments were opposed to any Russian encroachment
westward towards Constantinople and control of the Straits. Not only
did this represent a premature division of the spoils but it would allow
Russia to upset the European balance of power by providing access
to the Mediterranean. Far better to wait and see what would happen
and, for the time being, to shore up Turkey's position. Another factor
was the protection of the route to India. Any Russian encroachment
towards the Mediterranean would threaten Britain's interests – as
Seymour reminded Russell on 31 January:

Among the duties which an English minister has to perform at

St Petersburg none, I apprehend, are more clear than that of watching the progress of Russian encroachment in the East, and of using such slight influence as he may be fortunate enough to obtain in endeavouring to check a progress which may ultimately bring Great Britain and Russia into collision in very distant latitudes.[16]

Seymour was also much vexed by hints that Russia was about to make fresh diplomatic overtures to Persia. It had come to his attention that the Oriental Department of the Russian foreign ministry was about to replace its diplomats in Tehran with officials 'capable of speaking Indian languages' and that this could be a prelude to the signing of a new treaty of understanding between the two countries. As he told the Foreign Office this would be 'disastrous' especially if Russia had gained undue influence in Turkey:

Under such circumstances Russia might be expected to revert with increased eagerness to her designs on the Indian possessions of Great Britain, and she would do so under infinitely more favouring circumstances than at any preceding period.[17]

In the months to come Seymour was to grow increasingly concerned about Russian intentions towards India, and Russia's territorial ambitions in Persia were taken extremely seriously in the Foreign Office. For that reason Turkey's integrity was of paramount importance. With those fears in mind Seymour was given a further taste of Nicholas's diplomatic offensive when they met again at a party given by the Grand Duchess Hereditary on 20 February. As Seymour reported the following day Nicholas was at his most charming and spoke in flattering terms of the confidence he placed in Britain and its ambassador. Once again, he turned the conversation to Turkey. 'I am not so eager about what shall be done *when the bear dies*,' he said, 'as I am to determine with England what shall be done upon that event taking place.' Seymour's reply was an accurate reflection of British policy.

But sir, I replied, allow me to observe that we have no reason to think that the Bear (to use Your Majesty's expression) is dying. We are as much interested as we believe Your Majesty to be in his continuing to live – while for myself I will venture to remark that experience shows me that countries do not die in such a hurry. I have seen by our Archives both in Turkey and Portugal that these two countries have for years been considered in a perishing state, and yet there they remain, and there Turkey will remain for many a year unless some unforeseen crisis should occur; it is precisely, Sir, for the avoidance of all circumstances likely to produce such a crisis that her Majesty's Government reckons upon Your generous assistance.[18]

Nicholas replied that the British government was misinformed, that Turkey was on its last legs, 'that the Bear is dying, you may give him musk, but even musk will not keep him alive and we can never allow such an event to take us by surprise'. All that was needed, he continued, was 'a general understanding . . . between gentlemen'.

The conversation was a prelude to a longer discussion the following day when Seymour was bidden to read to the tsar Russell's confidential despatch warning that 'it would hardly be consistent with [the] friendly feelings' for Britain to commit itself to any firm action over Turkey. 'The great difference between us is this,' explained Seymour, 'that you continue to dwell upon the fall of Turkey and the arrangements requisite before and after the fall, and that we on the contrary look to Turkey remaining where she is and to the precautions which are necessary for preventing her condition from becoming worse.'

The conversation then ranged over the familiar ground that Russia had no territorial ambitions in Turkey but was prepared to act to protect its own interests and that, therefore, an understanding had to be entered into with Britain. The tsar also warned that he remained suspicious of France and that when he spoke of Russia's interests he included those of Austria. Towards the end of this lengthy and repetitive discourse Nicholas then gave Seymour a glimpse of his concept of dividing up the Ottoman Empire. The Danubian principalities, Serbia and Bulgaria, would become independent under Russian protection – thereby giving Russia control of the Balkans – while he would 'have no objections to offer' if Egypt and the island of Candia (Crete) became British possessions. Somewhat taken aback by the proposal, Seymour pointed out that Britain already had a strategic interest in Egypt as it provided the overland route to India across the isthmus of Suez to the Red Sea. He contented himself by noting that 'the English views upon Egypt did not go beyond the point of securing a safe and ready communication between British India and the Mother Country.'[19]

With that the conversation drew to a close and Seymour reported its contents to Russell the next day. Although he conceded that he had difficulty in remembering everything said by Nicholas and was conscious of 'having forgotten the precise terms employed by him with respect to the commercial policy to be observed at Constantinople', Seymour's letter confirmed British fears that Russian threats towards Turkey had to be taken seriously. Far from assuaging them, Nicholas's conversations with Seymour only served to heighten British concern. Although Aberdeen had been sympathetic to Russian demands over the Holy Places and was prepared to prevaricate, other members of his Cabinet would not sit back and allow the tsar to dictate policy.

Unfortunately for Nicholas he believed that Britain would fall in line with his proposals. In this he might have been cheered by Seymour's diplomatic sympathy and discretion but his biggest mistake was to misunderstand Aberdeen's position. While it was true that the prime minister decided the direction of Britain's foreign policy and was not keen to interfere directly in the French and Russian row over the holy places, Aberdeen was in charge of a divided Cabinet. Palmerston and Russell, backed by the influential Whig peer Lord Lansdowne, were eager to stand by Turkey, while Aberdeen and his chancellor of the exchequer, William Ewart Gladstone, wanted to avoid the possibility of being dragged into a war against Russia.

Matters were also complicated by Lord John Russell's position. He had agreed to join the coalition Cabinet on condition that he would not be required to stay at the Foreign Office for any length of time as he wanted to lead the government in the House of Commons. Aberdeen agreed to the arrangement as Russell's support was essential for the maintenance of the coalition but, even so, it stored up trouble for the future. During his brief eight-week spell at the Foreign Office in 1852 Russell had been responsible for writing the despatch which rebuffed unequivocally Nicholas's overtures. This set the tone which his successor, Clarendon, was bound to follow. Second, he asked Lord Stratford de Redcliffe (formerly Sir Stratford Canning) to return to Constantinople as Britain's ambassador.

On the face of it the decision could not be faulted. Not only was Stratford Britain's most experienced diplomat but there was little about Turkish affairs which he did not know. A cousin of George Canning, he had shown a precocious interest in foreign affairs while at Eton and in 1810, at the age of twenty-four, had found himself in charge of the embassy in Constantinople. With Britain fighting for its life against Napoleon Stratford was forced, as he put it, 'to steer by the stars' while interpreting Britain's policy – which was to check French influence at the Porte and to conclude a rapprochement between Russia and Turkey. The resulting Treaty of Bucharest, signed in May 1812, resolved the differences between the two countries and freed Russian forces on the Danube to join the war against Napoleon. It also made Stratford's name and cemented British influence at the Porte: from that moment onwards he was known in Constantinople as the 'Great Elchi', the ambassador par excellence.

Stratford left Constantinople in 1812 vowing never to return – he disliked many aspects of Ottoman society – but following appointments in Switzerland and the United States he heard with dismay that he was to be sent again to Turkey in 1825, and he remained there for another four years. A career in politics beckoned, but his grasp of Ottoman affairs forced him to accept another mission to Constantinople in 1842. For the next sixteen years his astuteness and firmness allowed Britain to emerge as the controlling force in Turkish politics, so much so that successive Sultans dared not act without his approval. For example, when Mehemet Ali Pasha, the Sultan's brother-in-law, murdered his Christian mistress and went unpunished Stratford said that 'an English ambassador can never admit to his presence a cruel assassin' and as a result of the protest the man was dismissed from his post as minister for the navy.

Inevitably, perhaps, his pre-eminence and his ability to act without reference to London made him many enemies. While foreign secretary in 1830 Aberdeen attacked him for his 'political inclinations'; Nesselrode feared him as an opponent while Nicholas I openly hated him because he exerted undue influence at the Porte. (He had refused to accept him as ambassador in 1832.) In 1852 Stratford was at home on leave in London and did not expect to return to Constantinople. Russell, though, persuaded him otherwise and he set out for Constantinople by the overland route through Paris and Vienna.

By then Nicholas had set in train the second string of his offensive towards the Porte. While he had convinced Seymour that he was only interested in achieving a peaceful accord he had arranged for a diplomatic mission to proceed to Constantinople. This was to be led by Prince Alexander Sergeevich Menshikov, whose orders were to achieve a solution to the question of the Holy Places, one which would recognise Russia's rights of protection, if need be by compulsion.

A bluff soldierly man with little imagination, Menshikov had fought against Turkey in 1817 and 1828 and had little respect for his opponents. Besides, he was accustomed to getting his own way and had a high opinion of his own abilities. (Seymour informed Russell that the prince had a 'peculiar turn of thought constantly shewing itself by sarcastic observations which make him a little dreaded by St Petersburg society'.) When he arrived in Constantinople on 16 February on board a steam-powered warship, the *Gromovnik* (*Thunderer*), his great rival Stratford had not yet returned to Turkey but, as Kinglake noted with no little awe, 'the Emperor Nicholas was obliged to hear that his eternal foe . . . was slowly returning to his embassy at the Porte.'[20]

2

Menshikov's Mission

Our diplomacy has for some time been too inactive in Turkey.
It is time that Russia's interests should be better protected when
attempts are made to dispossess us of our rights.
              Senior Russian Army Officer in conversation with
              Sir George Hamilton Seymour, 3 February 1853

D espite his protestations to Seymour, Tsar Nicholas was determined to regain Russia's position at the Porte, if need be, by
force. On 7 January 1853 he had laid secret plans for a pre-emptive
military strike against Constantinople before France or Britain could
intervene: this would involve a naval expedition to the Bosphorus
consisting of 28 warships and 32 transports. On board would be 16,000
men with cavalry and artillery support and the entire force would be
assembled and held in readiness at Odessa and Sevastopol. However,
Nicholas's advisers argued that such a move would antagonise the rest
of Europe and bring with it the threat of wider hostilities. From the
veteran field–marshal Count Paskevich came the counter–proposal to
occupy the principalities of Wallachia and Moldavia until such time
as the Porte agreed to Russian demands.

At that stage Nicholas was happy enough to accept the advice. He
believed that Britain was not overly concerned with the question of
the Holy Places and would not, therefore, intervene. Under those circumstances France was unlikely to act unilaterally to protect Turkey.
There was also the example of Austria which had exerted its influence
at the Porte to reassert territorial hegemony over Montenegro.
Alarmed about the possibility of Ottoman military intervention in
this fiercely independent principality, Austria had despatched a mission

to Constantinople headed by Field-Marshal Count Leiningen. He demanded that no further Ottoman intervention take place without reference to Vienna and the Austrian government backed up the request by mobilising its forces in Croatia and Dalmatia. When the Porte started procrastinating Leiningen threatened to break off negotiations and, unnerved by the Austrian threat, the Turks agreed to withdraw from Montenegro. Nicholas drew two lessons from that experience: first, his support for Austria during the crisis persuaded him that he could rely on Vienna; and, second, the Porte was liable to change its mind when faced by a mixture of talk and bluster.

With that in mind, Nesselrode provided Menshikov with precise written instructions on 28 January. First, he was to demand full and immediate satisfaction with regard to Russia's protective rights over the Holy Places and the Ottoman Empire's Orthodox population. This would be enshrined in a sened – or convention – which would guarantee Russia's rights, including the control over the Orthodox Church's hierarchy in Constantinople and Jerusalem. Second, if this failed to materialise he was to break off negotiations and threaten to leave immediately. Three days' grace would be allowed for the Turks to change their mind and, if they did not, Menshikov was permitted to reveal the extent of Russia's military preparations. Third, if the Porte conceded to the demands Russia would offer a secret defensive alliance against France. Finally, Menshikov was to demand the re-negotiation of long-standing differences on the frontier between the Caucasus and Turkey.

To make sure that the Porte fully understood the Russian position Nesselrode provided Menshikov with three letters which were to be delivered in stages to Mehemet Ali, the Sultan's Grand Vizier. The first was a letter of introduction from Nicholas to the Sultan outlining the purpose of the mission; the second contained the draft treaty; the third, the most far-reaching and ambitious, demanded the creation of a special relationship with the Orthodox Church which would allow Russia to exert its influence within the Ottoman Empire. The first article made it clear that Russia did not just want a reversal of policy over the guardianship of the Holy Places: it wanted complete control over the church:

> The Imperial Court of Russia and the Ottoman Sublime Porte, desiring to prevent and to remove forever any reason for dis-agreement, for doubt, or for misunderstanding on the subject

of the immunities, rights and liberties accorded and assured
ab antiquo by the Ottoman emperors in their states to the
Greek-Russian-Orthodox religion, professed by all Russia, as
by all the inhabitants of the Principalities of Moldavia, Wallachia
and Serbia and by various other Christian population of Turkey
of different provinces, agree and stipulate by the present Convention that the Christian Orthodox religion will be constantly
protected in all its churches, and that the ministers of the Imperial
Court of Russia will have, as in the past, the right to make
representations on behalf of the Churches of Constantinople
and of other places and cities, as also on behalf of the clergy,
and that the three remonstrances will be received as coming in
the name of a neighbouring and sincerely friendly power.[1]

Menshikov was a curious choice to lead a diplomatic mission of such
delicacy and complexity. Aged sixty-six, he had spent his career in the
armed forces, first as a cavalry officer and then as Alexander I's Chief of
Naval Staff, and he had little experience of diplomatic negotiation. In
both services he had gained a reputation as a forceful and determined
officer who believed in discipline and he was used both to obeying
orders and to having his own orders obeyed. True, he had served on the
tsar's Council of State and had been Governor-General of Finland but in
January 1853 he had admitted to friends that he regarded the mission to
the Porte as his 'last official action' before retiring from public life.

But it was not just his military career or his lack of diplomatic
experience which told against him. Menshikov was an intellectual
lightweight, much given to 'witticisms and jokes', who commanded
little respect and did not care what people thought about him. As a
soldier he was respected for the courage he had shown in the field
but at court he was considered a decent enough fellow, no doubt,
fond of a good story, but hardly the best person to convince the Porte
that Russia had time-honoured claims to protect the Christians in the
Ottoman Empire. Also, during the 1828 campaign against Turkey,
he had been emasculated by an exploding Turkish cannon shell and
it would have been natural enough for him to harbour a dislike for
the Ottoman Empire and all things Turkish.

At the time conventional wisdom had it that another veteran,
Count Alexei Orlov, would have been a better appointment. Not
only was he a recognised diplomat but in 1833 he had been responsible

for brokering the Treaty of Unkiar Skelessi which ended years of Russo-Turkish squabbling and which gave Russia diplomatic primacy at the Porte. Described by his contemporaries as a skilful, if feline, operator, Orlov knew how to negotiate with the Turks. He did not expect quick answers, he recognised the importance of playing a waiting game, he understood when to press a point and when to abandon it, when to flatter and when to be firm. He also had a good conceit of himself and his abilities, even telling Seymour that the tsar had made a fatal error in not sending him to Constantinople:

> Menshikoff [sic] is unquestionably a very clever man, but he is reserved — suspicious — and he is not a diplomatist — he does not know what he may do — he allows himself to depend too much or to be too restricted by his instructions.[2]

As one diplomat to another Seymour sympathised with Orlov's position but in his report to Russell he chose to paint a different picture of Menshikov, one which argued that 'the emperor could not have made a better selection in the interests of conciliatory measures than he has done':

> The Prince [Menshikov] is a remarkably sensible and well-informed man with more independence of character than perhaps belongs to any of the Emperor's associates . . . he has — [however] particularly good manners and, as I have already stated, is believed to be one of the number of those wise counsellors who would be opposed to any unnecessary extension of an already overgrown empire.[3]

Seymour was still enjoying the tsar's confidences and a mixture of sycophancy and self-importance led him to agree with Nicholas's choice. In time, though, Seymour came to see that his original estimation was wrong and, later in the year, he wrote to the Foreign Office admitting that Orlov would have made a better ambassador. (Palmerston was not so sure: to him the veteran Russian diplomat was 'civil and courteous externally, but his inward mind is deeply impregnated with Russian insolence, arrogance and pride.') Orlov was Nesselrode's original choice but in despatching his special mission Nicholas was not looking for tact: Menshikov's orders were clear-cut and brooked no possibility of negotiation.

Fatefully, though, he was also given permission to use whatever means to ensure the success of his mission, that 'if Turkey did not yield, then the ambassador extraordinary must threaten the destruction of Constantinople and the occupation of the Dardanelles'.[4] To sweeten the medicine he was also permitted to spend £1000 a month on entertainment but, as the British Embassy in Constantinople warned the Foreign Office, 'whilst the Russian Government have neglected no means for rendering this Embassy influential and agreeable to Orientals, they have been equally careful to impart to it the most powerful of influences amongst Turks, intimidation'.[5] It was the traditional Russian way of handling the Turks – holding out the olive branch with one hand and wielding the big stick with the other. As his assistant Menshikov took with him Nesselrode's son, Count Dmitri, but no one was left in any doubt that the elderly prince would have total charge of the negotiations.

Menshikov gave immediate notice of his intentions when the *Gromovnik* arrived in the waters of the Bosphorus on 16 February. Protocol demanded that he should present his credentials first to the Grand Vizier and then to the foreign minister but, much to the horror of the diplomatic community, Menshikov ignored the reception which was awaiting him at the Porte and made it clear that the visit would proceed on his terms. Worse was to follow. When he met the Sultan later in the day he condemned Fuad Effendi for his 'duplicity' in making concessions to the French and refused to have any dealings with him. With Stratford still en route to Constantinople British interests were in the hands of Colonel Hugh Rose, the chargé d'affaires, who lost no time in reporting to Russell:

A painful situation was caused here by the following incident which occurred yesterday.

Prince Menschikoff paid his official visit to the Grand Vizier at the Porte but purposefully omitted to pay it to Fuad Effendi who was ready to receive him.

I have entered into communication on the subject with the Russian Embassy. My representations were received, I am bound to say, in the most friendly manner and I have hopes that this inauspicious commencement to the Russian Ambassador's mission may not lead to the untoward results which were at first anticipated.[6]

Before Menshikov's arrival Rose's opposite number in the Russian Embassy, Monsieur d'Ozorov, had confided that the mission would 'embrace all unsettled claims and differences between Russia and the Porte, including the long-standing one as to the frontier between the Caucasus and Turkey'. He also made it clear that the main points of the talks would be passed on to Britain under the terms of a 'parfaite entente [which] existed between our Governments respecting the Russian negotiations about to take place'. Once the mission was in Constantinople, though, he refused to speak to Rose because Russian aims were 'secret'. Then, to add insult to injury, d'Ozorov revealed that Menshikov had met the Austrian ambassador to discuss the situation with him. Britain, it seemed, was being frozen out.[7]

Rose, though, was a capable diplomat who had already served a term as consul in Beirut where he had built up an impressive network of intelligence agents. He was also ambitious and resented the fact that his next appointment would be as consul in Egypt: however, he had been led to believe that if he shone during Stratford's absence he would be permitted to stay in Constantinople. Accordingly he set about talking to 'well-placed contacts' in the Greek Church who told him that Menshikov's sole purpose was to solve the question of the Holy Places and the legal position of the Ottoman Empire's Greek Christians:

The Porte should abstain for the future from taking any part in the selection of the Greek Patriarch, or the affairs of the Greek Church, and that these matters should be left to the Greek Church and the Emperor of Russia; further, that the Cupola of the Holy Sepulchre should be maintained, that is, that the Cupola should belong to Russia.[8]

This disclosure came close to revealing Menshikov's intentions but throughout the period of negotiation neither Rose nor Stratford were able to learn the precise details of the demand for a sened, or convention. Not that they did not try their utmost − at one stage a spy was even infiltrated into the Russian Embassy to eavesdrop while hidden in a wardrobe.

Rose reported the outcome of his meeting in a lengthy despatch on 5 March but he was not entirely convinced by the explanation. The matter of the cupola had been simmering for many years − it was slowly rotting and there had been constant wrangling between the two churches over the responsibility for repairing it – and Rose did not believe that Menshikov had come to Turkey simply to discuss an architectural problem or the election of the Patriarch. Besides, any Russian demand for precedence in the Church of the Holy Sepulchre would break the treaty of 1740 and 'war with France would follow'. In a subsequent despatch he argued that the Russians were using the Holy Places as a smokescreen and that their real intention was to coerce the Turks into a treaty which would restore their pre-eminence at the Porte. His fears were fuelled the next day when the Russians responded to his complaints about the treatment of Fuad Effendi:

> M. d'Ozeroff said that Fuad Effendi had acted in a manner which rendered it impossible that the Russian Embassy should have anything to do with him. Prince Menshikoff also said subsequently that Fuad Effendi was a *'coquin'* [rogue] and a *'menteur'* [liar] and had told *'mensonges'* [lies] to the Russian Embassy. And both these gentlemen said that the affront was directed against Fuad Effendi and not in any way against the Sultan.[9]

Rose could see the drift: the Russians hoped that by concentrating on Fuad Effendi and by demanding his replacement they would terrorise the Porte into submitting to Menshikov's demands. He was also alarmed by reports from the Danube of Russian military troop concentrations and he began to fear that, if Menshikov were rebuffed, there was the strong possibility of a Russian *coup de main* (surprise attack). On 7 March he sent a worried despatch to London claiming that the Russian 5th Corps' cavalry, commanded by General P.A. Dannenburg, had pushed up to the Moldavian frontier. A few days later his suspicions seemed to be confirmed when he heard that the Russians had demanded the dismissal of the Serbian minister in Constantinople: as he told London, 'the threat which accompanied it shews how varied are the real objects of Prince Menshikoff's Mission, how different they are from those which were announced and how unscrupulous are the reasons employed for carrying them out.'[10]

In some desperation he took his fears to his French opposite number, Vincente Benedetti. Like Rose, Benedetti was in temporary charge of the embassy following the return of de Lavalette on 25 February and it is possible that both men were out of their depth. (At the time Stratford was in Paris where his talks with the Emperor

had persuaded him to report to Clarendon that 'French and English
interests in the Levant are sufficiently identical to admit of a general
co-operation between the two governments respecting them'.) In
Constantinople that fond hope was about to be tested to the full
by Rose and Benedetti. Following a brief conference they sought
an audience with Mehemet Ali, the Grand Vizier, in an attempt
to thwart the Russian threats. As Rose told Clarendon, it was not
a happy meeting:

> The Grand Vizier said that the Russian government evidently
> intended to win some important right from Turkey which would
> destroy her independence and asked me to request the British
> Admiral to bring up his squadron to Vourla Bay from Malta.
>
> Feeling the immediate conviction that if the Sultan, who
> always yields to intimidation, were not supported by me on
> this occasion, he would call to his councils a Ministry selected
> under Russian influence, I informed His Highness that I would
> tell your Lordship that I felt convinced that the safety of Turkey
> required the presence of the British squadron in these waters. M.
> Benedetti said the same as regards the French squadron.
>
> But these assurances did not tranquillise the Grand Vizier's
> mind; he thought that Turkey would be lost before the answer
> could arrive from England and France.[11]

To add to the feeling of gloom Mehemet Ali confirmed Rose's
intelligence about the Russian troop movements along the border.
He also pointed out that two more Russian warships had arrived in
Constantinople bringing with them Vice-Admiral Vladimir Kornilov
of the Black Sea Fleet and Adjutant-General Nikapotchinski as well
as other senior military and naval officers. He was convinced that
Menshikov and his retinue would assume overall command for a
concerted military and naval attack if Russia's demands were not
met. The evidence concentrated Rose's mind and he determined
on an immediate plan of action: Britain would come to the Sultan's assistance by despatching ships from its Mediterranean Fleet to
Turkish waters. In the same despatch he informed Clarendon that
he had ordered a squadron of British warships to leave Malta and to
proceed to Vourla Bay. This would be a relatively straightforward
deployment, he explained, because a squadron of six ships was due
to be detached from the Mediterranean Fleet for a cruise to Corfu,

Athens and Smyrna on 20 March; if it left a week earlier, it could proceed first to Vourla Bay on Turkey's eastern coast.

It was a high-risk strategy. Because the newly developed telegraph from London only reached as far as Belgrade and most correspondence was by ship – Rose's despatch left Constantinople that night with the senior naval officer, Lord John Hay, on the steamer *Wasp* – he was forced in some desperation to act unilaterally and hope that the government would back him up:

> I have used all the exertions in my power to protect the rights and independence of the Porte; but it is my duty to submit my conviction, unfortunately a general one, that if the Porte do not receive prompt and energetic assistance from Her Majesty's Government, her independence and rights, and with them the balance of power, will be dangerously compromised by the Mission of Prince Menshikoff.[12]

Rose's actions caused consternation in both London and Valetta. The Royal Navy was not used to receiving orders from mere chargés d'affaires and the commanding officer at Malta, the bluff and hot-tempered Vice-Admiral Sir James Whitley Dundas, a veteran of the wars against Napoleon, refused to alter his plans without confirmation from the Admiralty. That it would not be forthcoming was evident from the response of the First Lord of the Admiralty, Admiral Sir James Graham: he promptly told Clarendon that he resented Rose's interference and that it was not a diplomat's right to treat admirals 'with impunity'. Clarendon was similarly nonplussed when he received Rose's despatch. Not only was the use of force not on the Cabinet's agenda but Aberdeen hoped that Stratford would be able to secure a diplomatic solution to the problem. At that stage, too, the British prime minister was still interested in the expressions of Tsar Nicholas's sincerity which Seymour had reported from St Petersburg and he was not inclined to pay any heed to Rose's warnings. A week later, therefore, on 15 March, the order to Dundas was cancelled, 'the aspect of affairs here [Constantinople] having become more pacific'. Only the French decided to stick to their guns. Following Benedetti's request a French squadron left Toulon for Vourla Bay on 25 March, a move which greatly enhanced France's prestige at the Porte.

When the news of Rose's request reached St Petersburg on 29 March, Seymour was summoned to the Russian Foreign Ministry to explain why the British were about to deploy naval forces in Turkish waters at the request of 'an English diplomatic agent'. Anxious not to 'irritate' Nesselrode, Seymour replied that Rose had been within his rights but that he would seek assurances from Clarendon that Britain was not intent on intervening with a naval force. These arrived on 5 April, together with the news that Rose's orders had been countermanded, allowing Nesselrode smoothly to claim that 'even a practised diplomatist might have been misled . . . and doubly so at moments of great excitement'.[13] In the days that followed Nesselrode and Orlov continued to insist that Russia had pacific intentions in Turkey and that the blame for the crisis could be laid at the feet of Napoleon III whom he believed to be 'bent on sowing disruption among the allied powers' by building up French power at the Porte.

Even though the British warships did not proceed to Vourla Bay Rose's intervention did concentrate minds at the Admiralty. Until then France had been perceived as the enemy and British naval strategy was centred on the need to maintain a superior battle fleet both to protect global trading routes and to control the English Channel. During a period of French bluster in the 1840s the Admiralty had evolved a so-called 'Cherbourg' strategy to destroy the main French naval base and thereby to pre-empt an invasion. Now, with considerable reluctance it has to be said, Sir James Graham and his colleagues had to bend their minds to the threat posed by Russia. Because any war would be a distraction from the navy's main task Graham produced a version of the Cherbourg strategy which he believed would bring victory at minimal cost. Basically, the navy would destroy the Russian Black Sea Fleet in Sevastopol: this would prevent an attack on Constantinople and leave southern Russia open to invasion. At the same time the Baltic fleet in the Gulf of Finland would be attacked, a move which would threaten St Petersburg and attract Sweden into the war on the allies' side. In other words, at that stage Graham envisaged any conflict as a naval war with the limited objective of destroying Russian sea power – just as Nesselrode had forecast at the beginning of the year.

Rose's intervention had also changed the pace of the negotiations in Constantinople. Aware that time was no longer on his side Menshikov increased his pressure on the Porte to comply with his demands. Here he was not helped by his own incompetence – the maps of the disputed Caucasian-Turkish border had been left behind in Odessa, but that

was a side-show. None the less he knew that Nicholas expected him
to build on his initial successes: so far Menshikov had succeeded in
having Fuad Effendi replaced as foreign minister by the pro-Russian
Rifaat Pasha and in unsettling the Sultan. By revealing the extent of
Russia's military preparations and by acting in a brusque and officious
manner he had also managed to instil considerable fear at the Porte.
He knew, too, that Rose and Benedetti were no match for him and
he had been cheered by Britain's refusal to deploy Dundas's squadron.
And yet, despite all the cajoling and the threats, the Sultan had refused
to budge on the question of a new treaty to guarantee Russia's rights.
One reason for Turkish obstinacy was a traditional unwillingness to
be rushed; another was a growing belief that Britain and France would
not stand aside and leave them to their fate. The deployment of the
French fleet and Stratford's imminent arrival seemed to suggest that
these hopes were not misplaced.

On 17 March the 'Great Elchi' had left Paris; six days later he
reached Vienna for talks with the Austrian foreign minister Count
Buol-Schauenstein and on 5 April he arrived back in Constantinople.
Acting on Rose's request the Porte greeted him with the same honours
that had been accorded to Menshikov. It was an astute move, for not
only was Stratford more than a match for the Russian ambassador but
he brought with him the British Cabinet's authority 'to request the
commander of Her Majesty's forces in the Mediterranean to hold
his squadron in readiness' in the event of a Russian threat to attack
Constantinople. Everything would now change – just as Rose hoped
it would when he sent his last official despatch to Clarendon following
his meeting with the Grand Vizier:

> But still although the Russian government may contemplate
> nothing but the employment of intimidation towards Turkey,
> I venture to think that nothing would justify our abstaining from
> considering the present hostile attitude of Russia as a most serious
> reality and acting accordingly.
>
> The safety of our vast commercial interests and of European
> policy as well as the maintenance of peace are compromised by
> Russia's present military and naval position.
>
> To judge of the Porte's present disposition she will not give
> way either to intimidation or unprovoked aggression.
>
> I venture to think that the only certain and safe means of
> preserving all these great interests would be the presence of a

British squadron, or of British and French squadrons, in Besika Bay [close to the entrance to the Dardanelles].[14]

The commercial interests which Rose mentioned were by no means insubstantial. As he had pointed out in an earlier despatch of 17 March the British financial house of Hazlewood was about to invest two or three million pounds in a Turkish bank and in the last year alone 1,741 British merchant vessels had passed through the Dardanelles. According to Rose this was evidence of Turkey's willingness to allow Britain 'to trade with her on more advantageous terms than any other Power' and he ended his report with the thought that 'Turkey's fall would be the signal for general war and confusion, the triumph of socialism and anarchy, and the ruin of British trade and interests.'

This, too, was Stratford's general belief – Turkey had to be supported and induced to introduce reforms – but for the time being the policy of the Aberdeen coalition was one of wait and see. On the one hand they were still receiving reassurances from St Petersburg that Nicholas had no warlike intentions towards Turkey; on the other they were being provided with evidence of Menshikov's coercion in Constantinople. Aberdeen had no quarrel with Russia, yet he understood the importance of protecting British interests; he disliked the Ottoman Empire but he was not convinced that its dissolution was imminent. Today Aberdeen's policy might be called appeasement and it contrasted with Palmerston's belligerent criticism of Russia's tactics. But at the time, faced by a divided and suspicious cabinet, it is difficult to see what the prime minister could have done, other than to compromise and await the outcome of events.

Unfortunately, and although Aberdeen had a healthy disregard for public opinion, especially when it was expressed as an emotional reaction to complicated events, there was little doubt that Britain was divided over the drama unfolding in Constantinople. The main feeling was distinctly anti-Russian. Not only was Nicholas's regime a police-state but the tsar had established himself as the main opponent of the liberal sentiments which had helped to create the year of revolutions in 1848. Huge crowds in London had cheered the exiled Hungarian patriotic leader Lajos Kossuth when he addressed them in October 1851 to denounce Russian despotism. Yet here was the oppressor of the Hungarians and the Poles carrying out the same tactics against the Turks. Compared to the French decision to send a naval squadron to the Aegean the British response seemed to be querulous and pusillanimous, as sections of the press did not hesitate to say.

In 1853 the British press was still hampered by the existence of a stamp duty as well as taxes on advertisements and paper. These 'taxes on knowledge' kept newspaper prices high (as much as 5d) and only *The Times* enjoyed pre-eminence, selling 50,000 copies a day, more than all its London rivals combined. In general, the inclination of its editor, John Thadeus Delane, was to support Aberdeen's government. As a younger man – in 1841 at the age of twenty-three he had been appointed editor – Delane had admired the foreign policy of the Peel government as it had been conducted by Aberdeen and he welcomed Aberdeen's coalition government in December 1852. By way of reward, on Christmas Day, *The Times* had revealed exclusively the composition of the new Cabinet and, as Clarendon conceded a few months later, 'as its circulation is enormous and its influence abroad very great a Government must take its support on the terms it chooses to put it'.

In February those terms were to be fully tested when Delane chose to publish a series of leading articles which recommended the early partition of Turkey. To Rose in Constantinople their publication had made his position 'very difficult and done injury to British and much good to anti-British interests and influence':

> Whilst I am making known to them the very friendly sentiments towards Turkey expressed by her Majesty's Government, a translation of the 'Times' is placed before their eyes in which with bitter cleverness, Turkey's disgrace, ruin and partition are announced to the world; and this, too, at a time when Russia is endeavouring to establish here a commanding influence and effect a secret treaty with the Porte, by means of the diplomacy of an extraordinary Embassy, the union of two, if not three Corps d'Armées ready for war, Russian advanced guards on the Turkish frontiers, and a fleet of twelve sail of the line and large steamers ready to sail for Constantinople.[15]

Rose's despatch of 17 March revealed the extent of his irritation. Until Stratford arrived he believed that it was his duty to shore up the Turks' morale and to prevent them from signing a treaty with Menshikov. How could he do that, he asked Clarendon, if *The Times* insisted on proposing a different policy, one which angered the Grand

Vizier and other Porte officials? The foreign secretary replied that he sympathised but had no means of controlling Delane's editorial policy. That much had been made clear by the aptly nicknamed 'Thunderer' in 1852 during an altercation with Lord Derby over criticisms of Palmerston's foreign policy. When the prime minister complained that *The Times* 'must share in the responsibilities of statesmen', Delane responded with a strongly worded leader defending the press's freedom to discuss topics which politicians would prefer to ignore:

> Governments must treat other governments with external respect, however bad their origin or foul their deeds; but happily the Press is under no such trammles, and, while diplomatists are exchanging courtesies, can unmask the mean heart that beats beneath a star, or point out the bloodstains on the hand which grasps a sceptre. The duty of the journalist is the same as the historian − to seek out truth, above all things, and to present to his readers not such things as statecraft would wish them to know but the truth as near as he can attain it.[16]

However, it is doubtful whether Rose's position was being undermined in the way he suspected. While Mehemet Ali was confiding his fears to Britain and France, and in so doing making the case for naval intervention, his colleague Rifaat Pasha was attempting to negotiate a workable settlement with Menshikov on the question of the Holy Places.

The talks had opened amicably enough on 16 March when Menshikov used Nesselrode's first note to demand satisfaction over the question of the Holy Places. Rifaat asked for time to consider the request but within a week Russia's intentions were made clear when Menshikov produced Nesselrode's third letter. On 22 March he introduced the demand for a sened which would give Russia complete control over the Orthodox Church within the Ottoman Empire and was pleased to note that 'during the perusal of these documents Rifaat's face grew visibly sombre: he seemed to me deeply affected and could not for some moments pronounce a word'. The foreign minister's dismay was understandable but he nevertheless insisted on making a distinction between Russia's requests for satisfaction over the Holy Places and the demand for a sened which he believed to be unworkable.

The following day he told Menshikov that he was ready to settle the points regarding Russia's interests in the Holy Places and the discussions continued into the following month. By then Stratford was back in Constantinople and his presence had a steadying influence. To Menshikov's surprise Stratford supported Russia's complaint about the Holy Places and urged Rifaat to find an early solution. The Great Elchi had little time for either man – Menshikov he thought a fool, Rifaat a drunkard – but his sole purpose was to broker an agreement in the hope that it would assuage Russia's demands for a sened whose undisclosed terms he rightly feared.

Under his calm guidance the talks continued and on 5 May Rifaat announced that the Porte would revise the firmans (edicts) regarding the Holy Places and restore Russia's privileges. As Kinglake put it, the question of the rival keys and stars had been settled and the long drawn-out quarrel between the 'rival churchwardens' was at an end. For Clarendon in London the crisis seemed to be passing: as he wrote to Stratford, Britain had been 'quite right in showing confidence in the pledged word of the Emperor of Russia'.[17] However, both he and his ambassador failed to understand the strength of feeling which lay behind Russia's demands for a sened. To Stratford it was unimportant – he still did not know its precise terms – as he believed that it would merely conform to the terms of the Treaty of Kutchuk-Kainarji or that its demands would be too vague for an immediate settlement. They also underestimated the Porte's resistance to the Russian proposals. When the terms of the sened were discussed on 10 May Rifaat argued that they would breach Ottoman sovereignty and should, therefore, be resisted. However, the Sultan was not prepared to make it a sticking point. That same day Menshikov was told that, while the Russian demand was unacceptable, the Porte would do its utmost to ensure the privileges of the Orthodox Christians:

> The Sublime Porte will devote all its attention to maintaining and to conserving for the future, in conformity with its rights of independence, all the religious immunities which have been spontaneously granted to its Christian subjects and particularly to the Greek subjects and monks.[18]

Menshikov was not taken in by the obfuscation. Accordingly he instigated the second of Nesselrode's instructions and threatened to break off discussions within three days. On 13 May the Sultan attempted to heal the breach by sacking Mehemet Ali as Grand Vizier and replacing him with Rifaat, but Menshikov was not appeased: either the Porte agreed to the sened or Russia would break off diplomatic relations. The following day he retired to the *Gromovnik* and allowed a period of grace for the Sultan to change his mind. A week later, on 21 May, no answer having arrived, he ordered the steamer to weigh anchor and return to Odessa.

When the news reached St Petersburg Nesselrode discussed the situation with Seymour and conceded that the crisis was entering a new and dangerous stage. As Seymour reported:

> At the close of our conversation Count Nesselrode, who is evidently much pained by the events on which he had been commenting to me, observed that it could not be denied that the state of affairs was very alarming and that the position of the Emperor was one from which it was impossible for His Majesty to recede and that he would not conceal from me that a continued objection to the terms offered to the Porte would be followed by the issue of orders for the entrance of Russian Armies into the Principalities.[19]

As the mastermind behind Menshikov's mission Nesselrode knew that the Sultan's refusal to accede to the demands for a sened would anger the tsar and that an uncertain future lay ahead. By then, too, Seymour had grown suspicious of Nicholas's protestations. A few days earlier, on 20 April, he had attended a dinner at the Russian Court during which Nicholas insisted on a toast to the health of Queen Victoria's fourth son and eighth child, Prince Leopold.

Afterwards, though, he took Seymour on one side and spoke to him privately: 'He would repeat that he had no intention of being trifled with and that if the Turks did not yield to reason they would have to give way to an approach of danger.'

3

Getting into Deep Waters

By the occupation of the Principalities we desire such security
as will ensure the restoration of our dues. It is not conquest that
we seek but satisfaction for a just right so clearly infringed.
Tsar Nicholas I, Proclamation, 2 July 1853

When Menshikov returned to St Petersburg to announce the
failure of his mission Nicholas is reported to have said that
he felt 'the five fingers of the sultan on my face'. The remark was
probably true. The tsar would not have been human had he not
felt anger at the rejection of his plans; being Nicholas he was also
furious at being outfaced by Stratford, a man for whom he entertained
the greatest contempt. For his part Menshikov attempted to excuse
himself by claiming that the Great Elchi had 'bewitched' the Sultan
and that Rifaat had assured him that 'it was only the disapprobation
expressed by Lord Stratford de Redcliffe which prevented the Porte
from accepting the Prince's Note.'

But, in truth, Menshikov only had himself to blame. The British
ambassador could hardly be condemned for the lack of diplomacy
and intemperate behaviour which had helped to steel the Turkish
backbone. While Stratford had exercised considerable tact in solving
the tiresome question of the Holy Places by advising the Turks to
agree unilaterally to the Russian demands, he had merely supported
Mehemet Ali's contention that there was a distinction between the
question of keys and stars and Menshikov's demands for a sened.
That support and the possibility of British naval intervention had
been enough for the Sultan to ignore the Russian demands. Nicholas,
though, was tired of words. Now he wanted action.

Shortly after Menshikov's return Nicholas and Field-Marshal Paskevich outlined the plans for implementing offensive operations against the Turks. These centered on Russian forces occupying the Danubian principalities to protect the rights of the Orthodox Christian population but the later stages of the plan would include a naval blockade of the Bosphorus and outright war against Turkey. Although Nicholas admitted that he was 'not yet of a mind to proceed to such extreme actions', orders were sent to Prince M.D. Gorchakov, commander of the Russian 4th and 5th Corps, to make preparations to cross the River Pruth, which formed the frontier between Russia and Moldavia, and begin the invasion of the principalities. On 31 May the Nicholas sent a courier to Constantinople 'to apprize the Turkish Government that eight days were allowed for reconsideration of the terms proposed, but that if at the expiration of the term satisfaction were not afforded, His Majesty, however unwillingly, must give orders for the advance of his forces.'[1]

On the same day Nicholas summoned Seymour to his palace at Tsarskoe Selo for a meeting which resulted in what the British ambassador was pleased to call 'a long and extremely interesting conversation'. During its course the tsar underlined his belief that Stratford, his 'personal enemy', had been responsible for directing Turkish policy and that his interference was a breach of trust between the two countries. 'Sir Hamilton Seymour,' he (Nicholas) said, 'has had several conversations with the Emperor who spoke to him with a total absence of reserve. Sir Hamilton Seymour must have written a report of those conversations – I have nothing to add to the information of which the English Government is in possession.'[2]

Seymour concurred that Aberdeen's cabinet had indeed been assured that Nicholas wanted a peaceful solution and was not intent on war, but he warned that the situation could change if Russia insisted on making bellicose preparations:

> I replied that I thought it highly probable, that in this event the public would not fail to reproach the Government with their extreme confidence in the intentions of the Emperor of Russia which had led to the neglect of those precautions which usually resorted to when the safety of Turkey was menaced.[3]

He then continued to tell the tsar that if the government were to be censured in this way, 'it is probable that a change of Government under existing circumstances must have very disastrous effects – that is a point which I leave to Your Majesty's consideration'. Although he did not say so Seymour was offering a broad hint that, if Nicholas were guilty of bad faith, Aberdeen might fall and his place could be taken by Palmerston.

Following that digression – which the tsar chose to ignore – Nicholas returned to the attack by placing the blame for the crisis solely on Britain. The British government had been made privy to his plans and he had been led to believe (or at least had allowed himself to believe) that there was no conflict of interest between the two countries, yet Stratford had conspired with the Porte to thwart them, revealing himself to be 'more Turkish than the Sultan's own Ministers'. Therefore, said Nicholas, 'England must necessarily be a party to any war which might break out in consequence of a refusal by the Sultan to accept the conditions offered by Prince Menshikoff.' While admitting that any conflict would 'paralyze commerce in the North and would lead to utter destruction in the South', Nicholas told Seymour that, unless Constantinople yielded to his wishes, he had no option but to fight for them:

> You see what my position is. I am the Head of a People of the Greek religion, our co-religionists of Turkey look up to me as their natural protector, and these are claims which it is impossible for me to disregard.
>
> I have the conviction that good right is on my side, I should therefore begin a War, such as that which now impends, without compunction and should be prepared to carry it on, as I have before remarked to you, as long as there should be a rouble in the Treasury or a man in the country.[4]

To his credit Seymour stood by his diplomatic colleague in Constantinople by pointing out that Stratford's aim had been the resolution of the Holy Places question, but the tsar was unmoved by that argument. Then Seymour turned the conversation to the terms of the sened which he believed to have no basis in law. Not so, rejoined Nicholas, the demands were guaranteed by the reaty of Kutchuk-Kainarji. Here he was taking a risk as neither he nor Nesselrode had been convinced of the exact articles of the treaty when the sened was drawn up.

I took the liberty of replying [Seymour told Clarendon] that having looked into the treaty of 1774 I had been unable to discover anything of the kind – I added that perhaps His Majesty would allow me to call upon the Chancellor in his name and ask him to show me the Article or Articles referred to. The Emperor rejoined with much good humour that I was quite at liberty to do so, that I might if I pleased, call for the originals of the Treaties.[5]

With that, Nicholas concluded the audience and Seymour left the palace to call on Nesselrode who confirmed that his master was indeed intent on securing a sened enshrining Russia's privileges even if that meant war. (The question of the Treaty of Kutchuk-Kainarji was not raised although in the weeks to come Seymour was to spend much time and trouble investigating its terms.) The chancellor also made it clear that Britain, through Stratford's actions, must accept some of the blame for the new impasse.

A week later Nicholas underlined the seriousness of the position to the French in an audience with their ambassador, de Castelbajac. In a surprising change of tack he told the ambassador that Britain was the cause of the current friction. If Stratford had not interfered the Russian proposals would have been accepted and military action would not be an issue. As matters stood, though, he had no alternative but to invade Wallachia and Moldavia and to hold them hostage until he was 'given satisfaction'.

This was a very different message from the assurances which he had presented to Seymour. Although Aberdeen was loath to take any action he had to respond to the changing situation. Nicholas had promised that he did not want war; yet Menshikov's diplomatic mission had been little more than crude coercion. Now the tsar was threatening to invade the principalities to ensure that his demands would be met by Turkey. On 28 May the cabinet decided to do nothing until they received reports from Constantinople and St Petersburg. When Seymour's despatches arrived apprising them of the tsar's threats, it was clear that Britain could no longer stand aside. Given a free vote, the cabinet decided on 30 May to order Dundas's squadron of six warships to proceed to Besika Bay close to the entrance of the Dardanelles; furthermore Stratford was given local authority to order them to protect Constantinople in the event of a Russian attack. In this way, argued Clarendon, 'I reasoned this as the least measure that will satisfy public opinion and save the government from shame hereafter, if, as I firmly believe, the Russian hordes pour into Turkey from every side. It may do some good to ourselves, which should not be our least consideration.'6

For Clarendon it was one of the most momentous orders he had given in the course of a public career which had already spanned four decades. In 1820, just out of his teenage years, George Frederick William Villiers had been sent to St Petersburg as an attaché where he showed a natural aptitude for diplomacy. Postings in Dublin and Madrid confirmed his talent, but following his elevation to his uncle's earldom in 1838 he threw himself into a political career, emerging as a leading free-trader in the Tory Party. Spoken of as a future prime minister – he enjoyed the support of the influential *Edinburgh Review* but the post never attracted him – he made his name in Ireland where he served as lord–lieutenant between 1847 and 1852. It was a difficult time, made worse by famine in the country areas and the violence which accompanied it, but despite the problems and personal danger he emerged from the experience with enormous personal credit. Appointed foreign secretary in Aberdeen's government in February 1853 his experience and canniness in public office spoke for themselves.

However, Aberdeen thought that the deployment of the British squadron was dangerous and loaded with implications, because the ships would not be able to shelter in Besika Bay once the winter gales arrived. Then they would either have to withdraw, thereby signalling an ignominious climbdown, or they would have to enter the Dardanelles in breach of the Straits Convention. It was still possible that a diplomatic solution would be found by involving Austria – who did not welcome the prospect of a Russian occupation of the mouth of the Danube – but the deployment of the warships inevitably increased tensions. By the end of June British and French naval forces were in Turkish waters while two Russian Army Corps were positioned on the borders of Turkish-owned possessions. The talking continued but by sanctioning the naval and military deployments each country had given notice that they would be prepared to use them if it became necessary. Indeed Nicholas chose the moment on 10 June to complain to Seymour and de Castelbajac that, while he 'conceives himself authorised to occupy the Danubian Principalities if he thinks proper, he would consider the consequent entry of the Dardanelles by an English or French fleet as a breach of Treaty agreements.'7

Although Seymour counselled Clarendon that such an explanation 'would be sought in vain in any Treatise upon the Law of Nations', he did admit that the turn of events had disconcerted him. Following the audience with the tsar, Nesselrode had elaborated on the reasons for the Russian ultimatum. 'You have known me,' he said, 'two years – you have seen that I am not disposed to violent measures (*à caper les vitres*). Well, I declare to you that I could not advise the emperor to recede. His dignity would be lowered, his position would be compromised. It would be a triumph for the Turks, and a humiliation for Russia – the inevitable result would be a war with Turkey – the insolence of the Turks would become such that friendly relations with them would become impossible.'[8]

Nesselrode also made it clear that the orders to invade the principalities would be given as soon as the expected rejection of the ultimatum reached Odessa. To do otherwise would harm Russia's standing and anything which was seen to damage that reputation also affected Nicholas. Besides, he said, adopting a 'warmth of manner' which Seymour believed he had 'assumed for the occasion', was it not the case that Russia was being treated as an international pariah? When French warships had blockaded the Ottoman port of Tripoli in Syria in August 1852 to demand the return of naval deserters not a word of blame had been heard from the international community, but when 'Russia sought temperately for redress of a serious grievance and exceptions were instantly raised – instantly Russia was charged with a wish to destroy the independence of Turkey.'

Seymour responded that the threatened invasion of the principalities was out of all proportion to the refusal of the Porte to accede to Russian coercion. He also reiterated Britain's position: 'as regards Her Majesty's Government there was no wish to raise a crusade against Russia; that as I have said before, all that was desired was, whilst making allowance for the position taken up by the Emperor, to provide for the security and independence (*de sauvegarder*) of Turkey.'

Nesselrode, though, was not to be moved. He concluded the interview by reminding the British ambassador that the tsar was intent on gaining satisfaction from the Porte and that not even the presence of a British fleet would 'deprive us of the means of marching our armies into Turkey.' And there the matter rested. Seymour had to accept that Russia intended to send forces into the principalities, both to protect the interests of the Greek Orthodox Christians and to exert pressure on the Porte to accept the terms laid down by Menshikov. As he told the Russian chancellor when they met a week later, suddenly both countries seemed to be getting into deep waters. Nesselrode did not disagree: he considered the deployment of the fleet 'very unfortunate' and 'he did not see how the Emperor could have the appearance of making any concession under menace.' Seymour reported:

> I replied that I thought the best course which could be followed would be that the two Fleets should withdraw from the Coast upon a clear understanding that there should be no attempt made at occupying the Principalities.
>
> Count Nesselrode made use of some expression signifying the impossibility of the Emperor renouncing his intentions – but the declaration was made in fainter terms than have been lately employed by the Russian government.
>
> The state of the case, I said, M. le Comte, is plainly this. The English and French Fleets have joined for a common purpose; the great object should be to prevent their junction by common action; to prevent this prudence suggests that the Principalities should not be entered, and that time should be given for the settlement of all difficulties by negotiation.[9]

Curiously, the decision to send Dundas's squadron to Besika Bay helped to calm nerves in London. At last something was being done although, as ever, Aberdeen warned Clarendon that the country seemed to be drifting towards war. In a sense he was right. Having committed the fleet to Turkish waters in support of the Porte the ships could not be withdrawn without enormous loss of prestige. Even though it was in the throes of modernisation the Royal Navy was the world's most powerful naval force and the main executor of Britain's foreign policy. It was unthinkable that it might be deployed and then not used effectively.

Inevitably, perhaps, the question of the deployment of the Mediterranean Fleet was discussed widely in the British press and Aberdeen found himself at the centre of considerable controversy. With the strength of a rip tide running up a beach, press opinion was increasingly in favour of Britain punishing Russia by initiating action in support of Turkey. To a certain extent this enthusiasm mirrored official government policy that Turkey's integrity had to be maintained and the Straits kept open, otherwise Britain's imperial holdings in the east might be jeopardised. That being said, Britain had little desire to go to war to maintain the status quo, the foreign policy of the day being based on the peaceful economic expansion provided by the post-Napoleonic settlement of 1815. While it was also policy to signal British intentions by making full use of its superior battle fleet, any military or naval operation would inevitably attract unwelcome increases in defence spending: for that reason alone Aberdeen was keen to solve the crisis through diplomacy.

Those restraints notwithstanding, Britain was gripped by war fever in the summer of 1853. Suddenly it became chic to support the Turks against the Russians and the London press took up the cry that 'something had to be done'. The uproar gave Rose in Constantinople further cause for concern. Having voiced his disapproval of *The Times*'s comments on Turkey he had taken the opportunity on 10 March to send a detailed report to the Foreign Office offering his frank view of the current state of the Ottoman Empire. It was an extraordinary document and one which can have done little to persuade the cabinet that Turkey was a cause worth saving. Far from supporting the British line that Turkey had to be propped up – 'the hope of her friends' as he put it – Rose painted a gloomy picture of an Islamic empire in decline, of a sick man whose death was imminent. Partly this seemed to be a result of the Koran's teachings 'which enjoins polygamy' and partly it was due to the weakness of the armed forces. To Rose, the two were not unconnected:

> Nearly the whole of the Turkish Army, except some of its officers, are either unmarried, or do not take their wives from home. Consequently the flower of the best Mussulman youth of Turkey does not increase the population during five years, the term of their service. And when they do return to their homes these young soldiers are only too often enfeebled and demoralised by wounds, and sickness, an arduous service and the vices of Turkish military life.
>
> Polygamy, besides restricting and diminishing the sources of population, produces, indirectly, another cause which checks population. Mussulmans themselves and Europeans of long experience in Turkey are of the opinion that the unrestricted use of women, allowed by the Koran, gives rise to an unnatural desire for further excitement; and all declare that the prevalence of a horrid vice in Turkey arises in a great measure from that cause.

Abortions, effected either from motives of economy or convenience with the view to prevent the undue increase of children, or for the purpose of preserving the shape, are another depopulating cause. The seclusion of women, also ordained by the Koran, increases this moral pestilence, as I have mentioned, especially in the Turkish Army. There are only too many and too disgusting proofs of this.[10]

Only by weaning themselves away from 'the influences of an immoral and unnatural law' could Turkey be saved and that could only happen if the great powers decided to intervene in the affairs of the infidel empire. 'In short,' he warned Lord John Russell, 'the cross is rising and the crescent is on the wane.'

Rose's deliberations on Turkey would have been music to Tsar Nicholas's ears. Here was an intelligent British officer, with ample experience of the Ottoman Empire, predicting a similar outcome to the one he foresaw. True, Rose based his argument on a belief that Islam had enfeebled the empire and that only the triumph of 'Christian vigour' could revive it, but his conclusion was the same: 'if the Powers which are interested in the destiny of Turkey would act with the disinterestedness which has always guided the councils of Great Britain with regard to Turkey, so great and so good a solution of her history would not be impossible.'

It was not as if Turkey were a particularly close ally or, as Rose had demonstrated all too clearly, if much were known about the country and its people. Indeed, in the past it had been considered a potential enemy – in 1827 a British fleet led by Vice-Admiral Sir Edward Codrington had destroyed an Ottoman force at Navarino during the Greek War of Independence – and there were historical prejudices about Turkish massacres of Christians in the Balkans. Thomas Carlyle called the average Turk 'a lazy, ugly, sensual, dark fanatic', and even Queen Victoria was dubious about the wisdom of supporting Constantinople 'without having bound Turkey to any conditions'. She, too, was concerned about French intentions and viewed the cross-Channel alliance with some suspicion: 'Who can say it is impossible that our own shores may be threatened by Powers now in alliance with us?' she asked Aberdeen.

While there were longstanding fears about French intentions, Turkey was another matter. To the public it was a distant and romantic country about which little was known but as it was being threatened by Russia it required British support and protection. It might be an Islamic state which had persecuted Christians but such was the antipathy towards Russia that these doubts paled into insignificance. At a diplomatic level there was also a belief that, given time and patience, Turkey could be saved from itself. Both Stratford and Rose thought that Turkey could be saved by reform although they admitted that the process would be slow. By way of unremitting pressure Stratford had used his influence to persuade the Porte to abolish executions for apostasy* but, as he pointed out to Aberdeen, such compromises were impossible 'without the employment of very decided language'. On another occasion when he suspected the Sultan of profligacy at a time of financial shortages he personally intervened to halt the construction of a new summer palace on the shores of the Bosphorus.

Small wonder that there were those in London who believed that Stratford was too powerful for his own good and that his influence over the Porte was antipathetic to Britain's interests. Clarendon's wife Katherine thought him 'a dreadfully unsafe man'; Graham, the first lord of the Admiralty, remarked that he was 'a Bashaw [pasha] – too long accustomed to rule alone', and the suspicion grew that the British ambassador in Constantinople was using his not inconsiderable prestige to force the Turks to stand up to Nicholas's threats. Certainly, that was the impression nurtured by Kinglake when he wrote his account of the war but far from adding to Stratford's reputation – Kinglake's intention – his adulatory comments left the impression to later generations that the Great Elchi had dragged Britain into an unnecessary conflict:

> Lord Stratford had brought to a settlement the question of the Holy Places, had baffled all the efforts of the Emperor Nicholas to work an inroad upon the sovereign rights of the sultan, and had enforced upon the Turks a firmness so indomitable and a moderation so unwearied, that from the hour of his arrival at Constantinople they resisted every claim which was fraught with real danger – but always resisted with courtesy – and yielded to every demand, however unjust in principle, if it seemed that they might yield with honour and safety.[11]

---

* Under Islam law, Muslims who converted to Christianity, without legal dispensation, were liable to be punished by death.

In time that came to be the accepted view – that 'entrusted with
the chief prerogative of kings and living all his time at Therapia, close
over the gates of the Bosphorus, he [Stratford] seemed to stand guard
against the North, and to answer for the safety of his charge' – but
it is not entirely accurate. While it is true that Stratford had used his
authority to solve the question of the keys and the dilapidated cupola
the real muscle had been supplied by the cabinet's decision to deploy
Dundas's squadron. More than any other factor, that was the move
which encouraged the Sultan to ignore Menshikov's demand for a
sened, and there is no evidence to suggest that Stratford subjected
the Sultan to any undue pressure. None the less, throughout the
summer of 1853, London gossip insisted that Stratford was deliberately
misrepresenting British policy. As Clarendon wrote to Cowley in Paris
on 8 July, 'my fear is that he will never consent to any arrangement
that does not humiliate the Emperor of Russia.'[12]

To those who knew him only through his office Stratford could
appear aloof and austere, a careerist who had allowed himself to
become too immersed in the shadowy world of international diplomacy and who had come to believe the myth of his omniscience. It
did not mean that he was indifferent to unkind gossip. Far from it:
he worried constantly about his relationship with Rose, whom he
mistrusted, and his dealings with the British military commanders were
not always happy. And in old age, when historians were claiming that
he had to bear some of the blame for the war with Russia, he left a
sad little note in his private papers excusing himself: 'To this charge
I would not hesitate to plead guilty if it had any foundation for the
truth. But the fact is that throughout the whole of my diplomatic
career I have been, as occasion served, an instrument of peace.'[13]
As evidence he pointed to a letter he had written to Clarendon in
May 1853 which he believed encapsulated the whole problem:

> What Russia requires of the Porte would bear a strange appear-
> ance if the principle involved in it were applied to other countries
> less anomalously situated. What would be thought in Europe if
> France or Austria were to demand a guarantee from Great Britain
> for the protection and good treatment of the Roman Catholic
> priesthood in Ireland? What if Her Majesty's Government were
> to interfere in a similar way on behalf of the Protestants in
> France? Is there a canton in Switzerland endowed with so little
> spirit and foresight as to submit without a struggle to France

asserting her right to take part in the protection of all Roman Catholic churches and priests in that country? In Turkey the dignitaries of the Greek or Ottoman church exercise in some degree the power of civil magistrates. Russia, overstepping the spiritual limit declared by herself, includes these powers in the spirit of privilege, for the ultimate maintenance of which she seeks a treaty right.[14]

In fact the solution to the impasse in Constantinople was supplied by Russia. When Turkey refused to answer Nicholas's ultimatum the order was given to the Russian southern army corps to cross the River Pruth and occupy Wallachia and Moldavia. 'So the Rubicon is passed and we must now see whether the Emperor will be more amenable inside the Principalities than out,' wrote Clarendon to Cowley on 2 July. 'I have come to the belief that he will not.' War was still not certain but the move inflamed further outbreaks of anti-Russian sentiments in the British press: as Clarendon admitted, 'Our pacific policy is at variance with public opinion, so it cannot long be persisted in.'[15]

Much of the intensity in the debate was being fanned by Henry Reeve of *The Times* who had earlier excited Rose's disgust by arguing for the partition of the Ottoman Empire. It was said of Reeve that he combined the best elements of the historian, the diplomat and the politician – he was widely travelled and enjoyed a number of close friendships with the leading politicians of his day, including, most importantly, Clarendon, with whom he had corresponded on matters of state since 1846. In 1840 he had joined the staff of *The Times* to guide its foreign policy and was one of Delane's chief leader writers. In this latter role he had a fair conceit of his abilities: when *The Times* introduced its new Applegarth presses, which were capable of printing two hundred copies per minute, Reeve visited the printing works to ponder his authority, 'for by this instrument my own thoughts and opinions are propagated and diffused over the habitable earth, with a power that seems irresistible.'[16]

At the same time he was a senior civil servant who was appointed Registrar to the Privy Council in April 1853. To read his journal is to be given an insider's guide to mid-nineteenth century society. Writers and artists were regular guests, amongst them John Millais and Anthony Trollope, but his most rewarding friendship was with Clarendon. In mid-March 1853, when Rose acted unilaterally to call up Dundas's squadron, Clarendon called Reeve to the Foreign Office to outline the dangers of escalation and to explain the government's reasons for countermanding he request. Later in the day he sent Reeve a précis of the meeting and, as a result, *The Times* urged caution in its subsequent leader:

> If there is not discretion and moderation on both sides, the whole affair may be complicated and dangerous, but there ought not to be any real difficulty; a European war over the tomb of our Saviour would be too monstrous in the nineteenth century.[17]

Throughout the crisis the foreign secretary gave him regular briefings, often over breakfast, and Reeve put the information to good use. Early in the crisis *The Times* supported Aberdeen's government but as the drama in Constantinople began to unfold Reeve's attitude started to harden. Not only did he believe that the Ottoman Empire should be partitioned and its European holdings held in trust by the great powers, but he began to criticise Russia's territorial ambitions. For that reason *The Times* supported the decision to order the fleet to Besika Bay. The support for a tougher line encouraged Palmerston to urge the Cabinet to be more decisive. On 28 June the home secretary wrote to Clarendon suggesting that Britain should warn St Petersburg that any military deployment would be countered by a British show of strength:

> I cannot help but think that such a communication would make the Emperor pause, if when he received it he had not ordered his troops to march; and would make him accessible to reason if he had ordered them to advance.[18]

Although Palmerston remained the fiercest interventionist in the Cabinet the time was not yet ripe for Aberdeen to abandon hope that Russia and Turkey would see sense, and the suggestion fell on deaf ears. Besides, the advice from Stratford was still 'the gaining of time for further negotiation with a view to peace'. Contrary to what was being said about him in London, the British ambassador to the Porte was not intent on humiliating the Russians by stiffening Turkish resolve. He understood that the rejection of Menshikov's demands had helped to fan national pride and that as a result a pro-war faction could take control of the government. In that case war with Russia would be inevitable and Britain would be drawn into it through its offer of naval support. Although Stratford was against what he called 'shilly-shally' he was hardly a warmonger and his best efforts were bent towards finding a form of words which would be acceptable to both Turkey and Russia.

Far from encouraging Turkey to continue its rejection of any Russian demand Stratford believed that the best hope for the future lay in the great powers combining their diplomatic efforts. To that end he had spoken to the ambassadors of France, Austria and Russia on 22 May and had reported back to London that 'this kind of confederacy [is] just the way to impress Constantinople'. [19] The outcome was to be the Turkish Ultimatum and this was to form the basis of a proposal known as the Vienna Note: it was the last and best chance for peace.

4

The Thousand and One Notes

I see little chance of averting war, which even in the most
sacred cause is a horrible calamity; but for such a cause as two
sets of Barbarians quarrelling over a form of words, is not only
shocking but incredible.

The Earl of Clarendon, to Sir George Cornewall Lewis,
9 October 1853

Despite the Aberdeen government's suspicions about Stratford's
real motives the general belief in the summer of 1853 was that
war could be averted and that diplomacy would settle the quarrel
between St Petersburg and Constantinople. Nicholas I's decision to
invade the principalities had been widely denounced in the British
press and by politicians such as Palmerston, but Aberdeen counselled
that it should not be considered an act of war. Following a meeting
with Nesselrode in St Petersburg Seymour reinforced his prime
minister's interpretation when he reported that 'it is now given
to be understood (for I cannot say that it is directly stated) that
the occupation of the Danubian provinces will afford a fresh and
favourable opportunity for negotiation'.[1]

Three days later Seymour discussed the situation with British
merchants working in the Russian capital. They had much to lose
if war were declared but remained confident that Russia would be
unable to afford a conflict with any European power, especially
Britain, mainly because the economy depended on foreign imports.
Not only would Russian merchant ships be at risk on the high seas
but any naval blockade of the Baltic would cut off Russia's lifeline to

the rest of the world because the Russian navy would be incapable of countering that threat.

From this point onwards Seymour started sending regular despatches to London describing Russian warship movements and the state of the Baltic fleet: a typical report, on 16 September 1853, noted an increase in its size and power, 'the broadsides of the Russian line of Battle Ships and Frigates being now as heavy as those of the Queen's Ships'. In this instance Seymour was being over-pessimistic – for all its size, the Russian navy was not on a war footing – but it was still useful intelligence. The Baltic fleet consisted of 24 capital ships plus numerous smaller gunboats in three divisions (squadrons) based at the heavily fortified bases of Kronstadt (the first and second divisions consisting of 17 ships of the line, 6 frigates and 20 armed steamers) and Sveaborg (the third division consisting of 8 ships of the line, a frigate and 3 steamers). A number of small gunboats of the rowing fleet guarded the bases at Vyborg, Rochenshalm, Riga and the Abo Skerries. Even if war did not break out it was an article of British naval policy to contain the threat of any Russian expansionism in the Baltic and, as we have seen, Admiral Sir James Graham considered the region to be integral to his contingency plans in time of war.

However, the immediate problem to be solved was the Russian military presence in the principalities. Nicholas had ordered the move to put pressure on Turkey to agree to the terms dictated by Menshikov but the invasion had also disrupted the regional strategic balance. The Austrians were displeased by the deployment because any conflict in the area would disrupt trade along the Danube, the main conduit into Europe. In theory Austria was Russia's ally and Nicholas took Vienna's support for granted, but the Austrians were now suspicious of Russian territorial intentions in the Balkans. Even so, they were in a difficult position. If they threw in their lot with Britain and France their proximity to Russia would force their army to bear the brunt of the fighting. Yet, full-blooded support for Nicholas would only make them more dependent on Russia. There was also a question of national pride. Four years earlier the Austrians had been forced to ask for Russian help in quelling an uprising by Magyar nationalists and there was a lingering sense of shame and resentment. Nicholas had forgotten the old dictum that personal indebtedness can often spoil the closest of friendships.

And so it proved. When Britain and France put pressure on the Austrians to involve themselves in the crisis they were happy to make hasty arrangements for a governmental meeting in Vienna which would 'take into consideration the question as at present in dispute with the Porte before they should be resolved by one of those five powers by force of arms'.[2] Convened by the experienced Austrian foreign minister Count Buol-Schauenstein, who had learned the art of diplomacy under the guidance of the great Count Metternich, the meeting had the twin aims of ending the Russian occupation of the principalities and of settling the dispute over the protection of the Orthodox Christian communities within the Ottoman Empire. Each was dependent on the other. Russia's invasion affected wider European interests but the withdrawal of that force depended on reaching an amicable agreement on the Russian claims to protect their co-religionists. Because France was also involved in the latter question any solution would require their approval. As Buol put it: 'We are seeking to pacify on every side and above all to avoid a European complication, which would be particularly detrimental to us'.[3]

The settlement proposed by Buol and his team was contained in a document, the Vienna Note, which was signed on 31 July and despatched immediately to Constantinople and St Petersburg. Inevitably it was a compromise in that it favoured Nicholas's contention that he had the right to be the protector of the Ottoman empire's Orthodox Christian subjects. As the tsar had long argued, these claims were justified by the treaties of Kutchuk-Kainarji and Adrianople and they had formed the basis of the demands made by Menshikov in Constantinople earlier that year. This might have been acceptable to the Porte. On 10 May Rifaat had told Menshikov that 'the Sublime Porte will devote all its attention to maintaining . . . all the religious immunities which have been spontaneously accorded and granted to its Christian subjects and particularly to the Greek subjects and monks.'[4] However he had also insisted that the Porte would never agree to any treaty which appeared to infringe Ottoman sovereignty. Unfortunately that is precisely what the Vienna Note now proceeded to do by introducing a clause which permitted both Russia and France to approve any change in Ottoman policy towards the Sultan's Christian subjects:

> The Sublime Porte, moreover, officially promises that the exist-
> ing state of things shall in no wise be modified without previous
> understanding with governments of France and Russia and
> without prejudice to the different Christian communities.[5]

Despite this apparent infringement in the Vienna Note, the initial soundings were favourable. Nicholas, to whom its contents had been revealed by Brunnov in London, was eager to accept its terms. As Seymour reported to Clarendon on 5 August the tsar had sent his acceptance by telegraph to Warsaw from whence it would be taken by *Feldjäger* [king's messenger] to Vienna:

> It is my agreeable duty to acquaint Your Lordship that upon waiting upon the Chancellor this morning, he had stated that he had the satisfaction of informing me that the Emperor signified his acceptance (acceptance pure and simple) of the Projet de Note which had been received from Vienna . . . the satisfaction at this result, at the termination of an arduous affair, which the Chancellor expressed, was very visible in his countenance . . .
>
> Count Nesselrode said a few words regarding the fresh proof offered by the Emperor of his love of peace, and for himself would only observe that it must be in my recollection that he had taken a more cheerful view of affairs from the time that intelligence had been received of the occupation of the Principalities.[6]

In other words, explained Nesselrode, by ordering the invasion of Moldavia and Wallachia Nicholas had concentrated the minds of the European powers and forced them to act as arbiters in his quarrel with Constantinople. Seymour was happy to agree with the sentiment but he ended the interview by passing on the British government's 'hope that the occupation would cease as soon as the Note should be signed'. Nesselrode was taken aback by the request. To him it smacked of British suspicions that Russia would not keep its word, and he replied that he could do nothing until the Turks themselves had signed the Note, and 'in the mean time he could only state that the Emperor was desirous that the occupation of the Principalities should not be prolonged *by one day beyond the term which was absolutely necessary*'.

A week later, in response to a request from Clarendon, Seymour inquired once more about the dangers inherent in prolonging Russia's occupation of the principalities. Nesselrode replied that Russia would only move once Turkey had signed the Note and not before. 'This does not look like a desire to protract affairs,' Count Nesselrode said. 'Now, let me proceed further. You wish to see us out of the Principalities. I beg of you not to speak to us upon that subject: we are persuaded that you are anxious to be able to withdraw your ships from Besica [sic], I entreat of you to believe that on our side we are just as desirous of leaving the Principalities. These things are better not spoken of, they will come naturally and of themselves.'[7]

Somewhat ominously, he ended the meeting by admitting that he entertained 'considerable misgivings' about the Porte's willingness to sign the new agreement. Until they did, he reiterated, the tsar was unlikely to order the withdrawal of his forces before the onset of winter made such a move impractical. Of course not, that was understandable, countered Seymour, but Nesselrode must realise that if the Note proved to be a 'non-conclusion of affairs' the British and French fleets would have no option but to enter the Dardanelles before the approach of winter storms. Once again the dangers of the military and naval deployments were becoming all too clear: neither side could withdraw them without losing face or agreeing to a mutually acceptable form of words. Even though Seymour admitted that he felt happier than at any other time during the crisis he cautioned Clarendon that peace still depended on the Porte adding its agreement to the Vienna Note.

For two weeks nothing was heard from Constantinople where there was growing resentment over outside interference in the country's domestic politics. Nicholas's rapid acceptance of the Note had encouraged Aberdeen to inform Queen Victoria on 6 August that matters seemed to be moving towards a favourable conclusion. Clarendon, too, had high hopes that the Porte would accept the compromise mainly because it headed off the threat of a forced agreement, or sened, with the Russians. The Porte, though, was in no hurry to respond but when they did, on 14 August, it came as a bombshell. Stratford was summoned by Reshid Pasha, recently reinstalled as Grand Vizier, and told that the terms of the Note were inadmissable mainly because the European powers had taken 'upon themselves to draw up a note without the knowledge of the party more immediately involved'.[8]

Not only did the Porte reject the proposal as running counter to their national interests but they demanded significant amendments to its wording. On this point Reshid refused to be moved. Considered a liberal and the main architect of reform in the Ottoman Empire, Reshid was close to Stratford but he was aware, at the same time, of the danger of appearing to be over-influenced by the western powers. Naturally, the turn of events was not to Russia's liking. Nicholas had accepted the Vienna Note with some alacrity but here were the Turks apparently abrogating an agreement brokered by the great powers and plunging Europe once more into crisis. Privately, Nicholas thought that the note should have been presented to the Porte as a *fait accompli* and that further Russian concessions would only add to Turkish insolence and make war inevitable. The tsar's thinking was revealed to Seymour by Nesselrode:

> The Note was not ours – we had no hand in drawing it up, nor indeed did it suit us, but we accepted it in the state in which it was received out of deference to the wishes of our allies and beyond this point we have not, you will allow, been encouraged to proceed.
>
> You have seen the newspapers of England, France and Germany, that in acting as we have done our motives have been misconstrued, and that we have been represented as having been compelled by the Allied Powers to abate our pretensions and to accept a compromise which is unacceptable to us.[9]

As a result, added the chancellor, the tsar would write to the British government through Brunnov rejecting the Turkish demands and insisting that Russian forces would remain in the principalities. Ending his despatch to Clarendon, Seymour gloomily remarked that the Porte's rejection of the Vienna Note had had 'the untoward effect of completely inverting the positions of the Emperor and the Sultan in the estimation of my diplomatic colleagues'. Whereas earlier in the year Nicholas had been widely criticised for threatening Constantinople, now the Porte was being blamed for refusing to accept a compromise peace settlement.

In London, though, Clarendon was quite certain who should shoulder the bulk of the blame. Stratford. To some extent he understood the difficulties of the British ambassador's position. During an earlier appointment as in Ireland Clarendon knew only too well the problems faced by the man on the spot and the difficulties of getting the Cabinet to understand the complexities of any distant situation, but from the very beginning of the negotiations he had doubted if the British ambassador would remain neutral. On 29 August that distrust seemed to be confirmed when Cowley passed on information from a confidential despatch written by de la Cour, the new French ambassador in Constantinople:

Lord Stratford has obeyed his instructions and called upon the
Ottoman government to accept the Vienna Note, but he lets it
be seen at the same time that his private opinion is at variance
with his official language, and he does not bring that personal
influence to bear which would have been so useful at the present
moment.[10]

Without any contemporary evidence to describe Stratford's deport-
ment during his discussions with the Porte the French ambassador's
observations have to be taken at face value. Certainly Stratford was
used to getting his own way with the Sultan, but in this instance de
la Cour was wrong to suggest that his British opposite number had
unduly influenced the Porte. (In any case, the French ambassador was
involved in secret meetings to encourage the Turks to resist Russian
demands.) Rather, the failure of policy lay in the Vienna Note itself.
No government worth its salt would agree to its terms and Reshid
was right to complain that the terms of the Note ran counter to
Turkey's interests. He and his fellow counsellors also knew that they
could count on the intervention of British and French warships in the
event of further Russian pressure. They were also encouraged by the
favourable reports from their ambassador in London which spoke of
a rising tide of popular support for the Turkish cause.

When he presented the Note Stratford might well have offered
subtle hints that its terms were unacceptable but such subterfuge was
unnecessary. The Porte, stiffened by the promise of Franco-British
naval support, was united in its resolve to reject the peace terms.
Clarendon, though, continued to insist that Stratford was to blame.
Ideally, he would have liked to sack him and replace him with Cowley
but that would have weakened the Paris embassy at a time when it
was essential to retain good relations with Napoleon III. He also
suspected that Stratford coveted his own job and might resign to
involve himself in politics at home. If that were to happen Aberdeen's
coalition would almost certainly collapse, leaving the field open to
Palmerston or Russell:

Stratford throughout has been and will be our great stumbling
block. His conduct in exciting the Turks has been bad, but the
course he pursues towards his colleagues is worse – he mistrusts
them with or without a cause, shows them no confidence, and
then if they don't confide in him and venture to do anything

off their own bats, or in obedience to their instructions, he fires up, and complains and thwarts them in every direction. I am always expecting his resignation with a fine flaming despatch for the Blue Book, which said book he has evidently had his eye on for a long time past.[11]

Throughout the summer Clarendon confided his fears about Stratford to Cowley in Paris and in some frustration pointed out that he could find nothing in the Vienna Note which ran contrary to Turkey's interests. However, by the middle of September he was coming to the conclusion that the Russians might be the real troublemakers. A few days before writing to Cowley he admitted to Reeve of *The Times* that, despite his earlier doubts, Stratford had 'honourably endeavoured to get the Note accepted and that we have no cause to complain about that'. This marked a sea-change in the foreign secretary's policy. Reeve was about to leave for Constantinople – where he would meet Stratford – and he left with the distinct impression that British attitudes towards Russia were hardening. On 12 September Clarendon revealed his growing fears to another old friend and confidant who was both politician and man of letters, Sir George Cornewall Lewis, the distinguished editor of the *Edinburgh Review*:

We can't press the Turks too hard about the Note – 1st because public opinion at home would be against it, and 2nd, because, if we did, they would certainly refuse and say they would fight it out single handed. We should still have to help them because otherwise Russia would be established at Constantinople in twelvemonth.[12]

One reason for the change of heart was Clarendon's dawning realisation that the promises of naval support had strengthened the Porte's opposition to Russia and that Britain would have no option but to honour them. Another was the publication in the Berlin newspaper, *Zeit*, of comments by Nesselrode which suggested a more 'violent interpretation' of the Vienna Note than its authors had anticipated. It took the form of a letter from the Russian chancellor to his ambassador in Berlin of 26 August and was published in *The Times* on 22 September:

It is for Austria and the Powers to declare to the Porte, frankly and firmly, that they, after having in vain opened up to it the only road that could lead to an immediate retraction of its relations with us, henceforth leave the task to itself alone. We believe, that as soon as the Powers unanimously hold this language to the Porte, the Turks will yield to the advice of Europe, and, instead of reckoning on her assistance in a struggle with Russia, will accept the Note in its present form, and cease to compromise their position so seriously for the childish satisfaction of having altered a few expressions in a document which we had accepted without discussion. For of these two positions only one is possible – either the alterations which the Porte requires are unimportant, in which case it is very simple that we refuse to accede to them; or they are important, and then the question arises, why should the Porte unnecessarily make its acceptance dependent on them?

Instead of being allowed to advise on Turkish policy towards the Orthodox Christians Nesselrode insisted that the terms of the Note would allow Russia to interfere directly on behalf of their rights and privileges. This went beyond the demands made by Menshikov earlier in the year and as Clarendon told Seymour, 'even Nesselrode himself would admit that we can no longer recommend the Vienna Note to the Porte':

It would now be highly dishonourable to press its acceptance to the Porte, when they have been duly warned by the Power [Russia] to whom the Note is to be addressed that another and totally different meaning is to be attached to it by that power.[13]

Seymour was equally gloomy about the unfolding situation. In a final attempt to broker a solution Buol had produced another version of the Vienna Note which tempered Russian claims to interfere directly in the affairs of the Ottoman Empire but it, too, was stillborn. Nicholas and Nesselrode travelled to Olmütz to discuss a compromise agreement embodied in a diplomatic *projet d'note* with the Austrian foreign minister and the Emperor Franz Josef, as well as the ambassadors of Britain, France and Prussia, but Seymour was not convinced that anything would come of the conference. Although both Austria and Prussia were dubious about Russian expansionism, especially in the Balkans — where they themselves hoped to gain spheres of influence — neither was in any position to influence events at Constantinople. As Seymour told Clarendon after the Russian entourage had left St Petersburg for Berlin on 13 September en route to Olmütz, the tsar was now only interested in the fate of the Sick Man of Europe and would agree to almost any note which did not compromise Russia's position:

> The Emperor is possessed, I really believe conscientiously possessed, with the notion that the fall of the Turkish empire being inevitable, and the idea is one which is uppermost in his thoughts that he appears unable to restrain himself from speaking of it to all those who approach him.[14]

When he reached Olmütz, though, the tsar appeared to change his tune. During a relaxed meeting with the Earl of Westmorland, the British ambassador to Vienna, he told him that, while he was keen to protect the interests of the Greek Church, he wanted 'nothing which could in any way prejudice the independence or the rights of the Sultan, or which would imply a desire to interfere with the internal affairs of the Porte'.[15] Westmorland was not fooled by the change of tack: the tsar was evidently happy to compromise for the good reason that any agreement with the European powers would allow him to increase pressure on Turkey for the right of protecting the Orthodox Christians. (Even at that stage he was convinced that neither Britain nor France would be in a position to offer Turkey any worthwhile military protection.)

At the tsar's request Buol produced a new proposal which would see the Russians withdrawing from the principalities once the Turks had agreed to the Vienna Note. After this latest plan had been accepted by Russia and Austria it was presented to the British and French ambassadors, but by then there was a weary acceptance within the British camp that confrontation with Russia was perhaps inevitable. On 20 September Turkey officially rejected Buol's *projet d'note* and four days later Clarendon confided to Stratford, 'the only likelihood now is war'. In the same despatch he authorised the British ambassador to call up Dundas's squadron to Constantinople where it would lie off the Golden Horn to offer protection to the Sultan. A few days later the French followed suit, with command of their squadron being given to Admiral Hamelin.

Initially, Napoleon III had been minded to accept the new version and to put pressure on the Sultan to accept it, but Aberdeen would have none of it. It reawakened the old fear that Turkey would be unable to withstand Russia, Constantinople would fall, and Russia would command the Straits and thereby gain access to the Mediterranean. At the back of Aberdeen's mind, too, was the fear that France would use the opportunity to pursue its own territorial ambitions in the region and he was determined to prevent that. Here Cowley was useful. The British ambassador enjoyed a good relationship with the emperor and was soon able to report that the French recognised the validity of the Porte's objections to the original Vienna Note and the *projet d'note* prepared by Buol:

> The Emperor's object in sending the French fleet into Turkish waters was to aid in maintaining the integrity and independence of the Ottoman Empire. That right is still uppermost in his mind and although His Majesty regrets the failure of the negotiations which have taken place and would willingly have pursued them further had there been a chance of a successful issue to them, His Majesty recognises that a persistence in them would be useless in the present temper of the Turkish government.[16]

There was still a slight chance that peace might hold. On 6 October Aberdeen told the Queen that while 'it may be very agreeable to humiliate the Emperor of Russia', he was of the opinion that 'it is paying a little too dear for this pleasure, to check the progress and prosperity of this happy country, and to cover Europe with confusion, misery and blood'. Victoria was inclined to agree: she had long warned of the dangers of becoming 'dupes of Russian policy' and she was opposed to any policy which might drag her country into war. With that in mind the prime minister told Graham to prepare for a defensive war which would involve the Royal Navy in the Dardanelles and the Baltic while French land forces, backed perhaps by British finance, would take part in any land operations on Turkish soil. There were also hurried and increasingly frenetic attempts to find a solution through diplomatic lines of communication and despatches hurried between the capitals of Europe. 'When everyone else is dead I intend to write an Oriental romance to be called *Les mille et une notes*,' quipped Stratford's secretary as another despatch reached him from London, Paris, Vienna or St Petersburg.

By then, though, the diplomatic efforts were being overtaken by events – as Aberdeen had feared. Despite the flurry of political activity the Porte declared a state of war on 4 October by delivering an ultimatum to the Russians to quit the principalities within a fortnight. Stratford did his best to get the Porte 'to hold back its manifesto and summons as long as it possibly could do', but they knew only too well that the White Ensigns of the Royal Navy's battle squadron were near at hand to check the tsar's ambitions. 'Things get worser and worser,' Clarendon told his wife. 'The beastly Turks have actually declared war.'

His displeasure was not misplaced. At that stage Clarendon was still unsure about the wisdom of being sucked into a war on Turkey's behalf but when the Cabinet met to discuss the situation on 7 October it fell to him to provide a lead. During the year he had enlivened cabinet meetings by providing running commentaries on the ambassadors' despatches and by all accounts had proved a good mimic. The Duke of Argyll, no mean orator himself, remembered that 'his readings of the character of each diplomatist were as good as a play, and were a real help in enabling us to judge how far we could trust each separate estimate of the situation at the separate courts'.

On this occasion, though, Clarendon's thespian skills were over-shadowed by the claims of *realpolitik*. Palmerston continued to argue that Britain's policy should be 'the Relinquishment by Russia of inadmissable Pretensions and her Retirement from Turkish Terri-tory' and that the Royal Navy should enforce those aims. Russell, too, was in bellicose mood: a memorandum to Aberdeen proposed immediate naval operations against Russia in the Baltic and the Black Seas. This had the support of *The Times* which was now fully engaged in promoting a more robust foreign policy. It reminded its readers of Britain's naval superiority and proposed that, to protect the country's honour, 'we are not ashamed to show what we *can* do, if the occasion should unhappily require it'. Only Gladstone continued to argue a pacific line. The trouble was that Aberdeen's cabinet, itself an uneasy coalition, was still hopelessly divided, and once more it adopted a compromise. Under Clarendon's guidance it was agreed that, in the event of a Russian attack against Turkey, Dundas's ships should be allowed to enter the Black Sea.

Aberdeen thought it was a sensible solution but it sent alarm bells ringing at Balmoral in the Scottish Highlands where Queen Victoria and her court were spending the autumn. On 10 October Prince

Albert produced a sombre memorandum which summed up all his wife's misgivings about the direction of Britain's foreign policy: 'The Queen might now be involved in war, of which the consequences could not be calculated, chiefly by the desire of Lord Aberdeen to keep his Cabinet together; this might then break down, and the Queen would be left without an efficient Government, and a war on her hands.' Sir James Graham was also at Balmoral, and he went even further, asking Aberdeen if he fully understood the dangers of offering such unqualified naval support to the Turks: 'Are we bound in that case to be dragged into hostilities by a Barbarian whom we are unable to control?'[17]

It was a question which the prime minister could not answer. Throughout the crisis Aberdeen, and to a lesser extent Clarendon, had made little secret of their detestation of Ottoman rule, yet by the end of the first week of October they had aligned Britain to support Turkey in any conflict which might break out with Russia. It was a muddled progress which would become even more confused as autumn turned into winter.

5

Phoney War

The task which is imposed upon Her Majesty's Government
of preserving Turkey from injury, or it may be, absorption, and
of averting war from Europe is one of the most honorable and
arduous which could be undertaken.

Sir George Hamilton Seymour to the Earl of Clarendon,
12 November 1853

Turkey's declaration demanding the removal of the Russian forces
from the principalities was met with scant surprise in St Petersburg. Not only had it been long expected but the diplomatic community seemed to be resigned to its being not a case of avoiding
hostilities but when they would commence. Seymour believed the
war was inevitable and even if the 'thousand and one notes' prompted
by the Olmütz proposals could be redrafted to both parties' satisfaction the result would 'bear the character rather of a truce than
of a renewed peace.' On 4 October he wrote a long and gloomy
despatch to Clarendon forecasting an impending 'interruption of that
peace which Europe has enjoyed for the last forty years'.[1]

His mood was not helped by the unseasonal weather in the Russian
capital. Two days earlier, on Sunday 2 October, St Petersburg had
been shaken by a mighty storm whose intensity had threatened to
break the banks of the River Neva. The wind blew from the north
for the best part of the day and, according to Seymour's anxious report
to the Foreign Office, it 'increased in violence after midnight to such
a degree that it became probable that a great part of the town would
be laid under water'. Fortunately, the wind abated in the early hours

of the morning but when dawn broke the bridges over the Neva were seen to be impassable to traffic and on some of them the iron lamp posts had been bent and 'even broken off'.

Seymour was too sanguine a man to make any Shakespearean connection between the disorder in the heavens and the impending collision between Russia and Turkey but he admitted to Clarendon that it had been a night of 'great anxiety'.

> Now as before I believe that His Majesty began this deplorable quarrel, and even took military possession of the Principalities, neither with the idea of over-running the rest of Turkey, of adding to his already overgrown possession, or of involving himself in disputes with his allies; but I cannot doubt that His Majesty entertains most exaggerated ideas as to the influence to which he is entitled in the country of a feeble but independent Sovereign, and that the time is fully come when some demonstration must be made which will have the effect of shewing where the limits to his authority are traced.[2]

For that reason he expressed considerable satisfaction that the government had given orders for the joint British and French fleet to sail from Besika Bay into the Golden Horn as a 'barrier . . . opposed to Russian ambitions'. However, within a week the imminence of war was once more uppermost in his mind. On 10 October he met de Castelbajac who showed him a despatch from Paris which said that a conflict was certain unless Nicholas succumbed to pressure from Austria or Prussia during his visit to both countries. (The despatch also revealed that senior French army officers had been ordered not to accept an invitation to a Russian military review held by the tsar to mark his visit to Warsaw.) Although Seymour was impressed by the French resolve to maintain 'the integrity and independence of the Ottoman Empire', he wondered if it would hold once hostilities broke out. Once again, in his subsequent report to Clarendon, he questioned whether de Castelbajac's admiration for Nicholas would cloud his judgement and therefore weaken Franco-British solidarity in St Petersburg. It was amusing to hear the French Minister indiscreetly admit that Nicholas had started calling Napoleon III 'Der Kerl' (the fellow) but, wondered Seymour, was that really the right way for one sovereign to describe another? Moreover, should Napoleon III's ambassador in

St Petersburg have been retailing the gossip to his British opposite number?

However, the meeting did reveal one interesting piece of information. According to the advice of the Quai d'Orsay, when the conflict did come 'it had better be directed in the first instance against the South-Eastern provinces of Russia because it was in that quarter that she is most vulnerable'.[3] It was the first time that anyone had bruited the possibility of a land campaign on the Russian mainland, let alone in the Crimea: at the time British and French assistance was confined to the naval protection of Constantinople and the Dardanelles. Back in London, though, Clarendon did not comment on Seymour's intelligence and the matter was allowed to drop. That same day he had received a despatch from Cowley confirming that the limit of French assistance would be the deployment of Admiral Hamelin's squadron to maintain 'the integrity and independence of the Ottoman empire' and that seemed to settle the strategic issue for the time being.

During the period following Turkey's declaration Seymour fluctuated wildly between a belief that war was inescapable and a feeling that Britain could broker an honourable agreement which would not only prevent a war but limit Russia's 'easternmost' ambitions. On 14 October he was in good spirits following a meeting with Nesselrode who assured him that Russia would not provide a *casus belli* by beginning offensive operations, and that Nicholas was keen to wait for a peaceful solution. Two weeks later, after fighting had started, this position would be reinforced in a diplomatic circular to all the main embassies in St Petersburg but Seymour was the first ambassador to be apprised of Russian intentions.

The tsar's apparent unwillingness to open the offensive certainly suited Aberdeen who had told Palmerston that he regarded war with Russia 'with the utmost incredulity'. Although British public opinion was largely in favour of aiding Turkey and halting Russia, the prime minister still hoped to avert war. On 10 and 12 October the Cabinet met to discuss a draft note by Clarendon which would put pressure on the Porte to agree to a truce. Based on a memorandum by Stratford – who had used all his ingenuity to persuade the Sultan not to start hostile operations – it called for a breathing space to allow further discussions to take place between Russia and Turkey:

Considering the assurances of support already given to the

measures actually adopted by Great Britain for the protection
of Turkish territory, it is indispensable that all further progress
of hostilities should be suspended for a reasonable time during
the course of the negotiations in which Her Majesty's Government are engaged for the re-establishment of friendly relations
between the Porte and Russia upon the understanding that no
hostile movement is made upon the part of Russia.[4]

As Nesselrode had already assured Seymour that Russia was anxious
to avoid war the Cabinet's Note seemed to offer an olive branch.
However, despite Stratford's ministrations the Porte only agreed to
a temporary truce: not only did they insist on Russia leaving the
principalities but, as Stratford warned in a despatch of 5 October,
they believed that most of Europe supported them in their aim:

It must be admitted that the Porte has had reason to derive an
increase of courage from circumstances which have occurred
since the departure of Prince Menschikoff. She has seen the
Four Powers acting together on her behalf. She has heard the
voice of all Europe condemning her adversary. She perceives that
the public sentiment of England and France is almost universally
in her favour. She hears from all sides that the occupation of the
Principalities by Russia constitutes a cause of war; and she has
not only put herself into a state of respectable defence, but she
has appealed with perfect success to the zeal of her Mussulmen
and to the loyalty of her Christian subjects.[5]

In St Petersburg the tsar cautiously welcomed the British initiative
but his protestations of peace were becoming increasingly thin. Now
aged fifty-seven, he had ruled for some thirty years and in that time
had come to believe that the absolute nature of his monarchy placed
him beyond doubt or blame. 'In his painful indecision, his religious
scruples on one hand, and his humanitarian scruples on the other; in his
wounded pride, in the face of national feeling and the dangers which
pursue his empire; in the violent struggle with these various feelings,
the Emperor Nicholas has aged ten years,' noted de Castlebajac.
'He is truly sick, physically and morally.' The French ambassador
added that Nicholas had allowed himself to be over-influenced
by the pan-Slavists, ultra-nationalists who dreamed of the creation

of a Greco-Russian Orthodox Empire which would control both
Muscovy and the Ottoman Empire. Because this was anathema to the
chancellor, Nesselrode was slowly being sidelined from the evolution
of Russia's policy towards the Porte. Seymour had been informed of
countless intrigues to oust the chancellor from office but he still clung
to the hope that Nesselrode would be powerful enough to influence
Nicholas's thinking.

Without him in office Seymour's access to the tsar would be
circumscribed and throughout October he made a point of keeping in
constant touch with Nesselrode in an attempt to determine Nicholas's
thinking. This proved to be no easy matter. As 1853 drew to a close
the tsar's attitudes towards Britain seemed to be hardening: gone was
the harmony which had attended his January talks with the British
ambassador and in its place was a new feeling that he was being
humiliated by the British. Not only were they guilty of 'interference in
an affair which belonged only to the Russians' but they were dragging
France along in their coat-tails. 'The blind hate of the English knows
no limits . . .' Nicholas told his sister Anna. 'It seems Louis Napoleon
had condemned himself to march at their bidding.'[6]

However, Seymour still clung to the hope that something could
be salvaged from the wreckage. Earlier in the year he had used
nautical imagery to describe the impasse when he told Clarendon
that Nicholas had allowed the 'vessel of state' to 'run upon a bank' and
that it was his and Nesselrode's intention to undo the damage. What
he failed to understand was that Nesselrode, now seventy-three, was
gradually being out-manoeuvered at court. None the less, with his
long experience of European politics and his innate understanding
of Britain's position the Russian chancellor remained Seymour's last
best hope. Early in the evening of 14 October the two men enjoyed
a further private discussion which Seymour reported in great detail
to Clarendon:

Nesselrode proceeded to speak with much feeling of the horrors
of war in general – particularly of one between two powerful
countries, two old allies like England and Russia, countries
which, whilst they might be of infinite use to one another, possessed each the means of inflicting great injury upon its antagon-
ist, and ended by saying that if for any motives known to him war
should be declared against Russia by England it would be the
most unintelligible and the least justifiable war ever undertaken.[7]

Nesselrode also confirmed that Russian field commanders in the Danubian principalities had been ordered not to commence offensive operations and had been told to negotiate with their Turkish opposite numbers should a local truce be declared. By way of response Seymour confirmed that Britain was actively engaged in calming Turkish fears and that even as they spoke Stratford 'has been labouring to arrest the progress of war and according to the news from Constantinople . . . has actually determined the Porte to an armistice'. Having weathered the summer row which threatened to undermine his position in Constantinople the Great Elchi was continuing his attempts to force the Sultan to agree to a truce followed by international arbitration. Although the hope was faint he told Clarendon on 21 October that he had been encouraged by a note from Reshid Pasha agreeing to postpone the commencement of hostilities. In the same despatch, though, he voiced his fears that in the long term this concession would not hold unless the Russians could be persuaded to withdraw:

It seems to me almost impossible in the present state of affairs that any proposition short of a complete surrender of the Russian views should be able to avert the declaration of hostilities. It is not reasonable, though less satisfactory, to look forward to the natural effects of the approaching season [winter] for some opportunity not indeed of preventing war, but of restoring peace before any considerable loss may have been sustained by either side.[8]

This, too, was Seymour's hope: that 'this unhappy quarrel' could be solved before winter called a halt to the campaigning season. However, in common with his colleague at the Porte he was afraid that Nicholas would never agree to withdraw his forces from the principalities. Although Nesselrode had assured him that Nicholas welcomed the involvement of the European powers in finding a diplomatic solution, the tsar was not prepared to be humiliated and would not withdraw from the principalities merely to comply with requests from Britain and France.

Inevitably, perhaps, that intransigence was to lead to war. Two days after Reshid Pasha had assured Stratford that hostilities would be postponed Turkish forces took the initiative. On 29 October Stratford sent a further despatch to Clarendon advising him that fighting had already broken out. Turkish troops under the command of Omar Pasha had crossed the Danube into Wallachia and had taken up a strong position along the northern side of the eastern frontier between Kalafat and Ruschuk. Initially there was only skirmishing between the two forces but first blood was drawn by the Turks on 2 November at the Danubian island of Oltenitsa. This was a heavily defended Turkish position covered by artillery and the first Russian attack was easily beaten off. Although both sides reinforced their positions the Russian 4th Corps, commanded by General Dannenberg, was forced to retire towards Bucharest. Further Russian attempts to cross the Danube were halted by Turkish successes at Macin, Kalafat and Giugevo and the Russian forces were soon in disarray. Gratifying though these victories were to the Turks, Stratford gloomily, but perceptively, predicted that they were but an overture to a much large conflict:

> It requires but little sagacity to perceive that the war which has all but commenced is likely to prove a contest of no ordinary importance and perhaps of no ordinary duration. The Porte is bringing forward all the remains of its strength, and together with the nation, feels that the issue of the struggle must determine its future destiny. It is evident, on the other side, that Russia, weary of a precarious and disputed influence in the Levant will exert its colonial force to secure a complete and recognised supremacy.[9]

When the news of the fighting reached St Petersburg Seymour hurried to visit Nesselrode who advised him that if the war led to the dissolution of the Ottoman Empire 'its reconstruction would be found impracticable.' It was a dismal meeting very different in tone from one held five days earlier, on 18 October, when Nesselrode had furnished the kind of gossip which allowed Seymour to have a clearer idea of the finer points of court politics. He admitted that it had been a mistake to send Menshikov to Constantinople, that he lacked tact, and that the silver-tongued Orlov might have been a better choice. (Later that day Seymour discussed the matter with Orlov who sarcastically claimed that his rival, as he himself had forecast, had allowed himself 'to depend too much, or to be too much restricted by his instructions.')

Demonstrating the diplomatic smoothness for which he was renowned, Nesselrode then took the opportunity to introduce some unwelcome information: that he had been told that all was not well with the relationship between Britain and France. Such a situation would have suited Nicholas who still clung to the hope that Britain might be separated from French interests in the Ottoman Empire but Seymour merely nodded and said that he too was aware of the rumours and counter-rumours which were sweeping through St Petersburg. At the end of the month, though, he informed Clarendon that he had been told by 'an impeccable authority' that France and the Netherlands were colluding to partition Belgium 'at some future and opportune moment' and that such a move would inevitably lead to war between Britain and France because Britain was bound by a treaty of 1839 to guarantee Belgium's neutrality. The story had its origins in the correspondence between Nicholas and his sister in the Netherlands but Seymour dismissed it as the repetition of earlier fears for, in April 1852, there had been genuine concern that France was on the point of seizing Belgium but had been forced to back down by Britain.

It was not just in St Petersburg that the rumour machine was working overtime. On 24 October Cowley told Clarendon that the Russian embassy had been spreading similar stories:

> Both here and in St Petersburg it seems to be the game of Russia to endeavour to make it appear that England is dragging France in her wake for her own interests and specious warnings are given to the latter to be on her guard, for that the day will come when Great Britain, having secured the best bargain she can for herself, will leave France to get out of the difficulties of the situation as best she can.[10]

This, too, seemed to be part of Nicholas's policy of planting seeds of doubt and discord but, like Seymour, Cowley would have none of it. Having reported the matter to Clarendon he advised that it be ignored as nothing more than 'miserable gossip'.

Of greater import to both ambassadors were Russian hints that any declaration of war against them by the European powers would inevitably harm relations with the United States of America. Nicholas had also let it be known that he would favour an American solution to the row over the Holy Places and was happy for them to act as mediators. Both were serious considerations. While the US had not yet emerged as a major industrial power to rival Britain (and would not do so until the period of reconstruction which followed the American Civil War), relations between the two countries were in one of their seasonal troughs. A long-running dispute over the boundaries of Oregon territory had not been agreed until 1846 and there was continuing concern in London about US territorial claims over Canada. In 1845 the journalist John L. O'Sullivan, editor of the *Democratic Review*, coined the phrase 'Manifest Destiny' to describe his country's territorial ambitions: that it was 'our manifest destiny to overspread the continent allotted by Providence for the free development of our yearly multiplying millions'. This would include not only taking possession of Texas and California but also of Canada and the countries of the Caribbean.

Although it was a settled assumption of British foreign policy, especially since the war of 1812, that a war with the US would be more trouble than it was worth, the relationship between London and Washington was never particularly easy throughout the nineteenth century. With their own country still undeveloped and with large tracts of open land beckoning, most Americans did not concern themselves with foreign affairs. They also retained a healthy suspicion of John Bull and British imperial motives, yet the more astute politicians understood that America's continental isolation was dependent in part on British support. The ships of the Royal Navy kept the sealanes free and Britain supported the Monroe Doctrine which allowed the US to have hegemony of the New World allied to the premise that it would not interfere in the affairs of Europe. The arrangement suited London perfectly for, as long as it worked, the colonial pretensions of the French or the Spanish could be kept at bay. Any dislocation in the arrangment would undoubtedly be to Britain's disadvantage. For that reason Cowley was disconcerted by a report from Madrid containing 'curious details respecting the demeanour and language of Monsieur Soulé, the new Minister for the United States to Spain':

Monsieur Soulé stated that there were but two Nations in the world of any real importance, the United States and Russia – that everybody else was rotten (pourri) and that all other nations must, for their own safety, seek an alliance with one or other of these Leviathans.[11]

Pierre Soulé was an emigré French republican who had taken American citizenship and entered politics to become the influential senator for Louisiana. He was hardly likely to feel any friendship towards France or indeed Spain whose kings he referred to as 'tyrants', yet against the odds he had been selected as the US Minister in Madrid. When the ambassadorial choices were being being made by President Franklin Pierce in March 1853 Soulé had let it be known that if he could not get Madrid he would plump for St Petersburg. However, the idea was vetoed by Nesselrode who acted on his Washington ambassador's warning that the Louisianan had a 'well-established reputation of bright red republicanism'.

A firebrand with a quick temper and a tendency for melodrama, he was unsuited to be the head of a diplomatic mission. Shortly after his arrival he wounded and crippled the French ambassador, the Marquis de Turgot, in a duel following an unkind comment about his wife's décolletage and he made open contact with Spanish republicans. But there was more than mischief-making in his actions. At the time the US was in favour of seizing Cuba from the Spanish – a move which was opposed by Britain, France and Spain following the signing of the Tripartite Convention in 1852. As Cowley told Clarendon in a later despatch dated 3 November 1853 the unrest in Europe could prevent the allies from combining to halt US expansionism: 'It is not in my humble opinion improbable that Monsieur Soulé's bombastic tone at Madrid may have its source in the knowledge that the Eastern Question has produced an intimacy, inimical to Great Britain, between his own country and Russia.'[12]

Clarendon took heed of the warning from Paris and wrote to the US Minister in London, James Buchanan, advising him that Britain could not stand by and allow the US to expand its possessions by purchasing or seizing Cuba. Inevitably the despatch brought an angry response from Buchanan who asked 'why England should object to our annexation; we extended the English language, Christianity, liberty, and law wherever we went on our own continent'.[13] All might have been well had Cuba been the only point of disagreement but London was already engaged in a long-standing dispute over the possession of Nicaragua and the Mosquito Coast Protectorates. The year before had seen a confrontation between a British and a US warship off the Bay Islands, after the bombardment of the British settlement at Greytown; now Clarendon was forced to warn the Cabinet that if Cuba were invaded Britain would almost certainly find itself at war with the US.

However, for the time being, this transatlantic squabble was a sideline to the main issue. With the fighting in the principalities confined to skirmishing along the Danube there was still some hope that a peaceful outcome could be engineered. The ever-hopeful Buol had convened another meeting of ambassadors in Vienna to draft a further mediation proposal which might prove acceptable to the Porte. That was certainly Aberdeen's wish and, echoing the queen's misgivings, he warned the Cabinet not to be lured into a confrontation 'the consequences of which cannot be foreseen and may be most calamitous'.

The prime minister distrusted both the bellicose warnings being sounded by Russell and Palmerston and the increasingly shrill note of the British press that Russian expansionism had to be halted. Here he was heartened by reports from Cowley in Paris that Napoleon III's ardour for military glory was once more cooling, and that he was coming round to the belief that a diplomatic triumph could strengthen his own, and France's, international reputation. But Aberdeen was fighting a rearguard action. Clarendon insisted that the latest Buol plan would not be accepted because Britain could not support any proposal which was unacceptable to the Turks.

With very little news coming from the war zone on the Danube, Seymour spent much of his time comparing notes with the French ambassador, de Castelbajac, of whom he said, 'a better man in his private capacity, or a more obliging colleague in his official capacity I never met with'. Because communications with the principalities were poor – on account of the distance and the paucity of the transport system – news from the battlefront took time to reach St Petersburg and the two ambassadors decided to pool their information. Even so the information they received was scant and Seymour was forced into dependence on news in the *Journal de Saint-Petersbourg*, copies of which were sent on to Clarendon. Not that he accepted the news wholesale. When news arrived of a major Russian naval victory – the sinking of an Egyptian sailing ship by a Russian warship under the command of Kornilov – he passed on the information with the disdain which any former naval cadet might feel for such an ill-earned success:

As regards his [Kornilov's success] on the late occurrence I imagine it to have been such as must attend any commander who with a stout English-built steamer (the *Vladimir*) and with a crew capable of pointing a ten-inch gun should engage a vessel of the force of the captured Egyptian.[14]

Although his naval career had been stillborn – the jibe against

Kornilov could be forgiven because few observers held the Russian navy in any high regard – Seymour was aware of the importance of the Black Sea to Russian strategy. Without control of its waters Prince Michael Gorchakov's position on the Danube was insecure. First, the Russian forts in the Caucasus could not be reinforced and their garrisons could become untenable if a Turkish fleet were free to transport land forces and supplies across the Black Sea from Constantinople. Second, it was also possible that the Turks would use the sea to reinforce their army in the principalities and that in the event of all-out war Britain and France would use their naval superiority to land their own forces in the region, probably at Varna. Should Austria then decide to attack across the Wallachian frontier Gorchakov's forces would be caught in a unprisable pincer.

For that reason Seymour continued to press Nesselrode on Britain's determination to use its naval power to protect its interests, reminding him on 16 November that these were not just in the Black Sea region but also included the routes to India:

> England has interests which make it extremely desirable that even the Easternmost limits of Russia should not be extended, since every step taken by a Russian Army in an Easternmost direction brings it nearer to the Indies.[15]

Seymour's comment was central to Britain's position as the world's leading power. To maintain that primacy the government relied on the Royal Navy to guard its oceanic trade routes and to protect its more vulnerable imperial holdings. The one exception was India. Its northern frontier was shared with China and Russia and, while no threat was perceived from the former, the Foreign Office greatly feared the latter's intentions. Recent increases in Russia's own imperial holdings in Bokhara and Kiva had strengthened these fears and fifteen years earlier British lives had been lost in an attempt to preserve Afghanistan as a buffer state to forestall Russian ambitions. For that reason the British were rightly concerned about any Russian move into the Ottoman Empire.

Nesselrode, too, was well aware of the relevance of British sea power and he was anxious to avoid its use in the enforcement of a trading embargo. On 11 November he asked Seymour if Britain would hold up the delivery of rails for the St Petersburg railway which was under construction. The response was crucial as Russia depended on British industrial expertise and Seymour was suitably circumspect. Unless sanctions were instituted against Russia, he conjectured, there would be no interruption to trade between the two countries. A month later, though, on 5 December he was forced to change his tune: Nesselrode was told that 'in the event of hostilites breaking out, very effectual blockades would be established'.[16]

By that time the two countries were drifting inexorably towards war. The Turkish military successes had emboldened the Porte sufficiently to ignore Stratford's Note and Seymour reported from Russia that Nicholas now accepted that the rest of the world was ranged against him. Even Nesselrode 'was at a loss' when he met him on 26 November:

> Count Nesselrode observed that it appeared that it was a fixed resolution on the part of Her Majesty's Government to find fault with every act of the Russian cabinet – Russia had been accused in the most violent manner from every quarter and when her voice was heard in reply a shout was raised against her. It comes really to this – all that was done by Russia was wrong, all that was done by the Porte was right.[17]

The following day Britain and France cemented Russian pessimism about their neutrality by concluding a defensive alliance with Turkey and, with the joint fleet already in the Bosphorus – the warships had arrived on 24 November – it was becoming increasingly difficult for Aberdeen to continue hoping that the peace might be kept. Three weeks earlier, on 4 November, he had told Palmerston that 'peace is still our object' but by the end of the month he was finding it difficult to keep his Cabinet together. Palmerston was openly opposed to any policy which smacked of appeasement and within and without parliament his bellicose statements were met with acclaim. 'Peace is an Excellent Thing & war a great Misfortune,' he declared, echoing Polybius. 'But there are many things more valuable than Peace and many Things Much worse than war.'[18] Russell, too, was opposed to Aberdeen's policy, and even Clarendon had thrown in his lot with the war party within the Cabinet.

Whipped up by sections of the press, most notably *The Times* and the *Morning Post*, war fever gripped the country. Small wonder that the normally phlegmatic Aberdeen said that 'in a case of this kind I dread public support'. Only a miracle, or at least only a determined diplomatic effort, could avoid a calamity and time was running out.

6

The Affair at Sinope

Know that we have against your force
And against your barbaric fleet
Both ships with white wings
And paddle steamers!
And our sailors no less than yours
So inured to the varying elements.
And where numbers may be wanting
Russian hardihood will triumph!
'Hurrah!', popular song composed in honour of the great
Russian naval victory at Sinope, Journal de Saint-Petersbourg,
19 December 1853

Even before the crisis began Russia was considered to be the largest military power in Europe, its army the heirs of the men who had stopped Napoleon in his tracks in 1812. On paper at least there was much to the conceit, but the reality was somewhat different. Its total manpower was one and a half million strong – at least ten times the size of the forces at Britain's disposal – but many of these were irregular formations which were not part of the regular army's order of battle. As things stood in 1853 this consisted of the Imperial Guard, the corps of Grenadiers and six army corps consisting of three infantry, one cavalry and one artillery division. Conscription was in force throughout the empire for all able-bodied men aged between twenty and thirty and landowners were forced to make financial contributions towards the army's upkeep. The results were haphazard and uneven with only the Guards units being fully manned and trained mainly because ceremonial was included amongst their duties.

Moreover, the soldiers were poorly equipped, especially the infantry which, for the most part, used obsolete flintlock muskets. Only four per cent of the infantry were equipped with modern percussion rifles similar to the Minié rifles used by most British infantrymen. (This used a cylindro-conical bullet instead of a conventional spherical ball, was more reliable and achieved superior penetration and longer range.) Although the allies were not privy to the information, the Russian infantry possessed only 52.5% of the weapons it was authorised to use and there was a serious shortage of muskets, carbines and rifles. Moreover, most weapons were in a sorry condition due to bad discipline and a shortage of spare parts. In brief, the Russians were embarking on a war in which the raw courage of its soldiers would have to make good the deficiencies of the army's commissariat service.[1]

Nor were those the only problems. As has been noted, the Russians were operating with lengthy lines of communication with the fronts which had opened up in the principalities and in Asia Minor. The army's commander, Prince Paskevich, had his headquarters in Warsaw, his General Staff reported to the tsar in St Petersburg, and poor roads were the only means of communication between them and the projected battlefronts along the Danube and in the Caucasus. Supply and resupply would create tremendous logistical problems, as would the development of a workable chain of command. Paskevich, a veteran of Austerlitz and Borodino, was also concerned about the strategic balance. Any deployment of forces to the south would weaken the northern corridor to St Petersburg and he feared that Austria or Prussia — or the two combined — would see an opportunity to gain by Russia's difficulties. Nicholas thought that his commander-in-chief was being unnecessarily pessimistic and that Austria would not dare to attack Russia while its armies were deployed against Turkey. None the less, he allowed him to retain substantial numbers of Guards regiments to control the western frontier.

Despite the difficulties the Russian forces were by no means unsuccessful after hostilities had broken out. Following the early setbacks Gorchakov was replaced by Paskevich and the year ended with substantial victories in the Caucasus theatre of operations in Asia Minor. Although it had been overshadowed by the fighting along the Danube the control of the Caucasus was central to Russia's claims on the Ottoman Empire and for years the region had been the target of attack from the forces of the Islamic leader Shamyl. Following

Russia's invasion of the principalities the Turks had entered into a defensive pact with Shamyl and the presence of these formidable allies helped to tie down Russian forces. Even so, despite the presence of European military advisers to the Turkish army, the Russians had taken control of the region through the efforts of the experienced Prince Bebatov, who won a stunning victory at Bayezid in Armenia. Only the threat posed by Shamyl prevented the victory from being exploited. Although outnumbered, another Russian army led by Prince Andronikov forced the Turks to flee again at Akhaltsike on 14 November, the victory being gained at the point of the bayonet, a tactic much favoured by Russian commanders. This was a battle from the past with Andronikov's men attacking at speed in tight formation and showing great resolution in engaging the Turks under fire. It was followed five days later by a similar rout at Ongulsi where Bebatov's cavalry overran the Turkish camp and captured its artillery.

When the news of the victories in Asia Minor reached St Petersburg on 12 December Nicholas ordered the city to be illuminated and a *Te Deum* to be celebrated in honour of his armed forces. For the Russians it was a great moment, one to commemorate, but a disgruntled Seymour reported that, much against his will, he too was caught up in the festivities: 'I found to my distaste that I was taking part, my house having been illuminated in the coarse manner employed here.'[2] Bad though that was for him – the lights and the pandemonium in the streets disturbed his sleep – it was made worse by the knowledge that the Russians were also celebrating a great naval victory in the Black Sea. That really was too much for the British ambassador to bear.

If any one event was destined to propel Britain into war it was the action at Sinope, a run-of-the-mill Ottoman harbour on Turkey's Black Sea coast. Its moment in history came on 30 November when a Turkish flotilla of seven frigates, three corvettes, two steamers and a number of transports under the command of Admiral Osman Pasha was sheltering in its roads. They were carrying reinforcements and supplies to Batoum for the Caucasus front but a week earlier their presence in the Anatolian port had been noted by a squadron of Russian naval vessels under the command of Vice-Admiral Paul Nakhimov. This was precisely the threat which Kornilov had feared – the Turks were using the Black Sea to reinforce their armies in the Caucasus and the principalities and behind them they had the support of British and French naval power.

For Nakhimov it was a tantalising situation. Realising that his squadron of three warships was too weak to engage the Turkish flotilla and the land batteries which guarded Sinope, he dared not attack without first getting reinforcements. Here geography came to his aid. The Russian Black Sea naval base at Sevastopol was only a hundred miles away while Constantinople and the British and French squadrons lay over three hundred miles to the west. Although Osman was able to send a message requesting reinforcements, time was on the Russians' side. From Sevastopol a fresh naval force of six warships under the command of Vice-Admiral Novosilski hurried across the Black Sea to join Nakhimov. Later in the day, once the action had begun, they were joined by three more steam-powered frigates commanded by Menshikov. The result was to be a turning-point in the history of naval warfare.

For the first time the guns of the Russian warships used shell projectiles instead of cannon shot and the results were devastating. Although the new shells were unpredictable and frequently inaccurate, those which did penetrate their targets caused immense damage. Within the course of a one-hour engagement Osman's flotilla was completely destroyed and a number of transports, including one British-registered ship, were in flames. So intense was the inferno that fire from the burning ships quickly spread to the shore and the whole port area was soon alight. Within a short time, even the shore batteries were silent and by evening Sinope was aflame, its harbour littered with the blackened hulks of Osman's ships. 'The shore of the bay was lined with wrecks and strewed with corpses,' noted Captain Adolphus Slade, RN, a few days later. 'Havoc had done her worst. Not a mast was standing, not a timber was left whole. We found above a hundred wounded in various cafés, in every stage of suffering; some in agony, many of them frightfully disfigured by explosions.'[3] Several thousand Turkish sailors had been killed – the exact number was never known – and hundreds more, including Osman, taken prisoner.

For the Russians it was a stunning victory. Nakhimov had used initiative, daring and superior force to destroy an enemy squadron carrying men and materiel to the battlefront. As a young officer in 1827 Nakhimov had served with the joint British, French and Russian fleet which destroyed an Ottoman fleet at Navarino Bay in tactical circumstances similar to those he found at Sinope. The lesson had obviously not been lost. His move also restored command of the Black Sea to the Russian Navy and thereby issued a direct challenge to the British and French naval squadrons anchored in the Golden Horn. Moreover, Nakhimov had settled the issue before those superior naval assets could intervene. Nicholas was entitled to order a public celebration when the news reached St Petersburg twelve days later: coupled to Andronikov's achievement at Akhaltsike it was a matter for noisy congratulation.

Naturally, news of the action had provoked the opposite effect when it reached Constantinople on 2 December. In the midst of the battle and screened by the smoke from the blazing flotilla, a small Turkish steamer, the *Taif*, had managed to escape to tell the sorry tale. Stratford's first inclination was to order Dundas's squadron into the Black Sea. Not only was he anxious to exact retribution on the Russians but naval pride, too, was at stake. The Royal Navy was to a certain extent the guarantor of Turkey's safety yet here was a Russian naval force able to act freely within reach of its guns. Much as the Great Elchi would have liked to order Dundas to set sail immediately, he realised such a move could be considered an act of war, and one which he was unable to initiate unilaterally. On 4 December, therefore, he sent a strongly worded despatch to Clarendon reminding him of Britain's obligations:

> It is painfully evident that the peace of Europe is exposed to the most imminent danger; nor do I see how we can either with honor[sic], or with prudence taken in its larger and truer sense, abstain longer from entering the Black Sea in force at every risk and thereby redeeming the pledge which has in fact been given, not only to the Porte but to all Europe by the presence of our squadron here.
>
> God knows that we have carried forbearance and the love of peace to an extent productive of much embarrassment and fraught with perilous contingencies.[4]

In order to assess the damage, though, one naval steamer, HMS *Retribution* under the command of Captain James Drummond, RN, was despatched to Sinope and when it arrived on 8 December Stratford's worst fears were confirmed. Drummond reported that 'a most destructive and sanguinary action' had taken place and that as a result the Russians had enjoyed a 'complete and entire' victory. Difficult though the news was for Stratford to bear, it caused a sensation when it appeared in the western capitals on 12 December.

From Paris Cowley reported that the French government believed that 'the affair of Sinope and not the passage of the Danube should be the signal for action of the Fleets':

> I found the French Minister greatly chagrined by this intelligence
> – not so much on account of the loss to the Turks, as to the moral
> effect which must be produced by this act being committed, as it
> were, under the guns of the French and English fleets.[5]

There was a similar reaction in London when *The Times* and other newspapers published the story of the battle in their editions on 12 and 13 December. Reeve was particularly shocked: during his visit to Constantinople he had been received 'most kindly' by Stratford who had sat up with him 'half the night' to explain why it was absolutely essential for the Royal Navy to guarantee Turkey's independence. Anything less would compromise Britain's position and Reeve's first leader on the subject underscored the point that the Russians had broken their word. Nicholas had promised not to start hostilities beyond the activities in the principalities, yet at Sinope his warships had taken an unfair advantage and thousands had perished as a result of his perfidy.

The language of outrage said it all. 'Has the British bosom ceased to throb in response to the claim of humanity?' asked the *Morning Advertiser*. 'Has justice ceased to occupy her throne in the English heart? Has the national honour – that which used to be the glory of every Englishman in every part of the world – lost its hold on the minds of the people of these realms? It is impossible.' Even *The Times* reported that 'the carnage was frightful' and 'sustained with heroic courage by the Turks'. Not only had the dastardly Russians inflicted a heavy and bloody defeat on the Turks but they had cocked a snook at the Royal Navy (there was even a wild rumour that the Russian warships had used subterfuge by flying a British flag). Far from being a well won and tactically sound naval action, devised and executed by one country in a state of war with another, Sinope was transmogrified by the press into a 'massacre'. It was nothing of the sort but the images of bloody battle flocked in like locusts and the London-based writers had a field day.

Reminding its readers that *The Times* had long argued that a 'sterner alternative' to diplomacy might have to be found unless the Russians gave way, Reeve argued on 13 December:

The English people are resolved that Russia shall not dictate conditions to Europe, or convert the Black Sea, with all its various interests encompassing its shore, into a Russian lake. They desire that a course of consummate hypocrisy should be punished by a signal defeat, and that a stop should be put to these aggressors. The Emperor of Russia, who began this war without a pretext, is carrying it on without disguise, and it therefore becomes the imperative duty of the Four Powers, who have so recently recorded their determination to put an end to it, to take all measures which that object may demand.

Although Aberdeen attempted to keep calm, the firebrands in his Cabinet could not contain their indignation. Palmerston told Clarendon that Sinope was a stain on Britain's honour and that something had to be done. The foreign secretary had in fact already sent a despatch to Seymour demanding an explanation from the Russians but it was not until Boxing Day that the ambassador was granted an audience with Nesselrode. It was not a comfortable meeting. Seymour began by reinforcing Britain's disquiet over Sinope in particular and its general abhorrence of Russian aggression towards the Porte, as manifested by Menshikov's mission and the invasion of the principalities. 'Turkey must be defended from aggression,' Seymour reminded the chancellor. 'Her Majesty's Government are pledged to defend her and the obligation must be discharged.' He went on:

Now as to the application of this, the victory over the Turks has produced a very painful effect in England. It may be regarded as an intentional insult to the maritime powers . . . these ships were charged with provisions for Batoum and they have been destroyed in a Turkish harbour – which is Turkish territory – which England is bound to protect.[6]

Seymour's protest got to the heart of his country's objections about Sinope – the belief that the victory had been won by duplicity and that it was an insult to a great maritime power whose ships were supposed to be preventing such an outrage – but Nesselrode refused to accept it. Before the ambassador could underline the overriding necessity of Britain protecting 'the independence and integrity of the Ottoman Empire', Nesselrode interrupted to say that the Turkish ships were carrying men and materiel and were, therefore, legitimate targets. It was an argument which Seymour had difficulty in parrying and five days later he wrote to Clarendon asking if the Russians did not have a point, that they were unlikely to have courted Britain's displeasure through an unnecessary naval action: 'I would submit to Your Lordship that the Russians are rather to be regarded as having been reckless in their wish to inflict injury upon an enemy than as having sought an occasion for converting doubtful friends into open opponents.'[7]

By then, though, attitudes in London were beginning to coalesce. Hope of a diplomatic solution had not been abandoned but a decision had to be taken over the future employment of Dundas's squadron: either it could remain at Constantinople, a symbol of British hesitancy, or it could enter the Black Sea and thereby provoke the Russians. As the dilemma continued to tease the Cabinet, though, London was treated to a bizarre political sideshow initiated by the home secretary. For some time Palmerston had been uneasy about the plans for further parliamentary reform being prepared by Lord John Russell and on 14 December he abruptly resigned from government. Ostensibly his reasons were the planned reforms to extend the franchise – Aberdeen had written to him suggesting that his opposition to reform made it difficult for him to remain in the Cabinet – but, inevitably, rumour had it that the real reason was his chagrin with British pusillanimity over Sinope. To complicate matters it was also widely believed that Prince Albert had engineered the resignation by suggesting to Aberdeen that Palmerston had to go.

There was some truth to the rumour. Palmerston was disliked at court – 'he will be a source of mischief to this country as long as he lives,' Victoria had said of him – and Albert had indeed suggested to Aberdeen the stratagem of bearding him over the reform question. But the plan backfired. So popular was Palmerston, embodying as he did robust John Bull attitudes, that it was easy to believe he was the victim of a wider plot. Was not the Prince Consort a member of the House of Coburg and a kinsman of the tsar? Did he not, therefore, have a vested interest in ruining the one politician who was prepared to stand up to Russian bullying? 'Above all,' pondered the *Daily News*, 'the nation distrusts the politics, however they may admire the taste, of a Prince who has breathed from childhood the air of courts tainted by the imaginative servility of Goethe.'[8] That was the interpretation placed on Palmerston's resignation by some sections of the press and London society was rocked by stories condemning what was considered to be the secret influence of the Prince Consort.

The episode had an equally eccentric outcome when Aberdeen allowed Palmerston to retract his resignation on Christmas Eve. The official reason was that Palmerston had not understood the finer points of 'the intended Reform Bill' and that any change to the franchise would be deferred until 1855, but the crucial factor was the hysteria over his decision to quit the government. Quite simply, Aberdeen knew that his own position would have been untenable had Palmerston demitted office and the matter was quickly, if not discreetly, papered over. As Albert's most recent biographer has described it, 'the entire affair had been dishonest, and everyone in politics could decrypt the language'.[9]

Palmerston's short-lived absence from public life was only a temporary diversion from the crisis in the Black Sea. From Vienna came the welcome news that even at this late stage Buol hoped to find a fresh solution by involving Austria, Britain, France and Prussia as mediators between Russia and Turkey. The first indication was that Nicholas might accept the idea but Seymour was less certain – 'the answer I apprehend will be of an evasive nature,' he told Clarendon. Stratford, too, was inclined to pessimism, informing London on 17 December that the Porte was unlikely to forgive the Russian action at Sinope:

We have learnt from an occurrence which cannot be sufficiently deplored that the Russians are willing as well as able to attack and destroy the Sultan's means of defence even in the fancied shelter of port. They have committed direct aggression in the Ottoman territory. Their commander was indeed most careful not to land and be excused the rigours of his violence by presuming that the Turkish squadrons had in view an insurrection in Circassia [the mountainous area of southern Russia to the north of the Caucasus] and by endeavouring on that presumption to put his attack in the light of a defensive operation.[10]

Although there were still unfounded suspicions that Stratford was continuing to conduct diplomacy on his own terms – Victoria believed that the British ambassador exhibited 'a desire for war, and to drag us into it' – he was stymied by the primitive communications, there being no direct telegraphic line between London and Constantinople, a problem which would grow as the crisis deepened. When the Cabinet sat down to discuss the situation in the week before Christmas they were not in possession of the full picture and were unaware how the tsar or the Sultan would respond to Buol's new initiative. Furthermore, anything they decided would not be unanimous. Palmerston was not privy to the discussion and Russell suddenly threatened to resign unless Britain acted decisively. By way of protest he stayed away from the Cabinet meeting of 22 December at which it was finally decided to send the Royal Navy into the Black Sea. The warships' task would be to act in concert with the French squadron to require all Russian vessels other than merchantmen 'to return to Sebastopol'.

At previous meetings on 17 and 20 December there had been a fair degree of obfuscation on this point. First Clarendon proposed that Stratford should be allowed to use his judgement as to the deployment of Dundas's squadron, then it was agreed that the Royal Navy should not let slip the opportunity to impose its will on the Black Sea. The British and French squadrons would only use force in the last resort and their task would be made easier by Russian unwillingness to engage in a large scale naval action, but the dangers inherent in the orders were only too clear.

From St Petersburg Seymour warned that such a deployment would be a further humiliation to Russia and that Nicholas was coming under increased pressure to show his resolve 'by sending off the French and English ministers and by declaring war upon the two countries'. Furthermore, having discussed the situation with de Castelbajac, the British ambassador doubted if the move would achieve anything because 'Britain and France are in no position to despatch troops to the Principalities without Prussian and Austrian support.'[11] And he ended the despatch with the thought that, as time was running out, any further discussions with Nesselrode would amount to little more than 'fencing'.

He was closer to the mark than he realised. The Russian chancellor had fallen foul of Nicholas who accused him of misrepresenting British and French policy and for the time being he had been sidelined from the tsar's deliberations for appearing 'anti-slavonic'. Shortly after the new year began he fell ill and sent a note to Seymour saying that the crisis had exhausted him and 'the fact is that this Eastern Question will be the cause of my death'. In the event Nesselrode did not die until 1862 but his domination of Russian foreign policy was fast coming to an end. It was also the end of the line for Seymour. Within days of the news of Britain's naval deployment reaching St Petersburg, Russian society had also taken its revenge on the British ambassador: 'I and my family are completely excluded from its Pale'. It was not yet war but, as Clarendon admitted to his wife on 2 January, it was only a matter of time before it was declared:

> However, for my part, I am getting in favour of war. Of course, a patch up would be the least troublesome thing now; but I believe it would only be playing the Emperor's game and allowing him to make monster preparations for monster objects.[12]

Three days later he expressed the same feelings, only more vehemently, in a letter to Stratford which showed the dramatic change in his thinking. Here was laid bare all the frustration that had been building up at the Foreign Office since Sinope. Using Stratford's phrase, Clarendon declared that shilly-shally had to make way for positive action and willy-nilly Britain would have to make the running:

> The hesitancy and delay must have produced a very bad moral effect, despairing to the Porte, encouraging to the Czar. However, allowances must be made for the French who wish to be thought equal if not superior to us but who know the real inferiority of their ships and crews and fear to make it public.
> I have no reliance on the Turks, their senseless boasting, their want of foresight and indifference to good advice make them bad allies, unless behind walls where they can't always be.
> Sebastopol *must* be the point at which all our efforts should be directed.[13]

So, within the space of a few months Clarendon had come to the view that, far from being avoidable, war was inevitable and that it should be pursued with the object of breaking Russia's power in the Black Sea. Moreover, given the perceived weaknesses of the allies, it would have to be a British-led affair.

In St Petersburg Seymour started making preparations for his departure and it was agreed that the Danish embassy should look after the interests of British citizens in the event of war. When he broached the matter with Nesselrode, the Russian chancellor replied that British subjects would not be in any danger and gave his word that their safety would be ensured by the authorities. 'All we ask is that the English should conduct themselves with reserve and prudence,' he said. 'In other words conduct themselves as they always have done here.'[14]

For both men it was a melancholy end to a long and mutually agreeable diplomatic relationship.

7

Drifting towards War

My noble friend has given us a new phrase in Parliamentary
or diplomatic language; we are not at war, nor at peace, and
we are not neutral, but we are drifting towards war.
The Earl of Derby in the House of Lords, 14 February 1854

Dundas received the orders to advance into the Black Sea on
3 January and five days later the joint British and French
fleet passed through the Bosphorus charged with the responsibility
of ensuring that all Russian naval vessels should be 'required to
return to Sebastopol'. Using the authority vested in him Stratford
ordered a naval force to proceed to Sinope under the direction of
Dundas's second-in-command, Rear-Admiral Sir Edmund Lyons in
HMS *Agamemnon*, the navy's first screw battleship. Built in 1849 she
was capable of 11 knots and was armed with 91 guns; the Royal
Navy had seven other similar ships, the French had nine and the
Russians none. For that reason their entry into the Black Sea sent
an unmistakable signal to St Petersburg that Britain and France were
determined to use force to defend the Ottoman Empire.

In that sense the warships provided a deterrent. They could, and
did, provide convoy assistance to Turkish merchantmen reinforcing
the Caucasus front and they also persuaded Menshikov to keep his
battle fleet at Sevastopol, but they were not capable of winning any
war with Russia single-handed. Clarendon had warned his colleagues
that the deployment could lead to an outbreak of hostilities 'at no
distant period' but it was still unclear how the allies would be able to
defend Constantinople or force Russia to withdraw her army from
the principalities.

In truth, Britain was hopelessly unprepared to fight a major war in
Europe. A generation had elapsed since Wellington's victories against
Napoleon, recruitment was a perennial problem – the army was not a
popular calling amongst the labouring classes – and all too often those
who volunteered did so as a means of escape from other problems.
Writing of the army he knew in 1846 an experienced recruiting
sergeant concluded that over two-thirds of its number had been
driven to its ranks through unemployment and the rest were 'idle
– bad characters – criminals – perverse sons – discontented and
restless'.[1] Only one in a hundred had genuine ambition or came
from respectable backgrounds. As a result far too many ordinary
soldiers were inadequates or social misfits whose failings were often
exacerbated by alcohol.

> You must not look upon the soldier as a responsible agent, for
> he is not able to take care of himself, he must be fed, clothed,
> looked after like a child and given only just enough to make
> him efficient as part of the great machine for war. Give him
> one farthing more than he really wants, and he gives way to
> his brutal propensities and immediately gets drunk.[2]

Captain Henry Clifford of The Rifle Brigade was not an exception
in harbouring ambivalent thoughts about the men who served under
his command in the Crimea. On the one hand he regarded them as
noble creatures, capable of enduring great hardship provided that
they were well led; on the other, he abhorred the insobriety which
was such a feature of army life. A report from a parliamentary select
committee into drunkenness in 1834 revealed a sorry state of affairs,
with the Scots castigated in particular for being 'the most drunken
country on the face of the earth'. Soldiers in Scottish regiments (not
all of them native Scots) were estimated to drink an average of four
gallons of whisky a year: in a diary entry of 1846 the commanding
officer of the 79th Highlanders noted that before a route march in
Ireland his men were 'nearly all drunk, they could hardly stand'.

To put the problem in perspective, drunkenness was also rife in
civilian society, especially the drinking of spirits. However, whereas
a drunk could stagger home from a public house and, provided that
he did not commit an offence, he was never reprimanded, other than
by the self-inflicted punishment of a hangover. Not so in the army.
An inebriated soldier would be placed under arrest and once sober

punished by his commanding officer. This could range from a fine of a penny a day for a specified period up to 168 days, confinement to barracks or, in the worst cases, by flogging. In 1846, following the death of a trooper in the 7th Hussars through 'the disgraceful practice of flogging', the number of permissable strokes had been reduced to fifty and its use steadily declined. However, many traditionalists in the army still held to the view that it was the only way to maintain good order and discipline; and it was not abolished until 1881.

In an attempt to cut back on drunkenness and crime there had been some reforms but all too often the changes were introduced piecemeal. Under the direction of Lord Howick, secretary-at-war in the late 1830s, there had been several improvements to barrack life including the provision of reading rooms, savings banks and the introduction of healthier provisions but it was only a modest beginning. As Britain readied itself to go to war early in 1854 public expenditure on the army had dropped from £43 million in 1815 to £9.5 million a year which exacerbated the severe recruitment problem. Most regiments were under-strength, desertion was rife, voluntary enlistment was haphazard and there were no viable reserves. It was all a far cry from the triumphs of 1815 when the country's armed forces had made Britain the paramount power in Europe.

Not that the army had any immediate intention of soldiering in Europe; instead, with the growth of Britain's world empire, military horizons shifted from Flanders to India, South Africa, the West Indies and Canada. By 1850 most soldiers expected to be one of the several thousand who served in India, increasingly seen as the real home of the British Army. Most were infantrymen: in 1846, of a complement of 100,600, there were 23,000 in India and 32,650 in other parts of the empire. Only 44,980 were stationed in Britain and available for service elsewhere.[3]

Even the officers seemed to belong to a different age. Commissions were still purchased, with the result that officers came from exclusive and wealthy upper-class backgrounds and training was confined to the age-old reliance on the barrack square and serried lines of infantry. Brave, stalwart and loyal those swells might have been – most regimental officers rode to hounds, indulged in field sports and placed a premium on personal courage – but modern tactical thinking was the realm of the enthusiast and in most infantry and cavalry messes such fanatics were unwelcome. Sir Garnet Wolseley later wrote:

Almost all our officers at that time were uneducated as soldiers, and many of those placed upon the staff of the Army at the beginning of the war were absolutely unfit for the positions they had secured through family and political interest . . . they were not men whom I would have entrusted with a subaltern's picket in the field. Had they been private soldiers, I don't think any colonel would have made them corporals.[4]

Wolseley had direct experience of the failings of the officer class: the future field-marshal served as a young officer with the 90th Foot (Perthshire Light Infantry) in the Crimea and the experience left a distinctly unfavourable impression.

The senior echelons were also somewhat long in the tooth. The Duke of Wellington had held the post of commander-in-chief until his death in 1852, aged eighty-three, and his subordinates were scarcely younger. Lord Raglan, who fought with him at Waterloo, was Master-General of the Ordnance and aged sixty-five. Sir John Burgoyne, Inspector-General of Fortifications, was seventy-one and many other senior infantry generals, such as Brown of the Light Division and de Lacy Evans of the 2nd Division, were well beyond modern retiral age. Indeed, of the army's generals in 1854, thirteen on the active list had over seventy years' service and thirty-seven had sixty years. Under normal circumstances advanced years need not be a barrier; indeed, age can bring the benefit of experience. Admiral Lord Rodney might have been a gout-ridden sixty-three when he broke the French line at The Saints in 1782 and Admirals Hood and Howe were even older (sixty-seven and sixty-eight respectively) at the Glorious First of June in 1794, but they were energetic and robust commanders with a lifetime's experience of naval warfare.

In contrast the military leaders of 1854 were not only advanced in years but unversed in modern military science. The army's last experience of war against a European power had been the war against Napoleon's France. In the intervening years its experience had been limited to small-scale operations against inferior native opposition and, as a result, its thinking, its equipment and its tactics had ossified. Even its redcoats and bearskins owed more to Waterloo than to the realities of modern warfare in a little known theatre of operations far from Britain.

Like the British, the French army lacked the expertise of fighting the armed forces of another major European power and its engagements also had been limited to colonial warfare. But there was a difference. Between 1830 and 1847 the French had been involved in a long drawn out struggle in Algeria which forced the army to rethink its tactics. It was a hard fought war against determined opposition led by the Emir of Mascara, Abd-el-Kader who proved a subtle opponent. In its early stages a succession of French commanders failed to curb the Algerian leader and it was not until the appointment of Marshal Thomas Bugeaud in 1840 that the Armée d'Afrique was reorganised to take account of the local circumstances. Realising that he was involved in a war of movement which favoured the mobile and elusive Algerian *gouma* irregular horsemen, Bugeaud told his officers that they had to remove the encumbrances of a European campaign and prepare for a different kind of war in a roadless and featureless landscape:

> You drag thousands of wagons and heavy artillery with you which slows your movements. Rather than surprise the Arabs with rapid offensive marches, you stay on the defensive, marching slowly. Your enemies follow you and attack at their convenience. All this is going to change!
>
> To begin with, no more heavy artillery, no more of these heavy wagons, no more of these enormous forage trains . . . the convoys will be on mule-back and the only cannons permitted will be light ones.[5]

Although it was not the end of the campaign it was the beginning of the end and Bugeaud's reforms paved the way for Abd-el-Kader's marginalisation from the fighting after the decisive Battle of Isly in 1844. During that time the French army prospered, and a younger generation of officers with direct experience of modern infantry tactics were promoted to senior positions of command. No less imbued with Napoleonic martial spirit than their forebears they had a good conceit of their abilities. Whereas most British generals looked back to Waterloo or the Peninsula campaign, the Algerian veterans were too young to have any memories of those heady days. There was also a difference in style which had nothing to do with past glories and rivalries. Most French officers believed that they were professionals who had been promoted on merit while their British colleagues were gentlemen who owed everything to family wealth and influence.

Differences in approach were not the only problem. The allies had

to consider how best to deploy their armies in order to fulfil their
obligations to Turkey and, as Britain drifted towards war in the
early months of 1854, there was a good deal of flustered thinking in
political and naval and military circles. Protection of Constantinople
in the event of attack was one consideration, the clearing of Russian
forces from the principalities another. Unfortunately the options were
complicated by a common British and French belief that the Turkish
army was a broken reed and that the Russians would sweep it aside
in a spring offensive across the Danube.

Although their combined strength was 300,000 the Ottoman forces
were considered to be hopelessly equipped, badly disciplined and led
by undependable officers. As Rose in Constantinople had already
warned London, a combination of drink and homosexual excess had
left the Turkish army 'vicious, corrupt, lethargic and timid'. There
was also a British fear that the Porte might still enter into a separate
agreement with the Russians in the event of Constantinople being
besieged: Cowley warned the French foreign minister Drouyn de
Lhuys, that 'no Turk is to be trusted', and that the French commanders should treat with some suspicion their opposite numbers in
the Ottoman army. Most of the doubts were fanned by ignorance
and prejudice and were far removed from reality. The better Turkish
units, recruited from the hardy mountainmen of Albania, Bosnia and
Bulgaria, were experienced and battle-hardened soldiers. They were
also well led. Omar Pasha, their supreme commander, had won his
spurs suppressing rebellion in the Balkans, fighting in what would
nowadays be referred to as low-intensity warfare, and many of his
regimental officers were British, Irish and European mercenaries.
Omar was himself a soldier of fortune. Having started life as Michael
Lattas, the son of a Croatian army officer, he converted to Islam
and joined the Ottoman army. His marriage to a wealthy heiress
provided him with the patronage to become military governor of
Constantinople but he was a skilful and courageous soldier in his
own right.

The Turks also had a good conceit of themselves and a poor view of
their allies: after inspecting a British unit, a Turkish minister remarked
that, although the redcoats were 'very fine to look at', they would
probably run away once battle began. The mutual disdain was not
just unfortunate; it helped to cloud the allies' initial tactical thinking.
The British and French believed that if the Russians chose to attack
Constantinople the Turks would be unable to meet the challenge.

In that event a line of defence would have to guard the Straits and that would involve a landing at Gallipoli.

However thought had to be given, too, to mounting an attack on Russia itself, either against its Baltic ports or against Sevastopol, its main base in the Crimea. An opportunity to assess the latter option was taken by Captain Drummond when he took the 28-gun paddle-wheel steam frigate HMS *Retribution* into Sevastopol Bay on 6 January. Ostensibly his mission was to inform Menshikov officially that any Russian warship sailing outside territorial waters would be stopped by the Royal Navy; but he also demanded the return of two British engineers, and also used the occasion to report on the Russian defences. Having fired a courtesy salute and handed over the order to Menshikov, Drummond showed considerable resolution by ignoring Russian threats and taking his ship as close in to the roadsteads as he dared.

His observations made pessimistic reading. The fortress was secure from attack from the sea, being defended not only by shore batteries numbering some three hundred guns but also by the broadsides of three lines of warships which would seal the entrance to the inner harbour. Only a land force supported by the navy would have any chance of taking Sevastopol from the land side to the north but it would require overwhelming strength and firepower. Writing from St Petersburg a few days later, Seymour backed up Drummond's findings when he reported on Russia's not insignificant military strength:

A military acquaintance of mine who has examined the works of Sebastopol and Cronstadt considers them such as to render these two places all but impregnable.

With regard to Sebastopol he is of the opinion that it might have been taken early in last summer from the land side, but that the fresh works which have been thrown up, and the additions made to the garrison, would render any attempt upon it unavailing.[6]

None the less Sevastopol did not drop out of the list of Britain's strategic options; but as the crisis deepened Sir James Graham on 15 January informed Clarendon that the sooner Britain sent an ultimatum to St Petersburg the better: 'I do not think that peace is any longer possible'. As a sailor he was convinced that, in the event of war, the Royal Navy's command of the Black Sea could only be secured by destroying the base at Sevastopol, and he had already advised Dundas that the Crimean stronghold should be attacked by sea 'should any opportunity present itself'. Later still, on 1 March, he re-emphasised the point to Clarendon with a note, scribbling on the base of his own copy the words: 'delenda est Sebastopol':

> The operation which will ever be memorable and decisive is the capture and destruction of Sebastopol. On this my heart is set: the eye-tooth of the [Russian] Bear must be drawn, and till his Fleet and Naval Arsenal in the Black Sea are destroyed, there is no safety for Constantinople – no security for the peace of Europe.[7]

The foreign secretary was inclined to agree with the first Lord and had already mentioned the possibility to Cowley in Paris who replied on 29 December that any such proposal would receive the ready support of Napoleon III and his foreign minister:

> How I rejoice at your determination about Sebastopol. It was but the other day that I said both to the Emperor and to Drouyn that if we let slip this occasion to *do up* the Russian navy in the Black Sea, we should repent it bitterly. You may depend upon it, that if the present business is made up, before two years are over, the Russian fleet will be before Constantinople, ere we shall know anything of the matter. She will never give us another chance of getting there before her. Therefore I say burn and destroy everything and at every hazard, and send double the ships to do it if necessary.[8]

It was easy enough for a British diplomat in Paris to make such warlike noises: but as Drummond had warned, it would be no easy matter to attack such a well defended fortress. In any case, the immediate priority for the military commanders was the defence of Turkey from Russian attack. As part of the naval and military preparations, Burgoyne, the army's senior engineer, was sent to Constantinople to report on the Turkish capital's defensive needs. Although he had strict instructions to limit his research to that immediate area and 'to turn his back on the Black Sea', he shared Graham's and Clarendon's concerns about the threat posed by Sevastopol. Before leaving for the east he prepared two papers for the Cabinet outlining his thoughts after studying an up-to-date map of the Russian fortifications. 'Sebastopol was not open to attack by Sea,' he warned, 'unless the land Defences be taken by an Army equal to cope with the Russian garrison.'[9] This would mean the creation of an allied army of at least 30,000 to match the Russian forces inside the heavily fortified base. Without them any naval attack would be 'madness'.

However, despite the manifold problems attached to its capture the Russian base remained a primary target. It was also clear that success would depend on a combined naval and military operation – something of which neither the Royal Navy nor the army had any recent experience. When Wellington commanded the army in the Peninsula War he had been forced to rely on a fleet of 265 transports, each of around 400 tons of which half carried food and fodder. Even so, it had been a close-run victory. More recently, an indication of the difficulties involved had been exposed when the French began operations in Algeria in 1830: it had taken over a year to collect together a fleet sufficiently large to transport an army of 30,000 men, their supplies, artillery and cavalry. In both cases Spain and Algeria were closer to home base than the Crimea would ever be.

When the papers were discussed by the Cabinet at the beginning of February Palmerston agreed with Burgoyne's assessment but put forward the possibility that the investment force should consist of Turkish forces backed by the British and French fleets. He also suggested an expedition into Circassia to encourage them to rise against the Russians, thereby opening up a second front. Other ministers, including Lord John Russell and the Duke of Newcastle, the secretary for war and the colonies, wanted to limit the military deployment to protecting Constantinople. Aberdeen had little to offer other than the hope that all might not yet be lost, although he was prepared to sanction the formation of an expeditionary force, its destination and purpose to be decided later. The multiplicity of ideas and the absence of any consensus within the cabinet were a foretaste of the muddle yet to come.

While senior British and French commanders made contingency plans for war – Burgoyne was accompanied by a French engineer officer, Colonel Ardent – the politicians and diplomats played their final moves to keep the peace. In Vienna there was still some hope that Buol would engineer a last-minute compromise which would suit both St Petersburg and Constantinople. In Paris, too, Cowley reported with some disgust that Napoleon III was keen to make a direct appeal to Nicholas, emperor to emperor, requesting an immediate halt to the fighting followed by a new round of peace talks. It was a vain hope. The tsar had lost nothing of his contempt for Napoleon III and, in his reply of February rejecting the approach, he raised the ghosts of 1812 and the French army's disastrous retreat from Moscow.

By now it was becoming increasingly difficult to see how war could be avoided. As Seymour had predicted, the Russians had been enraged by the Royal Navy's deployment in the Black Sea, regarding it not just as a breach of the Straits Convention but also as a direct challenge to their own fleet. On 22 January they responded through Brunnov, who passed on a demand to the British government requesting the immediate withdrawal of Dundas's squadron. If that were not forthcoming then Brunnov was to ask for his passport and break off diplomatic relations. On this matter Britain would not budge and just over a week later the Russian ambassador formally took his leave of Aberdeen. The final rupture came on 3 February while the prime minister was still trying to convince his Cabinet that war was not yet inevitable.

It was a curious time. Britain was not at war but was taking naval and military precautions which were soon being discussed at length and with considerable accuracy in the pages of *The Times* under the heading 'The Preparations for War'. On 8 February the Cabinet agreed to send 10,000 soldiers to Malta to form an 'expeditionary force now preparing for the East' and behind the scenes the first steps were taken to find a commander. The army's commander-in-chief was Lord Hardinge who had succeeded Wellington in September 1852 but it was inconceivable that, despite his experience, the army's senior officer should lead such an expedition. Of course the army lacked officers with practice of modern warfare. While soldiers such as Hugh Gough and Charles Napier had won names for themselves in India they, too, were advanced in years; indeed the latter was to die that spring, his health having been impaired by a chill while serving as a pall bearer at Wellington's funeral. There was another black mark: both men had commanded the presidency forces of the Honourable East India Company, the great professional rivals of the regular British Army.

With no Wellington (and certainly no Marlborough) in sight the army turned to the next best thing, someone who had served under the Iron Duke. The choice fell on Raglan who, as Lord Fitzroy Somerset, had been Wellington's military secretary in the Peninsula and who had an unblemished, if unspectacular, military career. Although best known as an administrator – he had served with the British Embassy in Paris and as Military Secretary before being appointed Master-General of the Ordnance – he was a sound tactician and, as many newspapers pointed out, all his professional knowledge of warfare had been gained at Wellington's side. There were other attributes. He had a reputation for personal bravery, having lost his right arm at Waterloo and the incident had entered military folklore. After his arm had been amputated without the benefit of any anaesthetic he asked for it to be returned so that he could retrieve a ring given to him by his wife. According to Hardinge, in a letter to Newcastle of 8 February, he also enjoyed 'personal qualifications most desirable in a chief who has to co-operate with a French force. His temper and manners are conciliatory, and he would command the respect of Foreigners and the confidence of our own force.'[10] All this was true. Raglan was loyal, self-effacing, yet possessed of an iron will. One further virtue marked him out: the ability to speak French fluently. (However, while in the Crimea, he proved incapable of addressing one French commander, Canrobert, as anything other than Kant-Robert. And in common with other officers of his generation he had difficulty in adjusting to the fact that the French were his allies, regularly referring to them as 'the enemy'.)

Quite simply, despite his years, there was no other general of similar stature and the feeling within the army was that he was 'just the man for the job'. When Hardinge first broached the appointment Newcastle expressed considerable doubts about Raglan's lack of experience as a field commander but these were obviously shortlived. On 21 February, two weeks after he had first been approached, Raglan's appointment as 'General Officer Commanding the Forces East of Malta' was confirmed by the Cabinet and preparations began in earnest to construct the army which would be under his command. Because it was thought that the forthcoming campaign would be short and sharp, similar perhaps to a small colonial war, Raglan was permitted to remain Master-General of the Ordnance.

Across the Channel there was also no little controversy about the appointment of Leroy de Saint-Arnaud as the commander of the French expeditionary force. Too young to have served under Napoleon I, he had first come to the fore fighting with the Foreign Legion in Algeria where he won the reputation of a first-class fighting soldier. He had also supported Napoleon III's coup in 1851 and as a result had been appointed minister of war. But he was a sick man, slowly dying of cancer of the stomach, and the suspicion remained that he owed everything to political favouritism while other contenders such as fellow Algerian veterans François Canrobert commanded the 1st Division and Pierre Bosquet the 2nd. The feeling in French political circles, as expressed by Adolphe Thiers was that Napoleon had favoured those soldiers who had helped him to come to power or who had won their reputations in Algeria fighting with the Foreign Legion or the Zouaves:

> Nothing can be more pitiable. With the single exception of Vaillant, [the minister of war] who is a man of honour and patriotism, besides being the first engineer in Europe, there is not one I would hire as a clerk. There is neither sense nor honesty in the whole gang.[11]

Even the British were unimpressed. Although the French commander-in-chief spoke good English – another reason for his appointment – Clarendon informed Stratford that he had 'no confidence of any kind in Saint-Arnaud. He is a regular charlatan and Napoleon I would never have sent such a man to command for France far away from home at such a time.'[12]

One other British institution was also making preparations for the coming conflict and in so doing would change the reporting of modern warfare. Early in February Delane summoned to his office in Printing House Square William Howard Russell, a stocky and forceful Irishman who had made his name as a journalist by covering Irish politics. Although Delane had several military officers under contract to provide him with news, it was not a satisfactory arrangement and he had already been advised by his manager, Mowbray Morris, that *The Times* would disappoint its readership 'when we offer nothing better than reports from other journals, however authentic'. To make good that deficit he decided that when the army left, William Howard Russell would accompany them. At first the Irishman was unwilling to follow what might still be a fool's errand but Delane convinced him that the war would be over in no time and that he would be back in London by late summer. With Russell suitably convinced, arrangements were made immediately for him to accompany the Guards Brigade when they left for Malta, en route to 'the seat of war'. As it turned out he did not return until two years later and he came back as much of a household name as any of the war's military commanders.

While the preparations were being eagerly debated in the public prints, war was still not a foregone conclusion. On 14 February, rising in the House of Lords to answer Lord Clanricarde's question on the current state of affairs with Russia, Clarendon admitted that he was at a loss to know how to reply:

> The question has been asked whether we are at peace or war. It is one that is very difficult to answer distinctly. We are not at war, because war is not declared; we are not strictly at peace with Russia (a laugh). My noble friend may laugh; but he must know perfectly well that I am correct in saying that we are not at war with Russia, although diplomatic relations with that country are suspended . . . I consider that we are in the intermediate state; that our desire for peace is just as sincere as ever; but then I must say that our hopes of maintaining it are gradually dwindling away, and that we are drifting towards war.[13]

A more direct answer was not long coming. On 27 February 1854 Clarendon sent an official demand to Count Nesselrode through Seymour demanding that the Russian forces be withdrawn from the principalities by the end of April, 'refusal or silence' being 'equivalent to a declaration of war'. Only six days' grace would be permitted. That same day Drouyn de Lhuys despatched a similar ultimatum through his ambassador, de Castelbajac. This time there could be no turning back.

8

'Our Beautiful Guards'

To Arms then my Comrades – with Heaven's assistance,
Ye Muscovite demons of blood take your fill!
May the war-cry be heard for Revenge and Resistance,
While Sword, Flame and Famine have power to kill.
Army-Surgeon James William Graves, 'The Turkish Appeal
to the Friends of Liberty', April 1854

Nicholas I refused to honour the British and French ultimatums with a reply after the official courier, Captain Blackwood, arrived in St Petersburg on 13 February. When Seymour presented the official British papers to Nesselrode the following day the Chancellor calmly assured him that the tsar would never declare war on either Britain or France. It was possible that he still could not bring himself to believe that Aberdeen would go to war to prevent the dismemberment of the Ottoman Empire. To his way of thinking this was a regional matter which concerned his country and Turkey alone. It was also possible that he hoped the great powers would be unwilling to break the long peace since 1815. If Europe were to be involved his main worry was Austria which had reinforced its army on the Wallachian border. Paskevich continued to warn that the Austrians posed a real threat but the tsar was more sanguine. Although Buol had attempted to find a diplomatic means of breaking the deadlock between St Petersburg and Constantinople, and although Vienna was the cockpit for the last-ditch peace talks, he believed that Emperor Franz Josef would never declare against him. Partly, this was a result of the Holy Alliance; partly, too, it was due to the gratitude which he hoped the Austrian emperor still felt for Russia's support in 1849. But the main reason was that Austria had no need to antagonise Russia over Turkey's possessions in Europe. To further their own territorial ambitions all they had to do was sit back and await the outcome of events.

But the tsar's main problem lay in his failure to read the signals which he was receiving from Paris and London. He expected Napoleon III to be antagonistic; hence his abrupt dismissal of the French emperor's peace overture. Britain, though, he continued to misjudge and his impressions might have been confirmed by the arrival in St Petersburg of a curious delegation from the British Society of Friends, or Quakers. Led by Joseph Sturge, a Birmingham corn merchant and pacifist who was renowned for doing good works, the Quakers had high hopes of making their voice heard. Not only was Nicholas himself interested in the movement but his brother and predecessor Alexander I had expressed great admiration for their work during his state visit to London in 1814.

Sturge was accompanied by two other leading Quakers, Robert Charlton, a businessman from Bristol, and Henry Pease, a Darlington-based railway developer. The party left London on 20 January and, travelling by way of Ghent, Düsseldorf, Berlin, Königsberg and Riga, they arrived in St Petersburg just under a fortnight later. Their mission was quite simple: to attempt to persuade the tsar to opt for peace. Writing to his niece from Berlin on 26 January, Pease acknowledged that it was a faint hope but with Europe on the brink it was the party's duty as pacifists to do all in their power to persuade him:

> As to our reward, dear, what can I say, the case is an awful one, I do not expect to see fruit. It may be that the most High permits the Emperor to be thus warned, and I do not doubt it is right that a Christian community as Friends [*sic*] should maintain this testimony against war: it is of no importance, comparatively, how the bloodshed is prevented if only it be so.[1]

On their arrival in St Petersburg the Quakers found to their discomfort that they were being treated as an important last-minute peace delegation from London. Wisely, perhaps, they did not make contact with the British Embassy for fear of giving substance to that belief and conducted their negotiations with Nesselrode through Russian Quakers. A week later their efforts were rewarded when they were received in the Winter Palace by Nicholas – 'a fine powerful tall frame, with an unmistakable countenance which one thinks quite capable of saying "Siberia" although by no means incapable of genuine kindly relaxation'.

In fact it was pure theatre. After listening to them and commenting that he was in favour of peace Nicholas shook hands with the three men who were then conducted into the presence of the empress. 'I have seen the Emperor with tears in his eyes!' was her breathless salutation. Pease was right that little would come of the meeting. The mission did not bear fruit, nor could it have hoped to, but it was a well-meant gesture and if nothing else it demonstrated considerable fortitude to have undertaken such a difficult and uncomfortable journey across Europe in the depths of winter. At home their efforts were satirised in the press – *Punch* called them the 'Doves of St Petersburg' – but even an increasingly cynical Seymour was prepared to give them the benefit of his not inconsiderable doubts. 'His Imperial Majesty received them with great affability, commending the zeal which had prompted them to undertake a long and painful journey, and assuring them that no-one was more intent upon Peace than himself!'

Four days later Captain Blackwood had arrived in St Petersburg with his ultimatum and the Quakers left on their homeward journey. Seymour, too, was on the move. Nesselrode asked him when he wanted his passports to be returned and on 21 February, having destroyed the embassy's cipher books the British ambassador left the Russian capital for the last time, still protesting that Britain was being dragged into an unnecessary war:

> I have long felt that I was struggling against a current which was too strong for me, while the pain of finding myself unable to give effect to the views of Her Majesty's Government has been heightened by the conviction which I shall ever entertain that very different results would have been obtained if those upon whose assistance I had in various degrees a right to count had not been, I cannot even say lukewarm supporters, but the secret opponents of my efforts.
>
> I have seen a most dangerous policy adopted by a Cabinet which considered my timely warnings as exaggerated or absurd.[2]

By then, though, Britain and France were both on a war footing.

Following the Cabinet's decision to deploy troops to Malta the first regiments in the expeditionary force were making preparations for departure amidst scenes of wild public enthusiasm. On 14 February the 1st Coldstream Guards left St George's Barracks in Trafalgar Square for Waterloo Station en route to Chichester and the troopships waiting at Southampton Water. They would form a Guards Brigade under the command of Brigadier-General H.J.W. Bentinck and the sight of these familiar redcoated soldiers leaving for what had become known as the 'seat of war' left a profound impression on the watching London crowds. Later they would be joined by their fellow foot guards regiments, the 3rd Grenadiers and the 1st Scots Fusilier Guards, and as *The Times* reported the following day the thrill of fife and drum was almost too much for the watching crowds to bear:

> Even the occupants of the omnibuses and cabs joined in these manifestations, and so great was the excitement to which the event gave rise that for some time the thoroughfare was entirely suspended. At Waterloo-bridge the tollkeepers were completely overwhelmed by the torrent of people accompanying the troops, and who were not to be stopped in their farewell greetings by any number of turnstiles. The men appeared to be in the highest of spirits, and marched cheerfully along to the familiar air of 'The Girl I Left Behind Me'.

A week later the Coldstreamers were on their way to Malta and they were followed in quick succession by the Scots Fusilier Guards – 'our beautiful guards', Queen Victoria called them – and the 2nd battalion The Rifle Brigade. Suddenly the Channel ports were busy with traffic as troopships began the lengthy task of moving the men and supplies of Britain's hastily assembled expeditionary force into the Eastern Mediterranean. Eventually the force was to consist of five divisions of infantry (including the Light Division) and a cavalry division together with supporting troops including seven batteries of field artillery.

It was no easy task moving such a large force and the government moved quickly to commandeer a number of ships taken up from trade including modern steamers such as the *Himalaya, Jason, Golden Fleece* and *Ripon. The Times* claimed on 14 February that these ships ensured that '20,000 men could be carried from Southampton to Constantinople without pressure or inconvenience in less time than it takes the Russians to march 300 miles' but as the soldiers themselves discovered, choice of ship determined the comfort or otherwise of their passages. A small sailing ship such as the *Asia* (710 tons) would be lucky if it carried a company of infantry or a troop of cavalry, whereas the modern steamship *Himalaya*, taken up from the Peninsula & Orient line, could carry an entire regiment to the Bosphorus in under two weeks. Even so, as Troop Sergeant-Major Henry Franks found out when the 5th Dragoon Guards embarked on it at Queenstown (Cobh) in Ireland, conditions were not just basic, they were a matter of rank. Franks wrote:

> The Officers occupied the Saloon and First Class cabins; the Non-commissioned Officers were each allowed cabins of the Second Class; and as for the Privates, well, I am afraid I must admit that the accommodation was not all that could be desired. About half of the men were supposed to be 'on Guard' each night, and the remainder got themselves stowed away in various places, but they seemed quite contented, and made no complaint, for it must be taken into consideration that we were all new to both sea voyages and campaigning. England had been at peace for about forty years, and therefore we cheerfully put up with many things and matters that at the present day would never be required of us.[3]

Just as bad were the conditions for the horses. Although Franks remembered that his regiment lost only one horse during the voyage, other regiments were not so fortunate. The 11th Hussars were forced to shoot injured horses after being caught in a storm and it proved difficult to load and unload the horses from ships which were not built as specialist troop transports. Some of the slower sailing ships took up to two months to reach Turkey and the conditions on board were horrendous for man and beast. During the deployment the Cavalry Division lost over 150 horses, a crippling number for a force which, in common with the rest of the army, had been hard pressed to bring itself up to strength for the campaign. As would become all too evident in the months to come, Raglan's expeditionary force had to go to war on a wing and a prayer.

At the time, though, the people of Britain were supremely self-confident. As so often happens in times of national emergency the armed forces became the focus of a great deal of interest and suddenly soldiers became very important people indeed. It was not just in London that crowds gathered to bid fond farewell to the departing regiments. In Manchester Timothy Gowing noticed that 'one could have walked over the heads of the people' when his regiment the 7th (Royal Fusiliers) set off from their barracks for service in Turkey. The son of a Baptist minister, he was an educated young man, yet he, too, was swept along by the seemingly inexorable tide of enthusiasm for the war:

> We had been blessed with peace for 40 years. The soldiers had degenerated in the eyes of the public; they were looked upon as useless and expensive ornaments. But suddenly a change came over the people, and every sight of the Queen's uniform called forth emotions of enthusiasm from all conditions of men. Our highest mortal interest – 'Honour' – was now at stake, and the pulse of the whole country beat high for her soldier sons.[4]

That sense of honour was not just an idle concept. Britain basked in the splendour of being the world's leading industrial nation. Its growing empire also provided self-confidence and a determination to impose order on the rest of the world – as foreign secretary Palmerston had reminded parliament four years earlier, 'half civilised Governments, such as those of China, Portugal, Spanish America, all require a dressing down every eight or ten years to keep them in order'. Although the word 'jingoism' was not yet in currency it summed up the national mood; the euphoria was widespread and the British people regarded the forthcoming campaign as a moral crusade. Although they had forgotten the harsh realities of warfare, and understood little of the need to curb Russia's territorial ambitions, they responded to the mood which was so vehemently expressed by *The Times* on 27 February 1854:

> It is not our business to inquire very exactly into the character of this enthusiasm, or to ask how far everyone of the multitude, or even if the many gentlemen who were there, understands the question at issue. The prevalent feeling is an honourable and a just one. It is that England has bound herself to assist a weak neighbour against the violence of a strong one, and that, for one reason or another, she has, in effect, been slow to fulfil her

pledge, and has now to make up for that lost time. It is, in fact, the people's quarrel, and a just one. Whether that people might not have spoilt their cause ere this by over much zeal it matters little now, when all are agreed, and nothing remains but to fight it out with Russia. But does anybody know England and doubt the result? It is no mere mob that leads this metropolis, nor does the metropolis lead the nation against its will. It is the whole nation that speaks in this way, and it is the whole nation that in heart and spirit goes with every regiment chosen for service from its barracks to the ocean steamer and thence to the seat of war. That nation, if not the most populous, is the most powerful, because the most determined, energetic and persevering people in the world. It never says what it does not mean, and never means what it does not carry out. Having once begun – having once cheered on these fine fellows to the work, whence so many of them will not return – it will certainly do its part, and will persevere in a noble cause to the utmost farthing, to the last inch of ground and the last drop of blood. England has been long making up her mind, but from that mind, so made up, she will never withdraw. Year after year she will send forth new fleets and new armies, if need be; and fight her battle single-handed, as she has done before, if that too, be necessary. For the honour of the civilised world, we cannot believe she will ever again be placed in that predicament; but even if it should be the case, she will not flinch from a quarrel in which she believes HEAVEN will still be her friend.

War fever was also breaking out in Russia. Shortly before leaving St Petersburg, Seymour reported that an English traveller in the country had found 'the peasantry greatly exasperated and clamorous for war' and that he himself believed that most Russians 'have been led to believe by the village Priests and vagrant Monks that their religion is in danger and that the Turks are massacring the Greeks in all directions'. The middle classes, too, were caught up in the patriotic fervour. In Moscow the governor, Count Sagrewski, had raised 600,000 roubles for the war effort and all over the country there had been reports of mysterious visions and apparitions which portended a great Russian victory. More prosaically the Russian Northern Fleet began preparing for the expected onslaught in the Baltic and one of Seymour's last despatches to London contained the information that plans were being laid to scuttle ships off Kronstadt to hinder any British bombardment from the sea.[5]

The Royal Navy was also on the move although its mobilisation was hampered by the same chronic manpower shortages which afflicted the army. This was especially true of the naval force which would be required to fulfil Graham's plan for waging a naval blockade of the Gulf of Finland. From St Petersburg Seymour had reported that the Russian Northern Fleet was reaching a state of preparedness for war and Graham feared that it would soon be in a position to enter the North Sea to attack British shipping and even the British coast. If that were to happen the Royal Navy would be hard pushed to oppose it as the bulk of the fleet had been committed to the Mediterranean. In some desperation a fleet of six screw-powered three-decker battleships and six steam frigates was hastily put together along with assorted smaller vessels; command was given to Vice-Admiral Sir Charles Napier who had already warned the Admiralty of the threat from the Baltic once the winter ice had broken.

One of the warships, HMS *Cumberland*, had just returned from three years service on the North American station, but without consulting captain or crew Graham ordered it to join Napier's fleet which had set sail from Spithead for the port of Kiel on 10 March. The senior members of *Cumberland*'s crew were then dispersed throughout Napier's ships and provided much needed experience as petty officers for the woefully undermanned force. In an attempt to solve the navy's recruitment problems – which had come into being in the years following the Napoleonic wars – Graham had introduced the Register of Seamen which was supposed to contain the names of all British seagoing men capable of serving in the navy. When it was first produced in 1839 it contained 175,000 names but by 1852 it had dropped to 150,000; even then only about one in twenty-five had ever served under the White Ensign. As a result there had been a flurry of activity and, before the summer of 1853, far-reaching reforms had been introduced. Under the terms of an Order in Council and the Continuous Service Act sailors' terms of service were regularised to ten years, pay was increased, pensions and paid leave were introduced and conditions on board improved.

These reforms would pay dividends for the navy in the long term but were of little immediate help to Napier. When his ships left British waters they only got under weigh thanks to the efforts of a small band of trained men but the remainder was a motley collection of coastguards, former fishermen or dockyard riggers whose best years were behind them. On board the battleship HMS *Nile*, for instance, the first Sunday church service revealed a disproportionately large number of bald heads and greying hairs when caps were removed for prayers. Matters were just as bad on HMS *Monarch* which had only eight able seamen out of a ship's company of 850. 'The *Monarch* is in a most deplorable state; she ought not to have been sent to sea,' noted Napier. 'There is hardly a man in her who knows the ropes.' So grim was the problem – the press gangs of an earlier age had disappeared – that when he arrived in the Bight of Kiel on 16 March Napier was forced to enlist seamen from Sweden and Denmark to ensure that his ships would be fully operational.[6]

A tall imposing Scot with a face full of whiskers, 'Black Charley' Napier was one of the best known naval commanders of the day and a sailor whose career seemed to have been blessed by the Nelson touch. He was certainly not a run-of-the-mill Victorian naval officer. While his service in the Royal Navy mirrored those of many of his contemporaries – he was a veteran of the Napoleonic wars, having commanded the frigate HMS *Thames* in the Mediterranean in 1811 – he was something of a maverick and much was expected of him in the Baltic. During the short-lived war against the United States he had been involved in the unorthodox amphibious attacks on Washington and Baltimore in the Chesapeake Bay area in 1814 when British forces burned down the White House and the Capitol and he enhanced his reputation for derring-do during the post-war peace.

His name came to the fore in waters thoroughly familiar to the Royal Navy – off Cape St Vincent – but it was made fighting under the *nom de guerre* of Carlos Ponza. At the time Britain was involved in a game of diplomatic cat and mouse while her ancient ally Portugal was caught up in a messy civil war. Following a period of unrest in 1820, during which the Portuguese Royal family was first expelled and then reinstated as a constitutional monarchy under King John VI, the country had been plunged into a state of anarchy. His death in 1826 provided the impetus for all-out warfare between his two sons – Don Pedro who was supported by the aristocracy and the liberal establishment and who wanted to place his infant daughter Maria de Gloria on the throne, and Don Miguel who was backed by the army and the church.

Officially Britain pursued a policy of neutrality after Miguel seized power in 1828 but Palmerston resented Miguel's increasingly authoritarian domestic policies. He was also concerned that France might take the opportunity to intrude in this traditional area of British strategic interests and turned a blind eye when a number of British naval officers, including Napier, resigned their commissions to fight for Pedro's cause. Napier commanded a 'liberation' squadron which defeated the Miguelite fleet off Cape St Vincent in July 1833 and he then proceeded to capture Valenza and Lisbon.

Seven years later he was in action again, having resumed his commission, when the Royal Navy seized Beirut and Acre and ordered the surrender of the Ottoman fleet during the Second Turko-Egyptian War but the buccaneering mystique of Carlos Ponza and the fall of Valenza never left him. Shortly before his departure Black Charley was entertained to dinner in the Reform Club and it fell to his old friend Palmerston to remind those present that when it came to winning a war they had in front of them a gallant commander who had already saved the 'liberties of Portugal'. The inference was obvious: anyone who was capable of standing up to petty tyranny in Portugal would make short work of the tsar and his northern ports. During the siege of Valenza, said Palmerston, the British envoy Lord William Russell had paid a visit to Napier's headquarters to see for himself how matters were proceeding:

Lord William Russell told me that they met a man dressed in a very easy way (great laughter), followed by a fellow with two muskets on his shoulders. (Renewed laughter.) They took him first for Robinson Crusoe (roars of laughter); but who should these men prove to be but our gallant Admiral on my right hand, and a marine behind him. (Laughter.) 'Well, Napier,' said Lord W. Russell. 'What are you doing here?' 'Why,' said my gallant friend, 'I am waiting to take Valenza.' 'But,' said Lord William, 'Valenza is a fortified town, and you must know that we soldiers understand how fortified towns are taken. You must open trenches, you must make approaches; you must establish a battery in breach; and all this takes a good deal of time, and must be done according to rule.' 'Oh,' said my gallant friend, 'I have got no time for that. (Cheers and laughter.) I have got some of my blue-jackets up here and a few of my ship's guns, and I mean to take that town with a letter.' (Laughter.) And so he did. He sent a letter to the Governor to tell him that he had better surrender at discretion. The Governor was a very sensible man (cheers and laughter); and so surrender he did.[7]

On that happy night in the Reform Club hopes were high that Black Charley would be able to repeat his exploits in the Baltic. Fuelled by drink and patriotic bonhomie those present took comfort in the commanding presence of a figure who seemed to epitomise Britain's resolve in the face of Russian threats. Others were less sure. 'I am anxious to get Napier under weigh,' Graham told Clarendon on 8 March. 'He is too fond of demonstrations on shore, of dinners and speechifying. We must now get to work in earnest.' Even Napier's captains had their doubts. Like his father, Henry Byam Martin was destined to become an admiral but in 1854 he was serving, somewhat reluctantly, in Napier's fleet and what he saw of his commander he did not particularly like:

> The selection of Sir Charles Napier to command the Baltic Fleet is remarkable – and one which both the profession and the public appear to view with distrust. He has had very little experience and has shown no capacity for the command of a fleet – and he is said to be wanting in the two most necessary qualities for command, discretion and nerve. He has gained notoriety as a lucky and successful buccaneer; but I doubt if the Russians are to be intimidated by a *name*.[8]

Byam Martin was right in one respect. As was the case with so many of the army's commanders, Napier's best years were indeed behind him (he was sixty-eight), but age had not atrophied his ambition. As early as the summer of 1853, when Russian forces had invaded the principalities, he had warned Aberdeen of the danger posed by Russia's Northern Fleet. With that in mind he decided to deploy his ships at Köge Bay, south of Copenhagen, where he would be able to guard the exits to the North Sea in the event of a Russian breakout. At the same time he sent a steam squadron under the command of Rear Admiral James Plumridge to reconnoitre the approaches to the Gulf of Finland – an aggressive deployment which seemed to justify the noisy confidence shown in him by the members of the Reform Club. His next move would depend on Nicholas's answer to Clarendon's ultimatum, which had demanded the withdrawal of Russian forces from the principalities and an answer within six days.

The response never materialised and on 28 March, two days after the ultimatum expired, Britain and France declared war on Russia. Forty years earlier the two unlikely allies had been involved in a fight to the death: now they were marching off to war together in the first European campaign to break the peace settlement of 1815. Shortly after Napier's fleet left home waters a French squadron of nine ships of the line, six frigates and nine steamers, commanded by Vice-Admiral Parseval Deschenes, left for the Baltic. At the same time the first French army units began embarking at Marseilles: they would eventually form four infantry divisions and two brigades of cavalry.

At least Napier was certain what his duties would be in the event of hostilities. The same could not be said with any confidence about the army's role. As it became increasingly clear that Russia would not back down, Raglan busied himself with intelligence reports which came from British and French sources in the Balkans and from the embassies in Constantinople. These seemed to suggest that the Russians had decided to concentrate their spring offensive on Dobruja, the marshy coastal strip between the Balkan Mountains and the western Black Sea coast. Although the heavily fortified towns of Silistria and Shumla and the old Roman defences of Trajan's Wall blocked their path, the Russian high command believed that a concentration of force would enable their army corps to cross the Turkish border and seize Constantinople before the British and the French could intervene. At the end of March two Russian army corps crossed the Danube at Galatz and Tulcea and began besieging Silistria on 14 April.

Faced by the Russian onslaught and the possibility of Turkey being invaded, Raglan had to consider appropriate counter-measures but, first, everything hung on Burgoyne's and Ardent's findings. Initially, the two engineers believed that military assistance should be confined to the protection of Constantinople and the Dardanelles with 'a scene of operations at Gallipoli' – the neck of land which guards the Sea of Marmara and the seaward approaches to Constantinople – and they were unenthusiastic about operations elsewhere. In fact the French had already despatched 15,000 troops to Gallipoli in two divisions under the command of Generals Canrobert and Bosquet and, predictably perhaps, they had commandeered the best accommodation. True to form, too, they quickly established a decent restaurant for the use of officers.

From the sea Gallipoli presented a pleasing prospect, its houses following the curve of the hillside against a startlingly blue sky, but it was only illusion. Shortly after arriving, in one of his first despatches to *The Times*, William Howard Russell called it 'a wretched place – picturesque to a degree but horribly uncomfortable'. And when the first French soldiers landed they found a labyrinth of noisome hovels, worse than anything they had encountered in North Africa. Even the hardened veterans of the two regiments of the Foreign Legion were shocked by the conditions when they arrived in the middle of May. In the original French war plans they were not intended to play any role in the expeditionary force – Saint-Arnaud argued that the legion's responsibility was to garrison Algeria – but Napoleon thought otherwise. He believed that their presence might encourage Polish officers in the Russian army to desert and he may have been right. A number did cross over to the allied lines and served their new masters well. Amongst their number was Captain Chodasiewicz of the Tarutin Regiment who went on to write a popular account of the campaign under the anglicised form of his name, Hodasevich. He was also well rewarded for his trouble: in return for providing the allies with intelligence about the Russian defences he was made a staff officer and paid 9s.6d. per day.[9]

Serving with the legion was the future Marshal François-Achile Bazaine who took with him to Gallipoli his newly wedded wife Soledad, together with her piano. She was not the only wife to go to war – both the French and the British armies were accompanied by substantial numbers of wives and assorted camp followers – but she was the first of their number to gain public recognition. When a son of Marshal Ney lay dying of the cholera which was to sweep through the allied camp later that summer, Soledad Bazaine brought him into her husband's quarters and comforted his last hours with a programme of Mozart's and Beethoven's sonatas. The touching scene was much remarked upon in the obituaries for this unfortunate scion of a famous family.

The first British soldiers were due to arrive from Malta in mid-April. Reacting to the presence of the French generals, Newcastle had appointed 'a British officer of corresponding station with a force of corresponding strength' to command the forces in Gallipoli; otherwise this would have been Stratford's responsibility. The position fell to Lieutenant-General Sir George Brown, the Adjutant-General, another veteran of the Peninsula who was known throughout the army for his insistence on his men wearing correct uniform, however trying the conditions. An irascible Scot with a touchy temper, he also entertained a low opinion of the French and that lack of tact had already cost him the appointment as Raglan's second-in-command, Hardinge having argued that Brown did not 'possess those qualities of judgement, temper, skill and foresight' to deal successfully with a potentially touchy ally.

Following an uncomfortable journey by coach across France to Marseilles, and then by ship to Malta, Brown and his advance party of riflemen and sappers arrived at Gallipoli at the beginning of April and began making preparations for the arrival of the main British force. Their journey was a further example of the problems the British would face in transporting their army to Turkey – although most of the senior commanders were spared the lengthy voyage they still had an overland journey across France – 'very fatiguing' according to Raglan who followed a similar route – before the sea crossing to Malta and thence to Gallipoli. The selection of Raglan's staff and the senior divisional officers also proved to be prolonged and time-consuming. Moreover, it was a practice open to patronage and as always happens in the event of hostilities senior officers indulged in a good deal of jockeying for position, it being a maxim of the Victorian army that warfare, death and disease were the best means of rapid promotion.

In this respect one example will stand for many – the case of Prince George, the Duke of Cambridge, a grandson of King George III and a cousin of Queen Victoria (and it may be added, at one time considered a potential husband, in spite of the young queen finding him 'very ugly, his skin in a shocking state'). In 1852 he had been considered a potential successor to Wellington as commander-in-chief – a suggestion vetoed by Albert who claimed that his kinsman 'would carry no weight with the public' – but despite the disappointment the thirty-five-year-old soldier was determined to use the forthcoming conflict to further his career. 'Very busy all day at Horse Guards with a view to being employed with the Army to go to Turkey,' he confided to his diary on 11 February, as if the only criterion would be his power of persuasion and not any known military ability. However, two days later found him at Buckingham Palace 'in a great state', telling his cousin that it would be a disgrace to his Royal name were he not granted an appointment in Raglan's army. 'We agreed with him and promised to do all we could,' promised the queen and that same evening she put the matter to Aberdeen over dinner. Despite admissable doubts as to the wisdom of sending a member of the Royal family to the battlefront the prime minister informed Newcastle that he would take responsibility for any appointment given to Cambridge, provided that it was not as second-in-command to Raglan. On 15 February Cambridge was given command of the 1st Division.[10]

Others had been equally busy promoting their cases. Command of the Cavalry Division was awarded to Lieutenant-General the Earl of Lucan who had lost little time in contacting Hardinge with a plea for advancement. Once again family position and influence outweighed any military competence for Lucan had been on half-pay since leaving the army in 1837. During that time his only skirmishes had been with his tenants on his Irish estates in County Mayo whom he had subjected to a savage policy of evictions. True, as a young man he had seen active service, having commanded the 17th Lancers, but his position owed everything to the £25,000 his family had paid the War Office for the privilege. Under his command the regiment had prospered, but at a price. Lucan was a martinet who did not suffer fools gladly: although the 17th Lancers enjoyed Wellington's praise for its smart turnout it was won through Lucan's uncertain temper and deep purse.

One fact retrieved Lucan's appointment. He was something of an expert on the Russian army, having been seconded as a staff officer in 1828 during the war against Turkey and he was familiar with the terrain in the Balkans. As the British Army only possessed the most rudimentary maps of the region Lucan's experience could be invaluable and it certainly counted when the appointment was made. Although Lucan had only requested a brigade he was given the Cavalry Division, whose Light Brigade would be the eyes and ears of the British expeditionary force. Given the lack of experience throughout the army's senior command the appointment made some sense. Lucan might have been arrogant and short-tempered; he had not worn uniform for seventeen years, but at least he knew about Silistria and the Danube plain.

Unfortunately, there was another contender for the position – his brother-in-law, James Henry Brudenell, the Earl of Cardigan, one of the most notorious men in the British Army. His reputation had been won for all the wrong reasons. In 1833, as a result of a vindictive campaign he had waged against a fellow officer, he was court-martialled and relieved of his command of the 15th Hussars. Two years later family influence and the payment of £40,000 had bought him command of the 11th Hussars but the early humiliations had not taught Cardigan any restraint. Although his new regiment was renowned for its smart appearance, especially for the men's tight cherry-coloured overalls, its panache came from a ruthless regime. Floggings were commonplace, officers were expected to conform to exacting standards or transfer to other regiments and in 1840 Cardigan put himself beyond the law by wounding one of their number, Lieutenant Harvey Tuckett, in a duel. Cardigan chose to stand trial before his equals in the House of Lords and while he was acquitted in February 1841, public scandal continued to be his companion.

Even before he had been charged he caused outrage by persecuting another officer, Captain John Reynolds, who had ordered a bottle of Moselle wine for a guest during a regimental dinner. In normal circumstances this would have been regarded as nothing worse than a minor breach of etiquette – Cardigan had ordered champagne to be served – but Reynolds was already suspected of being an outsider and something less than a gentleman. The reason? He had served with the army in India and was therefore considered to be a troublesome middle-class career officer. (In fact he and his cousin, Richard Reynolds, another target of Cardigan's scorn, came from a wealthy landed family.) The row became public knowledge as the 'black bottle' affair (Reynolds had been accused of ordering porter, an unforgivable sin) and Cardigan found the words being thrown at him whenever he appeared in public in London or Brighton. Out of spite Cardigan refused Reynolds permission to transfer to a new posting at the Royal Military College, Sandhurst and the affair was only settled by Raglan's intervention, one of many 'disagreeable visits' he recorded in his diary. Even so, that was not the full sum of Cardigan's notoriety. In 1844 he had been accused of having an affair with the wife of Lord William Paget who took legal action against him – unsuccessfully as it turned out, but the court appearance only added to the earl's infamous reputation.

All this was bad enough for any senior British Army officer and sufficient cause to prevent further advancement; sadly for Raglan there was one other disqualification but this, too, was overlooked. Cardigan had been married to Lucan's youngest sister – they had parted company in 1844 – and the two men were sworn enemies. It was inconceivable that they should serve together in the same division, let alone that one should take orders from the other, but social standing was all that mattered. Without consulting Raglan, whom he knew to be a family friend of the Brudenells, Hardinge awarded the Light Brigade to the hot-headed hussar officer. The news was not calculated to win approval throughout the army; indeed, it caused dismay in the junior ranks – 'two bigger fools could not be pulled out of the British Army,' noted Captain Henry Portal, 4th Light Dragoons.

Compared to this potentially explosive appointment the remaining posts were filled with a welcome lack of rancour. Brown was given the Light Division, Burgoyne was named as Chief Engineer and the other divisional posts went to officers who had cut their teeth fighting Napoleon: Sir George de Lacy Evans (2nd), Sir Richard England (3rd) and Sir George Cathcart (4th). To complete Raglan's staff the mild-mannered Sir James Estcourt became Adjutant-General and Lord de Ros, another officer without experience, Quartermaster-General. While these senior appointments were admittedly elderly there was a goodly number of efficient infantry brigadiers including William Eyre, Colin Campbell and J.L. Pennefather, all of whom were to show dash and courage leading their men in battle. Command of the remaining cavalry unit, the Heavy Brigade, was given to James Scarlett, a kindly man who had a reputation amongst cavalrymen of being good with horses, though his proficiency as a soldier was open to question.

A week after the formal declaration of war, on 5 April 1854, Hardinge ordered Raglan to the seat of war, his first duty being to secure the safety of Constantinople. Although the commander-in-chief conceded that the distance between London and Gallipoli meant that Raglan would be permitted to exercise his own 'judgement and discretion' it was still made clear that he would come under the government's overall direction:

Her Majesty having been graciously pleased to appoint Your Lordship to the command of a detachment of her army to be employed upon a particular service, I have to desire that you will be pleased to take the earliest opportunity to assume the command of that force, and carry into effect such instructions as Your Lordship may receive from Her Majesty's Ministers.[11]

Having finalised his staff – including the appointment of four aides-de-camp all of whom were family relations (Major Lord Burghesh, Captain Poulett Somerset, Captain Nigel Kingscote and Lieutenant Somerset Calthorpe) – Raglan left for Paris on the evening of 10 April. Accompanying him was the Duke of Cambridge and several hundred well-wishers gathered to give him a rousing send-off. For the first time since 1808, when a British expeditionary force landed at Mondego Bay to begin the campaign in Portugal against Napoleon's armies, British forces were once more on the move against a major European power. As *The Times* recorded the occasion, Raglan would enjoy the command of 'the finest army that has ever left these shores'.

9

Uneasy Partners

I feel uneasy about the Chief Command. Raglan under Saint-
Arnaud would never do! Marlborough and Eugene co-operated
successfully, and so have other great generals – why not small
ones?

The Earl of Clarendon to Lord Cowley, 27 February 1854

It was only to be expected that from the very outset of the campaign Britain and France would experience difficulties in working
together in common cause. Recent history was one reason. Waterloo
still rankled in many French officers' minds, while Raglan and his senior commanders did not find it easy adjusting to the idea that a former
enemy was now an ally. For the Royal Navy it was worse. They had
spent much of their time and energy since 1815 preparing for further
hostilities with France, whom they considered their main European
rival. Lack of precedent was another factor. When Wellington had
fought Napoleon he had enjoyed the loosest of arrangements with
his alliance partners, preferring informal consultation to hard and
fast agreements. Even so, he had little respect for his allies in the
Peninsula and concurred with his brother Richard's assessment that
he 'would not trust the protection of a favourite dog to the whole
Spanish army.' His soldiers had been equally unimpressed. 'What an
ignorant superstitious, priest-ridden, dirty, lousy set of poor devils are
the Portuguese,' wrote Private Wheeler of the 51st Foot. 'Without
seeing them it is impossible to conceive there exists a people in Europe
so debased.'[1]

Given that uneasy background the establishment of a reliable working relationship was essential. However, the matter was complicated

further by national pride and prestige. While Britain enjoyed naval supremacy she was sending smaller land forces. The amphibious nature of the operations clearly gave Britain hegemony at sea but on land France enjoyed supremacy and therefore had solid grounds for requesting overall command. Aware of this discrepancy Napoleon III insisted from the very outset that a French officer should be appointed supreme commander of the allied forces and that the Turks should come under France's direct control. This was unpalatable to the British but the minister for war, Newcastle, fudged the issue by urging Raglan to keep the two armies 'separate as much and as long as possible'. His preliminary orders provided for the defence of Constantinople on a line between the Black Sea and the Sea of Marmora and in making the necessary deployments he was ordered to 'consult' Saint-Arnaud and Omar Pasha so as not to impede their own operations. As for the French, Saint-Arnaud was left in doubt about the paramountcy of his position. 'Leave me the care of looking out for the interests of the country,' Napoleon . . . told him before Saint-Arnaud left Marseilles, 'we will be the dupes of nobody.'[2]

Unfortunately, the formal agreements did little to clear up the muddle. On 12 March Britain, France and Turkey had signed a tripartite treaty agreeing to send military aid 'in defence of the Ottoman territories in Europe and Asia against Russian aggression' but the question of overall command was left open to 'joint consultation', with article IV conceding that the three armies would remain the responsibility of their national commanders. The later Convention of London, which ratified the agreement on 10 April, also shed no light on the issue. As the campaign progressed, the failure to create a watertight system of overall command and control was to prove vexatious to all three allies.

Raglan arrived in Paris on 11 April where he and Cambridge were met by Cowley and the French Minister of War, Marshal Jean Vaillant, before being whisked off in the imperial carriage to meet Napoleon III at the Tuileries. During the week that followed, Raglan and his staff were fêted as honoured guests. They had dinner with the emperor, visited the opera and inspected the might of the French Army on the Champs du Mars. They were even treated to enthusiastic crowds and shouts of '*Vive l'Angleterre!*' – an occurrence so unusual that it was reported in the French press – but little or nothing was said about the evolution of a common strategy. Indeed, when Raglan met Saint-Arnaud the question was politely ignored and the French marshal spent most of his time discussing the potential shortcomings of the Ottoman army. (Before leaving London Raglan had been advised by Clarendon that the Turkish forces had been 'enfeebled by abominations'.) The meeting ended amicably enough and Raglan's despatches from Paris leave the uneasy impression that both men preferred to bypass the topic rather than face it head on before the campaign began in earnest.

For the easy-going and courteous Raglan it had been an agreeable interlude. He had enjoyed inspecting the French forces, in particular the cavalry which, as no mean horseman himself, he found to be efficient and well-mounted and he seems to have taken pleasure in Napoleon's company, the two men having met during the emperor's exile in London. Cowley, too, proved useful by providing him with gossip from the old Royalist faction who distrusted Napoleon III and his military ambitions. He also passed on the intelligence that Napoleon's half-brother, the Duc de Morny, was suspected of consorting with the Russians and showing them allied war plans. On this point he had already written to Clarendon on 6 March: 'I am more than ever for the independence of our troops, or we shall be betrayed by some blackguard or other.'[3]

To a certain extent there was a degree of snobbishness in the British position – Saint-Arnaud was considered by the British Embassy staff to be a vulgar *arriviste* who spent too much time in dubious company – but Cowley could see that the Russians were propagating the idea in the French press that a war in the east would only protect British imperial interests. Throughout the negotiations which had led to war the British ambassador had warned Clarendon that a separate French deal with Russia was not impossible. 'I cannot but fear that these practices have had a certain influence on the Emperor and his Government,' he wrote on 19 January. 'Not that they partake the opinions of these writers, but because they see that the arguments employed by the latter have had their effect upon the Public and that the war in the East would be decidedly unpopular.'[4]

As Wellington's nephew Cowley's suspicions about the strength of the alliance were perhaps understandable but he was right about the most important element of the entente between the two countries. From the outset Napoleon had made it clear to the British ambassador that France should be considered the senior partner. In private discussion with Raglan, Cowley reminded him that he had already written to Clarendon on that vexed subject. As far as the French attitude towards the question of command was concerned nothing had been settled, nor was it ever likely to be. As Cowley wrote:

> Your Lordship will naturally enquire how this came to be, and I can only answer that it proceeds from the natural defects of the French Government and of the French character. There is no unity of action among the Members of Parliament, no concert, no interchange of opinions. Each Department acts for itself without reference to others, and each Minister is jealous of an interference with what he considers his Prerogatives, as he is determined to make use of them. Hence, when two or more Departments are concerned in the same business, all is confusion . . .
>
> Then comes into play the vanity of the French character, the rivalry of the military and naval professions at Constantinople and the dislike of both to be under the direction of a civilian. In short, if Your Lordship saw behind the scenes, as I sometimes do, you would be astonished that in complicated questions with the French Government, any progress is made at all.[5]

These gloomy prognostications only served to make Raglan more uneasy about his relationship with his former enemies. Perhaps, he reasoned, a way of working together would be found once the armies were together in the field. After all, Newcastle had merely told him that he only had to 'consult' the French and certainly did not have to take orders from them.

On the morning of 18 April Raglan travelled by train to Chalon-sur-Saône, the shortcomings of the French railway system quickly being revealed to him when he was obliged to travel to Lyons by river steamer. Normally he would have continued on to Avignon by the same method but the Rhone was low and he and his staff had to take to carriages to complete their long and bruising journey across France. When they eventually reached Marseilles on the evening of 20 April a gale in the Mediterranean imposed a forty-eight hour delay to his sailing, so it was not until a week later that he arrived at the fledgling British base of operations in Gallipoli. There he found that Brown was doing his best under difficult circumstances. The French, having arrived first, had settled in the more salubrious Turkish quarter, leaving little room for the British and there was already friction between the two camps. Raglan's first General Order addressed the problem by reminding his men of the need for co-operation 'with an Ally to whom it has been the lot of the British nation to be opposed in the field for many centuries', but it was to prove an uphill task. There was a regrettable tendency for British officers to voice their dissatisfaction at the superior French facilities at Gallipoli and Brown was predictably dismissive of his fellow commanders. Saint-Arnaud he described as 'a strange flighty fellow and one it will not do to take at his word', while Prince Napoleon, who led the French 3rd Division, was 'the least prepossessing specimen of Royalty'.[6]

There were also differences of style. The French officers considered themselves to be more military and professional, whereas they thought the British hopelessly, though endearingly, amateurish. In contrast to their own bemedalled and caparisoned commanders, most of the senior British officers seemed to be uninterested in appearances. Raglan wore a simple frock coat, Cambridge arrived wearing a tweed jacket and Lucan preferred a hunting coat to a uniform jacket. As Russell reminded his *Times* readers, this was simply a matter of differing attitudes to fashion:

> Frenchmen live in their uniform, while everybody knows no real British soldier is quite happy without his mufti. He must have his wide-awake [hat] and shooting jacket, and dressing-gown and evening dress, and a tub of some sort or other, a variety of gay shirting, pictorial and figurative, while the Gaul does very well without them.[7]

However, Russell also pointed out that, whereas the French battalions travelled lightly, it was noticeable that copious amounts of luggage and, in some cases, their servants followed the British army's formations. Cambridge, for example, was accompanied by his own French chef and some of the cavalry officers brought with them their hunters and hounds, almost as if they were engaged on an exotic sporting expedition.

Fortunately, the soldiers themselves were prepared to be friendly and at brigade and unit level there was a good deal of co-operation. Despite difficulties over language British and French soldiers were soon visiting each other's camps to compare uniforms and equipment and offering one another entertainment in the form of readily available cheap alcohol. As Russell put it, 'when raki and wine have done their work . . . English and French might be seen engaged in assisting each other to preserve the perpendicular'. Shortly after Franks's regiment arrived, one of their number, an Irishman called Johnny Martin, 'a fine built young fellow . . . also fond of drop of whiskey', did what he could to cement the new entente:

> It so happened that Johnny had wandered out of his own camp and found himself in the camp of a Battery of French Artillery, only about a hundred yards from our own lines. Although not able to speak French, he had by some means made the men know how matters stood, and the warm-hearted Frenchmen brought him to the canteen, and soon placed before him some lunch, or what he called 'a jolly tuck out' washed down by a plentiful supply of French brandy, to which Johnny paid due attention.[8]

The upshot was one very drunk trooper of dragoons who narrowly avoided a flogging after 'staggering back to his own camp' but the incident was not untypical of the fraternisation amongst the rank and file during the first days of the campaign.

More serious were the differences in provisions and equipment. With their recent experience of campaigning in Algeria the French had arrived with adequate supplies of tents, building equipment, transport and ample medical equipment including ten field hospitals. Not so the British who depended on a Commissariat Department run largely by civilians and controlled by the Treasury. Its Commissary-General was James Filder, a civil servant who had been brought out of retirement at the outbreak of war to be responsible for the provision of Raglan's army. During the Peninsula War Wellington had based his logistics on mule trains which supplied the army from a network of magazines spread across Portugal. However, it was an expensive process and had been disbanded after 1815 as part of the cutbacks in defence expenditure and Filder and his staff were forced to begin again from scratch.

As a result the arrangements for supplying the British forces proved to be woefully defective and even the usually mild-mannered Estcourt was moved to complain that the Commissariat lacked any discernible organisation. This was mainly due to the fact that it had to produce a new system but the absence of objectives was also to blame. When the army set out for Gallipoli a short sharp colonial-type campaign in the Danubian provinces was envisaged which, it was

thought, would be concluded before the onset of winter. Even if
Sevastopol had to be attacked, that, too, could be accomplished
quickly and efficiently. The miscalculation would cost the British
Army dear.

After arriving in Gallipoli on 28 April Raglan proceeded to
Constantinople where he stayed for a few days at the British Embassy.
Stratford pressed an invitation on him to make free use of his quarters
at Therapia but the British commander preferred to be closer to his
forces who were being quartered on the opposite, Asian side of the
Bosphorus at Scutari. There he and his staff moved into a simple
wooden house standing in front of the beach 'where all the filth
of Constantinople is driven either by the wind or the current'. As
Raglan told his daughter Charlotte in the same letter, the stench was
unbearable and within a week one of the aides reported that his chief
was feeling 'seedy' from the privations of diarrhoea.

It was hardly surprising that the British high command should
have suffered such deprivations. Although the old cavalry barracks
looked comfortable from the outside the appearance was deceptive.
Inside, the British soldiers and their families were forced to endure
unimaginable squalor. 'The dilapidation! the dirt! the rats! the fleas!'
wrote an enraged Fanny Duberly, the young wife of the paymaster
of the 8th Hussars, whose letters and diaries provide one of the most
colourful accounts of the campaign. In the town itself she discovered
that things were even worse: 'horribly filthy beggars [were] hovering
everywhere . . . refuse of every description . . .'[9]

Not everyone was so disgusted. Those with a classical education
had not failed to hear the echoes of a past which had only existed
for them in dusty textbooks. 'On Friday [28 April] we reached Cape
Matapan, and came among the Cyclades,' noted Captain Anthony
Sterling who had come out of retirement to serve as Brigade Major in
Colin Campbell's Highland Brigade, 'and poor Haidee was mourned
over by the poetical part of the company.' Their journey had hardly
been propitious – the paddle wheels of their steamer, the *Tonning*,
had failed and they suffered the ignominy of being towed into port
by the steamer *Trent*. Although 'fagged to death' he was enamoured
by 'Stamboul' and was well pleased by the situation of the brigade's
base at Scutari:

Nothing can be more picturesque than the situation of our camp
[Sterling wrote on 29 April]. An immense and beautiful barrack

(square 230 yards to the side) crowns a hill close to the sea; from this hill a sloping, undulated, grassy descent leads down to a brook, which enters the Sea of Marmora, about half a mile down the coast; on the other side of the stream the ground again rises, and the view is closed by a green elevation, on which the Brigade of Guards is encamped, and behind their tents, far off snowy Olympus of Asia Minor makes a silvery distance. On the right hand is the sea, with an island or two; and Stamboul, variegated and brilliant as the Arabian Nights. On the left, a long Turkish cemetery, in a cypress grove, with its white Moslem tombstones upright, and mixed among the russet stems of the trees. The encampment stretches along the side of this space next to the sea.[10]

Encamped close by were the regiments of the Light Division and throughout May they were joined at regular intervals by the remaining British forces. The arrival of the 93rd Highlanders caused a particular stir with their bagpipes and kilts – the Turks thought they belonged to Raglan's harem – but the concentration of frequently bemused British and French soldiers was soon causing problems to both armies. With its minarets and domes, its alien sights and smells, its narrow alleys and exotic promises, Constantinople was both a fascination and a temptation. Behind the façade officers like Hugh Annesley of the Grenadiers found 'streets filthy beyond description' but even so the enticements proved too much for too many of the men. It did not take them long to discover backstreet bars and brothels and throughout the month there was a dismal increase in drunkenness and venereal disease. On one night alone, from a force numbering 14,000, 2400 men were reported drunk and incapable.

It was not to be wondered at, therefore, that Raglan was anxious to make a move but to do so he had to make an accommo-dation with his allies. The first talks were scarcely promising. No sooner had Saint-Arnaud arrived in Constantinople than he began conniving to place the Turkish field forces under his command. On 11 May he called on Raglan to inform him, quite wrongly, that the Sultan had agreed to this happening. To settle the issue a meeting was called two days later in Constantinople. Through-out the talks Raglan and Stratford argued that each of the allies had agreed to act under separate commands and they remained unmoved by Saint-Arnaud's compromise proposal to place individual

Turkish units, including the Bashi-Bazouk cavalrymen, under French control.

It was not the end of the matter. Saint-Arnaud continued to lobby the Porte – his meetings were reported by Rose, since 13 April acting as British liaison officer with the French – and Raglan found himself in the undignified position of having to seek his own audiences with the Sultan. Following a warning from Stratford that Saint-Arnaud was due to meet the Sultan on 23 May, Raglan made sure that he, too, was present. Although it was inconclusive – Raglan repeated the Newcastle formula that he was only obliged to consult and reminded his allies that he was under orders from his own government – Saint-Arnaud refused to let the matter drop. In this respect Stratford proved a good friend for he had already been advised by Clarendon that he was to do all in his power to ensure the safety of the British expeditionary force in Turkey:

> If Her Majesty's Government are to give effectual aid to Turkey and to engage in active operations, it is absolutely necessary that we should know upon what we can depend, and that we should not be spectators or sharers in defeat caused by imbecility and cowardice.[11]

Although his message was aimed mainly at the Turks, Clarendon remained unhappy about the whole question of directing the alliance's military and naval forces in the area of operations and had already told Stratford to order the Turks not to engage in any aggressive act until war had been declared. On the other hand he had to avoid making the French jealous of British prestige even if that meant flattering them whenever possible: 'They would then have the satisfaction of believing that they were on a footing of perfect equality with us and their vanity would not require them to play a lesser role.' The Great Elchi replied on 29 June that he was well aware of the situation but he still thought it better to thwart French efforts to gain the upper hand at the Porte: 'Our friends of the Seine are determined not only to have the lion's share in all joint dealings with the Turks but also to have it served out to them first.'[12]

Not only were there potential problems with the allies but the British command structure was not all that it could be. In theory Dundas and Raglan had separate command of the navy and army and were expected to act in concert but the practice proved to be rather different. Both men belonged to the aristocracy – Dundas was born a Deans but in 1808 married his cousin Janet Dundas, daughter of Lord Amesbury and took her surname; his second wife was Lady Emily Moreton, sister-in-law of Admiral Lord Fitzhardinge, for many years a lord of the Admiralty – but both were very different in their approach to the war. Raglan was an appeaser but he could be firm when required. Dundas, though fiery in his personal dealings, was thought to be over-cautious. He had already made it clear that he was not prepared to risk his ships in front of Sevastopol's guns, even though Graham continued to insist on an assault. On 13 June he wrote again to Lyons reminding him that the destruction of the Russian naval base was a priority:

> Sebastopol is the point to which our views and ultimate efforts must be directed, and I am persuaded that you will never lose sight of it. Every preparation should be quietly made which is necessary to the disembarkation in the Crimea; so that if at any moment the opportunity should present itself the means may not be wanting.[13]

Of this thinking Dundas was less sure and, ominously for the British cause, it led to a cancerous rift with Lyons who favoured a more aggressive approach. And as if that were not sufficiently awkward for the British, Dundas did not particularly like Raglan.

Strains in the relationship became evident as soon as the British forces began moving to Turkey. The navy had responsibility both for the deployment and for the movement of forces within the theatre of operations. For example, Raglan had to apply to the naval officer concerned, Rear-Admiral Edward Boxer, for the use of the steam frigate *Caradoc* and there were constant clashes between the navy and army over the transport of men and equipment. All this led to unnecessary vexation and bad feeling. Raglan did his best to smooth over matters but even he was prone to feel dismay, exclaiming in obvious irritation about Boxer's pedantic observance of regulations: 'I am powerless. No man can make him a man of arrangement.'

Dundas had also fallen out with Stratford simply because the British naval commander resented coming under the political direction of the British ambassador in Constantinople. Disagreements ranged from relatively minor matters, such as the provision of Turkish coal, to the more weighty question of sharing information with the Admiralty and the Foreign Office. When an increasingly touchy Dundas sent reports back to London in June, claiming that his greatest enemy was not the Russians but the British ambassador – the accusations were repeated and soon became common knowledge in London – an indignant Stratford was forced to remonstrate with Clarendon:

> I cannot refrain from expressing the painful impression which parts of Admiral Dundas's correspondence have lately made upon me. The tone generally, and the language sometimes, is such as to make me feel that I am corresponding with an antagonist rather than with a colleague. This is not as it ought to be, and the interests of the public service are exposed to dangers from the indulgence of such feelings.[14]

Clarendon was sympathetic. As tactfully and as firmly as he could, however, he reminded Stratford that although Dundas was a 'hot-tempered' man he also had his pride. Perhaps Stratford should treat him with greater subtlety and make him feel that he enjoyed the ambassador's total confidence:

> He [Dundas] thought you did not treat him as an equal and that your orders were opined to him in a tone which he had a right to resent. I am perfectly certain that that was not your intention and I have many times requested Sir Js Graham to assess him of it but at the same time however I cannot say that I myself should like to be addressed in the style of some of your letters.[15]

Having gently chastised him Clarendon ended the letter by reminding Stratford that the problem was finite as Dundas would be replaced at the end of the year by Lyons. Fox that he was, Stratford had already opened his own lines of communication with Lyons whom he believed to be a 'superior' officer, writing to him as early as 13 March that 'it would be particularly interesting to me to have an interchange of thoughts with you'.

In the short term those differences of opinion meant that although the allied naval and military forces conferred it was often difficult to reach a consensus about how best to aid the Turkish forces along the Danube. On 18 May a conference took place with Omar Pasha at the small Black Sea port of Varna and it was agreed to begin moving British and French forces there to support the Turks' flanks in the lower

Danube. The Turkish commander made a favourable impression on Raglan who expressed himself 'much pleased' with his military professionalism and sound arguments. However, when Raglan and Saint-Arnaud returned to Constantinople, the French commander suddenly started backtracking on the decision taken in Varna and decided that his forces were not ready to advance to contact with the enemy.

On one level he was probably right. Despite the relative ease which had accompanied the French deployment in Gallipoli, Saint-Arnaud still lacked the cavalry and artillery which were essential if the Turks were to be given sufficient support. The British, too, were still in the process of receiving the bulk of their forces, including the Cavalry Division, and were hamstrung by an inefficient commissariat. Nevertheless, Saint-Arnaud's indecision was also due to fear of failure at a time when nothing less than a resounding military victory would satisfy his fellow countrymen. Early in the morning of 4 June he called on Raglan at Scutari to tell him that he had changed his mind. Only Canrobert's 1st Division would proceed to Varna while the remainder of the French army would deploy in a defensive line behind the Balkan Mountains. If the British followed suit they would be able to protect the French left flank and by so doing retain allied solidarity 'to aid and succour the Turks in our own way'.

Courteously, but firmly, Raglan demurred. He had given his word to Omar and intended to keep it. Besides, British troops were already being moved and plans had been laid to send incoming troop transports direct to Varna. Having promised to furnish the Turks with direct assistance in the principalities Raglan intended to keep his word and he refused to be swayed by Saint-Arnaud's new argument. Later, when he looked at the paper prepared by Saint-Arnaud, Raglan was able to understand more fully the French commander's fears: 'It is important,' he had written, 'not to give battle to the Russians, except with all possible chances of success, and the certainty of obtaining great results.'[16]

The following day Saint-Arnaud's senior aide, Colonel Trochu, returned to Scutari to reinforce his master's determination and to advise the British that General Bosquet's 2nd Division was already on the march north. Once again Raglan was determined yet courteous. The French could do as they pleased but he intended to stick to the original plan and deploy his forces in Varna. Five days later Rose crossed the Bosphorus with some important news: Saint-Arnaud had 'consented to revert to the original intention of placing the main body of the Allied Armies in Bulgaria'. Raglan had won the first round and the uneasy partnership made preparations for advancing to contact with the enemy. 'It is of essential importance,' wrote Newcastle in a letter congratulating Raglan's circumspection, 'that a joint move should be made, both with a view to preserve an harmonious co-operation with our French allies and also to ensure the effective conduct of the operations in which you are about to be engaged.'[17]

No such disunity encumbered the Russian forces as they opened their campaign – but that did not mean an absence of difficulties. Not only were the Russian forces operating with lengthy lines of communication but they had been hamstrung by Paskevich's concern for the safety of the western frontier. As a result the investment of Silistria was not conducted with the vigour expected by Nicholas and for his pains the elderly field-marshal was constantly criticised by the tsar. Although Paskevich's fears of an Austrian or Prussian attack on the Russian homeland were exaggerated he was not insensible to the threat posed by both countries. A week after the siege of Silistria began Austria and Prussia signed a defensive alliance, a move which led Paskevich to warn that 'if we are going to find all Europe ranged against us then we will not fight on the Danube.' Nicholas's response was perhaps predictable. As he could not bring himself to believe that the Austrians would intervene he ordered Paskevich to redouble his efforts: a victory at Silistria would be the best means of dissuading his erstwhile ally from entering the war:

> If the Austrians treacherously attack us, you have only to engage them with 4 Corps and the dragoons; that will be quite enough for them! Not one word more, I have nothing to add![18]

Unfortunately it was easier said than done. Silistria was heavily fortified, its inner casements guarded by a semi-circle of well constructed forts and earthworks. By the end of April Gorchakov, the field commander, had finally managed to get his siege artillery into position on the high ground to the south-west and the Ottoman garrison of 12,000 troops was surrounded. Gorchakov hoped that bombardment of Silistria's defences would wear down the opposition and allow his superior forces to assault the town itself, but it was a vain hope. Not only did it prove difficult to dislodge the earthworks through artillery fire but they were manned by well disciplined Egyptian and Albanian troops. In the key Arab Tabia earthwork which protected the Abd-el-Mejid fort they were commanded by two experienced British officers, Captain Butler, Ceylon Rifles, and Lieutenant Charles Nasmyth who reinforced his Bombay Artillery officer's salary by writing reports for *The Times*. Gradually a pattern set in – artillery bombardment followed by infantry assault – but despite the best efforts of the Russian army, the Ottoman forces refused to budge.

> At night our [Russian] soldiers generally work on the trenches and the Turks throw themselves upon them to stop them; then you should have seen and heard the rifle-fire. The first night I spent at the camp this terrible noise woke me up and alarmed me – I thought an assault was taking place – and I very quickly saddled my horse; but those who had already spent some time at the camp told me just to keep calm; this cannon-fire and rifle-fire was quite normal and they jokingly called it 'Allah'.[19]

The observer was an aristocratic young Russian second-lieutenant, Count Lev Tolstoy, who had already seen service with the Russian forces in the Caucasus. Later his experiences of warfare in the Balkans and the Crimea were to furnish him with the raw material for the battle scenes in his novel *War and Peace* but at the time his letters to his family offer few suggestions that he was witnessing a crucial engagement. (In one letter he described artillery fire as 'a truly beautiful [spectacle] especially at night'.) It was, though, a crucial battle for the allies. If Silistria fell the Franco-British forces would be forced into action before they had reached full strength; but if it held it would give them valuable breathing space. Everything hung on the endurance of the garrison and the strength of their defences for Omar was not prepared to commit his reserves in any attempt to raise the siege.

It was a gamble but by then the Russians, too, were risking everything. They had lost control of the Black Sea and were facing an enemy who was being steadily reinforced by two powerful allies. It was also becoming increasingly clear that their army in Bulgaria was suffering from supply and resupply problems and that these would be exacerbated if the vital base at Odessa was destroyed by British sea power.

A few days after the allied agreement to redeploy to Varna, the Russians suffered a setback. On 10 June Paskevich and a group of staff officers were observing the bombardment of the Arab-Tabia when they too came under fire. A Turkish shell exploded near them and although it seemed to cause no damage at the time the Russian commander claimed that he had been injured and would have to retire. Whether or not he had been hurt is open to doubt. Perhaps he had only succumbed to nerves but, mindful of his marshal's past service, Nicholas was prepared to forgive him. Paskevich retired from the field with his reputation intact and command passed to Prince Michael Gorchakov whom Tolstoy had already seen in the trenches, 'a slightly ridiculous figure, very tall, standing with his hands behind him, cap on back of head, bespectacled, and speaking like a turkeycock'.

Under his command the Russian forces rallied for a final assault on the fortress. Despite their courage and forbearance the Ottoman forces could not hold out for ever and without reinforcements their plight was desperate. Even the phlegmatic Butler, who kept a daily diary until his death from a head wound, expressed disgust with the ferocity of the fighting, much of which was close-quarter combat. Having witnessed the 'terrific slaughter' of Turkish troops he was dismayed to see their comrades taking a terrible revenge: 'Numbers of the townspeople went out and cut off the heads of the [Russian] slain to bring in as trophies, for which they hoped to get a reward; but the savages were not allowed to bring them within the gate.'[20]

Given the nature of the fighting, the need for a quick Russian victory and the improbability of reinforcements arriving in time, few would have given the Ottoman garrison any chance of holding out. As it turned out, though, the siege of Silistria provided a grim foretaste of the fighting which lay ahead for both sets of armies.

10

Opening Shots

For the peace, that I deem'd no peace, is over and done,
And now by the side of the Black and the Baltic deep,
And deathful-grinning mouths of the fortress, flames
The blood-red blossom of war with a heart of fire.
                                    from Alfred Tennyson, Maud (1854)

It was left to the Royal Navy to open the British account in the war
against Russia in 1854. Although a handful of British officers were
serving in the Ottoman army at Silistria and in Asia Minor, the first
shots fired in anger by allied forces were those of the guns of a joint
British-French squadron consisting of six British and three French
ships which bombarded the Russian port of Odessa on 22 April. It
was not one of the greatest actions in the annals of either navy but
it ended almost four months of frustration. Ever since entering the
Black Sea to impose the blockade, Lyons had been anxious to engage
the Russian fleet but there was little chance of drawing their warships
out of Sevastopol. There had been some naval activity including the
capture of a Russian merchantman by a British frigate but for the most
part it had been a question of routine patrolling. For the bellicose
Lyons it was a period of unnecessary restraint made worse by the
fact that he had been unable to capture the troublesome Russian
steamer, the *Vladimir,* which had spent a profitable time attacking
Turkish shipping off the coast of Asia Minor.

Odessa ended all that. Following the official declaration of war the
British steam-frigate HMS *Furious* arrived off Odessa to pick up the
British consul and other British subjects. Although a flag of truce was

flown, and despite the fact that such diplomatic truces were traditional
in warfare, the Russian shore batteries opened fire on *Furious* and her
ship's cutter which had attempted to enter the harbour under a white
flag. This breach of etiquette provided the allied fleet with the reason
for the first naval action of the war.

At 5.30 in the morning, two British (*Samson*, *Tiger*) and two French
warships (*Vauban* and *Descartes*) followed one another around in a
continuous circle, their guns opening fire as they came in range of
the harbour and its well-defended mole. A well-aimed Russian shot
set fire to *Vauban* which had to retire, but the attack continued as
Furious, *Terrible*, *Retribution* and *Mogodar* brought their guns to bear
on a target which one British naval officer compared to Brighton
from the Channel. By the end of the action twelve hours later the
main magazine on the Imperial Mole had exploded, several Russian
warships had been sunk and Odessa's fortifications had been largely
destroyed.

It was an action which brought together the old and the new.
Amongst the British warships was the sailing frigate *Arethusa*, a veteran
of Nelson's navy, and this was destined to be the last time that a British
capital ship would fight purely under sail. Good use was also made of
the Royal Navy's new rocket-boats which covered the squadron's
main attack and joined in the bombardment with their 24-pounder
projectiles. Fired from metal pipes, these were the navy's first missiles
and were responsible for the destruction of Odessa's main arsenal. The
deployment of the modern screw warships and the rocket-boats was a
timely reminder of the strength of the allied naval force in the Black
Sea. It also gave much needed substance to Graham's order to make
'an early impression' on the Russians.

Having drawn first blood Lyons sailed to reconnoitre Sevastopol
which he believed could be attacked in the same way – 'the bare
idea of our not striking a successful blow is painful' he told Graham
– but the Russians refused to be tempted out of harbour. In any case
the port was so heavily defended that neither Dundas nor Hamelin
were prepared to risk their ships in what at that stage they believed
would be a fruitless gesture against a heavily armed garrison. Some
idea of the dangers facing the allies' Black Sea fleet came on 12 May
when the 16-gunned British steamer *Tiger* ran aground off Odessa
in thick fog. Following a brisk bombardment by Russian field guns
the crew was obliged to surrender and they were taken ashore as
the first prisoners-of-war of the conflict. Not that their lot was an

unhappy one. The ship's officers were entertained by 'the good society of the place' while the sailors became firm favourites of their Russian counterparts for the simple reason that they had money to spend and the Russians did not. It was all too good to last, though, and *Tiger's* crew was exchanged for a group of Russian prisoners a month later.

In Britain great things were expected of the Royal Navy – and not just in the Black Sea. Napier's Baltic Sea fleet had left Portsmouth watched by Victoria and Albert who later informed his brother Ernest that it will be 'magnificent, unless it be too heavy for that shallow sea' and a jingoistic press warned the British people to expect news of 'tremendous victories'. How these were to be achieved was less certain. Napier had bragged that he would 'treat the Russians to the old Nelson trick in the Baltic' – a reference to the expedition of 1801 which had secured the dissolution of the League of Armed Neutrality during the war against Napoleon. However, in making the boast Napier seemed to have forgotten that Nelson's objectives were only partially successful. Although he won the Battle of Copenhagen, subsequent dilatoriness prevented the Royal Navy from reaching Reval and Kronstadt before the onset of the winter ice.

Still, Napier was not an officer to let the lessons of history concern him too much. Indeed, apart from his promise to be in Kronstadt or heaven by the end of the summer he seems to have had little clear idea about how to pursue the naval war in the Baltic beyond following Graham's general orders to blockade the Gulf of Finland and to investigate the possibility of attacking the Russian fortifications at Sveaborg (an island off Helsinki), Bomarsund (Aaland Islands), Reval (Estonia) and Kronstadt in the Gulf of Finland. These orders had arrived from Newcastle following the declaration of war and it had been made clear that the question of tactics would be left to Napier's discretion.

I have to request that you will direct him [Napier], in the first instance, to establish a strict blockade of the Gulf of Finland, and at the same time to pay particular attention to the state and fortified condition of the Islands of Aaland, and to ascertain the exact strength of the garrison at Bomarsund and the nature of its approaches; but you will particularly enjoin upon him that his principal object must be to prevent the Russian fleet from passing his line of blockade, having first clearly ascertained that he has left no Russian ships which could pass through the Sound [the passage between Denmark and Sweden] or Belt [the passage between Zealand and Funen].[1]

In an attempt to make sense of Graham's thinking Napier had taken the advice of a veteran of Nelson's time, Admiral Sir Thomas Byam Martin, who warned him that the fortresses at Sveaborg and Kronstadt were heavily defended and that it would prove difficult to tempt the Russian fleet to meet him in battle in deep waters. Like his son Henry, the older Byam Martin was none too impressed with Napier's understanding of the problems facing him; so much so that he took the trouble to send a memorandum to the Admiralty expressing his fears and warning that Napier 'was by no means at ease, but on the contrary very nervous'.

At the time the elder Byam Martin's warning was ignored (but not forgotten) mainly because Graham was confident that Napier would not only prevent a Russian break-out but in so doing he would also encourage Sweden to join the Franco-British alliance. This was a matter dear to Graham's heart – 'my darling project of a northern maritime confederacy against Russia' – and he was convinced that a stunning naval victory in the Baltic would achieve it. If Sweden were to supply troops to reinforce Napier's attacks on the Russian fortifications their reward might be renewed hegemony over the Finns. This would certainly put paid to Russian naval ambitions in the Baltic which was Britain's main concern, but Sweden's King Oscar I was not convinced. In common with his Scandinavian neighbours he enjoyed good relations with Russia and was not prepared to jeopardise them at Britain's, or France's, request. Through his wife he was related to Napoleon III but even this family link failed to persuade him. Like Austria's Franz Josef, Oscar decided to hedge his bets and await the outcome of events.

It was a sensible precaution. Ever since arriving in the Baltic the state of unpreparedness in the British fleet had become painfully obvious to Napier and his senior officers. Under normal circumstances it took the Royal Navy six months to a year to train up a warship's crew to a state of operational fitness but such a timetable now was impossible. Not only were most of the crews raw recruits but the older men were incapable of fulfilling such essential tasks as manning the top-masts. For Lord Clarence Paget, commanding HMS *Princess Royal*, the manpower problems seemed to be so insuperable that any type of offensive operations were unthinkable, at least in the immediate future:

> Daily did we practice at the target, and what with the noise of the guns, and the hammers of the artificers, of whom there were about 100 on board, for a fortnight we were in the confusion of Babel; but still we could not get men, men, men! I wrote and wrote to the Admiralty, stating that if they did not assist me by placing 200 coastguards on board, I should be taken by the first Russian frigate we fell in with. This really alarmed their Lordships, and eventually they completed me with that number, many of whom are admirable, but alas! some have turned out to be worn out and very useless folk.[2]

It was not as if Paget were without social or political connections. He was the eldest son of the Marquess of Anglesey and had served as Secretary to the Ordnance Board. He was also considered to be a professional and capable naval officer; yet, he, too, had difficulty persuading his superiors at the Admiralty that the shortfall in crew strength and the lack of training could cost the Baltic Fleet dear when it eventually went into action against the Russians. When that might be was still a matter of conjecture and, good commander that he was, Paget bent his energies to training his crew in gunnery and manoeuvring *Princess Royal* in battle conditions. Neither exercise was particularly easy: Admiralty injunctions to conserve shot curtailed realistic gunnery instruction and a shortage of signalling officers made station-keeping at sea a hazardous business. There had already been a number of collisions – hardly the best example with which to impress the watching Swedes – and several captains (though certainly not Paget) avoided firing their guns because of the mess it made on their ships' decks.

On 12 April there seemed to be a breakthrough when Rear-Admiral James Plumridge returned from a reconnaissance of the Gulf of Finland. From its approaches he had seen the remarkable sight of the Russian fleet's Sveaborg squadron outside the harbour stuck firmly in the ice. If that were so it was a heaven-sent opportunity. Plumridge's steam frigates were capable of breaking the ice to enable Napier's battleships to attack them at reasonably close quarters. However, when Napier arrived five days later he decided against immediate action. While there was merit in launching a surprise attack – the Russian warships would have been helpless – there was no shortage of perils to threaten the British fleet. Not only had the Russians destroyed all lighthouses and other aids to navigation, but to engage the Russian squadron Napier would have had to take his own ships within range of the Sveaborg shore batteries. This need to attack at close quarters was not just due to a lack of accurate range-finding; there was also a deep-seated naval code that enemy ships had to be engaged at the closest range possible.

If Napier had decided to follow form he would have been prepared to put his ships at risk by accepting Nelson's famous dictum that 'no captain can do very wrong if he places his ship alongside that of an enemy'. However, he was concerned about running aground, a danger made more acute by the absence of local pilots. He was also mindful of Graham's injunction that he was to prefer caution to 'some rash act of desperate daring, which may lead to a great disaster':

> I have great respect for stone walls, and have no fancy for running even screw line of battle ships against them. Because the public may be impatient you must not risk the loss of a fleet in an impossible enterprise. I believe both Cronstadt and Sveaborg to be all but impregnable from the sea. Sveaborg especially.[3]

Compared to his certainty that Sevastopol had to be destroyed at all costs if Russian power in the Black Sea were ever to be neutralised, Graham was curiously reticent about attacking Russia's Baltic naval bases. One reason was certainly the fear of running aground in the shallow waters of the Gulf of Finland – Napier had two survey ships with hydrographers aboard but they lacked the complete range of skills which local pilots would have provided. Another was Graham's lingering concern that Napier might be tempted to repeat his Portuguese adventures with a dramatic gesture in the Baltic – even his 'Kronstadt or heaven' boast was a repetition of a well publicised braggadocio of 1833 concerning the taking of Lisbon. On this point he need not have worried. Napier decided not to attack the icebound Russian squadron and instead took his fleet to the Elfsnabben, south of Stockholm, to pay a courtesy call on King Oscar. Even the serious-minded Paget was prepared to give his commander-in-chief the benefit of not inconsiderable doubts:

Doubtless the Commander-in-Chief had some positive information which had induced him to give up the idea of attacking
the Russian squadron, bearing in mind our qualities of steamers
for such work . . . It was perhaps fortunate that the Press was
not made acquainted with the details of this first and significant
opening of the campaign.[4]

Just as Graham's fears were groundless, so too did Paget have
no reason to be alarmed about adverse publicity. Before leaving
Spithead Napier had agreed to supply *The Times* with news about his
exploits with the result that, throughout the summer months, Delane
published a bland succession of reports about British naval successes
in blockading the Russian coast. True, the actions amounted to little
more than merchantmen being stopped and searched and occasional
raids being mounted against small and lightly defended harbours, such
as Brahestad and Uleaborg in the Gulf of Bothnia, but at least they
reminded the public that the Royal Navy was taking the war to the
Russians.

While it was one thing to attack fishing settlements, these skirmishes
were hardly the stuff of derring-do and the public mood began to
change. Aberdeen's Cabinet was attacked for lack of resolve and, as
happens in any war when there is a call for something, anything, to
be done, the politicians began to put pressure on the service chiefs.
In turn they felt honour-bound to signal that displeasure to the
commanders at sea or in the field. In his despatch of 2 May the
Secretary of the Admiralty reminded Napier that their Lordships were
becoming somewhat irritated by the lack of action. Napier was stung
to reply on 20 May that his movements were circumscribed both
by his crews' inexperience and by inclement weather. Besides, he
argued, their Lordships seemed to be giving him contrary advice:

In their Lordships' letter of 2nd of May, commenting on a
paragraph of my letter of the 19th April, they appear to think I
have been going too slow; when I passed the Belt their Lordships
thought I was going too fast. I am perfectly aware that steam
makes a great difference in naval operations; but steam has no
effect upon fogs, and has not prevented two collisions, and very
nearly a third, which must have disabled half-a-dozen ships; and
their Lordships will observe by my last letter that fogs detained
me ten days in Elfsnabben, and a fog was nearly the cause of

the loss of part of the fleet; and it therefore behoves me to be careful and act with judgement in operations with this fleet.[5]

If the Admiralty thought that Napier would take criticism lying down, they were greatly mistaken. For one thing he was a Scot, blessed − or cursed − with all the virtues and drawbacks of that frequently prickly race. Dark of complexion, hence his nickname 'Black Charley', and powerfully built, he was argumentative, quick to take offence and with a marked tendency to be aggressive. To him black was black and white was white and to compromise was the work of the devil. In time of war those characteristics had stood him in good stead: *fier comme un écossais* 'proud like a Scot', he was the epitome of the Scottish warrior, proud, combative and an inspiration to his men. The obverse was less attractive. Napier could appear rude and vain, always keen to place himself and his actions in a good light yet much given to self-doubt. Fuelled by whisky, of which he was inordinately fond, he developed a split personality: the acclaimed warrior who secretly doubted his martial abilities, the public hero who was a private boor. With Napier there could be no middle way and that refusal to make any concessions to his high office, or even to his appearance, could be thoroughly disconcerting at a first meeting, not least for a Swedish naval officer:

He was wearing a blue tunic with short trousers and big shoes, a civilian hat with gold stripes, an enormously big handkerchief in all the colours of the rainbow hanging out of his tunic pocket. His movements and appearance as simple as possible. His face very badly washed, some yellow spots − probably from the egg at breakfast − round the lips and the lower part of his face. We shook hands and he greeted me with a 'You speak English, he?' and continued with two questions that − as he speaks Scottish in a rusty drivelling voice − I of course did not understand a word of.[6]

Napier's slovenly gait and his refusal to wear naval uniform were legendary − but the Swedish naval officer's off-hand description masked the inner tumult which Napier was enduring in the Baltic. From his flagship HMS *Duke of Wellington* he commanded a powerful, if inexperienced, fleet; great things were expected of it, yet he knew, too, that if he allowed it to be destroyed he would be sacrificed in

The Baltic Sea Area of Operations

turn by an ungrateful government. All his previous experience of naval warfare reminded him that an assault on the Russian ports was fraught with danger and that he would be achieving some kind of success if he managed to blockade them and prevent the Russian fleet from breaking out into the Baltic.

On the other hand there was growing public pressure for decisive action to be taken against the Russians and the presence of Napier's fleet in the Gulf of Finland seemed to provide just such an opportunity. With an improvement in the weather at the end of the month and with the arrival of Deschenes' squadron, Napier took his battle fleet east across the Baltic into the Gulf of Finland. There they were in full view of the inhabitants of Kronstadt — their sails and smoketrails on the horizon became a midsummer curiosity — but there was little chance that the Russians would risk a naval engagement. There was no need. Kronstadt was virtually impregnable from the sea, its garrison had been strengthened by the addition of Finnish conscripts and new gunboats were being hurriedly built for close-quarter protection.

To compound his difficulties Seymour had reported before he left St Petersburg that the Russians were developing a new type of undersea weapon — 'infernal machines' which could be detonated, so it was thought, by electricity. Before leaving Portsmouth Napier had doubted the veracity of the intelligence but he was soon to change his mind. At the beginning of June a Swedish resident of Helsingfors managed to make his way to the British fleet with the astonishing information that in 'the entrances of Sveaborg are placed under water boxes charged with explosives for the purpose of blowing attacking ships into the air. Chains are also stretched across the passageways. These he has seen and he knows the mechanic who laid down the explosive boxes.'[7] Seymour's information was correct: the Russians had indeed produced elementary undersea mines to defend the approaches to their main ports, including Kronstadt.

As soon as he began his reconnaissance on 26 June it became obvious to Napier that Graham was right, that it would be madness to 'knock [his] head against stone walls prematurely or without the certainty of great success'. The reconnaissance was the responsibility of Captain B.J. Sulivan of the surveying sloop Lightning and he provided Napier with a precise portrayal of the difficulties facing the Franco–British fleet. If his capital ships were to bombard Kronstadt they would have to do so from shallow waters under the Russian guns or he would have to rely on smaller and less well-armed ships with shallow draughts, which were in short supply. Both options were recipes for disaster. After three days lying off the granite-clad fortress Napier reported that an assault was 'perfectly impossible'. A reconnaissance of Sveaborg proved equally pessimistic: it too bristled with guns and its seaward approaches had been littered with so many obstacles that any attack would be suicidal.

Napier's report to the Admiralty would have made painful reading. While Graham was mindful of the dangers he was keen to see Napier's fleet make an impression on the Russian forces in the Baltic. His Cabinet colleagues Russell and Palmerston were both pushing Aberdeen to take up a more warlike stance and that very week *Punch* had added its own comment by publishing a cartoon showing two washerwomen, Joanna [Russell] and Georgeana [Aberdeen], above the caption: 'When's the fighting going to begin, Georgeana?' Graham's frustration was not alleviated by the news that one of Napier's commanders, Captain Hall of the steam frigate *Hecla*, had fruitlessly bombarded Bomarsund on 21 June. Far from praising him, Napier chose to reprimand Hall, wearily explaining his reasons in a despatch a week later: 'If every Captain when detached chose to throw away all his shot against stone walls, the fleet would soon be inefficient.'[8]

There was, though, a silver lining to the action. As *Hecla* engaged Bomarsund's defences a live shell landed on the deck close to one of the gun platforms. Without thinking twice Charles Lucas, the ship's mate, picked up the shell, its fuse still burning, and threw it overboard. In his despatch Napier hoped that the Admiralty would reward Lucas for his bravery and he received the doubly gratifying reply that not only did their Lordships approve of him censoring Hall but they had anticipated his wishes for Lucas.[9] In time the courage of *Hecla's* mate was suitably recognised: when the Victoria Cross was instigated by the queen at the end of the war for 'some signal act of valour or devotion to their country', Lucas was the first seaman to be decorated.

If a more detached view had been taken of Napier's operations Graham and his fellow sea lords might have been less impatient. The Russian Baltic Fleet showed no inclination to leave port and remained bottled up in their home ports; the Russians had been forced to deploy 30,000 soldiers who could have been sent to reinforce Paskevich's army and the Royal Navy had effected a total blockade of the Russian coast. These were substantial achievements but they were not sufficient to impress the sea lords. Although they shared

Napier's caution about attacking Kronstadt – rightly so in view of the port's defences – they were keen to report some success, any success, against the Russians. Somehow, the despatches detailing the shelling of fishing settlements or the capture of Russian merchantmen did not fit the bill. With public pressure growing for decisive action Napier was placed in an invidious position. Earlier, on 3 May, his quandary had been summed up by one of his senior captains, Henry Codrington – by no means an admirer of the commander-in-chief, or his methods:

> He is urged on, on the one hand by the state of excitement and high-wrought expectations which England has worked herself up about this Battle Squadron, and what great things it is to do, and especially about him, Sir C. Napier, personally and what deeds of successful daring he is to accomplish, and, by the by, no opportunity has been lost of heightening the public expectation as regards himself personally. On the other hand he now finds himself here brought face to face with difficulties which no one in England (not even the Ministry) have any idea of, and which they, not knowing the circumstances, or seeing the place with their own eyes, can imagine. He now sees his own character and the honour of the Flag at stake, not to say the safety of the Squadron and protection of the English coast, if we risked an attack without certainty of crushing resistance with so little loss to ourselves as to leave all our ships efficient. And, if the English flag, after all this fearful excitement at home, does suffer a reverse, then will come the question, 'Who's to be hanged for it?'[10]

Napier knew only too well that he would be the only candidate for blame should things go wrong. As his squadron sailed back down the Gulf of Finland he may well have regretted the bombast which accompanied its departure three months earlier.

The opportunity to make amends came on 2 July when Graham sent a despatch informing him that 10,000 French soldiers and marines were being sent to the Baltic under the command of General Adolphe Niel and would arrive at the beginning of August. It was not an easy voyage. The French troops were unused to lengthy journeys by sea and had to endure cramped conditions and spartan fare as they made their way from Calais to the Baltic. As happens in every campaign the enforced inactivity and the discomfort led to mutinous complaints from the rank-and-file and their officers were forced to take rigorous action to maintain discipline. 'Soldiers have the habit of moaning in such a way that they complain constantly: the chocolate is not thick enough or is too thick, the soup too salty, the tea insipid; they've always got something to say.' wrote Colonel Auguste Ducrot, French 3rd Regiment. 'I've adopted the policy of putting all who complain on bread and biscuit; it is the only way of making them see reason.'[11]

However, despite the grumbling, the French force added significantly to Napier's resources: together with a British contingent of one thousand marines and military engineers under the command of Brigadier-General H.D. Jones, Royal Engineers, they would provide a task force to attack either Sveaborg or Bomarsund. Napier, who had already suggested that Kronstadt might be vulnerable to an amphibious assault, replied that he would lay plans to attack Bomarsund, the fortress which guarded the main harbour of the Aaland islands. Consisting of three round towers and a heavily fortified citadel it presented a formidable obstacle but Napier was confident that he could bombard Bomarsund into surrender with his ships' guns and the artillery pieces which would accompany the amphibious landings.

Napier's tactics were relatively simple: the Franco-British fleet would isolate the island, thereby precluding the outside possibility that Russian warships might intervene, while the superior allied forces landed and laid siege to the fortress. As it turned out, everything went according to plan. On the morning of 8 August the first landings took place to the north where an advanced party of British engineers paved the way for a French marine brigade to come ashore. At the same time the main investing force landed to the south. Four days later the siege began with fire from the land-based French 16-pounder artillery pieces and a sustained bombardment from the fleet. Before the attack the French troops and sailors had complained long and loud about the difficulty of manoeuvring their guns into position – each piece required 150 men to drag it up the island's narrow roads – but, once in position, the results were impressive. The first objective, Fort Tzee, fell to the French the following day and the second, Fort Nottich, was captured by the British a day later following a heavy artillery bombardment. By 16 August it was all over as the Russian garrison commander ran up the flag of truce and surrendered his position and 2000 troops. A jubilant Napier sent a despatch to the Admiralty announcing that Bomarsund was 'a heap of ruins' and urging that at any peace talks the Russians should be prevented from rebuilding the base:

> It is impossible to contemplate the Fortress and the gigantic works in progress without feeling the conviction that Bomarsund was intended to eclipse Sveaborg and Revel and become the principal station of the Russian fleet commanding the Gulfs of Bothnia and Finland and holding Sweden in complete subjection.[12]

Bomarsund was the first allied victory of the war and the capture of the Aaland islands was hailed by the British press as 'a mortal thrust' against the enemy. Surely, speculated the leader writers, other triumphs would be in the offing. Why, the war might even be over before Christmas. The only people to be somewhat disconcerted by the attack was a curious group of travellers who accompanied the fleet on board five private yachts. Kin to the Travelling Gentlemen, or TGs who accompanied the allied army to the Crimea, they were well-to-do men of leisure, war tourists who experienced a vicarious thrill from watching, but not taking part in, the cut and thrust of battle. When the shooting stopped though, reality intruded, as it did for the Reverend R.E. Hughes, Fellow of Magdalene College, Cambridge, and one of the first men into the ruins of Fort Nottich: the sight and sound of the barrage might have been an invigorating experience but, as he and his brother discovered, for those on the receiving end it left in its wake the 'cold, clean silent forms of the dead':

> The shock of the surprise was fearful; the light linen cloths that shrouded the stiffened figures wavered and flickered in the draught, as if stirred by the breaths of those who could breathe no more. What did these fellows know about the Turkish question? And yet they had fought and trembled, they had writhed in agony, and now father and brother, maid and mother were weeping and breaking their hearts for them, and all about the Danubian principalities.[13]

Hughes's question which would be heard time and time again on both sides long before the war was over.

No such introspection clouded Napier's thinking. Elated by the fall of Bomarsund and spurred on by a tetchy Admiralty signal requesting information about his next plan of operations, he turned his attention to the two main goals in modern Finland – Abo and Sveaborg. However, both had been heavily reinforced, by Finnish recruits and by additional gunboats which could operate at will and possibly to great effect in the shallow waters of the gulf. An ambitious plan to repeat the Bomarsund operation had been drawn up by Brigadier-General Jones who was under Newcastle's orders 'to assist the siege operations in which the Fleets and the French Army are about to be engaged, with your scientific knowledge and experience, and to direct any operations which the British Forces may undertake on land.'[14]

These called for a landing by 5000 men and an attack from the sea – the mines notwithstanding – but as Napier was unsure he decided to follow the Admiralty's advice to convene a council of war on 12 September and to decide whether Jones's plans could be instigated 'before the winter sets in'. For the first time the equable relationship between the allies began to crumble. The French produced another plan which had been drawn up by their chief engineer, General Niel, which proposed an attack from the sea and they refused to countenance another landing, mainly because their army had been weakened by cholera. To add to the confusion, Napier, too, was wary of Jones's plan – in a rash moment he described it in a despatch as 'madness' and was forced to apologise – and as he informed the Admiralty on 13 September, without French support he had no option but to call off the operation:

Many absurd propositions have been made to me for attacking both Cronstadt and Sveaborg but I never will lend myself to any absurd projects or be driven to attempt what is not practicable by newspaper writers who I am sorry to say I have reason to believe are in correspondence with officers of the fleet who ought to know better.[15]

Showing an alarming inability to separate fact from fiction Napier seemed to have forgotten that he, too, had supplied *The Times* with stories earlier in the campaign, but despite its gruff good sense, that despatch was not met with acclaim by the Admiralty. The proximity of winter also concentrated minds. Within a fortnight gales had shaken the allied fleet and the French were making preparations to return, largely because Napoleon wanted to reinforce his army in the Crimea with the men from the Baltic[16]

When the French left a week later Napier decided to fall back on his earlier strategy of blockading the Baltic ports, but the campaign – and his naval career – was effectively over and Napier said as much in his despatch of 10 October:

> I should consider myself unfit for the command I hold were I much longer to expose these [ships] to the violent gales of the north – more particularly as their Lordships have directed me in their letters of the 23rd September – confirmed by their letters of 26th – to withdraw when in the opinion of the French admiral and myself, the presence of the combined fleet is no longer safe.[17]

It was far from being his, or the Admiralty's last word. Napier was destined to be a victim of that time-honoured gambit – the removal of political patronage and subsequent fall from grace, all because he was absent from the centre of events and could not defend himself from the attacks of lesser men. Criticised by his Cabinet colleagues and attacked by the press, Graham decided to place the blame for the failure of the Baltic operations squarely on Napier's shoulders. Having advised him to prefer caution to speculation or as he put it, 'some rash act', Graham now found himself attacking Napier for not doing enough to win glory for the allies. When the fleet returned to Portsmouth on 22 December Napier was effectively sacked, being told to strike his flag and come ashore.

This was manifestly unfair and Napier was to fight a long and ultimately successful battle to retrieve his name but it is difficult to see how he could have acted in any other way. His fleet was small, poorly trained and inadequately equipped. His objectives were never clearly focused and the orders from the Admiralty were frequently confused or contradictory. That being so, he had maintained a successful blockade of the Baltic and had captured a key Russian stronghold into the bargain. No ship had been lost and in any other circumstances he could have counted the campaign a reasonable success. But these were not rational days. The public wanted a triumph and Bomarsund was no substitute for Kronstadt, nor indeed the prize they most coveted, Sevastopol.

Had they known of a real naval disaster in the Pacific their views might have been tempered but unfortunately for Napier, the news of a farcical assault on the Russian Far East fleet at Petropaulovsk took several months to reach London and when it did most minds were focused on what was happening in the Crimea. In fact, this little known action is deservedly forgotten. On 29 August a small Franco-British flotilla of six ships under the command of Rear-Admiral David Price arrived off the Russian port and prepared to attack it by landing marines and shelling it from the sea. Before the plan could be put into effect, though, Price retired to his cabin and shot himself. Perhaps distracted by the calamity the Royal Navy's ships then compounded the disaster by accidentally shelling the allied forces on shore. As a result the attack was called off and that put a stop to any further naval operations in the Pacific. It was not the only bizarre naval operation of the war: in a separate action in the White Sea a Royal Navy frigate exchanged fire with a Russian monastery near Archangel.

With Aberdeen's government coming under increasing pressure from critics such as Palmerston to take the offensive to the Russians, everything now hung on events in the Crimea.

11

Varna Interlude

Never were tents pitched in a more lovely spot. When the
morning sun had risen it was scarcely possible for one to imagine
oneself far from England.
William Howard Russell, The Times, *July 1854*

At first sight the position of the allied base at Varna held out the
promise of great things. Omar Pasha had insisted that it was a
delightful spot and when the first troops landed they were struck by
the sheer homeliness of it all. True, Varna was a squalid little place
with a noisome open drainage system but, away from the port area,
the countryside was a lush profusion of flowered meadows giving
way to wooded hills in the distance. The waters of the Devna
lake to the west added a further touch of enchantment and, on
disembarking on 16 June, Sterling was reminded irresistibly of 'a
country something like the Brighton Downs'. And to complete the
sense of ease the British and French soldiers quickly discovered that
there was good foraging: the surrounding countryside provided fruit,
vegetables, rough shooting and plenty of wood and kindling. As the
profusion of allied forces disembarked in Varna's teeming harbour – 'a
picture which is seen perhaps only once in a man's lifetime' according
to Franks – spirits were understandably high.

The siting of the camps was orderly, too. The Light Division
marched eight miles inland to Alladyn (Aladeen) while the other
divisions were spread over a wide area around Varna and its lake. The
cavalry regiments were at Devna fifteen miles away to the west and
reached by a bruising march through a landscape which still managed
to enchant the dubious Mrs Duberly:

I shall never forget that march! It occupied nearly eight hours. The heat intense, the fatigue overwhelming; but the country – anything more beautiful I never saw! – vast plains, verdant hills, covered with shrubs and flowers; a noble lake; and a road, which was merely a cart track, winding through a luxuriant woodland country, across plains and through deep bosquets of brushwood.[1]

At that stage, too, despite differences of opinion amongst the senior allied commanders, there was a remarkable degree of co-operation amongst the allied forces on the ground. Raglan had been as fascinated by the polyglot confusion in Varna as Troop Sergeant-Major Franks had been, writing to his family that everyone had been mixed up together, the result being as amusing as it had been frustrating. Shortly after disembarking, Franks and the 5th Dragoon Guards' quartermaster came across a noisy mob surrounding a French soldier who was ineffectually beating a Turkish porter. Watching the scene was a well-built British sailor who obviously regarded the Frenchman's efforts with some disdain. To Franks's amusement, the sailor – 'as fine a specimen of the British Bluejacket as you could meet with' – pushed his way through the crowd and said, 'here Frenchy, let me show you.'

He then drew his right hand to his shoulder, and gave that unfortunate Turk such a blow – à la Tom Sayers [sic] – which caught him under his ear, fairly lifted him off his feet, and left him sprawling in the gutter. Then turning to the Frenchman, he thus addressed him – 'There, you blooming lubber, that's the way to hit him.' As may be surmised, the Turk did not wait for another blow, but as soon as he could scramble up again he took to his heels. The Frenchman gave a look at the old soldier, and said, 'Mon dieu'.[2]

It was hardly the best manifestation of the Franco-British entente but it certainly exemplified Palmerston's view that every so often foreigners should be given a taste of the British stick. Not that the French themselves felt that they were in way beholden to the British. In Sterling's hearing Saint-Arnaud said; 'J'ai le flair militaire; les Anglais n'ont pas fait la guerre depuis 1815.' ('I understand military matters intuitively; the English have not been at war since 1815.')

On a very fundamental level that may well have been true. Although the move to Varna had been a colourful and invigorating experience it had given further proof that all was not well in the British Army's commissariat system. Tents, baggage and supplies had been landed on the wrong side of the bay with the result that many troops had spent their first nights in the open and there was a woeful absence of transport, especially horses, failings which meant that the British forces would be unable to offer immediate support to the Ottoman army on the Danube. As the well-connected Guards officer Alexander Gordon told his father, the prime minister, the Commissariat was working out of kilter with the army and the result was confusion:

> They have no horses or mules for the transport of tents, provisions or baggage – and instead of setting to work to get them they are engaged in objecting to everything proposed and thwarting Lord Raglan in everything. Until you send out an order that Lord R. is to command the army and not Commissary General Filder we shall not get into ready working order.[3]

Even Sterling, who was generally well disposed to the Commissary officers, was moved to note: 'Nothing so hopeless as an army without transport'. It was not the last time that those particular complaints would be heard.

Aware that the combination of a luxuriant country and the summer heat would encourage men to relax regimental officers did their best to keep their men fit with drills and exercises. True to form, Cardigan was a stickler and the Light Brigade was confronted with a busy schedule of parades but the debilitating climate made life difficult for the soldiers, many of whom found solace in the cheap local wine. Once again drunkenness became commonplace and once again the army's response was flogging the culprits *pour encourager les autres*. Although Sterling was appalled by the widespread drinking and most especially by the failure of the Highland Brigade's men to 'carry their liquor like gentlemen', he had some sympathy for them: 'Drink is the only Christian vice we have much chance of indulging in here; gluttony is out of the question; and there is not a woman visible.'

Inevitably discipline became difficult to maintain and even the officers were affected by the general air of relaxed indifference to events elsewhere. One of Raglan's orders of the day forbad officers to grow moustaches; another banned the wearing of civilian clothes. It was to no avail. Cavalry officers started wearing turbans and loose fitting jackets and trousers and Airey caused a sensation by appearing at a conference wearing a red flannel suit. Civilians, too, mingled with the troops. Some were 'war tourists' ('loafers' to Franks), well-to-do young Englishmen who had come out to the seat of war at their own expense, anxious to share in the excitement. Others were professionals, correspondents like Russell or the writer A.W. Kinglake. Even Delane had been made welcome when he arrived for a short visit. 'Pray inform him as much as you can properly and give him right ideas,' wrote Clarendon to Stratford. 'He is a man very open to civility.'[4] The French were at turns suitably disgusted or uncomfortably impressed by these manifestations of what they took to be their main ally's curiously unwarlike preparations.

An end to the waiting appeared to come on 19 June when a huge explosion was heard on the north-eastern horizon. This was the detonation of eight thousand pounds of explosives which had been placed by Russian engineers in a mine under the main defence works of the Silistria garrison sixty miles away. Throughout the night artillery fire could be heard as Russian gunners pounded the defences prior to what most allied officers believed would be a decisive infantry assault. It was not to be. On 22 June Gorchakov received a communication from the tsar ordering him to raise the siege and to remove his 50,000-strong army back into Russian territory. The campaign in the Danubian provinces which had sparked the allies' intervention was at an end and, as Russell reported, many thought that the war was at an end too:

> It may be readily believed that the news of the Russian retreat caused a profound sensation. The prominent feeling among the men was one of disappointment, lest they should lose the chance 'after coming so far, of having one last brush with the Russians'.[5]

In Constantinople Stratford, too, was thrilled by the news, for the Ottoman victory seemed to vindicate his support for their cause. 'It would seem that man to man and horse to horse the pigmy steeds and weapons of this country are more than a match for the best productions of Russia,' he wrote to Clarendon on 6 July. 'No wonder the opinions of our officers show symptoms of change!'[6]

For Nicholas, though, the decision to withdraw had not been lightly reached. Gorchakov's army seemed to be on the brink of success – a British patrol sent to reconnoitre Silistria a few days later reported that the town was 'a rum sight, the town riddled with shot and shell . . . the Russian battery being within thirty feet of the Turkish one, the Turks must have fought like demons' [7] – yet its position had become untenable due to an unsung victory of diplomacy. Following Austria's decision to combine with Prussia, Franz Josef had ordered his army on to the Transylvanian border. The implication was obvious and on 2 June the Austrian ambassador in St Petersburg had demanded the withdrawal of Russian forces from the principalities. The note enraged Nicholas who is supposed to have reversed a portrait of the Austrian ruler and written on the back, '*Du Undankbarer*' ('You ungrateful wretch').

The strategic reality was that the tsar had had little choice but to comply. Ranged against Gorchakov was a combined allied army of Ottoman, British and French forces, all of which were being gradually reinforced through Varna. He had lost naval control of the Black Sea and as a result his forces in the Caucasus were having to be supplied over the high mountain ranges. In the Baltic, too, the allied fleet had been permitted to bombard Bomarsund and the inhabitants of his capital had suffered the indignity of seeing the masts of Napier's fleet off Kronstadt. Russia was isolated and it was essential, therefore, to safeguard the Imperial Army before the Austrians decided to intervene. Although Nicholas continued to rage against Franz Josef's perceived duplicity he agreed to withdraw his forces from the principalities on condition that they were not occupied by Britain or France. On 14 June Austria confirmed the new arrangement through a treaty with Turkey which allowed for joint Austrian and Ottoman forces to occupy the territories for the duration of the war.

None of this was immediately apparent to the allies. Raglan realised that fierce fighting was taking place at Silistria and the general view was that it would fall. However, on 24 June, while he was dining with his senior commanders, a letter marked 'urgent' arrived from Omar Pasha. It contained the good news that the siege had been raised, coupled with information that Russian forces might be moving south through the Dobrudja marshes between Silistria and the sea to drive a wedge through the allied armies. There was only one way to find out and Raglan ordered Cardigan to make an immediate reconnaissance, a move which, though necessary, had to be made without reference to Lucan. (There had already between a violent and unnecessary disagreement between the two headstrong cavalrymen over the chain of command.)

Cardigan's orders were quite explicit. He was to take a 200-strong patrol drawn from the 8th Hussars and 13th Light Dragoons and 'to patrol as far as he could in order to discover what the enemy's left was about', but, being the man he was, Cardigan decided to act according to his own volition. On 30 June he reached Karasou on the edge of the marshland and had found no sign of any Russian forces; on the contrary it was rumoured that Gorchakov's forces were heading north towards Bagadish and Tultcha on the Danube delta. To find out, Cardigan and his patrol took off in hot pursuit – and hot it proved to be, as one of its members, Captain Soames Jenyns, 13th Light Dragoons, reported later in a letter home:

We started to Bagadish and on next day north, but had to return for want of water. The whole country is deserted, not a soul to be seen, and the villages burned down and battered – such a desolate scene. We had only salt beef and biscuits and what we had on. No tents, of course, which in this hot weather on plains is no joke.[8]

In fact Jenyns was understating the difficulties faced by what came to be known as the 'soreback reconnaissance'. Each horse was weighed down by a trooper in full campaign order, some 25 stones in all, and as Cardigan himself admitted later, the terrain was almost devoid of water. At Bassora, close to Trajan's Wall, the patrol had reached the limits of its assignment and had concluded that the Russians must have crossed the Danube. At that point Cardigan should have retired, his task completed, but he chose instead to head south-eastwards towards Silistria and was effectively out of contact for another week. Indeed, so alarmed was Raglan that patrols had to be sent out to look for him.

Inevitably, given the harsh landscape and hot weather, there were casualties. When the patrol returned to Varna on 11 July it presented a pitiable sight. A number of horses had collapsed due to the heat and lack of forage, and the second-in-command of the 4th Dragoon Guards estimated that the survivors would be unable to see any further active service. The men, too, had suffered, to no advantage – or so it seemed to Fanny Duberly:

I was riding out in the evening when the stragglers came in; and a piteous sight it was – men on foot, driving and goading on their wretched, wretched horses, three or four of which could hardly stir. There seems to have been much unnecessary suffering, a cruel parade of death, more pain inflicted than good derived; but I suppose these sad sights are merely casualties of war, and we must bear them with what courage and fortitude we may.[9]

Given his poor reputation it was not to be wondered that Cardigan received his share of obloquy for the suffering and in time the numbers of casualties were greatly exaggerated. At the time, though, Raglan saw no need to censure his unruly subordinate and Jenyns, who had taken trouble to describe all the hardships, merely noted that Cardigan was a 'a capital fellow to be under at this work'. It was also acknowledged that Cardigan had been constrained by the desert conditions and that the lack of water had added to their privations. And Mrs Duberly was being no more than honest when she said that war brought its own dangers and setbacks and that these had to be confronted and endured.

Worse was to befall the French in the same region. For the ailing Saint-Arnaud the Russian withdrawal represented an affront to his military prowess. He had bragged that he would 'carry on this war with an activity, an energy that will strike terror into the Russians', but the raising of the siege of Silistria seemed to end those fond hopes. A chance to redeem them came from persistent reports that, Cardigan's findings notwithstanding, a Russian force had remained in the Dobrudja marshes. For the French commander the presence of 10,000 Russian forces and their artillery provided a 'beautiful climax' to what had been a lacklustre campaign. Against Raglan's wishes he decided to exploit it, using his newly raised force of Bashi-Bazouk Ottoman cavalrymen, the so-called 'Spahis of the Orient'.

This rag-tag collection of irregular cavalry had been the focus of Franco-British rivalry from the first days of the campaign. Saint-Arnaud regarded command of them as a precursor to bringing all Ottoman forces under French control; Raglan was not so sure about their abilities but he was under orders to raise a corps of irregular cavalry to augment his slender resources and, besides, he did not want to see the Bashi-Bazouks under French colours. He agreed, therefore, to an equal division of the spoils and some four thousand of their number were eventually attached to each army's command.

With their experience of campaigning in Algeria and the raising of the elite Spahis regiments, the French thought the Bashi-Bazouks could be trained as light cavalry skirmishers and under the direction of General Yusef regiments gradually came into being. Towards the end of July Saint-Arnaud decided that they should be the vanguard of a French force which would proceed into the Dobrudja to engage the imaginary Russians.

On 22 July the Bashi-Bazouks set off on their mission accompanied by the French 1st Division. Their mission quickly turned into a nightmare. Cardigan's 200 had suffered in the same region; for the much larger force of Bashi-Bazouks and French infantrymen it was much worse. Not only did they encounter the same heat and lack of water but at a halt on the coast they were suddenly and catastrophically hit by a cholera epidemic. Although the expedition pressed on towards the Danube they failed to make any contact with the Russians and still the epidemic dogged them. During the march back to Varna seven thousand men died and, as Russell reported in *The Times*, when the survivors straggled back to Varna the atmosphere was positively funereal:

> The result of this expedition was one of the most fruitless and lamentable that has ever occurred in the history of warfare.
>
> The details of the history of this expedition, which cost the French more than 7000 men, are among the most horrifying and dreadful of the campaign.[10]

Following the failure of Yusef's operation the French Bashi-Bazouks were disbanded. A similar fate almost befell those under British command. Raglan could never bring himself to believe that they would ever be a disciplined force and tried to keep them at arm's length. With some despair their commanding officer, Colonel W.F. Beatson, kept up a barrage of correspondence in an effort to convince the high command that with patience and effort the Bashi-Bazouks could be turned into a useful force:

> I have not the slightest doubt that the Bashi Bazouks could be made more efficient soldiers by proper treatment and regular payments; they have been heretofore treated like wild beasts and as a matter of consequence they have behaved as such.

Since I have been in command of them I have not had a
single crime brought to my notice.

The decapitation of enemies is an old Turkish custom but I
feel confident I could prevent it in the Bashi Bazouks after I
had shown them they were to be treated like soldiers both in
regard to reward and punishment.[11]

It was to no avail. So multifarious were their backgrounds and so
used to brigandage were these horsemen that military discipline sat
uneasily on their shoulders. Several times Stratford had reason to
complain to the Turkish authorities about their 'atrocious outrages'
and by November he was able to report to Clarendon that 'the
Porte has of late promoted the return to their respective homes
of those among them who at one time swelled the numbers of
the Ottoman Army in Bulgaria.'[12] Beatson's irregulars remained in
being but, such was their unruliness, they were never integrated into
the British Army.

The allied ground forces had yet to fire a shot in anger, the Russians
had withdrawn and an Austrian army had reclaimed the principalities.
Now that the threat to Turkey had evaporated there was little point
for the British or the French to retain such a sizeable and expensive
measure of military support in the region. That certainly was the view
of the Duke of Cambridge amongst others and for a brief season hopes
were high that the armies would be recalled. 'The Russians have made
regular fools of us, brought us out here and then cut away,' wrote
Captain Nigel Kingscote. 'Too bad!'

In fact there was never any intention that Britain or France would
give up the game. Writing home on 9 July Sterling put the matter
into military perspective when he pondered where the armies would
now be sent 'to bring Russia effectually to reason':

I do not intend to return home, however; my face is not set
that airt [point] of the compass. The diplomatists cannot work
without having an army here at present. Where shall we pass
the winter? Schumla? Bukarest? Scutari? or shall we, after all, go
to Crim-Tartary [Crimea]? There's a wale [scope for choice] of
places besides Circassia, and our own will has nothing to do in
it. Three or four penmen will arrange it. One thing is certain,
we shall not live in tents in the winter, but either in houses or
in mud-huts which we shall construct for ourselves.[13]

On that latter point Sterling's conjecture about accommodation proved to be wrong but he was right about the strategic need to keep the allied army in the region. The British and French governments were under popular pressure to gain a significant victory over the Russians but so far they had been thwarted. Napier had shown the impracticality of expecting such a victorious outcome in the Baltic and, in any case, the expedition to the Black Sea region had been costly: having moved the forces there something had to be done with them. However, the presence of a neutral Austrian army in the principalities meant that there could be no pursuit of Gorchakov's forces across the Danube or even an amphibious landing at the delta. The only hope lay in hitting Russia at some other point – Odessa or Sevastopol – and hoping that a quick victory would encourage Austria and Prussia to intervene on the allied side.

Besides, as Queen Victoria noted in her diary, the war was 'popular', with *The Times* leading calls for a decisive blow to be made against Russia to ensure a 'permanent peace'. In the House of Lords, Lord Lyndhurst captured the general mood when he described Russia as a 'barbarous nation' and called for its destruction. On 18 July Clarendon passed on the government's thinking to Stratford in a terse statement: 'We are still of the opinion that the Crimea should be our objective and that we shall have done nothing until it is achieved.'[12] The following day that same information reached the ears of Lieutenant-Colonel Edward Hodge, commanding the 4th Dragoon Guards, but it did not provoke the same optimism: 'I cannot say I wish to go to the Crimea. It will be bad work I know.'

One other factor intruded to make it necessary for the allies to move from Varna. Cholera.

> Whoever gazed on the rich meadows [Devno and Aladyn where British troops were encamped], stretching for long miles away, and bordered by heights on which dense forests struggled all but in vain to pierce the masses of wild vine, clematis, dwarf acacia and many-coloured brushwoods, might well be have imagined that no English glade or hill-top could well be healthier or better suited for the residence of man. But these meadows nurtured the fever, the ague, dysentery, and pestilence in their bosom – the lake and the stream exhaled death, and at night fat unctuous vapours rose fold after fold from the valleys and crept up in the

dark and stole into the tent of the sleeper and wrapped him in
their deadly embrace.[15]

For reasons which he never cared to explain Russell came to believe
that the sickness had been caused by eating the giant cucumbers which
grew in profusion along the lake shore. In fact the epidemic seems to
have started quite accidentally and little was done to control it. That
summer had seen a cholera epidemic in southern Europe and it made
its way into Bulgaria through the French transport ships. Once it took
hold in Varna a mixture of high temperatures and poor hygiene helped
it to sweep through the allied army and navy. Control of the disease
depends on a strict regime – all discharges from the patient have to
be disinfected, soiled clothing destroyed and drinking water must be
boiled. Sadly, in the summer heat lethargy set in: latrines were allowed
to overflow, basic rules of hygiene were ignored, as they often were at
home in Britain, and the medical services were quickly overwhelmed
by the huge numbers of victims. Then the situation was exacerbated
by an outbreak of amoebic dysentery.

From the standpoint of later years the inability of the allied armies
to control the epidemic is deplorable but, to a certain extent, the
measures taken were only a reflection of conditions at home. There
had been serious outbreaks of cholera in 1832, 1848 and 1853 and
Edwin Chadwick's *Report on the Sanitary Condition of Great Britain*
(1842) revealed the extent to which filth, disease-ridden water supplies
and lack of hygiene encouraged the disease. The modern mansions of
Belgravia in London stank of bad drains, a report on sanitary conditions
at Buckingham Palace had to be suppressed, so embarrassing were its
findings, and, according to one professional planner, even a city such
as Edinburgh with its wonderful architecture was unspeakably filthy
and unhealthy:

We devoutly believe that no smell in Europe or Asia – not in
Aleppo or Damascus in the present day – can equal in depth
and intensity, in concentration and power, the diabolical combination of sulphurated hydrogen we came upon one evening
about ten o'clock in a place called Toddrick's Wynd.[16]

Against that background it is not surprising that the army in the field
at Varna quickly succumbed to cholera. In an attempt to reduce the

effects of the epidemic Raglan ordered the British forces to disperse and the cavalry regiments moved away from the lake thirty miles west to Jenibazar. The decision helped the Light Brigade, which suffered relatively few casualties, but the two regiments of heavy cavalry at Kotlubie paid the price of poor personal discipline. Little attention was paid to the water supply and cholera quickly ran through the 5th Dragoon Guards. Within a week the disease had claimed 35 troopers and three officers and the commanding officer, Lieutenant-Colonel Thomas Le Marchant, was so enfeebled he had to be sent home. Even so, despite the suffering, the regiment was saved further casualties through the excellent work done by its medical officer William Catell. According to Franks this 'kindest of men' laboured 'for three successive nights in the Hospital Tents, and it was a miracle how he kept on his feet, as during that time he scarcely got any sleep'. Some men Cattell could not help. The regimental veterinary surgeon Fisher succumbed almost immediately after the first symptoms appeared. Each death was recorded by the meticulous Cattell:

> Duckworth was seriously ill but bore up with wonderful res-
> ignation; his features became so changed that F[isher], the vet,
> who went to sit with him became nervous. I met F. in a state
> of intense excitement rushing out of D's tent – 'Oh! I've got
> it', pressing his hand against his stomach, then 'What is it like?'
> He was sent to bed, diarrhoea set in and a week after he was
> buried in the ditch at Varna.[17]

In fact the medical services were woefully ill-equipped to deal with the outbreak. The hospital at Varna mentioned by Cattell was an old barracks into which the victims were packed with little chance of survival. Others were sent by ship to Scutari where conditions were little better and in both places the medical orderlies were either old soldiers or men with little training. Worse, they were frequently drunk and incapable, the order having been given to increase the rum rations as a preventative against the disease. Cholera also claimed the lives of British and French sailors in the ships lying offshore and by the time the epidemic eased the allies had sustained 10,000 casualties.

Cholera also claimed another casualty – the first public doubts about the direction of the war following Russell's reports in *The Times* about the conditions at Varna:

Horrors occurred here every day which were shocking to think of. Walking by the beach one might see some straw sticking up through the sand, and on scraping it away with his stick, be horrified at bringing to light the face of a corpse which had been deposited there with a wisp of straw around it, a prey to dogs and vultures. Dead bodies rose from the bottom in the harbour and bobbed grimly around in the water or floated in from sea and drifted past the sickened gazers on board the ships – all buoyant, bolt upright, and hideous in the sun. One day the body of a French soldier, who had been murdered (for his neckerchief was twisted round the neck so as to produce strangulation, and the forehead was laid open by a ghastly wound which cleft the skull to the brain), came alongside *Caradoc* in harbour and was with difficulty sunk again.[18]

Although Russell's description was tame compared to later reports filed by him and other correspondents, his despatches to *The Times* showed that this would be a war such as no others had been. Whereas the conflict against Napoleon and later colonial skirmishes had been reported once the action was over, this campaign would be fought under the gaze of disinterested professional war correspondents. Having arrived in Varna, Russell had made it his business to build up his contacts in the army and he had quickly become a familiar figure in his specially designed military-style uniform. In an attempt to curb his activities Raglan issued orders that Russell and his colleagues were not to receive any material assistance. (Saint-Arnaud was more forthright: he banned them altogether.) Although the commands were often honoured in the breach the suspicion remained in many military minds that the accompanying journalists were little more than unwelcome security risks who were to be ostracised. As Clarendon told Stratford this was an innovation which the army had failed to foresee before the campaign began:

Our 'own correspondents' have certainly contrived to keep our enemy informed of all he must want to know – his only disadvantage is 8 hours delay which is the time necessary for transmitting to St P[Petersburg] all that the newspapers contain and they generally publish as much as the Gvt knows for in one way or another some correspondents at Hd Qrs generally discovers and transmits every secret order or intended movement as well as every disaster and disharmony and the patriotic editors never think of keeping back anything injurious to the public service but on the contrary hasten to publish it all in proof of their superior means of intelligence. The press and the telegraph are enemies we had not taken into account but as they are invincible there is no use in complaining to them.[19]

It was a complaint which would be heard again and again and as the campaign progressed the calls for some form of censorship were to grow louder and more insistent. However, Clarendon's irritation with the correspondents had another source. He objected to receiving his best information about the campaign in the morning newspapers before Stratford's despatches had arrived. Most communications from the operational area had to be taken to Constantinople for despatch by sea to Marseilles and then overland to London. Urgent messages could be taken to the British embassy in Belgrade which had a telegraphic link with London but, otherwise, diplomatic and military despatches had to be carried by messenger and there were frequent delays. Unlike the painstaking Seymour in St Petersburg Stratford was lax with his correspondence and diplomatic bags frequently left Constantinople without his latest despatches.

There had been talk of extending the telegraph to the Ottoman capital but the Great Elchi did his best to frustrate it as he distrusted this new-fangled invention. He had already written to Cowley commiserating with him on this modern means of communication after Raglan had told him that the Paris embassy 'have sometimes four shocks from Downing Street a day'. Belonging to an older generation Stratford believed that there were times when it was best not to tell London everything but simply to report events once they had happened. Clarendon was not amused:

The messenger has again arrived bagless from you – panting as we are for news of every description it is a great disappointment not to have your despatches and not to have Rose's which are of great use to the War Department for collation with Raglan's. They often explain matters that would not be clear without them. The messenger says he left Constantinople at the usual hour. I am well aware how much you are occupied but I must beg of you not to allow this to happen again for the annoyance to the Queen as well as for the Govt is very great.[20]

It is not difficult to understand the Foreign Secretary's frustration. Newspapers such as *The Times* contained vivid pen pictures 'from the seat of war', not just from the correspondents but also from letters by serving soldiers, yet the government was being denied accurate background information from its diplomats. And as most despatches took up to two weeks to travel between the two capitals Clarendon was uncomfortably aware that the information he received was long out of date. Raglan could be equally tardy, on one occasion sending his despatches to Newcastle by ordinary mail instead of by Queen's Messenger, much to the latter's disgruntlement.

There was also the problem of security. In June Newcastle had sent Raglan a copy of the Foreign Office's cipher book with instructions that urgent messages were to be sent to Belgrade for telegraphic transmission to London. The order arrived with the suggestion that the cipher's principles were understood by Colonel Gordon and that he should be put in charge of it. However, as it was the government's only spare copy, Newcastle begged that it be properly guarded, adding that 'on your return from the East you will have the goodness to send the book under sealed cover to the Foreign Office.'[21]

The problems of communication were to rumble on until the late summer by which time more determined efforts were being made by the French to extend the telegraph line to Varna. By then both governments in London were concentrating their minds on what should be done with their armies in Bulgaria. By then, too, there had been changes in the British direction of the war, Newcastle having taken over sole responsibility for controlling Raglan as secretary of state for war; his prior joint responsibilities for the Colonies being given to Sir George Grey. Not that the appointment produced any greater flexibility: the British commander still had no responsibility for essential sea transport which remained in the hands of the Admiralty and it was not until December that responsibility for supply and resupply was transferred from the Treasury to Newcastle's office.

It was a curious period. From Clarendon's correspondence with his ambassadors in Constantinople and Paris the impatience is positively palpable. Newcastle, too proved to be an inveterate correspondent, bombarding Raglan with despatches and then fretting over the delays in the replies. Meanwhile in Varna Raglan and his staff had to wait for the arrival of reinforcements. The 3rd Division (Lieutenant-General Sir Richard England) had yet to be moved from Gallipoli, the siege train had not arrived, most regiments were still equipped with old smooth-bore muskets and were awaiting the arrival of the modern Minié rifle, and there was ongoing confusion about Russian troop strengths in the Crimea. Moreover, Raglan was still encountering difficulties in arranging a working relationship with his allies, especially with the French. Misunderstandings were an everyday occurrence. British staff officers were continually frustrated by their opposite numbers' refusal to provide accurate French troop levels, a failure which led Clarendon to inform Stratford that the government had lost all confidence in Saint-Arnaud. For their part the French continued to be dumbfounded by their ally's lack of professionalism. There was a fair degree of snobbishness in the British attitude. Captain Nigel Kingscote described the two French liaison officers, Colonel Lagondie and Commandant Vico, as 'a horrid bore . . . one is like a great fat cook [Lagondie], the other is a very good fellow but cannot speak a word of English [Vico]'.[22]

There was to be one more setback before the allied forces left Varna. On 10 August, following a hot dry spell, there was a serious fire which destroyed a large part of the British and French stores, including 16,000 pairs of boots and reserve supplies of rations. It took five hours for the blaze to be brought under control. Watching the conflagration in a state of despair Saint-Arnaud thought that it would delay the allied departure and his staff officers were not slow to place the blame on Russian agents. Just as bad, Russell noticed that the fire seemed to be the last straw for large numbers of disgruntled soldiers who took refuge from the disaster in alcoholic oblivion:

> The conduct of many of the men, French and English, seemed characterised by a recklessness verging on insanity. They might be seen lying drunk in the kennels, or in the ditches by the roadsides, under the blazing rays of the sun, covered with swarms of flies.[23]

Officers such as Sterling had constantly criticised the drinking and urged heavier punishments but the root cause was boredom, disillusionment and fear of the unknown, hardly the best emotions to engulf any army on the eve of battle with an enemy of unknown

strength. 'I do not think the army is fit to go Sebastopol,' wrote
Hodge in his diary on 17 August. 'The men are not the men they
were, and we have some hundreds of sick.'[24]

12

Hurrah for the Crimea!

L'heure est venue de combattre et de vaincre.
(The hour has come to fight and to conquer.)
Marshal Saint-Arnaud, Order of the Day, 25 August 1854

There was never any intention other than that the allies would attack Sevastopol. Although the decision was not taken until late June – by a somnolent cabinet on a balmy midsummer's evening in Richmond if Kinglake's version of events is to be believed – the Russian port and fortress had been considered a key objective even before hostilities had broken out. As early as 1 March Graham had begun promoting a 'memorable and decisive' attack on the base to destroy Russian naval power in the Black Sea and he approved thoroughly of the belligerent attitude taken by Lyons. How such an assault might be made he did not explain for there were still too many unknown quantities such as the effectiveness of the fortifications and Russian troop strengths. No thought had been given to the landing grounds or to the method of laying siege to such a powerful fortress but these doubts were cast aside amidst the clamour for Sevastopol to be destroyed by a combined attack involving the navy and the army.

On the same day that he had received his general orders to command the army in the east – 10 April 1854 – Raglan had received a classified communication from Newcastle requesting him 'to lose no time after your arrival in Turkey making careful but secret enquiry into the present amount and condition of the Russian Force in the Crimea and the strength of the Fortress of Sebastopol.' Although Raglan's first duty would be to defend Constantinople from Russian

attack, Newcastle insisted that Russian hesitancy would be no excuse
for British inaction:

> You must bear in mind that if the Russian General should make
> no demonstration of any further movement it may become
> essential for the attainment of the objects of the War that some
> operations of an offensive character should be undertaken by
> the Allied Armies.
>
> No blow which could be struck at the southern extremities
> of the Russian Empire would be so effective for this purpose
> as the taking of Sebastopol.[1]

Viewed on the maps in distant Horse Guards, Sevastopol looked
an easy enough target. Lying at the south-western end of the Crimean
peninsula it seemed to be relatively isolated and open to attack from
land and sea. (One short-lived proposal was to use warships to cut off
the peninsula from Russia at the Isthmus of Perekop, even though the
sea there was only three feet deep.) Encouraged by Lyons's view that it
was not unassailable, Graham stuck to his theory that Sevastopol could
be attacked and captured in a grand assault – just as the Royal Navy
had long planned to do to Cherbourg in the event of a threatened
cross-Channel invasion. At the same time, though, he was preaching
caution to Napier on the inadvisability of 'knocking your head against
stone walls'; as a result of the warning and of his own appreciation of
the dangers, Black Charley had decided against pressing home a naval
assault on heavily defended Kronstadt.

Sevastopol was another matter. There was a powerful allied fleet
which had command of the Black Sea; the expeditionary force at
Varna was deployed ostensibly on offensive operations and it was
reinforced by a substantial Ottoman army which had already repulsed
the Russians along the Danube. Silistria had fallen and Gorchakov's
forces had retreated. The combination of these forces and a growing
desire to halt Russian expansionism in the Black Sea region made
Sevastopol an irresistible target. As Clarendon had declared when he
explained British war aims to the House of Lords on 31 March, Britain
was going to war 'to check and repel the unjust aggression of Russia'.
If that objective were to be fulfilled, the threat posed by Sevastopol had
to be neutralised. And as was increasingly the case with the irresolute
handling of the campaign, much of the running was taken up by the
press. On 15 June *The Times* put the matter into sharp perspective

when it argued that the British government had to teach the Russians a lesson they would not forget: 'We hold, therefore, that the taking of Sebastopol and the occupation of the Crimea are objects which would repay all the costs of the present war, and would permanently settle in our favour the principal questions of the day.'

After some hesitation France, too, was prepared to support the proposals: ever since arriving in the region Saint-Arnaud had been keen to engage the Russians and earn *la gloire* for the French army; hence his enthusiasm for pursuing Gorchakov's army across the Danube. However, the successful assault on Bomarsund had encouraged Napoleon III to believe that Sevastopol was a less precarious target than had been originally believed and that with its rocket-boats and screw battleships the allied fleet would make light work of bombarding its defences.

Even the Russians expected an allied attack. Odessa had already endured bombardment from the sea and British warships appeared regularly along the coast, carefully outside the range of the bases' guns. Besides, it took only a week for copies of *The Times* to reach St Petersburg and the Russians could hardly ignore the bellicosity of its editorials. As early as 11 July, well before the allies made their fateful decision, the Russian commander in Sevastopol warned the tsar that he could not rule out the possibility of an attack on his base. This was the same Prince Menshikov who had led the mission to the Porte in March 1853. Now in charge of Sevastopol's defences, he was to show a similar lack of judgement in waging the war he had helped to start.

On 28 June the Cabinet met at Pembroke Lodge in Richmond to authorise Newcastle's despatch to Raglan ordering him 'to concert measures for the siege of Sebastopol, unless, with the information in your possession but at present unknown in this country, you should be decidedly of the opinion that it could not be undertaken with a reasonable prospect of success'. While the order was conditional in that Raglan was empowered to use his own judgement, Newcastle warned that the government would 'regret' any delay. When the despatch reached him a fortnight later Raglan was left in little doubt where his duties lay:

The difficulties of the siege of Sebastopol appear to Her Majesty's Government to be more likely to increase than to diminish by delay; and as there is no prospect of a safe and honourable peace until the fortress is reduced and the fleet taken or destroyed, it is, on all accounts, most important that nothing but insuperable impediments – such as the want of ample preparations by either army, or the possession by Russia of a force in the Crimea greatly outnumbering that which can be brought against it – should be allowed to prevent the early decision to undertake these operations.[2]

While Raglan was not lacking in courage he had grave reservations about putting Newcastle's orders into practice. All his training as a soldier told him that he had to obey his political masters; yet all his military experience warned him that he would be embarking on a perilous venture. Sitting in London the government was happy enough to recommend an amphibious assault – in a separate despatch Newcastle helpfully suggested Eupatoria as a landing ground provided that the weather were 'favourable' – but in Varna, without detailed maps and precise intelligence of the Russian troop strengths, Raglan thought it a risky business. He was also concerned about the morale of his army at Varna and about the delays in sending out reinforcements from Britain. When he mentioned his dilemma to Brown, who had also served under Wellington, the Light Division's commander is supposed to have retorted that if Raglan did not carry out the orders then the government would soon find a commander who would.

It was a measure of the man that Raglan was equal to the task in hand. The day after receiving the despatch, 18 July, he convened a Council of War which was attended by the main principals – Saint-Arnaud, Dundas and Lyons and the two French admirals Hamelin and Bruat. (No Turkish representative was invited.) The meeting lasted four hours and from the outset Raglan made it clear that they would debate not the wisdom of attacking Sevastopol but the ways and means of achieving that objective. Because no landing place had been identified most of the discussion centred on the means of transporting such large numbers of men and equipment – at that stage both the British and French armies consisted of four divisions plus cavalry and artillery (including a siege train), some 64,000 men. To get them ashore it was agreed to construct 'flat-bottomed lighters' lashed together with ropes and planks; and to ensure that the artillery landed first to provide immediate support. Their safety would depend on the fleet offering covering fire but, despite their continuing doubts, both Dundas and Hamelin agreed to support the plan. Finally, it was agreed that a reconnaissance party consisting of Brown, Canrobert and a number of artillery officers should leave immediately to investigate potential landing grounds on the peninsula.

From the point of view of initiating the campaign the meeting had been a success. Raglan had been firm and decisive and, despite his considerable doubts about the challenge ahead, allied unity had held firm. He had been ordered to attack Sevastopol and attack it he would, even though he admitted to Newcastle in his return despatch that he was laying his plans 'more in deference to the views of the British Government' than to his own views as a serving soldier. Later, Raglan was to be criticised for falling in so easily with Newcastle's orders but, schooled by Wellington, he knew he had no option. It was a simple soldierly stance, one that was shared equally by the men under his command:

> Various rumours were afloat in the camps as to the movements of the Russians, who had raised the Siege of Silistria, and recrossed the Danube into their own dominions; and also what effect this would have on the movements of our own Troops in the near future. Some people at home think perhaps that soldiers on a campaign would be most concerned or interested in the matter, seeing that it may be 'life or death' to any one of them before too long. The fact is, that the rank and file of an Army Corps in the Field, as a rule, know very little, and in many cases care less about what is taking place, or is likely to take place, with regard to the matter in hand. The soldier's duty is to move, when and where he is ordered, and not ask the reason why or wherefore.[3]

Franks's regiment, the 5th Dragoon Guards, had moved out of Kotlubie and returned to Varna and, following an adverse inspection by Lucan, they had been placed under the temporary command of Hodge's 4th Dragoon Guards. As Franks noted, it was a shrewd move: 'Knowing the state of affairs, the men of the 4th came – unasked by us – to our Lines, and gave our men a hand with the horses and saddlery, and after a day or two things began to look brighter, and, as the sailors say, "more ship-shape". There is an old saying, that when things are at the worst they mend, and in our case it was made manifest.'

To begin with Raglan and Saint-Arnaud confined their plans to their senior staff officers and it was not until 25 August that the orders were passed down to the army, much to Franks's satisfaction. Other soldiers were equally pleased to be on the move, glad that a decision had been made and thankful to leave behind them their disease-ridden quarters at Varna. Many had been touched, too, by the prospect of action and the age-old romantic allure of combat. 'Hurrah for the Crimea!' was the reaction of a young cavalry officer, too young ever to have experienced the horrors of war. 'We are off tomorrow. Take Sebastopol in a week or so, and then into winter quarters.' It would be as easy as that. The French concurred. Although Saint-Arnaud remained suspicious of the decision to attack Sevastopol, he issued a bombastic order of the day promising his men victory within three weeks and the prospect of undying glory.

However, before the armies could move, their destination had to be settled. When Brown and his party returned from their reconnaissance aboard the steamer *Fury* they had recommended a landing ground at the mouth of the River Katcha, seven miles north of Sevastopol and this had won conditional acceptance. Their mission had been accomplished with little incident. Through their telescopes Brown and Canrobert had seen parties of Russian sightseers in their best clothes perched on the cliffs watching the comings and goings of the British warship as it manoeuvred in front of their eyes. Although the Russian guns had opened fire and one shot had damaged the midshipmen's mess while *Fury* was lying one mile off shore, there was no sign of any Russian naval response. According to one of Raglan's aides who accompanied the party, their arrival off the coast had 'created no stir' in the Russian garrison.

One reason for the lack of concern shown by Menshikov's command was the reasoning that the allies would not risk a landing so late in the season. Another was the Russians' belief that they would be able to withstand any assault. Because the allies' intentions were scarcely secrets to them – *The Times* had announced the departure from Varna well before a decision had been taken – the Russians had been slowly reinforcing the Sevastopol area and by the beginning of September Menshikov had some 56,000 soldiers and sailors under his command with another 8000 on their way, marching slowly south through the Ukraine. By September the military garrison consisted of the 14th, 16th and 17th Divisions, together with two regiments each of Hussars and Don Cossacks, artillery and a strategic reserve. Hopes were high that these forces could either engage the allied invaders on the landing grounds or defeat them once they had come ashore and thereby prevent the implementation of a siege.

The optimism was aided by the strength of Sevastopol's defences. As Drummond and others had already reported, the naval base was guarded by a series of ten coastal batteries numbering 533 guns (cannon, howitzers and mortars) which covered the roadsteads and the mouth to the South Bay, home to Black Sea Fleet. When war seemed imminent these had been reinforced and strengthened with the addition of four batteries to bring the number of guns up to 633. Also to be considered were the navy's 530 guns but, limited by the lack of steam power, Kornilov's and Nakhimov's squadrons were never likely to emerge to engage the allied fleet. Only from the landward side was Sevastopol vulnerable, its southern front covered by a series of redoubts and incomplete perimeter defences while north of the harbour there was only an octagonal fort, known to the allies as the Star Fort. Even so, confidence remained high: shortly after the allies began landing Kornilov told his wife that the Russian forces remained 'unconcerned and in the best of spirits'. As the commander responsible for the fortification of Sevastopol he was in a good position to know and his diary reveals a heady optimism that the threat to the city could be repulsed.

Faced by Sevastopol's defences the trick for the allies would be to land their forces beyond the reach of the Russian artillery while still close enough to the base to allow a surprise attack and the subsequent surrender of the garrison. However, not everyone was satisfied that an attack should be made that year. Burgoyne warned that the lateness of the season and the poor health of the troops at Varna put the whole operation in jeopardy. He was right to be concerned. Winter comes to the Crimea in November and the expeditionary force was not equipped for cold weather campaigning in the event of a lengthy siege. Moreover the cholera showed no sign of abating: during the second week of August there were 2624 cases and 345 of them had died. Burgoyne's fears were shared by Brigadier Tylden, the chief engineer who warned Raglan that 'the projected attack on Sebastopol, with our present resources at command is eminently hazardous, and will, at best, require a longer time to effect, than the present advanced season will allow.'[4]

Illness had also claimed senior commanders. Saint-Arnaud was barely able to attend conferences and when he did he was usually too distracted by pain to make any positive contribution. The Duke of Cambridge had retired temporarily to Constantinople, complaining before he departed that the invasion seemed 'terribly risky' and de

Ros, too, had succumbed not just to nervous and physical exhaustion
but also to sunburn. 'My nerves are alas like a child's, and they send
me into tears,' he informed Raglan towards the end of the month.
'A pretty bit of material you see for a QMG who ought to be
made of iron.' On 29 August it was decided that de Ros should
be repatriated and his place as quartermaster general was taken by
Airey. It was a momentous change. With him as his aide-de-camp
came a young cavalry officer who was destined to play a crucial role
in the campaign.

Captain Louis Edward Nolan was one of the most unusual cavalry
officers in the British Army. Born in Milan in 1818 Nolan came from
a military family – his father, an Irishman had served in the 70th Foot
– but his own career had begun as a cadet in the Austrian army. A
precocious horseman, he was sent at the tender age of fourteen to the
military engineering school near Vienna before being commissioned
in the 10th Imperial Hussars where he quickly rose to the rank of senior
lieutenant. The decision to accelerate his career was not misplaced:
by 1838 he had seen service in the Polish and Hungarian provinces
and had received plaudit after plaudit for his military. abilities and,
above all, for his skill as a horseman. If he was also known for being
over–zealous and headstrong then that was no bad thing, a touch of
arrogance never went amiss in the best cavalry regiments.

Then he had his head turned by his native country. In June 1838
Nolan was in London, one of the many thousands who witnessed
the glorious pageantry of the coronation of Queen Victoria and by
all accounts he was bewitched. Nothing would do for him but that
he serve in a British cavalry regiment; in time-honoured fashion his
father began badgering Raglan for a commission and on St George's
Day 1839 his son's wish was granted. Nolan was gazetted a cornet in
the 15th Light Dragoons (later 15th Hussars) and for a short period,
until his Austrian commission was cancelled, he enjoyed the unusual
distinction of being an officer in two armies.

There must have been times when he wondered if the decision
were a wise one. When his regiment was sent to India at the end of
1839 he became ill and was given two years' sick leave which he spent
at the depot in Maidstone. And when he returned to his regiment in
1842 it played no part in the Sikh Wars in the Punjab which provided
British soldiers with extensive battlefield experience. This was doubly
unfortunate. Not only did he miss battles such as Sobroan and Aliwal
in which the cavalry played important parts but later he would be

stigmatised as an 'Indian' officer, an unforgivable sin if one were serving under Lord Cardigan or some of the stuffier commanding officers. However, Nolan refused to let his Indian service hinder him. Far from it; while serving as a staff officer in Madras he bent his mind to the question of cavalry tactics and the result was the publication of two outspoken books which questioned the assumptions under which the British Army employed its cavalry arm.

The first, *The Training of Cavalry Remount Horses: A New System* (1852), was a radical re-examination of cavalry training systems while *Cavalry: Its History and Tactics* (1853), is an equally innovatory study of cavalry tactics whose aim was to replace the present 'blind adherence to exploded theories or antiquated usages'. An enthusiast for the *arme blanche* school of warfare (cavalry as attacking or pursuit force), Nolan believed that cavalry could drive off entrenched infantry positions and disintegrate the fleeing remnants provided that the original charge had impetus and direction. His views were widely read and caused no little debate in cavalry circles – he suggested that cavalrymen should be shorter than the regulation five feet ten inches – but not everyone warmed to the immoderate self-promotion he brought to the introduction to *Cavalry*:

> After long consideration of the whole subject, I honestly believe that the main principles are right. Without this conviction I would not publish at all, but with it I feel it to be a dereliction not to offer to my brother officers, and the service in general, the results of my practice and meditation.[5]

Throughout the book there is an underlying assumption that Nolan's methods were the only way forward while the tactics of the day were guided by a hidebound officer class who owed everything to family influence. In a service which relied on its officers displaying pluck in the field this was not the kind of language calculated to win Nolan many friends and there were those in Varna who thought him conceited and arrogant. Even Russell of *The Times* found him 'impetuous' and was 'astonished at the angry way in which he spoke of Lord Lucan and Lord Cardigan'. Cleverness of the kind demonstrated by Nolan was not an attribute valued at the time. His brigade commander Cardigan considered it a disadvantage for any aristocrat to be 'over-educated' and the Duke of Cambridge was equally contemptuous, being heard to remark to a fellow senior officer, 'Brains! I don't believe in brains'. That Nolan was in Varna at all owed everything to the reputation he had gained from his first book: on 11 March Newcastle had ordered him to accompany the expeditionary force as the staff officer responsible for purchasing remounts for the cavalry from Syria, a frustrating operation which only yielded 292 horses.

On 20 August the allied commanders convened again to lay the final plans for conveying their forces to the Crimea. A mixture of steamers and sailing ships towed by steamers would convey the men, horses and equipment; embarkation would begin four days later with departure fixed for 2 September. It was a wildly optimistic timetable for such a large force. In the first wave the French planned to take 24,000 infantrymen, 70 artillery pieces and 100 cavalry scouts while the British hoped to embark 22,000 infantrymen, 60 artillery pieces and the entire Light Brigade of 1000 cavalrymen. In addition the Turks hoped to transport 5000 men in their own warships although these would come under Saint-Arnaud's direction. Each navy would be responsible for conveying its own land forces: Hamelin had opted to carry them in his warships, gambling that the Russians would not risk an attack at sea, while Lyons used a variety of war and merchant ships.

It was a confused process. The French were forced to cram up to 2000 men into each of their warships whose decks became so crowded that the guns could not be manned. The British too lacked any strategic plans for embarking men and supplies: articles which would be needed immediately on disembarkation were loaded first and there were understandable difficulties in loading the Light Brigade's horses on hastily assembled rafts. As Dundas remarked with weary resignation: 'If the Russians have the spirit of a mosquito, they will now leave their harbour and try the issue.' Fortunately, although the allies could not have known this, the Russians had adopted a careless policy of wait and see.

There were even problems with the wives. When it was discovered that there would be insufficient food and shelter for the full complement of regimental wives, Raglan ordered their numbers to be cut, with the result that many found themselves in danger of being left behind. Not so the adventurous Fanny Duberly who followed Cardigan's advice to disobey orders and was smuggled board the troopship *Himalaya* where the crew received her 'very hospitably'.

For the French this was no problem: they had made suitable provision for their wives and *vivandières* – nursing assistants attached to each regiment. Indeed, with their experienced Commissariat department, the French fared better overall and were ready to sail by the agreed departure date. Even so they had not been unaffected by the muddle at Varna. The constant swell turned embarkation into an unusually lengthy and uncomfortable operation and the untamed cholera created scenes straight out of nightmares. Victims were thrown overboard with weights, but all too often these were not properly secured and soldiers were treated to the ghastly spectacle of bloated grimacing corpses bobbing about in the waters below them. In this respect the French were the worst offenders.

Curiously, despite the rigours and the delays, morale remained reasonably high. Partly this was due to a combined sense of expectation and relief. 'We are all in a great glee at the prospect of getting away so soon from this horrid place and of having something to do,' wrote Captain Kingscote to his sister, 'besides the bustle and activity of the embarkation gives one excitement.' There was a sense of awe, too, about the 'perfect forest of shipping of every kind' and the size and apparent invincibility of the invasion force. 'How they [the Russians] can resist such a force as ours I know not,' was a typical observation. 'Failure seems impossible.' More than the French, who were to remain uneasy about the practicality of the mission until they arrived in the Crimea, the British were banking on the capture of Sevastopol to curb Russian ambitions. On 23 August Clarendon wrote to Stratford reminding him that he had to do all in his power to ensure that the British forces kept up the momentum for an early and decisive victory:

> I am sure that until Sebastopol is taken there is no chance of an honourable nor consequently of a binding peace. If Sebastopol remains intact the command of the Black Sea and the fate of Constantinople are in the hands of Russia and England and France are disgraced.[6]

It was easy to be optimistic in distant London where *The Times* and other newspapers produced euphoric articles prophesying an early and easy victory. 'I will not believe that in any case British arms can fail,' wrote Newcastle to Raglan, quashing any uneasy thoughts that may have visited the British commander in Varna. The plan was to assemble

with the French fleet at Balchik Bay, fifteen miles to the north, but
the delays caused the first cracks in the alliance. When Raglan arrived
at the rendezvous on board *Caradoc* on 5 September he discovered
that Saint-Arnaud had already departed on the three-decker warship
Ville de Paris, taking with him 36 French and Turkish sailing ships
and steamers. With the British fleet and the slower French sailing
ships now spread out over a wide area the allied invasion force was
dangerously exposed – only the Royal Navy warships protected it
– but still Menshikov decided against making an attack, confidently
informing the tsar that he was ready to repel the threatened invasion
on land.

Eventually, on 8 September, *Caradoc* caught up with the *Ville de
Paris* off Cape Tarkanhut to enable a commanders' conference to take
place. It was no easy matter. Saint-Arnaud was not in a condition to
make a contribution, being prostrate in his bunk, and the one-armed
Raglan was unable to board the French warship. However, a meeting
had to take place as, unaccountably, the French were not at all sure
about using Katcha as a landing place. Accordingly Raglan deputed
Dundas, Rose and his military secretary, Lieutenant-Colonel Thomas
Steele, to attend in his stead. The French were represented by their
divisional commanders and Saint-Arnaud's military secretary Colonel
Trochu who played a leading role. During the discussions the French
strongly supported a proposal to postpone the attack on Sevastopol
until the following year and to use the interval to build a secure
base at Kaffa, a hundred miles to the east of the Russian port. It
was a tantalising prospect. With its secure port Kaffa provided a
safe anchorage and a protecting mountain range meant that it was
reasonably safe from Russian counter-attack.

The proposals had been written on a piece of paper which, to
Dundas's disgust, 'was not signed, and not stated by whom drawn
up, under whose sanction or from what person put forward'. It
also argued that any landing at Katcha was 'considered insuperable
by the English Press having indicated that spot as the one at which
debarkation was intended.'[7] Following a desultory discussion the ailing
Saint-Arnaud said that he would agree to any new proposal decided
by Raglan. It was decided to reconvene the following day on board
Caradoc but far from settling the issue this meeting only served to
complicate matters. Colonel Trochu suddenly dismissed the Kaffa
project and argued instead for the landings to proceed at Katcha.
His volte-face was surprising but as the British officers were well

aware of the importance of his position – Rose believed that the French military secretary wielded more authority than Saint-Arnaud himself – they were forced to take stock. Because there was indecision over the landing place Raglan agreed to a second reconnaissance even though he had been prepared to accept Brown's earlier findings.

To later generations, versed in the intricacies of the invasion of the European mainland in June 1944, the decision seems inexplicable. Here were the commanders of an allied task force composed of several hundred ships carrying an army of 50,000, almost within sight of their destination, dithering about the correct landing grounds. Logic screams out that these decisions should have been taken before the force put to sea, but in those early September weeks of 1854 reason was forced to take a back seat while Raglan decided tactics on the spot. He could just as easily have been Leicester or York in earlier campaigns in Flanders and Holland when Britain struggled to make war on the European mainland.

None the less it would be too easy to lay the entire blame for the muddle at Raglan's feet. He had been given a free hand by the Cabinet; the choice of landing ground was his (although he had been presented with a number of alternatives by armchair strategists); and at the time he enjoyed Saint-Arnaud's confidence. However, that very independence was partly to blame for his predicament. Newcastle had offered him the freedom 'to act according to conscience', yet at the same time he had made it clear that Raglan was directly responsible to him and would have to heed his orders. Hardinge, too, wanted to be involved in any 'military transactions'. For the mild-mannered Raglan whose even temper could either be admirable or exasperating, it was a case of being given enough rope with which to hang himself.

Lack of intelligence information also contributed to the muddle. Not only was Raglan unaware of the Russian's troop strength at Sevastopol – estimates ranged from 20,000 to 100,000 – but the maps of the interior were inadequate. While they showed geographical features such as the mountains to the north and the steppe to the south, they lacked sufficient detail to plan any general strategy. Some help had arrived in the person of Charles Cattley, formerly British vice-consul at Kertch, who had been commissioned by Newcastle on 3 August to provide the expeditionary force with personal information about the terrain of the peninsula. As a precaution he adopted the *nom de guerre* of 'Calvert' and later became a source of much useful intelligence gleaned from interrogation of Russian prisoners. On

Stratford's recommendation Raglan also employed a number of local people as spies, agreeing with the British ambassador that their use, though 'dangerous', was 'necessary, and something must generally be risked in the employment of them.'

That absence of accurate information proved to be an enormous stumbling block but the problems had already been foreseen. Although Clarendon had been an early convert to the idea of attacking Sevastopol, during the summer he had been sufficiently worried about the absence of any accurate intelligence to voice his concerns to Stratford:

> We are still unanimous and eager for attacking the Crimea but it is deplorable that we should be so totally uninformed about the numbers of Russian troops there or indeed anything about the country. I think if nothing better could be devised that parties might have landed from the ships and carried off a few people at different places on the coast for the purpose of questioning them.[8]

Stratford passed on the Foreign Secretary's suggestion to Dundas but received the dusty response that any such operation would endanger the British warships by bringing them within range of the Russian coastal guns. Knowing that the answer would not please Clarendon, Stratford turned to Lyons who had become a useful conduit of information about conditions in the Crimea. Having marshalled that intelligence Stratford replied to Clarendon outlining the position as he saw it:

> By dint of listening and questioning I arrive at the following conclusions.
>
> 1. That a landing may be affected under fire from the ships.
> 2. That the capture of Fort Constantine would decide the fall of Sebastopol.
> 3. That the fort is a mere square with bastions at the angles, unprotected by outworks and commanded from the neighbouring ground.
> 4. That if the fort were too strong for an assault there are heights looking down upon the town and shipping which might be taken without too much loss to the allies and with the loss of all the Russians.

It was a hopelessly over-optimistic view but Stratford felt duty-bound to present it as realistically as he could to the Foreign Secretary. Then, having rehearsed the arguments, he came to some unpalatable conclusions. A direct assault on the harbour and a *coup de main* against Fort Constantine which guarded it had already been disregarded by Raglan as too great a risk. Stratford agreed and having sketched out the operational possibilities he underlined the dangers accompanying them:

On the other hand no one seems to know with any approach to certainty what number of troops the Crimea now contains. The nature of the ground between Sebastopol and the place of landing is a matter of conjecture, not of knowledge. The season is late; the beach selected is narrow; the ships may be forced by weather to leave the coast after landing a portion only of the troops, and the troops at best are somewhat disheartened and not over-numerous.[9]

In other words, the allied commanders were being forced to work with hunches and guesses – not the best of methods, argued Stratford, to begin a difficult campaign.

Faced by those uncertainties and aware that he had to push ahead with the campaign Raglan had little option but to reconnoitre the area himself. On 9 September, accompanied by Brown, Lyons, Burgoyne and Rose, together with a French party consisting of Canrobert and Trochu, he set off on board *Caradoc* under the protection of *Agamemnon* and *Sampson*, to take a closer look at the Crimean coast. It was a curious voyage. Just as Brown had discovered earlier, the Russians paid little attention to their presence as they steamed past Sevastopol on the following morning, a Sunday which brought them within sound of the church bells. Later, Raglan reported that the flotilla came so close to shore that Lyons was able to doff his hat to a watching Russian officer on horseback and at Eupatoria to the north he was perplexed to see well-dressed crowds walking about 'without seemingly feeling any apprehension'. Colonel Calthorpe, Raglan's nephew and ADC, was more pragmatic: his soldier's eye saw a powerful fortress which seemed to be bristling with guns.

Throughout the day they steamed up and down the coast, inspecting possible alternatives to Katcha at the mouths of the rivers Belbec, Alma and Bulganek but it proved difficult to reach a decision. Canrobert

favoured Katcha while Raglan thought that it was too near to
Sevastopol and too open to counter-attack from the clifftops where
the presence of military tents suggested that Menshikov's commanders
had been reading *The Times*. Newcastle's suggestion of Eupatoria was
deemed to be too far away but just to the south there was a long
open stretch of beach which seemed to offer possibilities. It was big
enough to accommodate both armies, its left flank was protected by
a salt marsh and while it was some forty miles from Sevastopol it had
the advantage of being undefended. There was only one drawback.
Ominously, for what was to follow, it was called Calamita Bay.

None the less, it seemed to Raglan to provide the allies with
the best option of getting their forces ashore without attracting
interference from the Russians. The flat ground beyond the shore
also offered the bonus of a campsite and assembly point for the
march on Sevastopol which would follow the landings. There was
no disagreement amongst the party on *Caradoc* which returned to the
rendezvous off Cape Tarkanhut early the following morning. Orders
were then issued for the fleet to proceed to a new assembly point off
an old fort covering the salt marshes; the French would land to the
right and the British to the left, the dividing point being marked by
a buoy. As the town of Eupatoria would make an ideal base Raglan
ordered Steele and Trochu to secure its surrender. The Russian mayor
complied but not before fumigating the summons – as he was required
to do under his country's customs regulations – and gravely informing
the allies that they should consider themselves to be in quarantine until
further notice.

Raglan's orders galvanised the fleet. That same evening they set
off into a heavily oppressive night, the sea glassily smooth, the British
steamers puffing lustily ahead of the slower French sailing ships. Early
the next morning the task force had its first sight of the Russian
coast and so too did Russian observers in Fort Constantine see
the distant masts and trails of smoke. Confirmation of the allies'
intentions arrived at the day's end when the signalling station at the
mouth of the River Alma reported a huge fleet sailing towards the
north-east. Its destination could only be Eupatoria. From the shore
the convoy seemed to make an orderly progress but at sea there was
some confusion as ships failed to keep their station and in some cases
steam tugs had to take the slower sailing ships in tow. Even so, the
mood on board was one of happy confidence. 'Last night there was
a bright full moon, and we saw the ships almost as plain as by day,'

wrote Sterling from the transport ship *Emu*. 'The look-out man on Cape Chersonese will lift up his hands with astonishment when he sees us.'[10]

In fact the Russians seemed to have been overcome by paralysis. A huge invasion fleet had come into their coastal waters unopposed; it was obvious that its destination was Eupatoria, but Menshikov's only response was to send out a Cossack patrol to report on the landings. He was still confident that even if the allies did land it would not be a full-scale invasion but a probing operation to test his defences. Two days earlier he had noted that 'with the lateness of the season a landing is no longer possible' and he shared the general view that the allies would never dare land an army which would have to rely on the uncertain winter waters of the Black Sea for its supplies. Certainly the mood in the Sevastopol garrison was a mixture of excitement and apprehension. When the news of the landings at Eupatoria was announced most of the senior officers were attending a performance of Gogol's play *The Government Inspector* and the news 'ran round the house like electricity'. The theatre quickly emptied and a soldier in the Tarutinsky regiment spoke for many when he noted: 'There is no doubt that we will beat the enemy hollow.'

Menshikov was destined to face heavy criticism for his inaction, the theory being that he should have marched his forces to Eupatoria to oppose the allied landings. It has an attractive ring – during his reconnaissance Raglan had been worried about the presence of 'a good many camps' containing Russian troops – but the critics were simply being wise long after the event. Like Raglan, Menshikov was unaware of the allies' strength and he was unable to second-guess their intentions. If, as he believed, it was merely a raid, Sevastopol would not be threatened and the commitment of forces would weaken his garrison. If it were an invasion he preferred to consolidate his forces and prepare for the defence of Sevastopol, the loss of which was unthinkable. Accordingly, the day after the landings began, on 15 September, he sent a message to the tsar stating his intentions: 'Not having the means to attack the enemy on the open beaches that are covered by the guns of the fleet, I am concentrating my force on an advantageous position from which to give battle.'[11]

By then both sides were preparing to give battle, blissfully unaware of the other's true intentions. 'It is a remarkable expedition, and will have many historians to record our exploits, and recount our successes or our failure,' noted Sterling who had been promoted lieutenant-colonel before leaving Varna. 'The latter I think scarcely possible; but there is also a chance of it; and if that chance should turn against us, the memory of the defeat will be stamped in such characters of blood as will put half England in mourning.'[12]

PART II

1

Advance to Contact

By day or by night I can think of nothing but Sebastopol and I tremble to face the great moral disaster of the expedition being abandoned.

The Earl of Clarendon to Lord Stratford, 29 August 1854

Thursday 14 September 1854 dawned bright and sunny as the allied fleet made its way into the waters of Calamita Bay to begin the invasion of the Crimea. The French were the first to disembark at 7 a.m., unfurling a tricolour above the shallow shingle beach as the first men swept ashore, shouting encouragement to the boats following them. Without any sizeable cavalry force to land, three infantry divisions disembarked easily enough and by nightfall the French had established tented camps for themselves on the spit of land beyond the shore. It was just as well that they did because by evening the fickle Black Sea autumn weather changed from sunshine to grey skies and a steady drizzle.

Inevitably, perhaps, given the delays and last-minute changes of plan, the landings at Calamita quickly degenerated into a muddle. The buoy marking the division between the two landing beaches had shifted position with the result that the British had to move further south and did not start landing until nine o'clock. To begin with there was a holiday atmosphere to the process. The weather was good and apart from the brief presence of a Cossack cavalry patrol there was no sign of any Russian opposition. As the landing boats raced to and from the shore carrying the first cheering troops the ships' bands played and there was still enough hope in most men's hearts to banish their natural apprehension. 'For nearly a mile, flat-bottomed boats filled with armed men – our Light Division being first – were being towed by the sailors rowing in other boats,' remembered Sergeant-Major George Loy Smith, 11th Hussars. 'We saw them leap cheerily on to the beach. Grave thoughts now passed through my mind: how many of these fine fellows will never again leave that shore!'[1]

Once on the beach the regiments assembled and marched inland, the Coldstream Guards quickly finding that the countryside, so inviting when viewed from the sea, was barren and without shelter. As the thin afternoon rain became a deluge, Gowing's fusiliers tried to make fires as best they could from driftwood but, lacking shelter, it was a lost cause. Without tents and weighed down by their equipment the soldiers had to take cover wherever possible, at best constructing flimsy bivouacs or simply cowering beneath their greatcoats. Officers who had come ashore wearing full dress uniform saw their expensive gold braid being ruined in the steady downpour while the men cursed their heavy personal loads. Each soldier carried fifty rounds of ammunition, spare clothes and boots, a water canteen and three days' rations consisting of four and half pounds each of meat and biscuit.

The weather had improved by the following day but a heavy swell slowed down the landings and it proved impossible to get all the horses ashore without damaging them. Upset after the lengthy voyage they struggled as they were lowered on to the landing craft and not surprisingly there were casualties. 'The beach is a vast and crowded camp, covered with men, horses, fires, tents, general officers, boats landing men and horses, which latter are flung overboard and swum ashore,' noted Fanny Duberly who watched the landings from the deck of the *Himalaya*. 'Eleven were drowned today. I am glad to say we lost none.'[2] By then, though, things were beginning to improve with the first landings of tents, stores and ammunition which were stockpiled on the beach to await the arrival of transport wagons which would have to be secured from the local farmers.

Airey and his staff were able to purchase 350 wagons together with 67 camels and 253 horses but these were hardly sufficient for providing supplies for some 27,000 men and the Light Brigade's horses. Once again the French had proved to be quicker on their feet, sending out patrols to forage and quickly stripping the surrounding countryside of farm animals, fruit and vegetables. Sometimes they paid for the supplies; more often they simply plundered. As Russell could not help but noting – and then reporting back to *The Times* – there was a clear distinction between the two armies, the French being well provided with tents but no cavalry, while the British lacked the former but had the latter. As for the Ottoman forces of whom Russell said, 'it is a great pity that it is not permitted us to hate the Turks', they had neither. And that was not the end of the failings. Shortly after landing the war correspondent encountered some British medical officers who were enraged by the lack of arrangements for the wounded and the sick, many of whom were still suffering from cholera:

> Do make a note of this! By—! They have landed this army without any kind of hospital transport, litters or carts, or anything! Everything was ready at Varna! Now with all this cholera and diarrhoea about, there are no means of taking the sick down to the boats.[3]

In fact provision had been made to take cholera cases back to Scutari on board the transport ship *Kangaroo* but the ambulance wagons had been left behind in Bulgaria because they had proved ineffective at Varna. It was not that the British were indifferent to the fate of their soldiers while the French had made adequate provision. Shortly before the declaration of war the Director-General of the Army Medical Department had sent out a team of doctors to Constantinople to study the conditions 'at the seat of war' and as a result of their findings preparations had been made for a short war in the principalities. Envisaging a summer campaign the doctors thought that wounded soldiers could be taken by ambulance wagons to casualty clearing stations at Varna for onward transportation to Constantinople. Provision had also been made to send the worst cases back to Britain 'in any steamers which may from time to time be returning to their country'. As *The Times* had reported as early as 15 February, medical supplies including 1000 yards of adhesive plaster, 1000 lb. of lint, 12 large medicine chests and 30 panniers for their carriage would accompany the first troops travelling eastwards. Civilian surgeons had also been enlisted for the duration of the war and there turned out to be no shortage of volunteers, anxious for a little excitement and the opportunity to improve their own medical expertise.[4]

Under the circumstances it would have been difficult for the Army Medical Department to have laid contingency plans for an invasion and prolonged campaign in the Crimea: even as the troops were landing, senior British officers were convinced that the fighting would be over within a few weeks and that the troops would be back home for Christmas. So too were the French: buoyed up by drugs and the anticipation of battle, Saint-Arnaud had already written to his wife forecasting the fall of Sevastopol after *'une belle bataille'*. Not that the French came empty-handed. With their recent experience of campaigning the French came fully prepared for any contingency and were, rightly perhaps, dismissive of their ally's lack of military foresight.

Self-belief also coursed through Menshikov's mind, although, naturally, the Russian commander envisaged a rather different outcome. All along he had doubted that the allies would invade the Crimea but now that they had landed their objective must be Sevastopol. If they could be defeated in the opening battle the campaign would be over and they would be forced to retire with heavy losses. Having told the tsar that he intended to meet the threat once the allies had landed and begun their advance on Sevastopol, Menshikov now began preparations for the coming battle.

The first intelligence from the Cossack reconnaissance patrols suggested that the enemy strength was between 50,000 and 100,000. The size of the fleet warranted that estimate but the Russians had also been able to capture and interrogate eleven French soldiers who were able to confirm a figure of around 80,000. By then, too, the first infantry battalions had begun arriving at their defensive positions to the north of Sevastopol, the obvious line of the enemy's expected attack, and had been suitably awe-struck by the forest of masts and smoke trails of the huge allied fleet lying off the coast. The Tarutinsky regiment had already taken up position on the hills between the rivers Katcha and Alma and, responding to his men's natural alarm, Captain Ermalaeu told them that they had little to worry about as the British army was so inexperienced:

> The Englishmen go and return on the sea, but there is no fear that they will reach Sevastopol; they would be afraid to try; let them try on land, and we would give it to them in fine style. The French, we know, can fight, but the English, if they ever do make war, it's only with savages in a country a long way off.[5]

The news of the allied invasion did not reach St Petersburg until 23 September, by which time the first battle of the campaign had already been fought. Despite Menshikov's assurances that the allies would never dare to attack Sevastopol the landings had been long expected and there was a natural air of alarm in the Russian capital. Realising the fragility of Menshikov's position Nicholas ordered further reinforcements of infantry and cavalry to join the army in the Crimea. Only later would Menshikov be criticised for failing to oppose the landings: at the time most commentators were well aware of the imbalance in the size of his forces and supported his decision to engage them in a decisive battle before Sevastopol where 'we will be on home ground and we have fresh troops; the first storm will separate the enemy from his fleet and he may be cut off.'[6]

By then the news of the landings had also reached London. Heeding the warnings he had received from his masters at the Foreign Office about delays in his despatches, Stratford had immediately sent Raglan's signal by messenger to Belgrade for urgent onward telegraphic transmission to London. It arrived on Sunday 24 September and the following day Clarendon wrote back to Stratford claiming that the landings represented 'one of the greatest events of modern times and the precursor, I trust, of further triumphs over difficulties'. Warming to his theme he acknowledged that while the capture of Sevastopol would be 'difficult' its fall 'cannot be doubtful . . . [and] assuming that we are consequently masters of the Crimea, what is to be done?'

At that stage of the operation Clarendon believed that there were three options open to the allies once Sevastopol had fallen: to move the army into Sevastopol for winter quarters and to destroy its fortifications and naval base in the spring; to return the territory to the Ottoman Empire from which it had been appropriated by Catherine the Great in 1783; or to create an independent Crimea under local Tartar rule.[7]

Of the three Clarendon favoured the first option as it was the sole intention of the invasion. While there was much to be said for putting the area under Ottoman rule once more, he acknowledged that this would only store up problems for the future as Russia would inevitably attempt to reclaim it. For that reason he favoured the creation of an independent Crimea whose freedom would be guaranteed by Britain, Austria and France. This, too, was Stratford's view. He had visited the Crimea and had been much impressed by the sturdy independence of the Crim-Tartar population – as was Raglan who reported that the local headmen had refused all offers of compensation for the use of their wagons as they were no friends of the Russians.

France, too, wanted to destroy the naval base to prevent it ever being used again by Russia or Turkey. Following the news of the landings Cowley in Paris had instigated a similar conversation with Drouyn de Lhuys who was strongly of the opinion that the destruction of the base should precede any post-war treaty arrangements with Russia. Having received information from Saint-Arnaud that the allied armies would probably have to winter in the Crimea and be 'prepared for the sacrifices it will cost them' the French foreign minister passed on this intelligence to Cowley. While his words made sense, the optimism with which they were delivered show only too clearly how ignorant were both sides about the conditions facing the soldiers in the field:

> The climate of the southern portion of that peninsula was healthy and fertile; the Port of Sebastopol would be a constant refuge for the fleets. From no place could further enterprises in the East, to whatever point directed, be now advantageously undertaken. The moral effect of wintering on Russian ground would be immense and the armies would be removed from the chance of contemplating the cruelties and misgovernment still practised in Turkey which had made so unfortunate an impression upon them during the occupation of Varna.[8]

However, before the allies could develop a post-war peace settlement their armies had to capture Sevastopol and in the hinterland of Calamita Bay there was much muddle and confusion in the British camp. The landings had taken longer than expected, largely due to the problems of disembarking the Light Brigade and unloading the artillery pieces, but there was also an absence of any logistical organisation. Delays in rounding up the transport wagons meant that supplies and ammunition had to be dumped on the beach and the lack of transport forced commissary officers to decide on the spot which supplies had to be taken and which could be safely left behind. All the while further confusion was caused by files of cholera cases waiting on the beach to return to the transports. As the French historian, de Bazancourt, described the scene the British were delayed because 'an immense quantity of impedimenta retarded their operations interminably'.

That was also Saint-Arnaud's opinion and he told his wife that 'the English have the unpleasant habit of always being late', thereby preventing him from keeping to a timetable which would see the

Russians defeated and Sevastopol in his hands by mid-October. He asked Raglan to be ready to move on 17 September, three days after the landings; but the British inability to organise themselves meant that the move was postponed by twenty-four hours. To growing French impatience Raglan said that he would be ready on 19 September; by then there had already been a number of minor engagements with the Russians as patrols from both sides made contact with each other.

Some were potentially serious – during their foraging expeditions French Spahi cavalrymen came into contact with Cossack patrols – but one involving the British was pure farce. Shortly before midnight on 18 September a Light Brigade sentry panicked and opened fire into the darkness after hearing what seemed to be advancing cavalry. 'Thinking the Cossacks were attacking us,' remembered Loy Smith, 'the brigade was soon mounted and in line, ready. Lord Lucan and Lord Cardigan were in front.'[9] Soon the entire British camp was in an uproar. The sound of the shots and the jangle of harnesses and shouted commands as the Light Brigade lined up convinced the neighbouring infantry camps that they were under attack. The result was a flurry of shooting which was only stopped when the brigade-major rode round the vedettes (mounted sentries or scouts) ordering a general ceasefire. Amazingly, no one was killed although an officer's personal servant wearing a grey greatcoat was mistaken for a Russian and was shot in the leg by another officer as he bridled up his master's horse.[8]

The Russians, too, were jittery. Sent to reconnoitre a village in the valley in which a French patrol was thought to be present, Captain Chodasiewicz decided to be prudent. Like any soldier in his first contact with the enemy he was seized by the familiar emotions of fear, fear of the unknown and fear of fear itself:

> I picked out two men that I considered the most to be depended upon. We began to descend the slope towards the village, crawling on our bellies, and I must confess that I felt a strange sensation of cold; my heart beat faster at the thought that in a few minutes we should be engaged in a martial struggle. I tried, I know, to hide this feeling, of which I was ashamed, from my men. After all, I don't think it was cowardice – it might have been the effect of the cold night-dew through which we were crawling.[10]

Before giving the order to fire, Chodasiewicz decided to investigate further and crawled forward to challenge the sentries. It was as well that he did because they were men of the 2nd Moscow Regiment: under Russian military law, had he ordered an attack, he would have been reduced to the ranks and, if he survived the war, exiled to Siberia. It had been a narrow escape.

Encounters such as those described by Chodasiewicz and Loy Smith are common before battles when both sides are attempting to probe each other's defences, and they can take a toll on soldiers' spirits. However, by the following morning Raglan's army was at last ready to move off and march on Sevastopol some thirty miles away. Saint-Arnaud's plan was to engage the Russian forces, already reported by the captain of HMS *Terrible* to be assembling on the River Alma, and then to advance on the city itself. More detailed plans would be settled once the size and disposition of the Russian forces were known more accurately. And so they set off towards Sevastopol in a mood of high optimism with bands playing and colours flying. Ahead lay unknown numbers of enemy soldiers and the prospect of bloody battle, but in the bright morning sunshine the allied soldiers were confident that Saint-Arnaud was right, that there would be a short sharp campaign and that most of them would be home in time for Christmas.

First, though, they had to get there and it proved to be no easy matter to march the army and their 128 artillery pieces up the coastal plain towards the Russian naval base. With their superior numbers the French claimed the right of the line, which meant that their flanks would be protected by the sea and by the British to the left. Behind them came the 7000-strong Ottoman forces. To protect the force Raglan divided his infantry into two columns – the Light, 1st and 4th Divisions on the extreme left, with the 2nd and 3rd in the middle. Responsibility for protecting the columns and for providing advance reconnaissance fell to the Light Brigade, Scarlett's Heavy Brigade being still at Varna. The 11th Hussars and 13th Light Dragoons rode at the head of the columns while Lord George Paget's 4th Light Dragoons brought up the rear. Flank protection was provided by the 8th Hussars and 17th Lancers under Lucan's command.

Four miles separated the two flanks as the army set off into a strangely verdant landscape, 'as green and smooth as a racecourse'. Like many other facets of the campaign, though, the easy-going terrain was an illusion. As the sun climbed higher in the sky it became an enemy, and although the men were only carrying light packs their uniforms were totally unsuitable for marching in hot weather. Tight red tunics and heavy ornamental shako helmets helped the soldiers to cut fine figures on northern parade grounds but in the heat and dust of the Crimea they were a curse. Also, unlike the French with their experience of Algeria, the British infantrymen were unused to route marching. In desperation men started discarding their helmets and greatcoats and those who were unable to continue simply fell out of the line and became stragglers. Bringing up the rear Paget wrote later that he had never seen such a scene of despair as he passed by growing mountains of equipment and collapsing men: 'This went on gradually increasing until ere a mile or two was passed the stragglers were lying thick on the ground, and it is no exaggeration to say that the last two miles resembled a battle-field!'[11]

One problem was the cholera which was still claiming further victims. Another was the lack of water: in the haste and confusion of departure men had been unable to fill their canteens and were desperate to slake their thirsts. The high temperatures and undulating landscape also affected the weary columns. When Mary Evans had won the ballot which allowed her to accompany her husband's regiment, the 4th Foot (King's Own Royal Lancaster), she had considered herself fortunate. On the line of march she was not so sure: 'The marching conditions were frightful. My feet were sore and blistered but I had to keep up with the men.'[12]

With their wagons and ample supplies the French *vivandières* in their smart blue uniforms fared better but, as happened throughout the campaign, the British regimental wives suffered the same privations as their husbands. Several had died of cholera at Varna and only the hardiest, or the luckiest, had managed to accompany their husband's regiments to the Crimea. Officers' wives such as Fanny Duberly, or Lady Erroll whose husband served in the Rifle Brigade, fared better both because of their husbands' rank and because they could afford home comforts. But for Mrs Evans and the other regimental wives it was a case of making the best of increasingly difficult conditions.

Respite came in the late afternoon when they reached the River Bulganek, shrunk to a stream in the late summer heat, and its brackish waters offered the first drink of the day for hundreds of thirsty British infantrymen. The countryside began to change, too, the plain giving way to a series of ridges and hollows on the southern side. There the allied commanders had their initial view of the opposition – groups of Cossack riders in skirmishing order on the first high ridge. Raglan realised that they could be the advance patrols of a larger Russian force and ordered Cardigan to investigate with a patrol of four squadrons drawn from the 11th Hussars and 13th Light Dragoons.

This was what the Light Cavalry was supposed to do and Cardigan eagerly led his men up to the crest of the hill as the Cossack horsemen retreated before them across the valley. There they made for the higher ground and opened fire with their carbines which the British soldiers were relieved to discover were less accurate than their own weapons. 'It was now that the first shot of the campaign was fired,' remembered Loy Smith. 'A Cossack in front of the 11th raised his carbine and fired. It was instantly taken up by the whole line. Our trumpets now sounded the "Fire".' As the desultory firing continued between skirmishers from both sides Lucan rode up to the position to take overall command, a move which, though correct militarily, was bound to cause friction. With the enemy in sight Cardigan wanted to engage them immediately before Russian reinforcements could arrive and had already given the order 'Draw swords – skirmishers in – Trot'; whereas Lucan preferred to draw up a plan of operations before commencing offensive operations.[13]

The argument probably saved many lives. As the two men continued their battle of words Airey rode up with an order from Raglan 'suggesting' that they should retire. This was one of the problems with the British commander-in-chief: while his gentlemanly behaviour made him many friends, his orders always sounded like polite requests and failed to convey any urgency. A touch of steel was required and Airey provided it by turning Raglan's words into a direct order. There was good reason for it. Airey had been with Raglan at the rear and had been able to see what the two cavalry commanders could not see. To Lucan and especially to Cardigan the Russian cavalry presented an irresistible target for a charge in line. But behind the Cossacks lay a considerable danger – a Russian force of some 6000 men consisting of a brigade each of infantry and light cavalry, two batteries of artillery and several more squadrons of Cossacks. If the Light Brigade had charged at that point they would have endured heavy casualties; just as bad, they would have drawn the allies into battle before they were fully prepared.

With Airey was his ADC, Nolan, who had jumped at the opportunity of seeing some action and caused considerable comment by demonstrating coolness under the Cossacks' fire while talking to his friend Lieutenant Irwin, 13th Light Dragoons. According to the latter's trumpeter, Corporal Powell, 'the brave and dashing Captain Nolan . . . says to Adjutant Irwin in my hearing "The Russians are dam'd bad shots"; the bullets were then flying over us; we were quite close to each other; Captain Nolan, as cool as a cucumber, dismounted, looks round his horse, remounts and rejoins Lord Raglan.'[14] It was not just bravado. Like many other officers in the expeditionary force Nolan saw battle as a chance to win personal acclaim and promotion. He was already smarting under the fact that, while he was Airey's ADC, he remained a captain, not the best rank, he believed, for the position. Before leaving Varna he had sent Stratford a coy letter pressing his claims for promotion:

> It is usual to give an officer a step in rank if he has been sent on a special service by the Government, but the name of one so little known as I am will most probably be overlooked and forgotten at home unless a reminder is put in by some person of influence in fairness to my claim. The Duke of Newcastle employed me, and if in writing to him, you, My Lord, would kindly say a few words on the subject I feel confident that I should get the unattached Brevet Majority in the first gazette.[15]

Stratford was indeed in constant contact with Newcastle but he decided to keep Nolan's letter on one side and to await the outcome of events. While the headstrong young officer had acquitted himself well in purchasing remounts – against the odds, it must be said – the war had not begun and his conduct in battle would be quite another matter.

On this occasion there would be no chance for Nolan or his brother officers to win their spurs on the Bulganek. Lucan was forced to concede that Raglan's order to retire must be obeyed. The assembled cavalry squadrons retreated by squadrons in line – 'one really would have thought it only a little cavalry review', thought Calthorpe – while the gunners of 'I' Troop and 'C' Troop, Royal Horse Artillery (RHA) gave covering fire from the flanks. During the exchange of fire five cavalrymen became the army's first battlefield casualties of the campaign, including two who had a foot blown off – Sergeant Joseph Priestly, 13th Light Dragoons and Private Williamson, 11th Hussars. The latter entered the British Army's annals of understatement by riding up to his troop commander, his leg in tatters, and asking permission to fall out. Raglan would surely have approved.

As Cardigan's cavalrymen withdrew they were treated to obloquy from both sides. The Cossacks rode after them with jeers and taunts, which was only to be expected, but as they returned to make their bivouacs with the main body of the army in the Bulganek valley they were given the same treatment by their fellow infantrymen. The behaviour was not to Cardigan's liking – he had already complained loudly in the presence of his men that he was tired of being continually frustrated – and not even the arrival of a polite message of thanks from Raglan could mollify him. For Lucan it was worse. An infantry officer quipped that henceforth he should be known as Lord Look-On and the name stuck. (The army was not alone in bestowing nicknames: throughout the navy Dundas was 'Damn'd Ass'.)

There is no doubt that Raglan was correct in his decision to withdraw the Light Brigade. Not only did he need to preserve them as a screen for the main force but any engagement with the enemy could have led to a pitched battle and the infantrymen were in no position to fight after a bruising day's march. Even though Cardigan had been denied a scrap and was still smarting at what he took to be Raglan's unnecessary interference, the encounter on the Bulganek had at least brought into sharper focus the Russian troop dispositions at the next river crossing – the Alma.

Shortly after the allies began landing Menshikov had determined his plan of action. Not that he had discussed it with his colleagues or produced any coherent plans: he ran his army as a personal fiefdom, there was no command and control system and orders to individual battalion commanders came direct from central headquarters. In fact his plans were relatively simple. He had decided to commit the majority of his land forces to defend the northern approaches to Sevastopol at the valley of the River Alma which offered him a good defensive position. If he could hold it and inflict a heavy defeat the war would be won because the allies would have to retreat and fight their way back to Calamita Bay. Once there they could either surrender or fight a holding action while attempting a difficult withdrawal to the ships waiting offshore. Even if a decisive victory were not gained the allies would be held up sufficiently long to allow the Russians to strengthen the defences of Sevastopol. Accordingly, Menshikov decided on a show of force on the hills above the Alma while keeping behind a small reserve of infantry and armed sailors to guard the town.

Much of this was known to Raglan and Saint-Arnaud. Lookouts

on French warships had seen the grey-coated Russian army assembling on the high steppe five miles away and following the clash on the Bulganek the two commanders must have realised that the Alma was the best place to make a stand. Unfortunately they had neither accurate maps nor detailed intelligence to back up that guesswork. As the two armies settled down for the night, building bivouacs and lighting camp fires, Saint-Arnaud rode over to Raglan's temporary headquarters, a post house on the Sevastopol road to the rear of the British lines. By this time the French commander-in-chief was showing his illness and the buoyancy which had accompanied the landings had all but evaporated. Earlier he had written to his wife voicing his worries about who would replace him but during his meeting with Raglan he rallied sufficiently to present his plans for the coming engagement.

Like Menshikov's they were reasonably simple; unlike the Russian commander's, though, they were accompanied by a rudimentary sketch map (which proved in the end to be wildly optimistic). All that was required, argued Saint-Arnaud, was a pincer attack on the Russian positions. The French would engage the Russians on the left flank towards the high ground at the river mouth while the British would attack the right from the centre and wheel the Russians round. If the pincer movement succeeded the enemy would be prevented from withdrawing and his lines of reinforcement and resupply would be cut off. With his customary courtesy Raglan listened to the proposals and, according to Kinglake who was allowed to accompany the headquarters group, he seemed to agree with them. It was decided that General Pierre Bosquet's 2nd Division would form the vanguard and advance at 5 a.m. the next morning followed by the remaining allied divisions two hours later. Covering fire would be provided by the warships lying off the coast.

For most of the men in both the armies the following day would bring a new experience: a setpiece battle in which they would kill or perhaps themselves be killed. While most of their commanders could hark back to their past careers and their memories of battle in the wars against Napoleon, many of the young men who would do the actual fighting were ignorant of the intricacies of armed combat against the army of a major European power. However much they were able to disguise their emotions the majority would have been frightened, scared that they might not have sufficient courage or worried lest they be badly wounded. As the heat of the day gave way to a humid night they lit fires, cooked their dinners and waited. Some slept, others went through the rituals of cleaning their muskets or attempted a rough and ready toilet. On the Bulganek and above the Alma innumerable fires punctuated the night: it was a sight which touched the soldiers of both sides:

> As it became dark we could see plainly enough the enemy's fires on the River Boulganak (*sic*). I lay down in my hut of branches [bivouac], and tried to sleep, but in vain, notwithstanding the fatigue of the previous day. I rose about 3 o'clock; it was still dark; the soldiers were collected around the huge fires they had kindled with the plunder of the village of Bourliouk, and orders had been given to burn all the huts of branches, which had added to the number of fires. After a short time I went up the hill (for our own battalion was stationed in a ravine), to take a peep at the bivouac of the allied armies. Little, however, was to be seen but the fires, and now and then a dark shadow as some one moved past them. All was still and had little appearance of the coming strife. These were both armies lying, as it were, side by side. How many, or who would be sent to their last account, it would be impossible to say. The question involuntarily thrust itself upon me, should I be one of that number?[16]

Captain Chodasiewicz was doubtless not the only soldier to have asked that question of himself. Be they highlanders from Perthshire or the Transylvanian Alps or men from the farmlands of Tipperary, Wiltshire or the Loire, similar thoughts would have coursed through the minds of everyone on the five-mile stretch of land straddling the road to Sevastopol.

2

The Alma: The Infantry Will Advance

God does not abandon the righteous and we therefore await
the outcome calmly and with patience.
Vice-Admiral V.A. Kornilov, diary entry on the eve of battle,
19 September 1854

That a set-piece battle was fought at all at the River Alma owed
more to the throw of the dice than to any carefully constructed
stratagem. Menshikov's thinking was obvious: he wanted to deploy
his forces to block the allied advance on Sevastopol and believed he
could accomplish this within three weeks. The allied response was less
easy to discern. Although both commanders went to bed in apparent
agreement that Saint-Arnaud's plan would be adopted, Raglan wanted
to inspect the lie of the land and the Russian troop dispositions before
he decided how to initiate the assault. After all, that was a lesson he
had learned from his mentor, Wellington, who once remarked that
there was 'a great deal of difference between fighting in a position
which I choose or one which the enemy chooses to fight'. Knowing
that Menshikov had already selected his position Raglan wanted to
inspect it before committing himself and his army.

Other experiences from the war in the Peninsula informed Raglan's
way of thinking. The long lines of communication and shortage of
reserves meant that he had to husband his resources; there were
continuing concerns about the army's logistics and well-grounded
fears that the Treasury would fail to deliver the vital assets needed
to finish the war; there was an absence of reliable information about
the terrain over which he would be fighting. He was also tired, having

endured a 'wearisome' march. Being a cautious man, not given to rash gestures, Raglan preferred to wait and to see.

At first light the dawn brought only confusion and once again the timetable dictated by the French had to be altered because the British forces were in no position to move off at the agreed hour. A soldier in the 3rd Zouaves in Bosquet's 2nd Division complained to his parents after the battle that they had been held up by '*Messieurs les Anglais*' but this was not due to any undue tardiness on the part of the British. Aware that his baggage train and reserve supplies had to be protected Raglan had ordered part of the army to face east to prevent a possible flank attack and it took time for such a large force to wheel round into the line of march. The growing heat also added to the difficulties faced by the infantrymen, sweating beneath their colourful red or green uniform jackets and the equally exotic headwear of ostrich feathered caps and rigid shakos.

The delay caused the French to halt – they used the time to brew up mid-morning coffee – and it was not until 10.30 a.m. that the allied army was able to advance on a broad front towards the River Alma. Ahead of them lay a landscape that might have been created for warfare. Taking full advantage of the high narrow escarpment above the winding river, Menshikov had concentrated his forces on the slopes of Kourgané Hill which dominated the road to Sevastopol. On the shoulder above the village of Bourliuk two fortified earthworks – known as the Greater and Lesser Redoubts – had been constructed for use by artillery and infantry. Below them, in the centre, guarding the pass, were five battalions of infantry from the Borodino Corps under the command of General P.D. Gorchakov while the high ground to the west, Telegraph Hill, was held by the Tarutinsky and Brest-Bialystok regiments. This was the centre-piece of the Russian defences: the allies would be obliged to cross the river and press home their attack against well-defended positions on higher ground.

Only to the west had Menshikov left matters to chance. Here the escarpment gave way to 350-feet sheer cliff faces flanking the river and so steep and barren were they that Menshikov believed them to be inaccessible. As it was dead ground only one regiment and few guns were deployed to guard them, Menshikov having reasoned that no commander in his senses would commit men to a difficult assault against such a precipitous position. Later he claimed not to have known – but should have taken the trouble to discover, given the fact that the Russians were fighting on home ground – that there was a narrow, almost perpendicular path up the cliff face and that the approaches were by no means impregnable to determined troops.

But as Menshikov and his staff watched the allied armies halt one mile short of the river they were confident that the expected assault would be stopped in its tracks, secure in the knowledge that they held the high ground and that it would be up to the enemy to dislodge them. Indeed, so carefree was the moment that the Russians had allowed a party of Sevastopol's prominent citizens to take a picnic to the battlefield so that they could watch the expected defeat of the allied forces. From a hastily improvised grandstand on the Telegraph Hill they sat in elegant rows, watching the preparations through opera-glasses with glasses of champagne within easy reach. At the time watching battles was a common enough practice, little different from spending a day at the races, and the party, which included women, was in high spirits as they watched the two armies square up to one another across the Alma.

It was a moment which none of them, participants or spectators, would ever forget; yet there was an air of unreality about the preparations in the mid-day heat as the two allied commanders met to confer, Saint-Arnaud smart in his dress uniform, Raglan at ease in a blue frock-coat looking for all the world as if he were about to take a morning ride in Rotten Row. On rising ground in front of their armies the two men discussed the situation after first viewing the Russian positions through Raglan's field glasses which had a specially adapted gunstock, thereby allowing them to be used with one hand. What the commanders said is open to question, for neither man recorded the conversation, but from what followed it is clear that Raglan rejected Saint-Arnaud's idea for a flank attack because his cavalry force was outnumbered and that, therefore, he would be unable to dislodge the Russians. Instead, as he reported to Newcastle, he decided to press home a frontal assault on Kourgané Hill once the French had engaged the Russians on the right. In other words, the tactics would evolve as the battle progressed, hardly the most encouraging sign from a general schooled in the Wellingtonian tradition of maintaining command and control throughout a battle. As one disgruntled French trooper put it, 'a battle, after all, is like a surgical operation – nobody knows if they will come out if it alive, but once the necessity for it has been recognised, and the hour has come, it is best to get it over with.'[1]

In fact the hour was already at hand. Shortly after one o'clock the

The Battle of the Alma

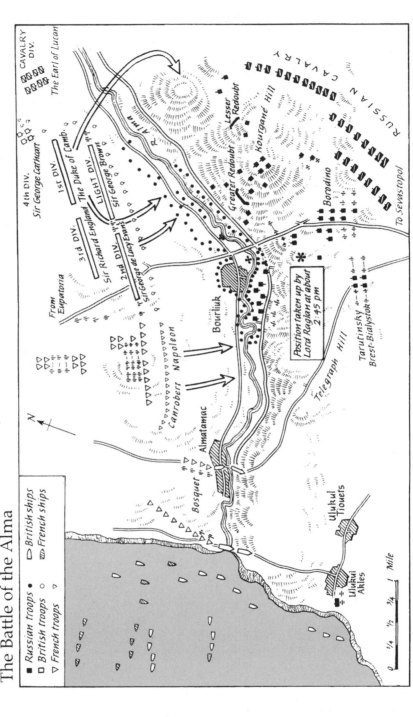

Russian troops ■   ▷ British ships
British troops □   ⊲ French ships
French troops ▽

4th DIV.
Sir George Cathcart

CAVALRY
DIV.

The Earl of Lucan

1st DIV.
The Duke of Camb.

LIGHT DIV.
Sir George Brown

3rd DIV.
Sir Richard England

2nd DIV.
Sir George de Lacy Evans

From
Eupatoria

Alma

Lesser
Redoubt

Greater Redoubt

Kourgane Hill

RUSSIAN CAVALRY

Borodino

To Sevastopol

Bourliuk

Position taken up by
Lord Raglan at about
2.45 pm

Tarutinsky
Brest-Bialystok

Telegraph Hill

Camrobert Napoleon

N

Almatamac

Bosquet

Ukukul
Tiouets

Ulukul
Akles

0 ¼ ½ ¾ 1 Mile

order to advance was sounded and the first units of the allied army moved forward to cross the river. On the British left was the Light Division supported by the Duke of Cambridge's 1st Division; to the right was the 2nd Division followed by the 3rd while Cathcart's recently arrived 4th Division supplied the reserve together with the cavalry. 'I know that I felt horribly sick − a cold shiver running through my veins,' remembered young Timothy Gowing who was seeing action for the first time, 'and I must acknowledge that I felt very uncomfortable.'[2] To their left the French advanced steadily towards Telegraph Hill while Bosquet's independent division, made up of experienced colonial troops and legionnaires, started scaling the perpendicular path which Menshikov had unwisely chosen to ignore.

Shedding their backpacks by the river bank the French made early progress. Bosquet's men forded the Alma and in two brigades made their way unopposed up the cliff road behind the village of Almatamac where they found the Plateau Hills unguarded. The few Russian soldiers who attempted to stem the tide of Zouaves and *tirailleurs* (skirmishers) were given short shrift. Having crossed the river 'under a hurricane of iron and lead' remembered Colonel Cler, 2nd Zouaves, his men charged 'and after a short, sharp struggle the enemy was compelled to abandon their formidable position'.[3] At the same time Canrobert's 1st Division crossed at the White Farm while Prince Napoleon's 3rd Division attacked to the west of the village of Bourliuk in front of Telegraph Hill.

While the French pressed home their attack the British divisions were forced to play a waiting game, Raglan having decided that it would be foolhardy to begin the assault until his allies had made sufficient progress. In any other circumstances it should have been a welcome respite, a quiet moment before battle was joined, but for the patient ranks of infantrymen Raglan's order provided many of them with their first taste of action. While green-tunicked riflemen engaged Russian skirmishers on the river banks the Russian artillery on Kourgané Hill fired their first rounds into the unprotected ranks of the 2nd and Light Division. Having deployed from column into line the infantry, drawn up by battalion, made a tempting target and the Russian heavy gunners took advantage of it. Gowing's 7th Fusiliers were positioned directly in front of the Great Redoubt and they took the full brunt of the heavy iron balls which started falling in their midst:

As soon as the enemy's round shot came hopping along, we simply did the polite – opened out and allowed them to pass on; there is nothing lost by politeness even on a battlefield. As we kept advancing, we had to move our pins to get out of their way. Presently they began to pitch their shot and shell right amongst us, and our men began to fall.[4]

Under fire men were supposed to keep their ranks, on pain of punishment, but it would have been suicidal if they had not behaved as Gowing's fellow fusiliers did. As the barrage continued men kept up their spirits by joking about the enemy's cannons, giving them nicknames as the balls bounced through their midst 'bounding along the ground like cricket balls'. Not to be outdone their officers refused to take cover and casually presented themselves as targets, personal leadership of that kind having been set at a high premium in the army of the day. Following the tradition begun by Wellington in the Peninsula, Raglan and his staff moved along the British line in full view of the enemy, a tactic which served the double purpose of stiffening the men's resolve and allowing him to gauge the enemy's dispositions.

While it is a moot point whether unnecessary exposure to enemy fire is always a good thing – to some soldiers it smacks of vanity and exhibitionism and can endanger lives – there are times when frightened men will take comfort from the cool behaviour of the officers commanding them. The Alma was such an occasion and after the battle many of the survivors remembered with gratitude the sight of the Light Division's short-sighted brigade commander Sir William Codrington casually riding his white Arab charger in front of his men as they waited for the order to advance. According to Kinglake, who managed to remain in contact with most of the commanders during this first phase of the battle, the tone was set by Sir Colin Campbell, whose Highland Brigade would attack the heavily defended Russian right. As his men waited under fire and as casualties mounted, Campbell addressed them with 'a few words – words simple, and, for the most part, workmanlike, yet touched with the fire of warlike sentiment':

Now, men, you are going into action. Remember this: whoever is wounded – I don't care what his rank is – whoever is wounded must lie where he falls till the bandsmen come to attend him. No soldiers must go carrying off wounded men. If any soldier does such a thing, his name shall be stuck up in his parish church. Don't be in a hurry about firing. Your officers will tell you when it is time to open fire. Be steady. Keep silence, fire low. Now men, the army will watch us; make me proud of the Highland Brigade![5]

The most fortunate casualties were those who received direct hits from the Russian artillery fire: they died instantly and were beyond suffering. For those who received abdominal wounds or had limbs torn off there was a long slow wait for the orderlies to pick them up off the battlefield and then an uncertain future as doctors patched them up behind the lines. Many survived the operations only to die a few days later from post-operative infection, for battlefield surgery was still a dirty business. Surgeons operated with unsterilised instruments, wounds were dressed with lint from discarded linen, and operating tables were usually encrusted with the blood and detritus from previous patients. Then, together with those suffering from cholera, many were despatched by ship to the unsuitable British Military Hospital at Scutari which had been established in a Turkish cavalry barracks and where conditions quickly became overcrowded and insanitary. It sounds appalling – and it was – but the conditions were only marginally worse than those endured in civilian hospitals at home where antisepsis was still in its infancy.

For those who survived that barrage, though, there was another hazard. As the British skirmishers advanced, Cossack cavalrymen set fire to the buildings in the village of Bourliuk and the resulting smoke and flames obscured the view of the advancing riflemen. It also meant that the 2nd British Division would be unable to cross the Alma and attack in line but, as a military tactic, it was double-edged because the smoke drifted back on to the Russian lines. 'It would have been wiser,' noted a laconic officer whose men had been blinded by the conflagration, 'as those with battle experience said at the time, not to have created a smokescreen for the enemy's benefit since this enabled him to fire on us without any loss on his side'.[6]

This was not strictly true as the Russian gunners had not only caused casualties but they had also added to the confusion as the British infantry divisions wheeled into line – an easy enough manoeuvre on the parade-ground but one which caused problems on the sloping ground and vineyards where Raglan had ordered his army to halt. At one point during the re-formation the flank regiments of the Light and 2nd Divisions – the 7th Fusiliers and the 95th (Derbyshire) Foot – became hopelessly entangled and had to be extricated by Codrington, a Coldstream Guards officer who had arrived in the Crimea at his own expense and had been rewarded with the unusual appointment for a foot guards officer of commanding a light infantry brigade.

The temporary confusion had been noted by the Russians watching on Kourgané Hill – and, presumably, by the spectators eagerly scanning the battlefield from their grandstand on the Telegraph Hill – raising hopes that the artillery fire had halted the advancing redcoats. But already the battle was beginning to slip away from the Russians as Menshikov's command and control system started yielding to the pressure of battle. When news of Bosquet's successful attack reached the Russian commander he rode across to take stock of what was happening on his left flank. All was confusion. Under fire from the advancing Zouaves and the guns of the allied fleet the unit guarding the position, the Minsky Regiment, had begun to retreat, the men unnerved by the range and accuracy of the French Minié rifles. Although the commanding general Kiriakov had promised Menshikov that the French would be seen off at bayonet point his idle boast owed more to the champagne drunk before the battle than to any military reality.

Forced to take action, otherwise the flank would be turned, Menshikov ordered up reinforcements of seven regiments of infantry and four batteries of artillery but by the time they were in position it was one o'clock and Bosquet's men were on the plateau. Worse, throughout the morning, Menshikov had been forced to leave his position on Kourgané Hill and ride four miles to oversee the operation. Not only did his behaviour smack of panic but it was insane for an overall commander to behave in this way after battle had been joined. Once again, as he had done in Constantinople earlier in the year, Menshikov had behaved hysterically and in so doing he had compromised his position. Fortunately for him though, Bosquet's advance was not matched by Canrobert's and Prince Napoleon's divisions, both of which were still struggling under heavy Russian fire from Telegraph Hill.

If the Russians were to have any chance of retrieving the situation this was it. Although Bosquet's division was on the plateau its position was precarious and depended on a successful assault on the hills by the two divisions under the command of Canrobert and Prince

Napoleon. Yet these formations had not made the progress expected by Saint-Arnaud and were pinned down by heavy Russian fire in the vineyards below the Russian positions. Without artillery support their future was uncertain but neither commander seemed able to act decisively. Had Menshikov moved against Bosquet by committing the remainder of his artillery and infantry on the Telegraph Hill the French attack would have faltered and the British line would have been exposed. But Menshikov was still in the saddle, too flustered and too excited by the events to take a measured view of the battle's progress.

All this was in stark contrast to Raglan's conduct. In the midst of the storm his small headquarters was a quiet haven. Staff officers were told not to rush, excited comments were met with polite restraint and he maintained a serenity of demeanour which was both reassuring and, for his divisional commanders at least, maddening. Yet beneath the quiet resolve Raglan could see that the stalemate had to be broken. The French attack on the hills had faltered and his own divisions were pinned down by accurate artillery fire. If the Russian heavy cavalry attacked from Kourgané Hill, as well they could have done, the Light Brigade would be unable to defend the flanks and his army could be caught in a pincer movement. A kindly man, Raglan was also strangely moved by the sight of his men stoically enduring a bombardment which, as he later told Stratford, was as heavy as any he had experienced at Waterloo.

The tactical fragility of the battle, his men's predicament and a late French plea for help convinced Raglan that the time had come to act. At three o'clock in the afternoon he gave the time-honoured order: 'The infantry will advance'. Later in his official dispatch Raglan gave a more measured reason for his order – from his position he divined that the Russians were not as formidable as previously thought – but to all intents and purposes he was using his soldier's judgement, reading the battle as it unfolded in front of him. And then, having given the order, he rode up the post road to take up a position on a low rise on the Telegraph Hill where he could get a clear view of the advance and the effect it would have on the enemy on Kourgané Hill.

With him went his staff, as well as Kinglake who was astonished to hear Raglan worry that Shadrach, his charger, appeared to be nervous under the fire of the Russian guns. By the time they reached their position on the spur they were well ahead of the British advance and almost within reach of the Russian lines – an unusual position

for any commander to direct a battle. 'In a minute more,' noted
Calthorpe, 'we were among the French skirmishers, who looked
not a little surprised to see the English commander-in-chief so far in
advance.'[9] The wonder was that Raglan did not fall victim to enemy
snipers for he certainly offered them an easy target.

The sight which Raglan and his staff witnessed was as old as war
itself: a frontal assault by 10,000 armed men on a heavily defended
position. From afar it made a stirring spectacle, the men dressing
into ranks to the sound of bugle calls, the regimental colours flying
and the steady voices of command, almost as if the serried infantry
battalions were on parade and not about to fight for their lives. Even
the battalions in the 3rd Division, waiting in reserve, were touched
by the splendour of the occasion as their fellow soldiers pushed
forward. 'Look well at that,' an officer told Elizabeth Evans, 'for the
Queen of England would give her eyes to see it.'

At close quarters, though, the infantrymen's view of battle was not
so noble. Artillery fire continued to rain down on them and as they
crossed the river, itself no easy task with its hidden depths and sudden
shallows, they could see the flame from the cannons' mouths. Once
on the other bank they found not an unyielding slope, as they had
expected, but a steep rocky terrain interspersed with vineyards. For
the Light Division's regiments on the left it was worse: they crossed the
Alma to find themselves confronted by a rocky ledge which seemed to
mock Brown's insouciant order to his light infantrymen to advance in
line. In the midst of the noise and confusion Codrington acted calmly
and decisively. It was his first experience of combat but he was equal
to the occasion; he eased his horse on to the ledge and bellowed
out the uncompromising order: 'Fix bayonets! Get up the bank and
advance to the attack.'

In open order the regiments stumbled up the bank and carried out
their brigadier's command. Gowing and his fellow fusiliers on the
flank could hardly see what they were doing but still they pressed
ahead up 'the dirty rugged hill'. By now they occupied a front
only a quarter of a mile long and, to the Russians on Kourgané
Hill waiting to receive the attack, they presented a frightening,
unstoppable force.

The mass of English troops, notwithstanding our devastating fire
of shot and shell that had made bloody furrows through their
ranks, closed up once more and, with new forces, protected

by swarms of skirmishing riflemen and supported by a battery firing from behind the smoking ruins of Bourliuk, crossed the river and drove back the brave Kazansky [regiment], forcing our field battery to limber up and depart.[7]

General Kvitsinsky wrote the description long after the battle in order to defend his handling of the 16th Division's defence of Kourgané Hill. At the time he was incensed by suggestions that his superior officer, General Paul Gorchakov, had ordered a later and almost successful counter-attack by the Vladimirsky regiment, but his words do give an accurate account of what was happening from the Russian point of view. As the British forces came within range they opened fire with devastating effect, their modern Minié rifles with its distinctive 'ping' causing heavy casualties in the ranks of the defending Kazansky regiment in the Great Redoubt. Accurate over 500 yards the Minié was a muzzle-loader which fired an elongated bullet and although a heavy weapon it was much superior to the obsolete muskets used by the Russians. Used effectively, as it was by the 7th Fusiliers who bore the brunt of the engagement with the Kazansky, it was a formidable battlefield asset.

Even so, the course of the battle still hung on the ability of the British infantrymen to hold the ground they were slowly winning from the Russians in the Great Redoubt. As Wellington said of Waterloo it was hard pounding but by dint of their superior firepower, and the support of the 7th Fusiliers on the flank, Codrington's four battalions (19th, 23rd, 33rd and 95th) gradually drove back the defending Kazansky regiment. A turning-point of sorts came when the Russians began moving off their guns, leaving the men of the Light Division in possession of the redoubt. The battle was not yet won but with the French attack in stalemate the British infantry had won a decided advantage, provided always that they could protect their position.

In his description of the fighting Kvitsinsky mentioned the arrival of a new force supported by artillery: this was the attack of the 1st Division. After much dithering, for it was his first experience of battle and he had to be urged by Airey to carry out his vague orders 'to support the front line', the Duke of Cambridge committed the Guards Brigade and the Highland Brigade into action at half past three. The attack of the 1st Division provides the Crimean campaign with one its many celebrated images. The Guards regiments, the Grenadiers on the right, Scots Fusiliers in the centre and Coldstreamers on the left, advanced with a parade ground precision which would not have disgraced Horse Guards; while to their left, on the eastern slopes of Kourgané, the kilted Highlanders – 42nd (Black Watch), 78th (Cameron) and 93rd (Sutherland) – pushed ahead with their customary eagerness, anxious to be in a fight.

They represented the cream of the British Army, the Guards regiments proud of their discipline and commitment to excellence, the kilted Highlanders jealous of their reputation as fighting soldiers. The Scots were also led by one of the finest commanders in Raglan's force. A veteran of the Peninsula and the Sikh Wars, Sir Colin Campbell was a professional soldier who actually cared for and understood his men, but the rigidity of the army's caste system meant that this Glasgow-born son of a carpenter only occupied the middling rank of brigadier-general.

However, before they could fulfil their obligation to support the British advance, the men of the Light Division in the Great Redoubt were facing a new danger. Using an initiative which had been conspicuously absent Prince Gorchakov had ordered up the Vladimirsky regiment to attack the British left flank. Slowly and ponderously the 3000 men advanced in column, bayonets fixed, but what happened next was an admirable example of the fog of war obscuring well-meant intentions. First, the advancing Russians were mistaken for French soldiers and the order was given to hold fire; then a bugle call sounded the order to retire. No satisfactory explanation was ever given but Codrington's men began to obey it in droves – just as they had been trained to do. And as they made their way pell-mell down the slopes they ploughed into the advancing Guards Brigade, the Scots Fusilier Guards taking the brunt of the collision.

For the second time in the battle the initiative seemed to have passed to the Russians but neither Menshikov, who was still on his horse to the rear, nor his second-in-command Gorchakov was able to take advantage of the confusion. As the Guards continued their advance the centre of their line was plugged by a company of Scots Fusilier Guards – the commanding officer of the Grenadiers rejected the offer of men from the 95th because it was a socially inferior line regiment – and the whole line made its way to within one hundred yards of the Russian line. 'The fire was so hot,' Hugh Annesley told his mother later, 'that you could hardly conceive it possible for anything the size of a rabbit not to be killed.' Minutes later he was shot in the cheek, losing twenty-three teeth and part of his tongue.

Once again the battle had been reduced to hard pounding between two sets of infantrymen but events elsewhere were beginning to affect the course of the battle. From his position below Kourgané Raglan had requested two nine-pounder artillery pieces and ordered them to fire at the Russian positions above the pass. Astonishingly the second shot hit an ammunition wagon and the explosion had far-reaching consequences. Thinking that they were in danger of losing their own guns the Russian artillerymen began retreating from their positions, allowing the British gunners to turn their attention to the Russian reserves. As they began to find their range they, too, began to falter.

For Prince Michael Gorchakov watching on Kourgané Hill this was enough to convince him that any counter-attack would be pointless. For de Lacy Evans, though, the respite was enough to allow the 2nd Division to push up in support of the beleaguered 7th Fusiliers. For Bentinck's Guards and Campbell's Highlanders the climax had also arrived and the battle was won on the slopes of Kourgané Hill where both brigades attacked the Russian positions with a clinical parade-ground precision which Colonel Sterling reported in a matter-of-fact letter to his family the following day:

> The men never looked back and took no notice of the wounded. They ascended in perfect silence, and without firing a shot. On crowning the hill, we found a large body of Russians who vainly tried to stand before us. Our manoeuvre was perfectly decisive as we got on the flank of the Russians in the centre battery, into which we looked from the top of the hill, and I saw the Guards rush in as the Russians abandoned it. The Guards were not moved on quite so soon as our Brigade, and suffered far more, poor fellows. The end was killing and wounding a many [sic] innocent Russians and a many [sic] innocent English, and making the Russians leave that; but it was very glorious; and we have to do the same thing on new ground tomorrow, and perhaps once more before we reach the port of Sebastopol.[8]

In fact Sterling's hopes for an end-game were not to be realised but as the cheering Highlanders stood on top of Kourgané Hill there was little doubt in his mind that the British Army had carried the day.

True, the French divisions also won their way up on to the plateau, and Bosquet's rapid ascent took the Russian left by surprise, but to all intents and purposes the victory owed everything to the resolve and courage of the British infantrymen aided by one timeous shot from a nine-pounder gun.

By four o'clock the Russian army was in full retreat and the civilian spectators had long since left the battlefield, according to Russell, having been obliged 'to fly for their lives in their carriages'. Menshikov's army was in complete disarray and the first battle to be fought on the European mainland in half a century was at an end, scarcely three hours after it had commenced in earnest. It was a satisfying moment for Raglan and his first taste of action since he lost his arm at Waterloo all those years ago. With his staff he left his exposed position and rode over the post road to climb Kourgané Hill to confer with his divisional commanders. At the summit he was greeted by cheering Highlanders many of whom were meeting their commander for the first time.

Carefully averting his eyes from 'the hill opposite, over which the Russians fled, quite thick with dead and wounded, abandoned packs and broken arms, the work of the Highland Brigade', Raglan thanked Campbell for his work that afternoon. By way of reply the Scottish general asked permission for him and his staff to wear the Highland bonnet in place of the usual cocked hat worn by staff officers, an honour which singled them out from the other brigade commanders. (Sterling's letters make it clear that there was little love lost between the officers in the two brigades.) Raglan's eyes filled with tears and he could not speak, but simply nodded his permission.

'With all its horrors, war has its romance,' noted a satisfied Sterling. But as the mopping-up operations began it was difficult for a disinterested observer such as Russell to find any sense of glamour:

> One who has not seen, cannot conceive the relics of a great fight, especially on such a field as that of the Alma on which there had been an army bivouacking for several days. There was an immense accumulation of camp-litter on the hill-sides. There was a sickening, sour, foetic smell everywhere, and the grass was slippy with blood.[10]

At the time it was difficult to compute the casualties because many of the men who survived the battle succumbed to wounds or cholera, either in the Crimea or on board the ships taking them to Scutari. In his report Raglan lists 362 killed, the Russians listed 1755 and the French 60, but these were all inflated later and it is generally accepted that the Alma claimed over 5000 lives.

As a battle the Alma may not rank highly in the annals of the British Army; none the less it involved eight cavalry regiments, three regiments of foot guards, and twenty-six line infantry regiments, all of which carry the Alma as a battle honour. Also the battle itself spawned many well-known examples of Victorian military art such as the stirring, though fanciful, depiction of the Scots Fusilier Guards advancing under fire with their colours flying proudly. The French, too, regarded the Alma as a glorious victory; all their four divisions took part in the action and afterwards an exultant Saint-Arnaud wrote to his wife that he had beaten the Russians 'completely'. Only the Russians saw it in a different light, acknowledging that while it was a defeat it had not been a decisive success for their opponents. Moreover, they soon came to see that out of the disaster they would be able to retrieve a tactical respite of sorts.

Like others who had taken part in the battle, combatant or otherwise, Russell had been unable to piece together what happened on the banks of the River Alma. Not finding one single position which could give him the best view – unlike Kinglake he was not close to Raglan – he was forced to do what every journalist has done ever since. Although his eyes were swimming with tiredness he rode around the battlefield, wearing a homemade uniform of rifleman's patrol jacket and gold-braided cap, and interviewed whomever he could in order to piece the story together. In the Great Redoubt a Royal Engineer officer fashioned a makeshift desk for him and Russell sat down to write his first battlefield report for *The Times* from the seat of war.

Later he was to express his dissatisfaction with his early cliché-ridden efforts – 'How was I to describe what I had not seen?' – but an eager audience at home awaited his reports. War was popular and it sold papers: when the news of the victory on the river Alma reached London on 1 October it produced tremendous excitement and it did not take long for *The Times* to prophesy an allied victory and the early fall of Sevastopol.

3

Missed Opportunities

Lord Raglan says we ought to be kept in a bandbox. Did any one hear of cavalry in a bandbox doing anything?
Captain Edward Lewis Nolan to William Howard Russell,
21 September 1854

For the cabinet in London the first news of the victory on the Alma arrived through Stratford in the Constantinople embassy. He had sent Raglan's battlefield despatch to Belgrade for onward telegraphic transmission to London and it arrived, written in French, on the morning of 1 October: '*Les armées alliées ont attaqué la position de l'ennemi sur les hauteurs au defens de l'Alma hier, et l'ont emporté après un combat acharné environ une heure et demi avant le coucher du soleil.*'★ Following the long uneasy silence and the growing concerns about the lack of communication, it provided blessed relief. 'Raglan has covered himself with glory,' replied a jubilant Clarendon, 'and his calmness and judgement in the field, as well as the modesty and the terseness of his despatch would, I am sure, have made the old Duke proud.'[1]

The official despatch, written the day after the battle, was brought to London by Lord Burghersh whose steamer arrived in Marseilles on 7 October. From Paris, Cowley arranged for a special train to take him to Boulogne and Raglan's text was published in full in *The Times* on 10 October. 'Your fame is now established in history,' was Newcastle's

---

★ 'Yesterday the allied armies attacked the enemy's position on the heights above the river Alma, and carried it an hour and a half before sunset after a fierce battle.'

response in a private letter written that same day. 'God grant that you may live many years to enjoy the reputation you have won.'[2] From her Highland holiday home at Balmoral, Queen Victoria described the news as 'glorious' although she added the cautionary note that she could not feel 'quite sure of its truth' − a further indication of the disquiet which she and her government had felt about the lengthy delays in receiving accurate reports from Raglan's army.

The French, too, had reason to celebrate. Not only had the entente held firm but if Saint-Arnaud were to be believed, their army had taken part in a glorious passage of arms. The jubilant French commander had also penned his report the day after the battle and it, too, was published in full, together with eye-witness reports, in the French press. Whatever else it was, it was certainly colourful. The French Army was hailed as true sons of Jena and Austerlitz, much was made of Bosquet's attack and the overwhelming impression was that the Zouaves, *tirailleurs* and *légionnaires* had triumphed over the Russians with some British help on the left flank. Saint-Arnaud had had the good grace to praise Raglan's bravery − 'In the midst of cannon and musket fire he displayed a calmness which never left him' − but the publication left a sour taste and Cowley was forced to lodge an official complaint with Drouyn de Lhuys. 'When these reports went back to the East,' he told the French foreign minister, 'not all the calm or prudence that the commander-in-chief could exercise would prevent young officers from showing their indignation at such language. Answers would be made, quarrels would ensue and all cordiality cease between the two armies.'[3]

By then the news had also reached the tsar's court although it was to be some days before the extent of the defeat became generally known. One of Menshikov's aides had ridden from the battlefield with the simple instruction to tell the tsar exactly what he had seen. Not unnaturally perhaps, Nicholas was unwilling to accept the young man's version of events particularly as they seemed to portray the Russian troops in a bad light. 'I can hardly understand it,' wrote Nicholas of his army's supposed lack of courage, 'knowing from earlier reports how good they were and what spirit they were in.'[4] That impression was confirmed by Menshikov's own report and the feeling grew in St Petersburg that all was lost in the Crimea and that it would only be a matter of time before Sevastopol fell to the allied armies.

Initially, that, too, was Stratford's belief and following receipt of

Raglan's despatches he sent a breezily optimistic letter to the foreign secretary:

> All our anxieties now point to the last scene at Sebastopol. I am led to suppose that there will be no more fighting till after the passage of the Balbek and the attack on Fort Constantine where we may or may not be able to take up a position clear of the guns. That the Russians will make a vigorous resistance I have no doubt. It is most unlikely that they will make a desperate one. Their discipline and ruse in a position with which they are familiarised must tell in their favour. Nevertheless I have little doubt that our people will prevail. They may be detained, they may be staggered – they may suffer an enormous loss but if anything can take the place, I verily believe that they will take it. Still, it is a nervous and tremblingly anxious struggle![5]

In the weeks to come Stratford's despatches to London were to betray a bewildering oscillation of emotions, ranging from triumphalism to bleak despair, but for the time being Raglan's victory had put him in a good humour not least because it seemed to vindicate the wisdom of his opposition to Russian expansionism. 'Allow me to say that I have read your printed despatches with an unbounded delight and admiration,' he told Raglan. 'Every step you take adds something to our national glory, and to the appreciation of English characters by foreigners.'[6]

On the plateau above the Alma, though, things were not so clear-cut. In fact, as light faded on the evening of 20 September there were elements in the British Army who felt that Raglan had failed to capitalise on his success and that the defeat of the Russian Army could have been turned into a decisive rout. That belief was particularly strong in the Light Brigade whose 1000 cavalrymen had been forced to play a watching role, idling in a field by the Alma while the infantry attacked the heights opposite them.

From the very outset Raglan had determined to use his light cavalry as a reconnaissance force, the role for which they were best equipped, and at the Alma they were held in reserve to the left with the field artillery. No orders were given to them because, as Raglan explained later, he wanted 'to shut them up', reasoning that the battlefield offered no opportunities for the cavalry arm. He was also aware that the Russians had a superior force numbering 3000, many of which were heavy cavalry formations, and no field commander would dare risk a fragile material asset against superior opposition. This was prudence taking precedence over enterprise, yet Raglan was right to be so cautious. Scarlett's Heavy Brigade had not yet arrived and there was a serious shortage of remounts. In those circumstances it would have been folly to have committed the Light Brigade into action against the Russians.

However, that was not how the cavalry saw it. They still believed that they were the decisive factor on the battlefield whose spirit and determination could make victory complete by breaking the enemy's determination to fight. As the Heavy Brigade was still on its way from Varna there could be no question of integrating the lightly armed hussars and lancers into the attack on the Russian lines, but both Cardigan and Lucan believed that they should have been deployed as a 'pursuit arm'. This, too, was ideal for the light cavalry role for, in the aftermath of Ramillies in 1706, Marlborough's cavalry had ruthlessly chased the fleeing French forces for some fifteen miles, utterly destroying its appetite for further action.

Unfortunately for Raglan, that is precisely what was on Lucan's mind when he ordered the Light Brigade to advance up the slopes of Kourgané Hill with a battery of horse artillery. 'We pushed on in haste,' remembered Private Albert Mitchell, 13th Light Dragoons, 'expecting to be called into play on the top of the heights.'[7] As Mitchell and his fellow troopers passed through the ranks of the dead and dying – 'many poor fellows we passed begged for assistance, but we could not stay to render any' – they could hear the cheers of the Highlanders and the Guards and suddenly realised that the battle was over. If so, there might still be a chance to pursue the defeated Russian army and the sight from the top of the hill seemed to confirm that fond hope.

Menshikov's army was swarming back southwards in the direction of Sevastopol and from the heights it seemed to be in complete disarray. One officer in the 17th Lancers wrote later that the Russians were 'running as hard as they could go, throwing away their knapsacks, arms and even their coats to assist them in their flight'.[8] In fact, although there was a rout, there was still some order to the Russian retreat. A handful of commanding officers managed to control their men so that the regiments leap-frogged one another, offering cover to the flanks and rear, and to the south of Telegraph Hill the Uglitz Regiment, as yet untested, had taken up a new defensive position. The allies' response was to use their artillery. From the heights of Kourgané the six guns of the horse artillery battery opened fire on the Uglitz position, breaking the column and creating heavy casualties. At the same time Canrobert's guns opened fire on the retreating Russians from Telegraph Hill. For the disillusioned Captain Chodasiewicz this was the bitter end:

> We passed numbers of unfortunate men who cried out to us for help we could not give them. Some asked for water to quench their intolerable thirst, while others begged hard to be put out of their agony by a speedy death. These sights and sounds had a very visible effect on the morale of the men, as they saw how little care was taken of them when they most required it. They exclaimed amongst themselves while passing through these horrors, 'Happy is he who a merciful Providence permits to die on the field of battle.'[9]

Other Russian officers also had harsh words to say about the effects of the allied artillery fire and of the complete lack of medical facilities to succour the wounded men. Kornilov, who had fretted in Sevastopol until the sounds of gunfire and his own growing impatience called him to the battlefield, was shocked by what he found: 'There were neither hospitals nor field dressing stations, nor even stretcher-bearers,' he wrote in his diary that night, 'and this explains the large numbers of wounded left on the field of battle.' Despite the attempt to cover its retreat this was a badly demoralised army and long after the fighting had ended there was relief mingled with some scorn that the allies had not exploited the position:

> The enemy took the heights, yet he used them only to direct artillery fire on our troops withdrawing from the area of the bridge [over the Alma]. He then sat there, rejoicing at his victory over what he imagined to be the advanced guard of our army; his mistake saved us and Sevastopol. For who could have thought that our handful of men *was* the Crimean Army, particularly since it was customary at that time to talk of the Russian million-strong force? It is frightful to think what might have happened, had it not been for this cardinal error of the enemy's.[10]

Had Lucan been able to read Kornilov's account he would have felt fully vindicated. Like every other cavalryman on the Kourgané heights that afternoon his instinct was to give chase to the fleeing Russians. Raglan must have sensed his impatience for he sent over Adjutant-General Estcourt with strict instructions that the cavalry was not to attack. Instead Lucan was to take two regiments – 8th Hussars and 17th Lancers – to escort some field guns on the left while Cardigan followed suit on the right with the 11th Hussars and 13th Light Dragoons. This took the Light Brigade forward towards the plain and, sensing an unmissable opportunity, Lucan ordered his men to pursue the Russian stragglers, a number of whom were brought back, most of them wounded.

Raglan was not amused. Not only was Lucan disobeying orders but he was risking the Light Brigade. A second command to break off the pursuit was despatched, then a third, before a furious Lucan deigned to obey. In protest he released the prisoners and later that night he sent a terse formal message of complaint to his commander-in-chief: 'Lord Lucan trusts that Lord Raglan has that confidence in him, as commanding the cavalry, that he would allow him to act on his own responsibility, as occasion should offer and render advisable, for otherwise opportunities of acting will frequently be lost to the cavalry.'[11] But if Lucan was angry, so were his men and, unfairly, some of them blamed him. The impetuous Nolan went further, telling Russell: 'It is too disgraceful, too infamous. They [the generals] ought to be—!' Coming on top of the enforced restraint shown at the Bulganek a few days earlier it was too much for some cavalrymen to bear and more than one was heard to call Lucan a cautious ass.

Added to the fact that Cardigan was equally furious, because Lucan seemed to be intruding on his area of responsibility by directing the Light Brigade, the cavalry was not in a particularly happy frame of mind following the war's first serious encounter. Typically, Raglan attempted to soothe the two commanders' ruffled feathers with a plea for them to co-operate but on the question of pursuit he was adamant that he had taken the correct option. He realised that the Russian cavalry were still massed to the south-east and still posed a threat. He also knew, but Lucan did not, that the French had refused to support any move to attack the Russian rearguard. With a few hours of daylight remaining Raglan reasoned that a pursuit force of cavalry, horse artillery and infantry could combine to attack the Russians along the Sevastopol road but only if the French joined it. But Saint-Arnaud would have none of it. Exhausted by the battle and desperately ill – only a cocktail of opiates and his own determination had kept him in his saddle – the French commander declined to offer any assistance, arguing that his men would have to retrieve their packs from the banks of the Alma and then tend to the wounded.

Raglan was disappointed – and would have been doubly so had he known that Saint-Arnaud would write to his wife boasting that he would have won the war then and there if cavalry had been available – but, shorn of French support, pursuit would have been too risky a business. Besides, so far away from home and with scant resources, he preferred caution to chance. And he had already seen grim evidence of the effects of battle as he rode down Kourgané Hill and recrossed the Alma. Calthorpe remembered 'a horrible scene – death in every shape and form' and Kinglake noted the strain on Raglan's face as he passed by the scores of wounded crouching in the ruins of Bourliuk waiting with various degrees of patience for what treatment could be provided. Elsewhere burial parties were at work, hurriedly shovelling corpses into makeshift trenches. While the British had come to the Crimea prepared to fight a war, as Albert Mitchell and many other soldiers discovered that night, little thought had been given to the consequences of battle:

> By this time, the greater part of the army was asleep, and then it was that we heard around us the groans of the wounded and the dying; some calling for the love of God for a drop of water. Others were praying most devoutly, well knowing this to be their last night in this life. We had already seen sufficient to harden our feelings, and make us callous to human suffering, but I lay some time thinking very seriously and praying to God for protection from all dangers.[12]

And so the day ended with the victorious allies resting and taking stock while the Russians made good their escape. Later Kinglake, so solicitous of Raglan in the aftermath of battle, would criticise him for failing to adopt 'a sterner method', claiming that the allied army could have 'drunk of the Katcha that night'. While it is true that more could have been done to exploit the success it is unlikely that the battle-weary troops could have marched the seven miles suggested by Kinglake. Certainly the British forces could not have done it alone and Saint-Arnaud's unwillingness to commit his own troops made any pursuit impossible. Not that Raglan was not keen to push on to Sevastopol. According to Lyons, who visited his headquarters the next day and who reported the British commander-in-chief's words, Raglan had once again been stymied by his French allies:

> With the troops perfectly fresh and fit to march on and the weather very fine, I [Raglan] sent to Maréchal St-Arnaud to propose that we should march on to Sebastopol and assault the place at once (to take our ground above the town, I forget which was the expression) and the answer to me was that the French troops were fatigued and cannot move on any further. That cannot be the real reason, as the march has not been long enough to fatigue the troops – but however as they cannot move of course I cannot either.[13]

Lyons, of course, was not a disinterested reporter, being one of the allies' more bullish commanders and an enemy of the kind of procrastination advocated by Dundas. Indeed, Stratford was strongly of the opinion that Lyons and Raglan would make an ideal partnership and lost few chances of promoting the suggestion – 'Sir Edmund too – what more can be said than that he is worthy of you?' he reminded the British commander-in-chief in the days following the Alma. 'In reading your letters and tracing your progress I seem to breathe again the air of my younger days of Waterloo and Trafalgar.'[14] Newcastle was prepared to go further, advising Raglan in a despatch of 9 October that if Dundas failed to support the army in its operations Lyons should be persuaded to disobey them.

Fortunately this was never put to the test but a comment made by Clarendon to Stratford that same week shows that Lyons' star was in the ascendant: 'What a fellow Lyons is! He makes one proud of one's country and what fine fellows there are too under him; so there are also under Sir C. Napier and it is melancholy that two such splendid fleets should be under such inefficient Crs in Chief for Napier is not a bit better than Dundas is.' [15] By then, of course, Napier would soon be on his way back to Britain and disgrace while Lyons was on the verge of supplanting Dundas.

Despite that elevation and his later need to paint himself in a good light, Lyons' account of his meeting with Raglan is a fair reflection of what had happened. Twice that day Raglan had attempted to persuade the French to move and on both occasions he had been rebuffed, hence the admiral's description of finding his colleague tired and 'dispirited'.

A more commanding personality might have pursued the point
– Saint-Arnaud was dying and in no position to be decisive – but
Raglan was too courteous a man to force a colleague to act as he
did not choose. Had he been a Wolfe, far less a Wellington, matters
might have been different but as he was the commander on the spot,
the choice of the British government, and nine days short of his
sixty-sixth birthday he was hardly likely to start changing his ways.
Besides, he was also mindful that he was under orders to preserve
and maintain the entente with his French allies. Not only did this
mean acting in concert with them in military operations but, when
the occasion demanded, bowing to their wishes. To Raglan, despite
his obvious disappointment, this seemed to be such an occasion to
defer to his touchy allies. Rather than complain, though, he confined
his disappointment to an ironic comment about the French army's
penchant for bugle calls. 'Ah! there they go with their infernal
toot-toot-tooting,' he protested to his staff, 'that's the only thing
they ever do!'[16]

Instead of moving forward, the allies used the time to tend to their
wounded. With fewer casualties and better facilities the French fared
better than the British could ever hope to do. Providing that they
did not succumb to cholera or to gangrene, those who were treated
by the banks of the Alma stood some chance of surviving. Not so
those who were despatched by transport ships to Scutari. Over a
quarter of their number died during the four-day voyage and once
in Constantinople their chances of survival were to prove little better.
'Numbers of men wounded at Alma have been five days without
having their wounds looked at by a medical man, and many men
died from their wounds mortifying,' wrote Captain Henry Clifford
to his parents. 'All this is the fault of the Heads of the Medical
Department, for quantities of medicine etc have been provided and
sent out as far as Scutari and Varna.'[17] Inevitably, given the presence
of the accompanying correspondents, the plight of the wounded was
soon being reported in the London press and the revelations would
ensure that the war was remembered for its blunders and the neglect
of the ordinary soldier.

However, all that trouble lay some weeks in the future. At this
time the country was still basking in the glory of a famous victory
and as early as 2 October *The Times* had optimistically published a
story under the headline 'Fall of Sevastopol' which was supposed
to be based on 'decisive intelligence'. In fact it derived from an

ill-advised piece of boastfulness in Boulogne by Napoleon III who told departing reinforcements that the flags of the victorious allied army were already flying from the city's ramparts. Unfortunately, even those in positions of authority were inclined to believe what they wished to believe. Claiming that the decision to attack Sevastopol was his and his alone, Sir James Graham wrote to Raglan on 8 October that he could not have anticipated 'so grand a result in so short a time' and that Wellington would have been proud of him. Even Newcastle felt confident enough to state that Sevastopol might have fallen and wrote to Raglan expressing the hope that 'may have' would have become 'will have' by the time his letter arrived.

Raglan was furious and rightly so. After reading *The Times*'s stories he reminded Newcastle that the operation to attack Sevastopol, was 'one of extreme difficulty, and of no certainty' and that to talk of easy victories did his troops very little justice. Prudently, Clarendon advised circumspection. If the mood of elation turned to ashes, he warned an increasingly ebullient Stratford, then there would be no winners either in the army or in the government:

> Public anxiety is, if possible, on the increase and one thing and one thing alone is spoken of – the newspapers ever since the commencement of the war have never missed an opportunity of doing mischief that the fall of Sebastopol is a fait accompli and as a matter of not the merest doubt, so that if we fail no allowance can be made for the generals and if we succeed little credit will be awarded to them.[18]

In fact while these letters were flying to and fro between London and the army in the field, Raglan was wrestling with an increasingly intractable tactical situation. The march south had recommenced on 23 September but while the troops were in good humour and full of confidence, there was still no definite plan about what should be done next. It was not until the next morning, when they were beyond the River Katcha and in sight of Sevastopol itself, that the allied commanders sat down to confer. By then Saint-Arnaud was desperately ill and to Raglan's eyes at least he was obviously at death's door. By then, too, the ailing marshal had been told that in the event of him being incapacitated Canrobert carried the emperor's warrant to take over command. This glum information had been withheld from him until after the armies were safely ashore and in fact Saint-Arnaud had written to his wife a fortnight earlier that he would be 'obliged to leave the party, and as soon as I have established the army in the Crimea, I will ask the emperor for a replacement.'[19]

Despite the concern raised by the marshal's predicament the conference ended on an optimistic note mainly because a plan had been proffered and accepted by the allied commanders. Drawn up by Burgoyne in a succinct memorandum it called for an allied attack from the south, making use of Balaklava and the other nearby bays as supply bases. The obvious alternative – a direct attack on the north side – was out of the question not just because it was covered by the Star Fort but also because naval intelligence had revealed a rapid reinforcement of the landward defences. Raglan was inclined to agree, arguing that he had 'always been disposed' for such an operation and he knew, too, that his worries about resupply would be eased by seizing the southern bays. The French were happy to concur as they, too, had evidence from a Polish deserter that the Russians had moved naval guns to the northern defences to counter the anticipated allied assault.

Inevitably, given the future course of the war, the decision to attack from the southern uplands has left history with another 'what if?', the argument being that Raglan was wrong not to commit his forces to an immediate assault on Sevastopol. At home in London *The Times* certainly thought that he should have done so, arguing a year later that the British commander 'had not sufficient spontaneous energy to take it [Sevastopol]'. Other armchair strategists have also criticised him for lack of foresight and initiative in pressing home an immediate *coup de main*. There are substantial attractions to the argument. Menshikov's army was in disarray, there was a certain amount of panic in Sevastopol, a bombardment by the allied fleet could have been decisive and, from a military point of view, there is much to be said for continuing the momentum of a successful battle. That was certainly what Captain Chodasiewicz and his fellow defenders in Sevastopol expected:

> In the town the people were as busy as ants, working day and night at their defences. The greater number of wives and families of the naval officers were at this time in the town. As it was not known where the enemy might be expected, they were afraid to retire to Simferopol [town to the north]. In fact, all seemed to be seized with a kind of panic. Korniloff [*sic*] appeared to have the power of multiplying himself, for he was everywhere, promising large rewards to all if they could only keep the town.[20]

A bold commander might have been prepared to risk everything for the prize but the ever-prudent Raglan was not that kind of soldier.

Besides, he was unhappily aware that he had little in the way of accurate intelligence about his enemy's movements. Was Menshikov's army in Sevastopol or was it preparing a fresh assault on his flanks or rear? What was the true state of the Russian defences at the Star Fort and how many men and guns defended them? Where were the Russian reinforcements? Obviously the capture of the Star Fort held the key to the capture of the city but what good would come from it if the allies lost precious men and resources in the assault? These doubts crowded in on the information which Raglan did have. Reports had come in that Kornilov had ordered ships of the Black Sea fleet to be sunk across the harbour approaches and that their guns had been removed to fortify the city's defences. There was also sufficient intelligence from the warships lying offshore that the Russians were rapidly strengthening their fortifications. Given those doubts and the growing certainty that any attack on the northern defences was beset with dangers Raglan was justified in accepting Burgoyne's plans. Once again discretion was the order of the day.

And so the allies set off for the southern coast, making a flanking movement to avoid marshy ground, and slowly heading over territory with names which would soon become as familiar to the British Army as the positions on the western front in Flanders would be to their successors sixty years later: Traktir Bridge, Fedioukine Hills, Canrobert's Hill, Kadikoi and, most prominent of all, the base at Balaklava. Not that the deployment was uneventful. At one stage the cavalry lost its way and in so doing led Raglan and his staff into firing range of the Russian rearguard. Only Raglan's coolness, some luck and the covering fire of the horse artillery retrieved the situation, but it was an indication of the dangers facing the allied army, dispersed as it was over several miles of exposed countryside. Only a sudden thick fog and Menshikov's failure to exploit the situation saved them from attack.

On the morning of 26 September Raglan had reached the village of Kadikoi and was able to look down on the narrow inlet of Balaklava which would be the British forces' lifeline to the outside world. To Henry Clifford, it was a charming sight, 'a most beautiful harbour, not more than two miles round – a basin in its shape, where the water is almost like a mill-pond, though deep enough for any line-of-battle ship to come within stone throw of the shore'.[21] Bitter experience would expose the inadequacies of the harbour but on that late September day of 1854, when the fall of Sevastopol was thought to be within reach, Raglan was sure that the port and the surrounding saucer-shaped plateau would provide an ideal base for operations.

That same day Saint-Arnaud surrendered to the inevitable and resigned his command. The steamer *Berthelot* took him back to Constantinople but he was destined not to survive the voyage. Shortly before arriving he died of heart failure exacerbated by cancer and cholera and also by the demands of the campaign. The *Berthelot* continued its voyage to Marseilles taking with it the marshal's body and some electrifying news. 'The steamer brings the intelligence that the investment of Sevastopol was completed on 2nd,' an exultant Cowley telegraphed to London that same night, 'and that the Allied Armies would probably be in possession of the place on the 8th'. For a brief moment it seemed that the war might indeed be over but in distant Paris they were not to know that in their positions 'before Sebastopol' the allied armies were experiencing the first hint of winter weather with the Russian fortress as secure as it had been a month earlier.

Once again the absence of reliable information from the battlefront made it impossible for either government to understand what was happening. (In the first week of November a Queen's Messenger actually lost Raglan's despatches whilst travelling through France.) After receiving Cowley's despatch and the subsequent disclaimer Clarendon wrote once more to Stratford berating him for his tardiness in communicating news from the Crimea. The ambassador replied in measured tones that while 'no one was more anxious than myself to meet the wishes of Her Majesty's Government in that respect', he refused to pass on the first wild rumour which came his way:

In most instances, be it observed, I have no official advisers on which to rely. Other sources of information, such as private letters and oral narratives, are subject to much uncertainty and in stating what is derived from them under circumstances of so deep and delicate an interest, I have to guard myself, and, what is more, to guard Your Lordship from the effects of mistake and exaggeration. Of the incidents which attended the progress of Her Majesty's Army from Alma to Balaclava I had no reliable information until I received intelligence of Lord Raglan's arrival at the latter place. At this very moment I am in total darkness of

the very important occurrences which took place between the
24th and 28th instant.[22]

Stratford was right to defend his corner and to warn against the
danger of over-optimism, but his words arrived at a time when the
British government was desperate for good news from the Crimea
to divert attention from the alarming stories which were beginning
to appear in the London press. Suddenly, without warning, the first
cracks were beginning to appear in the public solidarity which had
cheered the troops off to war with such ardour earlier in the year.

4

Ladies with Lamps

Together with the lightly wounded, lie many badly wounded, hopelessly ill and dying people. Oh, for the sake of God do not think I am exaggerating!

Pyotr Alabin, Kamchatka Regiment, letter home following the Battle of Inkerman, 5 November 1854

When *The Times*'s 40,000 readers opened their copies on the morning of 12 October 1854 they received an unwelcome surprise. Following the euphoria of the victory on the Alma the newspaper's report from the seat of war made unpleasant reading: instead of heroics, they were treated to the harsh reality of the aftermath of battle and the suffering of the soldiers. Here, laid bare, was the first stark evidence of the revolting conditions faced by the sick and wounded at the British Military Hospital at Scutari, which stood on the opposite of side of the Bosphorus from Constantinople. While wounds and death are an unavoidable in war, and while it is true that British soldiers were not immune to suffering and official indifference, in the past they had died like flies far removed from public gaze. Now, thanks to the presence of reporters the people of Britain could understand what was being done in their name and, to do them justice, the mid-Victorian British public showed that they cared.

The credit for revealing the horrific conditions at Scutari is usually given to William Howard Russell but, in fact, the writer in this issue of the paper was Thomas Chenery, an Etonian barrister, who acted as the local correspondent for *The Times* in Constantinople. Delane had met him on his return from the Crimea at the beginning of the month when he had witnessed at first hand the deficiencies of the so-called hospital ships and the absence of facilities at Scutari and he was desperately anxious to bring them to the attention of the British public. Spurred on by Delane, Chenery's first report was unsparing in its criticism 'that no sufficient medical preparations have been made for the proper care of the wounded':

> Not only are there not sufficient surgeons – that, it might be urged, was unavoidable – not only are there no dressers and nurses – that might be a defect of system for which no one is to blame – but what will be said when it is known that there is not even linen to make bandages for the wounded? The greatest commiseration prevails for the unhappy inmates of Scutari, and every family is giving sheets and old garments to supply their want. But, why could not this clearly foreseen event have been supplied?

It was a question which would remain unanswered until the end of the war but, having been asked, Chenery's plea and Delane's leading article suggesting the establishment of a fund for 'creature comforts' demanded a response. It came the following day with the publication of letters offering various sums of money to buy comforts for the wounded. One letter in particular stood out and helped to change the course of the war. Written by Sir Robert Peel, a son of the former prime minister, it proposed the creation of a privately funded scheme to assist sick and injured soldiers. The same issue carried a further report from Chenery comparing the humiliating British position with the foresight of the French:

> The worn-out pensioners who were brought out as an ambu-lance corps are totally useless, and not only are surgeons not to be had, but there are no dressers or nurses to carry out the surgeons' directions and to attend on the sick during intervals between his visits. Here the French are greatly our superiors. Their medical arrangements are extremely good, their surgeons are numerous, and they have also the help of the Sisters of Charity, who have accompanied the expedition in incredible numbers. These devoted women are excellent nurses.

From there it was to be only a short step to the introduction

into the fray of Florence Nightingale and her nursing sisters and
to the beginning of the long-running scandal of official indifference
towards the soldiers serving in the Crimea. At long last, too, those
in government were becoming dimly aware of the fact that the army
sent to the Crimea was prepared for the wrong kind of war, that no
number of colonial campaigns against inferior opposition could have
prepared the soldiers for a lengthy war against a major European
power. Before the year was out Clarendon admitted to Stratford that
he was 'very sorry to say that the deficiencies have been deplorable –
nothing but want of arrangements could have caused the destitution
of the army'.[1]

The letter that brought into focus the charge of official indifference
was published in *The Times* on 14 October. Written by 'A Sufferer by
the Present War' it asked why the British had no 'sisters of charity'
similar to those employed by the French. Its publication did enough
to capture the interest of the superintendent of the Establishment
for Gentlewomen During Illness who had trained as a nurse at
Kaiserwerth and Paris. Known as Florence after the city of her
birth, Miss Nightingale was the daughter of a wealthy Hampshire
family and had faced considerable parental opposition to pursue a
career in nursing. As a product of the Victorian moneyed classes
she might not have turned that training into a career – much of her
youth was idle and unproductive, but she was determined. Now that
same stubbornness – allied to an occasionally shrill and self-righteous
belief in her abilities – came to her aid. Having read *The Times* she sat
down in her Harley Street office and wrote to her friend Mrs Sidney
Herbert, wife of the secretary at war, setting out a proposal for the
creation of a nursing service which might be 'of use to the wounded
wretches'.

As chance would have it, Herbert, a family friend, had also written
to her that very day proposing that she should accept a commission
from the government to go out to the Crimea as the head of the
army's nursing services. The letters crossed but the combination of
ideas was the first step towards an improvement of the lot of the
British soldier. Sidney wrote:

> There is but one person in England that I know of, who would
> be capable of organising and superintending such a scheme and I
> have been several times on the point of asking you hypothetically
> if, supposing the attempt were made, you would undertake to

direct it. The difficulty of finding women equal to a task after all full of horror, and requiring besides knowledge and goodwill, great energy and great courage will be great. The task of ruling them and introducing system among them is great; and not the least will be the difficulty of making the whole work smoothly with the medical and military authorities out there.[2]

She accepted immediately and three days later the Cabinet approved her appointment as Superintendent of the Female Nursing Establishment of the English General Hospitals in Turkey with a preliminary budget of £1000. Then, from the Herbert's home in Belgrave Square, she set about appointing her band of nurses, the majority coming from religious nursing orders although, according to Florence Nightingale, their only inducement was financial reward. Far from being the saintly ladies with lamps of legend they were a motley crew; few were literate, and Nightingale was forced to issue strict injunctions about the need to remain sober and to avoid sexual relations; however, this 'Angel Band', to use Kinglake's description, was to assure their superintendent of an undying place in the pantheon of Victorian heroes.

Her oft-told tale has a curiously British ring, of an enterprise begun badly and ending tolerably; of initial bumbling, ineptitude and, above all, disavowal giving way eventually to something approaching hope. In that respect her experience has become an exemplar of all that was inefficient and amateurish about the war against Russia and there is good reason for that being so. The correlation of Chenery's despatches and Florence Nightingale's offer of help was certainly a turning-point which led not just to improvements at Scutari but also to the later investigations into the army's handling of its casualties. As Clarendon admitted, the move owed everything to publicity and the growing power of the press:

If the veil had been lifted up here [London] from the last 2 months of cholera and the whole truth had been told about the sufferings of the poor in their ill-provided dwellings a picture far more harrowing even than that from Constantinople might easily have been drawn. But cui bono?[3]

The foreign secretary's dry observation was not far off the target. Little had been written about that summer's cholera outbreak in

London simply because such epidemics were a regular occurrence
but the reports from Scutari had generated a different response. In
the parlance of a future age *The Times* had a campaign on its hands
and Delane was to make full use of the dreadful conditions facing the
soldiers to consolidate his growing readership. For his pains he faced
opprobrium too: his rivals jealously argued that either *The Times* was
exaggerating the problems at Scutari or its fund-raising was simply
a means of increasing sales. As the *Illustrated London News* angrily
huffed, *The Times* was 'cursed with too much zeal and too little
discretion'.

As was so often the case with this war, those in positions of authority
had imagined that the situation was fully under control. Shortly after
the Alma, Stratford wrote to Clarendon informing him that the
Russian prisoners would be housed in the old arsenal building at
Scutari but that the sick and wounded would be treated alongside
their British counterparts. Because he imagined that the arrangement
would be temporary – the fall of Sevastopol being imminent – his
early despatches on the subject were reasonably buoyant:

> While upon this subject [Russian prisoners] I am happy to state
> that the wounded and sick from Her Majesty's Forces have
> received the most cordial expressions of sympathy as well as
> from the Ministers of War and Marine as from His Majesty
> the Sultan himself and what is still more gratifying, the British
> soldiers have displayed the kindest and most considerate feeling
> towards the Russian prisoners, even supplying their wounded
> with food before they partook of their own meals.[4]

A month later, following the publication of Chenery's reports,
Stratford was still trying to convince the Foreign Office that while
there had been initial problems the medical staff had the situation
under control:

> When I last visited the hospital and barracks, agreeably to what
> I knew to be Lord Raglan's wish, I found an appearance of con-
> siderable improvement in the state of the arrangements, though a
> number of additional patients had just arrived. Those with whom
> I conversed, and they were not few, spoke with cheerfulness and
> contentment; and the medical attendants assured me that, with
> the assistance they had already received, they were sufficiently

numerous to attend, not only to the British, but to the sick and wounded Russians, who occupy the part of the barracks, occupied in general by the officers and soldiers of Her Majesty's Army.[5]

Comforting though it was for Stratford to write in this vein – stalwart British soldiers, lions in the field but lambs in the house, prospering in an overall air of calm efficiency – he only saw what he wanted to see. (To be fair, though, the Great Elchi would soon change his tune.) The reality facing the British wounded was far removed from 'cheerfulness and contentment'. As Fanny Duberly herself observed, the four-day voyage by transport ship from Balaklava to Scutari was a season in hell which began as badly as it ended:

We have no ambulance wagons; they are nearly all broken down, or the mules dead, or the drivers are dead or dead drunk; as well one as the other, as far as usefulness goes. Our poor Cavalry horses, as we know full well, are all unequal to the task of carrying down the sick; and the French have provided transports for us for some time . . . why can we not tend to our own sick? Why are we so helpless and broken down?[6]

So insistent did the question become that a worried Clarendon asked Cowley to confirm or deny that the French Army had a superior medical system. The reply was not encouraging. On 22 October Cowley confirmed that each French division had 46 doctors, 104 nurses and seven administrative officers; moreover each ambulance wagon of the type described by Mrs Duberly consisted of '*5 caissons, portant chacun 2000 pansements et tous les éleméns d'un petit hôpital chaque caisson est attelé de 4 chevaux.*'[7] In view of the superiority of the French system and the controversy in the press Cowley suggested that the information should be restricted to the Foreign Office.

By then it was too late for official discretion. Travelling on board the steamer *Vectis* Florence Nightingale and her party – consisting initially of 38 nurses – had arrived in Constantinople on 4 November, 'much fatigued' due to a stormy passage from Marseilles. Stratford informed the Foreign Office that 'they were immediately conveyed, under proper attendance, to Scutari where they were at once accommodated with apartments'. It did not take them long to get the measure of the place. Nightingale's first letter home described in graphic detail the

appalling state of the hospital, the blocked privies, the filthy floors
and overcrowded conditions. Here were sheltered the victims of the
cholera outbreaks and shortly the hospital would have to cope with
the sick and the wounded from the fighting in the Crimea:

> In all our Corridors I think we have not an average of three
> limbs per man – and there are two ships more 'loading' at the
> Crimea with wounded . . . We have four miles of beds – and
> not eighteen inches apart. All this fresh influx has been laid
> down between us and the Main Guard in two corridors with
> a line of beds down each side, just room for one man to step
> between and four wards.[8]

Nightingale found ample evidence that, far from being in the
satisfactory state described by Stratford, everything at Scutari was
thoroughly inadequate. Again, so familiar have become the fetid
scenes at the dilapidated Selimiye Kislasi barracks that the authors
of contemporary accounts seemed to take a vicarious pleasure in
recording the muddle and the sufferings of the men. It was not
just the absence of medical supplies or an inability to cope with the
hopelessly insanitary conditions that jarred – these were commonplace
in most civilian hospitals – it was the unyielding mismanagement of the
resources. The medical department was a law unto itself and composed
of doctors who thought that they knew best. The Commissariat and
Purveyors departments were responsible for feeding and clothing the
sick and wounded but so labyrinthine were their administrations
and so timorous the civilian officials who manned them, that their
obsession with red tape and responsibilities produced an atmosphere of
indecision and paralysis. Worse, they combined to hinder Nightingale
and her nurses; the doctors because they resented their presence and
the administrators because the nurses were an unwarranted intrusion
in an already complicated world. Later, Florence Nightingale would
say of them: 'Their heads are so flattened between the boards of Army
discipline that they remain old children all their lives.'[9]

Even Stratford, who does not normally emerge with much credit
from this episode, could see that the main problem at Scutari was
not so much the filth, squalor, vermin and lack of basic hygiene –
all of which could be cured – it was the complete absence of any
recognisable management. A fortnight after the arrival of the nurses
he said as much to Clarendon:

The prime cause of what is amiss in the working of the establishment [Scutari] appears, in my humble judgement, to be the want of a superintendery authority to whom the heads of subordinate departments may refer in cases of embarrassment or differences of opinion.[10]

Fortunately, this was Florence Nightingale's greatest strength and her ability to bring a sense of cohesion to the nursing services at Scutari was to be her finest achievement. By no stretch of the imagination was she the 'Lady with the Lamp' but she was a doughty fighter. This Stratford seemed to realise and in the same despatch he suggested that her problems would be eased, though certainly not solved, if the growing numbers of Russian prisoners could be sent to Malta or even to Britain. As they were sharing the facilities at Scutari their presence only added to the general muddle but it was to be another year before the British dealt adequately with the problem.

As it was, Nightingale and her party had other and more immediate difficulties on their hands. Not only were they given a grudging welcome but the absence of facilities meant that they could make little immediate impact. Their accommodation was both rudimentary and disgusting – in one of their rooms lay the corpse of a Russian officer – and the doctors paid them no heed. Just as bad, they obstructed them under the erroneous belief that there was not much wrong with the system. In response to *The Times's* first reports Stratford had written to Dr Duncan Menzies, the army's Deputy Inspector-General of Hospitals at Scutari, on 24 October asking him to provide a list of 'wants as are most urgent' so that he could arrange their supply, either from local sources or directly from Britain 'where every readiness exists to supply them'. Menzies' reply two days later was breathtaking in its refusal to face facts:

I now beg to state that having consulted with the officers at the head of the Apothecary and Purveying Departments, as to what further supplies of medicines and stores may be required for the comfort and sustenance of the sick and wounded, I have to observe that I find as far as the present wants extend, we are satisfactorily supplied, and more expected daily from England and Varna . . .

I feel extremely obliged for the interest Your Lordship has so kindly taken in assisting us on this important occasion, and as the Government appears desirous of every information, I beg to observe that the sick and wounded, in this Hospital, up to the present time, have wanted for no surgical appliances and they have received every care and attention which their situation so imperatively demanded.[11]

Although Menzies' response makes sorry reading, in the context of the times he had little option but to respond as he did. The army's medical department was badly funded – his immediate superior's budget was £1000 a year – and although surgeons were considered socially superior to the personnel in the Commissariat and Purveying departments, they were still not considered gentlemen. Even Palmerston, the darling of the middle classes, was to say of them after the war that the greatest deficiencies in the Crimea had been caused not by people of his social standing but 'where there were persons belonging to other classes of the community – in the medical department, the Commissariat department, the transport service, which have not been filled by the aristocracy or gentry.'[12]

This lack of respect meant that they were touchily jealous of their positions and fearful of any outside interference, most especially from a female, which might put them in a bad light. Their medical opinions were also typical of an age when a civilian doctor could happily admit that he almost died of blood-poisoning after undergoing an operation in a hospital whose walls were 'reeking with germs'. And in a notably heartless profession – mid-Victorian doctors were not noted for the delicacy of their sensibilities – military surgeons were reckoned to be a particularly callous bunch. Menzies' colleague Dr John Hall, who commanded the army's medical staff on the Crimean front, warned his colleagues not to use anaesthetics while operating because 'however barbarous it might appear, the smart of the knife is a powerful stimulant; and it is better to hear a man bawl lustily, than to see him sink silently into the grave'.[13]

Much of that was to change with the arrival of the nurses, not just because they helped to introduce reform but through The Times Florence Nightingale had access to the funds which would buy the necessities for improvement. Through her almoner John Cameron MacDonald, The Times's business manager who accompanied her to Scutari, she was able to buy the scrubbing brushes and soap which would clean up the wards, the food which aided recuperation and the boilers which introduced a hygienic laundry service. In a letter to Sidney Herbert she described herself as 'a kind of General Dealer in socks, shorts, knives and forks, wooden spoons, tin baths, tables forms, cabbages and carrots, operating tables, towels and soap, small tooth combs, precipitate for destroying lice, scissors, bed pans and stump pillows'.[14] And there was much to the conceit: the initial improvements at Scutari came not from the Government but from the shocked readers of *The Times*.

There was also support from Stratford who finally convinced the Turkish authorities to provide much needed beds and furniture. He also persuaded them to make improvements to the building itself although it would not be until the arrival of a government Sanitary Commission in the spring that Scutari's drains would be cleared and its walls distempered. Even so, for all that he enjoyed an uneasy relationship with Nightingale, who thought him too self-important for his own good, Stratford, too, was smitten by the nursing superintendent's crusading zeal:

Hospital matters still present uncomfortable difficulties [Stratford told Clarendon on 5 December 1854]. The Turks, I believe, are willing but their notions differ immensely from ours. They ordered the quay at Scutari to be set to rights. Scarcely was this done, when a northerly wind sprang up and demolished the improvements. They sent workmen to repair the hospital. The workmen got no wages and struck. Miss Nightingale came gallantly to the rescue – and she also wrote to me. I did not like to see the Government disparaged by the advance of private funds, and therefore I have made arrangements for paying the wages myself, applying at the same time to the Porte.[15]

It would still take time and effort to right the wrongs at Scutari – the sanitary conditions were not changed until the intervention of Hospital Commissioners – and countless problems still faced Florence Nightingale. (Not all of them were germane to the situation: she was to be accused of employing too many Roman Catholics and at least one nurse was to be sent home for drunkenness. She was also what might be called a bossy-boots.) But had she not arrived in Constantinople when she did the disaster would have been much worse, for on top of the hundreds of cholera patients came the wounded from the first great battles of the war at the Alma, Balaklava and Inkerman.

For them conditions were truly appalling. The lack of ambulance
wagons made their journey to the base hospitals at Balaklava a grim
business during which many died of shock. Then there was the
equally appalling voyage to Constantinople: as late as January 1855
Newcastle was still making irritated representations for this situation
to be improved:

> My attention has been again called to the discomfort and incon-
> venience experienced by the sick and wounded from the Army
> in the Crimea . . . and I trust that ere this arrangements have
> been made for fitting up some of the Vessels now in the
> Black Sea as hospital ships for the purpose of being employed
> in the transport of the sick and wounded from Balaclava in
> pursuance of instructions from the Lords Commissioners of the
> Admiralty.[16]

In common with his Cabinet colleagues Newcastle was shocked by
the reports of the suffering that reached London. But like them he was
powerless to make improvements because everything depended on his
orders being obeyed in the Crimea. That would soon be remedied.
On 12 December orders were finally given to the firm of R.S. Newall
and Co. to begin the construction of a telegraph line from Balaklava
to Varna and, as Newcastle told Raglan, 'It will also in some degree
alleviate that great and almost overwhelming state of anxiety with
which the French and English nations now look for intelligence
from the Seat of Active Warfare in which both countries are at
present engaged.'[17] Once in use it was certainly true that the more
rapid means of communication with London made it more difficult
for allied leaders to hide behind the fog of war.

In an attempt to bring some order to the base hospitals at Balaklava
Florence Nightingale also paid a visit to them but her efforts were
cut short by illness. In fact two other notable women were already
at work there — Elizabeth Davis, no friend of Nightingale's, and the
remarkable Mary Seacole, a widow from the West Indies. Known as
'Mother' to the troops, Many Seacole had set up a rough and ready
nursing station which, according to Russell, attracted men 'who had
a faith in her proficiency in the healing art, which she justified by
many cures and by removing obstinate cases of diarrhoea, dysentery
and other camp maladies.'[18]

He was right to be so fulsome in her praise, for she was a natural healer who had already won the admiration of many of the soldiers in the Crimea by tending to them while working in Jamaica before the war. Against all the odds and at her own expense, she had made her own way to the Crimea where she quickly made her presence felt at Balaklava by providing a wide range of medicines and other comforts for the troops. Not only did she bring relief to the wounded on the battlefield but her cheerful personality and undaunted refusal to give in to the prevailing bureaucracy helped to make life tolerable for those in her care. Her perseverance is all the more remarkable given the fact that Florence Nightingale rejected her offer to serve at the Scutari hospital.

It should not be thought, though, that all the medical care in the Crimea was in a state of antiquated chaos or that all officials, military or civilian, were indifferent to the misery of the troops. Some innovations did work and lives were saved as a result. On 23 November Newcastle told Raglan that he intended to provide a sanatorium on the island of Rhodes for soldiers suffering from chest wounds as 'those removed to a milder climate during the approaching winter would be attended with advantage.' Following representations by Stratford the Porte agreed to investigate this possibility on 5 January 1855 and, although it came to nothing – Stratford reported that it would take three months to construct a suitable hospital at a cost of £3000 – it did lead to the foundation of a sanatorium at Smyrna.[19] A fortnight later Newcastle also arranged for the despatch of railroad equipment and engineers 'for laying down a line of railroad between Balaklava and the heights above Sebastopol'[19] which could be used to bring up siege equipment and remove the wounded. Built at cost by the firm of Peto, Brassey and Betts it entered service on 26 March 1855 and as Russell noted 'the British Army had developed the first hospital train'.

Another successful, though sadly uncelebrated, innovation was the prefabricated hospital at Renkioi in Turkey. Designed by the engineer Isambard Kingdom Brunel it provided 22 modular wooden ward units which were kept cool by an ingenious though primitive ventilation system. There were also separate buildings for kitchens and laundry but what made the hospital so practical was Brunel's attention to detail. After a prototype had been constructed in the grounds of Paddington Station the prefabricated buildings were despatched to the Crimea with detailed instructions for their construction. According to Brunel, although the units would be interconnected, each provided a hospital in miniature:

To ensure the necessary comforts, and particularly to provide against the contingency of any cargo of materials not arriving in time, each building contains within itself two ward-rooms, one nurse's-room, a small store-room, bathing room and surgery, water-closets, lavatories and ventilating apparatus.

Its distance from Scutari meant that Brunel's hospital was not used to full capacity after it became operational in August 1855 but it helped to change the way in which armies would regard their field hospitals. Visiting US officers took note of it and Brunel's plan was later to be used by the Federal army during the American Civil War. And at a time when muddle seemed to be winning the day, far from being obstructed, Brunel was encouraged by the War Office to complete his work as quickly as possible. 'It is most gratifying to be able to state that from everybody I have received the most zealous and cordial assistance,' he told Sir Benjamin Hawes, Under-Secretary for War, 'and found it sufficient to mention the object of my enquiries to obtain every assistance I could possibly require.'[20]

Tending the sick and wounded at base hospitals was one thing: providing immediate care on the battlefield was another and in this respect, the French had come to the Crimea fully prepared. Their field ambulances operated by orderlies and *vivandières* were infinitely superior to the haphazard British medical orderlies, many of whom were of pensionable age, heavy drinkers, or both. Raglan did his best 'to arouse the Medical Department to a sense of duty' but he was hamstrung by the fact that the doctors did not come under his direct command. None the less, this unsatisfactory state of affairs did not provide him with any protection from his political masters at home. Stung by the public outcry over the conditions in the Crimea, Newcastle vented his and his Cabinet colleagues' anger on the commander-in-chief in a lengthy letter written on 6 January 1855:

I have for some time been painfully apprehensive that there has been either a want of foresight or of ability on the part of some of your Lordship's staff which has led to an amount of suffering and sickness amongst the officers and men under your command which might and ought to have been avoided . . .

In a recent instance it is stated that the sick sent to Scutari have been allowed to embark without a Medical Officer to assist them on board and without help in their distress other than that which they could afford to each other. Such suffering, if it has existed, is cruel because it could have been prevented under proper arrangement . . .

I could multiply complaints of a like nature but I think it only necessary to give your Lordship an outline of those most deserving enquiry.[21]

In time Raglan's name was to become associated with the blunders and mismanagement of the army in the Crimea and he was to be written off as an accomplice to the slaughter — just as the British generals of the First World War were to be condemned for the carnage on the Western Front. As a verdict it is less than fair. Raglan was operating within a set of circumstances which did not brook any change and as Newcastle's letter shows, the government was happy to use him as a scapegoat. Inevitably, too, he fell victim to the *canard* that the French forces were superior in every way — Newcastle constantly made invidious comparisons — yet within five years they, too, were to be exposed. At the Battle of Solferino in 1859 the French army was found to have only one doctor per thousand men and the suffering of the wounded French and Austrian troops on the Italian battlefield was to lead directly to the foundation of the International Red Cross.

Had the British politicians known of the conditions facing the Russians, their criticisms might also have been less shrill.[22] In fact all the hardships visited on the British soldiers at Balaklava and Scutari were familiar to the Russian wounded inside Sevastopol. By contrast with Britain, though, there was no free press to report the reality of the war and most Russians had little idea of the difficulties facing their men in the Crimea. However, those who did know and who cared enough to do something found that their work was hindered by an indifference and obfuscation as reckless as anything encountered by Florence Nightingale.

Although Nicholas Pirogov was one of Russia's top surgeons, an innovator with military experience who believed in the use of anaesthesia during operations, red tape prevented him from reaching Sevastopol until the middle of November. By then it was almost too late. Waiting for him was a scene of Scutari proportions, thousands of wounded men, 'all lumped together, lying on dirty mattresses, soaked with blood'. With an energy which equalled his more famous British counterpart Pirogov quickly introduced a strict and competent regime. The Russian military hospital had been established in the House of the Nobles' Assembly and there Pirogov and his assistants carried out over five thousand operations. Although witnesses to his work also saw 'a vat from which amputated arms and legs peeped out', the whole scene was suffused by a wondrous calm.

In addition to his skill with the knife Pirogov encouraged the employment of nurses. Just as the British had been roused to compassion for the men in the Crimea, so too had the Russians and Pirogov was helped immeasurably by the nurses belonging to the Orthodox Sisters of Charity, a nursing order founded and paid for by the Grand Duchess Elena Pavlona. Like their British counterparts they served as nursing sisters to the sick and wounded; unlike them, as Pirogov remembered, they continued working even 'when bombs and rockets shot over or fell short and were flying around the Nobles' Assembly'. As one of them put it later, their inspiration came from a sense of self-sacrifice and from the knowledge that because British nurses had responded to the call, 'surely we weren't going to do nothing?'[23]

As for the Turkish soldiers, they were to suffer even more from official indifference. Not only was medical provision noticeable by its absence but British liaison officers, such as Captain Adolphus Slade, noted that the Turks cared little about how their men were treated: 'Devoid of resources, with no public to stimulate their rulers, the Turkish sick, all more or less influenced by the dogma of fate, in general died where they had sickened.'[24] No Pirogov or Mary Seacole attended them: they were just part of the human detritus of war, expendable commodities who had made the transition to paradise by fighting their religion's cause.

5

Balaklava: A Cavalryman's Battle

Was there a man dismayed?
Yes, they were damned afraid,
Loathing both shot and shell,
Into the mouth of Hell.
Sticking it pretty well,
Slouched the six hundred.
Ewart Alan MacKintosh, 'The Charge of the Light
Brigade: Brought up to date' (1917)

The first indication of possible delays to the investment of Sevastopol came on 15 October when Stratford informed Clarendon that 'the difficulties of getting the heavy guns into position and completing the trenches have been found, I believe, to be greater than we originally expected.'[1]

With typical candour Raglan had informed the British ambassador that there would be a deferment and that no one in government must expect the easy victories forecast by the newspapers. Equally typically, for he was under continuous pressure from the Foreign Office to provide London with up-to-date information from the front, Stratford passed the gloomy news to London with the result that Clarendon quickly became convinced that the siege would soon be running into difficulties.

He was right for, following the victory at the Alma, the allies had once more become querulous and indecisive. When Raglan first arrived at Balaklava and the French moved into their base at Kamiesh, he and Lyons believed that an immediate assault might take the city because the Russians were in disarray, but when he put the idea to the French, Canrobert replied that he would not attack before an artillery assault, otherwise 'the safety of the whole army would be compromised'. Without allied support any British attack would be fruitless and although Cathcart told Raglan that he was convinced that he 'could walk into it, with scarcely the loss of a man, at night or an hour before daybreak', it was agreed to prepare for a formal siege. The plan was put forward by Burgoyne and supported by the French: the watching Russian soldiers inside Sevastopol could scarcely believe their good luck.

After the war was over the general opinion amongst the senior Russian officers inside Sevastopol was that the allies 'would have taken it easily' had they committed all their forces to an immediate attack. On 25 September Menshikov had taken the bulk of the Russian army away from the city eastwards with a view to reinforcing it before regrouping and driving the allies back into the sea from their bases at Balaklava and Kamiesh. From a strategic point of view the deployment was understandable as the Russian commander did not want to bottle up his army in a city about to be besieged, but it left Sevastopol scantily defended. Fewer than 18,000 men remained, most of them sailors, and only twelve artillery pieces were left to guard the exposed northern front. Just as bad, there was an air of mutiny amongst the defending troops.[2]

In the aftermath of the battle Captain Chodasiewicz spoke of widespread disenchantment not just amongst the Russian troops but also in the high command. When Menshikov inspected his regiment he looked 'downcast and bad-tempered', as well he might, considering the difficulties of his position. However, two men under his command were to rise to the occasion – Kornilov, the aggressive naval commander, who had wanted to attack the allied fleet, and Lieutenant-Colonel Franz Edouard Ivanovitch Todleben, an enterprising engineering officer who was to emerge as the real saviour of Sevastopol. When he arrived in August Menshikov had been inclined to ignore him but the Alma changed all that.

Both men were to play a key role in the days which followed and it was due to their determination – plus allied dilatoriness – that the siege of Sevastopol was to be so long and so costly. In his memoirs Todleben conceded that the odds were stacked against him and that he had to work against time to reinforce the city's defences. From Kornilov's letters to his wife the sense of desperation is equally unmistakable. 'There is no retreat,' he constantly told his men. 'In front of us is the enemy and behind us is the sea.' Not that he was unequal to the task. Far from it: now a battery commander in the garrison, Tolstoy remembered that the admiral's presence in Sevastopol was positively talismanic:

> It is only now that the tales of the early days of the siege of Sebastopol are no longer beautiful historical legends for you, but have become realities: the tales of the time when it was not fortified, when there was no army to defend it, when it seemed a physical impossibility to retain it and yet there was not the slightest idea of abandoning it to the enemy – of the time when Kornilov, that hero worthy of ancient Greece, making his rounds, said, 'Lads, we will die, but will not surrender Sebastopol!' and our Russians, incapable of phrase-making, replied, 'We will die! Hurrah!' You will clearly recognise in the men you have just seen those heroes who gladly prepared for death and whose spirits did not flag during those dismal days, but rose.[3]

Although he had been anxious to mount a naval attack on the allies, Kornilov had been forced to concede to Menshikov's decision to strip the Black Sea fleet of its guns and to scuttle ships across the harbour entrance. Hotly disputed at the time, the decision was correct as the sailors released from naval duties were able to join Sevastopol's defenders.

If Kornilov was a walking inspiration to the men, then Todleben gave them the means with which to defend the city. Under his direction the existing bastions and trenchworks were reinforced and new protected artillery batteries sprouted along the perimeter. On the vulnerable south-eastern front the Malakov tower was protected by a complicated trench system which connected it to the Little Redan and Great Redan on either side. By the beginning of October Kornilov felt confident enough to tell his wife that the city's defences were 'becoming more imposing to look at'; better still, the appearance of trench systems in the allied lines to the south meant that the threat of attack had passed and a formal siege was about to begin.

By the middle of the month the tactical situation was to determine the future direction of the war: the allies hoped to secure the destruction or the surrender of Sevastopol through bombardment while the Russians wanted to use part of their forces to defend the city and the bulk to attack the enemies' bases. The opportunity to strike first fell to the allies but it was not be a straightforward operation. Although Burgoyne had been bullish about attacking Sevastopol he now admitted that he was surprised to find that the city's defences were stronger than he had anticipated. At a war council on 7 October he gloomily conceded that the position was one of 'extreme difficulty' mainly because there was almost three miles of dead ground between the British positions and the Russian defences. Despite the difficulties and a growing fear that the siege might not be completed before the onset of winter it was agreed to make preparations for a massive artillery assault on the city which would take place ten days later.

The allied plan was to use the artillery against the Malakov and the Redans while the ships' guns would try to silence Fort Constantine and Fort Alexander. During the next few days British and French forces took the high ground on Mount Rodolph, Green Hill and the Woronzow Height. This brought them closer to Sevastopol's defences and provided them with the necessary elevation for their heavier field pieces but there were still considerable doubts if the attack would achieve anything. Burgoyne was not alone in being surprised at the efficacy of Todleben's preparations. Calthorpe spoke of the defences springing up overnight, 'as if by enchantment',[4] and two days before the attack Stratford made his equally worried observation to London that the success of the artillery assault was by no means a foregone conclusion.

As it turned out, the doubts were settled by a lucky Russian shot. The allies had hoped to begin their bombardment at 6.30 in the morning but for reasons which have never been explained, but which were probably due to lax security, the Russians opened fire first. Two hours later they had their reward when two shells fell on the French magazine. Following a tremendous explosion the French guns began to fall silent, the gunners too unnerved by the accident to be able to continue. However, the British continued firing and all might have been well had the ships' guns been effective. But here, too, there was muddle. Not only did Dundas and Hamelin postpone the barrage until 1.30 but their ships lay too far off-shore for their fire to be effective.

While the artillery kept up a barrage into the next day it was obvious that they were making little impression on the Russian positions. In his despatches from Constantinople Stratford tried to strike an optimistic note when he wrote to Clarendon describing the assault, but it was difficult for him to be anything other than sober about the allies' chances:

Before the month was out, though, the failure of the artillery to breach Sevastopol's defences had been put into perspective by the news of an even greater calamity – the first reports of the loss of the Light Brigade.

So firmly is this action entrenched in the British conscious-ness that it is often thought of as a display of pluck and cour-age rather than as a dreadful blunder which should never have happened. Indeed, the charge of the Light Brigade soon came to be regarded as something glorious in its own right, an inci-dent which achieved nothing except the memory of undying heroism; and its story has been told many times, not just by the participants but also by those who observed it. But memo-rable though it undoubtedly was – for all the wrong reasons – it contributed only a small part to the fighting at the Battle of Balaklava.

It was a day which began well but ended badly. On the morning of 25 October the British forces were on the eastern extremity of the besieging army and their positions to the south of Sevastopol on the heights above Balaklava were exposed to attack by Menshikov's field army. An inner line of defence was formed by Royal Marines and naval artillery and the outer line on the Causeway Heights was guarded by Turkish troops in hastily constructed earthworks. Beyond them lay the North Valley and Fedukhine Heights and overlooking the South Valley was a force consisting of Lucan's Cavalry Division and Campbell's 93rd Highlanders, and some Turkish and English troops also under Campbell. These included the guns of 'W' Battery Royal Artillery commanded by Captain Barker; and to the rear there were two Turkish battalions and a force of Royal Marines.

As a defensive deployment it was completely inadequate and inevitably the Russians took advantage of its failings. A field force under Lieutenant-General Pavel Liprandi, consisting of 25,000 infantry, 34 squadrons of cavalry and 78 artillery pieces had been assembled around the village of Chorgun to the north-east of Balaklava. Its objective was relatively simple: to concentrate ex-treme force on a weak British position which, if successful, would allow the Russians to threaten Balaklava. The assault began at 6.00 a.m. with an artillery barrage and Liprandi intended to fol-low it up with a three-pronged infantry attack on the Causeway Heights and the Turkish redoubts. At worst a victory would

The Battle of Balaklava

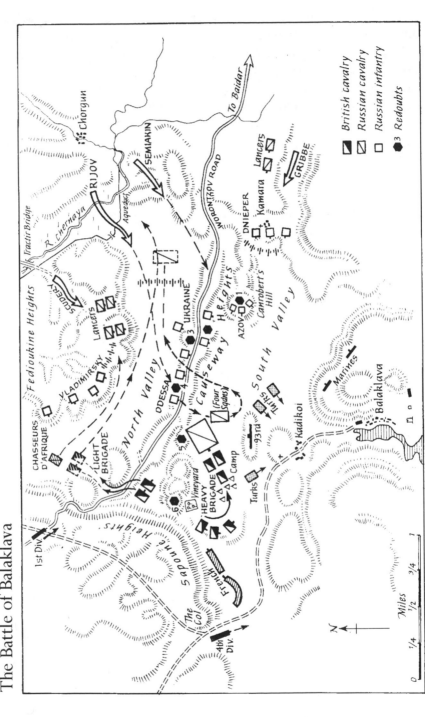

give Russian forces a tactical advantage; at best it could win the war.

For the first hour or so the battle was an unequal artillery duel between the Russian and Turkish guns. Firing roundshot to devastating effect, the Russian heavy guns (18-pounders and 12-pounders), although dated, caused terrible damage to the Turkish positions. British positions were also hit by the heavy fire: as a trooper in the 4th Light Dragoons was killed, an officer recalled 'the slosh that sounded as it went through the centre of his belly'.[5] Soon, the Turkish resistance began to crumble as Russian cavalry and infantry moved forward to overwhelm their positions. Watching from the cavalry camp, Fanny Duberly condemned their 'brutal cowardice' but the troops, mainly Tunisians, had been outnumbered and had shown considerable mettle under the blistering Russian assault.

From his command position on the Sapouné Heights above the Woronzoff Road, Raglan could see the Russian forces advancing up the North Valley and sent orders for the 1st and 4th Divisions to move into the South Valley. At the same time Lucan was ordered to move his cavalry to the north to cover Campbell's exposed position. As the advance guard of Cossacks and Ingermanlandsky hussars of Major-General Rijov's 6th Hussar Brigade reached the causeway cross-roads they could see Barker's guns but not the 93rd Highlanders who had taken cover from the artillery fire and were hidden from the Russians' view. This was all that stood between them and Balaklava. For the advancing 400 cavalrymen it was too good an opportunity to miss and they took full advantage of it.

This was cavalry against infantry (and a few Turkish guns) and its outcome depended on which side won the battle of wills. At Waterloo, Picton's Union Brigade had broken d'Erlon's lines and had driven off the French infantry but in the same battle French cavalry broke the 69th Regiment's square and captured its colours. Everything depended on the resolution of the defenders and the determination of the attackers: if the first held firm there was every chance that infantrymen had little to fear from charging horsemen. Precisely the same happened at Balaklava. 'Remember, there is no escape from here,' Campbell famously told his Highlanders. 'You must die where you stand.'

That said, the Highlanders stood up and opened fire. The first volleys failed to halt the Russian charge but when they wheeled round to the left in an attempt to outflank the Highlanders, the close-range fire from the Minié rifles succeeded in driving them off. From the hills above, Russell had a grandstand view and he, too, was to commemorate the action with words which passed into history:

> The ground flies beneath their [Russian] horses' feet; gathering speed at every stride, they dash on towards that thin red streak topped with a line of steel. The Turks fire a volley at 800 yards, and run. The Russians come within 600 yards, down goes that line of steel in front, and out rings a thundering volley of Minié musketry. The distance is too great; the Russians are not checked, but still sweep onwards with the whole force of horse and man, through the smoke, here and there knocked over by the shot of our batteries above. With breathless suspense every one waits the bursting of the wave upon the line of Gaelic rock; but ere they come within 150 yards, another deadly volley flashed from the levelled rifle, and carries death and terror into the Russians. They wheel about, open files right and left, and fly back faster than they came.[6]

The 'thin red streak' emerged again as the more felicitous 'thin red line' in Tennyson's lines about the battle and established itself as a cliché of Victorian jingoism. That should not detract from Russell's report which, although somewhat breathless, was written in the excited aftermath of battle and remains an accurate enough account of the Highlanders' repulse of the Russian charge. Later, Liprandi tried to gloss over the incident by claiming that British heavy cavalry was present and assisted in the defence. Certainly, Scarlett's heavies were in the area but their moment of glory came a few minutes later in a different part of the field.

As the Heavy Brigade moved to the west to help protect the Turkish guns they stumbled across the rest of Rijov's force on the ridge of the Causeway Heights. Cossack lance-heads on the skyline gave Scarlett the first clue that his force was in any danger but he was ill-placed to meet it. Not only was the going rough – a mixture of scrub and deserted vineyards – but his force was strung out over half a mile in two columns, the 6th Inniskilling Dragoons in the van, followed by the Royal Scots Greys and the 5th Dragoon Guards, with the 4th Royal Irish Dragoon Guards bringing up the rear. With the Russians having the benefit of the higher ground, the odds seemed to favour them but Rijov ordered his front ranks to spread out for a pincer attack and the delay was fatal.

Unlike his opposite number who had fought in the war against Napoleon, Scarlett had never seen action before, but he did not lose his nerve. Facing him was the rump of Rijov's force, some 1600 cavalrymen, and he had less than half that number under his command. While the first squadrons of Inniskillings and Scots Greys struggled to get into line Lucan and his staff appeared with orders to engage the enemy immediately. The charge was sounded and following a brief delay as the leading squadrons finished their parade-ground preparations the Heavy Brigade lumbered into the enemy's centre. Behind came the 4th and 5th which hit the flanks and following behind were the Royals. The entire engagement lasted only a few minutes and neither side sustained heavy casualties – a result of poorly sharpened swords – but, none the less, the heavies broke the Russian line. Franks of the 5th Dragoon Guards described the action:

> Some of the Russians seemed to be rather astonished at the way our men used their swords. It was rather hot work for a few minutes; there was no time to look about you. We soon became a struggling mass of half frenzied and desperate men, doing our level best to kill each other. Both men and horses on our side were heavier than the enemy, and we were able to cut our way through them, in fact a good many of them soon began to give us room for our arms, and to quote Mr Russell's words, 'The Heavy Brigade went through the Russians like a sheet of pasteboard.'[7]

Like many other men in the Brigade, Franks could not understand why the Russians had given way with such ease. One reason was the impetus of the attack: Franks noted that it had taken no time at all to cut through the Russians. Another was the shock caused by Hodge's 4th Dragoon Guards as they hit the left flank: Rijov described the hand-to-hand fighting as being as ferocious as any he had seen in over forty years of service. But the deciding factor was artillery. 'C' Troop Royal Horse Artillery galloped down from the heights and opened fire, according to one gunner 'with admirable results, the 24-pounder howitzers making splendid practice'.

The combination of cavalry and artillery proved to be too much for the Russians who withdrew hurriedly into the North Valley to re-form behind a battery of eight artillery pieces. They would be in action again before too long. Raglan despatched a terse note of congratulation to Scarlett and as Russell told the readers of *The Times*, 'there arose a great shout from the spectators'. It was only half-past-nine and the day was far from over.

Now began the series of events which would seal the fate of the Light Brigade. As Scarlett's men launched their attack, Cardigan's force was less than half a mile away on rising ground further up the valley. They had a grandstand view of the operation and many of their officers were impatient to exploit the heavies' success. Even Loy Smith 'felt certain' that Cardigan would give the order to attack. Indeed, at that very moment he was being berated by Captain William Morris, in temporary command of the 17th Lancers, 'to charge the flying enemy'. Cardigan would do no such thing and he did not appreciate being harangued by an 'Indian' officer – Morris was an experienced soldier who had fought in the First Sikh War.

His excuse for the inaction came straight out of the military text books but it also owed much to the enmity he felt towards his brother-in-law. Lucan had ordered him either to remain in his position 'and to defend it against any attack of Russians' (Cardigan's version) or to 'attack anything and everything that shall come within your reach, but you will be careful of columns or squares of infantry' (Lucan's version).[8] According to the evidence of those who were present there was a moment of opportunity but Cardigan passed it up. An exasperated member of Canrobert's staff who observed the incident merely noted that the Light Brigade's commander might be brave but he lacked initiative. Lucan shared that view. He sent his brother-in-law a brief note asking him to 'remember that when he [Lucan] was attacking in front it was his [Cardigan's] duty to support him by a flank attack, and that Lord Cardigan might always depend upon receiving from him similar support.'[9]

Raglan was now in a quandary. The first part of the battle was over and it had ended in stalemate. The Russian cavalry had retired but the Russians were still in a position to threaten Balaklava. On the Causeway Heights as far as Number 3 redoubt there was a force consisting of eleven infantry battalions and 32 guns, while, to the north, the slopes of Fedioukine Heights were occupied by eight battalions, four cavalry squadrons and fourteen guns. Anxious to

The Charge of the Light Brigade

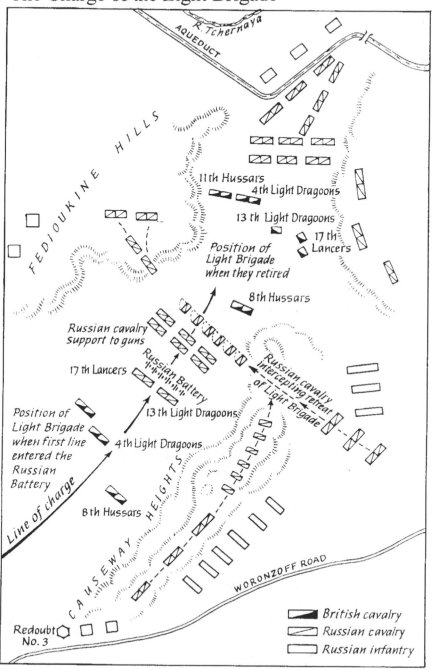

R. Tchernaya

AQUEDUCT

FEDIOUKINE HILLS

11th Hussars
4th Light Dragoons

13th Light Dragoons

Position of
Light Brigade
when they retired

17th
Lancers

8th Hussars

Russian cavalry
support to guns

Russian cavalry
intercepting retreat
of Light Brigade

17th Lancers

Russian Battery

Position of
Light Brigade
when first line
entered the
Russian
Battery

13th Light Dragoons

4th Light Dragoons

8th Hussars

Line of charge

CAUSEWAY HEIGHTS

WORONZOFF ROAD

Redoubt
No. 3

British cavalry
Russian cavalry
Russian infantry

exploit Scarlett's success Raglan wanted to drive the Russians off the Causeway Heights but to do that he needed infantry and there was still no sign of Cambridge's and Cathcart's divisions.

However, Raglan saw no reason to tarry and at 10.15 he ordered Lucan to deploy his brigades for an assault should the opportunity arise: 'Cavalry to advance and take advantage of any opportunity to recover the Heights. They will be supported by the infantry which have been ordered. Advance on two fronts.' Accordingly Lucan ordered Cardigan to move the Light Brigade into the North Valley to face east while the Heavy Brigade remained in support behind them protected by a ridge. As Lucan understood the order he had acted in accordance with Raglan's wishes: to await the arrival of infantry before supporting a two-pronged assault on the Causeway Heights. After all, the British commander had shown considerable miserliness in using his cavalry and was unlikely to risk them in a hopeless attack against heavily guarded infantry and artillery positions.

That was one interpretation of the order but, from his position above the cavalry, Raglan wished them to move forward to take any advantage of attacking the enemy. Instead he was treated to the sight of the Light Brigade dismounted and taking their ease in the morning sun. His impatience was exacerbated by the tardy arrival of the infantry. It was almost eleven o'clock yet the first units of the 1st Division were only beginning to file into position in the South Valley. Meanwhile the Russians themselves were consolidating their positions in the North Valley: any opportunity to attack had been lost forever.

With the two commanders thinking at cross purposes a member of Raglan's staff shouted out that the Russians seemed to be moving captured guns from the redoubts captured earlier that morning. These lay to the right of the Light Brigade but, fatally, they were hidden from Lucan's sight. To lose guns to the enemy was a sign of defeat and Raglan was not going to let that happen. With considerable impatience – onlookers saw his empty sleeve twitch, an ominous sign – he gave his orders to Airey who scribbled them on a piece of paper. It read: 'Lord Raglan wishes the cavalry to advance rapidly to the front – follow the enemy and try to prevent the enemy carrying away the guns. Troop Horse Artillery may accompany. French cavalry is on your left. Immediate.'

Then, having read the order, he summoned the worst possible officer to deliver it to Lucan – Airey's hot-tempered ADC, Captain

Nolan. According to several witnesses, including the reliable Rose who committed his recollections to his diary that night, Nolan was 'much excited' and had been 'talking very loud against the cavalry . . . and especially Lucan'. There was nothing new in this behaviour. He had already discussed with Russell the shortcomings of Raglan's handling of the cavalry and he was openly contemptuous of Lucan. But as he was considered to be the best horseman in the army, well capable of riding quickly down the steep escarpment, Raglan chose him and not his duty ADC. That choice and Raglan's parting words – 'Tell Lord Lucan the cavalry is to attack immediately' – sealed the fate of the Light Brigade.

Not surprisingly Lucan was non-plussed by the order. Contrary to the previous command it made no mention of the heights and ordered an attack without infantry support. While he could not see the guns being removed he clearly knew that this was happening as his subsequent report makes it clear that he had to 'prevent the enemy carrying away the guns lost by the Turkish troop'. Yet the orders seemed imprecise and when he questioned them he received the arrogant riposte from Nolan that he should attack immediately.

'Attack, sir! Attack what? What guns, sir?'

'There, my lord, is your enemy!' responded Nolan, vaguely waving his arm westwards to where he supposed the redoubts might be. 'There are your guns!'

The gesture was imprecise and pointed to the battery guarding Rijov's cavalry further up the valley. So taken aback was Lucan by Nolan's insolence that he refused to answer and rode over to Cardigan to order him in person to charge that position. With no mention of the heights in Raglan's last order, and given Nolan's gesture, he clearly believed that there had been a change of plan and that the Light Brigade would have to attack the guns under the enfilading fire of Russian guns on either side of the valley. As a soldier he knew only too well that there would be times in a battle when one unit had to sacrifice itself for the good of others. Perhaps that moment had arrived; the Light Brigade would attack first followed by Scarlett's heavies.

In spite of their mutual antipathy the final exchanges between the two cavalrymen were restrained. When a 'greatly excited' Nolan arrived to confirm that action was imminent Cardigan sent his ADC, Lieutenant Henry Fitzhardinge Maxse back to Lucan to point out that 'the heights which flanked the valley leading to the Russian

battery of heavy guns was covered with Artillery and Riflemen.'
Lucan understood this and it says much for the man that he was
prepared to give the unwelcome order in person. He rode over to
the Light Brigade position and when Cardigan repeated his concern
about the fire from the flanks Lucan quietly responded that it was
Raglan's wish. There was no other option.

Having gained permission from Morris to ride with the 17th Lancers
Nolan had one more contribution to make to the debacle. As the
Light Brigade trotted forward he suddenly charged ahead gesticulating
wildly with his sword and shouting incomprehensibly. Either he was
trying to change the direction of the charge or he was caught up in his
eagerness to hasten the attack. Both have been put forward as reasons
for his impetuous behaviour but the truth will never be known for
he was killed immediately by a Russian shell splinter. No one in the
leading lines would ever forget his blood-curdling scream – 'more
like a woman's wail than a man's' according to Cardigan – as the
shrapnel ripped into his chest mortally wounding him. He was to be
the first of the 107 men and 397 horse who would be killed within
the next 25 minutes as they rode the one and a half miles towards
the Russian guns.

Despite the enfilading fire the bulk of the cavalrymen reached their
target and sabred the Russian gunners. They also engaged the waiting
Russian cavalry but with no way out of the valley they were forced
to return through the same gauntlet of deadly fire. It was not just the
British who thought it folly. A Russian cavalry officer had the same
reaction as Bosquet who famously remarked that it was magnificent
but not war:

> It is difficult, if not impossible, to do justice to the feat of these
> mad cavalry, for, having lost a quarter of their number and being
> apparently impervious to new dangers and further losses, they
> quickly reformed their squadrons to return over the same ground
> littered with their dead and dying. With such desperate courage
> these valiant lunatics set off again, and not one of the living –
> even the wounded – surrendered.[10]

The Charge of the Light Brigade has received more attention than
any other action undertaken by the British Army in the Crimea. It
was immortalised by Tennyson who conjures up a stirring picture of
British resolve in the face of overwhelming odds. But it was not just

a heroic blunder. It was totally unnecessary and it cost Raglan the use of his cavalry forces. For the participants who survived, it achieved nothing apart from the dubious honour of being hailed as the 'noble six hundred.' Indeed, had it not been for the brilliant flanking attack by the French Chasseurs d'Afrique (4 Regiment) on Russian artillery positions on the Fedioukine Heights the tragedy would have been even greater. There was also a bizarre coda to the action: the spectacle of Cossack horsemen rounding up the surviving riderless horses of the Light Brigade and, according to a watching officer, 'true to nature' offering them for sale. A few minutes earlier these gallant horsemen from the steppes 'frightened by the disciplined order of the mass of [British] cavalry, did not hold, but, wheeling to their left, began to fire on their own troops in an effort to clear their way of escape.'[11]

Inevitably, the recriminations began almost as soon as Cardigan rode back towards the start line at around 11.30 a.m. ahead of most of the surviving members of his brigade. Later in the afternoon he was summoned by Raglan to explain why he had attacked the Russian artillery position 'contrary to all the usages of warfare, and the customs of the service'. It was a telling moment. Raglan, who had ridden down into the valley with his staff, was clearly angry but the haughty Light Brigade commander merely responded that he would not be blamed as he had received the orders from his superior officer. And Lucan, indeed, was held to be responsible. Later that evening Raglan summoned Lucan to his quarters and with cold contempt exclaimed, 'You have lost the Light Brigade.' That sense of outrage also informed his despatch to Newcastle: Lucan was accused of making 'a fatal mistake' and would therefore have to accept the blame. However, as the war was still in progress there could be no question of punishing Lucan and, two days later, Airey assured him that Raglan's report would be fair. For the time being the matter would have to rest.

Viewed dispassionately, the weight of the evidence implicates Lucan. He failed to question Nolan who, having been in Raglan's company, knew the import of the order. If Cardigan had not been so contemptuous of his brother-in-law he, too, could have asked for greater clarification but for both men that would have been out of character. Instead, Lucan ordered the Light Brigade to attack down the North Valley in the mistaken belief that the action would somehow fulfil Raglan's order to prevent the removal of the Turkish guns. And then, having made the fateful order, he failed to support

Cardigan, first by refusing to deploy his horse artillery and secondly
by withdrawing the Heavy Brigade.

Of course, he was not acting in isolation. Raglan's order was
muddled and made little sense when read in conjunction with the
preceding order. Nolan, too, must shoulder some of the blame.
Although he was privy to Raglan's thinking he made no attempt to
explain it to Lucan. It is possible, too, that he was so determined to
see the cavalry attack that he allowed impatience to get the better of
his judgement. There is evidence to suggest that, before riding down
the escarpment, he shouted that he would give the lead to Cardigan.
As happens so often in warfare a combination of mistakes and errors
of judgement sent men to certain death. However, for the men of
the regiments involved – 4th Light Dragoons, 8th King's Royal Irish
Hussars, 11th Hussars, 13th Light Dragoons and 17th Lancers – it was
fortunate that their sacrifice was suitably chronicled. Russell watched
the action and confided to the readers of *The Times* that in his opinion
there had been 'some hideous blunder'. Three weeks later Tennyson
penned his famous lines:

> 'Forward, the Light Brigade!'
> Was there a man dismayed?
> Not though the soldiers knew
> Some one had blundered:
> Their's not to make reply
> Their's not to reason why,
> Their's but to do and die:
> Into the valley of Death
> Rode the Six Hundred.

The first indication of the disaster reached Constantinople three
days later and a worried Stratford wrote immediately to Clarendon
to assure him that the setback was only temporary:

> True or false, the impression still prevails that the allied armies
> will finally succeed in carrying the place, though not perhaps,
> without a second, or even a third assault, owing the nature of
> the ground which, as it has been described to me, is highly
> favourable to the besieged.[12]

It would take time, though, for these assaults to be planned.

Above left: Mars made manifest:
Britain's bullish minister of war,
Lord Panmure.

Above right: Lord Palmerston,
Britain's prime minister, who
believed that the dispatch of battle
fleets was a necessary ingredient
of his country's foreign policy.

Right: The Earl of Clarendon,
British foreign secretary. 'Things
get worser and worser,' he told his
wife. 'The beastly Turks have
actually declared war.'

Left: Napoleon III, Emperor of France. His ambition was to break the consensus of 1815 which kept France in check. The Crimean War provided the means.

Below: Count Walewski, France's foreign minister, a bastard child of Napoleon Bonaparte. Greatly distrusted by his British colleagues.

Peacemaker: Count Bourqueney, the French diplomat who worked with the Austrian foreign minister, Count Buol-Schauenstein, to broker the Paris peace treaty.

Count Karl Robert Nesselrode, Russia's foreign minister. 'He does not have the devil in him and without the devil a diplomat can go nowhere.'

Nicholas I, Russia's autocratic ruler, who saw himself as the constable of Europe.

Lord Cowley, Britain's ambassador in Paris. The French government stood in awe of him – and not just because he was Wellington's nephew.

The Great Elchi, Lord Stratford de Redcliffe. No Western diplomat knew more about the Ottoman Empire than Britain's ambassador to the Porte.

Sir George Hamilton Seymour. He gained the trust of Tsar Nicholas over the vexed question of the 'sick man of Europe'.

The general who did not want to command an army: Sir James Simpson considers his prospects.

Field Marshal Lord Raglan, commander-in-chief of the British forces in the Crimea. 'Everyone who knew him loved and respected him, and justly so.'

Britain's man in Kars and one of the neglected heroes of the Crimean War, William Fenwick Williams.

A stern and professional Scottish soldier: Sir Colin Campbell, the general who might have won the war more cheaply had he been born into the nobility.

Black Charley Napier, who claimed that he would be in hell or Kronstadt before Christmas. He failed to reach either destination.

The only naval commander to display the Nelson touch: Admiral Sir Edmund Lyons.

Lacking the Nelson touch: Admiral Sir James Dundas, ineffectual British commander of the Black Sea Fleet.

Death claimed him before he could claim victory: Marshal Leroy de Saint-Arnaud, commander-in-chief of the French forces.

Known as 'Robert Can' to the British, General Canrobert succeeded Saint-Arnaud in command of the French forces.

General Pierre Bosquet, a forceful battlefield commander whose attack on the allied right helped to win the Battle of the Alma.

Likened in appearance to a wild boar, General Pelissier brought a sense of purpose and direction to the French forces during the final stages of the Siege of Sevastopol.

Above: Lord of all he
surveyed throughout
the Ottoman Empire:
the Sultan Abdul Mejid.

Left: Michael Lotis, a Croat soldier
of fortune who gave loyal service
to the Ottoman forces, which
he commanded under the
nom-de-guerre of Omar Pasha.

Emasculation by Turkish gunners in the war of 1828 war did not encourage Prince Alexander Sergevitch Menshikov towards a high opinion of his enemy.

The military engineer who saved Sevastopol: Lieutenant-Colonel Franz Edouard Ivanovitch Todleben.

Leaving the girls behind them: the 4th Dragoon Guards depart for the seat of war.

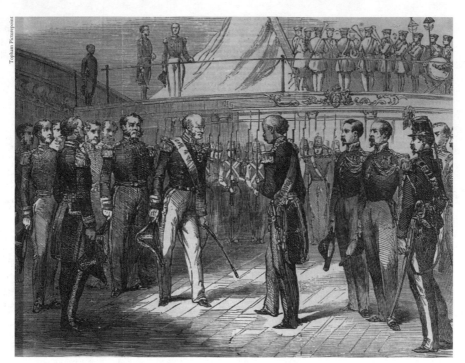

Allied council of war (i): France's Admiral Baraquay d'Hilliers is greeted by Britain's Admiral Dundas, 4 February 1854.

Allied council of war (ii): British and French generals confer in Paris before leaving for the front, 22 April 1854.

A long and narrow inlet well protected by the surrounding hills and Russian artillery: the north and south sides of Sevastopol Harbour.

British troops in the field. Tents were sent to the Crimea because the planners thought that the war would be over before Christmas.

The Battle of Balaklava: Russian artillery on the heights, 25 October 1854.

British light cavalrymen fighting their way into the history of military incompetence. Cardigan' men engage the Russian guns in the 'valley of death'.

Right: Leo Tolstoy, a young Russian gunner officer who used his experience of war to help him write the battle scenes in *War and Peace*.

Below: Ladies with lamps tend a wounded soldier. Press exposure of the soldiers' suffering led to a revolution in military medicine.

Above: British troops reform after beating off the Russian attack at Inkerman, 5 November 1854.

Left: An uncertain alliance. Raglan, Omar Pasha and Pelissier ponder the next move.

Jolly good fellows all. Survivors of the Battle of Inkerman toast their good fortune at a celebratory Christmas lunch.

General Sir George Brown and his staff in conference in the field before Sevastopol.

Left: William Howard Russell of
The Times, 'honoured by a good
deal of abuse for telling the truth'.

Below: Smiles all round, but
the delegates to the Paris peace
conference in March 1856
added to the problems they
were attempting to solve.

Raglan knew that he dared not risk his two infantry divisions in any attempt to move Liprandi's forces from the Causeway Heights. Even if the redoubts were recaptured they would need to be defended by men who might otherwise be more gainfully employed in besieging Sevastopol and he dared not expose Balaklava to further attack. In any case the loss of the Light Brigade had been so traumatic an event that the allies seemed to be incapable of further action that day. Only the Russians were happy. To them the Battle of Balaklava was a victory which not only gave them possession of the high ground but also avenged the humiliation of the Alma.

The battle was over – that night a survivor recalled feeling the first touch of night frost – but the celebrated charge of the Light Brigade would be fought and refought several times over as the two rival field commanders attempted to clear their names. They were already storing up ammunition. Shortly after the battle Lucan sent a copy of Raglan's order to Stratford for safe keeping. With it was a letter from an unnamed staff who had witnessed the charge and who clearly believed that the blame lay with Cardigan and Nolan. Both were forwarded to Clarendon:

> Now comes the sad part of the affair; our Brigade of Light Cavalry was upon our left, orders were sent to them to 'follow the enemy', hanging upon his flank and rear, so as to take advantage of a charge. This order was either misunderstood [by Cardigan], or delivered incorrectly by poor Captain Nolan.[13]

Writing to his wife the following day Lord George Paget forecast that 'the destruction of the Light Brigade . . . will be the cause of much ill-blood and accusation'. He was not far wrong. Far from exonerating Lucan, Raglan's report accused him of misconstruing an order and when it was published in *The Times* it caused an uproar. Lucan demanded complete vindication and professed his willingness to be court-martialled. It was to no avail. He was sacked from his command at the beginning of 1855 and returned home in relative disgrace. By then Cardigan, too, was back in Britain, having been sent home an invalid. He, too, was destined to defend his name when Calthorpe published an account of the war which claimed that he had failed to rally his brigade after the charge.

Both men stayed on in the army, Lucan to become a field-marshal and Cardigan Inspector-General of Cavalry. It was no bad reward for two soldiers who had no solid military distinction other than participating in a battle which was neither victorious nor, *pace* Tennyson, particularly glorious.

6

Inkerman: An Infantryman's Battle

The Guards, all must admit, set a glorious example; for if
they had to die, they acted upon the old 57th motto, 'Let
us die hard.'

Sergeant Timothy Gowing, letter home after
the Battle of Inkerman

The first frost felt by the light cavalryman in the wake of the
battle for Balaklava was a reminder that winter was not far away.
Two days earlier, acting on the advice of Calvert who knew the area,
Raglan passed on his intelligence officer's warning to Newcastle that
'in such weather no human creature can possibly resist cold during the
night unless in a good house properly warmed; and in day-time unless
properly dressed'.[1] It was a problem which would come to preoccupy
Raglan's mind in the weeks ahead but the day following the action
to preserve Balaklava brought more pressing difficulties.

Raglan was uncomfortably aware that the allies' tactics would now
have to be governed by the ground available to them. As their first
task was to besiege Sevastopol the bulk of the army, some 35,000
men, were encamped outside the fortress, the British on the right,
the French on the left. However, the presence of Liprandi's force
meant that the flank had to be guarded and this fell to the so-called
observation army made up of those not engaged in the siege. It faced
east to guard the right flank: in the centre were the French and
the Turks with the Brigade of Guards on the left and Campbell's
Highlanders on the right covering Balaklava. Buoyed by their success
it was always possible that the Russians would counter-attack from

Sevastopol and, indeed, that is precisely what they did the following day.

Taking advantage of the fact that the British siege line stopped short of Sevastopol Bay the Russians launched an attack from the Karabelnaya suburb in the afternoon of 26 October. Consisting of six battalions of infantry supported by four artillery pieces its target was the 2nd Division on the Home Ridge. Although the picquets were overcome the onslaught was stopped in its tracks by artillery fire and by the determined resistance of a unit of guardsmen under the command of Captain Goodlake who was later awarded the Victoria Cross.

Known as 'Little Inkerman' the skirmish exposed the weakness of the allies' right flank but, despite Raglan's promptings, the French were loath to detach troops to defend it. When their chief engineer visited the area he thought it too remote to defend adequately. Beyond it lay the broken ground of Mount Inkerman – Cossack Mountain to the Russians – which overlooked the road to Simferopol, Sevastopol's link with the outside world. It was difficult ground to defend and the failure to reinforce this extremity almost cost the allies the war. As Sterling noted at the time, if the Russians had managed to take the ground 'they would have brought their offensive army into immediate contact with the garrison of Sebastopol . . . and the allies would have been forced to abandon the siege of the eastern part of the town, that is, of the Malakoff and Redan, the docks and the Karabelnaya suburb.'[1]

Raglan also realised that his depleted army was overstretched and needed to be reinforced. At the beginning of November Newcastle informed him that the 3rd, 62nd and 90th Regiments would be despatched together with a third battery train but everything depended on the availability of steam transports. The Admiralty was asked to give precedence to the despatch of troops but within a few weeks the navy's resources would be overburdened by fresh demands for clothes and hutting equipment to protect the soldiers against the Crimean winter. Canrobert, too, had asked for reserves and had been promised an additional three divisions of infantry. To meet the need for transport Cowley reported that Napoleon had ordered the withdrawal of the French fleet from the Baltic. With the Crimea rapidly becoming the focus of the war the French could see no reason to remain in northern waters especially as winter was approaching and there was no hope of achieving any success. This was the order which eventually sealed Napier's fate:

The Emperor, to whom I had written, informs me that he has sent orders to Admiral Parseval to consult with Sir Charles Napier on the possibility of attacking Sveaborg but as His Majesty is convinced that no effect can be produced by the fire of ships upon fortifications at a greater distance than five hundred yards, he is of the opinion that an attack should not be undertaken, if the ships cannot approach within that distance.[2]

The Russians, too, had been busy reinforcing their army. At the beginning of November two fresh divisions, the 10th and 11th, had arrived from Bessarabia and they were to play a key role in the next battle of the war. There was good reason for the urgency. By 2 November French engineers had pushed their siege trenches to within two hundred yards of the outer defences at the 4th Bastion. The best way of breaking that siege would be to use Russia's numerical superiority to drive the enemy back to the sea but, to add to the Russians' woes, the inspirational Kornilov had been killed during the first allied bombardment.

With the arrival of the fresh divisions Menshikov had a field army numbering some 107,000 men whereas the allies had around 70,000, many of whom were debilitated by illness and the shock of battle. Although he remained the same irresolute commander who had dithered at the Alma, Menshikov was under enormous pressure from St Petersburg to attack the allied lines and to break the siege of Sevastopol. The arrival of two of Nicholas's younger sons was a clear sign that the tsar wanted to see the siege lifted and the allies defeated – a not impossible feat given Liprandi's success during the fighting for Balaklava. Menshikov had every incentive to attack the allies. All he needed was a sensible plan of action but, as he never tired of telling those around him, life had not blessed him with an understanding of battlefield tactics.

However Menshikov knew only too well that fight he must and that further obfuscation would only lead to his removal as commander-in-chief. There was one crumb of comfort. The fighting at Little Inkerman had revealed a potential weakness in the allied lines on the southern edge of Mount Inkerman at a position known as Shell Hill. Although the attack had been beaten off, the 2nd British Division was obviously overstretched and the broken country – a mixture of scrubland and ravines – made reinforcement difficult. Also, but this was unknown to him, the division had lost its commander, the gifted de Lacy Evans, who had injured himself falling from his horse and the formation was under the temporary command of Brigadier-General J.L. Pennefather, a fiery soldier who believed in leading from the front. With several advantages at his disposal Menshikov moved his head-quarters into the ruins of the village of Inkerman on 4 November.

A battle was in the offing – Calthorpe reported that Raglan knew from deserters 'that large reinforcements are daily arriving to the Russian Army' – and the Russians seemed to have the upper hand both in terms of numbers and tactical dominance. But just as there were chronic administrative deficiencies in the British forces, so too was Menshikov's army in a state of disarray. After the war several officers revealed their feelings of inadequacy while fighting in the Crimea: this was particularly true about the state of their equipment. As in every war, fear of the enemy's bogey-weapons had produced panic in Russian infantry formations and these anxieties had been compounded by the failure of their own weapons. Following the Alma it was obvious to every Russian infantryman that the allies' Minié rifle was superior to anything they possessed and those fears had grown with each passing engagement. 'I am convinced that they will cut us down as soon as we fight in the open,' admitted one Russian staff officer after noticing that front-line regiments 'melted' under concerted allied fire.

Also, little attempt had been made to provide food and fodder for men and horses, nothing was to be had locally and the infantry divi-sions, especially those arriving as reinforcements, were ill-equipped to withstand a long campaign. Absence of decent rations and the sheer monotony of what was on offer damaged morale on both sides during the war in the Crimea – in the Caucasus the Russians were better provided – and the effect on the ordinary infantryman about to face the shock of battle was a profound disincentive. 'There was general depression everywhere,' stated one officer after the battle of Inkerman, 'and all knew that in the whole Russian Army there were hardly three or four names in which anyone had confidence or which were in any way popular.'[3]

A popular general is one who wins battles with the least expense to his own forces and, sadly, for the Russians, there were none of that calibre in Menshikov's army. The commander-in-chief himself seemed to be terrified by the thought of fighting and he had no confidence in his subordinates. In turn, they revealed their supposed lack of worth by refusing to take any initiative and by attempting to cover their tracks once the action was over. The muddle was exacerbated by poorly phrased and imprecise written orders and by a complete absence of battlefield maps. When divisional commanders asked why there were no plans of the area over which they were about to fight, they were simply advised to use their eyes.

As if these deficiencies were not enough, there was bad blood between Menshikov and his second-in-command, General P.A. Dannenberg who had arrived with the reinforcements from Bessarabia. Already Menshikov had pleaded with Gorchakov to send the soldiers but not their commander and had received the dusty response that he could not have the benefits of the former without the disadvantages of the latter. In any case it would have been folly to have sacked a corps commander at that stage of the war, even though the man in question, Dannenberg, was not exactly renowned for his soldierly skills in command of a large force. Like many others of his ilk he was a veteran of the campaign against Napoleon and the memory of that long-drawn out and bloody defence of the motherland was still powerful enough to guarantee status and promotion, regardless of what had happened in the intervening years. For all his learning, Dannenberg was a nervous and indecisive man and his self-esteem had not been helped by his already having been defeated by the Turkish forces. Exactly a year earlier, on 4 November 1853 Omar Pasha had routed Dannenberg's army at Oltenitsa in southern Romania: he would not have been human had he not been unnerved by the unhappy contiguity of the dates.

Even so, there was enough on the Russian side to suggest a successful outcome and Menshikov's orders, though sketchy and ill-formed, were sensible enough in theory. Basically, he called for an attack on three fronts, with the main weight concentrated on the exposed British position; 60,000 men and 234 guns would take part in the assault which would enjoy covering fire from two Russian warships. For the assault on Cossack Hill there would be an initial infantry attack supported by artillery which would be led by Lieutenant-General F.I. Soimonov. This would begin from inside Sevastopol at 6.00 a.m. the following day – 5 November – and it would take Soimonov's force across the Careenage Ravine south-east on to Shell Hill. There he would be supported by a second attack from Inkerman Bridge with infantry under the command of Lieutenant-General Pavlov. When the two converged on the ridge they would come under Dannenberg's unified command.

Meanwhile, on the left flank Liprandi's 12th Infantry Division, supported by cavalry, would attack the Sapoune Heights on the Chorgun sector, the force led by Prince Gorchakov; and from within Sevastopol itself an assault would be made on the allied siege lines. It might have worked but Menshikov's plan required careful timing and co-ordination, none of which were available to the Russian commanders in the short period available to them. Worse, Soimonov and Dannenberg then produced contradictory written orders which threw everything into confusion in the final moments before battle was joined. Soimonov had made it clear that he would adhere to Menshikov's plan for attack but then Dannenberg gave different orders for him to advance west of the Careenage Ravine on to the Victoria Ridge. This last-minute order was calmly disregarded and when the battle began Dannenberg was blissfully unaware that Soimonov would act according to his original instincts.

Even the Russian infantrymen were unaware until the final moments that they were about to go into battle. Pyotr Alabin felt that something was amiss when he saw horses being saddled; another officer in the Tarutinsky Regiment was equally prescient. 'No one knew where we were being taken so early, or why,' he noted in his diary, adding the telling observation, 'although the night-time meal and extra cup of vodka and our route towards the enemy positions forced us to make a guess.'

Anxious to be on his way Soimonov had assembled his troops shortly after midnight and by 2.00 a.m. the leading units of the Russian 10th Division were making their way in the dark across the Careenage Ravine and clambering up the slopes on to the ridge. All the previous day it had rained and as dawn came up there was a thick mist covering the high ground. As the Russian infantrymen of the Tomsky and Kolyvansky regiments began to deploy in columns to protect the field guns which were being dragged into position, they could hear the bells of Sevastopol summoning the faithful to church – for 5 November was also a Sunday. The heavy chimes and the thick mist gave them perfect cover as they halted just under a mile away from the forward picquets of the 2nd British Division on Shell Hill. There was no sign of Pavlov's troops who had been held up by the rebuilding of the Inkerman bridge and were still climbing up Quarry Ravine, but the Russians retained the element of surprise.

However, being so close to the British lines on Shell Hill – some

The Battle of Inkerman

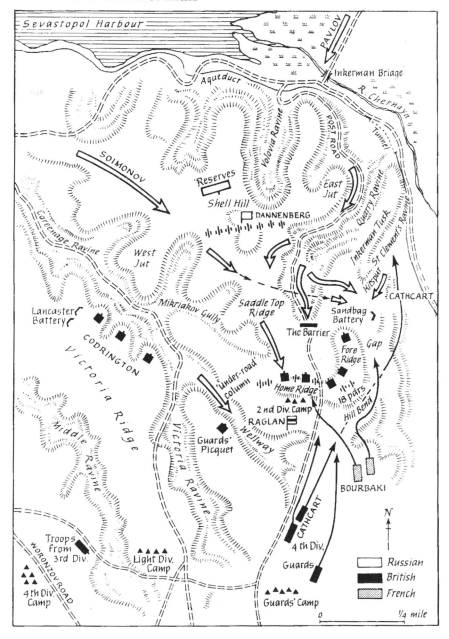

Sevastopol Harbour

PAVLOV

Inkerman Briage

Aqueduct

R. Chernaya

Tunnel

SOIMONOV

Volovia Ravine

POST ROAD

Reserves

East Jut

Shell Hill

Quarry Ravine

DANNENBERG

Careenage Ravine

West Jut

Inkerman Tusk

St Clement's Ravine

Kitspur

CATHCART

Lancaster Battery

Mikriakov Gully

Saddle Top Ridge

Sandbag Battery

The Barrier

CODRINGTON

Victoria Ridge

Middle Ravine

Fore Ridge

Gap

Under-road Column

Home Ridge

18 pdrs

2nd Div. Camp

Hill Bend

RAGLAN

Wellway

Victoria Ravine

Guards' Picquet

BOURBAKI

Troops from 3rd Div.

Light Div. Camp

CATHCART

N

WORONZOV ROAD

4th Div. Camp

4th Div.

Guards

Guards' Camp

☐ Russian
■ British
▨ French

0   ¼ mile

of the 2nd Division's picquets had already been taken prisoner – the Russians opened fire shortly after six o'clock and there was a brisk exchange of shots. Caught unawares, even though the Russian plan for an assault was common knowledge, Pennefather ordered reinforcements into the forward defensive positions and the battle settled down to become the confusion of dense mist, shouting and ferocious hand-to-hand fighting which participants on both sides were to remember with awe in the years to come.

> On our part it was a confused and desperate struggle. Colonels of regiments led on small parties, and fought like subalterns, captains like privates. Once engaged every man was his own general. The enemy was in front and must be beaten back. The tide of battle ebbed and flowed, not in waves, but in broken tumultuous billows. At one point the enemy might be repulsed, while, at a little distance, they were making the most determined rush. To stand on the crest and breathe awhile, was to our men no rest, but far more trying than the close combat of infantry, where there were human foes with whom to match, and prove strength, skill, and courage, and to call forth the impulses which blind the soldier to death or peril.[4]

Most battles are soldiers' battles in that positions have to be defended, fought for and held by men on the ground but there is good reason for the historians of the regiments who fought at Inkerman to describe it as 'a soldier's battle'. As Lieutenant-Colonel E.B. Hamley explained in his first-hand account of the fighting, once the battle was joined it was a case of every man for himself. A gunner officer in the 1st Division Hamley sent back his accounts for publication in *Blackwood's Magazine* and they provide some of the best descriptions of battle seen through the eyes of a professional soldier. Indeed, so popular was his story that an American publisher, Gould and Lincoln of Boston, brought out a pirated edition before Hamley's story was published in book form, late in 1855. In common with several other officers in the Crimea Hamley saw no harm in publishing his own version of events while deprecating the press coverage from Russell and other reporters. It was also good for the magazine's circulation, his editor John Blackwood noting that Hamley wrote in a 'cool, easy vein' and that sales were 'expanding'.

As it turned out, though, even Russell was flummoxed by the fog of war, telling *The Times* that 'one could scarcely see two yards before one'. Units on both sides fighting on Shell Hill in the early morning mist were unaware of the wider picture, only conscious of the fact that they were engaged in bitter personal battles with the enemy. Alarmed by the noise of battle and aware of the desperate plight facing the exposed British division, Bosquet rode up to the British lines to offer the support from his corps of observation. But the offer was gruffly refused by the British commanders, presumably because they felt it was a sleight on British military prowess.

By then reinforcements had arrived from Brown's Light Division, Cambridge's 1st Division and Cathcart's 4th Division and despite early Russian incursions into the British line, the tide of battle was beginning to turn against them. Raglan had arrived on the Home Ridge to assume direction of the battle and had quickly reversed the decision to turn down French help. A staff officer was sent to Bosquet with a polite request for reinforcement and two British heavy artillery pieces were ordered up. Both moves were effective. The sight of the advancing Zouaves lifted morale in the embattled British lines and Russian prisoners admitted that the accurate fire of the 18-pounder guns seriously checked the impetus of their attack when they came into action at 9.30 a.m.

By then, too, Dannenberg had assumed overall command of Soimonov's and Pavlov's forces but there was much confusion in the forward lines as some of the battalion officers did not recognise their new commander. There was further misfortune for them on Shell Hill: shortly before eight o'clock there was a sudden clearing in the mist and Soimonov was quickly picked off by sharpshooters – riding on his horse he was an obvious target – and in the confusion elements of the Ekaterinburg and Tomsk regiments began to withdraw. At that moment an insignificant and defensively worthless point, the Sandbag Battery, became the cockpit of the battle during its second and bloodiest phase. 'On came the Russian columns,' wrote Gowing, describing the Russian infantrymen as they stormed the walled embrasure:

> The bayonet was used with terrible effect by all regiments. The enemy, driven on by their brave officers, had to – and did literally – climb over the heaps of their slain countrymen and ours to renew this bloodthirsty contest; but they had to go back time after time much quicker than they came.[5]

For the Brigade of Guards this presented an opportunity to redress the balance after their embarrassments on the Alma and they were in a dangerously reckless mood. They had been brought up on to the ridge along with other reinforcements including three field batteries of artillery and two thousand infantrymen from the 4th Division. Along with them were two French battalions, sent by Bosquet to help the British drive back the Russians but it was the three regiments of foot guards which were first in action. What happened during the next hour was undoubtedly courageous and noble but it was futile and men died unnecessarily. Worse, it almost cost the allies the battle.

First, the Grenadier Guards charged and recaptured the Sandbag Battery, clearing the Russians from it at bayonet point; but finding it worthless as a defensive position they retired to higher ground. This allowed the Okhotsky regiment to retake the position, the Russian infantrymen whooping in triumph and waving their weapons as they streamed on to the rising ground. Then it was the turn of the Scots Fusilier Guards. They had already engaged a Russian column to the north of Sandbag Battery above the St Clements Ravine, firing a volley of Minié rounds into them before engaging them with the bayonet. Seeing that the Russians had retaken the walled embrasure they attacked it once again and cleared it, sending the Russians tumbling down the hill.

By then there was a bloodlust in the regiments which was difficult to quell. The guardsmen were slashing and stabbing with their bayonets, squelching over the bodies of the dead and dying, neither giving quarter nor expecting to receive it. After the battle Scots Fusilier Guards officers would recall with some distaste that they were so close to the enemy that they could smell 'that peculiar, strong leather-like smell', characteristic of Russian troops. For the Russians the sight of the big Scotsmen in their tall fur caps was a terrifying sight; even the Scots were appalled to be in such immediate vicinity of their enemy. One young Russian officer had a youthful face 'just like an Eton boy'.[6] Other accounts of the Scots Fusilier Guards' action are more prosaic: they speak of madness and men temporarily out of control.

By then, too, guardsmen were dying in droves and Bentinck's brigade, especially the exposed Grenadiers, was becoming dangerously overstretched. As the attacks and counter-attacks rumbled over ridge and down ravine a gap began to appear to the left of the Sandbag Battery. If Dannenberg could exploit it he would split the British line and victory would be his. Here he was helped by Cathcart who, in a moment of madness, disobeyed Raglan's order to support the Duke of Cambridge, by then with the Grenadiers in the Sandbag position. Seeing a chance to drive off the Pavlov columns which were attacking on the Russian left flank he ordered his men to charge down the ravine towards them.

The initial shock of the attack caught the Russians by surprise but to Cathcart's horror he saw that other Russian troops had swarmed on to the ground he had vacated. Then, to add to his problems the mist lifted again, leaving the red-coated soldiers an obvious target for the Russian gunners. As the British soldiers attempted to retrace their steps the two French battalions which had been waiting patiently in reserve moved into the gap with other units from the 4th Division and for the moment at least the Russian attack had faltered. For Cathcart it was too late: he was one of the 597 British soldiers who died on that muddled and murderous Sunday morning.

The fighting would not be broken off until mid-afternoon but the Russians' best chance had gone. The arrival of the two 18-pounders had the desired effect of discommoding the Russians on Shell Hill and, as Bosquet's men moved on to the right flank, the allied position was finally secured. The battle still ebbed and flowed. A determined Russian attempt to take the Home Ridge was beaten off by the 55th Foot and the survivors of the 21st and 88th Foot made a successful attack on the Russian artillery positions, forcing them to withdraw, but by one o'clock Dannenberg had had enough. As the pale winter sun broke through the mist and clouds it revealed to the retreating Russian soldiers a sight from the charnel-house.

There was little firing and everything became quiet as we crossed the [Inkerman] bridge on the way to our previous day's billets, taking our wounded with us on carts and limbers; the men marched listlessly and unhappily, looking round and asking the fate of their missing fellows. We took possession of the same huts, but whereas last night there had been six or seven of us in each now there were but two or three. Where yesterday there had been chatter, noise and mirth, today there was melancholy and emptiness.[7]

There was good reason for the soldiers' dismay: 10,729 Russians were casualties, killed, wounded or taken prisoner. Even for a large army it was a dreadful loss.

The allies were equally chastened. The British lost 597 killed and 1860 wounded; the French 13 killed and 750 wounded. When Bosquet saw the result of the carnage at Sandbag Battery he looked down at the broken bodies – British, French and Russian piled on top of each other – covered his nose and said, '*Quel abattoir!*' Even Hamley, no stranger to the effects of battle, was moved sufficiently by what he saw to remind the readers of *Blackwood's* that war was not a pretty business:

> Few sights can be imagined more strange and sad in their ghastliness than that of dead men lying in ranks, shoulder to shoulder, with upturned faces, and limbs composed, except where some stiffened arm and hand remain pointing upward. The faces and hands of the slain assume, immediately after death, the appearance of wax or clay; the lips parting show the teeth; the hair and the mustache [*sic*] become frouzy [*sic*], and the body of him who, half and hour before, was a smart soldier, wears a soiled and faded aspect.[8]

Inkerman proved to be a defining point in the war. The British were not defeated and the Russians failed to dislodge them from their positions. Canrobert could perhaps have committed his fresh French troops to pursue Dannenberg's retreating army but with so little knowledge of the Russian dispositions and force strengths it would have been a risky business. Besides, the failure to defeat the Russian field army meant that all available allied resources had to be bent to besieging Sevastopol. That was now Canrobert's priority and, as Kinglake noted, it was accepted as the main goal of all future allied plans.

Given the death toll, there were repercussions on both sides. Raglan was blamed by many of his officers for failing to bring any direction to the battlefield but it is difficult to see what he could have done. He showed great personal courage in keeping his staff on Home Ridge where they were subjected to intense Russian artillery fire – poor General Strangways, the artillery commander, had his leg blown off – and he did his best to plug the gap during the Guards' fight for the Sandbag Battery. It was not his fault that Cathcart disobeyed orders but Raglan's decision to deploy the 18-pounders was decisive.

Besides, Inkerman was a modern battle in that it was not fought over a concentrated area and at several points the action was obscured either by distance or the enveloping mist and smoke. Without reliable means of communication – the heliograph had still to be invented, the wireless was a distant dream – Raglan simply had no means of controlling the battle. It is still not easy for the modern historian to describe the action in its entirety.[9]

Menshikov, too, had obloquy heaped on his head. The two most important witnesses of his behaviour told their father that the 'disorder' originated from the Russian commander and that he was solely to blame for the failure. Nor could the tsar have been pleased to read the letter from the grand dukes which stated quite clearly that the Russian field commander was solely to blame: 'staggering though it is to relate, Menshikov had no headquarters at all, just three people who work at those duties in such a fashion that if you want to know something you are at a loss to know whom to ask.'[10]

In his official report Menshikov, who had not wanted to fight in the first place, blamed the superiority of the allies' rifles and the arrival of French reinforcements. He also claimed that Dannenberg had demonstrated insufficient aggressiveness and had misdirected Soimonov's troops. Unwilling to be the scapegoat Dannenberg, too, got himself off the hook by blaming Soimonov for disobeying orders and not attacking to plan. Gorchakov, too, was criticised for failing to attack the allied flank with more determination and he in turn placed the responsibility for failure firmly on Liprandi's head. However, for all the name-calling the Russian commanders had also been hampered by lack of communications. The original plan called for strict timing and firm handling but it was simply too ambitious for such an irresolute commander as Menshikov. Only the defenders inside Sevastopol were happy, secure in the knowledge that the hard-pressed allies would be unlikely to increase the tempo of their besieging operations.

As for the allies they were left to bury the dead, including the Russians, hastily shovelling the corpses into mass graves. There was a curious atmosphere in the British and French camps: elation that the enemy had been repulsed and dismay that conditions were deteriorating. Obviously the survivors had reason to rejoice that they were still alive, yet they were becoming uneasily aware of their predicament. Sevastopol was still unvanquished, the medical services' failure to treat the wounded and dying was obvious and the weather was beginning to show all the signs of a typical Crimean winter. Even the generals were dispirited: the battle had so depleted the allied army that Canrobert's plans for a fresh assault on Sevastopol's defences were postponed at the joint planning conference on 7 November. The normally sanguine Clifford, shortly to be promoted, told his parents that the situation was 'a difficult and critical one', and described the allies' position in stark terms: 'A large army quite at liberty and independent of the siege of Sebastopol has to be fought – winter is coming on – and we are far from our resources.'[11]

The first crisis of the war was rapidly approaching but back at home in London and Paris the battle of Inkerman was hailed as a glorious triumph. Certainly that was the view taken by Newcastle who wrote to Raglan on 27 November expressing the Queen's thanks for this 'important victory'. Newcastle also asked the British commander to pass on the nation's thanks to Canrobert for 'his cordial cooperation' but above all Victoria wanted to thank the ordinary soldier without whose efforts nothing would have been achieved:

> The Queen desires that your Lordship will receive Her thanks for your conduct throughout this noble and successful struggle, and that you will take measures for making known Her no less warm approval of the services of all officers, non-commissioned officers and soldiers who have so gloriously won by their blood, freely shed, fresh honours for the Army of a Country which sympathises as deeply with their privations and exertions as it glories in their victories and exults in their fame. Let not any Private Soldier in those ranks believe that his conduct is unheeded. The Queen thanks him – his Country honours him.[12]

The private soldier would have been forgiven had he asked for warm clothes, medical care and shelter in place of the well-meant praise, but it would take the onset of winter before the country's growing unease would turn into outrage. In the aftermath of Inkerman it was enough to give thanks and to hope for the best. By way of thanks, and perhaps to bolster morale, Raglan was appointed field-marshal. Other officers were allowed to go home, some on leave, others for good. Exhausted by the battle, Cambridge retired to Constantinople, Cardigan left the Crimea for ever, to relive the infamous charge for the benefit of London society. Changes in command were also necessary. Sir George Buller took over temporary command of the

4th Division and the bluff and likeable Scarlett was given the sorely depleted Cavalry Division. With the new year there would be other changes and fewer letters of congratulation. Inkerman would change everything.

The first voices of concern were heard from de Lacy Evans who bluntly told Raglan on 6 November that the siege of Sevastopol stood little chance of success and that consideration should be given to withdrawing the armies from the Crimea. The general was by no means a coward – he had risen from his sick bed to rally troops on the Inkerman heights – but he was realist enough to suggest the unthinkable. His proposal received no support and Raglan and his staff began the lengthy and time-consuming process of ordering up new equipment and munitions, knowing full well that none of it would reach the Crimea before the new year.

It was a time when spirits began to sink. Even the normally buoyant Clarendon was moved to tell Stratford that he feared a 'monster catastrophe': 'The only event at all like it that I know of is the embarkation at Corunna but there our numbers were small and circumstances light and we had the Spaniards to hold the walls.'[13] Sir John Moore's retreat to Corunna in the harsh winter weather of 1808–9 was another instance of the British Army transmogrifying an inglorious retreat into something more acceptable to public taste. It also produced famous lines of verse to commemorate the commanding general's death but the retreat, during which British regiments displayed extremes of great courage and disgraceful indiscipline, was not covered by the press. Any withdrawal from Sevastopol would not only be ignominious but it would be described in painful detail by Russell and his colleagues. In an attempt to raise the foreign secretary's spirits, Stratford sent a jaunty reply as he struggled to come to terms with the unfolding events in the Crimea:

> Let the reinforcements arrive in time, as, no doubt, they will, if Providence in its mercy shall favour the exertions of Her Majesty's Government and, in spite of recent disappointments and present difficulties, I hope, without presumption, to reckon upon a triumphal issue.[14]

It was the only hopeful despatch which Stratford was able to send in the second half of November. The rest all spoke of the privations

of the wounded and of the desperate need to bring comfort to the
troops in the field before Sevastopol where Providence in its mercy
was most notable by its absence.

7

Arrival of General Winter

It seems to me, God grant I may be wrong, that we are on
the verge of a monster catastrophe.
The Earl of Clarendon to Lord Stratford de Redcliffe,
13 November 1854

The mood in the allied camp following the fighting on the
Inkerman heights was a combination of elation and despair; yet
all were painfully aware that there had been no glorious victory. To
the north Menshikov's army was still a potent force, for all that the
piles of Russian dead, hideous in their death throes, spoke of defeat
and destruction. As for Sevastopol, it was still impregnable and seemed
likely to remain so for the duration of the winter. Added to the sense
of disbelief was the growing misery of the winter weather. The cold
nights and the heavy rain had intensified mightily, so much so that even
hardened veterans cursed the miserable conditions – the inadequate
leaking tents, the shortage of spare clothes and the monotonous diet.
For the wounded, suffering in Dr Hall's gaunt hospital tents, the misery
was compounded not just by recurrent outbreaks of cholera but also by
the deteriorating weather. A surgeon, Arthur Henry Taylor, wrote:

The weather is miserably wet and windy, and last night [10
November] our Hospital tent was blown down on top of the
sick, and gave a great deal of annoyance to the sick and a great
deal of trouble to us all. I had to get up myself during the night
and secure my own tent, the wind having blown up the pins on
the side, and it was nearly blown down on top of me.

Taylor was one of the army's assistant-surgeons who had arrived in the Crimea in October and was attached to the Royal Artillery Siege Train. His letters home offer a somewhat different account of the hardships endured by the army for, although he did not make light of them, he was at pains to defend his own profession. Called up to work in the general hospital in the aftermath of the fighting he found that 'the wounded were being carefully and speedily attended to, there was not a man that could possibly be found who was not dressed in the Hospital tent and given some nourishment as tea, coffee etc before midnight on the day of battle'. Displaying a natural pride in his professionalism, he also pointed out that he had done 'more practice in one day than any of the most celebrated practitioners in one year'.[1] This was not a case of a man wanting to put himself in a good light but merely the thoughts of a young doctor who was doing his best in dreadful circumstances.

Taylor's account is also painfully honest. The wind which was whipped up on 10 November was a harbinger of worse to come. For the next three days the Crimean peninsula was hit by a storm which began with a steady downpour accompanied by high winds and rose to a crescendo on the night of 14 November. The great storm was a disaster for the allies. It pulled down tents and scattered them without mercy, it left men soaked and shivering and, worst of all, it destroyed shipping in Balaklava's crowded harbour and its exposed roads. Even those on shore, such as the soldiers of the Highland Brigade who thought themselves secure, were given a rude buffeting.

> All the tents fell in about three minutes; in some the poles broke, in others the pegs drew. As to mine, the wind rushed in at the door, and split it right up; so my servant and I spent an hour lying on the wet canvas, to keep it compactly down, and to prevent the household goods from being blown away. Just at the first destruction of the tents, the air was loaded with all sorts of articles – Highland bonnets, shoes, chairs, bits of wood, and all the papers, news or official, in the camp. My box or trunk, which I pillaged, or rather bought from a pillager, to hold my documents, was blown open for a moment, and the wind had just time enough to whip off one document and pour in a shower of water.[2]

The day before, Sterling had told his friends at home that despite the hardships 'our hearts are high and it will take a deal of Ruskis to chaw us up': now he was left to lament the destruction caused by the hurricane. Up on the exposed plateau overlooking Sevastopol the besieging army suffered more grievously. A soldier in the Rifle Brigade saw a man being blown into the air, Raglan's farmhouse headquarters had part of the roof torn off and a French infantry battalion was forced to dig in only a few yards from its camp because the men could make no headway in the ferocious gale.

When the storm subsided the following afternoon the armies set about retrieving their possessions. Tents were hurriedly thrown up, searches were made for personal belongings – Sterling found his document three hundred yards away in a vineyard – and the dead buried, for in the bitterly cold winds men already enfeebled by illness died of hypothermia. At least the men on dry land could make reparation: the worst effects of the storm were felt at sea. All told, the British lost twenty-one transport ships and with them went their precious cargoes of stores and munitions. Even in the safety of the harbour Fanny Duberly saw the waters 'seething and covered with foam and the ships swinging terribly' – amongst them was the *Retribution* which was taking the Duke of Cambridge to Constantinople. It was saved by the captain's decision to jettison its upper guns to prevent it from capsizing.

The ships in the outer harbour and the roads stood little chance and one after the other they were swept to the shore and smashed, a dismal litany of hopeful names – *Progress*, *Resolute*, *Wanderer* and *Marquis*. The worst disaster was the loss of the steamship *Prince* which went down with the loss of almost all hands – only six were saved from the crew of 150 as it careered on to the rocky shore. It had arrived in Balaklava a few days earlier bringing with it the 46th Foot and much needed winter stores. The infantrymen had disembarked but the cargo remained on board and when the *Prince* went down it took with it 40,000 winter uniforms and boots, 'everything that was most wanted', according to the official report. More than any other loss, this was to cause the most havoc to the British regiments in the field.

In the aftermath the army did its best to restore order to the chaos in Balaklava but already the organisation was a cart without wheels and there were neither materials nor opportunity for repair. The sheer impossibility of reinforcing and resupplying the British expeditionary force became grimly apparent as inefficiency, mediocre bureaucracy and, all too often, sheer bloody-mindedness gripped the army's Commissariat Department. 'All life is a blunder, as we may see and feel,' wrote the normally stoical Colonel Sterling. 'All matters, weather included, look sad and murky.' For all of them, Highlanders, guardsmen, riflemen and line infantrymen alike, it was the beginning of a season in hell.

As the scale of the suffering became apparent, Raglan roused himself to action. No sooner had the storm blown itself out than he sent one of his staff officers, Captain Weatherall, to Constantinople 'to purchase articles of urgent necessity, warm clothing for the troops in particular'; and following his arrival Stratford was able to report that 'this Embassy is endeavouring to render him all the assistance in its power'. Despite suffering from a painful bout of rheumatism the British ambassador was equal to the task in hand. From Bucharest the British consul, Robert Colquhoun, reported that he had arranged for '70 bales containing 2184 fur coats and 5 boxes containing 545 dozen of woollen socks' to be shipped to Balaklava and that a further 18,000 fur coats would be sent by the end of December. To speed matters Stratford fired off a salvo to Rear-Admiral Edward Boxer warning him that the precious cargo was to be given immediate priority on its arrival in Constantinople. In a further attempt to be helpful he suggested that Weatherall should try his hand at purchasing large supplies of the rough woollen cloaks worn by shepherds in the Anatolian uplands. Although it proved to be an impractical suggestion at least Stratford was trying to get something done and the papers of the Constantinople embassy reveal a flurry of activity which lasted well into the new year.[3]

However, provision of quarters for the troops in the field took a longer time to resolve. With the September heat of the marching days long forgotten, the uniforms and lightweight tents were totally inadequate for the bitter cold days which had swept in after the storm. Writing to Newcastle on 15 November Raglan insisted that he could not 'send us too many stores of all kinds'. Three days later, before the despatch arrived, Newcastle insisted that he had ordered the Board of Ordnance 'for Huts for the troops [to] be prepared, without delay and sent to the Crimea'. They were supposed to accommodate 20,000 men but it would take time and sufficient transport ships before they could be despatched:

As however, it is of the utmost importance that no time should be lost on supplying shelter to these troops I have requested

Lord Clarendon to urge upon Lord Stratford de Redcliffe to purchase materials and engage native artizans in Constantinople for the purpose of making and erecting huts of a temporary nature which may hereafter be superseded by the frame houses ordered in England.[4]

Once again, logistic arrangements which should have been settled earlier were being left to last-minute happenstance. The despatches from that period reveal no shortage of verbiage about the difficulties facing the army – Raglan was both energetic and prolific in dealing with the organisational paperwork – but the reaction to the plethora of orders and complaints was an insurmountable inertia. With the inevitability of a dramatic tragedy the men in Raglan's army began to bear the full brunt of the mistakes made by an organisation clearly unfit to prosecute war so far removed from its home base. It was not that the supplies were failing to come through. Dozens of contemporary accounts describe the chaos at Balaklava where food, uniforms, forage and other supplies were left to rot on the quays either because the Commissariat officers were overwhelmed by the administration needed to account for them or because there was no way of distributing them to the troops. By the end of November the three-mile stretch of road from the port to the plateau was awash with mud and well-nigh impassable.

As had come to be expected the French fared better. They, too, had lost equipment in the storm but their home base at Kamiesh was both better organised and closer to the army's front lines. Within the confines of their base they had constructed a large hutted town complete with store-houses from which their well-organised *intendance* service was able to keep the troops well supplied and equipped. They were also able to help out their allies from time to time. Rose was astonished when a senior Grenadier Guards officer asked 'to procure him if I could, 6 pairs of sabots, wooden shoes, from the French Army, for the sick of the Hospital of his Battalion. General Canrobert gave me one hundred pair, with one hundred pair of the woollen socks which are worn with them.' There were many other untold instances of personal kindness and with an efficient administration to keep them tolerably happy the French soldiers could only view the plight of their allies with amazed pity:

Any soldier who has been in the Crimea knows the English

words 'bread' and 'boots' from having heard them so often: the
English will actually exchange their boots for something to eat.
In the absence of bread, which we are lacking in ourselves,
we give them what we can but we never take their money.
It's pitiful to see such superb men asking permission to gorge
themselves on the dregs in our mess tins.[5]

The compassion in the young French dragoon officer's letter is
self-evident. Here were good soldiers who had proved themselves
in battle being treated as if they did not exist. For although the
French were appalled by the privations facing the British soldier
they never lost sight of the fact that he was courage personified. In
conversation with Henry Clifford, General Brite of the French 1st
Division remarked that his troops would have collapsed before the
Russian attack a few days earlier. 'We are good in many things, but
we cannot stand without works in front of us, with death staring us
in the face. Your infantry is the finest in the world.'[6] While that might
have been so, there was no escaping the growing muddle which had
Fanny Duberly tearing out her hair in frustration:

If any body should ever wish to erect a 'Model Balaclava' in
England, I will tell him the ingredients necessary. Take a village
of ruined houses and hovels in the extremest state of imaginable
dirt; allow the rain to pour into and outside them, until the
whole place is a swamp of filth ankle-deep, catch about, on an
average, 1000 sick Turks with the plague, and cram them into
the houses indiscriminately; kill about a hundred a day, and bury
them so as to be scarcely covered with earth, leaving them to rot
at leisure – taking care to keep up the supply. On to one part of
the beach drive all the exhausted bat ponies, dying bullocks and
worn-out camels, and leave them to die of starvation. They will
generally do so in about three days when they will soon begin
to rot, and smell accordingly. Collect together from the water
of the harbour all the offal of the animals slaughtered for the
use of the occupants of above 100 ships, to say nothing of the
inhabitants of the town – which, together with an occasional
human body, whole or in parts, and the driftwood of the wrecks,
pretty well covers the water – and stew them all up together in
a narrow harbour, and you will have a tolerable imitation of the
real essence of Balaclava.[7]

This was not hyperbole but the voice of a disinterested and increasingly disgusted observer. In time the cavalryman's wife was to become one of the best-known writers of the war, not because her prose was particularly memorable – though it was certainly better than her husband's – but because she wrote truthfully about what she saw. Her account touched the hearts of many and it became something of a bestseller but it did her social life no favours. In return for exposing some of the worst horrors endured by the British soldier in the Crimea she was ignored by Queen Victoria when the regiments were welcomed back to Britain at the war's end.

The suffering of the British forces during that terrible winter has come to typify all that was rotten in the war in the Crimea and there is no shortage of descriptions of the deprivations endured by the soldiers. Quite apart from the senior officers who had returned home to the safety of a British winter and who were able to retail stories of the suffering, the newspapers were awash with the disgruntled writings of those who had to remain with their men in the army before Sevastopol. In addition to the reports written by Russell and others, a sizeable army of military correspondents was not slow in telling the British public what was happening to them and their men. Even Aberdeen could not claim to be ignorant. By then his son Alexander Gordon was Assistant Quarter-Master General and his letters home made no secret of the catalogue of despair. A letter suggesting the despatch of 'several hundred wagons for the conveyance of ammunition and commissariat supplies' was followed a few days later by another bemoaning the lack of reinforcements. 'Why was not winter clothing sent out sooner?' he asked plaintively.[8]

Queen Victoria, too, was no stranger to the suffering. Not only did she have the first-hand evidence of the Duke of Cambridge – whose departure from the Crimea she deplored as 'shameful' to his reputation – but she went out of her way to entertain those wounded at the Alma who had been fortunate enough to survive the voyage home. Her compassion was not just confined to the officers. Of especial interest was the well-being of those 'beautiful Guards' who had marched out of their barracks so hopefully in the early spring of 1854. Almost a year later, the men presented to her were a sorry sight. Having found that her words 'all stuck in my throat' when she inspected 32 Grenadiers, she was only marginally better prepared when 26 Coldstreamers were brought into her Servants' Hall:

I thought they looked worse than the others – more suffering & sickly, & less fine looking men. There were some sad cases; – one man who had lost his right arm at Inkermann [sic], was also at the Alma, & looked deadly pale; – one or two others had lost their arms, others had been shot in the shoulders & legs; – several in the hip joint, which impeded the action of the leg, rendering them unfit for service. A private, Lanesbury, with a patch over his eye, & his face tied up, had had his head traversed by a bullet, penetrating through the eye, which was gone, – through the nose, & coming out at the neck! He looked dreadfully pale, but was recovering well.[9]

The extreme winter weather was no respecter of nationalities. According to the accounts of the British liaison officer Captain Slade, the Turks were in a terrible condition and even the British, ill-equipped and suffering from shortages, were moved to help. 'The state of these poor people is shocking,' reported Raglan, 'and the consequences of their being huddled together, as they are now, cannot be otherwise than fatal to them and may extend much further.' In a letter to Stratford he begged him to make the problem known to the Porte. This the British ambassador did and HMS *Terrible* was deployed to tow a Turkish hospital ship to pick up the wounded and ill Ottoman soldiers from Balaklava.[10]

The Russians, too, had their own crosses to bear. Secure and relatively snug they might have been within the walls of Sevastopol but, as Tolstoy makes clear in his vivid *Sevastopol Sketches*, they still had to endure the torment of regular shell fire from the allied artillery batteries. And those in the field army outside the walls suffered almost as badly as the allies: the Russian soldier Alabin's description of the 'rain, mud and slush' which prevented supplies from arriving could have been written by any soldier in Raglan's army.

Faced with the knowledge that matters were going from bad to worse in the Crimea, Aberdeen was not in any hurry to reconvene parliament before Christmas. When it did open on 12 December, though, the increasingly shaky coalition survived the first attacks against its prosecution of the war. Government spokesmen were able to reassure parliament that supplies and reinforcements were on their way to the seat of war and that steps were being taken to remedy the deficiencies. A Militia Bill would enable militiamen – part-time soldiers raised for home defence, to transfer to the regular army and, controversially, a Foreign Enlistment Bill paved the way for the recruitment of non-British subjects in specially formed 'legions'. Most would come from Germany and to manage the recruitment a base was established at Heligoland and a depot at Bexhill both under the command of Colonel John Kinloch. Under the terms of the capitulations agreed with the government's German recruiter Baron Richard von Stetterheim, the cost to the British taxpayer would be £975 per 100 men and each recruit would be paid a bounty of £6, provided that he was more than thirty-five years old and over five feet two inches in height. Steps were also taken to raise a new division of 20,000 Ottoman troops which would be led by British officers although Stratford warned that the reinforcements would count for little unless the officers themselves were suitably experienced in leading native forces:

> Unnecessary though it be, Your Lordship will excuse my observing how greatly the future efficiency of the Ottoman troops will be depend upon the selection of their officers, not only in respect to military knowledge and ability, but in point of qualifications adapted to the management and addressed to the confidence of soldiers differing so widely from the British in language, customs and religion.[11]

With the government appearing to take action, however unpopular – the idea of enlisting mercenaries was attacked both inside and outwith the army – Aberdeen even enjoyed the backing of Delane but it was only the calm before the storm. The litany of anguish from the Crimea was too insistent to be ignored and middle-class public opinion united in a feeling of revulsion: while they were preparing to celebrate Christmas in the comfort of their homes their fellow countrymen were facing only too easily imaginable discomfort in the Crimea.

The upsurge in national resentment caught the attention of the press and it did not take long for the papers to profit from it. Ten days after writing in support of Aberdeen *The Times* turned its ample firepower not just on the government but also on Raglan, by then generally held to be wholly responsible for the army's difficulties. Until that time Delane had kept his powder dry but the flood of officers' descriptions and the growing bitterness of Russell's reports concerning the mismanagement of the army meant that he had little option but to go on the attack. The uneasy truce was broken on 23 December with a bitterly expressed leading article which lamented the unnecessary destruction of the 'noblest army ever sent from these shores'. A week later Delane placed the blame for the disaster squarely on Raglan's shoulders:

> There are people who think it a less happy consummation of affairs that the Commander-in-Chief and his staff should survive alone on the heights of Sebastopol, decorated, ennobled, duly named in despatch after despatch, and ready to return home to enjoy pensions and honours amid the bones of fifty thousand British soldiers, than that the equanimity of office and the good humour of society should be disturbed by a single recall or a new appointment over the heads now in command.

This assault *ad hominem* was to signal a change of attitude towards the hapless British commander-in-chief. From being the hero of Inkerman and the rock upon which British interests depended – and a newly appointed field-marshal to boot – he suddenly found himself in the unwelcome role of scapegoat. No sooner had the new year begun than Raglan found himself on the receiving end of a series of increasingly ill-tempered despatches from Newcastle. Following *The Times*'s attack on the British commander – an exultant Delane informed Russell that he had 'at last opened fire on Lord Raglan and the General Staff' – Newcastle obviously believed that he should follow suit. While making due acknowledgement of the local difficulties facing the high command surely there had been sufficient time to learn important lessons from the adversities facing them?

> I am grieved thus to address your Lordship in the spirit of complaint but when reports reach one from time to time, of some of the Regiments under your command, and even of men in the trenches being on half, and in some instances quarter rations for two or three days together whilst there is no deficiency of food, and stores at Balaclava; I cannot entirely attribute this state of things if it exists to the badness of the roads, or to the interruption caused by bad weather.[12]

The day before, 5 January, a similar letter of warning had been sent to Colonel Lord William Paulet who had been despatched to command the military hospital at Scutari. In it Newcastle provided general instructions for Paulet's 'special service' and made it clear that everything should be done to remedy the deficiencies which had been so graphically described in *The Times* and other newspapers. Although it was written in gentler terms than the missive sent to Raglan, the implication was clear. The government had been rattled by the constant stream of complaints and it expected its officers in Constantinople and the Crimea to impose stringent remedies. 'H.M's Government cannot too strongly impress upon your Lordship the importance they attach to the affording of every accommodations, and comfort to the sick and wounded of our Army,' intoned Newcastle. 'This is a sacred duty, for the due performance of which no exertion and no cost must be spared.'[12]

In time the correspondence with Paulet would become as testy as the despatches to Raglan but at the beginning of January the British commander-in-chief was fated to be the focus of Newcastle's ire. The catalogue of complaint was unyielding. Reinforcements for the Brigade of Guards had not been met at Balaklava, essential supplies remained at Varna, the horses lacked nosebags and, unaccountably, mistakes had been made in preparing names for listing in the *London Gazette*. For instance, Lieutenant-Colonel Charles Warren, 55th Regiment, should have been designated 'Lt-Col and Brevet-Colonel Charles Warren, severely wounded'.[14] As if such trivia over rank mattered at a time when the pride of Britain's armed forces were facing a far greater disaster.

To each of the complaints Raglan replied with his customary courtesy even though he knew that the shortcomings were more to do with the government's lack of foresight than with muddled local attempts to deal with a problem which, in the worst winter experienced by the Crimea in many years, was beyond any instant solution. What did upset him was the disloyalty of his subordinates who were obviously supplying Horse Guards with letters of complaint. Newcastle's letters are peppered with hints of 'private letters' and 'information drawn to my attention': in common with *The Times*, he was allowing his policy to be directed by the views of disaffected officers who publicised the army's shortcomings and Raglan's failure to counter them. 'Some of the letters written by Officers are too bad, it is a great shame to publish them, however great the mismanagement might be,' Clifford told his parents. 'I don't think it is the duty of *Officers* to write complaints in the public papers, whatever they may think or see.'[15]

Only once did Raglan loose his composure with Newcastle. His reply to the lengthy missive of reproach written on 6 January regretted that the complaints concerning 'the character and reputation of distinguished officers' had been made 'without inquiry from me or reference to them'. Otherwise he was patience personified, even when the requests were fatuous: in the midst of trying to manage an unmanageable campaign Raglan had received a request from the Society of Antiquaries for photographs to be taken 'of any ancient remains which may be observed on the route of the army'. In common with every other order received from London it was noted, filed and a staff officer was detailed to deal with it. Raglan was nothing if not thorough when it came to administration.

Unfortunately, although reserved and lacking pomposity, he lacked the common touch which soldiers often look for in their commanders. When he rode out amongst his army his lack of a recognisable uniform and the absence of a bodyguard meant that few recognised him. On the other hand Canrobert displayed considerable élan when he visited the forces; his smartly turned out cavalry escort drew admiring glances and it was not unknown for British soldiers to give them rousing cheers as they passed by their lines. The French general was also much appreciated for his oft-repeated comment that generals and infantrymen were all equal before the bullet. Raglan might have agreed – he was not incapable of showing the occasional tenderness towards his troops – but he would have died rather than express such a common sentiment.

The contrast in style only helped to underline more fundamental differences between the two armies. 'The organisation of the French is beautiful, ours a perfect disgrace,' noted a British officer, 'and I do therefore hope that, if we have another campaign, we may get rid of all the Peninsular heroes.'[16] It was not just that the French had retained their martial bearing – with their beards and their unmarked greatcoats most of the British Army did not resemble soldiers – they had better organisation and seemed to be prepared for a long war. One of the greatest differences between the two armies lay in the preparation of food: the French had huge messes to cook hot food and they were able to get it to their men in the forward trenches. This was certainly not the case in the British lines where infantrymen in the forward areas were more often than not on short commons. Just about every description of life in the trenches dwells on the inadequate rations and the failure of the transport system to get food and equipment to the men who needed it most. The experienced Bosquet simply expressed his astonishment that 'the English seem not to take very much interest in these transport aids'.

In a sense, though, the arrival of winter brought a feeling of equality to all the participants. Although the British troops were forced to endure hardships not of their making, and while the Turkish officers showed little interest in their own troops' suffering, the harsh winter weather was a great equaliser. Indeed, the Russians hoped that it would be more than that, that the great Generals *Janvier*, *Février* and *Mars* would come to their aid again, just as they had done when another Napoleon had attempted to invade their homeland. It seemed to be working too. On 9 January Sterling was sent to the forward positions occupied by the Light Division before Sevastopol and he returned that evening appalled by the 'sad misery amongst the men'. Although he had grown accustomed long since to the privations of the Balaklava garrison the conditions in the besieging army were horrendous and made worse by the complete absence of wood to light fires to keep themselves warm. As usual, it was the men who suffered worst of all, as Sterling described:

The consequence is, they cannot dry their stockings or shoes; they come in from the trenches with frost-bitten toes, swelled feet, chilblains, etc; their shoes freeze, and they cannot put them on. Those who still, in spite of this misery, continue to do their duty, often go into the trenches without shoes by preference, or they cut away the heels to get them on. None of the fine warm clothes have reached them yet. I heard of one company going in to the trenches fourteen men strong; all the rest, dead, sick, broken. One night lately, forty-five men went into the trenches, of whom nineteen were sent out during the night; nine died. If this goes on the trenches must be abandoned, or occupied by the French, lest we should be annihilated.

Sterling shuddered to think what would become of his beloved Highlanders if they were sent into the trenches. 'Alas,' he exclaimed, 'it makes me very sad to see such men lost in such a way.'[17]

With the worst of the winter weather came the unsettling rumour that Austria was about to throw in its lot with the allies. The French received the news with acclaim, hoping that the alliance would bring military reinforcements to the siege. The British commanders were not so sure: many feared that the new arrangement would lead to a peace settlement and that the army's suffering would have been in vain before they could defeat the Russians. The government shared those fears and on 12 January Newcastle reminded Raglan that his first duty remained the vigorous prosecution of the war:

> Her Majesty will not be advised to demit any cessation of hostilities, because the Government is convinced that negotiations for peace will be accelerated by vigorous prosecution of the operation in which the Allied Armies are engaged; and that important military successes are most likely to bring the war to an honourable conclusion.
>
> Without therefore giving your Lordship any new instructions in any way fettering that discretion as to the mode of conducting it, with which from the first you have been invested, I have to instruct you to continue all hostile operations against the enemy, without reference to the reports of negotiations which may reach you from various sources.[18]

It was to be a long hard slog before those hopes were realised, particularly as Raglan knew that his army was too enfeebled to begin a fresh assault on Sevastopol. Already the French were being asked to assist with the transport between the besieging lines and Balaklava and this extra work caused a good deal of friction. Added to the constant demands for food and equipment made by hundreds of starving British soldiers, the French began to feel that their allies were unable to prosecute the war on equal terms. Ahead lay the kind of command and control problems which Clarendon and others had forecast even before hostilities had begun. As the winter weather conditions scythed down Raglan's army the French grew stronger and in Constantinople they were slowly building up an army of reserves. Gradually they were waxing stronger and therefore becoming the dominant force while the British were 'toujours en retard', 'always late'. It was not a good omen for the future conduct of the war.

8

Muddle in Washington, Progress in Vienna

> We must, as long as Russia will not negotiate for peace, frankly
> unite with the policy of the sea powers and have the courage to
> say so on all sides.
>
> *Count Buol-Schauenstein to the Emperor Franz Josef,*
> *September 1854*

As the year drew to a close Tsar Nicholas had no reason to feel dissatisfied with Russia's position. In the Crimea Sevastopol was secure and the allies had failed to inflict a convincing defeat on the Russian field army. Despite the destruction of Bomarsund, the Baltic would not be troubled again until the spring and in the meantime Kronstad and Sveaborg were being reinforced. In the Far East, on Russia's Pacific front, allied naval forces had been driven off, and in the strategically important Caucasus region the Turks were bottled up in Kars and Erzerum. And from their observation of the forces outside Sevastopol Russian commanders were only too well aware of the desperate plight facing the allies in the Crimea. True, Russia had suffered the indignity of losing command of the Black Sea and of seeing foreign forces invading her territory but there was still considerable optimism that, come the spring, the position could be reversed. In that hope Nicholas was much encouraged by the renewal of peace talks, even though they had been instigated by the ungrateful Austrians.

From the outset of the conflict Austria had cast itself in the role of peace-maker, while at the same time reserving the right to protect its longer-term interests. Having forced the Russians to leave the principalities during the summer, their immediate strategic aims had been achieved but their foreign minister, Buol, was well aware that the allies' prosecution of the war posed sensitive problems for Austria's future well-being. The longer the fighting continued, the more shrill would become the demands for Austria to throw in its lot with the allies and, if that were to happen, the Austrians would be placed in a hazardous position. Not only would they have to contribute substantial ground forces to the war effort but, whatever the outcome of the conflict, they would incur Russia's wrath.

It was a difficult balancing act but Buol, with his wide diplomatic experience, including a spell as Austrian ambassador in London, was not unequal to the task. Tall and elegant, with aquiline features, he was a traditional diplomat who believed that he had to subjugate his own preferences to his country's wishes and in that respect he served Austria well. Crucially, he had the emperor's ear and was able to direct foreign policy with little political interference, largely because Franz Josef shared his foreign minister's fears about Russia. Buol's enemies, especially those in the army who doubted the wisdom of pursuing an over-aggressive foreign policy, thought him devious and shallow and they made much of the fact that the minister's great mentor, Count Metternich, had likened him to a knife with a sharp point but no cutting edge.

There was probably some truth to the jibe – Buol frequently allowed his concern about Russian expansionism to blind him to the wider picture – but he was alive to the conundrum which faced him, namely that Austria had to find a solution to the conflict without embroiling its armed forces. In this respect he was not helped by having to adopt a different posture when he dealt with each of the protagonists. He and Nesselrode had a good understanding and the Austrian ambassador in St Petersburg, Count Valentin Esterhazy, was a sound diplomat, but the Russian chancellor's movements were circumscribed by his uneasy relationship with the tsar. With France Buol had the ear of Drouyn de Lhuys who was increasingly anxious to extricate his country's armed forces from what was becoming an expensive adventure. Having rejected his earlier initiatives the Porte remained an awkward problem but Buol believed that the Sultan would respond to any plan which checked Russian threats against Turkey.

However, the British were an enigma and, with good reason, Buol did not trust them. Throughout the frantic negotiations which had preceded the war Clarendon had treated Austria with ill-disguised condescension. The British foreign secretary wanted Austria's military support – the necessity grew more desperate the longer the fighting continued – but he did not want to gain it at the price of pursuing peace before the war was over. As the need to check Russian expansionism towards the Mediterranean would have unwelcome repercussions for Austria's multi-national empire, especially for its holdings in the Balkans, Clarendon thought it better to remain secretive about Britain's war aims. On 27 September Clarendon explained the position to Russell:

> Nothing would alarm her [Austria] more than England and France taking up their permanent abode on the edge of the Black Sea, having the command of Constantinople and of the mouths of the Danube and being ready to revolutionise the Slaves [*sic*] and Hungarians if necessary.[1]

To that end Clarendon hoped that a *casus belli* would draw Austria into the war without the need for further diplomatic discussions. Here he pinned his hopes on the Austrian and Turkish forces which were occupying the principalities. After the Alma, in one of his last directives, Saint-Arnaud had pressed the Turks to make a demonstration across the River Pruth to attack the Russian forces in Bessarabia. The French marshal was thinking in military terms and his request was seconded by Raglan but Clarendon saw another advantage to the move. If the Turkish troops in Moldavia were to open a new front the fighting could draw the Austrian garrison into the conflict, especially if, as anticipated, Omar Pasha's army was forced to retire. A fresh Russian attack on the principalities would invoke Austria's treaty with Prussia and with it would come the prospect of a grand alliance to keep Russia contained once and for all. But everything hung on a sequence of events which would begin with Turkey attacking across the Pruth. In an attempt to force the Turks to take this course of action Stratford mounted a vigorous campaign in Constantinople to persuade the Turks to act, but he found no takers. Omar was uncomfortably aware that approaching winter made such a course of action impossible and, besides, he did not want to surrender any territorial advantage to the Austrian forces in the region.

For their part, Austrian commanders in Moldavia knew only too well that the failure of any Turkish demonstration would compromise

their own position. The result was stalemate. The Austrians made
no attempt to help the Turks move their forces and Omar was
quite happy to stay put for the time being. When the Earl of
Westmorland, the British ambassador in Vienna, pressed Buol to
end the Austrian obfuscation the foreign minister smoothly replied:
'I cannot but suppose that there had been some misunderstandings
upon this subject.' The deadlock was only broken at the beginning
of November when Raglan made urgent representations for Omar's
forces to be sent to Varna prior to reinforcing the allies before
Sevastopol. Not unnaturally this had the support of Austria because,
as Westmorland reported on 15 November, it removed from them
the untimely need to assist an attack which might drag them into a
costly war:

> Count Buol would consider any serious invasion of the Dobrudsha
> [sic] by the Russian army and their advance upon Varna or against
> the Balkans as the aggressive act which would lead to the casus
> belli which is contemplated in the Convention with Prussia, so
> that any portion of the Turkish army may be sent with safety to
> the Crimea. Count Buol is however persuaded that the Russians
> never would make so dangerous a movement as the one in ques-
> tion. He recommends that the Turkish reinforcements to the
> Allied Armies at Sebastopol should if possible be expedited.[2]

Shortage of transports meant that the Turkish forces could not
be moved until January 1855 but by then the question of Austrian
involvement was no longer dependent on diplomatic and military
manoeuvre. Instead everything hung on Russia's acceptance of an
agreement known as the Four Points which had been signed in Vienna
on 8 August by the Austrian, British and French governments. This
called for Russia to accept the following four demands as a basis for
a lasting peace agreement:

> 1. Russia to renunciate territorial claims in Serbia and the
> principalities and the substitution of guarantees by the European
> powers.
> 2. Freedom of navigation in the Danube.
> 3. Revision of the Straits Convention of 1841.
> 4. Joint European guarantees of rights for the Christians in
> the Ottoman Empire.

To no one's great surprise, Russia had refused initially to accept the conditions but that did not prevent Buol from continuing to promote them as a basis for negotiation. In keeping with its policy of no peace talks while the war was continuing, Britain remained lukewarm but the French were eager to maintain the momentum. With that in mind Buol concentrated the pressure on Drouyn de Lhuys and Count de Bourqueney, the French ambassador in Vienna. On 13 September Westmorland reported that, following discussions with the Austrian foreign minister and the French ambassador, it was proposed to work towards a peace conference 'which would have for its object to discuss and defuse in separate acts the questions of internal organisation which are referred to in the Four Articles.'[3]

Clarendon was not impressed. He had little confidence in Westmorland, describing him to colleagues as a foolish old woman who was out of touch with reality. This was somewhat harsh. Westmorland might well have been of advanced years – he was seventy and, like so many participants in the Crimea, he had fought in the Napoleonic Wars – but, having served previously as minister in Berlin, he was a fluent German speaker who had a good rapport with the Austrians. One other virtue gave him additional credibility in Vienna. He was passionate about music and had been responsible for establishing the Royal Academy of Music in 1827. His seven operas might have been politely received and quickly forgotten but there was no doubting the intensity of the delight he took in matters musical. In Vienna that counted for much.

Throughout October Westmorland worked assiduously with Bourqueney to bring Austria into the war on terms which would be acceptable to London and Paris, telling Clarendon on 2 October that he had not 'ceased to urge upon Count Buol the importance of a closer union of the Three Powers and the necessity of making every possible effort to secure the object of the Allies by conducting the present War to a successful conclusion.'[4] This was all very well but Clarendon was becoming impatient. Either the Austrians joined the alliance or they stayed outside and forfeited any claim to participation in the peace talks which would follow the successful conclusion of the war. Two days later Westmorland reported again, this time to explain Buol's reasons for holding out:

Count Buol remarked that while his government had never let it be understood that they would make a casus belli of the refusal of Russia to accept the Four Points, they had on the other hand never declared that they would not have recourse to arms to oblige Russia to sign a just and equitable peace, but it was impossible to disguise the very critical position in which Austria was placed, for although the assistance of Prussia and her German allies had been promised to her in case she should be attacked by Russia, that assistance could hardly be counted upon at the present moment if she took the initiative by declaring War and commencing hostilities, and she might find herself exposed alone to the attacks of Russia during a winter campaign.[5]

With the despatch came a proposal for a limited defensive treaty which Clarendon wanted to reject straightaway because it fell short of any real commitment to the war effort. However, in Paris, the plan was greeted with enthusiasm by Drouyn de Lhuys who had just received an extraordinary telegram from Buol congratulating him on the allied victory at the Alma. The French foreign minister wanted to exploit this diplomatic gaffe and he was much encouraged when the Austrian ambassador, Count Hübner, reported to him on 13 October that Russia had lodged an official complaint because the congratulations had been made in Franz Josef's name. Typically, the ambassador, better known for his social climbing than for any diplomatic ability, leaked the information to the French press. Surely this would provide the impetus to draw Austria into a defensive/offensive alliance for her own future safety.

Viewing the unfolding events from the British Embassy Cowley was aghast. He trusted neither the Austrians nor the French; the former because they would not pledge their active participation and the latter because he believed that they were working to a different agenda. In both cases his instincts were not misplaced. Buol was indeed hedging his bets. In France's case Cowley's intuition was sharpened by his close ties to the emperor. From his discussions with Napoleon III and his ministers he could see that the war against Russia provided France with a wonderful opportunity to smash for ever the constraints which had been put in place against her at the Congress of Vienna in 1815. A treaty with Austria would destroy the international order which prevented France from reasserting her authority in Europe: it would sunder the Holy Alliance and remove the Russian influence which kept French ambitions in check.

Cowley also had a good understanding of France's broader war aims.

These included the establishment of a separate Kingdom of Poland which would be ruled by Napoleon III's cousin, the Prince Napoleon. Wallachia and Moldavia would be combined into a new kingdom of Romania. Italy would be freed from Austrian domination and France would extend her borders to the left bank of the Rhine. With typical understatement Cowley found the proposals 'unfortunate' and hinted to Clarendon that the raising of the Polish question was 'more likely to throw her [Austria] back into the arms of Russia'. However, in the autumn of 1854 he was sufficiently alarmed by France's cynical manipulation to send a regular stream of warnings back to the Foreign Office.[6]

On 23 October the British cabinet met to discuss the Austrian proposals and duly rejected them. However, they did agree to pursue the idea of another conference in Vienna in the expectation that nothing would come of it. There the matter was allowed to rest, firstly because the British and French governments were increasingly preoccupied with the reports of the fighting from the Crimea and second, because France suddenly found itself on the brink of war with the United States.

This was one of the most bizarre episodes in a war which had already shown a tendency to throw up the unexpected. France had previously found reason to object to the presence in Madrid of the US Minister Pierre Soulé, not least because he had fought a duel with their own ambassador. In short, Soulé was a pest. His dislike of monarchical regimes and his revolutionary fervour were unlikely to be met with acclaim in most European capitals and he had already attempted to make political capital out of the European preoccupation with the Eastern Question. Then, at the very point when Drouyn de Lhuys was preoccupied by the negotiations with Buol, Soulé let it be known that he intended to visit France on his way back to Spain from a meeting in London. Ostensibly the request was made to enable him to visit his birthplace and to talk to French workers' leaders but the French Foreign Ministry was in little doubt that he was simply making mischief.

A week earlier, he and two fellow US diplomats – James Buchanan from London and John Mason from Paris – had met, first in Ostend and then in Aix-la-Chappelle, to discuss Cuba and to test possible British and French reactions to US annexation. The result of their deliberation was the Ostend Manifesto, which proposed a more energetic US policy towards Cuba, if need be with the use of military force. The meeting was supposed to be secret but so boastful had Soulé been in Madrid that the entire European diplomatic community knew what was about to unfold. Not wanting to support a diplomat who was working against Spanish interests and knowing that Soulé had already been in contact with republicans opposed to him, Napoleon III refused to grant the US Minister permission to enter France.

This was in keeping with diplomatic protocol: an ambassador required an invitation to make an official visit to another country and the French were within their rights. However, the hot-headed Louisianan senator was not the kind of man to accept the emperor's refusal meekly. On 25 October he arrived in Calais only to be turned away by the immigration authorities because he lacked the necessary papers. Washington reacted angrily. Mason was ordered to write to Drouyn de Lhuys informing him that the exclusion of the US Minister 'cannot but be regarded by the Government and people of the United States, not only as a most unusual and humiliating act towards the Minister personally, but as a national indignity of very grave character, only to be extenuated by facts established as conclusive proofs'.[7]

As the communications became more bad-tempered Cowley told Clarendon in some alarm on 29 October that the Soulé affair had the makings of a fully blown diplomatic crisis. The British foreign secretary had already had cause to remonstrate with the US over Soulé's activities in Madrid and six days earlier he had received a despatch from the Washington embassy warning that the United States was on the point of establishing a base at San Domingo 'in a position so menacing to the islands of Cuba and Puerto Rico'.[8] Clearly this would threaten British interests but, not wanting to complicate the already complex relationship with the United States in Central America, Clarendon preferred caution to further confrontation. However, to his horror, Cowley then reported that France was actively considering the possibility of going to war against the United States. During a heated meeting at the French foreign ministry on 29 October Drouyn de Lhuys angrily stated that he would 'prefer a war with the United States to the danger of allowing democratic principles to gain the upper hand in this country. A war with the United States could not be fatal to France but another revolution might be. It was the duty of the French Government to prevent, by all means at their disposal, the mischief which might arise were former revolutionists allowed to circulate freely throughout the country.'[9]

While it is difficult to see how France could have prosecuted a war against the United States – her navy was already overstretched by the operations in the Baltic and the Black Sea – Clarendon was sufficiently appalled by the crisis to urge Cowley to enter into immediate talks with Drouyn de Lhuys and to force him to see reason. The last thing the British wanted was a deepening transatlantic crisis: in the middle of a war which was not going their way, the allies could not afford any diversion which might affect Washington's neutrality. President Franklin Pierce had previously made it clear that a dim view would be taken of any attempt to interfere with American shipping on the high seas and Clarendon had already used up much patience convincing the president that the embargo of the Russian ports should not cause any trouble to US shipmasters provided that they kept to its terms. Shortly before the outbreak of hostilities he had reassured Buchanan on this point, telling him that 'the neutral flag shall protect the cargo except in the case of contraband'.

It was a sensible precaution because the Russian *chargé d'affaires* at Washington, Alexander Andrevich Bodisco, had been attempting earlier to play on the maritime rivalries which existed between the United States and Britain over the Cuban slave trade. Although Washington had decided against invading the island, Pierce's administration was still anxious to protect its territorial interests at a time when Spain, backed by Britain, wanted to emancipate Cuba's slaves. To the secretary of state, William Learned Marcy, this would make Cuba 'an African colony given over to barbarism' and he warned Buchanan in London that it was 'an act which, in its consequences, must be injurious to the United States'. In an attempt to find a solution which fell short of force – US planters in the southern states warned that the emancipation would be 'dangerous and pernicious' – Soulé was given authority on 3 April to offer Spain $120 million for outright possession of the island. Furthermore, he was told to 'direct [your] efforts to . . . detach that island from the Spanish dominion and from all dependence on any European power'.[10]

Washington's preoccupation with Cuba provided the Russians with a useful lever. Spurred on by Nesselrode, Bodisco had produced a paper proposing the enlistment of American privateers to attack British shipping: the wages would be provided by Russia and the lure would be booty and trade. Following his untimely death in January, Bodisco was succeeded by Edouard de Stoeckl who was travelling through America on his way to take up a junior diplomatic appointment in Hawaii but was forced to stay on in Washington to take Bodisco's place. With his fluent English and easy manners he soon became a favourite in Washington society, so much so that he was promoted ambassador in 1857, an appointment made soon after his marriage to a Massachussetts lady, Elizabeth Howard, whom he described to the Russian foreign office as 'American, Protestant, without property'.

Shortly after his arrival, Stoeckl went one step further than his predecessor. He suggested that funds should be made available to persuade a US merchant ship to break the blockade. When it was stopped by the Royal Navy the confrontation might provide the *casus belli* which would bring the US into the war on Russia's side. Stoeckl was well aware that the long-standing dispute over Cuba could provide a suitably tendentious background for the plan to work – throughout the period southern senators would routinely call for action to be taken against Britain whenever a US slave ship was searched by Royal Navy cruisers in the Caribbean. Senator James Henry Hammond of South Carolina was a typical, if overly bellicose, promoter of the cause: he thought that any seizure of a US merchant ship provided 'a just and ample cause for war'.

Nesselrode liked the idea of instigating trouble on the high seas, telling Stoeckl '*les idées qu'ils expriment ont fixé tout l'attention de l'empereur*' ('their ideas have become the focus of the emperor's thoughts') and asked him to continue investigating the possibility of employing a Yankee privateer to play the role of blockade-buster. Clarendon's guarantees to Buchanan had taken the gloss off the idea but on 10 April 1854 Nesselrode was again urging Stoeckl to keep up the pressure in Washington:

> *Cultiver nos excellentes relations avec les États Unis, les faire fructifier dans un commun intérêt et préparer ainsi les voies à une heureuse entente sur les questions que l'avenir peut présenter, c'est à quoi jamais user dorénavant les soins de la Mission Impériale à Washington.*[11]

On one level Stoeckl did not have to work too hard to fulfil that order because he enjoyed good relations with the White House. Described on his election in 1852 as a 'northern man with southern

---

★ 'Cultivate our good relations with the United States, make them yield a common interest and in this way prepare the path for a happy entente over the questions which the future might bring. From now on make sure you benefit from the care bestowed on the Imperial Mission in Washington.'

principles', President Franklin Pierce was inclined to favour Russia which he viewed as the greatest of the European powers and his secretary of state, Marcy, was distinctly anti-British. In July 1854, following the signing of a treaty between the two countries restating the principle that 'free ships make free goods', Marcy told the Russian ambassador to pay careful attention to Alaska as, despite a public avowal by Clarendon that Britain would not attack Russian-America, as Alaska was known, he believed that Palmerston had plans to send amphibious forces to invade the colony. Nesselrode was sufficiently impressed by the warning to pass it on to the local governor but the threat never materialised. The failure of the Royal Navy's operations against Petropaulovsk put a stop to further adventures in the Pacific and the harsh reality was that Britain lacked the resources to open another front.

None the less, the sudden impasse over Soulé was a vexation which the Foreign Office, concerned as it was about the siege of Sevastopol, did not need. That much became apparent when Buchanan visited Clarendon on 28 October, his first audience since the revelation of the Ostende Manifesto. Following the usual diplomatic niceties – 'bagatelle' to the American – the conversation turned to Cuba and to British press hostility, subjects which Buchanan 'treated in the jesting manner they deserved', because, as he explained to Marcy, the British seemed to be incapable of understanding the United States' sense of self-esteem. Small wonder that its President was so irritated by France's prohibition of a US official, a matter on which Washington was prepared to make a stand because it 'could not afford to submit patiently to such indignity'.

While Clarendon listened in silence, Buchanan explained that he did not blame Britain. The villain of the piece was Napoleon – 'a despot [who] regards the existence and the rapid advances of the United States as a standing censure upon his usurpation and his tyranny' – and as a result of his over-arching influence he might drag Britain into a war with the United States. Although Clarendon said that the idea of war was preposterous Buchanan was not convinced. Three days later he sent a lengthy despatch to Marcy outlining his fears that Napoleon was close to making an 'attempt to humble us by one of those bold strokes in which he much delights', and if that were to happen the United States would be isolated:

In case of a rupture between us and the Allies, or what is more probable, between us and France alone, he [Tsar Nicholas] could render us but little service. The contest would be purely by sea; because no European Power, it is presumed, would commit the folly of landing forces on our Continent, although I have been informed that individuals near the Emperor Napoleon express the belief that the Union is ready to fall to pieces on the slavery question.[12]

With Washington and Paris beating the war drums Clarendon made immediate contact with Cowley, asking him to come up with a solution, and was relieved to receive a placatory despatch the following day. Cowley wrote:

Finding the French Government determined to maintain the prohibition against Soulé, I suggested that it should have been explained as referring only to a stay in France, but not to his passage through France on his way to his post. I hope this may come to be adopted.[13]

It was. Somewhat pompously Drouyn de Lhuys declared that that explanation had always been his intention and Soulé was granted permission to return to Madrid on 10 November, travelling, albeit at a leisurely pace, through Paris and Bordeaux. A crisis had been averted, the allies could return to the more pressing business in the Crimea, and a relieved Clarendon telegraphed his thanks to Cowley:

Mr Soulé has doubtless earned for himself an unenviable notoriety, and the Government of the Emperor has on more than one occasion had cause to resent his conduct, but a rupture between France and the United States would at this moment be a deplorable waste, and by creating a diversion in favour of Russia would affect most prejudicially the great questions now pending in Europe.[14]

Then nemesis took a hand. On Soulé's return to Madrid the contents of the Ostende Manifesto were revealed in the *New York Herald* and there was outrage over its piratical proposal that, if Spain would not sell Cuba, then 'by every law, human and divine, we [the US] shall be justified in wresting it from Spain if we possess the power'. Against that background Drouyn de Lhuys had been right to feel so alarmed, but Soulé had over-reached himself. The threat of force inherent in the Ostende Manifesto put the United States in a bad light and the US press united against the minister in Madrid. The *Boston Atlas* spoke for many conservative Americans on 16 November when it attacked Soulé's 'reputation as a brawler, an intriguer, a manufacturer of revolutions and a fomenter of treasons'. Inevitably, Marcy came under pressure to sack him – which he did the following February and the mercurial Soulé disappeared from the diplomatic scene.

A crisis had been averted but it was not the end of the tensions between the allies and the US. While Buchanan, a genuine anglophile, was convinced that Britain would 'make any sacrifice' rather than go to war with the United States, the disagreements over Cuba and Central America remained a running sore throughout the Crimean War and, before the year was out, the US Minister in London was forced to concede that there was a growing irritation amongst some sections of the British public that 'their transatlantic cousins should seem to sympathise with the Russians rather than with themselves'.[15] Those suspicions certainly ruled out the United States as a possible mediator: at various stages throughout the war the House of Representatives discussed this possibility, but the matter was always dropped when it became clear that Britain would never agree to a close friend of Russia intervening in a European conflict. The matter was closed in December when the Foreign Relations Committee agreed that the most impartial mediators were the Austrians and that the matter should be left in Buol's hands.

In fact, a breakthrough was already in the offing. Following the Soulé impasse Buol, aided by the intervention of King Friedrich Wilhelm IV of Prussia, finally persuaded Tsar Nicholas to accept the Four Points unconditionally. With Russia agreeing to attend a peace conference in Vienna, Austria felt sufficiently confident to enter into the long anticipated treaty with Britain and France on 2 December. Its terms did not oblige Austria to enter the war but it did bring a change of alignment for the allies. Britain remained suspicious, with Clarendon warning the Cabinet that Austria might try to 'detach' France from its alliance with Britain. His fears were heightened by a lengthy despatch from Cowley pointing out that France would use the treaty to pursue its own agenda in Europe:

I cannot too often invite your Lordship's attention to the fact that the Emperor has, in his dealings with Austria, two objects in view – the one [to] obtain if possible her military cooperation in the war with Russia – the other by separating her from Russia to put an end to the Northern Coalition, the basic object of which, since 1815, has been to hold France in check.[16]

This was closer to the truth than Cowley imagined. On 10 December Edouard Thouvenel, head of the French Foreign Ministry's political section, received a note from the French embassy in Constantinople congratulating him for his part in securing the new deal: 'You have mortally wounded the Holy Alliance and given it a first-class funeral.'[17] At the same time, following an audience with Napoleon III, the British ambassador was obliged to report that the emperor was intent on using Austrian influence to sue for an immediate peace, a move which was against British interests. Not only would it bring the war to an unsatisfactory conclusion but it would prevent the allies from enlisting Austrian military support. Something had to be done to avoid that possibility and the result was a secret manoeuvre to sabotage the Austrian plan.

It was disarmingly simple. When the British Cabinet met on 13 December it agreed to enter into a secret agreement with France over the third point. While Austria would be told that Britain and France wanted a revision of the Straits Convention which would bring an end to Russian domination in the Black Sea, a confidential Franco-British protocol would call for the destruction of Sevastopol and the limitation of the Russian fleet to four warships – a draconian measure which would eliminate Russia's influence in Europe. Although Drouyn de Lhuys urged rejection of the British proposal, Napoleon was sufficiently pragmatic to accept it on 19 December. Obviously, at that crucial stage in the war, keeping the cross-Channel alliance intact was preferable to uncertainty of throwing France's lot in with Austria.

The story of the subsequent Vienna Conference does not bring much credit to British or French diplomacy. Both countries went into it with little prospect of achieving a solution, preferring instead to use it as a means of bringing Austria into the war. Even before it began Cowley warned Clarendon that Drouyn de Lhuys had hinted that 'the Negotiations, if begun, might easily be protracted to gain time, and that, in the meanwhile, every effort should be made to strike a serious blow in the Crimea'. He also passed on a warning that France's long-term aim was to bring other countries into the war in return for territorial gains – the German Confederation would be rewarded with Schleswig, Prussia with Holstein, and Sweden with Finland. With some satisfaction Cowley reported that the proposals should not be taken seriously and that Britain's French allies had much to learn in the field of international diplomacy:

> It is in vain, I grieve to say it, to hope that a French minister may be made to understand that such proceedings not only are not honest in themselves but lead generally to the very reverse of what is anticipated from them. I shall be more careful in future when I see any indication of such exuberant fancies on the part of Monsieur Drouyn de Lhuys to combat them at once.[18]

Clarendon was in a dilemma. He hoped that the conference would not reach an unnecessary compromise yet he wanted Britain's voice to be heard, if only to make sure that France did not make any political capital. As he did not trust Westmorland he argued that a senior figure be sent with plenipotentiary powers and the choice fell on Lord John Russell, whom Clarendon believed to be 'quite incapable of making a peace that would be inglorious or unsafe'. The former foreign secretary and prime minister was well equipped for the task but before he departed he was bombarded with advice about the necessity of preserving British interests by waiting for a decisive military victory before making any deals with the Russians. From Constantinople Stratford had been charged with representing the Porte's case and he argued that much more effort had to be put into the war before the allies could return the sword to the scabbard:

> To hear my new Austrian colleagues, one would suppose that the most sanguine hopes might be reasonably entertained. But, eagerly as I long for such a peace as Europe may own with satisfaction, I cannot entirely blot out the past, or entirely forget the character and policy of our antagonist, as to count upon his submission under present circumstances. What I am certain of is that the sincerity of Russia will be fairly tested under your auspices.[19]

Russell, too, was in a difficult position. By the time he set off for Vienna Aberdeen's administration had fallen and he himself had failed in an attempt to establish an alternative government. While he had

Clarendon's ear, the new prime minister, Lord Palmerston, did not trust him, thinking him too impetuous and given to being influenced by others. It was a fair observation. Russell went to Vienna convinced that Russia had to be defeated before there could be any peace talks but during the lengthy negotiations he would allow himself to be swayed by Buol's argument that Russia could be contained and Turkey protected by a defensive alliance consisting of Austria, Britain and France.

Before the plenipotentiaries met in Vienna – France was represented by de Bourqueney, later by Drouyn de Lhuys, Russia by their ambassador Prince Alexander Gorchakov, cousin to the general of the same name – there was another diplomatic coup. On 26 January, following lengthy negotiations in which the French took the leading part, the Italian state of Piedmont-Sardinia joined the war on the allied side and agreed to send 15,000 troops to the Crimea. For the country's ambitious prime minister, Camillo di Cavour, it was a shrewd move. With the support of King Victor Emmanuel II, who had come to the throne in 1852, he had begun the process of strengthening Piedmont-Sardinia by introducing democratic reforms and rebuilding its economy and, more importantly, its army. In addition to the obvious benefits introduced to the country, Cavour hoped that Piedmont-Sardinia's growing strength would convince the Great Powers that supporters of Italian unity were not the dangerous revolutionaries of 1848 but reliable statesmen. Entering the Crimean war on the allies' side was simply further proof that the Sardinians were mature and could be trusted.

The goodwill stood him in good stead. In return for sending forces under the command of General La Marmora, Cavour was able to encourage Napoleon III to support him in his dreams of uniting Italy under the auspices of Piedmont-Sardinia. As that would entail driving Austria out of the northern Italian states, Cavour needed military support and in France he found an ally in the summer of 1858 with the conclusion of a secret alliance at Plombières in the Vosges. A few months later, in the spring of 1859, French troops were fighting on Piedmont-Sardinia's side in its campaign to liberate Lombardy and the Veneto. Some of those soldiers had served together outside the walls of Sevastopol: as Cavour prophesied correctly at the time he agreed to help the allies in the Crimea, 'There is only one effective solution of the Italian question: cannon.'

Britain, too, gained from the agreement. Raglan's army demanded reinforcements and despite French interference it was agreed that, in return for a payment of £1 million, the Sardinians would come under British command. It was a welcome addition: despite the recent reinforcements the British Army before Sevastopol had begun 1855 little more than 25,000-strong. 'I believe we cannot muster more than 12,000 bayonets in the English Army,' Henry Clifford told his parents in one of the first letters he wrote in 1855. 'If the weather, with its consequent hardships, is to continue till the end of March, what will become of us?'[20]

9

'Pam' Enters the Fray

Incompetence, lethargy, aristocratic hauteur, official indifference, favour, routine, perverseness and stupidity reign, revel and riot in the camp before Sebastopol, in the harbour of Balaclava, in the hospitals of Scutari, and how much nearer to home we do not venture to say.

Leading article, The Times, *23 December 1854*

It was not just in the Crimea that the weather was bad. London, too, was suffering from the worst effects of a harsh winter and the damp freezing fog seemed to echo the air of concern that gripped the country. When parliament reconvened after its Christmas break on 23 January 1854 the atmosphere was sombre and concerned, almost as if the succession of bad news from the Crimea had sapped the government's collective will. Its handling of the war had already attracted the opposition of Richard Cobden and John Bright, and the two men were soon to continue the onslaught: early in the new session the latter used the language of the Old Testament to argue his case: 'The angel of death has been abroad throughout the land; you may almost hear the beating of his wings.' Disraeli, too, had added his voice to the chorus of complaint, chiding the government that while they had set out to fight a major war they had only provided for a small one.

Despite those attacks, Aberdeen's coalition had managed to survive, but it was a desperate kind of durability. Cracks were beginning to appear and as the conduct of the war had become such a public scandal it seemed to be only a matter of time before the government fell to bits. Lord John Russell had already called for the sacking of Newcastle and his replacement by Palmerston and although the secretary for war had been saved by the support of his fellow Peelites, Russell retaliated by signalling his intention to quit his office. When 1855 began that threat of resignation still hung heavily in the air but the catalyst for the government's destruction turned out to be not a Cabinet minister but a backbench Member of Parliament – John Arthur Roebuck. During the opening session the flamboyant barrister and member for Sheffield announced his intention to call for the appointment of a select committee of the House of Commons to investigate the conduct of the war in the Crimea. When the motion was debated two days later it was supported by two well respected MPs, Augustus Stafford and John Henry Layard, both of whom had recently returned from the war zone and knew only too well how badly matters were faring. Indeed, Layard was one of the few British politicians who knew anything about the region, having excavated the ancient Mesopotamian city of Nineveh and having served as an attaché at the Constantinople embassy under Stratford in 1849. In the resulting vote on 28 January, 85 government supporters deserted the Aberdeen coalition and Roebuck's proposal was carried by 305 votes to 148.

Worse, by then Russell had carried out his threat to resign, arguing that he could not vote against a motion which supported his belief that the war was being badly handled by the War Office. On the opening day of parliament he put his case succinctly to Aberdeen:

> I do not see how this motion is to be resisted. But, as it involves a censure upon the War Department, with which some of my colleagues are connected, my only course is to tender my resignation.[1]

Coming on top of Roebuck's initiative, the resignation left the Aberdeen coalition mortally damaged and for his pains Russell was the target of a great deal of Peelite obloquy, especially from those of Aberdeen's supporters who believed that he had carried out his threat in order to further his own career. Had he been able to garner the necessary support he might have achieved his wish to succeed Aberdeen as prime minister but his former colleagues were in no mood to serve him. Following the resignation of Aberdeen's ministry the Queen approached Lord Derby, the leader of the opposition who

had hoped to appoint a fresh coalition with Palmerston as secretary
for war. That, too, fell on stony ground as Palmerston would not
serve without Clarendon in the Cabinet and the fastidious foreign
secretary had already made it clear that he would not serve under
Derby. Clarendon also turned down the opportunity to form his own
government, as did the aged Lord Lansdowne who had no further
wish to remain in government.

The succession of refusals left the way open for Palmerston. Earlier in her reign Victoria had made it clear that an irreconcilable
gulf existed between her and the man she was about to ask to
form a government but, having listened to Clarendon's warning
that 'none other could take the helm', she was forced to ignore
her heartfelt feeling that 'Ld Palmerston is somewhat of a *trial*'.
Having been asked to form a government on 4 February he set
about the difficult task of creating a new administration. Of the
old Aberdeen coalition only Argyll (postmaster-general), Clarendon
(foreign secretary), Gladstone (chancellor of the exchequer), Graham
(first lord of the Admiralty) and Herbert (colonial secretary) agreed
to serve under him.

The greatest changes took place at the War Office where the
positions of secretary for war and secretary at war were combined
and the position given to Lord Panmure. A bluff and stubborn Scot
who had already served in Melbourne's ministry of 1835–41 and under
Russell between 1846 and 1852, he had some military experience,
having spent twelve years with the 79th Highlanders and knew many
of the officers serving in the Crimea. During his military service he
gained a name for being free with his money and had fallen foul of his
domineering father William Maule, the first Baron Panmure, who had
virtually cut him off from his inheritance. By the time he came to office
again Panmure's girth had encouraged the nickname of the 'Bull' and
although friends rallied to his side by propagating the more warlike
sobriquet of 'Mars', he was unable to shake off a reputation for being
something of a figure of fun. That opinion was unwittingly reinforced
when he sent off a despatch to Raglan's headquarters requesting the
staff to look after the interests of his nephew, an officer by the name
of Dowbiggin. For reasons which are not entirely clear, but which
obviously caused great mirth at the time, the despatch gave rise to
a popular and much-used catch-phrase. Whenever things seemed to
be going wrong, not an infrequent occurrence in the Crimea, young
officers would roar with laughter and say 'Take care of Dowb!' To his

credit Panmure was industrious and painstaking but he was frequently out of his depth. Recurrent and painful spells of gout did not help.

It was an untried team but the public loved it. 'Pam' was the man who would restore the country's fortunes and bring the war to a satisfactory conclusion. On 17 February *Punch* caught the mood with a cartoon showing Palmerston as a boxer about to take on Russia: 'NOW FOR IT! A set-to between "Pam, the Downing Street pet" and "The Russian Spider."' That was what the country wanted: an early end to the war and an end, too, to the blunders which had well-nigh destroyed the British Army. But no sooner had the new government taken office than it was plunged into fresh disarray with the resignations of Gladstone, Graham and Herbert who opposed the acceptance of Roebuck's proposal for a committee of inquiry when it was debated again on 21 February. They were replaced by Clarendon's friend Sir George Cornewall Lewis (chancellor of the exchequer) and Sir Charles Wood (Admiralty), while Russell was told that he would succeed Herbert as secretary for the colonies once the negotiations in Vienna had come to an end.

In the Crimea the fall of the Aberdeen government and the replacement of Newcastle with Panmure was met with concern and uncertainty. To the soldiers in the field the political machinations in London were an unwelcome distraction but if Raglan thought that the new appointments would stop the constant stream of criticisms from Horse Guards, he was to be rudely mistaken. On 12 February Panmure put his name to a letter of complaint which exceeded anything written by his predecessor. Its opening tone was discouraging: 'I cannot find that your Lordship has been in the habit of keeping Her Majesty's Government acquainted in a clear and succinct manner with the operations with which you are engaged.' And its conclusion was downright rude: 'I see no reason, from anything which has come to my hand, to alter the opinion which is universally entertained here of the inefficiency of the general staff.' In between there was the familiar litany of complaints about uncaring inefficiency and a refusal to face facts, the implication being that Raglan was solely to blame for the army's misfortunes. By way of redress, Raglan was ordered to supply detailed fortnightly reports on the condition of each of the army's divisions. He was also told in no uncertain terms that Airey and Estcourt would have to be replaced as the government had lost confidence in their abilities as senior staff officers.[2]

It was a devastating critique made worse by the fact that many of the reforms put in place by the Aberdeen government were about to take effect. Faced by the unexpected and unfair tirade Raglan's response was dignified and restrained: a less equable commander might have resigned and taken the first ship home. As it was, Raglan decided to counter Panmure's intemperance with the patient and careful tact which accompanied all his despatches from the Crimea:

> My Lord, I have passed a life of honour. I have served the crown for above fifty years; I have for the greater portion of that time been connected with the business of the Army. I have served the greatest man of the age [Wellington] more than half of my life; have enjoyed his confidence, and have, I am proud to say, been regarded by him as a man of truth and some judgement as to the qualification of officers; and yet, having been placed in the most difficult position in which an officer was ever called upon to serve, and having successfully carried out most difficult operations, with the entire approbation of the Queen, which is now my only solace, I am charged with every species of neglect.[3]

The appeal fell on deaf ears. Panmure was not interested in Raglan's excuses: he wanted changes to be made and, above all, he wanted to see the immediate dismissal of Airey, Estcourt and Filder, the head of the Commissariat. So did Delane who went one step further by demanding the immediate sacking of Raglan whom he dismissed in a *Times* leader on 12 February (the date of Panmure's letter) as an 'aristocratic general' whose 'aristocratic staff view this scene of wreck and destruction with a gentleman-like tranquillity.' Now Raglan was facing two opponents – the government and the press. True to himself and loyal to his staff, Raglan refused to surrender to the clamour for sackings and stood by his colleagues. Campaigning was due to begin again with the arrival of the first spring weather and he did not need further disruptions. What he wanted, and what he would soon be receiving, were supplies and men and then more supplies and more men.

Panmure, though, was himself under pressure, telling Raglan on 19 February that he had to do 'something to satisfy the House of Commons' and that that 'something' had to be the dismissal of the three senior staff and Commissariat officers. Critics such as Layard demanded the move and so too did the press. It was clearly a time for sacrificial lambs but Raglan stuck to his guns. He was probably right to do so, not just out of misplaced loyalty, but because he believed that Airey and Estcourt had given of their best, only to be overwhelmed by a situation for which they were not prepared and which was immune to easy solutions. Had he known that Panmure had circulated his criticisms not just to Cabinet colleagues but also to the Queen who became a stern critic of 'the meagre and unsatisfactory reports [from the Crimea]' it would only have redoubled his resolve that he was right to stand firm in the face of the constant stream of complaints from London.

He was powerless, though, to interfere with other changes. Burgoyne was replaced as his senior engineer adviser by the same General Jones who had done so well to destroy Bomarsund the previous autumn. Lieutenant-General Lord Rokeby was given command of the 1st Division in place of Cambridge and Pennefather was given the 2nd Division. As had been agreed from the beginning of the campaign, the more forceful Lyons replaced Dundas, a move which delighted Stratford who had already asked the admiral 'to tell me, with that truthfulness which belongs to your character and profession that all is going on progressively and auspiciously towards the result we desire'.[4]

Most importantly of all, Raglan was given a Chief of Staff, a government appointment, who would be free to report independently to London. This would be Lieutenant-General Sir James Simpson, a Scot from the Borders, who had served with the Grenadier Guards in the war against Napoleon. Although badly wounded at Quatre Bras he stayed on in the army to command the 29th Foot (Worcestershire Regiment) in Bengal and served under Charles Napier in the campaigns to pacify the Kachhi hill tribes. An experienced officer, he had been serving as commandant at Chatham when the call came to go the Crimea and he quickly emerged as a fair and sensible observer of the difficulties facing Raglan. When he arrived he admitted that he was prejudiced against the staff but his first letter of report, written on 16 April (a month after his arrival), described Raglan as 'the most abused man I ever heard of!' and proceeded to praise Airey and Estcourt as 'a very good set of fellows' who were by no means 'incompetent' or 'objectionable'.

The letter, which could hardly have been music to Panmure's ears, ended with the thought that Simpson had 'never served with an Army where a higher feeling and sense of duty exists than I remark in the General Staff Officers of this Army. It pervades all ranks, except among the low and grovelling correspondents of *The Times*.'5 As a field commander later in the war Simpson was to be found lacking, but his support for Raglan did much to stop the criticism from London. The appointment of an independent commission 'to inquire into the whole arrangement and management of the Commissariat Department' was also evidence that the government was trying to make good the damage in the Crimea. The three-man team was headed by Sir James McNeill, a distinguished Scottish surgeon, and it spent the rest of the year collecting evidence in the theatre of war before completing a damning critique in January 1856. A second commission was appointed to investigate the conditions in the camp hospitals and on board the hospital ships which ferried the wounded from Balaklava to Scutari and its findings managed to produce a number of reforms before the war ended.

But at least something was being done and being seen to be done. Even *The Times* caught the new mood and with the end of the winter season Delane called a halt to his attacks on aristocratic inefficiency. Layard, though, refused to give in. For the rest of the war he kept up his attacks on the government and called on them to end the system of purchasing commissions which, in his opinion, prevented promotion by merit and allowed the aristocracy and landed gentry to maintain a stranglehold on the army. He had a point: despite calls for Campbell to replace Raglan, or at the very least to be given a more senior appointment, Britain's most successful soldier in the Crimea was sidelined because he did not come from a 'suitable' background.

The French, too, were experiencing problems with their senior commanders. Canrobert might have received the plaudits of the troops when he flashed past them on horseback but his style of command left much to be desired. Just as Lucan had attracted a rude sobriquet because he was thought to look on instead of acting, so too did Canrobert come to be known as 'Robert can't'. As a nickname it got rather nearer the truth than the soldiers thought. Bosquet told his mother that the inactivity of the armies might encourage the Russians to take the war into Europe and if that happened then Canrobert was to blame. The British were also unimpressed: Sterling had spent much of January fretting about the loss of a watch which he had sent for repair in Constantinople but he broke off his ruminations to complain that Canrobert was simply 'too amiable' to be a serious commander.

At home, too, Canrobert was under attack. Throughout the war the French maintained tight censorship over the coverage of the war: all reports were sent to the War Ministry for approval before being published – and the authorities were amazed at the freedom afforded to Russell and *The Times* and his other colleagues. However, the muddles of the Crimea were rudely exposed to the people of France with the publication in early January 1855 of a pamphlet, *La Conduite de la Guerre en Orient*, which contained a virulent exposé of the conditions facing the French army in the Crimea. Although it was published anonymously many people, Napoleon III included, believed it to be the work of Prince Napoleon who had left the battlefront following his disgraceful inability to deploy the French 3rd Division in support of the British centre at Inkerman. Showing considerable tact, for the prince's behaviour was becoming a matter of scandal within the French army, Canrobert suggested that he should leave the Crimea to recover his health, although, in private, the French commander said of the emperor's cousin: 'This wretch may be a Prince, but he certainly isn't a Frenchman.' Karl Marx, who observed the war from afar, went further, stating that 'the man who is permitted to wear the uniform of a general of division has managed to throw a stain upon the military traditions of the name of Napoleon.'[6]

The prince angrily dismissed the charges that he was the author but, as he had made no secret of his criticisms of the conduct of the French forces while staying in Constantinople, it was hardly surprising that his name was linked with the document. And as he was a member of the Bonaparte family his fault-finding carried considerable weight, so much so that his uncle began to worry that the family's great name was being impugned. Uneasy questions began to crowd in on the emperor's troubled mind. What would his great ancestor have made of the muddle and the growing casualty lists? How had French military prowess fallen to such a low ebb following the promising start to the campaign in the Crimea? Perhaps the time had come to restore the name of Napoleon by going in person to the Crimea to take over the command of his country's embattled forces. On 28 February, following a meeting with the emperor, an alarmed Cowley reported verbatim Napoleon's determination to guide his country's military fortunes in the Crimea:

We must get out of the scrap in which we are in the Crimea. There is no plan of action there – no decision – not even a preparation for future operations. I do not pretend to be a military genius, but if I go I shall at least relieve the Generals from the responsibility which is weighing them down and of which I am not afraid. If something is not done, we shall go from bad to worse. Army after army will rot before Sebastopol. It is a duty which I owe to France at all events to do what I can to put an end to the state of things.[7]

This was not what the British government wanted to hear: Stratford had already passed on a rumour from the Porte that Nicholas was about to replace Menshikov and now Napoleon was making a similar threat. Not only was the emperor displaying a recklessness which would hardly solve the stalemate in the Crimea but he had evolved and circulated a new plan for destroying Sevastopol by cutting off its means of supply. This would require a huge army, made up mainly of French reinforcements from Constantinople, and it would require the British to play a secondary role. Passing through Paris on his way to Vienna a week earlier Lord John Russell had cautioned the emperor that his rightful place was in Paris, that 'the government of France were a great affair; the direction of a siege was in comparison a small affair', but Napoleon was not to be dissuaded. Russell wrote:

He told me very fairly his ideas. He had observed that every suggested operation was stopped by the objection of some other general; that if he were there he could order the best operation the military men could project to be undertaken, and if it were successful the Turks might occupy and defend Sebastopol while the allied troops might come away. Unless something of this kind were done the spring and summer might see our allies dwindling while the Russians would increase in force, and we should be obliged to embark with shame.[8]

It was to no avail. Napoleon was determined to go to the Crimea and not even Cowley, normally a restraining influence, could dissuade him. As the debate rumbled on the French, like the British, made some changes to their chain of command, the most important being the appointment of General Jean-Jacques Pélissier to command the army's 1st Corps and General Adolphe Niel to direct the operations at Sevastopol. Both appointments were to have far-reaching consequences. Niel was an ambitious, though relatively untried, engineering officer who had come to the fore during the siege of Bomarsund but his role in the Crimea was not just to direct operations: he had a line straight to the emperor and had been ordered to report on Canrobert's actions, or, as it turned out, his lack of action. Pélissier, too, had a hidden role. This fiery veteran of the fighting in Algeria was sent out as Canrobert's understudy and he made little secret of his ambition to take over command of the French army. Neither appointment was destined to give much confidence to a commanding officer who was already dithering about the allies' next move. Calthorpe spoke for both armies when he complained that the French commander 'never seems to know his own mind two days together'.

The Russians, too, were suffering from paralysis of the high command. Having failed to dislodge the allies on the Inkerman heights Menshikov had taken his army to the north of Sevastopol where they wintered on the Belbek. Despite the lack of action – in stark contrast to the Sevastopol garrison which had to endure frequent shelling – life was intolerable for most of the men. Although the Russian officers were denied the luxury of writing to the St Petersburg press to voice their complaints, many made their feelings clear in private letters to their families. These paint a drearily familiar picture of hardship, lack of resources and petty corruption while 'Prince Menshikov and his parish live in a state of near-insensibility'. Indeed, it seemed as if the Russian commander had lost any appetite for further fighting. He spoke of abandoning Sevastopol and no amount of encouraging correspondence from Nicholas was able to rouse him from his torpor. According to those closest to him on the Belbek he 'sat hidden, silent, secretive as the grave, just watching the weather'.[9]

However, Menshikov was not prepared to give up his position without a struggle and when news arrived from St Petersburg that former allies such as Paskevich, Nesselrode and Orlov were urging Nicholas to replace him, Menshikov decided to act. Following prompting from St Petersburg that he should consider an attack on the Turkish garrison at Eupatoria both to prevent further allied landings and to win a cheap victory to raise morale – Omar Pasha's army, recently arrived from Wallachia, was considered an easy target – Menshikov ordered a force of 19,000 men under Lieutenant-General Khrulev to assault the town on 17 February. It was a fiasco. The defending garrison enjoyed superior firepower from their own artillery pieces and from the guns of the allied fleet lying off-shore: over eight hundred Russians died in three hours of unequal action before Khrulev was forced to retreat. As the British liaison officer, Lieutenant-Colonel J.L.A. Simmons, Royal Engineers, told Stratford, the Russians soon ran off when HMS *Valorous* 'threw down some well-directed shells'.[10] When the news reached the Russian capital Nicholas decided that the setback was the last straw and that Menshikov had to go. He would be replaced by Prince Michael Gorchakov, the commander of the Russian forces in Bessarabia although the question of whether or not this was an improvement or a replacement of bad by worse was a moot point amongst many of the more cynical officers at the Belbek camp.

The letter of dismissal was signed by his son, the Grand Duke Alexander, but it was the tsar's last act. With the arrival of Austria into the allied coalition it seemed as if the world had turned against him and to the dismay of his family and closest associates it was obvious that the tsar's spirit had been broken by his army's inability to defeat an enemy whose own setbacks were a matter of scandal throughout Europe. 'Like an oak, broken by a whirlwind' – the observation of a maid-of-honour – Nicholas was finding the psychological strains of seemingly unending warfare difficult to bear. His health, too, was failing. In the second week of February he caught a bad cold yet, true to form, he disobeyed his doctor's orders and insisted on reviewing a detachment of troops bound for the Crimea. The temperature was well below freezing point and the tsar suffered accordingly: he was forced to take to his bed and pneumonia quickly set in. With all hope gone, he summoned Alexander, who was told to 'serve Russia' and to pass on the message to the defenders of Sevastopol that their tsar would pray for them in the next world. According the testimony of Nicholas's personal physician, Dr Mandt, it was a scene touched by nobility and courage. Nicholas knew that he was dying and was in great discomfort yet he refused to give in to self-pity. 'Never have I seen anyone die like this,' wrote Mandt, later. 'There was something superhuman in this carrying out of duty to the very last breath.'[11]

Nicholas had started the war as Europe's strong man, a colossus who held Europe's fate in his hands. With his death, the country was forced to hold up a mirror to itself and what it saw it did not particularly like. But before the pressing questions of the day could be dealt with – economic crisis, industrial backwardness, serfdom and an absence of democracy, to name but a few – his son Alexander II had to deal with a war which was draining Russia's exchequer. However, if anyone thought that he would be willing to accept peace at any cost they were mistaken for the new tsar's first message to the conference in Vienna was that he would 'perish rather than surrender'. When Russell reported to Clarendon the tsar's determination not to proceed with a treaty which would be detrimental to Russian interests he received a reply from the prime minister, Palmerston, reminding him that that there could be no peace unless Britain's original war aims had been met:

> I fear from all you have said to Clarendon, public and private, that there is no chance of the new Emperor of Russia agreeing to the only condition which would afford us security for the future; and though some few people here would applaud us for making peace on almost any conditions, yet the bulk of the nation would soon see through the flimsy veil with which we should have endeavoured to disguise entire failure in attaining the objects for which we undertook the war, and we should receive the general condemnation which we should richly deserve.[12]

Palmerston, of course, did not approve of what was happening in Vienna and only consented to the continuation of the talks if they kept Austria happy. For him and, to a lesser extent for Clarendon too, everything rested on the allies capturing Sevastopol and until that happened the events in Vienna were something of a sideshow.

In fact, no sooner had the conference begun on 15 March than it showed every sign of sinking into a diplomatic quagmire. One reason for the impasse lay in the interpretation of the Third Point and the Franco–British refusal to admit their intentions to the Austrians. Another was the fact that, despite their official titles, the main representatives did not have full plenipotentiary powers and had to be briefed by their respective governments. For example, Russell was bombarded by a succession of despatches from Clarendon reminding him that he had to stand firm against Buol; otherwise he would 'hustle' him into an unnecessary and incomplete peace agreement. Prince Alexander Gorchakov, too, had to report back to Nesselrode and although the French were represented by Bourquenay he was replaced in mid-conference by Drouyn de Lhuys. As for the Turks, their representative, Aali Pasha, newly appointed as Grand Vizier in succession to Reshid, did not arrive until the conference was well

under way. As Stratford told London, Aali and his foreign minister
Fuad (now appointed Pasha) had one abiding concern – the question
of the Orthodox Christians, a problem which hardly featured in the
allies' thinking:

> With regard to the diminution of the Russian fleet in the Black
> Sea and the free navigation of the Danube, the Porte has no
> objection to offer.
>
> As to the Fourth Point respecting the spiritual immunities
> and privileges of the Christians, Their Highnesses declared that
> the Porte is decided not to enter into any agreement thereupon
> with the Allies. Turkey, said they, declared war to [sic] Russia
> because this Power was encroaching upon the independence of
> the Sultan by demanding to interfere in the spiritual affairs of the
> Orthodoxes and how can now the Allies demand a concession
> which they declared themselves, more than once, both verbally
> and in writing, to be inconsistent with the Sultan's sovereign
> rights and independence?
>
> What relates to the revision of the Treaty of 1841 the Porte
> is ready to subscribe to the condition which the allies will
> propose.[13]

Unfortunately for the Turks, their plea would fall on deaf ears.
As the talks proceeded it quickly became obvious that its success or
failure would depend on the interpretation of the Third Point. Buol
had put forward a compromise which involved counterpoise – an
agreement which permitted the allies to station a naval force in the
Black Sea which would equal Russia's – but this was not agreeable
to Russell who insisted that Russia's naval force should be subject
to limitation. At the same time the British minister was aware that
there might have to be a compromise, for he could see no point
in demanding the reduction of the Russian fleet while Sevastopol
remained in Russian hands and the allies showed no signs of taking it.
This brought a sarcastic response from Palmerston that, while no one
wanted to persist with the fighting for its own sake, it was ludicrous
to reach a peace agreement which did not 'obtain that future security
for which we began the contest'. The conference adjourned until 17
April with the Third Point still unsettled.[14]

By then Drouyn de Lhuys had arrived in Vienna carrying a new
proposal to neutralise the Black Sea and to limit the size of the

Russian and Turkish fleets. This had been discussed with Clarendon and apparently agreed upon but no one had thought fit to inform Russell. A terrier of a man with a short fuse and easily goaded – early in his career his father warned him that he lost friends 'by not being courteous to them, by treating them superciliously, and de haut en bas, by not listening with sufficient patience to their solicitations or remonstrances' – Russell fired off a stinging rebuke to Clarendon expressing his astonishment at the turn of events:

I believe I am very unfit to be a diplomatist. The only use in sending me was to have some one to whom a certain latitude was to be allowed. I can now only obey implicitly your orders, and reclaim my liberty on my return to England. The prestige of power is a good thing, but the prestige of good faith is also valuable. This I am afraid, unless Drouyn on his arrival becomes aware of his error, you are about to lose. I have no doubt you have felt for my situation, but I must say it has been much aggravated by your conduct to me. Buol expressed his surprise that, having been sent here, no confidence in me should be shown.[15]

Russell has been much criticised for his vacillation in Vienna but he was ill-served by Clarendon who shared his prime minister's view that the conference was a waste of time, other than as a means of encouraging Austria to declare war on Russia. Throughout the negotiations he showed little interest in Russell's despatches, although to be fair to him, his attention was preoccupied by Napoleon's alarming decision to lead the French army in the Crimea. With the diplomatic game once more in stalemate and despite a growing war-weariness, the onus once more fell on the soldiers in the Crimea to take Sevastopol and in so doing to pave the way for peace. Hamley summed up their expectations:

Our present prospects, though much brighter, were no less dubious. Negotiations for peace were pending, while we were preparing for another attack with increased means, but with confidence diminished by former disappointment. A few days would see commenced, either the armistice as the preliminary of peace, or a bloody struggle with doubt beyond. Before our eyes was the great If, Sebastopol; – that once taken, we could venture to look forward either to a glorious return, or to a brilliant campaign.[16]

It was going to be a long haul and, as Hamley noted on 31 March 1855, fatalism and optimism seemed to be marching hand in hand as the armies faced up to an uncertain future.

10

Spring Stalemate

General François Certain Canrobert: 'Gentlemen, we are here
for the capture of Sebastopol.'
Admiral Edmund Lyons (dryly): 'Oh, that's it, is it?'
Opening words of allied council of war, March 1855

With the coming of spring there was a growing feeling in the
allied armies that the worst was behind them. Slowly the
harbour at Balaklava was being cleared of its noisome cargo of
rotting carcasses and some order was being restored to the landing
areas. Supplies, too, were reaching the men, many of them arranged
through *The Times*'s Crimean War Fund, and amongst them were
strange luxuries such as fur coats and rubber boots. 'We are all very
sensible of the kindness shown to us by the Ladies of England in
having sent us many little comforts which are not to be got here at
any price,' wrote Captain Nicol Grahame of the 90th Light Infantry.
'They also sent us Tracts of a religious nature which I am sure have
been great consolation to many a poor soldier in his last hours.'

The promised huts were also taking shape to replace the inadequate
tents and there were new carts and beasts to haul them – a veritable zoo
of pack ponies, mules, buffalo and camels. Workmen from the ends of
the Ottoman empire had also arrived to help with the construction of
the railway from Balaklava to the plain before Sevastopol. It had not
been an easy task rounding them up: amongst the Croats were Austrian
subjects and Stratford had been forced to bargain with Vienna for visas
to be given to them. There were also difficulties with the Bosnians
who were afraid of crossing the sea and Raglan was uncertain about

the willingness of the Turks to put in a hard day's work. None the less, Stratford was able to write on 4 February that 630 labourers had been sent to Balaklava on a boat towed by HMS *Terrible*, 'agreeably to Lord Raglan's request'.[1]

At long last a sense of military order was being restored and with the arrival of proper rations the army's health began to improve. In January over three thousand men had died from illness or as a consequence of their wounds: by April this had fallen to 582. Even Stratford felt confident enough to tell London that the army in the Crimea had turned the corner as far its physical shape was concerned:

> I am happy to feel myself warranted in stating, on the authority of private accounts, both oral and written, that a marked improvement has taken place in the state and the general appearance of things in that quarter, including, what is of much consequence, the health of the army.[2]

The changes also brought new arrivals. Encouraged by Prince Albert the photographer Roger Fenton had come out to the Crimea to record the campaign for posterity and although the results were carefully sanitised some of his images provide an intriguing glimpse into the army of the day. His portrait of Raglan shows a tired and drawn general and his views of Balaklava harbour give a good indication of its tight and confused confines. He himself knew only too well, though, that the public would not stand for the grim reality of war. Visiting the scene of the Light Brigade's hapless charge Fenton saw 'skeletons half-buried, one was lying as if he had raised himself upon his elbow, the bare skull sticking up with still enough flesh in the muscles to prevent it falling from the shoulders', but he knew he could never record the image with his camera.[3]

Other visitors included Alexis Soyer, the chef at the Reform Club, who had gone to Scutari at his own expense to advise on the menus to be given to the troops. This proved to be one of the more fruitful episodes in the war against waste and inefficiency. Soyer was an inventive and forward-looking French cook who had decided ideas about dietary requirements and whose suggestions helped to improve the feeding of the British troops. He also invented an efficient camp stove and taught the army cooks to conserve the water in which beef had been boiled as a stock for nutritious soup. Although Soyer was considered to be something of a comic turn by the army – he was

given to outbursts of singing while cooking and was highly excitable –
his intervention undoubtedly boosted the morale of the British Army.
He arrived with Florence Nightingale who fell ill and had to remain
in bed for a fortnight, racked by a fever which seemed to her to be
like an engine pounding inside her head.

With the clement spring weather there was also a fresh influx
of travelling gentlemen, come to see for themselves the conditions
which *The Times* had described so graphically. Most were impressed
by what they found. When Philip Rathbone arrived in Balaklava at
the beginning of April 1855, in place of the putrid hell-hole he was
'not prepared to find the harbour in so good a state. All dead animals
were towed out to sea, and no pains seemed spared to keep it clean.' A
member of the Liverpool family of Quaker philanthropists, Rathbone
admitted that he arrived in the Crimea expecting the worst but was
pleasantly surprised to discover that most of the muddle had been
countered and that conditions were better than he expected. Even
on the plain before Sevastopol he waxed eloquent about the scene
which stretched in front of him:

> I have never seen a more lovely day. The very few clouds that
> hung on the horizon only served to throw into relief the bright
> blue of the heavens – a blue such as we dream of when we speak
> of Italian skies, but never seen in England. In the distance lay
> our fleet mirrored in the still deeper azure of the Black Sea, and
> the same colour as pure and deep in the harbour of Sebastopol
> contrasted well with the brilliant white of the of the handsome
> buildings that surrounded it. Light puffs of smoke rose above
> different parts of the lines, and every now and then what seemed
> to be a little fleecy cloud would suddenly appear in the heavens.
> This was the bursting of a shell.[4]

Having been loaned a horse by a friend in The Rifle Brigade,
Rathbone made good use of it to traverse the British lines and
to inspect for himself the trench systems which had been thrown
up in front of the Russian defences. While out riding he also
encountered several of the allied commanders including Raglan ('a
very good-natured looking man with a particularly pleasant smile'),
Campbell ('a good-humoured Scotchman') and Canrobert ('a not very
intellectual Frenchman'). While in Constantinople he had also been
introduced to Stratford and was impressed by the 'terrible amount

of overwork' being done by the British ambassador and his staff at Therapia. It was quite unfair, he thought, that they were being criticised in the British press: 'Surely in times like the present our ambassador in Constantinople has quite enough on his hands without any supervision of hospitals at Scutari being added.'

On this point Stratford had already decided to fight his own corner. Stung by criticism in *The Times* that he had 'shown indifference to humanity by not visiting the Hospitals more frequently' and that he had failed to provide the army with sufficient accommodation, he wrote to the Foreign Office on 19 March pointing out that he had secured buildings for hospitals and offices at Scutari, Therapia, on the Bosphorus, Pera, the Golden Horn and, outside Constantinople at Smyrna, Rhodes, Salonica and the Dardanelles. As he said, the list spoke for itself, but as for the accusation that he was indifferent to the needs of the wounded, that was simply malicious journalism:

> I do not complain of these misrepresentations. I am not the only public officer exposed to calumny and I am content to accept my share of the general nuisance which unfortunately attends upon the still more pervading benefits of a free press.[5]

It cut little ice. At home in London Clarendon told the Cabinet that Stratford was inefficient, imperious and deaf to all requests for information, but this was mere obsession on the foreign secretary's part. By then in his sixty-eighth year Stratford pushed himself remorselessly, frequently staying up all night to finish his despatches, and insisting that his staff do the same. Sometimes they would be found at their desks still in evening dress as dawn broke, but despite the tension and the pressure the despatches to London were packed full with detail and tart observations. Little escaped his attention, whether it was the need to offer recompense to 'the wife of a poor man who died in consequence of having his arm blown off while saluting the British Consular Flag when hoisted for the first time at Diabekiev' (only £100, he noted, but 'the cost to Her Majesty's Government at the present rate of exchange will scarcely exceed seventy') or French plans to build a canal in the Suez isthmus, Stratford found time to deal with each and every contingency. He was particularly displeased by the French action which was being undertaken by a certain M. de Lesseps and lost no time in giving his opinion to the Porte:

The enterprise is vast, and its eventual effects so complicated, that the most ordinary prudence points it out as unfit to be decided off-hand between a private individual, however respectable [de Lesseps], and a provincial governor [Mohammed Said, Khedive of Egypt], however talented, having but little administrative experience.[6]

Having been told that the total cost of building the canal would be 230 million francs Stratford was appalled that it was even being considered at 'a time of war which fixes the attention and absorbs all the energies and resources of the Empire'. The Porte seems to have listened to his pleas for a delay because permission was not given to de Lesseps, a cousin of the Empress Eugénie of France, and work did not start on the canal until 1860.

Stratford was equally concerned by a report from his consul in Baghdad passing on information that Russia intended to make moves towards Bokhara with a view to threatening India's north-west frontier. The answer, he suggested to Clarendon, was to give every support to Dost Muhammad with whom the East India Company had signed a peace agreement the previous September. It would not be easy – the Afghan leader had already sent the British packing from his kingdom in 1842 and was held to be 'fickle, faithless and avaricious' – but Stratford was convinced that Britain had 'to reconsider our whole system of resistance in Asia to our natural enemies, the Russians'.[7] Not for the first time in the conflict the Russian threat to India was bruited as a good reason for inflicting a major military defeat in the Crimea.

All this Clarendon understood and appreciated but that did not stop him from sniping. In one letter to Russell he claimed that Stratford was intent on prolonging the war simply to force the Ottoman Empire to borrow more money from the British government so that it could meet the costs of the war, estimated to be £2 million a year. This was unfair. Stratford had informed the Foreign Office on 29 March that 'the Turkish Revenue is in a deplorable state . . . and there is a reluctance, difficult to be explained, in adopting measures to put the Revenue on a better footing' but that did not silence the constant criticisms. If the querulous Clarendon had been serious in those complaints it would have been easy enough to have replaced the ambassador but the last thing the government wanted was to see Stratford attacking them from the House of Lords. In any case the foreign secretary had more pressing problems on his hands.

From Paris Cowley reported the alarming news that Drouyn de Lhuys had decided to support Napoleon's decision to go to the Crimea. 'Perhaps it will do some good,' the foreign minister had reported during a meeting on 2 March to discuss the military position in the Crimea. Cowley was much taken aback. He still entertained hopes that his influence over the emperor would force a change of heart but, to effect it, he knew that he needed Drouyn de Lhuys' support. After expressing his 'alarm which a tort on a raison His Majesty's supposed project had in England' – a standard Cowleyism – the British ambassador skilfully changed tack. 'Did His Majesty mean that his decision was to be supreme with all four armies?' he asked. 'Was this fair by his allies?'

Drouyn de Lhuys responded that as far as he knew that consideration had not been taken into account. In fact Napoleon only proposed to lead the French army against Menshikov's field force while the British continued the siege but the presence of such an eminent figure would clearly have caused command and control problems with the allies. Raglan certainly thought so and told Russell in Vienna that Napoleon's presence would only add to the difficulties he was already facing. The French, too, were disturbed by the prospect for despite the decision to form a Council of Regency headed by Prince Jerome, the regime was obviously vulnerable to attacks by anarchists and other undesirables during the emperor's absence. Prince Napoleon had already made it clear that he would disobey the order to accompany his cousin and in the Crimea Canrobert confided to Rose that his staff feared that Niel was simply playing the role of John the Baptist.[8]

It was at this point that Clarendon decided to intervene. As a perfervid supporter of the view that the war would only be concluded by an allied military victory he realised that Napoleon's presence in the Crimea might obviate that aim. Not only would the professional commanders feel aggrieved and unsettled by the emperor's presence but, like Cowley, Clarendon feared that, willy-nilly, Raglan's position would be compromised. After all, it was not as if the allied coalition forces had worked together in total harmony. Clearly something had to be done and between them Cowley and Clarendon embarked on a diplomatic offensive which had the full backing of the French establishment.

While Cowley continued to implore Napoleon to change his mind Clarendon made arrangements to visit France on 3 March while the emperor was inspecting troops at Boulogne. The visit was a complete success in that the British foreign secretary persuaded Napoleon that the difficulties were insuperable and that he should not contemplate a trip to the Crimea until the last act was in sight. '*C'est le mot!*' exclaimed the emperor, '*le dernier coup de main.*' ('That's it, the last word.') Arrangements were also made for Napoleon and Eugénie to make a state visit to Britain in April and that seemed to do the trick. From the moment that he arrived with his entourage on Monday 16 April he was treated with regal solemnity: he was entertained at Windsor and invested with the Order of the Garter, a ball was held in his honour, he visited the Crystal Palace and he left with the feeling that he had been finally accepted into the European family of royalty. Even Victoria was charmed and in her journal she seemed to transfer to the French emperor some of the awe she had earlier expressed for Tsar Nicholas: 'That he *is* a very *extraordinary* man with great qualities there can be no doubt – I might almost say a mysterious man. He is evidently possessed of *indomitable courage, unflinching firmness of purpose, self reliance, perseverance and great secrecy . . .*'[9]

By the end of the month Napoleon was finally persuaded to drop his plan to go the Crimea – the range and accuracy of the Russian fire during the renewed hostilities may also have persuaded him to show some caution – and Cowley and Clarendon were left with the view that the combined operation to make the emperor change his mind had been one of the war's happiest and most fruitful examples of cross-Channel co-operation. Elsewhere, however, the certainties in the alliance were proving to be less productive.

While Napoleon and Victoria were doing their best to cement the Franco-British alliance the plenipotentiaries in Vienna were still unresolved about the Third Point. In an attempt to break the deadlock Buol had proposed a compromise which supported the concept of limitations and linked it to a reduction in the size of both the Turkish and Russian fleets. Any infringement would be a *casus belli* on the part of the allied powers, including Austria. Finally, it was agreed that Buol's proposals should be presented to Alexander Gorchakov as an ultimatum.

When the plan was presented to them both Russell and Drouyn de Lhuys thought it merited further consideration and they gave their measured support, Russell because he was becoming increasingly convinced that Sevastopol would not fall and that the allies faced the 'possibility of our having to get worse terms from Russia after another campaign'. But before the Austrian initiative could be taken any further the diplomats would have to consult with their respective governments. Unfortunately for his own position Russell sent on his despatches before he left Vienna on 24 April and these reached London in advance of him. The consequences were to be far-reaching. True to form Clarendon dismissed them as 'frivolous and fallacious' and began combining with Palmerston to achieve their rejection. It would not be an easy task because the war was becoming so unpopular that even the foreign secretary was forced to admit to Cowley that acceptance of an enforced peace might be the price Britain had to pay for its military failures.

Indeed, when the proposals were discussed by the Cabinet it was impossible to reach a consensus mainly because, although most members were aware that a peace without a victory would mortify Britain, there was a strong possibility that France might accept the terms. Despite the pleasant glow of unanimity which had surrounded Napoleon's visit many French people felt considerable disquiet about the wisdom of continuing the war. Their army had sustained heavy casualties yet it remained the senior partner in the field; the British had not covered themselves with glory, indeed, they had been exposed as bumbling amateurs, and besides, it was an expensive business which might require fresh loans. So, when Drouyn de Lhuys arrived back in Paris at the end of April he found Napoleon suddenly minded to accept the proposals. Only a month earlier Cowley had informed Clarendon that 'His Majesty is of the opinion that no honourable peace is possible until a decided success has been obtained by the Allied Armies', but this new compromise seemed to suggest that a way could be found out of the difficulties facing the allies in the Crimea.[10]

It was then that Cowley decided to act on his own initiative. First he met Drouyn de Lhuys on 2 May and told him that Britain's honour would be compromised by acceptance of the peace terms; then on the following day, suspecting that the French foreign minister had been offering weighted advice to the emperor, he met Napoleon at the Tuileries. It proved to be a decisive encounter. Napoleon was persuaded that the Austrian version of limitations was unworkable and would not suit French interests and agreed to discuss the matter again the following day with Drouyn de Lhuys and Vaillant, the war minister. Seeing his chance Cowley asked, quite undiplomatically but with great firmness, if he might be present.

The upshot was that any support for the proposal quickly ebbed away, largely because Drouyn de Lhuys was unable to counter Cowley's arguments but also because Vaillant made a providential observation which went straight to the emperor's heart:

> I am not a politician, but I know the feelings of the army. I am sure that if, after having spent months in the siege of Sebastopol, we return unsuccessful, the army will not be satisfied.[11]

It is open to doubt if that sentiment were entirely true, but it seemed to persuade the emperor. Buol's ultimatum was dropped by the allies with Palmerston telling Clarendon on 20 May: 'We should thank Austria for her offer, but her proposals to Russia are too harsh if we decide we want peace at any price, but not harsh enough if we think we can win the war.'[12] The Vienna Conference was as good as dead (it ground to a halt at the beginning of June), Drouyn de Lhuys resigned and although Russell was dissuaded from following suit his nemesis came later that summer when Buol revealed that the British plenipotentiary had provisionally accepted his peace plan. As Russell had not revealed his position he was forced to resign, having first attempted to argue his case in parliament. He was not to know that he had been stabbed in the back by Cowley's machinations in Paris. The British ambassador was fond of saying that French politicians could not distinguish right from wrong: in Paris during that first week of May Cowley seemed to experience a similar difficulty.

With Vienna dead in the water everything now hung on the allies gaining an early military victory so that Russia would be forced to sue for peace – just as Palmerston and Clarendon had planned. The signs, though, were inauspicious. Canrobert continued to be catatonic, calling for more men before any attack could be made, while Raglan continued to fret about the allies' inability to produce a concerted plan for a fresh assault on Sebastopol's fortifications. The indecision showed both commanders at their worst. According to Rose – not a completely disinterested witness as he was smarting from a British refusal to allow him to accept the award of the Légion d'Honneur – Canrobert believed that it would be madness to attack as the British were too weak and that 'even if he could take Sebastopol alone, he would not do so without the co-operation of the British Army'.[12]

For his part Raglan was unable to make any impact on the French commander's indecision and always demurred whenever Canrobert put another obstacle in the way of action – for example, at a war council held on 8 March, the French insisted that there should be no further attacks until Omar Pasha's forces were able to make a contribution.

As ever the stalemate in the allied camp had a variety of causes. Canrobert was being over-cautious because he was under the emperor's orders 'not to assault unless perfectly certain of the result being in our favour, but also not to attempt it if the sacrifice of life should be great'.[13] He also knew that even if Napoleon did not come out to command the French Army he would expect his ideas to be put into action and that meant conserving French forces and not risking the reserves which were slowly building up in Constantinople. Also, from a pragmatic point of view he feared that any assault on Sevastopol might invite retribution from Michael Gorchakov's field army and with the British still woefully weak he was not at all certain that they would be able to resist a fresh attack. Matters were complicated by Niel's presence – Canrobert admitted to Rose that the studious military engineer was Napoleon's spy – and they would be further muddied at the end of April when the telegraph line reached the Crimea, allowing instant access between the allied capitals and the armies' headquarters in the field.

Canrobert also wanted to make use of the 13,000 Turkish troops which would soon be arriving from Eupatoria but Raglan was less enthusiastic. He wanted to attack Sevastopol sooner than later because with each day that passed he could see the powerful additions which the Russians were making to the city's defences. And as time went on the British commander-in-chief was becoming uncomfortably aware that he was the junior partner. The French had eight full strength divisions in front of Sevastopol with 40,000 reinforcements promised while Raglan only possessed six sadly depleted divisions, many of whose best men had died during the winter to be replaced by untried recruits. On top of these concerns he would shortly have to deal with the commissioners who were being sent out to investigate faults in the medical and Commissariat departments and had been told by Palmerston in 'the most peremptory manner' that he had to support them.

Fortunately, with the cessation of the attacks in *The Times* Panmure had adopted a more conciliatory manner and Raglan was spared the

The Allied Positions Before Sevastopol

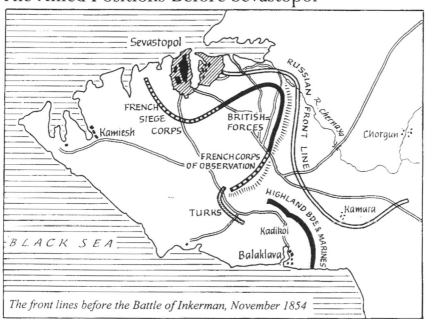

The front lines before the Battle of Inkerman, November 1854

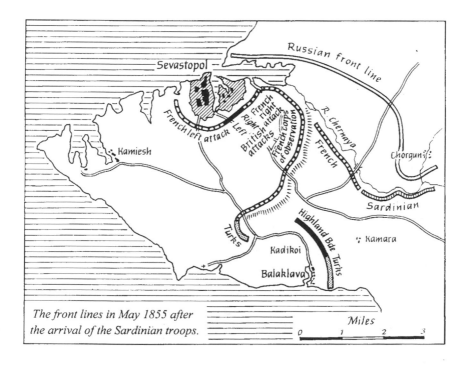

The front lines in May 1855 after the arrival of the Sardinian troops.

bile which had made their initial correspondence so disagreeable. By the end of March the secretary for war was showing an affability and understanding for Raglan's position that make his earlier criticisms even more wounding than he had probably intended them to be:

> Your Lordship has hitherto accomplished to my entire satisfaction the difficult and delicate task of maintaining friendly relations with our allies, but I feel it to be my duty to point out to you that a strong feeling pervades my mind that the policy of the French has been to cast on us the toil, and labour of the siege and the battle and that this might be pushed too far. England will ever court the place of honor [sic] and the pact of danger, but her strength and resources and the lives of her gallant sons are not to be wasted or sacrificed merely as a forlorn hope to an Army of more than treble her number, and which boasts itself to be superior also in skill and organisation.[14]

At the heart of Panmure's concern was a growing feeling in London that the French were dragging their heels over a decision to attack the Russian fortifications. This was indeed the case. Throughout the month and into April 1855 the three allies found little common ground in their strategic planning and when they did Canrobert always found an excuse to equivocate. The main difficulty lay in the tactics to be used and the targets to be attacked: on these the French seemed never to be able to make up their minds or to stick to a decision once it had been reached. A Wellington would have been more iron-willed in his approach but Raglan was over-courteous, even by his own exacting standards, with the result that Canrobert's staff had no concept of how his mind was working.

To be fair to the French, on 22 February they had lost heavily in a fruitless attack on the Mamelon Vert, a smaller defensive position in front of the Malakov Tower and they had been shaken by the strength of the Russian counter-attack during which large numbers of Zouaves were stranded and killed or made prisoner. Worse, the Russians showed themselves well capable of not just rebuilding the damage to the Mamelon but also making it more secure. Later bottles of brandy were found in the trenches, leaving the French with evidence that the Russian soldiers were either intoxicated or fired up by drink before doing battle with the enemy. The experience impressed Canrobert so much that, coupled with the uncertainty about his emperor's plans, he was unwilling to take unnecessary risks. It even convinced him that the Russians were stronger than the allies expected and he produced figures which, when seen in London, made Panmure think that Canrobert was in a funk:

> I grieve to learn the tone which has been adopted by General Canrobert, although it only confirms me in my opinion as to his want of enterprise.
>
> I cannot understand upon what grounds he calculates that on our opening fire the Russians will have 100,000 men disposable for offensive operations, over 20,000 for a sortie, 40,000 for an advance on the right our position and 40,000 for an attack on Balaclava.[15]

To that Raglan had no answer or if he had one he chose not to reveal it.

The main objective was the Malakov Tower, the huge stone fortified tower which was the linchpin of the city's defences. On that Burgoyne and Niel had agreed, but the difficulty lay in creating a timetable which would allow the allied artillery to assault both it and the great redoubts to the east, the Flagstaff Bastion and the Redan itself which bristled with guns. Clearly there would have to be a major bombardment which if successful would allow the infantry to break into the defences. But that depended on the allied guns and, as the soldiers in the trenches could see, the Russian positions appeared to be growing stronger by the day. Conferences were held throughout March and it was finally decided to begin the bombardment on 9 April and to use infantry to mount an assault on the Redan and the Mamelon and Malakov defences. Because the British were now pinned in the centre of the allied siege line — Bosquet's forces had moved to the right — the Redan would fall to them while the numerically stronger French would tackle the larger objective.

After the bitter winter interlude, with all its hardships, and the more recent battling with the Russians, much of it hand-to-hand, the allied soldiers faced the prospect of an action which, if decisive, could end the war and send them back home again. It would also relieve them from life in the trenches which, as many of them found to their cost, was uncomfortable, brutish and above all dangerous. 'This is not siege, neither is Sebastopol a fortress,' Sterling was told by Bosquet, a general whom the Scot thought looked like Napoleon but was 'totally without fanfaronnade' (boasting):

> The enemy's position from their right at Sebastopol Harbour to their left stretching away towards Balaclava is one entrenched camp. Behind them is a large military nation, with all its supplies, which they can pour into Sebastopol at pleasure. With our Engineer's plans, I do not see how we are to succeed. I command thirty-four battalions; of these sixteen are in the trenches every night. A fortnight more of this work will give me a terrible sick list. The remainder of my thirty-four battalions are under arms continually. We sleep neither by night nor by day. Last night we had a Lieutenant-Colonel killed, eighteen officers wounded, and a hundred men hors de combat. That will go on constantly and is a serious drain. *La partie est bien dure.* (The struggle is really hard.)[16]

Sterling sympathised. During his visits to the trenches he had been made uncomfortably aware of the fact that the Russian rifle pits were manned by sharpshooters whose fire made life extremely difficult for the advancing sappers. The only way to deal with them was to clear the positions with the bayonet, according to Gowing 'fearful work', which was entrusted to volunteers from several battalions in order to spread casualties.

> About 100 or 150 (sometimes 300 or 400) men would be formed up at the point closest to the pits to be assailed, all hands sometimes taking off their accoutrements. At a sign from the officers who are going to lead, the men creep over the top on all fours. Not a word is spoken but, at a given signal, in they go — and in less time than it takes to write this, it is all over; the bayonet has done its work. The defenders are all utterly destroyed or taken prisoners, while the pits are at once turned and made to face the enemy, or are converted into a trench.[17]

The timescale of the attack was probably not as limited as Gowing claims and the fighting itself would have been bloody and terrifying but there is a curious similarity of purpose in Gowing's description which would not look out place sixty years later in the trenches of the Western Front. Already life in the forward trenches was showing all the signs of conforming to modern industrialised warfare. In places the French were within fifty yards of the forward Russian positions and their sappers were busy tunnelling towards the Flagstaff bastion in the sort of operation which would also be repeated in Flanders. Mining was as old as siegecraft and the French sappers were an elite formation made up exclusively of officers; at times they were so close to the Russians that they could hear their conversations.

War, the bringer of change, also introduced other military innovations. It was suggested that Raglan should ascend in a balloon to view Sevastopol's defences but he politely declined. The French had experimented with observation balloons during the Revolutionary Wars but the idea was not adopted until the American Civil War when both the Union and Confederate armies used balloons to give commanders that vital glimpse to the other side of the hill which had been previously denied them. The use of the electric telegraph between government and military headquarters in the field presaged the introduction of the field telephone and the success of the Minié rifle marked the end of the close-quarter musketry engagements which had typified black-powder warfare. Finding that the British 9-pounders had to be fired within range of the heavier Russian guns thought was given to other means of breaching the defences. Amongst these was Robert Mallet's heavy mortar, a 42-ton monster which was designed to fire a 3000-pound projectile over a mile and a half. (It never went into service as each round cost £675 to fire.) Railways, too benefited from the war. The completion of the line from Balaklava to Kadikoi brought the steam-powered train into use for ferrying supplies and carrying out the wounded and in France Paris was connected directly to Marseilles by rail to enable the more rapid transit of troops to the Crimea.

Other ideas proved less workable. The indefatigable Earl of Dundonald produced plans for an adaptation of the fire-ship – specially built ships with a low draught which would pour out sulphurous fumes in advance of an allied naval attack on Russia's Baltic fortresses. He also thought that an armoured land vehicle could be used in front of Sevastopol but the suggestion was disregarded as being inhumane. However, another naval invention, the undersea mine, did come into service when the Russians succeeded in exploding two below the British steam frigates *Merlin* and *Firefly* off Kronstadt on 9 June 1855. During the war the Russians used two types of mine to defend their Baltic fortresses – an electronically fired weapon, triggered either from the shore or from contact with the ship's hull, and a rudimentary chemical contact mine.

Although they were little more than nuisances, they did prove that undersea weapons could prove effective in maritime warfare and the War Office asked William Armstrong, a Newcastle lawyer turned engineer, to design a similar weapon for British use. So shocked were he and his partner, James Rendel, by the obsolete round-shot artillery pieces used by the navy that they set about designing a new breach-loading rifled gun which fired elongated projectiles instead of cast-iron balls. Warships, too, changed to meet the changing face of warfare: the Russian victory at Sinope and the superiority of British and French screw-powered battleships signalled the end of round shot and sail and ushered in a new era in which steam-powered ironclads would become the standard warship.

However, in most respects, little had changed from the wars fought by Wellington. Soldiers were in sight of their enemy when they fought each other; at Balaklava, infantry and artillery received cavalry, and civilian spectators were present during the fighting – albeit at a discreet distance. Philip Rathbone, the Quaker, observed:

> After dinner we went out to watch the shells, like shooting-stars, flying over the city; but the moon being high they were not so bright as they otherwise would have been. Every now and then the sharp crackle of musketry broke in upon the slow boom of the cannon, sometimes with startling clearness and apparent proximity.[18]

The next day Rathbone was on his way back to Liverpool, having come to the conclusion that irresponsibility, overwork and under-payment were the main reasons for the army's sufferings. He had also heard soldiers talking 'as a matter of course' about the deaths of comrades; he had seen a man buried; watched shells exploding over the Malakov, and entered the trench systems in front of Sevastopol. All in all it had been an entertaining week, enlivened by roughing it in a tent yet made agreeable by such creature comforts as champagne and port with his dinner. Ahead lay a comfortable life as a well-to-do underwriter but like many others of his fellow countrymen (under conditions very different from those suffered by the soldiers) he could say that he had been to the Crimea and had stories to tell his grandchildren. His wife Jane hardly recognised him when he returned to Liverpool bearded and scruffy and a few days later she discreetly destroyed his prized souvenir, a Russian soldier's cap with hair and blood still stuck to it.

But, as it turned out, there was to be more to the connection than simple war tourism. Philip's brother William, a Liberal Member of Parliament and Unitarian reformer, founded the District Nursing Service and was a great patron and friend of Florence Nightingale. As well as supplying funds and support he gave her a *jardinière* to keep in her room and every week up to his death in 1902 he kept it stocked with flowers. In that case and in many others the Crimean War was a war which touched many hundreds of ordinary people as well as those who did the fighting.

11

Todleben's Triumph

Men! The tsar relies on us to hold Sevastopol. There is no
retreat – in front is the enemy and behind us is the sea.
*Vice-Admiral V.A. Kornilov, order of the day to the
Russian garrison inside Sevastopol, October 1854*

The long-awaited allied artillery barrage began in the early morning
of 9 April. As the mist started to clear 138 British and 362 French
guns began a sustained attack on the Russian fortifications and as the
day wore on they seemed to be doing considerable damage to Flagstaff
Bastion and the Mamelon. Within a week the French gunners were
able to claim that they had done an 'enormous' amount of damage
to both positions. The embrasures – fortified gun positions – had
been destroyed, the Russians had pulled away their artillery pieces
and, better still, they showed no sign of being in a position to repair
the damage. Unfortunately, the British had enjoyed no such luck at
the Redan, the heavily reinforced third bastion which seemed to be
impervious to the shells which rained down on it.

The whole point of the barrage was to soften up the Russians for an
attack by the infantry but with the enemy guns returning fire on the
allied trenches the conditions were not propitious. Even so, Raglan
thought that an assault was possible but it would have been a forlorn
hope without the support of the French. At a conference on 14 April
Canrobert declined to take part. Instead it was agreed to continue
the barrage, albeit at a reduced level, and to meet again to reconsider
the options open to the allies. By this time Canrobert was more or
less completely in thrall to Napoleon's wishes and the councils of war

held throughout April were to be carried out under the long shadow of the emperor's insistence that the operations should be widened. At the end of his visit to London Napoleon had revealed his strategy to his allies: Panmure, who was present, summarised them for Raglan with the added hint that 'Her Majesty's Government agrees with the Emperor that until fully invested, Sebastopol cannot be taken and that it cannot be effectually invested until the Russian covering army is driven from the position from which it communicates with the town':

> To effect this object we entirely concur in the proposal to divide the Allied forces into 3 Armies according to the document signed by Marshal Vaillant and myself referred to in His Majesty's despatch to General Canrobert. One of these three armies will maintain the siege, a second under your own command is intended to advance on the heights of Inkerman and McKenzie's Farm so as to interpose between the town and the Russian Army in the Field, and the third is intended to make such a diversion as shall engage the enemy's attention and by threatening or actually attacking his rear and you in your attack on his front.[1]

Panmure's despatch did not arrive until the beginning of May but when the new war plans were put forward they seemed to produce more questions than answers, particularly concerning the employment of the army of diversion. At the time the emperor's intervention and the effect it was having on Canrobert created an impossible situation for Raglan and his staff. The carefully contrived alliance between the British and French was becoming unstuck and to complicate matters the Turks were also showing a desire to run their own show. While Raglan wanted Omar Pasha to contribute men to the siege of Sevastopol the Turkish commander voiced a preference to concentrate his forces at Eupatoria for independent operations against the Russian siege army.

Each commander had a valid point. Although Canrobert was constrained by the emperor's influence and by the presence of Niel, he was in sympathy with the proposal to build up his forces, which would soon be over 90,000-strong, to enable the majority to maintain the siege while the remainder formed a field army to attack the Russians outside Sevastopol. At a further council the next day the arithmetic

produced by the allies envisaged the creation of two armies made up
of: besieging force: 90,000 (55,000 French, 20,000 British, 15,000
Sardinians); field force: 65,000 (40,000 French, 25,000 Turks).[2]

The Turkish representatives were happy with the outcome for
Omar Pasha had always argued that his men were unsuited to serve
in the trenches but Raglan was ill-at-ease. He could see the sense of
widening the scope of the allied operations in an attempt to cut off
Sevastopol from its supply lines into the Russian hinterland but that
would take time and the creation of a huge army. As he was not
privy to the reasons for Canrobert's prevarication he had to take
on trust the French commander's insistence that there should be a
postponement of offensive operations against Sevastopol until the
reinforcements arrived in May. To Raglan this seemed not only to
be inconsistent, given the French agreement to an assault, but also a
wasted opportunity. Long after the war was over Todleben seemed
to agree with the British commander-in-chief when he wrote in
his memoirs that following the bombardment he was 'continually
expecting the enemy to advance to the assault'.

The experienced Russian engineer clearly thought that the allies
had the chance to take the Flagstaff Bastion and with its loss the fall
of Sevastopol would have been a certainty, but he was writing with
the benefit of hindsight. At the time the Russians believed that they
had the capacity to withstand the bombardment and to continue the
siege on their own terms. After all, they were not cut off from the
outside world, reinforcements and supplies continued to pour into
the city and, despite the losses from shellfire, morale was high. For this
state of affairs they owed everything to the man who later believed
that they were staring defeat in the face.

Todleben had arrived in Sevastopol before the siege began, sent
by Gorchakov as an engineering adviser to Menshikov's garrison. He
received short shrift and the advice to take some leave – the Russian
commander was nothing if not consistent in his pig-headedness
– but the determined young military engineer decided to stay,
even though he understood that his report on the city's defences
would make painful reading. By the end of September the allied
advance after the Alma battle put paid to any thought of leaving
and the presence of his forceful personality and enthusiastic energy
was to give the defenders a head start in the direction of the
siege operations. Together with Kornilov, Todleben, a native of
the Baltic states, was to provide the Sevastopol garrison with real

hope that they could not only survive but in so doing drive off the allied armies.

Hamley, the gunner officer, had visited Constantinople before Christmas and when he returned in the middle of January the improvements to the Russian fortifications were all too evident. The Mamelon he described as a low rounded hill crowned with batteries, while lower down there were screens of trenches guarding the Russian sharpshooters. It overlooked the Malakov surrounded by 'an earthen parapet, pierced with embrasures, and surrounded on the slope outside with a dark line of abattis, or obstacled made of felled trees and pointed stakes'. With the help of a telescope he could see the zigzag trench systems and fieldworks, all two or three feet deep and protected by stone and earthen parapets. Also visible behind the Malakov were barracks for six battalions and beyond that the Simferopol road along which Russian soldiers were hauling large numbers of wagons. Hamley, a thorough professional, could not help remarking that, despite the intermittent fire, parties of Russian sappers were hard at work rebuilding and reinforcing their defences. In his professional soldier's view of the enemy's position, the fortifications presented a formidable obstacle to the allied gunners:

> The capture of the Mamelon and its two flanking hills beyond Careening Bay, would have been a work of infinite labour and difficulty; carried on under heavy artillery fire, and would have been but a step towards the attack of the Redan and Round Tower, each formidable achievements, and still the town remained for a separate siege: and this process demanded, if successful in all its separate particulars, many months to accomplish.[3]

The story of Todleben's triumph in effecting the fortification of Sevastopol is one of the epics of military engineering. Thinking that the allies would attack from the north he reinforced the Star Fort but when it became clear that there would be a formal siege he directed the strengthening of the formidable semicircle of redoubts which formed the basis of the city's southern defences. Built originally of earth – to Cathcart they had resembled 'a low park wall' – they had been transmogrified through sheer brute strength and persistence into solid fortifications whose 68-pounder naval guns provided a reassuring line of defence. There were also improved defences for the men – specially built bomb-proof shelters known as 'blindages', constructed from ships' timbers and protected by large iron cisterns filled with rocks and earth, which were proof against the heaviest allied bombardment.[4]

What was more, the defences were in a continual state of change and renewal. By March the Mamelon had been reinforced to take more cannon and the defences in front of the redoubts had been strengthened. Their construction and Todleben's attention to detail greatly boosted Russian morale. As Captain Chodasiewicz pointed out, if any gun embrasures were incorrectly sited they were immediately altered 'to enable the guns to be pointed in the right direction. Whenever a discovery of this sort was made the whole was changed during the night. If no changes were required, new and more formidable works were added.'[5]

There are several telling descriptions of what it was like to be under fire in the besieged town. Tolstoy's *Sebastopol Sketches*, published after the war, show the same keen eye for portrayal of what it was like to be on the receiving end of a barrage that he had brought to the earlier siege of Silistria:

> The stars were high in the sky but shone feebly. The night was pitch dark, only the flashes of the guns and the bursting bombs made things around suddenly visible. The soldiers walked quickly and silently, voluntarily outpacing one another; only their measured footfall on the dry road was heard besides the incessant roll of the guns, the ringing of the bayonets when they touched one another, a sigh, or the prayer of some poor soldier lad: 'Lord, O Lord! What does it mean?' Now and again the moaning of a man who was hit could be heard, and the cry, 'Stretchers!'[6]

For many of the reinforcements who had arrived in Sevastopol during the winter it was their first sustained experience of warfare. The sheer volume of noise of the guns and the unpredictable nature of the explosions would have been terrifying, adding to the stress which men already felt when going into action. As a watching British surgeon told his family, the booming of the guns produced a sensation of dread and excitement, almost impossible to describe to those who were not there.

Other British soldiers wondered if anyone could survive the bombardment, so heavy and sustained was it throughout. They were not to know their guns' limitations: artillery was a key weapon in siege warfare but the small calibre of the British weapons meant that it was not always effective. Despite the damage to the fortifications, which was clear for all to see, much of it was easily repaired, Todleben's revolutionary system of 'flying entrenchments' being reconstructed in a twinkling. And while the Russians did sustain casualties, particularly in the counter-battery duels with the allied gunners, these were not as heavy as might have been expected. It was a puzzling feature of artillery fire during the war that the casualty figures were not always commensurate with the effectiveness of the length and weight of the bombardment. Yet for every section of the fortifications or trench systems which remained relatively unscathed there would be others touched by dreadful carnage. In Arthur Henry Taylor's battery fifty men were killed on the first day, including experienced non-commissioned officers, and he spent twenty-four hours in the trenches tending the wounded. While this was part of his contract as a surgeon, it all seemed to be without point:

> What annoys and distresses everyone is that all was for no defined object as the Army were not prepared to storm the town . . . We say here that 'We did not take Sebastopol because the French would not fight by day, the English would not fight in the dark and the Turks won't fight at all.'[7]

Taylor was not alone in his bewilderment. 'The English have advanced their batteries to within 600 yards of the town, and they and their General all want to go in!' commented the French Admiral Bruat. 'The French have got within 60 yards of the town and their general won't go in!' The puzzlement was not just confined to the high command. What was the point, asked many British regimental officers, of raining down fire on the Russian positions and causing casualties, if the infantry were not to storm the battered fortifications? Even the Russians were bewildered: the bombardment lasted over a week, it clearly expended valuable munitions, yet the expected assault never came and was never likely to come while the allied command remained divided.

Inevitably perhaps, the end of the barrage and the obvious indecision led to frustration, especially amongst the British troops who were becoming increasingly aware that they were playing second fiddle. The growing French numbers, and the fact that the British regiments had lost most of their experienced men who were being replaced by untried recruits, were reminders of a growing inequality. On the other hand this was balanced by a suspicion that apart from the Zouaves, considered to be the elite of the French Army, the French *poilus* were inferior, or at least less determined, than the average British infantryman. (Of the enemy they thought even less: Hamley told his readers that 'the countenances of the Russians, short and broad, with thick projecting lips, pug-noses and small eyes, betokened a low order of intellect, cunning and obstinate.') Much of the scepticism was little more than misplaced patriotism and the traditional rivalry which existed between the two armies but as the ever-perceptive Henry Clifford told his parents on 31 March, the inequality of size did not mean that the British had no contribution to make:

> If the assault is made by us on the 'Redans' I think it will make a very big hole, not easily filled up, in our little army; but I am the last to wish to shirk any part of the work, and get the French, because they have more men, to do any of the dirty work for us. Depend upon it, tho' our loss may be very great, the work will be done when it is. The men are looking very well and are in good spirits . . .
>
> The excitement about taking Sebastopol is, of course, not so great now in England, and no doubt many look on it as hopeless. I don't wonder at it after so long a Siege. It will give France and England plenty to do yet to take it I think. We have got through one Army already, and this will be pretty well used up by the time Sebastopol changes hands.[8]

Clifford's summary was not far wrong and it goes some way to explaining Britain's military predicament in the Crimea. Ever since the end of the Napoleonic wars the army was not envisaged as having a role to play in Europe and it was very much a poor cousin of the Royal Navy. It was also largely out of mind and out of sight, with a substantial garrison in Ireland for internal security duties and various, mainly unpopular, garrisons scattered throughout the country. Apart from fighting against native opposition in the colonies where superior numbers and modern firepower were sufficient to achieve victory, it had little experience of warfare. Worse, its senior officers were still revelling in the afterglow of Waterloo with the result that it was not a progressive force. It might have had modern rifles but its ideas were still entrenched in a dogmatic conservatism. As a result, when its regiments were sent with the expeditionary force to the Black Sea they represented the best of the British Army and simply could not be replaced. Because successive governments had failed to provide any plan for a sustained campaign on the European mainland the army simply could not cope when it was called upon to embark on a war for which it had neither the manpower nor the resources. Small wonder that Clifford thought that Sevastopol would be the death of the British Army.

It was not just the soldiers who were concerned about the shortage of trained men. Palmerston worried incessantly about the lack of troops – he claimed that Raglan's army was 40,000 short of the complement voted by parliament – and he admonished Panmure that 'we shall disgrace ourselves if we do not make every effort to raise that amount'. Part of the problem was that Britain did not have a ready supply of reservists: soldiers enlisted for long service with the result that there was no pool of discharged soldiers who could be re-enlisted in time of emergency. The 1852 Militia Act had created a part-time militia of 80,000 soldiers but as it was intended primarily for home defence it could hardly be called a ready reserve. (To their credit many militiamen served in the Malta garrison and at Rhodes and other Mediterranean bases connected with the war.)

It was that shortage which had led the government to pass the controversial Foreign Enlistment Act and by the early summer of 1855 it was beginning to pay dividends. A British German Legion and a British Swiss Legion had produced 5659 men. Against Palmerston's wishes Poles, too, were also recruited: he thought the emigrés too 'rascally' and wanted them to enlist in the French Foreign Legion. Eventually the mercenary forces numbered 13,000 men but they were considered doubtful material. Their main purpose seems to have been the shoring up of numbers at a time when the imbalance between the British and French armies was becoming an acute embarrassment. In addition to Palmerston's concerns Clarendon, too, chided his Cabinet colleagues about the shortfall, telling Panmure that not only was it a source of alarm but that it allowed the French to adopt a superior and arrogant tone which could have serious repercussions at the end of the war.

Somewhat mischievously Napoleon III entered the debate by asking Cowley why the British did not introduce conscription. In France those men called up for service in the Crimea were allowed

to buy themselves out of the army once the war was over and
the emperor clearly thought that a similar system would benefit
Britain. Throughout the conversation Cowley told Clarendon that
he remained silent 'because I could not with propriety discuss the
value of British troops as compared with French'. He did remonstrate,
though, when Napoleon suggested that another solution could be
provided if each country played to its own strengths:

> What will be the state of things at the end of the war if we
> continue as we have begun? Why, that I shall have a navy of
> which you will be the first to be jealous and you will have
> expended millions to raise an Army which will then be useless
> to you. Whereas, if we each take the part that nature has assigned
> us, we may eventually assist each other materially at less cost and
> inconvenience.[9]

Cowley thanked the emperor for his suggestion but was too
courteous to utter more than diplomatic pleasantries. The truth was
that naval rivalry already existed between the two countries and this
would be exacerbated after the war. As for the army, the emperor was
both right and wrong. Britain never had any intention of creating a
large continental-style army but in the present impasse it did need
a larger army than the one commanded by Raglan. Unfortunately,
in its efforts to create it, the government found itself once more at
loggerheads with the United States.

From the very beginning of the proposal to enlist foreign legions
North America had been regarded as a prime recruiting ground and to
meet the expected rush a depot had been established at Halifax in Nova
Scotia. According to the Lieutenant-Governor, Sir John Gaspard Le
Marchant, the main problem would be accommodation and medical
facilities – at least 4000 recruits were expected in the spring of 1855
– but that turned out to be the least of the British government's
problems.[10] Responsibility for running the North American campaign had been given to the British minister in Washington, John
Fiennes Twisleton Crampton, a career diplomat who had served
in the St Petersburg and Vienna embassies before arriving in the
United States in 1845. His work in assisting his predecessor, Sir Henry
Lytton Bulwer, to conclude the Clayton-Bulwer Treaty, by which
Britain and the United States agreed not to make further colonial
acquisitions in Central America, ensured his promotion but it was

at that point in his life that his good fortune began to run out in Washington.

As any attempt by Britain to recruit in the United States would infringe the Neutrality Act of 1818, Crampton took legal advice to discover if there were any way of circumventing its articles. He found a solution but it was sailing close to the wind: he told Clarendon on 12 February that Britain could keep to the spirit of the act by employing agents to send the men to Canada without first signing them up in the United States:

> The outlay would not be considerable in any one instance; and if the Agent was to fail to fulfil his engagement as to the first batch of men, we should, of course, not employ him again and abandon the whole project as a failure. The thing must therefore be looked upon as an experiment; but it is one which I think likely to succeed, and of which the risk of trying is not great. Until otherwise instructed, I shall charge any money which I may advance to the Secret Service Account.[11]

With the help of Le Marchant he created a scheme for recruiting amongst disaffected European immigrants, mainly on the eastern seaboard. Here the British would be helped by a growing resentment against the rising tide of immigrants – between 1850 and 1860 their total numbers rose from 2.24 million to 3.09 million – and by the creation of a political party, the Know Nothings, which exploited widespread animosity against anyone not considered to be American-born. Local conditions also helped. The winter had been severe and unemployment was high and many of those seeking work were former soldiers who had served in the 1846–8 war against Mexico. Between them the two men hatched a plan whereby an ebullient Nova Scotia politician, Joseph Howe, would supervise the recruitment through a series of agents with the active assistance of Britain's consuls. On 10 April Le Marchant reported that the first seventy recruits had arrived in Halifax from Boston and only four had been rejected. It was a promising start.

All might have been well had Crampton used discretion but the whole enterprise was so amateurish that it was bound to attract the interest of the authorities. One of Crampton's first actions was to employ two agents: Henry Hertz, a Dane, to work in Philadelphia with Consul George B. Mathew; and Max Strobel, a Bavarian, to work in New York with Consul Anthony Barclay. Neither troubled themselves to keep their activities secret – according to the New York police the agents were a mixture of 'boarding house runners, saloon-keepers and riff-raff' – and in May Hertz was arrested. Howe, too, proved to be no diplomat and his indiscreet, albeit enthusiastic, methods soon attracted the interest of the New York District Attorney. One of his agents, Angus McDonald, had brazenly opened a recruiting office at 36 Pearl Street, and was immediately arrested when he started pamphleteering for volunteers. Other agents were rounded up, border controls were tightened and Marcy, the secretary of state, began to put pressure on Crampton.

Unhappily for US-British relations Crampton denied all knowledge of the recruiting when he was summoned to meet Marcy on 12 March. Marcy also accepted Crampton's promise that he would use his best endeavours to put a stop to any recruiting should he ever find evidence of it. Ten days later, when confronted with confirmation of Angus McDonald's activities, he repeated the disclaimer but the New York District Attorney was already making investigations; by May the trail led from Hertz to Crampton and Howe. All this Clarendon knew, although when questioned by Buchanan he denied any knowledge of the plot, and on June 22 Panmure called a halt to recruiting in the United States.

Ironically the scheme had produced little more than seven hundred recruits at a cost of £5250 to the British exchequer. But it was not the end of the matter. Hertz admitted everything at his trial that autumn and, stung by the fact that Crampton had lied to Marcy, the United States made a vigorous protest to Clarendon. In the first week of July he made an official complaint to the Foreign Office that 'numerous attempts have been made since the commencement of the existing war between Great Britain and Russia, to enlist soldiers for the British Army within the limits of the United States; and that rendezvous for this purpose have been actually opened in some of the principal cities':

> The President will be much gratified to learn that Her Majesty's Government has not authorised these proceedings; but has condemned the conduct of its officials engaged therein, and has visited them with its marked displeasure as well as taken decisive measures to put a stop to conduct so contrary to the laws of nations, the laws of the United States and the comity

which ought ever to prevail in the intercourse between two friendly nations.[12]

By then the US authorities had incontrovertible evidence that Crampton was involved in illegal recruitment but Clarendon refused to budge. The British government had taken stringent measures 'to guard against any violation of the United States' Law of Neutrality', he explained; the agents were acting in a freelance capacity and the potential recruits had only been paid to travel to Nova Scotia. As they had not been recruited in the United States, no law had been broken. Clarendon's confident readjustment of the facts did not mollify Marcy and during the late winter and spring of 1855–6 the row over recruitment would bring Britain and the United States once more to the brink of war.

Although the shortage of British troops in the Crimea and the growing French numbers made Raglan the junior partner, he was still able to exert his influence at conferences mainly because Canrobert was so diffident. April had seen a series of inconclusive plans following the failure to exploit the second artillery barrage and Canrobert seemed to the British to be overburdened by his responsibilities, not least by the emperor's interference in his plans. On the one hand he was required to prevent unnecessary French casualties; on the other he was under orders to continue the siege and to make preparations for an attack on the Russian field army. To the French this was prudence but to the British it smacked of pusillanimity.

An opportunity to redress the balance came at the beginning of May when, after much prevarication, Canrobert agreed to join an allied attack on the port of Kertch which covered the Sea of Azov and was an important conduit for supplying Sevastopol. The idea had been mooted by Lyons early in the campaign but the first order for action was not made by Panmure until 26 March:

> It has not failed to attract my attention and I have already alluded to the subject in my private letters to your Lordship that a great portion of the supplies of Russia are drawn from the direction of Kertch and from the Sea of Azoff by Arabas.
> Sir Charles Wood has written to Sir Edmund Lyons more than once upon this subject and it will be most important feature in war [sic], if by a combined operation by Sea and Land we can reduce the defences of Kertch and so cut off the

enemy's defences between Anapa and his Army. We should in
such case get possession of the Sea of Azoff with our Gun Boats,
and effectually sweep the road which reaches along the borders
of the Sea.[13]

It was an attractive proposition. Not only would it put a stop
to one of the Sevastopol garrison's supply routes but, because it
would be an amphibious operation, it would involve the Royal
Navy at a time when the British contribution to the war seemed
to be faltering. Initially Bruat and Bosquet warmed to the idea and
although Canrobert was dubious, on 29 April he gave his agreement
for a squadron of French warships and 8500 soldiers to join the
expedition which would be under Sir George Brown's command.
Amongst the British forces taking part would be the Highland Brigade,
the Rifle Brigade and the Royal Marines.

Here was a chance to impose a defeat on the Russians and Brown
was exultant: Fenton, the photographer, noticed him 'dancing and
kicking and emptying a tumbler of champagne' after receiving the
order to start on 3 May. 'You would have thought they were all
schoolboys,' the photographer told his wife. 'No one knows where
they are going.'[14] In an attempt to maintain that secrecy the allied
fleet sailed north-west past Sevastopol as if heading towards Odessa but
then doubled back towards Kertch. It was not to reach its destination:
the new telegraph line to Paris brought orders from Napoleon for
Canrobert to bring up the reserve forces from Constantinople. As
Bruat's ships would be required the expedition would have to be
recalled.

At 2.15 a.m. Canrobert sent an aide to Raglan giving him the
information. The two men had already spent the past few hours
debating the situation because Canrobert feared that the Russians had
reinforced Kertch and Raglan told Lyons later that he thought he had
managed to overcome the French commander-in-chief's concerns.
This time, though, Canrobert would not budge and a fast despatch
boat was sent to the fleet ordering Bruat to return. By the time it
arrived the allies were two hours' steaming time from Kertch and
making preparations to attack. Even then Bruat might have turned a
blind eye but he was no Nelson and, to the fury of his British allies,
he agreed to turn back. Without the backing of the French, Brown
could not continue and, to the accompaniment of much ill-disguised
criticism of the French, the fleet turned back to the Crimea.

The decision caused immense bad feeling between the allies. The normally placid Raglan was reported to be 'hurt and irritated', Brown had come close to punching the French General d'Autermmare and in his report to the Admiralty Lyons spoke of the 'great mortification of the French and English Admirals and Generals who, having arrived with the Forces off the Straits of Kertch under very propitious circumstances, considered success certain.'[15] When told of the recall in London, Panmure replied that the decision proved that Canrobert was 'utterly incapable of high command'. The bad feeling could not be hidden from Canrobert and when he presented a new plan to the conference on 9 May there was little chance of it being adopted even though overall command would have been given to Raglan. As summarised by Rose, who had been briefed by Niel, the strategy would have entailed moving more French troops into the trenches and it would rest on four main principles:

1. Leave siege intact.
2. Attack Russians on the plateau to the east of the post road from Belbeck to Inkerman.
3. Invest Sevastopol from the north.
4. Attack Simferopol.

In a separate despatch Rose also made it clear that Colonel Trochu had told him that Niel was pulling the strings, that it was not limited to his 'arme speciale, the Engineers, but that it is extended to the Military and Naval expedition against Kertch'. Rose also noted that Canrobert looked shattered and despondent, drained of all will to continue in command. On 13 May he told the British liaison officer, whom he liked and respected, that 'no event in his life had caused him such sincere regret and sorrow as his recall of the expedition because it had put him wrong with his friends, the English officers'.[16] There was to be no respite and, knowing that his position had been damaged irreparably, Canrobert tendered his resignation three days later, telling the Emperor that his 'health and spirit, tired by constant tension, no longer permit me to carry the burden of immense responsibility'. He added that Pélissier should succeed him and although Napoleon thought that the position should be given to Niel, Canrobert's proposal was accepted by Vaillant. Never comfortable in supreme command Canrobert showed great spirit and humility by asking to stay on in the Crimea as a divisional general in Bosquet's Second Corps.[17]

Pélissier's appointment was greeted with enthusiasm in the British camp. They had grown weary of 'Robert Can't' and the anger roused by the Kertch debacle had to be lanced if allied co-operation were to remain intact. The new French commander-in-chief quickly made an impact by reorganising his army into two corps and by making it plain that he was not going to be railroaded into accepting the emperor's plans for three armies to wage the war – a scheme which Panmure now agreed was 'wild and impracticable'. Short, stocky and bad-tempered – Fenton thought that he looked like a wild boar – Pélissier also won plaudits for putting Niel in his place and by adopting a no-nonsense approach to concentrating on bringing the siege to a successful conclusion. Rose, who had liked Canrobert, told Clarendon that the time had probably come to adopt a more rigorous approach to the war and that Pelissier was the man to do it:

> General Pélissier will never allow a half and half execution of his orders; if it can be done, it must be done. He is of a violent temper and rough manner, but I believe him to be just and sincere; and I think that in all important matters these two qualities will triumph over his ebullitions of temper. He has a quick conception, plenty of common sense, and a resolute mind, which thinks of overcoming, not yielding to difficulties.[18]

Pélissier began the task of mending bridges by agreeing to make a second raid on Kertch although he still insisted that the main target of the allied operation must be Sevastopol's defences. And it was left to Todleben himself to have the last word on this unhappy episode. Canrobert, he said in his memoirs, had failed to stand up to the advice given to him by his engineering officers and had shown 'extreme indecision'. Ironically, of Todleben, as an engineer, it could be said that this specialist branch of the army was the sole reason why the walls of Sevastopol remained unbreached at the beginning of the summer of 1855.[19]

12

Spring Cruise, Summer Success

When the war broke out, it was supposed that, because we had
steam as a propelling power instead of sails, we were about to
see great results obtained by means of our Navy. But ships were
meant to meet and vanquish ships, and we were beginning to
see that this was not a naval war.

Admiral Lord Hardwicke, The Times, *11 October 1855*

T he revival of the plan to attack Kertch gave the Royal Navy much
needed and welcome employment. Ever since the first bombardment of Sevastopol the previous October, during which British
warships led by Lyons in *Agamemnon* attacked Fort Constantine, the
fleet had been mainly involved in transportation and convoy duties.
Kertch provided an obvious means of redressing the balance and the
second expedition left with high hopes of achieving a comparatively
easy victory.

At dawn on 24 May 1855 sixty ships of the allied fleet made a
rendezvous off Cape Takil and, following a brief bombardment,
the troops were able to make an unopposed landing. The town
fell quickly and, having destroyed the government buildings and
an arsenal, the allies were able to march to Yenikale on the other
side of the peninsula. There the destruction continued and it was
made worse by the pillaging which accompanied Brown's order to
raze any buildings which might be useful to the Russian war effort.

William Howard Russell, who accompanied the expedition, was
shocked by what he saw, telling his readers that attempts 'to prevent
outrage and destruction were of the feeblest and most contemptible

character'. While it was true that the Turkish troops were the worst offenders, killing civilians without mercy and raping the Russian women, the British and the French were not without blame. Houses were ransacked, the booty taken to the waiting ships and, disgracefully, Kertch's museum was sacked and destroyed. With its collection of early Hellenic art it was an important repository, yet such lofty considerations did not impinge on the thoughts of the soldiers who looted it. Later, Russell came across a hastily written note in the museum condemning 'la guerre des barbares' but by then it was too late. Age-old statues and tablets lay in shards and the remains of one civilisation lay shattered at the hands of those who followed in its wake:

> The floor of the museum [he wrote on 28 May] is covered in depth with the debris of broken glass, of vases, urns, statuary, the precious dust of their contents, and charred bits of wood and bone, mingled with the fresh splinters of the shelves, desks, and cases in which they had been preserved. Not a single bit of anything that could be broken or burnt any smaller had been exempt from reduction by hammer or fire.

It was a shocking incident, deprecated by Raglan and by Brown who sent in fifty British cavalrymen to patrol Kertch and to prevent further outrages, but the damage had been done. When the news reached St Petersburg the Russians were rightly outraged. So too was the US minister, Thomas H. Seymour, who informed Marcy that 'the atrocities of the allies at Kertch and other places in the Crimea, which they have easily overrun, exceed in enormity the atrocities the British were guilty of in the war of 1812 against us'.[1] Seymour had arrived in the Russian capital in April 1854 and, although he had been handicapped by his inability to speak French, he had received a warm welcome. Nicholas told him that he wanted to see more of the US flag in the Baltic and had pressed his hand 'with a force and warmth which in our country would be called a good republican grip'. Seymour knew where he stood, too, having been told by Marcy that his mission in St Petersburg was to ensure the good health of relations with Russia:

> Between no two Nations on the Globe are the relations of peace and amity likely to be enduring. It is scarcely possible

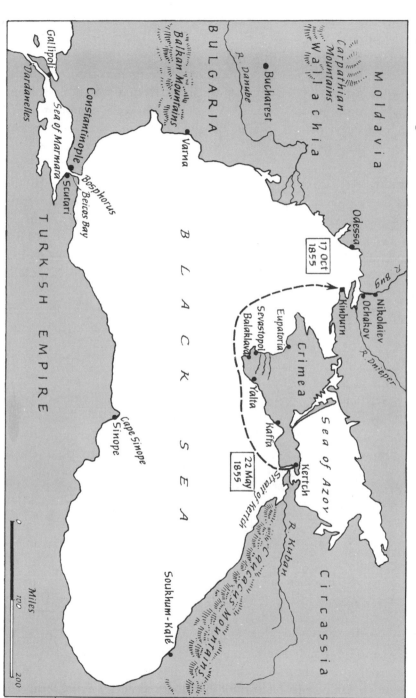

Operations Against Kertch and Kinburn

that the political policy of the one would interfere with that of the other.[2]

Seymour's anglophobia coloured all his comments from St Petersburg during the war and his report about Kertch was an easy oversimplification but the acerbic US minister had a point: not only had the British and French soldiers behaved badly but their officers had failed to stop them or their Turkish allies.

Despite those shortcomings, the expedition demonstrated that a maritime strategy could play a major part in defeating armies. Lyons was able to take his warships into the Sea of Azov and within weeks of the fall of Kertch all Russian supply ships had disappeared from the coast and the thoroughness of the blockade meant that Sevastopol had to rely on the increasingly unreliable overland route for their supplies. More than anything else, this pleased Pélissier who told Napoleon that he had 'struck deep into the Russian resources'. However, if he thought that the success at Kertch would mollify the emperor, the reply from Paris on 30 May merely told him to concentrate his mind on the matter in hand:

> I am glad that it [the Kertch expedition] was successful; but nevertheless, I can't help regarding as *fatal* anything which today tends to scatter your forces. The course to follow is easy to indicate: (1) defeat the Russian army in order to surround the fortress;(2) the place being surrounded, take Sebastopol;(3) the place taken, evacuate the Crimea and destroy all the fortifications or at most leave the Turks there alone.[3]

In conclusion Napoleon reiterated the fact that Pélissier was under orders to carry out his emperor's plan, although he remarked somewhat ambiguously, that 'the means of achieving this result are naturally up to your particular calling'. Once again Napoleon was intent on directing events in the Crimea while leaving the implementation to his commander-in-chief. It was not a recipe for harmony but fortunately Pélissier was his own man and refused to be diverted by Napoleon's constant interfering by telegram which had worn down his predecessor. Having told the British that omelettes cannot be made without breaking eggs he insisted that all of the allies' energy should be concentrated on breaking the siege by attacking the Russian defences. On this point he had been cheered by a successful French assault on the Russian trenches and counter-approaches on the night of 22 May. Although it cost some two thousand casualties it proved that the Russian defences could be broken by a sustained and determined infantry attack. With the supply line to Kertch broken an effective assault on the Mamelon Vert could pave the way for the breaching of the Malakov and the Redan. Raglan concurred and at a council of war on 28 May it was agreed that, following the customary artillery barrage, the French would attack the Mamelon Vert while the British would take on the new defensive systems in front of the Redan, known as the Quarries.

The optimism in the Crimea was matched by the Admiralty's confidence that a second expedition into the Baltic could inflict serious damage on the Russian war effort. Napier's successful destruction of Bomarsund suggested that Sveaborg and Kronstadt were not impregnable and that if they fell it would be possible for the allied fleet to threaten St Petersburg itself. Once again the chimera of an effortless way of winning the war came into focus, and once again the Admiralty laid plans for sending a fleet into the Baltic. When the First Sea Lord introduced the Naval Estimates on 16 February 1855 it was agreed that only steam-powered ships should be deployed and that the fleet should also include small gun boats and mortar vessels. There would also be a change in command. Napier having been disgraced, unfairly so (he was later to be vindicated), the Baltic Fleet was put in the hands of Rear-Admiral Sir Richard Dundas who proved to be a more sober and judicious commander than either his predecessor or his namesake in the Black Sea. It also helped his cause that he was a member of the distinguished Scottish house of Melville, his father having been for many years the First Lord of the Admiralty.

Planning for the expedition was put in the capable hands of Captain Bartholomew Sulivan, the fleet surveying officer whose charts and sketches had played such a vital role in the previous year's operations. A Cornishman, he had accompanied Charles Darwin on the *Beagle* expedition of 1831–6 and was highly regarded as a hydrographer and surveyor. After Wood succeeded Graham at the Admiralty he asked Sulivan to report on the Russian fortresses at Sveaborg and Kronstadt and to recommend the type of forces which should be engaged. This Sulivan did, providing an accurate summary of the Russian strengths and recommending that these could be engaged by naval forces alone without the need of troops. When Clarendon crossed over to France at the beginning of March to try to dissuade Napoleon from carrying out his threat to go to the Crimea he took Sulivan's report with him. Its recommendations were warmly received by the emperor, partly because he believed that the failure to take the fortresses was a stain on allied honour, and partly because he hoped that a naval success would finally encourage Sweden to join the alliance against Russia.

On 20 March the first British warships left Spithead for Kiel, with the rest following a fortnight later. Although they were seen off with some enthusiasm a sober leader in *The Times* warned that better things were expected of them than the partial success won by Napier, more especially as they were facing 'a third-rate naval power':

> It [the Baltic Fleet] is to attempt more, to run more risk, to follow further and closer, to care rather less for losing ships and men, and rather more for inflicting losses and disgraces on the enemy. In a word, the force is stronger and the duty more terrible than last year; and if the scene today should attract a smaller number of gazers than last year, they will doubtless see it less of a holiday spectacle and more as an operation of war.[4]

In addition to threatening the Russian fortresses Dundas's fleet was also charged with the responsibility of imposing a blockade, a thankless task which none the less denied Russia strategic supplies. Various coastal stations were attacked and destroyed but the main targets remained Sveaborg and Kronstadt, both of which had been the subjects of careful reconnaissance by Sulivan in HMS *Merlin*. He proved to be a meticulous operator, taking his vessel as close in shore as he dared – on one occasion *Merlin* struck a mine, an incident which was much dramatised at the time – and he was not above going ashore to get local information. On one island, Hogland, he found that the local fishermen were willing to be helpful and he admitted that he was disconcerted by the arrival of a pretty young woman, 'nicely dressed in a pink skirt and black jacket, with a shawl on her head.' On another occasion, in Estonia he found that the German-speaking Balt nobility were more English than the English. Invited to dinner he was driven to a nearby country house which he found to be quite bucolic and idyllic:

> It really all seemed like a dream: three miles inland in an enemy's country, and going over all this quite English-like scenery with a nice young lady speaking as good English as I did, except

with a slightly foreign accent . . . we had a splendid dinner, but
more plain meats, game etc than I expected. Coffee and tea were
carried out under a tree, and we left about ten, just at dusk, the
baron driving me at a rattling pace in a light phaeton with the
English horses and a thorough English-dressed groom, leather
belts, boots and all.[5]

And then it was back to the business of war. The arrival of a
French fleet under Admiral Pénaud on 1 June raised allied hopes that
Kronstadt might be attacked but Sulivan's report was disappointing.
Not only had the Russians reinforced their fleet – Sulivan counted 34
steam gunboats – but they had strengthened the seaward defences with
44 electrical undersea mines and 950 chemical contact mines and a
seemingly impregnable barrier. These had to be swept from the chan-
nels but it would be a difficult and dangerous task: the chemical contact
mines were moored a few feet below the water and were triggered
when the fuse, a glass tube containing chlorate of potassium and sugar,
produced a flame to fire the main charge, eight pounds of explosive.
Under the circumstances Sulivan could not recommend an attack and
on 4 June Dundas explained his reasons to the Admiralty:

> The barrier itself, in the parts examined, appeared to consist of
> irregular rough frames of timber, firmly secured in the ground,
> and filled with stones, and with a narrow opening between each
> frame, sufficient only to admit row-boats of light draught; but the
> size of the frames appeared to increase in an easterly direction,
> and in the deeper portions of the channel, where stones were
> showing above water, it seems probable that the obstructions
> may be still more substantial. Under these circumstances and in
> the absence of a powerful and numerous flotilla, sufficient to
> oppose that of the enemy, no effectual attempt could be made
> to remove such obstructions: and no serious attack appears to
> me to be practicable with the means at my disposal.[6]

This was a description which would have been familiar to Napier
but this time the Admiralty took a more sanguine approach to the
Baltic Fleet's chances of success and Kronstadt was permitted to be
left alone. 'I can see the admiral is very doubtful and I dare not
urge him to try it,' noted Sulivan, 'unless with a force to give
every probability of success.' With the Royal Navy's global fleet

overstretched Dundas did not have the resources to attack Kronstadt, even though Sulivan knew that such an assault was not altogether hopeless, given the right weapons. In this respect the British had placed considerable faith in the French invention of floating batteries – squat, heavily-armoured vessels with shallow draughts which could approach the enemy's defences to fire their heavy 30-pounder guns secure in the knowledge that ten centimetres of wrought-iron plating would offer them adequate protection from explosive shells. These innovations gave notice that warships would now be able to attack heavily defended sea fortresses with some hope of success, but those that had been built were sent to the Black Sea and would not be ready for deployment against the northern Russian bases until the following year.

For the watching Russians the decision to abandon an attack on Kronstadt came as a relief, for although the defences had been strengthened the fortress's fall would have left St Petersburg undefended. Not that the population seemed to be worried. As they had done when Napier's fleet arrived the previous summer the masts and smoke trails became something of a summer attraction. One Russian captain, anxious to impress the ladies of St Petersburg, held a ball on board his warship and allowed his guests to view the enemy from the bridge. Amongst those who ventured out to look at the masts of Dundas's fleet was the US ambassador, Thomas Seymour. He had just finalised arrangements for an American military commission headed by Major Richard Delafield to visit the Crimea, but when he reported back to Washington it was the arrival of the Royal Navy which excited his immediate attention.

> The British and French fleets have attempted nothing against Cronstadt yet – but for want of better employment they have been devastating the coast below, destroying peaceful villages, and winning by slow but sure degrees that kind of fame which is most closely allied to infamy.[7]

On this occasion Seymour was entitled to express his disgust. Because it was taking considerable time to assess the risk of attacking the Russian strongholds and because many captains became so bored by the thankless task of investigating breaches of the blockade, they became over-zealous in their duties. Some Finnish fishing villages were put to the torch and their inhabitants killed, and there were several incidents of naval parties mounting an attack after approaching small ports under the flag of truce.

All this might have been written off as one of the consequences of total war but there were occasions when British captains exaggerated their roles, not just in their despatches to Dundas – who dutifully passed them to London – but also in correspondence and conversation with the press. With the fleet was J.W. Carmichael of the *Illustrated London News*, an artist distrusted by senior officers due to his tendency to over-elaborate every incident he witnessed. When sailors from HMS *Nile* went ashore to investigate a settlement Carmichael's illustration was accompanied by a description stating that their cutters came under heavy fire from 3000 enemy soldiers. On seeing it Sulivan could not resist commenting: 'Well, this celebrated battle consisted, I hear, of two muskets being fired by militiamen on shore, for which fire was opened on villages, houses, church and hall. Worse, the Royal Navy was making itself look ridiculous in the eyes of the Russians who knew only too well the truth of the assertions.'[8]

However, despite these exasperating incidents (the concomitant of any campaign in which men eager for battle are forced to hold their fire while waiting for a major encounter), the sight of Dundas's steam-powered fleet was a powerful reminder of Britain's naval supremacy. Within a few days Alexander II would learn of the fall of Kertch and of the clear-cut effectiveness of allied sea power in the Black Sea. The lesson was not lost on him: even with a relatively small fleet the British were able to take command of the Black Sea and the Baltic, exercising a control that was so complete that every Russian warship was condemned to remain in port for the duration of the war.

However, Kronstadt's reprieve did not mean that Dundas was ready to go home without inflicting a blow on the Russians. Sulivan's survey of the Sveaborg defences convinced the allied naval command that a bombardment could be engaged upon without too much risk and that its downfall would neutralise the northern coast of the Gulf of Finland and threaten the Finnish capital of Helsingfors, only three miles away. Built by the Swedes to protect their northern approaches, the huge fortress had been surrendered to the Russians in 1809 and by the time of Sulivan's survey it was not in the best repair. During the previous year a test-firing of its guns had resulted in some of the fortifications falling down and although the Russians had repaired the damage and added to its defences the fortress was still considered to be vulnerable.

Sulivan reckoned that it would be possible for the mortar and rocket boats to get close in to the target through the approaches while the capital ships provided cover.

That proved to be the case. Early in the morning of 9 August the allied fleet lined up in attack formation two miles off shore while their gun and mortar boats, flanked by Lancaster-armed British boats wheeled into the attack, circling the Russian positions and sending a wall of fire into the fortress. The assault began at seven o'clock and continued throughout the day. At a few minutes past eleven the arsenal in Fort Vargon exploded and an hour later there was a similar 'monster explosion' which seemed to the watching reporter from *The Times* to resemble 'a volcano in a state of eruption'. Despite their best efforts the Russian gunners failed to hit any of the gunboats and when the bombardment halted the next day there had been no allied casualties. The greater part of Sveaborg had been destroyed and, convinced that an invasion was at hand, the inhabitants of Helsingfors fled the city only to return a few days later once the fleet had left. Two days later Dundas was able to report that, all told, the allies had fired 1100 tons of iron shells and that his ships had succeeded in destroying Sveaborg as a naval base for the Russian fleet:

> Considering the extent of injury which had now been inflicted in the enemy, and reflecting that few buildings of importance remained to be destroyed on the island of Vargon, and that those still standing upon Svarto were at the extent of our range and in positions where no shells had yet reached them, I was of the opinion that no proportionate advantage was to be gained by continuing the fire during another day with fewer mortars and smaller objects over a larger extent of ground.[9]

Sveaborg does not stand high in the long list of British naval successes. While it was a thorough and cheaply won victory it did not bring the war any closer to a conclusion and Dundas's fleet had been unable to make any impact on Kronstadt. But, at the time, Sveaborg was good for morale and raised expectations that Sevastopol was equally vulnerable – for in the minds of politicians and the public the Crimean fortress was always the real target of the allied war effort. Hopes were high, therefore, that Sevastopol and Kronstadt could be equally threatened and that their fall would force the Russians to sue for peace. Watching the bombardment from HMS *Duke of Wellington*

The Bombardment of Sveaborg

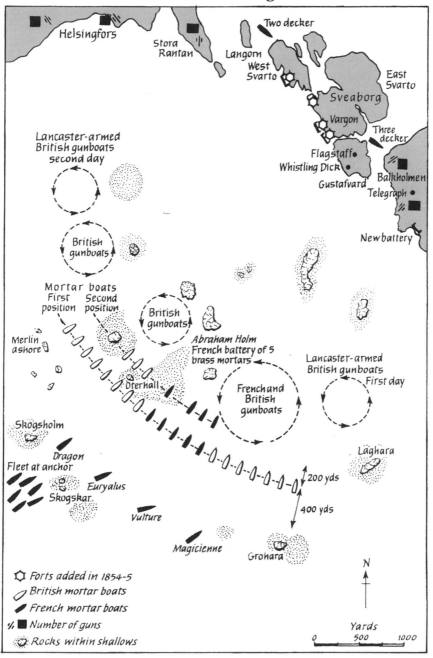

Helsingfors

Stora Rantan

Two decker

Langom

West Svarto

East Svarto

Sveaborg

Vargon

Three decker

Lancaster-armed British gunboats second day

Flagstaff

Whistling Dick

Balkholmen

Gustafvard

Telegraph

New battery

British gunboats

Mortar boats
First position   Second position

British gunboats

Abraham Holm
French battery of 5 brass mortars

Lancaster-armed British gunboats
First day

Merlin ashore

Oterhall

French and British gunboats

Skogsholm

Läghara

Dragon
Fleet at anchor

200 yds

Euryalus
Skogskar

400 yds

Vulture

Magicienne

Grohara

N

☆ Forts added in 1854-5
◁ British mortar boats
◀ French mortar boats
// ■ Number of guns
⬭ Rocks within shallows

Yards

0   500   1000

William Don, a young Scot later to be a doctor, was convinced that he had witnessed a breakthrough in naval warfare:

> The ruin wrought at Sveaborg by our mortar fire brought home to the Tsar and his advisers the certainty that, if the war went on, Cronstadt would next year meet with a similar fate. If that happened and St Petersburg was menaced, not all the official lying in the world could conceal it from the Russian public. There is the best ground for inferring that the bombardment of Sveaborg was a more important factor in ending the war than even the fall of Sevastopol itself[10]

Don had a vested interest in making that claim but he was right about allied intentions. The experience at Sveaborg had settled once and for all Nelson's argument that warships should not attack sea fortresses: Sulivan's gunboats, mortar vessels, armoured batteries and blockships had seen to that. When the fleets sailed back into home waters before Christmas, plans were already being laid for a renewed attack on Kronstadt in the following spring using a massive force of the new coastal vessels. By then it would be possible to concentrate naval force in the Baltic and the French believed that troops could be landed in the Baltic states to invade Russia itself. All that, of course, would depend on Sevastopol falling to the allies.

Meanwhile, the Admiralty suddenly found itself deflected by a need to reinforce its North Atlantic and West Indian stations due to fresh tensions with the United States. Despite Clarendon's bland and not completely truthful assurances, Marcy had refused to let drop the matter of Crampton's involvement in illegal recruiting. In a strongly worded letter to Crampton on 5 September the secretary of state claimed that he had incontrovertible evidence that the British ambassador and his consuls had been acting illegally and that their involvement in the recruiting programme infringed the sovereign rights of the United States as well as its municipal laws. That being so, it was insufficient to make excuses: the British government had to admit its involvement in the plot:

> The information in the possession of this Government is so well established by proof, and corroborated by so many publick acts, that the President feels warranted in presenting to the British Government this conduct of Her Majesty's Officers as

disrespectful to the United States and incompatible with the friendly relations between the two countries.

Among the solemn duties imposed upon the President is that of maintaining and causing to be respected the Sovereign Rights of the United States, and to vindicate before the world their good faith in sustaining neutral relations with other Powers; and from this duty he will not allow himself to be diverted, however unpleasantly it may affect his personal or official relations with individuals.

The course which the President would deem it proper to take towards the implicated officers within the United States depends, in some measure, upon their relation to their Government in this matter.

In his covering letter to Clarendon Crampton expressed 'surprise and regret at Marcy's attitude' and reminded the foreign secretary that it had been his 'constant care to avoid and to inculcate upon others to avoid any act which could possibly constitute a violation of the stringent municipal law in the United States on the subject of Foreign Enlistment'.[11] Having received the correspondence the foreign secretary decided to adopt that line and went on the offensive. Buchanan was summoned to the Foreign Office to be told that the British government was becoming increasingly impatient with the constant demands from Washington:

> Her Majesty's Government feel confident that even the extra-ordinary measures which have been adopted in various parts of the Union to obtain evidence against her Majesty's servants or their agents by practices sometimes resorted to under despotic institutions, but which are disdained by all free and enlightened governments, will fail to establish any well-founded charge against Her Majesty's servants.[12]

Having thus placed the United States on a par with tsarist Russia, Clarendon went on to accuse the United States government of supplying arms and ammunition to the Russian war effort and of making arrangements for American medical personnel to serve in the Russian army inside Sevastopol. There were also rumours that three hundred Kentucky riflemen had been smuggled into Russia to help the war effort and in August Cowley had passed on an intelligence report

that a number of American engineers had travelled to St Petersburg
through Berlin taking with them a 'model of a submarine infernal
machine'. There was sufficient evidence, he claimed, to back up these
accusations but 'Her Majesty's Government has been silent on the
matters which they did not think indicative of the general feelings
of the American people'.

Buchanan replied that Britain, too, had received some munitions
from US suppliers and that the government had been vigilant in trying
to put a stop to skippers attempting to break the blockade. Indeed,
the US consul in Liverpool, the novelist Nathaniel Hawthorne, had
been instrumental in stopping an illegal shipment through a merchant
called Field and that everything possible was being done to keep
within the letter of the law. (This was quite a concession. Hawthorne
had already admitted his preferences: 'I hate England; though I love
some Englishmen, and like them generally, in fact.') Besides, added
Buchanan, these matters should not detract attention from the case in
hand, namely, that there was sufficient proof to implicate Crampton
and the British consuls.

The quarrel rumbled on throughout the autumn by which time
the British government had made its position clear by strengthening
its naval power off the coasts of the United States. One reason for
the deployment was the need to show the British flag; the other
was intelligence from New York that a powerful armed steamer
was being built with Russian funds. Once constructed this would be
manned by privateering crews and it would be used to attack Cunard
steamers on the North Atlantic route. Clarendon also claimed to have
evidence that the US government was intent on taking advantage of
Britain's pre-occupation with the war by fomenting trouble in Ireland.
According to information gathered by Crampton and his consuls, Irish
sympathisers, with the tacit approval of the United States government,
had laid plans to infiltrate three hundred republican terrorists into
Ireland to cause trouble while most of the British garrison was fighting
the Russians in the Crimea:

In the latter part of July last my attention was called by Mr
Barclay, Her Majesty's Consul at New York, to the existence
of Clubs composed of the Irish population in that City for
the purpose of enlisting and drilling volunteers to effect an
insurrection in Ireland; it being their intention to embark in
small parties in almost every ship going to Liverpool, and on

reaching Ireland to divide themselves among all the counties; and it was stated to Mr Barclay that many of those composing the Irish Militia Regiments as well as the Police Force in that country had been corrupted and that their aid was counted upon by the conspirators of New York in the projected rebellion.[13]

While Crampton admitted that much of the 'evidence' was flimsy and even hysterical – in Cincinnati the consul Charles Rowcroft reported a suspicion that one of the witnesses in the Hertz trial was the doorman of the United Irish Party headquarters and 'one of those active in carrying out the plot to entrap me into a violation of the Neutrality laws' – there was a sudden outbreak of anti-British feeling amongst the Irish populations in New York, Boston and Philadelphia in the autumn of 1855. To Crampton the issue was clear: Irish republicans in the United States were taking advantage of the old dictum that England's difficulty was Ireland's opportunity and, at best, the United States was turning a blind eye to their activities. If so, then the administration was surely guilty of breaching its own Neutrality Laws by allowing Irishmen to combine against a foreign power. 'It is, however, not the less true,' he advised Clarendon, 'that the continued toleration of numerous associations professing the most hostile intentions to Great Britain is calculated to have an injurious effect upon the friendly relations of the two countries.'[14]

Buchanan replied that the idea of Washington involving itself in any plan to unsettle Ireland was preposterous and, as for the armed steamer, he had no information to suggest that New York shipbuilders were working for the Russians. On the latter complaint he was mistaken. A modern steamer was being built for Russian service but it was later diverted into Rio de Janeiro by the Royal Navy while sailing into the Pacific. These threats seemed to suggest to 'the silent and attentive' Clarendon that Britain had sufficient reason to strengthen its naval presence in the North Atlantic:

They [the warships] were sent there because it is the duty of those who are charged with the conduct of the affairs of this country to be on their guard against all dangers which may appear on any part of the Horizon.[15]

So convinced was Buchanan by Clarendon's firmness that he warned Marcy that Britain would not hesitate to go to war and they would do so with the backing of France. For that he once more blamed Napoleon III. To the US minister the French emperor was a despot who 'regards the existence and the rapid advance of the Republic of the United States as a standing censure upon his own usurpation and his tyranny. He has annihilated liberty in France and looks upon its continued existence in our own country with extreme jealousy.'[16] As France had come close to declaring war on the United States in the previous year Buchanan counselled that it might do so again in concert with Britain, once the war against Russia had been concluded.

The recruiting affair had clearly touched a raw nerve and anti-American sentiments were being expressed in the popular press. The same was true in the United States. Earlier in the crisis the *New York Herald* had accused the US government of working 'to get up a difficulty with Great Britain to influence the approaching elections and the presidential contest of 1856', but by November it too had been gripped with war fever, its issue of 17 November carrying the sensational headlines: 'Great War Excitement/The United States the Battle Ground of European Parties/The Great Celto-American Invasion Project'.

Under the circumstances Buchanan proposed that he should stay in Britain longer than he had intended to do at the outset of his appointment. His decision was hardly a sacrifice to the public good; this time-served political servant, nicknamed 'Old Public Functionary', had plans to seek the Democratic nomination in the forthcoming presidential elections and it suited his purpose to be outside the United States during this long drawn out and increasingly tense confrontation.

13

Trench Warfare: Massacre in the Redoubts

Is that Peninsula doomed to be the grave of our most gallant fellows?

Consul Robert Colquhoun to Lord Stratford de Redcliffe,
1 July 1855

The third bombardment of Sevastopol began in the late afternoon of 6 June 1855 and once again great things were expected. It continued throughout the night and by dawn the following day the allied batteries were still blazing away as the British and French infantry waited in their lines for the rockets which would be the signal to attack. Fanny Duberly spoke for many in the British camp when she hoped that 'this time the guns will not play an overture for another farce'. Others were not so sanguine. Riding beside her as the French infantry moved up to the attack, Bosquet found tears coursing down his cheeks. '*Madame,*' he said, turning to her, '*à Paris on a toujours l'exposition, les bals, les fêtes, et dans une heure et demie la moitié de ces braves seront morts.*'*

Inevitably there would be casualties, just as Bosquet had foretold. The very nature of the frontal assault would bring a heavy bill: for all that the artillery pieces and howitzers had done sterling work in bombarding the well-defended Russian positions, the fortifications would still have to be won by infantrymen attacking across open and defended ground.

---

* 'Madame, in Paris there are always exhibitions, balls and parties taking place; but in ninety minutes' time half of these brave fellows will be dead.'

Why then had Pélissier taken the decision to push ahead with the assault when he knew that there would be an uncomfortably large casualty list? First, he believed that concentrated force was the only way of ending the siege. Diversions of the kind suggested by the emperor were useful but, none the less, secondary considerations: in his mind the direct approach was to be preferred even though, as he admitted to Bosquet, the 'conquest of the enemy counter-approaches will cost us definite sacrifices'. His thinking was clear. Because the Russians had invested so heavily in Todleben's defences, these had to be the main target. Destroy them and the enemy's will to resist would crumble.

Second, it is clear from the despatches between Paris and Kamiesh that Pélissier was becoming increasingly irritated by Napoleon's continual interference and by Niel's unthinking support for any imperial *diktat*. Here the French commander-in-chief had the backing of his old friend Vaillant but, even so, he was running a considerable risk by disobeying orders and effectively running his own show. Occasionally, Napoleon's exasperation at being so far removed from the battlefront got the better of him. Three days before the attack began he begged Pélissier to remember that an engineer was the best soldier to handle a siege and that an infantry attack on the Russian lines would only succeed 'after fierce and bloody struggles which will cost you your best troops'. Fortunately, Pélissier had the backing of Raglan, Kingscote noting that the two commanders were in complete accord during the planning of the attack.

The idea behind the attack was that, once the artillery had softened up the Russian positions, the French would assault the Mamelon Vert defences. Then it would fall to the British to begin their offensive against the new Quarries defences in front of the Redan. The British knew what to expect. During the campaigning in the Peninsula British infantrymen had put their lives in the balance attacking the French in entrenched positions whose names were emblazoned on the colours of many of the regiments serving in the Crimea – Badajoz, Ciudad Rodrigo and San Sebastian. The memory of the 'forlorn hope' was still strong – the infantrymen who formed the first line of attack – and those who remembered knew only too well that siege battles produced appalling carnage balanced by incredible gallantry. At Badajoz Wellington lost more soldiers than in any battle of the Peninsular War, save only Albuera and Talavera. Then the French were only armed with muskets; at Sevastopol most the Russian sharpshooters were now equipped with rifles which swept the field with a fearsome density and range. Raglan and his senior commanders knew that the forthcoming offensive would take a dreadful toll on their weakened and untried infantry, yet, like Pélissier, they were committed to it.

At 6.30 in the morning of 7 June the attack went in, a shower of rockets from the French lines marking the first stage of the battle. The French, whose zig-zag parallel trenches had taken them closer to the Russian lines, attacked first, advancing rapidly and with great momentum towards their target. For the watching Henry Clifford it was an awe-inspiring spectacle, line after line of whooping French soldiers streaming up to the attack:

> The Russian sharpshooters in the Rifle Pits took to flight at once, and many of them were turned over before the French reached the 'Mamelon'. It was as splendid as it was awful to see the brave Frenchmen rushing up under such fire and my heart beat as I never felt it before and the tears ran down my face when in less than ten minuts after they left the trenches I saw the 'tricolor' flag flourishing over the parapet of the 'Mamelon'.[1]

There was more to the French initiative than sound and fury. So complete was the attack that the Mamelon was soon in their hands – the honour of taking the position fell to Colonel Brancion of the 50th Regiment – but the French over-reached themselves. Sensing that the Russians were about to yield before the intensity of the attack the French officers urged on their men to assault the Malakov itself. With their blood up it was difficult to quell the urge – soldiers at the sharp end of a battle often prefer instinct to judgement – but it was a tactical error. Regrouping behind their fortifications the Russian infantrymen mounted a spirited counter-attack which forced the French to retreat. Once more they were forced to set about retaking control of the Mamelon by clearing the Russian trenches at bayonet-point. By the evening the position was safely in their hands and in honour of the gallant colonel whose regiment had taken it, the Mamelon Vert was immediately renamed the Brancion Redoute.

By then, too, the British had achieved their objective, having successfully stormed the Quarries, sweeping the Russians from their positions and capturing their naval guns. According to Kingscote, the battle had provided 'one of the grandest and most soul stirring sights ever seen'. For those who survived the spectacle had indeed been impressive, the rattle of rifle fire and the sound of bugles heard above the rumble of artillery, and in front of them the flash of fire from the Russian redoubts. But Bosquet's tears had not been misplaced. There was a shocking price to be paid for the triumph: the French lost 5443 casualties, the British 671.

Not without reason, though, the capture of the Russian advance defences was a tremendous filip to morale and those who had taken part in the battle were confident that another attack would surely break down the resistance from the Malakov and Great Redan. An excited Rose, his mind still reeling from witnessing the battle alongside Pélissier, wrote immediately to Clarendon, claiming that the Russians 'must now, more than ever, think that the time is come to leave a Fortress which is doomed, and fall back on Russian resources'.[2] If that were to be the outcome the momentum had to be maintained but already Pélissier was under renewed pressure from the emperor to call off the assault. Unlike Raglan who had received a courteous message from his political masters, praising him for the victory and for maintaining the 'best feeling' with the French, Pélissier received nothing but cold water from Napoleon III:

> I wished before sending congratulations on the brilliant success to learn how great the losses were. I am informed of the figure by Saint-Petersburg. I admire the courage of the troops but I would observe to you that a battle fought to decide the entire fate of the Crimea would not have cost you more. I persist then in the order which I had the Minister of War give you, to make all your efforts to enter resolutely into a field campaign.[3]

This was the last message which Pélissier wanted to hear but, being in constant contact with Paris through the telegraph system, he could hardly turn a blind eye. When the occasion demanded, he could claim that there had been hold-ups in the reception and sending of signals − a common problem − but it would be impossible to ignore the emperor's order to conserve French forces for a battle with Gorchakov's field army. His response was typical of the man. In a fit of carefully contrived pique he told the emperor that, 'at the somewhat paralysing end of an electric wire', he was caught between insubordination and loss of self-respect, that the army's blood was up and that a fresh assault could win the day. Unless he were allowed to continue he would have no option but to resign. It was a risky strategy – battlefield commanders who offer their resignation frequently find it being accepted by their superiors at distant headquarters – but Pélissier clearly believed that he had no other option. At that critical stage, any French backsliding would put him in a poor position with his allies.

On 10 June General H.D. Jones and General Niel met with the senior sapper and gunner officers to study the Russian defences and to plan the next stage of the attack. It was decided that the siege operations had to continue and five days later Raglan and Pélissier held a council of war at which it was agreed that the French should mount their offensive against the Malakov while the British attacked the Great Redan. It was a risky business. Both targets contained artillery pieces and provided well-built embrasures for the Russian infantry: unless these were neutralised the allied infantrymen would attack the walls under punishing fire. For that reason the artillery barrage would have to be heavy and sustained.

At first the signs were good. When the guns opened up on 17 June they produced a wall of fire all along the line and later Todleben admitted that the Russian defences were in a parlous state. 'I don't remember any of the preceding bombardments having been even a little like this one,' claimed an officer in the Malakov. 'This time it was pure hell. It was clear that they had prepared themselves for something out of the ordinary.'[4] Even the Russians' ability to reconstruct Todleben's flying entrenchments seemed to have deserted them. Over six hundred allied guns took part in the barrage in addition to the fire provided by the fleet lying off-shore and the watching infantrymen began to grow in confidence. Surely this latest assault was the endgame for it seemed that no one could survive before its onslaught. Even the date was propitious – the following day would mark the anniversary of Waterloo.

And yet, as so often happens in a battle, the outcome would be decided not by events on the battlefield but by equally tortuous incidents elsewhere. Two days earlier Pélissier had seen fit to sack Bosquet who disapproved of the plans to attack the Malakov. Little love was lost between the two men who had been rivals in Algeria; they might have been able to tolerate one another in the Crimea but for two errors of judgement on the part of Bosquet. First he failed to hand over to Pélissier a plan of the Russian defences found in the uniform of a dead Russian officer and, second, he had sent a stream of bitter despatches back to Paris criticising Pélissier's conduct of the war – both unpardonable offences in a subordinate officer. Pélissier had little option but to replace him but the move unsettled the army on the eve of a vital battle.

Also, the row may have unsettled the French commander-in-chief and interfered with his judgement. For reasons that remain unclear he suddenly decided to bring forward the French attack to 3 a.m. and to order the infantry to go in without the preliminary bombardment. Although Jones was present when the decision was taken he did not demur and as a result Raglan was left with no option but to comply. Any other consideration was out of the question as the British had been accused many times before of tardiness on the eve of battle. The last thing Raglan wanted was a fresh rupture and, late in the evening, he was forced to issue fresh orders to his men to bring them up to the start line in time to meet the new timetable.

Then fate took a hand. The night was cloudless and together with the brightness of the fires from the Russian lines, it provided no cover for the British troops as they marched into position in the forward trenches. It was impossible to conceal their movements and the Russian defenders were quick to assess the danger. Artillery pieces were redeployed and primed and infantrymen poured into the entrenchments. Even then a concerted attack might have succeeded but when a stray shell was shot over the French lines the officer commanding the division on the right, General Mayan, gave the order to advance, having mistaken its firey trail for the rockets signalling the beginning of the attack. Seeing what was happening Pélissier ordered the remaining two divisions to attack but by the time the rockets had been fired the French were moving forward in broken order, the planned co-ordinated attack reduced to a desperate rush against the concentrated fire from the Russian lines.

It was an appalling sight. The lines in front of the Malakov became a killing ground as the French infantrymen walked into a hail of bullets and ball. Rudimentary landmines exploded beneath their feet while shrapnel and grapeshot thinned their ranks. Still they stumbled on; some managed to engage the enemy with the bayonet; others fell like ninepins before the weight of the artillery fire. Smoke enveloped the battlefield, adding to the confusion, and wounded men screamed out for mercy from God or help from their mothers, anything to gain release from the hell in which they found themselves. This was the face of battle which few had expected to encounter only an hour or two beforehand.

Watching the plight of his allies Raglan was strangely moved. To join in the attack was to produce inevitable British casualties, yet to have left the French to their fate would have been a stain on British honour. Attack they must, whatever the consequences. As he told Panmure in his next despatch he considered it to be his duty to attack for had he not done so, he was 'quite certain that, if the troops had remained in our trenches, the French would have attributed their non-success to our refusal to participate in the operation'. Pride and duty: combined, they were powerful considerations.[5]

Brown was given the order to attack but with the lack of time available to him, he was denied the luxury of planning its timetable and execution. If the French were to be assisted the British forces had to attack immediately and this they did in two flank columns which left their trenches and advanced steadily across the quarter of a mile between them and the Russian defences. Led by General Sir John Campbell (4th Division) and Colonel Lacy Yea (Light Division) they were soon in difficulties. As had happened to the French they came under withering fire from the Russian batteries – after the battle Raglan told Panmure that he 'never had a conception before of such a shower of grape as they poured down from the Russian works', far worse than anything he had experienced in the Peninsula – and, predictably, this led to heavy casualties. Amongst the first to be killed was Campbell, gunned down as he left the security of the trenches; his second-in-command met a similar fate immediately afterwards.

First into the breach were the 'forlorn hope', riflemen drawn from the Rifle Brigade and the 33rd Foot, who cleared the way for the combat engineers and naval parties with their ladders and sacks but, shorn of artillery support, the two columns were soon halted. Men took cover in shell craters as best they could while the bullets and shell splinters rained over them. After the battle the survivors likened the experience to running into a deadly hail storm and in many versions of the fighting the soldiers are described as running forward with their heads down as if they were in the teeth of a living gale. Amongst them was a young Midshipman called Evelyn Wood who carried the memory of the attack into a ripe old age which had seen him transfer to the army, win a Victoria Cross and rise to the rank of field-marshal. Commanding one of the ladder parties he rushed forward with his men only to see them cut down by rifle-fire and he himself was wounded twice in the arm before he managed to escape back into the trenches. There he fell unconscious only to regain his senses when he heard a surgeon say, 'I'll have your arm off before you know where ye are.' Happily that severe treatment proved unnecessary and the young sailor survived.[6]

Wood was one of the lucky ones. Just as Clifford had observed with a sense of agonised awe the fate of the French a week earlier, so too was Hamley moved by the fate awaiting his fellow countrymen:

> In vain the officers stood up amid the iron shower and waved their swords; in vain the engineers returned to bring up the supports; the men could not be induced to quit the parapets in a body. Small parties of half a dozen, or half a score, ran out only to add to the slaughter. The party of artillerymen, whose business it was to follow this column and spike the guns, sallied forth, led by their officer, and, of the twenty, only nine returned unwounded; and the sailors who carried the scaling ladders, and the naval officers who led them, also suffered very severe loss.[7]

Some soldiers managed to enter the Redan and there were reports that parties of French infantrymen had fought their way into Sevastopol but the attack was slowly turning into a disaster. Thankfully help was at hand. Raglan was observing the battle from the mortar batteries in the forward trenches and the scale of the tragedy was only too obvious to him. He ordered the artillery to give covering fire in an attempt to silence the Russian batteries and to enable his men to retire in a semblance of order, and it was a measure of the man that he took the same risks as his own troops. Then, seeing that the attack had failed, he rode hurriedly over to Pélissier's headquarters where the commanders agreed to order their men to retire.

For both armies the failure of the attack was hard to take and with typical candour Pélissier accepted the blame for the setback when the commanders met for a post-mortem a few days later:

> General Pélissier [has also] expressed his great regret that he sanctioned the change [of plan] and freely admits that it was a most objectionable one, having been the cause,
>   1. that the abattis laid down in front of the Enemy's defences were not destroyed.
>   2. that the Allied Troops had to march for some hundred yards to the Assault of the Russian Works under a heavy fire of

Artillery and musketry, without any cover, such an operation being entirely opposed to the experience of sieges, and of the rules and custom of war.[8]

Amongst the French regimental commanders, though, there was a strong feeling that they had been asked to bear the brunt of the fighting and that their British allies had not pushed their attack with enough determination. While this was unfair – so fierce was the Russian fire that the assault parties stood no chance of reaching their objectives – some British officers felt that the plan of attack was suicidal and should never have been attempted. Garnet Wolseley had been present in the trenches close to Raglan's positions and had entertained high hopes of success but at the end of the day, like so many other British officers, he admitted to feeling 'humbled in spirit by failure'. But while leading his commander-in-chief out of the trenches they came across some of the wounded and the young officer was forced to witness an unbelievable scene:

> On the first stretcher that Lord Raglan encountered lay a young officer – I withhold his name and regiment for the sake of the old and historic corps to which he was a disgrace. As to himself I hope his hateful and undistinguished name has been forgotten as he himself should be. Lord Raglan, going up to him in the kindest way, said in the most feeling and sympathetic tone and manner, 'My poor young gentleman, I hope you are not badly hurt?' or some words to that effect. This brutal cur – I subsequently knew the creature well – turned upon him, and in the rudest terms and most savage manner, denounced him as 'responsible for every drop of blood that had been shed that day.' Wounded though this ungenerous officer was, I could with pleasure have run my sword through his unmanly carcass at the moment.[9]

While Wolseley admitted that his later military experience made him see that Raglan was out of his depth in the Crimea, he realised that the man's courage and natural dignity could never be called into question.

As dawn broke over the battlefield the French began making their way back to the safety of their trenches and both armies were left to compute their casualties. The figures were unacceptably high – the British lost 1500, the French 3500 – and for Raglan the defeat could not have come at a worse time. As bad luck would have it, the British soldiers were dying at the very time that Roebuck presented his report to parliament on the mishandling of the British Army in the Crimea. It had harsh words to say about the administrative and operational failures and, when it was debated, there was a renewal of the attacks on Britain's commander-in-chief. To add to Raglan's discomfiture he had been informed by Panmure that his pre-war post of Master-General of the Ordnance had been abolished as, henceforth, the department's duties would be taken under the direction of the minister for war. Despite Raglan's protests – he believed that its work was beyond the powers of a secretary of state – Panmure was adamant. Because the system had failed the army in the Crimea, it had to be changed.

The criticisms at home and the loss of the Ordnance Board added to the sense of despair which enveloped Raglan after the failure of the attack on the Great Redan. A Coldstream Guards officer is supposed to have noticed the change and to have pronounced that Raglan was a dying man. The story might be apocryphal but it was undoubtedly true. Not only was Raglan bowed down by a sense of failure but he was suffering the first symptoms of a debilitating illness. On 23 June he was diagnosed as having severe diarrhoea and the death of Estcourt from cholera the following day only added to his gloom. Raglan continued working at his despatches, but his staff could see that their chief was getting weaker and on 26 June he took to his bed. Two days later he was dead, whether from dysentry or simple exhaustion it was difficult to tell. Those close to him felt that it might even have been from heartbreak.

So unexpected was the news of Raglan's death that it sent a profound shock round the British camp. Since the beginning of the campaign he had been a constant and reassuring figure. His calmness under stress and his many kindnesses were legendary; even those who had only caught a glimpse of him in cocked hat and unostentatious frock coat felt that they knew him well, and the feelings of loss were entirely genuine. 'Everyone who knew him loved and respected him and justly so,' wrote Clifford on 30 June, 'for his manners were most pleasing and he was gifted with the most sensitive feelings and kind heart.' [10] That was all true but it was Raglan's fate to leave an uneven reputation to history. Soon he would be castigated as an incompetent blunderer, the scapegoat for the army's shortcomings in the Crimea. The failure to take Sevastopol, the loss of the Light Brigade, the catalogue of disasters in the Commissary and Medical departments, the disastrous losses in front of the Great Redan: all these would be laid before his memory as evidence of his military culpability and with the presence of reporters on the scene there was no little confirmation. All that was true, but it was not the whole story.

As the commander-in-chief Raglan had to accept some of the blame for the direction of the campaign but it would be ungenerous to place the whole opprobrium on his head. When he took the expeditionary force to the Crimea, in effect, Raglan was commanding the same army that had served Wellington so well. True, its weapons had changed with the introduction of the Minié rifle but its tactics, uniforms and equipment had hardly altered at all. With no other example to follow, for he had never been a Sepoy General, Raglan followed Wellington's style of command, even to the extent of refusing to wear a uniform and paying strict attention to his despatches. Like his great predecessor, too, Raglan was prepared to show himself to his troops in the heat of battle. He led his men to the Alma and was present in the trenches when his men attacked the Great Redan, meeting one near-miss in the trenches with the exclamation, 'Quite close enough!' He might have lacked Wellington's ability to utter timely words of encouragement but his presence at the point of danger certainly raised morale. It was also necessary for the direction of the battle. Despite the power of the British and French rifles most of the combat against the Russians took place at close range and Raglan was rarely so divorced from the action that he was unable to make decisions on what he was able to observe.

The worse that can be said of him was that he was indecisive and failed to communicate his ideas, or sometimes his orders, to his subordinates. As for the more general failings, such as his inability to understand the changing face of warfare, these were the shared blunders of a society which held its army in little regard – even Wellington, who was not known for his love of the ordinary British soldier, deprecated his country's lack of care towards its army. The best that can be said about Raglan was that he was responsible for maintaining the French alliance; as a commander he was an honourable man who did his best when his country asked it of him. He also cared about his men and in battle guarded their lives jealously. 'One of the last times I rode with him, the men ran all sides to cheer him,' wrote his military secretary Colonel Steele in a letter of condolence to Lady Raglan. 'He was mobbed by soldiers who never give a cheer unless it comes from the heart, and with these he was greeted on all sides.'[11] Even Panmure, never a great admirer, got close to the truth when he sent a brief letter of condolence to Raglan's headquarters staff:

> I feel it to be scarcely possible to estimate the loss which the country has sustained by Lord Raglan's death, as he not only possessed the finer qualities of a soldier but in his courteous and conciliatory manners, his calm and equable temper enabled him to maintain with rare success the kind feeling which has existed between us and the allies of all nations.[12]

It was no bad epitaph but unfortunately for Raglan's reputation that generosity was not shared by subsequent critics who preferred to view his career from the standpoint of later ages and, in so doing, to belittle all that he accomplished. With full military honours his embalmed body (a final service by the French who also mourned his passing) was taken to the steamer *Caradoc* on 3 July. On arrival in Britain it was taken for burial at the family home, Badminton House, and privately buried. No public statue was ever raised in his honour.

His successor was Major-General Simpson who made no secret of the fact that he did not regard the promotion as a particular honour. 'I feel it very irksome and embarrassing to have to do with these Allies!' he famously told Panmure, and he lamented the absence of Raglan's soothing diplomacy in dealing with the obstreperous Pélissier. Within weeks he was asking Panmure to replace him with the 'most eminent and best known soldier we have'. Unassuming his stance most certainly was, but it hardly smacked of the kind of firm leadership which the British forces in the Crimea needed at such a critical moment in the war.

14

Sevastopol Falls

Thank God there were no women or brandy left in the Town.

Captain Henry Clifford, postscript to letter written to his father, 14 September 1855

Raglan's death, and the succession of Simpson to command the British Army, changed the complexion of the war in the Crimea. Responsibility for directing the allies' tactics fell to Pélissier who felt that he had much to prove following the failure of the June attacks on the Russian defences. From Paris he faced constant criticism for the loss of life, which Napoleon felt was avoidable, and in his immediate area of operations two of his subordinates, Bosquet and Niel, were still making trouble behind his back. As his position continued to be under threat, the pressure to end the siege became more pressing and he complained constantly about the unwelcome interruptions. Some relief came his way in July when Napoleon recalled Canrobert to Paris – although demoted, he remained popular with his men and his presence in command of a division was thought to have an unsettling effect on the French high command.

In his place came the experienced General Patrice de MacMahon, a soldier of Irish descent who had cut his teeth in Algeria and who was known to be a strict though fair disciplinarian. Popular with his men, he brought initiative and fresh thinking to a campaign which was in danger of settling into stalemate. The bombardment of Sevastopol continued apace and was gradually wearing down the Russian defences – having been wounded on 22 June and forced to withdraw, Todleben no longer directed the defences – but it was a long and laborious business. Everywhere, in the front-line trenches and in the high command, war-weariness was setting in. Men were exhausted and there was a feeling that the war might go on, if not for ever, then at least for another winter. Even Sterling found his optimism draining away as the British gunners continued to fire at the enemy line without much noticeable effect:

> It is very strange at night, with the peaceful stars looking down, to see these earthly meteors scattering destruction, and to hear their horrid noises, when, but for them, everything would be still and beautiful. Sometimes our own shells burst as they issue from the guns; and then the pieces do much mischief as the men in the trenchments are exposed towards the rear, though covered towards the enemy. All these dangers exist equally in a battle; but there, the excitement of advancing, and the confident feeling of overthrowing the enemy, prevents one thinking of the shot flying around. The passive and long-continued endurance in a siege is very trying.[1]

The stresses and strains of the war had also forced changes on the British Army. A Highland Division had been formed with command going to Sir Colin Campbell (a move greeted with great satisfaction by Sterling), and the remaining divisions all had new commanders – 1st (Rokeby), 2nd (Markham), 3rd (England, succeeded by Eyre in August) and 4th (Bentinck), while Scarlett retained command of what remained of the Cavalry Division. With the exception of Campbell none were inspirational leaders and they were not given a lead by Simpson who did nothing to disguise his bewilderment at commanding an army which he had never wanted to lead in the first place. Even his despatches were gloomy and uncertain and by the end of July Panmure was chiding him constantly about their 'disheartening' tone and asking him if he wanted to be relieved:

> If you feel unable to bear the weight of responsibility, which I am aware is not small, I advise you to give it up, and everyone will give you credit, and on your retirement a still further mark of the Queen's favour may be conferred [on his appointment Simpson had been promoted lieutenant-general]; but I strongly

recommend you not to hesitate in the matter. Either buckle up your reins vigorously for the work, or at once claim the consideration which your long and honourable services entitle you to receive. I have written you plainly as a friend, and you will, I know, accept what I write as such.[2]

Panmure did his best but his correspondence with Simpson makes dispiriting reading. The men were friends and fellow Scots and Panmure knew only too well that Simpson was being afflicted by the 'black dog', those cyclical bouts of depression not uncommonly found in the Celtic countries. The government insisted that Simpson use the telegraph on a daily basis to report on the local situation and this new-fangled contrivance added to the feeling that he was being subjected to an unwelcome and unlooked-for obligation. By the middle of July he was forced to concede to Panmure that 'these four armies can never carry on any joint and united operation in their present condition' and begged once more to be relieved of his command.[3]

Such a heartfelt and despondent plea could not be ignored and the government was already facing up to the dilemma of who should be appointed in Simpson's place. Hardinge, the commander-in-chief, asked not to be considered both on account of his age and his infirmity – he was seventy and had difficulty walking – and, in the absence of any outside candidate, Panmure concentrated on the generals already serving in the Crimea.

Unaccountably, Campbell was not given any lengthy consideration yet he was the most experienced of the divisional commanders. Partly, his lack of social contacts counted against him but there was also a growing feeling that he was too hotheaded and too boastful about the fighting qualities of his Scottish troops – to his three Highland regiments had been added three Lowland battalions: 1st and 2nd battalions 1st Foot (Royal Scots), and the 71st Foot (Highland Light Infantry). Not having been in action since October the previous year they were in fine condition, being composed almost entirely of older and more experienced soldiers, and Campbell pressed constantly for their employment to assault the Russian lines. However, as the greater burden (and casualties) had fallen on the battalions of the 2nd and Light Divisions, Simpson argued that they should be granted the glory of being the first troops into the Redan. For maintaining morale and *esprit de corps* there was some logic to the argument, but from a purely tactical point of view it was highly questionable: not only did the battalions contain far too many unblooded recruits but, having seen the calamitous consequences of the earlier assaults, they were naturally timorous.

Of the other commanders there was not much to be said in their favour. The old-fashioned martinet Brown had ruled himself out through illness, the royal-blooded Cambridge had failed to make his mark in the first battles of the war, while Markham's experience of warfare had been in India; so the choice as Simpson's successor fell to the short-sighted Major-General Sir William Codrington of the Coldstream Guards. A member of a notable English family – a kinsman, Christopher Codrington, endowed the library of All Souls, his father Sir Edward commanded the British fleet at Navarino and his brother was a rear-admiral serving under Lyons – Codrington was a compromise candidate who had little or no battlefield experience. His first taste of action had been at the Alma where he had led a brigade in the Light Division, demonstrating bravery but not much tactical sense in front of the Russian guns.

Initially the appointment was made as a contingency in the event of Simpson becoming physically incapacitated and for the time being the querulous commander-in-chief was allowed to retain his position. That being the case, the summer of 1855 was marked in the British camp by inactivity, growing doubts and a paralysis of thought. Clarendon summed up the position when he told Palmerston that the commanders had no other idea in their heads than to prepare for a second winter in the field. Newcastle, the deposed secretary of state for war, went even further. When he visited the Crimea he reported back that Simpson was a 'raving lunatic' and that no one in command had any clue how to bring the war to a successful conclusion.

Some attempt had been made to reorganise the army's logistical back-up with the introduction of a Land Transport Corps, led by officers from the Indian armies, and a civilian Army Work Corps, an army of navvies employed on trench construction. Neither unit solved the problem. Many of the men in the transport corps had little experience of working with horses and, initially at least, were not amenable to military discipline. As for the navvies, both Raglan and Simpson complained that not only were they insubordinate and unwilling to work but they caused considerable resentment because they were paid at a higher rate than the infantrymen who protected them in forward positions. That was missing the point, argued Panmure; the new corps would relieve soldiers from a task which they did not do well:

> There may be various works to be performed which may be executed by the navvies which would otherwise press heavily upon the energies of the soldier, whose strength should as much as possible be husbanded by his being released from any but military duty.[4]

In theory Panmure's ideas for a non-military corps to dig trenches and build defences were perfectly sound. However, the navvies objected to being led by engineer officers and spent much of their time drinking in the canteens which had begun to spring up at Kadikoi. When told about the constant drunkenness Panmure insisted that the drinking dens be closed but he managed to cause unnecessary offence by ordering that alcohol should not be given to troops before they went on sentry duty. Instead they were to be given a hot meal. This kind of interference, well-meant as it undoubtedly was, simply added to the friction between Panmure and the headquarters in the Crimea. Judging from the restrained comments made by Raglan and Simpson both men had had difficulty keeping their feelings in check in their correspondence with Panmure.

No such lassitude invaded the French camp although by the end of July Pélissier was disinclined to share his thoughts with Simpson, stating that he would only confide his plans to his pillow. In fact not much had changed. The Malakov remained the target of his ambitions but he needed to bring his forward positions closer to the Russian fortifications before he could be sure of a successful assault. This was proving to be a time-consuming and dangerous business: the British sapping operations had been confounded by the solid rock foundations beneath the Great Redan and the French had suffered heavy casualties while reinforcing their forward trenches. Their miners had proved adept at pushing their tunnels towards the Russian lines but, as visitors to the French positions admitted, it was dangerous and enervating work. Hamley wrote:

> In the parapet of a trench near is a portal six feet square, opening on a steep path descending into the earth. An officer outside tells you it is forbidden to enter here, but the sergeant who accompanies you obtains the permission of the engineer

officer, and, descending, beckons you on. The passage narrows
to little more than a yard square, along which you crawl for a
considerable distance. A few men are squatting in the gallery,
which is lit at intervals by candles. The heat grows stifling as
you advance, and the roof seems ready to close on you. The
rifle-shots, French and Russian, are now crossing each other
unheard above you; and, a few yards further on, you are actually
beneath the enemy's ramparts. The sappers working here can
never be sure that in the next minute the Russians, delving 'a
yard below their mine,' will not 'blow them to the moon,' as
Hamlet says; or pour upon them, through a sudden aperture,
sulphurous vapours; or drown them with torrents of water. You
breathe more freely after emerging from the narrow gallery of
the French mines.[5]

Hamley's graphic description of the risks undertaken by the French
engineers might have excited readers of Blackwood's Magazine but
there was a growing feeling at home that the fall of Sevastopol was
long overdue. Any ennui felt by Simpson's army in the Crimea was
more than matched by a growing impatience at the War Office and
war-weariness amongst the public at home.

The Russians, too, were tiring of the war. While the fighting was
far removed from St Petersburg – the summer masts of the allied
fleet provided the only reminder of hostilities – the embargo had
affected the Russian economy. Imports of cotton from the United
States through Britain had dried up, as had the supply of British-built
machinery. Not only did this hinder the war effort but it also hit
the lucrative cotton textile industries which had sprung up around
Moscow in the 1820s. While Russian industrial expansion had been
miserable compared to what had taken place in western Europe, the
country's economic links were increasingly with the outside world.
Wheat exports and world prices were vital issues, Russia had been
supplied with loans by western banks and there had been a measure
of currency reform with the introduction of convertible paper money
based on the silver rouble. All these reforms were being placed in
jeopardy by the war: not only did the fighting reveal the strength of
Britain and France but it also brought Russia to the brink of financial
collapse. By contrast, Britain was able to earmark £46.7 million for its
military budget in 1856, 50.2% of total government expenditure.[6]

For his part, Alexander II proved to be more flexible in his approach than his father ever had been, but his willingness to concede diplomatic points did not make him any less trenchant in his prosecution of the war. As he had shown through his instructions to Alexander Gorchakov in Vienna he was not prepared to make peace at any price, and he was also aware of the tactical situation facing the allies. Sevastopol's fall might be a bitter blow but it would not signal the end of the fighting. For the time being at least, in the summer of 1855, he insisted that the battle continue. Following the repulse of the allied attack in June the tsar had informed Michael Gorchakov that there must be no more defeatist talk of abandoning the city.

Inside Sevastopol, though, the position was less assuring than it had been earlier in the year. It was becoming increasingly difficult to make good the damage caused by the allied barrage and many of the reinforcements who had arrived before the fall of Kertch had succumbed to illness. Faced by a growing allied army the defenders had three options. The first was to continue the siege, the second to partially abandon Sevastopol by withdrawing to the north, and the third to attack the French and Sardinian forces on the high ground along the River Chernaia. Of these the first was quickly dismissed and although the second was discussed it was considered to be defeatist. At a council of war held on 9 August, therefore, it was agreed to go on the offensive, even though Michael Gorchakov warned the tsar that there was little hope of success.

Doubts had been expressed about the ability of the Russian gunners to engage the enemy before mounting an infantry assault and the Russians knew only too well that the French and Sardinians were well dug in on the Fedioukhine heights. But attack they must. Gorchakov had been under a constant barrage of advice from the tsar who had warned him that, unless he dislodged the enemy, all the Russian reserves would be sucked into Sevastopol, 'that bottomless pit', a further letter adding: 'Your daily losses inside Sevastopol emphasise what I have told you many times before in my letter – *the necessity to do something to bring this frightful massacre to a close.*'[7] Just as the Simpson was under unrelenting pressure from Panmure 'to do something', so, too, did Michael Gorchakov come to dread the arrival of despatches from St Petersburg.

The decision having been taken, Gorchakov elected to attack the allied lines on two fronts on the morning of 16 August, the corps being commanded by Liprandi and General-Adjutant N.A. Read, a Russian soldier of Scots descent. However, so unsure was he about the wisdom of fighting this battle that he produced an outline plan which gave little more than general directions to the two commanders. Following an initial artillery barrage, they were to advance towards the Chernaia and to await further instructions, each stage of the battle thereafter to be determined by Gorchakov's reading of the situation. The only information vouchsafed to the two commanders was that Read's men were to engage the Fedioukhine heights while Liprandi was to clear the allies from Telegraph Hill before moving against the Sardinian positions on a point known as Gasfort Hill. What happened thereafter would be revealed as the battle progressed.

The attack, already questionable in outline, was made unworkable by a Russian security failure. Gorchakov's plans were discussed openly in St Petersburg and the intelligence was passed to the British ambassador in Berlin who immediately informed Simpson. The plan was also revealed in the *Zeit* newspaper, a breach of security as bad as anything published by Russell in *The Times*.[8] By then the Russian troop movements were being observed by the allies who, although used to false alarms, were aware that something was afoot and the allied generals Herbillon and La Marmora were left in little doubt of the Russians' intentions. To frustrate further Gorchakov's ability to control the battle, low cloud made semaphore communication impossible and he and his staff had to ride between Liprandi's and Read's headquarters to direct the operations.

Inevitably, there was muddle and although the Russian troops gained their first objectives, the bungles soon began to multiply. Confusion over an order to begin the battle meant that Read's troops attacked the Fedioukhine heights ahead of schedule and without suitable reinforcements. They also had to attack the French positions uphill and, caught in disciplined fire, they quickly lost impetus. At the same time Liprandi's corps had made good progress against the Sardinian position on Gasfort Hill but no further orders came from Gorchakov. At this point – it was only eight o'clock in the morning – the one chance to win the battle was lost. Seeing that a gap was opening between the Sardinian and French lines La Marmora quickly moved troops into the area and the allied positions remained secure.

Determined fire from the superior French rifles settled the issue and by ten o'clock the battle was over. The following day a dejected Rose reported that he had missed the action as he had been visiting Eupatoria at the invitation of Lyons and had not been at Pélissier's side during the battle. In an attempt to understand what had happened he interviewed as many French officers as he could but his subsequent report makes scanty reading.[9] That lapse and the minor supporting part played by the British cavalry and artillery meant that the Chernaia battle has received little attention but Gorchakov's handling of the battle was to have far-reaching consequences. For the Russians it was a dreadful defeat made worse by the casualty list – 2273 dead, 1742 missing and around 4000 wounded. The allies had fewer than 2000 dead or wounded, of which the Sardinians only lost 14 killed.

The battle also settled once and for all Napoleon's theory that the Russian field army had to be defeated. Now that it had been, the allies were allowed to concentrate on ending the siege of Sevastopol. Pélissier gave orders for the bombardment to intensify and, as Russell reported, for the remainder of the month the city faced almost constant shelling:

> The fire which opened at daybreak on Friday continued the whole of Saturday and yesterday, but slackened this morning [20 August] by order. I should not wonder if it were to be again increased tonight, in order to favour the progress of the French works. This has already been considerable, and the French seem duly sensible of the service our cannonade has rendered them. It enabled them, I heard a French officer say on Saturday evening, to do in four hours what they previously could not have done in fifteen days. I believe that the three days' fire has enabled them to do what they otherwise would probably have never done.[10]

Russell's pride in the British gunners was not misplaced: the concentrated fire certainly helped the French to push their forward trenches right up to the Malakov. What he could not see, but what was all too obvious to the imagination, was the effect of the barrage inside Sevastopol. By then it was proving impossible to make good the damage to the defences and on the very day that he told the tsar about the defeat on the Chernaia, Gorchakov was forced to concede that the bombardment might force him to order the evacuation of Sevastopol.

However, Alexander ordered that there was to be no retreat and, as Gorchakov was too weak-willed to act on his own volition, the two men were responsible for thousands of unnecessary deaths during the final bombardment of the city. Although accounts differ it is not unreasonable to suppose that the barrage at its height caused at least two thousand casualties a day, most of them infantrymen guarding the main defensive positions. The allies had at their disposal eight hundred artillery pieces and three hundred mortars and between them they caused a huge amount of damage and loss of life. On 5 September Gorchakov wrote to the tsar admitting that the enemy's bombardment was 'unbelievable' and that whole areas of the city had been destroyed:

> This infernal fire, much of which is counter-bombardment, clearly indicates that the enemy intends to destroy or neutralise our guns and make a ground assault. It is impossible to repair the fortifications and the best that one can do is to try to keep the powder magazines and the shelters intact; the broken parapets are filling the ditches and we are for ever keeping the embrasures clear. The losses among the gun crews have been heavy and can hardly be replaced.[11]

Gorchakov did not need to be a mind-reader to gauge the allied intentions. The ferocity of the barrage and the concentration of French troops close to the Malakov were obvious signs that an attack was imminent; all that remained in question was when it would take place. That had been decided two days earlier when Pélissier finally revealed his plan of action. It came as little surprise that the Malakov would be the main target: 25,000 French troops would be concentrated on it while a general attack, supported by naval gunfire, would be made along the whole front. Bosquet would command the attack and the French 1st Division, led by MacMahon, would be first into the breach, supported by the Imperial Guards and a brigade of Sardinian troops. The attack would take place on 8 September and would be preceded by the artillery fire which Gorchakov had found so incredible.

To the British was given the same objective which had cheated them in mid-June – the heavily defended Great Redan, still two hundred yards from their lines, despite the best efforts of the sappers. Again, the shock troops would be provided by the 2nd and the Light Divisions with the Guards and Highlanders held in reserve, all under Codrington's command. The signal for attack would be the sight of the French tricolour flying over the Malakov and the firing of four signal rockets. All this was agreed without comment by Simpson who kept to the same plan of attack which had failed on the previous occasion: following the cessation of the bombardment and the French signal to attack, the ladder parties would rush forward under covering fire followed by one thousand stormers in advance of the main force of three thousand infantrymen.

Pélissier was determined that the attack should succeed and his engineers had gone to considerable pains to improve the forward trench system. Wherever possible trenches had been widened and the improvements camouflaged by gabions – large wicker baskets used in mining operations. Some were sufficiently wide to permit the passage of small field artillery pieces. In contrast the British trenches were still as narrow as ever and in some places the men would have to advance in single file, a considerable inconvenience and danger for a force of 5000 troops. They would also have to attack across two hundred yards of open ground whereas the French were but a few strides from reaching their first objective. The mood in the British camp was sombre. Before the attack Sterling spoke to a fellow officer in an English line regiment and was appalled to be told that raw recruits on sentry duty had already abandoned their posts under Russian fire:

> The heart is out of them. They ought to employ Eyre or C[Campbell] for the assault, if they wish to make a sure job of it; but then Codrington would not get the credit, and he has friends about headquarters, where C. and Eyre are not in good odour; I wonder why; they are the two best here, and, in fact, the only good ones that I see among the higher ranks. God help us! – we are in strange hands.[12]

The colonel's premonitions of disaster were not misplaced and within days he was right to condemn the biggest disgrace 'which has befallen the British arms'. The British infantry did indeed suffer grievous casualties when they attacked the Great Redan and, to the shame of many fine regiments, men did crack under fire. But before that happened there was the 'splendid' (Clifford's word) French attack on the Malakov. This was the defining moment of the battle.

In previous attacks the allies had launched their assaults at dawn but on this occasion Pélissier decided to wait until mid-day. The morning of 8 September began with a preliminary bombardment which then halted for two hours before beginning again for half an hour before twelve noon. Then, exactly to timetable, MacMahon's 1st Division, led by the Zouaves, leaped out of their trenches and rushed the short distance to the Malakov's defences. It was a ferocious assault which took the defenders by surprise – many were eating their mid-day meal, a select few were on parade to be awarded gallantry medals – and so taken aback were the Russian gunners that only six artillery pieces were able to open fire.

Once inside the defences there was hard hand-to-hand fighting on the ramparts and along the bastions but within ten minutes the Malakov tower had fallen to the French and the tricolour was flying bravely from its summit. The Kornilov bastion, too, had fallen but elsewhere on the front, on the far left, the French and the Sardinians were facing determined opposition. So too, were the British infantrymen. Seeing the French flag, the first stormers of the 19th and 97th Foot had not waited for the word of command but had rushed forward towards the Great Redan. Once again the Russians were taken by surprise, but not for long. Enfilading rifle fire and grapeshot from the bastions cut the attackers down and the assault quickly faltered in front of the salient. A follow-up charge by the 23rd Foot managed to reach the ditch but there they had to face a Russian counter-attack, the men of the Selenginsky Regiment beating them back at bayonet-point.

In the confusion any hope of retaining command quickly vanished. Senior officers had been killed in the assault, the sappers failed to get their ladders to the walls and in the narrow trenches it proved impossible to move men quickly into the attack. One of the assaulting engineers left a graphic description of the confusion, panic and terror which had invaded the ranks of the British assault force. These were merely multiplied when Codrington ordered his reserves to support the men on the salient:

> There was little of that dash and enthusiasm which might have been looked for from British soldiers in an assault; in fact, it required all the efforts and example of their officers to get their men on, and these were rendered most ineffective from the manner in which the various regiments soon got confused and jumbled together. The men, after firing from behind the traverses, near the salient, for half-an-hour at the enemy – also firing behind his parados and traverses [rear and forward defence works] – began to waver. I rushed up the salient with the view

of cheering them on, and the officers exerted themselves to sustain them; the men gave a cheer, and went at it afresh. The supports of reserves, ordered to follow, struggled up in inefficient disorder, but were unable to press into the work, as the men in advance, occupying the salient, *refused to go on*, notwithstanding the devoted efforts of the officers to induce them to do so.[13]

The description, written by Lieutenant Rankin, Royal Engineers, was quoted with evident approval by Sterling when he published his own letters from the Crimea. At the time, two days later, he contented himself with the observation that the men of the Light Division were entirely ill-equipped to lead the operation, mainly because they had spent too much time in the trenches. As a result, they were understandably cautious about exposing themselves to Russian fire, with the unhappy result that they did not press home their attack and in some instances the younger men, mainly callow recruits, actually refused to continue fighting. This was confirmed by Captain Grahame who admitted later that he 'could not get the men to stand' because 'when a panic struck the men . . . the Devil himself could not stop them'. For this failure Sterling blamed Codrington and Simpson, the former for not exposing himself to his men before the Great Redan, the latter for his blunder in not selecting the Guards and Highlanders for the attack.

Campbell's division was in fact ready to renew the assault the following day but they were not needed and the Scottish regiments ended the campaign as relative bystanders. Ironically, they were to provide the British public with a reminder of British pluck in the face of adversity: photographed by Roger Fenton, the stern, bewhiskered Highland soldiers, staring their disapproval at the world's frailties, seemed to typify all that was good and courageous about the army. Queen Victoria was particularly fond of them and in time was to make great pets of her kilted and ostrich-feathered Highlanders, lions in the field but lambs in the house.

It soon became clear why Campbell would not have to test his men in an assault on the Great Redan. Although the French had only captured the Malakov it was the key to Sevastopol and with its capture Gorchakov knew that his position was untenable. In fact he had already made preparations for that eventuality. At the beginning of July Russian military engineers had begun the construction of a long pontoon bridge between the two shores of Sevastopol harbour. There had been suspicions that it would be used to bring up reinforcements but by the later afternoon of 8 September its purpose was all too clear. At 5.30 p.m. Gorchakov decided that his position was hopeless and ordered the remains of his army to retreat across the bridge into the northern side of the city.

It was a brilliant operation. As the troops made their way across the pontoon bridge rear parties maintained their fire on the allied lines and as they, too, began to retire, systematically, they blew up the ammunition stores and sank the remaining ships. Then, when all but the most severely wounded were safely across, the bridge itself was destroyed. Exhausted by the battle the British and French regiments were not ordered to make pursuit and the crisp frosty night was lit up by numberless fires. For the survivors who expected a further assault the next day, sleep proved impossible as explosions and desultory rifle and artillery fire split the night. Several thousand were beyond caring: in the final battle of the war the Russians lost 13,000 men, the allies 10,000.

Both sides claimed it as a victory. The Russians insisted that, although they had surrendered ground they had not been defeated and were ensconced within powerful new fortifications; the allies had taken Sevastopol, or at least part of it, but had not inflicted a conclusive defeat on Gorchakov's army. Shortly before leaving the Crimea Newcastle, who had watched the battle, reported his disgust at the failure of the allied command to exploit their success but the truth was that the armies were exhausted and dispirited. The capture of the enemy's defence works should have been an occasion for rejoicing but soldiers like Clifford merely felt the emptiness of victory – 'I stood in the Redan more humble, more dejected and with a heavier heart than I have yet felt since I left home' – as they stood on the previously impregnable parapets and looked at the scenes of death and desolation below.

Inside the city the scenes were equally distressing. Many of the ruined buildings housed the Russian wounded and their plight was worse than anything faced by the British soldiers. Even hardened surgeons were appalled by what they saw. 'Never saw I such a scene of misery,' wrote Arthur Henry Taylor two days later. 'Dead, dying and wounded lay without attendance, shrieking and calling for drink, squalid, starving, dirty and miserable in the extreme. None of the doctors (shame on them) remained behind with them. I gave my brandy and water to them, though I wanted in badly myself, as far as it went, and reported their state to headquarters.'[14] Their plight was living proof of the old military adage that next to a battle lost there is nothing so pitiable as 'a battle won'.

15

The Forgotten War: Kars and Erzerum

Veeliams Pasha chock adam dur – Williams Pasha is no end
of a man.
Ottoman soldier to Dr Humphrey Sandwith, 28 November 1855

I f any incident was calculated to raise the ire of the British ambassador in Constantinople it was the conduct of the fighting in Asia
Minor where Colonel (acting Brigadier-General) William Fenwick
Williams was engaged in a long drawn-out and badly supported campaign against superior (though numerically inferior) Russian forces.
Fought in the mountainous areas where Armenia borders Georgia,
the advantage should have been with the Ottoman army. Not only
did they have the support of the robber baron Shamyl, for many years
a thorn in the flesh of Russian forces, but as Humphrey Sandwith, a
British doctor in the Ottoman forces observed, 'Here you have Turks
posted on their own soil in the midst of a Mussulman population. At
the summons of the fiery crescent thousands of warlike tribes will rush
to the standard of Islam.'[1] Alas, matters did not turn out in that easy
way, hence the presence of Williams at the head of the Ottoman
forces in Asia Minor, and, hence, too, his troubled correspondence
with Stratford and the Foreign Office to make the Porte understand
the importance of holding out against the Russians.

It was to be a long drawn-out affair, not just because the Russians
held the upper hand, but because Williams was forced to fight lethargy,
corruption and cowardice in an attempt to make the Ottoman forces
to face up to their responsibilities. In both instances he would be forced
to admit defeat but that did not make him a lesser man for, in many

respects, Williams was one of the unsung heroes of the fighting against Russia. Born in Canada of Welsh stock he was a military engineer who had considerable experience of the area in which he was fighting, having been seconded to the Ottoman army earlier in his career. Like Beatson, whose Bashi-Bazouks never fulfilled their promise, he was to find himself in the unenviable role of leading ill-disciplined troops and their venal commanders in a campaign which was badly supported by the Porte and virtually ignored by their British and French allies.

Following the Russian victories in the field, which had given them the upper hand in Asia Minor in the early winter of 1853, the Ottoman forces had been reinforced with Armenian conscripts and there had been a change in command. Abdi Pasha had been sacked and replaced by Ahmed Pasha, although whether this was an improvement was open to doubt as the latter was a lazy and scheming official whose prime interest lay in lining his own pockets. He was also surrounded by sycophants and spent so much time and money in Constantinople ensuring the security of his position that what happened to his troops went by the board. Like their allies at Varna they too had been hit by cholera in 1854 but little had been done to help them. Indeed, conditions were so bad that visiting British doctors described the hospital conditions as being too disgusting for publication and added that the numbers of the dead were kept secret, their names remaining on the Ottoman muster rolls to allow the senior officers to claim their salaries and allowances.

This shameful behaviour did nothing for the army's morale and although the campaigning season of 1855 had opened with the Royal Navy capturing key Russian forts on the eastern coast of the Black Sea the army was in desperate straits. At the end of July the Russians defeated the Ottoman forces at Bayezid near the border with Azerbaijan and advanced towards the key towns of Kars and Erzerum with the intention of capturing the port of Trebizond through which the Turks were supplied. By then, though, the fighting at Silistria had ended and reinforcements were rushed to Asia Minor; Trebizond and Batoum were secured but the inland garrisons remained under threat. The outcome was almost settled on 7 August when the Russians forced the Kars garrison into an unnecessary battle at Kurekdere. Lacking any coherent chain of command, the Turkish infantry was annihilated. The watching reporter from *The Times* was left in no doubt who was to blame for the disaster:

With a vivid impression of the whole engagement, from the first cannon shot to the last straggling discharge of musketry, I can use no language too strong to express my mis-approbation of nearly four-fifths of the Turkish officers present. In accounting for the defeat of an army numbering nearly 40,000 men of all arms by a hostile force of less than one half that number, it is not sufficient to say that the management of the whole battle on the side of the Turks was a series of blunders from first to last; strategical errors might have protracted the engagement, and added to the cost of a victory, but downright cowardice alone – which no generalship could have reduced – gave the day to the Russians.

So pusillanimous was the conduct of the Ottoman commanders that the man from *The Times* ended his despatch with the urgent plea to send out allied officers to turn the rabble into an army capable of engaging the Russians with some hope of success: 'I, for one, earnestly entreat that Downing Street and the Tuileries will no longer leave Asia Minor to the mercy of intriguants and imbeciles.'[2] Unless they did, Russia would take control of the region and with it the vital overland route to Persia, through which they would be able to carry out their long-standing threat to India's north-west frontier.

As this danger was well enough understood in London arrangements had already been made to send Colonel Williams as the British Commissioner to assist the Ottoman forces in Asia Minor and, in Clarendon's words in the letter of appointment, 'to keep me fully informed of the operations in which the Turkish Army is engaged'. As it turned out, though, he was to do rather more than that by taking over responsibility for directing the defences at Kars and Erzerum. He was not the first European in the field. Prior to his appointment an Irishman, Guyon Pasha, had advised the Ottoman commanders but, although a capable and resourceful soldier, he had been sacked following the defeat at Kurekdere. There were also a number of mercenaries amongst the junior officers, mainly Poles, Hungarians and Italians but they were judged by Dr Sandwith to be 'of a most seedy, questionable aspect . . . a queer lot with whom it would be unpleasant to be too intimate'.[3]

When Williams arrived at Kars on 24 September he was confronted by good and bad news. First, the Russians had been unable to maintain their pressure on Kars due to the intervention of Shamyl's forces from

Daghistan to threaten Tiflis. Having destroyed as much as they could, General Bebatov's Army of the Caucasus withdrew to meet the new threat, leaving Kars and Erzerum to be defended by badly demoralised Ottoman troops. This eased the immediate pressure on the garrisons but Williams was not enamoured by what he found when he inspected the army available to him. Although he estimated that he had a total strength of 14,600 infantrymen, mostly armed with flintlocks, and three battalions of *chasseurs* with Minié rifles, their equipment was deplorable. In his first report to Stratford he described their 'ragged and threadbare' uniforms, and worn greatcoats as 'embarrassing to the soldiers' and made an immediate request for the provision of 20,000 pairs of boots and 10,000 shirts and drawers.

As for the cavalry, he had four regiments composed of 2222 men and horse but they were 'in a wretched plight as to clothing and accoutrements' and the horses were 'small and in bad condition'. Not only would they need to be reinforced but Williams recommended that the three senior cavalry pashas should be sacked immediately and replaced by European officers. Only the artillery passed muster. The Horse Artillery possessed 36 guns, the Foot Artillery 42 guns and the Mountain Artillery 84 guns, all of which were in good working order. Moreover, the senior gunner officer, Tahir Pasha, had been educated at the Royal Military Academy Woolwich and had shown considerable élan and courage at Kurekdere. The Ottoman batteries had been the only unit to inflict heavy losses on the enemy.

But it was not just the condition of men and materiel that concerned Williams. The hospital services lacked facilities, bandagings and medicines – although that would soon be put to rights by Dr Sandwith who had been sent from his practice in Constantinople to join Williams in Kars – and the accommodation for the men was horribly basic:

> Kars cannot accommodate more than 10,000 within its walls, so as to avoid danger from disease. It would be very desirable to have European officers for overlooking the drills and sanitary arrangements during the winter. No attention paid by the Turks to practice in ball-firing – a most essential thing.
>
> Men much neglected as to their comforts. The great copper cauldrons dangerous from want of tinning. Butter rancid and musty – as bad as possible – though used for pilaff.

That was by no means the end of Williams' catalogue of despair.

On speaking to the men he found that most were owed two years' wages, desertion was rife, the wounded and maimed had been forced into beggary and 'drunkenness prevails to a great degree among those of higher rank'. He ended by listing those officers whom he considered to be too useless or too cowardly for further service and recommended that the Sultan issue a firman which would empower his officials to put to rights the calamitous plight of its army in Asia Minor.[4]

Williams' report caused consternation when it arrived at the British Embassy at Therapia. It could hardly be forwarded to the Porte as a straightforward comment on the condition of the Kars and Erzerum garrisons for Williams had not minced his words. The references to cowardice and corruption and the fact that names had been named meant that its production at the Porte would provoke a diplomatic row. Held up for principal censure was the overall commander, or mushir, Zarif Pasha, whom Williams had scolded for his 'fraudulent and negligent' leadership. For that reason alone Stratford knew that he needed to be circumspect and while that requirement presented no problem to the Great Elchi, he was irritated by Williams' bluntness. Not only did the report sound peremptory and brusque to the point of rudeness – Stratford knew all there was to know about the scale of corruption and venality in the Ottoman army – but it arrived when the ambassadorial staff were engaged with the consequences of the first battles in the Crimea. Soon they would be coping with the emergency at Scutari and Stratford clearly believed that these issues had to take priority: he had already been greatly irritated when three staff officers travelling out to join Williams had arrived in Constantinople demanding to be allowed to visit the Crimea before resuming their journey to Kars. They were Colonel A.T. Lake (Madras Engineers), Major William Olpherts (Bengal Artillery) and Captain Henry Langhorne Thompson (68th Bengal Native Infantry).

None the less, Stratford was prepared to take issue with the Porte and on 29 November, somewhat later than he had promised Williams, he lodged an official complaint, couched in the best diplomatic language. Asking that the communication be shown to the Sultan, Stratford insisted that Britain could no longer tolerate their ally's inaction and demanded that those most culpable should be brought to book. The letter was addressed to the Porte on behalf of Her Majesty's Government:

The Porte is earnestly requested to bear in mind that the Sultan's allies are making great sacrifices, incurring a heavy expense, and shedding profusely their best blood in His Majesty's cause, that they are in consequence entitled to require the correction of abuses subversive of all efficiency in the Ottoman armies, and to expect the condign punishment of officers or functionaries convicted of having wilfully persisted in corrupt practices ministering to their personal profit, and fatal to the interests of the Empire, or of having neglected their duty in presence of the Enemy, and given an example of cowardice to the troops under their command.[5]

In his reply Reshid Pasha the Grand Vizier, insisted that the matter would be investigated but little was done and Williams and his staff were left to battle on as best they could. It proved to be an uphill struggle and over the winter Williams sent a series of increasingly anguished despatches to Stratford and, when these went unanswered, to Clarendon in London. When the foreign secretary upbraided his ambassador, Stratford replied that he was unused to being ordered as if he were a junior commissariat officer and, besides, he had the more pressing problem of the wounded at Scutari on his hands. So slow was the progress in repairing the building and putting it to rights in the wake of the arrival of Florence Nightingale that, throughout December, Stratford's attention was taken up with the need to bully the Porte into action. On 5 December he reported that the withdrawal of Turkish labour due to lack of funds had left him with no option but to pay the men from his own pocket. Surely that had to take precedence over Williams's plight in Kars?[6]

Naturally Williams was not placated and on several occasions throughout the winter he was forced to make representation to Clarendon and Raglan, complaining that he was being ignored. Not so, replied the British ambassador after receiving a curt despatch from the Foreign Office shortly after Christmas: Williams had simply 'rushed to the conclusion that I gave him no support, and under this inconsiderate impression he has made a deliberate appeal to Your Lordship and Lord Raglan'. On the contrary Williams had not been forgotten, representation had been made to the Porte but 'winter, distance, roads scarcely passable, the extent of the evil to be cured, the scarcity of trustworthy officers, the greater interest of operations elsewhere' had combined to forestall the despatch of relief supplies. And to complicate matters the lack of punctuality in the sailing of the mail packets to Trebizond meant that letters were delayed or lost en route. It was a case, he said, of the old proverb about taking the horse to water, for the machinations of the administration of the Ottoman Empire were impossible to circumvent:

> I regret the existence of such obstacles, and blame the Turkish ministers for not surmounting them with more activity. But can I wonder? No! – corruption, ignorance, prejudice, want of public spirit, and the instincts of selfishness engender the same consequences, wherever they prevail in long habitual exuberance. Such cankers, wide-spreading and deep-rooted, have ever been the harbingers and instruments of ruin, except in those few and favoured states where public opinion proclaims the danger and suggests the remedy in time.

It was a theme to which Stratford would return: the need, at the war's end, to bring the Ottoman Empire into the same state of grace enjoyed by its principal ally, Britain. Meanwhile Williams would have to be patient for it was beyond Stratford's power to unravel the skein of jealousy and rivalry which surrounded the empire's governance. The general would just have to accept that 'while the Seraskier [Minister of War] asserts that he has sent ample supplies to the army in Roumelia, the generalissimo [Omar Pasha] complains of being neglected, and all is contradiction and uncertainty except one painful fact, the suffering of the soldiers.'[7]

Stratford's carefully considered argument was of scant comfort to Williams. He was faced with the defence of Kars and Erzerum and although plans for the defence of the former had been laid down by Guyon much work remained to be done if it were to withstand a further attack by Bebatov's army. At first inspection the signs were not unpromising. Kars was dominated by a craggy rock on which stood a sixteenth-century fortified castle which dominated the town and the river which bisected it. On all four sides the outer defences were provided by small forts, or tabias, linked together by breastworks and redoubts and there was sufficient artillery for Tahir Pasha's gunners to provide a decent field of fire. Most of the credit for the fortification of Kars must be given to Williams's second-in-command, Lieutenant-Colonel C.C. Teesdale (Royal Artillery) and, later, to Colonel Lake but the British Commissioner made sure that every able-bodied man, himself included, took a hand in the work.

Watching the effort being made by the soldiers Dr Sandwith wondered if it were worthwhile. Kars was strategically important in that its fall would enable the Russians to push through to the Anatolian coast but it was little more than 'a true Asiatic town in all its Asiatic squalor':

> The streets are narrow and dirty, the people sordid in appearance, and the chief employment of the women appears to be the fabrication of *tezek*, or dried cow-dung for fuel, cakes of which are plastered over the walls of every house.[8]

Was that really worth defending? Williams was in no doubt that it was and he brought to his duty an almost messianic conviction that was inspirational to those who served him – 'no sign of despondency clouded that honest face' noted Sandwith in his diary at the beginning of 1855. By then Kars had been secured as the first line of defence and thought was being given to the protection of Erzerum, over a hundred miles to the south-west, to which Williams returned on 11 November. By then, too, the Porte had acted to acknowledge the role played by Williams. It had long been a source of irritation to him that, although he had been given the temporary rank of brigadier-general in the British Army, his position was unclear and that left him in a limbo with his Ottoman colleagues. At Stratford's prompting – although he was to receive no thanks for his help – the Sultan eventually agreed to give Williams the title of Pasha. What was more, Williams was permitted to keep his surname, a unique honour in the Ottoman army as all infidels honoured in this way normally had to take an Islamic *nom-de-guerre*. However, far from being grateful, Williams continued to bombard Constantinople with complaints about the lethargy of the Porte in making adequate provision for his duties.

On 21 January 1855 a clearly exasperated Stratford told Clarendon that while he was sympathetic, Williams had to understand that the Ottoman administration was reaching breaking point. It had to maintain two armies in the principalities and in the Crimea, its naval forces were fully engaged with Lyons in the Black Sea and, as a result, its exchequer was feeling the strain. The war was costing the Ottoman Empire 310 million piastres (£2 million) a year and most of this was being met by loans from the British government. As Stratford explained, this was 'extremely discouraging and there is a reluctance,

Kars and Erzerum

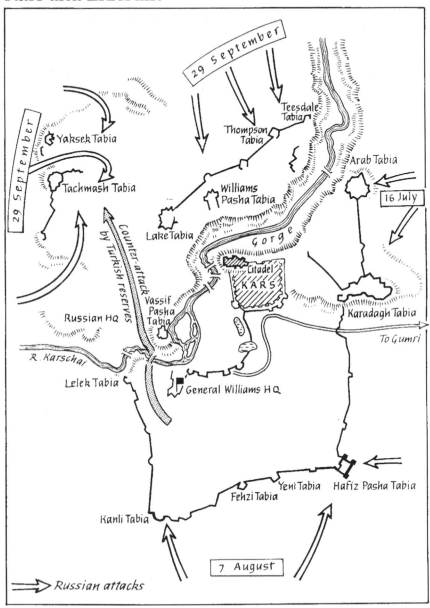

29 September

29 September

29 September

Yaksek Tabia

Tachmash Tabia

Teesdale Tabia

Thompson Tabia

Arab Tabia

16 July

Williams Pasha Tabia

Lake Tabia

Gorge

Counter-attack by Turkish reserves

Citadel

KARS

Russian HQ

Vassif Pasha Tabia

Karadagh Tabia

To Gumri

R. Karschai

Lelek Tabia

General Williams HQ

Yeni Tabia

Hafiz Pasha Tabia

Fehzi Tabia

Kanli Tabia

7 August

Russian attacks

difficult to be explained, in adopting measures calculated to put the Revenue on a better footing':

> Bearing these in mind with reference to objects, circumstances and resources, I would submit that, although there has been much to blame and to deplore in the conduct of the Turkish authorities, there is less room for wonder at past delinquencies, than reason to hope that British influence has cleared the way for their correction in future.
>
> Let it be remembered that the war began in hesitation and weakness even on the Danube; that the Army in Asia was naturally a secondary object; that the known defences and abuses of Turkish administration were no less rife in the military than in other departments, that officers of knowledge and capacity were scarce, that the deficiencies of the line were necessarily supplied by hordes of undisciplined fanatics, that the Sultan's revenue was altogether inadequate, and that all these general causes of evil were aggravated, as to the Army in Asia, by distance, by almost unpassable roads, and at times by the rigours of a severe climate, to say nothing of personal intrigues and official jealousies, which are not confined to the army.[9]

Throughout the spring of 1855 Stratford was forced to deal with a torrent of correspondence from Williams concerning conditions in Asia Minor, much of it copied to London. When the Porte appointed Vassif Pasha to take command of the Ottoman forces under Williams's direction Clarendon immediately questioned his qualifications. Stratford wearily replied that although Vassif was somewhat elderly he was reckoned to be a conscientious soldier. In any case he could hardly be held responsible for the appointment: 'The object of changes in office or command, throughout Turkey, when taken at the best, is not the promotion of known desert, but the removal of tried demerit. On such occasions the chances are quite as much in favour of change for the worse as change for the better.' A week later he was forced to reprove Williams for calling Vassif's predecessor, Shukri Pasha 'a drunkard'. This was not the general of division, he replied, but 'another Shukri Pasha, having the rank of Brigadier'. With that he insisted that there had to be a halt to the stream of protests and criticisms emanating from Williams's headquarters:

It appears from the close of General Williams's despatch that he
was still under an impression that I had neglected the public interests entrusted to him. I have endeavoured to prove elsewhere
to Your Lordship the utter groundlessness of this charge, and
I abstain from further comment or explanation. Many other
questions besides that of Kars command my attention, and
compel me to look rather to objects and results than to phrases
and paragraphs.[10]

Stratford's despatch seemed to settle the issue, in as much that
Clarendon instructed him to agree with the Porte a contract of
Williams's duties. While it did not stop the complaints, which would
become more aggravated when fighting recommenced in the early
summer, it did at least provide the general with a more secure position,
for it settled Williams as the sole commander in Kars and put Vassif
and the other pashas under his direct control:

Williams Pasha enjoys the high consideration of the Sublime
Porte and is counted as one of the Chief Commanders of the
Imperial Government. His Excellency Vassif Pasha will not look
upon Williams Pasha as a stranger but will consult with him
frankly on subjects of reform and military matters; and he will
do whatever is necessary to be done there, and report upon what
is requisite.[11]

Williams could not have asked for more but his vexation throughout the campaign in Asia Minor is understandable. To all intents the
defence of Kars was a sideshow compared to the need to end the siege
of Sevastopol and Williams was not the first commander to feel that
he was being ignored while precedence was being given to events
elsewhere. Cut off in the Anatolian highlands and increasingly aware of
his predicament should the Russians renew their attack, his feelings of
frustration shine through his correspondence with the outside world.
Not only did he feel isolated and exposed but he was never entirely
sure how his allies would behave in the heat of battle.
    At the beginning of February he was given a brutal reminder of the
tenuousness of his position when a Kurdish chieftain called Yesdeshia
Bey (also known as Izzideen Shere Bey) started a rebellion in the
mountains of Anatolia. This was war to the knife, similar to the kind of
fighting which the British Army experienced in their long drawn-out

campaigns against the Pathans on India's north-west frontier, and the Porte was determined to stamp it out. A force was drawn up from the army of Asia Minor under the command of Mehemed Cavakli Pasha and it was ordered to put down the revolt immediately because, as Sandwith noted, any revolt by the Kurds led to an outbreak of bloodletting:

> Whenever any warfare has broken out in Kurdistan it has been marked by the most savage cruelty; the prisoners who fall into the hands of the victors are often murdered wholesale in cold blood, their noses, ears and hands are cut off, they are impaled or skinned alive, while the young girls are carried into captivity.[12]

While Williams agreed that the Kurds posed a problem he felt that Mehemed Cavakli Pasha's deployment was an unnecessary distraction which would weaken his capacity to defence Kars. A letter of complaint was despatched to Clarendon who took up the matter with the Porte on 17 February:

> You will observe how impossible it is for the Allies to act with any confidence of success or to provide for their own responsibility if the principal functionaries of the Porte exhibit so lamentable a want of fair dealing and common sense.[13]

This was strong language but the Porte was not moved, the Grand Vizier replying a few days later that he could not 'interfere with orders issued direct from the Porte to its own officers on internal matters'. But by then the crisis had been solved. Taking matters into his own hands Williams had sent an experienced Polish officer, Mahmoud Effendi, into the Kurdish camp to persuade Yesdeshia Bey to call off his revolt. As guarantee of British good faith the Kurdish force was told to cross the mountains and to place itself under the protection of the British consul at Mosul on the River Tigris. The plan worked – 'the word of an Englishman has such magic power in the east,' noted Sandwith – and the Kurds enjoyed a brief respite from their centuries-old struggle to gain an autonomous homeland in the highlands of Anatolia.

With the coming of spring Colonel Lake arrived in Kars to take over direction of its defences. Rumours were already strong that a the Russian army, now led by the experienced General Muraviev, was on the move from Georgia and would soon be threatening Kars.

On 7 June Williams moved his staff back into the town, to take up his headquarters in the lea of the castle. A week later the first Russian formations were seen to the east and on 16 June an attack was made by a small force of infantry and cavalry backed by 48 artillery pieces. It was clearly more of a sighting shot or reconnaissance in depth than a serious attack. None the less, the garrison was suitably impressed:

> The army of the Caucasus which had now set down before Kars was acknowledged to be one of the finest and best disciplined forces which the Russian empire could boast of and it well deserved its character. It was commanded by General Mouravieff [sic] in person, an officer of talent and energy who, during a long period of arduous service, had won for himself a name of which any soldier might be proud.[14]

In the months to come Lake and his fellow commanders were to have no reason to doubt that judgement. Not only did the Russians show tremendous courage but they arrived fully equipped for the task of maintaining a lengthy siege. Muraviev also deserved the encomium. Finding that the defences of Kars were well able to withstand attack from outside he decided to start a blockade, cut the communications with Erzerum and wait for the arrival of siege guns and heavy mortars. July saw little more than a flurry of skirmishes — an attack against the defences on the high ground to the east was beaten off, the Turkish troops displaying considerable gallantry and determination — as the Russians consolidated their positions outside Kars. To Williams's exasperation he was unable to do anything to restrict those activities. He did not want to risk his infantry outside the defence works and his cavalry, led by an Austrian officer, Baron de Schwartzenberg, was 'in such a defective state, that it was utterly useless, except for outpost duty; there was scarcely one officer to it that knew his duty.'[15]

There was another break to the interlude when the Russians attacked the southern defences between the Kanli Tabia and the Hafiz Pasha Tabia but these were again beaten off, mainly due to the resolution shown by the field commander Feyzi Pasha, an Hungarian known also as General Kméty, who rallied his men to beat off the Russian attack. While this was encouraging, the garrison of Kars was beginning to suffer. On 1 September Williams was forced to put his men on half rations, desertion became commonplace, cholera re-appeared and the weakest cavalry horses were removed to be slaughtered. Two days later Williams managed to smuggle out a message to James Brant, the British Consul in Erzerum begging him to pass on news of the garrison's plight to Constantinople:

> I would therefore represent to your Excellency the necessity of stimulating the Turkish Government to hasten forward succours, for if Kars be taken, Erzeroom [sic] must of course fall, and the losses these events would occasion the Turkish Government are such as would be beyond its power to repair, and, besides, an enormous sacrifice of blood and treasure, a very large army, and a year's campaign, would be required to recover the two cities, which in the hands of Russia might become impregnable.[16]

There was to be a glimmer of hope on 23 September when news arrived of the fall of Sevastopol, a move which many believed would lead to the lifting of Muraviev's siege. The optimism was increased when the Russian army appeared to be re-deploying but to the consternation of the garrison this was merely the prelude for an attack six days later. Again, this was to be a ferociously contested encounter, the main attack being made against the northern and north-western defences, in which both sides offered no quarter. At one point the Russians managed to encircle a blockhouse, the Tachmasb Tabia, but the intervention of reservists and the concentrated fire from the other forts drove them off:

> This horrid carnage continued until the Russians, stopped by a mound of dead bodies and dislocated by the repeated discharges of grape, were brought to a standstill. The Turks there leaping over the breastwork and led on by the gallant Kméty, finished with bayonet the utter rout of their assailants.[17]

As dusk fell Lake saw to his satisfaction that the Russians were retreating back to their lines but the defending garrison lost one thousand men, the Russians six times that number, although the fact remained that Muraviev's army had not budged. Furthermore it was only too evident that it was well equipped for the task in hand. As the first winter snows appeared the tents were taken down and replaced by huts, and the smoke from numerous fires proclaimed the

Russians were warm and well fed – unlike their increasingly wretched opponents in Kars. On 19 November Williams sent a last despairing message to the outside world:

> Tell lords Clarendon and Redcliffe that the Russian Army is hutted, and takes no notice of either Omar or Selim Pashas. They cannot have acted as they ought to have done. We divide our bread with the starving townspeople. No animal food for seven weeks. I kill horses in my stable secretly and send the meat to the hospital, which is now very crowded.[18]

To add to Williams's consternation, as this curt despatch demonstrates, he knew that the allies had in fact decided to send forces in a last-ditch attempt to relieve him. His succession of despatches, passed through Brant to Stratford, had finally convinced the Porte that steps had to be taken to drive the Russians out of Asia Minor and the Turkish minister for Foreign Affairs had conceded that the fall of Kars would not only give Russia a strategic foothold in Anatolia but it would also give them a moral victory at a time when Sevastopol was still under siege by the allies. On 11 July Omar Pasha informed his allies that he intended to move his forces out of the Crimea to march to the relief of Kars and three days later his proposals were discussed at a council of war.

The Turkish commander-in-chief was in a difficult position. First, he depended on the British and French navies to transport his army across the Black Sea to Trebizond and, second, since arriving in the Crimea his army (25,000 infantry and 300 cavalry) was considered by Pélissier to be part of the allied order of battle and, therefore, a necessary component in the fighting to bring the siege of Sevastopol to a triumphant conclusion. When it became clear that Pélissier and Simpson were opposed to his plan Omar left the Crimea for Constantinople to persuade the Porte to put diplomatic pressure on London and Paris. That was the first delay. The second came from French fears that the presence of Williams and his staff in Kars was a cover for Britain to gain an economic and strategic interest in the area. The French also believed that they held the moral high ground in the argument as they were providing the bulk of the ground forces in the Crimea. Napoleon said as much to Vaillant on 2 August when Palmerston conceded that the British government might press for Omar's army to leave the Crimea. Napoleon said:

We have 60,000 men at the siege, the English have 12,000! The Turks for whom we are fighting are never in the trenches, no more than the Sardinians. They say that it was Lord Raglan who hindered Canrobert as well as Pélissier, from making a diversion which could have have permitted investment of the fortress, etc., etc. All this ought to be considered carefully. If now they still want to weaken the siege army by withdrawing Turkish troops, they will create a justified alienation in the French army. Furthermore, the great objective now is Sebastopol and not at Kars.

The point was reinforced three weeks later when Napoleon told Cowley that, while he was quite sensible of the gravity of the situation, he would not 'admit that the relief of Kars is to be put on the same scale with the capture of Sebastopol'.[19] That was enough. The Crimean port came first, events in Asia Minor second, and the decision to release the Ottoman forces was not taken until 29 September – far too late in the day to save Williams. Even then, Omar intended to bring relief to Kars by attacking Tiflis and landed his army on the Black Sea's eastern shore at Soukhum-Kalé. A second relieving force, led by Selim Pasha, landed at Trebizond on 22 October but only got as far as Erzerum and refused to budge.

With his supplies running out and his men falling to disease and cold Williams had no option but to offer his surrender to Muraviev. As Lake remembered, the choice was made for him because 'provisions were now running so short, that it was no longer difficult to calculate how many days or weeks the place could hold out in the possible event of no assistance coming from any quarter'. [20] To his surprise, Williams was greeted by his opponent not as a defeated general but as a brave soldier who had done his best:

General Williams [said Muraviev], you have made yourself a name in history, and posterity will stand amazed at the endurance, the courage and the discipline which the siege has called forth in the remains of an army. Let us arrange a capitulation that will satisfy the demands of war without outraging humanity.[21]

All this was true and Muraviev allowed Williams to lead his men out of Kars still carrying their arms. Paroles were given to the senior officers and Williams and his British staff were treated courteously during their brief period of imprisonment – they were repatriated the following spring – but that could not disguise the garrison's sense of betrayal. In his final despatch to Clarendon, Williams insisted that it was through no fault of the Ottoman soldiers that Kars had fallen:

> They fell dead at their posts, in their tents, and throughout the camp, as brave men should who cling to their duty through the slightest glimmering of hope of saving a place entrusted to their custody.[22]

Brave they had been undoubtedly, but it was their misfortune to have their fate bound up in allied disagreements about what should be done to end the war in the Crimea. Ironically, the fall of Kars, although considered to be only of minor significance at the time, was to return to haunt the allies when the final peace negotiations got under way in the spring of 1856.

16

A Second Winter

To those who know anything of the history of the two powers which have taken in charge the civilisation of Europe, and who would be glad to lend a hand towards assisting in American affairs, it is plain enough that both France and England will continue to push on their troops till they are glutted with conquest or crunched beneath the steel or snows of Russia.

Thomas H. Seymour to William L. Marcy, 27 September 1855

Having driven Gorchakov's army out of the south side of Sevastopol the allied commanders were at a loss about what should be done next. The battle had been expensive in soldiers' lives, ammunition and resources; so much so that it was difficult to avoid a general feeling that they had justified their presence in the Crimea by taking the city whose capture had eluded them for a year. This was particularly true in the French camp where there were smiles and congratulations all round. Pélissier was given a marshal's baton and, much to the irritation of the British, was appointed a mushir, or commander-in-chief, by the Sultan; Bruat was promoted to full admiral (but did not live long to enjoy the pleasure as he died at sea two months later) and Simpson was awarded the Légion d'Honneur. Even the much-reviled telegraph came into its own on 12 September when Pélissier received the thanks of a grateful emperor: '*Honneur à vous! Honneur à votre brave armée! Faites à tous mes sincères félicitations.*' ('All honour to you. Honour to your brave army. I send to you all my sincere congratulations.')[1]

At home in Paris there were sonorous celebrations allied to a sense of relief; a Te Deum was celebrated in Notre Dame, which had been decorated with the flags of the allied powers. Sevastopol had fallen and in many people's minds the victory and the part played by Pélissier's men symbolised a rebirth of French military might. For a few happy hours 1812 became just another dusty date in a long-forgotten history and it seemed possible that Sevastopol was but a springboard for even greater successes against the Russians. Two weeks after Sevastopol fell Rose sent a thoughtful despatch to Clarendon which captured the mood in the French camp:

> After 1815 the spirit of the French Army was lowered by a succession of reverses. The successes in Algiers against Barbarians, without artillery, were not sufficient to restore them the prestige they once enjoyed.
>
> But the share of successes which the French Army have had in conquering a Military European Power of the first order, in battles on the field, and in the Siege of a peculiarly strong and invested Fortress, a Siege without many parallels in History, have not only improved, very much, the experiences and military qualifications of the Officers and men of the French Army, but have raised their military feeling and confidence.[2]

To capitalise on that effect Napoleon insisted that the war must continue and that Russia must be humbled before there could be any peace settlement. Not only would that process isolate Russia from Europe but it would also restore France as a major power and destroy for ever the settlement of 1815. It might even be possible to realise Napoleon's dream of rebuilding the kingdom of Poland and placing his cousin on its throne.

There was much to recommend this way of thinking. France had been left exhausted by the Napoleonic wars and the nation itself had been humbled, its frontiers reduced to those of 1789. Napoleon III certainly believed that he had a mission to restore his country's fortunes by continuing the war, but he was already swimming against a tide of growing disapproval with the war. While his fellow countrymen had been happy and relieved to celebrate the fall of Sevastopol it could not be denied that the victory had been won at a cost. The casualties seemed to be disproportionate to any diplomatic or strategic gain and the need to keep the forces supplied for another winter was a strain on an already overloaded exchequer. France simply did not have the resources to continue the war and was unable to match the expenditure lavished on it by her British allies. London's well-filled purse was one very good reason why Napoleon was so desperate to keep the cross-Channel alliance in being.

He had little difficulty in persuading his allies to be assertive. Palmerston remained as bellicose as ever and, together with Clarendon, warned colleagues that the war was far from being over and might last another two or three years. Their message was clear and unwavering: Britain's war aims would not be altered and there could be no negotiated peace until Russia had been defeated. To achieve that goal Palmerston still thought that it would be possible to construct a grand European alliance similar to the coalition which had defeated Napoleon forty years earlier. As he told Clarendon on 9 October, 'Russia has not yet been beat enough to make peace possible at the present moment.'[3] Military pride was also at stake. Palmerston had refused permission for the church bells to be rung in celebration of the recent victory as it was all too evident that British troops had not distinguished themselves in the fighting.

The Turks were keen to see the allies continue the war in the Crimea as this would allow them to open operations in Asia Minor and to that end they insisted that Omar Pasha be allowed to withdraw his army from the Crimea. Russia, too, was adamant that the war was far from over. 'Sevastopol is not Moscow, the Crimea is not Russia,' said Alexander II in a proclamation to Gorchakov shortly after the fall of Sevastopol. 'Two years after we set fire to Moscow, our troops marched in the streets of Paris. We are still the same Russians and God is still with us.'[4] In military terms the Russian commander had merely made a tactical retreat into a new position which would continue to pose problems to the allies. The tsar also guessed correctly that his enemies had no intention of marching into Russia and that unless Gorchakov were defeated stalemate had returned to the Crimean peninsula. Given that unassailable position, the allies' only hope of inflicting a decisive defeat seemed to lie in the Baltic; Dundas's destruction of Sveaborg having given rise to hopes that a similar campaign in the spring of 1856 could crush Kronstadt and leave St Petersburg open to attack by sea and land forces. It was an idea which would exercise the minds of allied planners throughout the winter.

None the less, the continuing public bellicosity could not disguise the fact that there was also a growing desire for peace, especially in France, where Count Walewski, Drouyn de Lhuys's replacement as

foreign secretary, was playing a somewhat different game. An illegiti-
mate son of Napoleon Bonaparte, he was considered by Cowley to
be an intellectual lightweight who was too close to the emperor's
pro-Russian half-brother, the Duc de Morny, and therefore not to
be trusted. To Clarendon he was a parvenu, 'a low-minded strolling
player' whose 'view of moral obligation' was always 'subservient to
his interests or his vanity'. Palmerston shared that opinion and added
the thought that if anything were to happen to the emperor there
would be no shortage of French politicians of Walewski's ilk who
would be prepared to sue for peace with the Russians.

There were grounds for these fears. Although Cowley and Clarendon,
the British statesmen most directly involved, never lost their suspicions
about those who served the emperor – based largely on social snob-
bery, it must be admitted – they were right to pay close attention
to the new French foreign secretary, Walewski. At a time when the
allies were attempting to maintain a common front and continue the
war he was in secret negotiation with the Russians through the Duc de
Morny and a shadowy figure called Baron Hukeren, the adopted son
of the Dutch ambassador in Paris, whom Cowley described as 'among
the numerous speculating and political intriguers that abound in the
capital'.[5] Initially, Napoleon seems not to have known that covert
peace feelers were being made but by October he had given them tacit
approval. These were conducted on two fronts: through his friendship
with Prince Gorchakov, the duke made it known that France was
ready for peace while a similar message was passed by Walewski to
Nesselrode's daughter who was married to the Saxon ambassador in
Paris, Baron von Seebach. At the same time the Russian ambassador
in Berlin, Baron Budberg, alerted the Prussian government that the
tsar was ready to reopen negotiations. While, in themselves, these
clandestine talks did not lead to the reopening of peace talks, they
at least helped to pave the way.

Meanwhile, as had happened earlier in the year when the Vienna
conference seemed to hold out the hope of a cessation of hostilities,
the British and French governments urged their commanders in the
Crimea to continue the campaign. Having told Simpson that from
the Queen's palace to humblest cottage British hearts were beating
with pride at 'this long looked-for success', Panmure turned to sterner
matters:

The consequences of this event upon the morale of the Russian

Army must be very great, and I trust that in concert with Marshal
Pélissier you have devised means to take advantage of them and
to give the enemy no rest till his overthrow is completed.

In order to keep this object properly in view you must not
suffer your mind to rest upon any expectation of peace; your
duty as a General is to keep your Army in the best condition
for offence and to turn your attention to all the means in your
power for so doing.[6]

There was considerable mortification that the victory had not been
followed up with a further attack on the Russian position and Panmure
told Simpson that there were to be no celebrations in the army until
Russia had been finally defeated. A succession of despatches from
London attempted to goad the British commander into action but
without success. Simpson simply reiterated his and the French belief
that it would be folly to attack the Russian positions and he remained
unmoved by an unhelpful suggestion that he should think of 'applying
a hot poker' to make Pélissier do something positive. The impasse was
broken on 26 September when Panmure sent a peremptory telegram
to the British commander demanding action:

The public are getting impatient to know what the Russians
are about. The Government desire immediately to be informed
whether either you or Pélissier have taken any steps whatever to
ascertain this, and further they observe that nearly 3 weeks have
elapsed in absolute idleness. This cannot go on and in justice
to yourself and your army you must prevent it. Answer this on
receipt.[7]

From the evidence of the correspondence between the two men
it is difficult to know what Panmure wanted to achieve from this
telegraphic despatch. That he was anxious to hear Simpson play a
more martial tune was beyond doubt, yet the commander's own
letters betray a worrying timorousness that was not to be cured by
Panmure's mixture of threats and cajoling. In one letter he would
chide Simpson for playing second fiddle to the French and insist on
action, ending the despatch with an order that the British soldiers
were not to be given spirits before going on sentry duty; in another
he would reflect on the pleasure of discussing the campaign at some
future date over a bottle of claret. However, his latest despatch had

one obvious effect: the man who had gone out to the Crimea with no other thought than to report on Raglan, finally admitted that high command was too great a burden to bear. Two days later Simpson telegraphed his resignation, explaining that he could not remain in command while facing sustained criticism, and his offer to stand down was quickly accepted.

As Codrington was the designated successor, it should have been an easy matter to confirm his promotion, but during the final assault on Sevastopol Codrington seemed to have lost his nerve – Newcastle was particularly withering in his criticism – and renewed thought was given to the command of the army in the Crimea. Once again the candidates' claims were examined and during the hiatus, which lasted three weeks, Panmure was forced to address his orders simply to the British Headquarters in the Crimea. Despite doubts about his abilities Codrington was confirmed in command on 15 October but did not take over the office until a few weeks later: more than any other attribute, his ability to speak fluent French and his easy social skills seem to have counted in his favour. To soften the blow to the other commanders, on 10 December the army was divided into two corps, command of each going to Campbell and Eyre.

By then the British Army was in a much better position than in the previous year and relatively well equipped to face another winter. Each soldier had been given a new hard weather uniform consisting of two woollen jerseys, two pairs of woollen drawers, two pairs of woollen socks, two pairs of long stockings, one cholera belt, one comforter, a pair of gloves, a fur cap, greatcoat and waterproof cape. At Panmure's insistence – he was a great stickler for detail – each man was also given, and ordered to use, a tin of Onion's Drubbing, a new patented waterproof treatment for boots; and on 7 December four hundred field stoves specially designed by Alexis Soyer arrived at Balaklava. As an aid for observing the enemy in forward positions the army was supplied with a thousand trench telescopes of the kind which would be used in the First World War 'for looking at objects without exposing the viewer'.[7]

With better conditions, the supply problems having been largely solved, the army's morale improved. Before winter settled in there were race meetings and hurriedly improvised shoots for the officers and theatricals for the men. Despite Panmure's exhortations about keeping drunkenness at bay the independently owned canteens at Kadikoi did brisk business and, with the Russians content to keep their distance, the miseries of the last winter's discomforts in the trenches were soon forgotten. By contrast it was now the turn of the French to suffer. Cholera followed by typhus ran through their camp and, added to a general air of disaffection, there were calls from the veterans of the fighting to be sent home. As the casualties from illness began to mount these demands were met: on 13 November Rose reported that the French Imperial Guards regiments were to be withdrawn and that eight line infantry regiments were to return to Algeria. Despite promises to the contrary, these were not to be replaced.

Before the armies went into winter quarters at the beginning of November, the British in good spirits, the French in as sorry as state as their allies had been in the previous season, there were two noteworthy attacks on the Russians. Having despatched part of their cavalry to Eupatoria, French units led by General D'Alonville attacked a larger Russian force on 20 October and succeeded in compelling it to withdraw with the loss of many casualties. However, D'Alonville chose not to follow up the success, other than to continue the harassment of Russian stragglers, because, according to Rose, the French chief of staff, General de Martimprey, had ordered his subordinate commanders to rein in any propensity for offensive activities:

> I again perceived that he was opposed to any hostile operation against the enemy on a large scale. But whether he entertains this opinion because he thinks that the Enemy will leave the Crimea, without being forced to do [sic], or because he is of the conviction, which he lately expressed, that negotiations in the winter will bring about a peace, I know not.[8]

The other operation was far more aggressive and it was destined to be the last blow struck by the allies during the war. It was also the most successful, a combined forces' attack on the Fort Kinburn, a heavily defended Russian position which covered the confluence of the Rivers Bug and Dnieper. The brainchild of Lyons, it made full use of three newly developed French armoured steam batteries which, together with the allied gunboats and battleships, battered the fortress into submission. The French played a full role by committing 6000 men to the infantry force of 10,000, command of which was awarded to General Bazaine, as well as three battleships and a number of gunboats, although it remained unclear if Pélissier's enthusiasm for the assault was governed more by a succession of orders from Paris or by his newly developed infatuation with Bazaine's wife, Soledad. During Bazaine's absence, Pélissier's coach, captured from the Russians, was to be seen each day outside Soledad's quarters. It was not the only romance thrown up by the war: Canrobert had fallen for the daughter of Colonel Strangways, the British gunner commander killed at Inkerman, but as with Pélissier's fondness for Bazaine's wife nothing came of the wartime dalliance.

The attack on Kinburn, though, was a complete success. On 16 October the infantry and marine forces made an unopposed landing on the Kinburn peninsula to cut off the fortress from reinforcements and to attack the garrison should it decide to retire. The following day, having advanced under cover of darkness, the allied fleet commenced a heavy bombardment, using tactics similar to those employed at Sveaborg a month earlier. Having been infiltrated into the bay in front of the fortress the gunboats and steam batteries were able to produce a sustained bombardment which quickly silenced the Russian guns. Then the allied battleships steamed into line to fire an equally heavy succession of broadsides which left the garrison with no option but to surrender. The way was open to strike inland but Bazaine called a halt to the operation once the forts and Kinburn and Ochakov (on the other side of the estuary) had surrendered. Following the destruction of Sveaborg, the successful outcome of the Kinburn operation demonstrated that the allies now had the naval capacity to attack and defeat Russia's hitherto impregnable sea-fortresses.

As winter set in other activities included a reconnaissance of the Baider valley to ascertain whether or not an attack on the Russian positions at Simpheropol would yield results. Napoleon thought so but the French-led scouting party reported back that the Russians were entrenched on the high ground and that any attack would only result in unacceptable casualties. That fear lay at the heart of the allied command's thinking. With the fall of Sevastopol, France had recovered her honour and, just as importantly, her right to sit at the high table when European matters were being discussed. Pélissier did not want to pursue the war against the Russians and by the middle of October he had come to the opinion that the allied army in the Crimea should be reduced by almost half to 70,000 and that it should take up defensive positions on the Chersonese peninsula.

His thinking chimed in with the mood at home where the war was now decidedly unpopular. On 22 October Cowley reported a conversation with the emperor in which Napoleon argued that the war had become an expensive anachronism and that the presence of the allied armies would not encourage Russia to negotiate. That could only be achieved by diplomatic means. As evidence, he produced a report from Pélissier in which the marshal claimed that there was nothing for the allies to conquer in southern Russia – 'sterile plains which the Russians will abandon after some battles in which they will lose a few thousand men, a loss which causes them no decisive damage, whilst at every step the Allies with a great sacrifice of men and money and with nothing to gain will risk each day the destinies of Europe'.[9]

The gloomy mood in Paris appalled Cowley who recognised that any withdrawal would be a sign of weakness which Russia would surely exploit and in concert with Clarendon he put diplomatic pressure on Napoleon not to yield to his commanders' gloomy prognostications. It seemed to work for although the emperor was by then aware of French diplomatic efforts to make peace he agreed to keep his troops in the Crimea until the spring. The lure was a joint allied war council to be held in Paris in January which would be responsible for clarifying future operations against Russia in the Black and Baltic seas. While the decision saved the alliance it spelled doom for thousands of French troops. In the last three months of the war the French army lost more men from disease than they had done in the fighting. Between 25,000 and 40,000 (the numbers have never been computed) troops died of cholera or typhus between January and March 1856. Worse, the much vaunted French medical services, which had performed so well and so heroically during the campaign, were completely overwhelmed.

Ironically, the British were able to offer much needed assistance. Just as they had been helped during the previous winter so they returned the compliment in January 1856 by supplying surplus warm clothing, much of it paid for by the British public, to the suffering French soldiers. By then the number of soldiers available to Codrington had also swollen. With the withdrawal of Omar Pasha to Asia Minor his forces had been replaced by another Ottoman army corps of 20,000 troops under the command of Lieutenant-General Sir Robert Vivian, formerly adjutant-general, Madras Army. This included Beatson's Bashi-Bazouks but the passing of time had done nothing to cure their indiscipline: in August Stratford had been forced to intervene after the irregular force had fought with French troops in Gallipoli, leaving the ambassador to renew his call for its disbandment following the 'numerous testimonies of its capability for insubordination which have reached me from reliable sources'.[10]

However, Vivian had proved himself to be a capable commander of native troops, having spent most of his time in the army of the East India Company on active service in Burma. In May he had arrived in the Dardanelles to take command of the Ottoman forces assigned to the British Army – no mean sacrifice for a man who had recently left the army to become a director of the East India Company – and, Beatson's unruly cavalry notwithstanding, had turned his men into a reliable and disciplined formation. Together with the Foreign Legion battalions and the Sardinian forces, Codrington now had an army which was the equal of Pélissier's. As had happened so often in the past Britain had gone to war ill-prepared and was ending it tolerably well. The trouble was that there was nothing for its forces to do and its main ally was no longer interested in prosecuting an increasingly unpopular war.

The other ally, Turkey, was also proving to be troublesome. On 1 September Stratford returned from visiting the armies in the Crimea – part of his duties had been to present Orders of the Bath to British and French officers – to find that the Sultan had taken advantage of his absence to appoint his disgraced brother-in-law Mehemet Ali to the post of Kapudan Pasha, or minister of marine. The move had been engineered with the help of Omar Pasha and Stratford took it as a personal affront to his authority in Constantinople. Not only did Mehemet Ali lead an 'obnoxious personal life . . . notorious for corruption and branded with the criminality of indulging in dangerous intrigues against the Sovereign's authority' – he had been found guilty of murdering his Christian mistress and, at Stratford's insistence, sacked from public life – but his appointment showed a contempt for British attempts to introduce reforms at court. What was the point of bolstering the Ottoman Empire by taking its side against Russia, asked Stratford, if its rulers were deaf to Britain's demands that changes had to be made in its style of government?

A worse consequence is but too likely to ensue; and indeed the indications of its approach are already visible. If half that is rumoured to be true, the morals of the Palace are undergoing a melancholy decline. I hear of personal expenses threatening the Sovereign with serious pecuniary embarrassment, of indulgences calculated to impair a constitution naturally feeble, of vices no less pernicious than detestable, and of resentments kindled in a bosom, naturally just and generous, by the inconvenient fidelity of those who mark the progress of contamination and foresee its results.[11]

No sooner had Stratford returned than he sought an audience with the Sultan but, to his vexation, he was kept waiting a week. In that time Turkish attitudes had hardened and Stratford was to be confounded when he suggested that the appointment of Mehemet Ali was a backward step and one which would not win any favour in London. The Sultan simply replied that any British interference would be 'disagreeable' to him and that he was not minded to make any changes. If this was a setback to the Great Elchi then the tone adopted only made his position more embarrassing. The Sultan, he told Clarendon, was 'far less gracious than usual' and manifested 'a degree of impatience and ill-humour' which did not bode well for future relations between the two countries.[12]

The contretemps came at a particularly difficult time for Stratford. For the first occasion in his long career in Constantinople his prestige was being questioned and, to his great discomfort, the challenge was mounted with the support of the French. Seeing that the French army was dominant in the field, with Britain playing a lesser role, Stratford's enemies at the Porte understood only too well that a shift in power had taken place and they worked assiduously to take advantage of it. Here they were helped by the arrival of a new ambassador in the forceful Edouard de Thouvenel who was less overawed by the Great Elchi than his predecessor, Benedetti, had ever been: as Stratford told Clarendon, the new French ambassador was 'six foot three of Gallic intimidation'.

It was not just his presence that was discommoding. It soon became evident that Thouvenel was working to a different agenda, one which would put him on a collision course with British interests. First, he tacitly supported Mehemet Ali's appointment and then he let it be known that his British colleague had a very rough bedside manner in dealing with the sick man of Europe. He also made it his business to build bridges with Fuad Pasha and Aali Pasha who had quickly shown the direction of their thinking by agreeing to support separate concessions for French Catholics. All this was very vexing to Stratford. Not only was he attempting to thwart the claims of a French engineering consortium to build a railway from Belgrade to Constantinople, but he was already engaged in a long-standing confrontation with the Porte over the rights of Muslims to convert to Christianity, if that were their devout wish. This was a subject dear to Stratford's heart. He had been a lifelong campaigner to change the Islamic law which condemned Muslims to death if they were guilty of the sin of apostasy and, in 1844, had finally persuaded the Sultan to put a stop to its automatic implementation throughout the Ottoman Empire. To the British ambassador it was a barbarous practice which had no role to play in the modern state which he hoped Turkey would one day become but, despite the Sultan's edict, it had proved difficult to persuade the Islamic clerics.

Now, in the middle of October 1855, after an eleven-year period of grace Stratford received information that religious executions for apostasy had taken place in Aleppo and Adrianople. Confirmation came from Paris where Cowley had received a deputation of the Society of Friends of Religious Liberty who had first-hand knowledge of the executions. As they had already persuaded Walewski to make an official protest, they asked Cowley to do the same. No sooner had Stratford been instructed from London than he made an urgent appointment with Aali Pasha, the Grand Vizier, who furnished him with bland promises:

> There was the same declaration as to religious tolerance, administrative reform, and the necessity of European constitution, the same acknowledgements of benefits derived from the alliance, and the same assertion that blasphemy, alone of religious offences, was now, in practice, liable to capital punishment.[13]

By that stage of the war Stratford was becoming increasingly exhausted, the long nights working on his despatches having taken a heavy toll – he was in his sixty-ninth year – and he admitted to feeling depressed by the possibility that the fighting might drag on relentlessly. In place of the anxious optimism which had coloured his earlier despatches to Clarendon there was a new cynicism, a genuine war-weariness added to a belief that Britain was engaged in an unequal struggle. He felt oppressed, too, by the failure of the Porte to take seriously the fate of the garrison at Kars: it was already clear that neither Omar nor Selim Pasha would break through to its aid and Williams's surrender seemed inevitable.

Realising, perhaps, that his role as an interlocutor for the British generals was now approaching its end, Stratford turned his attention to the rights of Christians within the Ottoman Empire and he was to achieve some formidable successes. During the winter, under pressure from the allies, Abd-el-Mejid agreed a wide range of measures to protect the rights of Christians and all non-Muslims in his empire, including the abolition of the death penalty for apostasy. These changes would form part of the peace settlement and, freed from the need to deal with military matters, Stratford bent his energies and persuasiveness to the task and later admitted that he had to use some 'very decided language'. After all, the rights of religious communities was one reason why the allies had found themselves involved in the long and expensive war with Russia.

While Stratford spent January engaged in that Sisyphean task the allies met in Paris to discuss their war aims for the coming year. Britain was represented by Cowley and, from the army and navy, Cambridge, Jones, Airey, Lyons and Dundas; France by the emperor, Walewski, Princes Jerome and Napoleon, Vaillant and, from their forces, Canrobert, Niel, Bosquet, Martimprey, Hamelin and Penaud. Described as a Grand Council of War, it achieved little beyond a general agreement to continue fighting in the Crimea, Napoleon arguing that it seemed strange to maintain an army 200,000 strong, unless it was prepared to do something. Diversionary plans were discussed and discarded. Prompted by Newcastle's findings, the British delegates argued for an attack on the Russian holdings on the Black Sea's eastern coast while the French had drawn up ambitious plans to attack Kronstadt.

This was the brainchild of Canrobert who had led a diplomatic mission to Stockholm to bring Sweden into the alliance. Although King Oscar had only agreed to a defensive commitment, there was a secret understanding that Sweden would enter the war in the event of an allied attack in the Baltic. In January that seemed to be not improbable. Buoyed by the successful assaults on Sveaborg and the Kinburn forts, British and French naval planners believed that they could repeat the operations on a larger scale against Kronstadt. If that fell St Petersburg would be defenceless – although the large Russian-Finnish army would still have to be defeated. To meet that threat the French planned to invade the Baltic provinces and to take advantage of local anti-Russian sentiments. It found no takers. While Lyons and Dundas were in favour of a further naval campaign, the

Duke of Cambridge argued that a land operation was beyond the allies' resources:

> As regards the Baltic campaign, Niel read a long paper as to how Cronstadt was to be bombarded and taken by a fleet, and Canrobert read a very wild scheme for attacking St Petersburg by land with an army of 60,000 French and an equal number of troops not named, but which I believed were intended to be Swedes. However the scheme was so wild that he concluded by saying that it was impracticable, and that he might have saved us the time occupied in reading it. I believe that any plan of this description is so impracticable that it would not be entertained by anybody.[13]

And so it proved. The conference concluded on 21 January 1856 with the allies agreeing to launch one more attack on the Russians' lines of communications from Eupatoria. It would be a French-led operation with the British and Sardinians providing support from the Chernaia river.

For the allied armies in the Crimea it was a curious time; they were still at war, yet everyone knew that peace was in the offing. The chances for action were few and far between and despite exhortations from their respective governments neither Pélissier nor Codrington made any preparations for aggressive operations. Indeed, the British commander put the matter in perspective when he told Panmure in February that, while his men were still bullish, the chances of ever fighting the Russians were limited because of their defensive position on the other side of Sevastopol's wide harbour – 'a large mutual wet ditch', as he called it. Only one issue had been decided: in December the British and French governments decided to destroy the docks in Sevastopol and that at least gave welcome employment to the allied troops.

By then, many of the veterans of the war had also begun to go home. Bosquet and Niel had returned to Paris for Christmas and the British cavalry had withdrawn to winter quarters near Constantinople, taking with them the indefatigable Mrs Duberly. Another of the war's chroniclers, Colonel Sterling, had also applied successfully to go on leave, as a first step to resigning his commission and returning to civilian life. Passed over for promotion and angered at the decision to place a number of junior Guards' officers above him, Sterling left for Malta carrying with him a feeling of betrayal. 'Ah me, I am sick and belong to the classe dangereuse,' he complained. 'What else can an officer be, used as I have been? I declare I only wonder my brain is still sound.'[14]

While that blameless staff officer's frustrations were born of personal considerations they were not untypical of the army that spent its second winter in the Crimea. The veterans who had arrived with such high hopes in September 1854 wondered if their sacrifices had been worthwhile. Those who had replaced the estimated 20,000 British and 80,000 French casualties no longer had the fall of Sevastopol as their goal. It was an in-between time, a period of waiting for peace, yet not knowing for certain that the war was over. Even Sterling caught the mood. Like the man who spends long glaring hours beneath the desert sun and swears never again to break his back and split his head in the saddle and who then finds that a month of ease and town life fills him with impatience to inflict on himself the same torments, Sterling did not remain long at home. Despite his protestations to the contrary, in February he was back in the Crimea with his beloved Highland Division ready and willing to go to war once more.

'I do know war and I hate it,' he said, 'but I hate tyranny more, and would fight against it any day.' Time, though, was running out for such high-blown warlike sentiments: with the coming of spring, peace was finally not very far away.

PART III

1

Peace Feelers

I am neither warlike nor peaceable, but I say that if we cannot
have an honourable peace, we must have a bloody war.
Lord Panmure to Lord Granville, January 1856

It would take time for the British government to realise that it had
no alternative but to seek a negotiated peace. Lack of military success
in the war was one reason for the procrastination, the failure to take
the Great Redan being an unwanted affront to British pride; the
overwhelming need to inflict a military defeat on Russia was another.
There was also a possibility that Spain would join the alliance, having
offered on 7 October to provide 30,000 troops for service in the
Crimea. The overture was politely rejected as Britain did not want
to antagonise the United States any further over the matter of Spain's
possession of Cuba, but on the question of war or peace Palmerston,
Clarendon and Panmure were in full agreement: they did not want
to conclude the military operations in the Crimea and the Baltic.
The Russians were barbarians who had to be given 'a sound licking'
to curb their territorial pretensions and to make Europe a safer place.
They were not to know, until it was too late to interfere to any effect,
that France was intent on peace from the moment that the allied
armies marched into Sevastopol. Napoleon might have continued
to give a good impression of wanting to prosecute the war more
firmly and of maintaining the integrity of his cross-Channel alliance,
but the diplomatic reality was that his officials were paving the way
for peace talks. Observing from the sidelines, Buchanan told Marcy
that he was 'sorry to observe that I believe him [Napoleon III] to be

the controlling spirit of the alliance. His influence over the Councils of Great Britain is very great, if not commanding.'[1]

By applying pressure on the emperor, though, Cowley had managed to keep up the pretence that the alliance was still strong – as late as January 1856 Clarendon was confident enough to tell Palmerston that Napoleon would stick to his word because 'he has made up his mind that we are the only country that wish him long life and success' – but it was mainly façade. Not only had Waleswki been making secret contact with the Russians through central European diplomatic sources but, shortly after the fall of Sevastopol, Buol had reopened the question of the Four Points with the French ambassador, Bourqueney. As the unfortunate Westmorland had been recalled, Britain did not have an ambassador in Vienna, their interests being represented by a *chargé d'affaires*, Henry Elliot, an experienced but relatively minor diplomat, and it was left to the French to play the leading role in the negotiations with the Austrians. By the middle of October Bourqueney had returned to Paris where he briefed the emperor and Cowley on what had been discussed in Vienna.

Buol's proposals were, in effect, the same Four Points that he had peddled before, only this time they had been bolstered to take advantage of Russia's weaker position. The peace plan would be presented by Austria in the form of an ultimatum; if it were not accepted by St Petersburg the refusal would cause a rupture in diplomatic relations which would lead inevitably to war. For Buol it was a calculated risk but he was confident that the odds had shortened in his favour. From Prince Alexander Gorchakov, the Russian ambassador in Vienna, he knew that Nesselrode was not unwilling to listen to any proposals that the allies might put forward, provided always that they did not humiliate Russia. With France anxious to make peace because its armies had done enough to retrieve the country's position in Europe, and with Russia economically exhausted and not unsympathetic to an honourable solution, the way was open for Austria to operate as honest broker – on this occasion with some hope of success. That was precisely what Palmerston had feared all along, but although he complained that 'Austria will try to draw us again into negotiations for an insufficient peace', the tide was running against Britain. Her principal ally was intent on peace and the British government would have little option but to be part of the process.

The next few months, from October 1855 to the end of January 1856, were to be marked by a tortuous diplomatic dance in which

Austria and France were to take the lead while Britain did its utmost to disrupt the rhythm. It was not always a dignified procedure, for each participant was guided by national self-interest and only occasionally would they present a united front. On 14 October Cowley met Bourqueney with the emperor to listen to the Austrian proposals for a negotiated peace based on a revision of the Four Points. As the deal had already been accepted by Walewski, who was to persuade Napoleon to accept it three days later, Cowley was unsure of his ground. The British ambassador did not trust either party, the French because he realised that Walewski wanted a quick end to the war and the Austrians because he was suspicious of their motives. Cowley, who in fact admired Bourqueney, felt that Austria was only intent on improving its own position at the expense of the allies.

The revelation of the Buol-Bourqueney plan caused a flurry of excitement in London. Clarendon shared his ambassador's scepticism and felt that Britain was being railroaded into a peace treaty which was deeply flawed. He was also becoming increasingly concerned that Britain was being forced to 'play second fiddle' to France. While it made sense to keep the door open, he felt that the new conditions suggested by Buol did not go far enough. If the allies were serious about curbing Russian power, they should impose harsher conditions, such as forcing the tsar to surrender his authority over the Crimea, Circassia and Georgia. Not only would this protect Turkey's flanks, and in so doing offer further safeguards to India's borders, but such stringent demands were unlikely to be accepted in St Petersburg. As the British prime minister told Cowley, that would allow a breathing space which would give the allies the excuse to continue the prosecution of the war. Palmerston went even further. As soon as the campaigning season reopened in the spring he wanted to expand the allies' operations by attacking Russia through Finland and Poland in the north, and through Georgia in the south.

These were wild words – there was never any chance that such an extreme policy would be adopted – and Cowley was told to continue his discussions with the French while taking care not to offend the Austrians. It was a tall order but Cowley stuck to his task even though he realised that his political masters' obfuscations put him in a weaker position than he normally enjoyed in Paris. He feared, too, that his amicable relationship with the emperor might be weakened and that he stood in danger of being sidelined. During the tense days of negotiation in October and November his despatches betray a grim sense of irony allied to a genuine alarm that he was being outplayed by Walewski. On 19 November, following what had clearly been an unsatisfactory meeting with the emperor and his foreign secretary, he revealed his exasperation to Clarendon:

> I will only add that both the Emperor who has spoken to me on the subject, and Count Walewski, are most anxious that the proposal of Count Buol should be favourably entertained by Her Majesty's Government. I have not given either of them hopes that this will be the case, though I have assured them of the constant desire of your colleagues to meet the wishes of the Imperial Government, as far as your own sense of duty will admit it. I have dwelt more particularly on the great anxiety of Her Majesty's Government to avoid a repetition of the Vienna Conference by advancement of negotiations which can terminate in no practical result.[2]

It was, though, a losing game. Because Britain had not rejected the plan out of hand but had suggested certain modifications to it, Waleswki instructed his ambassador to return to Vienna to continue the negotiations but with two important revisions, both suggested by the emperor. Moldavia and Wallachia should be united into a single entity and Russia should concede territory in Bessarabia at the mouth of the Danube. Bourqueney arrived back in Vienna at the beginning of November and reopened negotiations with Buol, taking care to ensure that the Austrians thought that he was talking for both allies. 'Disguise it as we may,' an alarmed Clarendon told Elliot, the British chargé d'affaires in Vienna, 'they will be conditions offered to Russia by England and France, and that under present circumstances will in my opinion amount to national degradation.'[3]

To begin with the meetings were cordial enough as both men were confident they could broker an agreement which would appeal to all the belligerent countries. However, Buol could not bring himself to agree to the new French conditions. First, he feared that the union of the principalities could threaten Austrian security and, second, he wanted Russia to cede more territory in Bessarabia so that the Danube could revert to being an Austrian-controlled waterway. Anxious not to weaken his position at this critical juncture Bourqueney conceded both points in return for a new condition insisting that 'the belligerent powers reserved the right which belonged to them of bringing forward in the interests of Europe particular conditions over and above the four pledges' — the so-called Fifth Point. Having found common ground the two diplomats drew up a new agreement which would be presented to Russia in the form of an ultimatum. If the following points were not agreed within a set time, Austria would break off diplomatic relations with Russia, a move which would precede a declaration of war. On 14 November Buol and Bourqueney signed the *Projet de préliminaires de paix* (preliminary peace plan) which made the following demands:

1. Abolition of the Russian 'special or exclusive right of protection' over the Danubian principalities (Moldavia and Wallachia). Rectification of the Russo-Turkish frontier by Russia, ceding part of Bessarabia from a line drawn from Chotyn, southeast to Lake Salysk.

2. Freedom of navigation of the Danube and its mouths 'to be assured on a European basis'.

3. Neutralisation of the Black Sea, which was to be thrown open to the commerce of all nations. Abolition of military or naval arsenals. Mutual engagement by Turkey and Russia to preserve only an agreed and equal number of light boats for police purposes.

4. The preservation of privileges and immunities for the Christian *rayahs* or subjects of the Sultan.

5. The 'Fifth Point' giving the European powers unnamed *conditions particulières* (special conditions).[4]

Having initialled the agreement Bourqueney returned once more to Paris and on 18 November the papers were forwarded to London for approval. They met with a mixed response, the only common ground being a belief that the demands would never be acceptable to the tsar. Clarendon thought that there was much to recommend the new proposals, not because he believed they were sound within themselves but because he hoped the very stringency of the proposals would keep the war alive. Queen Victoria was also impressed. Possibly influenced by her new regard for Napoleon, for she was easily swayed by men of authority, she urged acceptance for the good reason that Britain might find itself isolated:

The terms of the Austrian Ultimatum are clear and complete

and very favourable to us, if accepted by Russia. If refused, which they almost must be, rupture of diplomatic relations between Austria and Russia is a decided step gained by us, and will produce a state of things which can scarcely fail to lead them to war. A refusal to entertain the proposal may induce and perhaps justify the Emperor of the French in backing out of the War, which would leave us in a miserable position.[5]

Only Palmerston remained obdurate, telling the French ambassador the Duc de Persigny – no friend of Walewski whom he considered an upstart – that the Buol-Bourqueney proposal was 'un protocole pour nous, mais sans nous' ('a protocol for us, but without us'). Personal honour was also a consideration. Throughout this anxious period Palmerston could never understand the wisdom of agreeing to a plan created by a country, Austria, which had not even been involved in the fighting. To him the matter was clear-cut: not only did Britain want to realise the original objectives of the war but Russian power had to be crushed. If that were to be achieved by continuing the war, then so be it, even if it meant fighting on alone with Turkey as Britain's only ally.

However, when the Cabinet discussed the new peace plan on 20 November Palmerston found himself over-ruled. Following a long discussion, the Buol-Bourqueney proposals were accepted, subject to what Clarendon later called 'some trifling alterations', and it was agreed that the ultimatum should then be sent to Russia. To all intents and purposes the decision paved the way for peace but as the matter of the alterations was left in the hands of Palmerston and Clarendon the negotiations were destined to drag on for another two months. On some of the lesser British demands the French and the Austrians were prepared to concede immediately. On Point Three, freedom of commerce in the Black Sea was made universal, and on Point Four, Jews were to be granted the same rights as Christians in the Ottoman Empire. On other more substantial alterations to the Fifth Point they were less willing to make concessions.

This was particularly true of the British demands which the French found most hawkish: in Point Three, the Sea of Azov should be included in the neutralisation of the Black Sea, and there should be an additional condition which would recognise the independence of the native tribes in the eastern Black Sea regions of Circassia and Mingrelia. And under the terms of the Fifth Point the allies should insist on the neutralisation and demilitarisation of the Aaland Islands in the Baltic as a means of protecting Sweden from Russian aggression. As the territory included the fortress of Bomarsund, destroyed by the allies in 1854, Palmerston believed that the claim could not be lightly refused by the Russians. All this he found 'very moderate' and Cowley was asked to inform Napoleon that the British initiatives were being made for the best possible motives.

That was not how the position was viewed in Paris. Waleswki was aghast at Britain's attitude and could not disguise his feelings. In a highly charged meeting with Cowley on the morning of 21 November he voiced his frustration – first seeming to agree to the Austrian proposal and then stymieing it by adding insuperable conditions. While he found the minor alterations acceptable he could not agree to the demands concerning the Sea of Azov or the Aaland Islands. The first would be unacceptable to the Russians as it concerned an inland waterway and would almost certainly be rebuffed as too humiliating a concession. As for the Aaland Islands, if these were to be included in the ultimatum, then there was no reason to omit the matter of Poland over which the emperor had decided opinions. In any case, there was no precedent for Austria making any territorial demands. According to Cowley, Walewski then 'got on his high horse' and insisted that, at this delicate stage of the negotiations, there could be no question of conditions:

> I said that Count Waleswki was totally mistaken if he supposed that out of deference to the Emperor Her Majesty's Government would subscribe to terms which they could not justify to the country . . . Unfortunately it appeared that in many essential points the opinion of Count Waleswki differed from that of Her Majesty's advisers. The first thing therefore to be done was to settle these differences of opinion between two Governments for how could they run the risk of recommending negotiations with such a wide divergence in their views?[6]

That same day Napoleon wrote a sympathetic letter to Queen Victoria asking, in the gentlest possible fashion, why Britain continued to place obstacles in the way of the Austrian initiative. Having taken advice from Palmerston and Clarendon the queen sent a non-committal reply reinforcing her government's view that they would not be bound to the Austrian ultimatum. She also expressed the opinion that the Austrians should not permit any counter-proposals,

an argument which had already been reinforced by Cowley during
a later meeting with Waleswki in the evening of 21 November:

> I should add that during my conversation with Count Waleswki
> I impressed upon him very strongly the necessity of requiring
> a positive declaration from Austria in case it was agreed that
> her ultimatum should be sent to St Petersburg, not to receive
> any counter propositions from the Russian Government nor to
> commit to any modification whatever of the terms to which
> France and England had given their adherence.[7]

Part of the problem lay in Britain's attitude to the Austrian government. As Cowley told Napoleon, there was considerable irritation in
London that the Austrians were using the ultimatum to gain favourable
terms at any forthcoming peace conference and this they would
achieve without firing a shot in anger: 'Austria wanted to obtain
a peace which suited her through the prowess and sacrifices of the
Western Powers.' This was especially true of Austrian demands for the
Danubian territory in Bessarabia, hence Palmerston's and Clarendon's
insistence on the inclusion of Britain's own particular conditions.
While Napoleon was sympathetic to Cowley's argument he feared,
too, that Austria might refuse to break off relations with Russia if
Britain continued to insist on imposing conditions. For that reason
he was not unhappy when, quite untruthfully, Walewski informed
Buol on 26 November that there was agreement with Britain over
the ultimatum and that preparations should be made for informing
St Petersburg.

The revelation of the French initiative infuriated Palmerston who
believed that, in an underhand way, Britain was falling victim to a
plot hatched between Paris and Vienna which would lead only to
humiliation. From the evidence of the diplomatic despatches between
London and Vienna there is ample reason for the suspicion as relations
between the two countries were anything but easy. The creation of a
workable peace plan might have been the primary concern of both
governments during the winter, but a number of niggling incidents
had combined to irritate the British cabinet and to lead them into
thinking that Austria was not entirely sincere. Amongst these aggra-
vations were the cases of Colonel Türr, an Austrian officer serving
with British forces, who was being court-martialled for desertion, and
the wrongful arrest of the British vice-consul in the port of Fiume. (He

was accused of stealing the property of Samuel Haire, an eighty-five year old Englishman who had died shortly after marrying his young chambermaid.)

Trifling in themselves, these cases were not the best accompaniment to negotiations which were becoming increasingly tortuous. Britain had also insisted that it did not want to make any further decisions until its new ambassador had arrived in Vienna and was able to deal directly with Buol. As chance would have it the choice fell on Sir George Hamilton Seymour who had been involved in the crisis since the very outset. It was a sensible selection but a heavy cold had delayed his departure from London and when he arrived in Vienna on 6 December he was still far from well.

In the nature of the intensely febrile allied relationship it proved impossible for either France or Britain to gain a diplomatic upper hand and by the time that Seymour set foot in the Austrian capital a compromise had been agreed. Britain dropped the demand for the Sea of Azov to be neutralised as a condition, while Waleswki agreed to the inclusion in the Fifth Point of Britain's demands for the Aaland Islands. It was the usual diplomatic expedient, a form of words which seemed to settle the disagreement between the two main allies, and each side assumed that they had won important concessions. The French believed that the Austrian ultimatum would usher in peace talks while the British continued to hope that the Russians would never accept such severe conditions, and that the war would continue. One final piece of duplicity marked the agreement: when the papers were sent to Vienna, Walewski omitted the British special conditions and informed Buol that there was complete allied agreement on the matter. That dissimulation was to be the cause of further bad feeling which almost scuppered the process in the new year. However, for all its drawbacks, the final text was despatched to Vienna on 16 December and that same day it was sent on to St Petersburg. The Austrian ambassador, Count Valentin Esterházy, was instructed to give the Russians eight days following its arrival to accept the terms unconditionally.

While the French and the British had been bickering and labouring to protect their best interests, the tsar was equally ambivalent about entering into peace talks. Although he was aware that the war was crippling Russia his armed forces had not been defeated decisively and he believed that he could negotiate from a position of considerable strength. Through Nesselrode and Alexander Gorchakov he knew

that the French entertained a strong desire for peace and to Tsar
Alexander this smacked of weakness. From his father he had inherited
a dismissive attitude towards Napoleon and he believed that a new
revolution could unseat a ruler whom he believed to be an impostor.
If the war continued to be unpopular, and if the failed harvest in
France brought fresh economic problems, discontent could easily lead
to revolution. 'This I regard as the most probable conclusion to the
present war,' he had told Alexander Gorchakov in October. 'Neither
from Napoleon nor from England do I expect a sincere desire for peace
on terms compatible with our views and as long as I live, I will accept
no others.'[8]

His resolve had also been stiffened by visiting his army in the
Crimea and inspecting freshly raised regiments in Moscow. Plans
had been laid for a new campaign in the spring and he was in
a belligerent mood which he took care to pass on to the army's
high command. By way of encouragement Michael Gorchakov had
received the icon of St Sergei which had been with Peter the Great
at the decisive Battle of Poltava in 1709 when the forces of Peter the
Great scattered the army of Charles XII of Sweden; more practically,
a plan had been drawn up to defend the Crimea against further enemy
incursions. The mood of 1812 was upon the tsar and, on his return
to the capital in November, Alexander cared little to hear talk of
peace. In Vienna Gorchakov was ordered to curb any enthusiasm for
further negotiations both in his unofficial discussions with the Duc de
Morny and in his direct contact with Buol and Bourqueney. At the
end of that month the tsar's resolve to continue the war seemed to be
justified when news arrived of Muraviev's triumph at Kars. Not only
was this the first military victory of Alexander's reign but it gave the
Russians a valuable bargaining piece which could be used to counter
the expected allied territorial demands.

The arrival of Esterházy in St Petersburg on 28 December punc-
tured that buoyant atmosphere. With the ultimatum the Austrian
ambassador gave the Russians until 18 January to agree to the Five
Points, otherwise a state of war would exist between the two countries.
On 1 January 1856 the tsar summoned a council of his most trusted
advisers to discuss the Austrian demands. All present were in favour
of peace but not at any price. First to speak was Count Paul Kiselev,
minister of the interior, who pointed out in moving terms that Russia
was being bled dry by the war and that further allied victories could
lead to an even more humiliating peace. If that were to happen Russia's

territorial integrity would be threatened and its frontiers weakened by the possible loss of Poland, Caucasus and Finland.

The theme was taken up by the others present – only Count D. N. Bludov, the president of the Imperial Council, wanted to fight to the bitter end. But despite the general feeling that the war had been lost no one was willing to accept the controversial Fifth Point which Nesselrode claimed would have 'threatening implications' for the future. And that line was eventually adopted. On 5 January the Russian reply was returned to Vienna accepting, with some modifications, the Four Points, but rejecting out of hand the Fifth Point. Faced by Russia's refusal to agree unconditionally to the ultimatum Austria had no option but to announce that Alexander Gorchakov would be presented with his passports and that diplomatic relations between the two countries would be severed on 18 January. As Nesselrode had feared throughout the war, Russia would then find herself fighting a country once regarded as its closest ally.

But there was more to Esterházy's mission than the simple delivery of the ultimatum: there was also the hidden French agenda. In presenting the allied response to the Austrian ultimatum in December Walewski had omitted Britain's special conditions and this allowed the Austrian ambassador to tell the Russians that the Fifth Point did not form part of any treaty between Austria and the allies. In other words, it need not present a serious obstacle once peace talks got under way. As this message had also been included in the secret negotiations with de Morny the Russians had no reason to disbelieve Esterházy's assurances. Indeed so confident was Gorchakov of France's primacy that he counselled the tsar to reject the ultimatum and to deal directly with Napoleon. That advice was rejected as being impractical – von Seebach, the envoy in Paris of the King of Saxony, had already approached Napoleon unsuccessfully during the second week of December proposing a separate peace treaty – but now the Russians were ready to cave in. On 15 January the tsar met once more with his advisers in the Winter Palace and in an emotionally charged atmosphere, agreed to accept the ultimatum, the general feeling being summed up by Bludov's tearful words, 'If we no longer have the means to make war, then let us make peace!'

For the Russians there was no other way forward. No one in the council wanted to continue the fighting, and although the Grand Duke Constantine argued that 'Russia was not conquered, she still had a numerous army gloriously tried; she had her recollections, her patriotism, her perseverance, the difficulties which her immense territory and her severe climate opposed to invasion'. Russia had simply run out of options. Not only was the country so exhausted that further fighting would only risk further humiliations, but Russia was also totally isolated. That same day had come from King Friedrich-Wilhelm a telegraph announcing that Prussia supported the Austrian proposals and that, if Russia rejected them, there would almost certainly be a break in diplomatic relations between the two countries. There was also a danger of civil unrest in Russia itself: if Alexander hoped that revolution might unseat Napoleon he was well aware that the same danger threatened his own hold on the throne.

The news of the Russian acceptance reached Paris on the evening of 19 January and the following day Napoleon announced it to the members of the specially convened allied Council of War. By then the conference had turned into little more than a debating chamber and the plans for further military activity in the spring were being laid with little expectation that they would be carried out. On the surface Napoleon's glittering array of commanders and statesmen was intent on prosecuting the war to a victorious conclusion but in truth the French knew that peace was imminent. In a gloomy despatch to Clarendon, Cowley said that the prevailing sentiment in France was 'far more Russian than English' and that Britain was perceived as being implacably opposed to a negotiated peace. When he mentioned this finding to Napoleon while they were out shooting, the emperor simply replied that he could not disagree, 'that unfortunately the opinion that Her Majesty's Government were determined on continuing the war prevailed throughout Europe'.

In contrast there was jubilation in Paris that the war would soon be over. The feeling was fuelled by the publication of another anonymous pamphlet which argued that France should take the lead in imposing a new order on Europe and that it should take the opportunity to forge new and stronger links with Russia. Entitled *Nécessité d'un Congrès pour pacifier l'Europe, par un homme d'état* (The Need for a Congress to bring peace to Europe, by A Statesman) it was thought to be the work of the emperor (a piece of gossip which Cowley refused to believe) and it enjoyed a wide currency, especially as it argued that France would be better served by working independently of its bellicose neighbour on the other side of the Channel. In a belated attempt to scotch the canard that Britain wanted to continue the war 'to retrieve the character of her Army after the failure of the two attacks on the Redan', Cowley

gave a dinner on 26 January for French officers raised by the Queen
to be Knights of the Bath and offered them a heartfelt final toast:

> Before we separate, allow me to propose one toast more. To
> the re-establishment of peace! I am not afraid to mention such
> a toast in the presence of so many soldiers, for they, who know
> what are the horrors of war, can appreciate, better than others,
> the blessings of peace. God grant that the negotiations which are
> about to open, may end in an honourable and lasting peace.[9]

The British ambassador undoubtedly meant well but, alas for the
alliance, his initiative rebounded on him. When the *Moniteur* reported
the occasion the following day, it translated Cowley's words as: 'To
the conclusion of peace and the legitimate hope which the new
negotiations give to the Allies, and particularly to the English nation,
of an early termination of the evils of war.' In vain did Cowley protest
to the editor, M. Fould: the version had been provided by Prince
Napoleon's secretary and any further correction would only make the
situation worse. As was the case with the particular conditions, Britain
had been outwitted by the French and in London at least there was
little expectation that a workable peace was in the offing. 'England
must consult her own interest and her own dignity,' Clarendon told
Seymour. 'We must not recede from any engagement we have entered
into and only hold the same language we have held throughout.'[10]

2

Tying Up Some Loose Ends

I don't like Austria. I detest her policy but I don't wish to quarrel with her.

Emperor Napoleon III in conversation with the Earl of Clarendon, 18 March 1856

A foundation for peace talks had been agreed but there was still no certainty that the war would come to an end or even that the negotiations would continue. This was especially true in London where Palmerston remained insistent that Britain's special conditions, encapsulated by the Fifth Point, had to be agreed by Russia before there could be any armistice. If that were not permitted, Cowley explained to the emperor, everything that had happened during the past two years would be in vain and Russia would have escaped scot-free. As he reported:

> I dwelt particularly upon the position in which the allies would be placed if, in following a contrary course, they found Russia willing to make peace on the basis of the Austrian Ultimatum and themselves obliged either to accept that peace, or to break off negotiations because Russia refused to entertain these particular conditions.[1]

That position had already been passed on to the Austrians by Seymour who showed to Buol Clarendon's despatch of 8 January insisting that Britain's demand be made clear to the Russians before there was any further negotiation. Four days later, before the Russians had even agreed to accept the ultimatum, the Austrian foreign minister replied that such a move was out of the question. Britain had accepted the Five Points and, as he interpreted the situation, the special conditions could only be discussed during the negotiations for a peace treaty:

> He [Buol] felt strongly the necessity of conforming strictly to engagements, of making acts conformable to words, the more so as Austria, from not taking part in the war in which the Western Allies are engaged, was the more bound not to recede from the position which she had taken up in their support.[2]

There was to be no let-up in the unhappy relationship between the two countries. For Buol, who had laboured under the impression that Britain had accepted his plan, the production of new obstacles was most unwelcome and he felt that Clarendon was not being entirely candid. All along he had been made to believe that the British would not specify their conditions and to reinforce that belief he had visited Seymour before Esterházy's mission to St Petersburg to inquire if Britain still adhered to the agreement signed on 14 November. Of course, agreed Seymour. Later he told Clarendon on 16 January exactly what had transpired during the meeting: 'I replied that I had no instruction upon the point but that I had no hesitation in expressing my firm belief that such was the case; that Her Majesty's Government had agreed to the Ultimatum and that I inferred therefore that the Paper which had led to it was included in the sanction.'[3]

As bad luck would have it, the Austrian ambassador in London, Count Colleredo, had put the same question to Clarendon but had received a somewhat different response. While the agreement stood, replied the British foreign secretary, he could not agree to further negotiations with Russia unless they had been apprised of Britain's conditions. Clarendon and Seymour were now working at cross purposes and the blunders were to place additional strains on the relationship with Vienna.

When the extent of his mistake became known – Clarendon sent Seymour an angry despatch on 8 January reminding him of Britain's position – the British ambassador was distraught, telling Clarendon that he was appalled to have caused 'the evil misfortune of incurring some portion of Your Lordship's displeasure.' His first thought was to tell Buol that a grave blunder had been made but that would have endangered the delivery of the ultimatum and put Britain in bad odour, not just with the Austrians but also with the French. Realising the impracticality of such a course he accepted the blame and vowed to make good Britain's position as best he could. 'It is only then right,' he told Clarendon, 'that I should admit that if the Austrian Government has exceeded its powers in making the propositions upon which the Russian Government is now deliberating, the error is to be attributed to me and *not* to Count Buol.'[4] His second thought was to offer his resignation, a suggestion which Clarendon brusquely brushed aside.

To retrieve the lost ground Clarendon told Seymour he should now insist that the Austrians accept the terms of the despatch of 8 January, namely that the special conditions should be made known to the Russians. Unless that happened, he warned, 'England and France, who have borne all the brunt of the war, are required to content themselves not with their own terms but with those of a power which has not spent a shilling or split a drop of blood in the contest which more nearly concerns her than it does any other.'[5] Because Buol already knew from Colleredo that the revelation of the British special conditions was a sticking point in London, his response was more measured than Seymour could have hoped. He simply expressed his regret and made the observation that Britain was under a moral obligation to back Austria's ultimatum. Any other move would simply play into Russia's hands.

Seymour could see he was in a precarious position. To some extent he was the author of the impasse but he was slowly coming to the conclusion that Britain was making unsustainable demands. He was also beginning to feel some sympathy for Austria, as in his opinion there could be no solution to the Eastern Question without that country's political involvement. This was certainly in keeping with his own view of conducting diplomacy: just as he had come under Nicholas I's spell while he was stationed in St Petersburg, so too did he find himself espousing the Austrian cause from Vienna. Following a further meeting with Buol on 22 January he made his feelings known to Clarendon:

> I feel only that Austria had some grounds for understanding that
> we are pledged to act as she calls upon us to do, and that her
> assistance is requisite for ultimately carrying out the objects upon
> which Her Majesty's Government are so deeply intent.[6]

For his pains he was told that he had 'adopted too much the opinions of Buol' and was in danger of forgetting his country's interests. However, in the middle of the predicament the unexpected news arrived from St Petersburg announcing Russia's acceptance of the ultimatum as a basis for peace talks. As far as Seymour was concerned that changed everything. In a long and excited despatch written on the night of 22 January he described the scenes in Vienna, using his not inconsiderable powers of observation to paint a picture of universal jubilation and relief. It was certainly as fulsome as anything he had written from St Petersburg in the anxious days before the rupture with Russia:

By the Austrian Cabinet it [the Russian acceptance] has been hailed as an ample compensation for short but very intense anxiety; those persons who had been the least backward in condemning Count Buol's rash policy (for so it was deemed) being as full of exultation as the rest at a result, which in the universal opinion, liberates Austria from all further demands upon her exertions.

The feeling is not less universal among the public and was unequivocally expressed upon the Emperor's first appearance at the Theatre after the news had arrived of the timely acceptance by Russia. His Imperial Majesty was received upon that occasion with an enthusiasm which could hardly have been exceeded had he been returning from a glorious campaign.[7]

Grasping the moment Buol told Seymour that he and his colleagues had been scrupulous in their dealings with the allies and with Russia. The time for further negotiation had passed and, that being so, the preliminaries to peace should be signed by all parties to the agreement. As for Britain's special conditions, his attitude remained unchanged: these would be discussed at the conference, not before; although, by way of concession, he promised Austria's support for Britain's demands over the Aaland Islands. As ever, Buol's main concern was that the revelation of Britain's special conditions might encourage Russia to refuse to sign the preliminaries to the forthcoming treaty.

That was not what Clarendon wanted to hear but he could see that there was no point in taking the matter any further with Buol. Although he was much vexed by Buol's attitude – but not as irate as Palmerston who regarded Austria's firmness as a personal insult – the British foreign secretary understood that there was little to be gained, and much to lose, by continuing to badger him. Instead he turned the focus of his attention to Paris and for the next fortnight it was the French who came under the most severe pressure from the Foreign Office. Because Palmerston and Clarendon had good reason to distrust Waleswki they worked assiduously on the emperor whom they regarded as their last remaining ally.

For a while Napoleon wavered, torn between his desire for peace and his reliance on the allied relationship. As a friend of Britain and an avowed admirer of Queen Victoria, it was difficult for Napoleon to resist Clarendon's increasingly strident blustering that England could not consent to be told what to do by a foreign power or to permit the exclusion from the negotiations conditions upon which they had insisted. He also had some fellow feeling for Clarendon's argument that national honour and the need to complete the original war aims meant there could be no peace without Russia agreeing to the special conditions. France would have to give way and support Britain, argued Palmerston, otherwise they would both be 'dragged down' by the Austrians and all the suffering in the Crimea and the Baltic would have been in vain.

In the tense days that followed it fell to Cowley to play the role of *un intime*, spending as much time as he could, or as protocol allowed, in the company of the emperor. From his despatches to London it is clear that there was little that the two men did not discuss openly, as if they were close friends and not the head of one state and the diplomatic representative of another. One meeting will stand for many during that curious interlude: with the demands for peace growing ever more vociferous in Paris, Cowley let slip to the emperor his strength of feeling both about the alliance and their personal friendship. 'What I wished to convey to His Majesty was this,' he informed Clarendon. 'That with the exception of himself I could not name a Frenchman who was a cordial supporter of the English alliance. I did not exempt from this sweeping statement even His Majesty's ministers.'

If that was an indelicate matter for an ambassador to raise with a sovereign ruler, then the emperor's response was equally blunt. Yes, he said, all that he knew, but perhaps Lord Cowley had not read Drouyn de Lhuys's interpretation of the alliance which he had drawn up while foreign minister in October 1853. At that he showed Cowley a letter which summed up for the emperor the stance he should take when dealing with London: 'Make use of England as long as it suits you, form your continental alliances without reference to her and shake her off whenever she stands in your way.'[8]

The emperor's candidness touched Cowley. Like many other Englishmen of that period (and indeed later) he was inclined to be sentimental about France and things French. He liked the country and its people – not its noisy middle classes or the 'liars and rogues' who made up the government but certainly the aristocracy and, at a suitable distance, the peasantry – and he was especially fond of Napoleon with whom he liked to think that he enjoyed a true rapport. He had no reason to think otherwise. Always an anglophile, the emperor warmed to men like Cowley and Clarendon and, as something of a parvenu, he enjoyed the fact that he had been accepted at the highest levels of English society. In an attempt to milk that relationship, and in so doing to break the deadlock, Napoleon had written an impassioned letter to Queen Victoria on 13 January telling her that his country's exchequer was exhausted and that his people simply wanted an end to the war.

Palmerston's response was to try to put more backbone into the French administration but it was too late in the day to insist that France should march in step with her British allies. Cowley was realist enough to see that the emperor was in an impossible position, telling London on 25 January that 'public opinion will not allow the conclusion of peace to depend upon these particular conditions'. He was also not to know that, the emperor's sentimental attachment to Britain notwithstanding, Napoleon had encouraged his government to look to the future and to the possibility of a closer relationship with Russia. Something had to give and, typically perhaps, it was left to Waleswki to cobble up a tortuous compromise. Through von Seebach he informed the Russians unofficially about the special conditions concerning the Aaland Islands and the Black Sea territories; at the same time he assured Britain, again unofficially, that France would support the claims at the forthcoming negotiations. Not only did Russia agree to the proposal – all along it had known about the British conditions – but the matter was settled once and for all when the tsar's advisers conceded that their acceptance of the ultimatum would provide the basis for the forthcoming peace negotiations.

In an atmosphere tinged by relief and anticlimax a protocol was signed in Vienna on 1 February agreeing to appoint plenipotentiaries to convene within three weeks to sign peace preliminaries, produce an armistice agreement and begin final negotiations. It was not the only event of note to take place that day. From Russia came the news that Paskevich had died. Throughout the war the Russian marshal had argued that Austria was the real danger and that troops should be reserved in the west to meet that threat. There had never been any possibility that the Austrian army would intervene and it is one of the war's many ironies that the old soldier should die on the very day that Buol's peace deal had been finally accepted by the belligerent powers.

As to where the conference should take place, each side had already put forward different proposals. Still riding on his success Buol nominated Vienna but this was unacceptable to Britain and Russia; Napoleon suggested Brussels as a compromise but this was vetoed by Clarendon as 'too Russian a city' – he remembered the Duc de Morny's machinations in the Belgian capital at the beginning of the war – and the deadlock was broken by the Russians who proposed Paris. With the tsar's desire to forge closer links with France there was an ulterior motive to the Russian preference but Britain lent ready support. The choice carried several risks as Waleswki would chair the proceedings with the ambitious Vincente Benedetti as his secretary, but Cowley's primacy at court suggested to Clarendon that Britain would enjoy 'the power of immediate appeal to the emperor'.[9]

There were still several loose ends to be tied up, the most important of which was the participation of Sardinia and Prussia. Both countries felt they had strong claims to be represented at Paris and both used the period between the acceptance of the ultimatum and the signing of the Vienna protocol to lobby the belligerent powers. Of the two, Sardinia had the stronger claim because its army had fought alongside the allies and Cavour had pressed these demands during King Victor Emmanuel II's state visits to London and Paris earlier in the month. During his discussions with Palmerston Cavour had been gratified to learn that Britain supported Sardinia's full participation at the conference but, as he had not yet agreed to peace, that would depend on further Sardinian participation in the war. Later, Palmerston kept his support to an agreement which limited Sardinian participation to points which only concerned its interests.

This was acceptable to France as Walewski was nervous about any Sardinian participation. His main fear was that Cavour would carry out a threat made on 6 January to raise the question of Austria's predominant influence in Italy and the Danube region. As the French foreign minister told Cowley, it was not a fitting moment to talk either about Italy or the future of the principalities. This could be left to the peace conference:

> The object of the Sardinian government [Count Walewski said] was to shew that the arrangement contemplated by the Ultimatum was in favour of Austria only; that, in fact, a peace, such as was thus shadowed [*sic*] out, would leave Austria the strongest Power in Europe; that she would be mistress in the Principalities with increased territory, and would dominate completely Italy. In short, that, unless something was done to relieve this latter country from her sway, the Balance of Power, to defend which the Allies had taken up arms, would be as much compromised as ever.[10]

There was logic to Cavour's argument but *realpolitik* had to take precedence. Within two years France would combine with Sardinia to oppose Austria but, at that stage, Walewski did not want to manufacture a fresh quarrel with Vienna. Buol had already announced that he did not wish to see the Sardinians in Paris as they were not a great power, but he was forced to bow to the wishes of the British and French governments, both of which entertained a sentimental attachment to the concept of Italian nationalism. For the Sardinians then, it was both a setback and a triumph. Cavour had not yet gained a name for himself in European diplomacy but he had been shrewd enough to understand that Sardinia's support for the allies in the Crimea had given him and his country added stature and that his presence in Paris would cement that authority.

The Prussians, though, presented a different difficulty. King Friedrich-Wilhelm's intervention had been instrumental in encouraging the tsar to bow to the Austrian ultimatum, and his foreign minister, Otto von Manteuffel, had lost few opportunities to remind the allies of that fact. Indeed, in conversation with Seymour as early as 8 January he made no secret that the reward for that support should be a seat at the conference table. Seymour wrote:

> [Manteuffel] has been able to convince himself, and he has pointed out to His Royal Master, that the price to be paid for his re-admission into the European councils is a warm recommendation to the Emperor of Russia to accept the proposition made to him from Vienna, followed by a withdrawal of the

Prussian mission from St Petersburg, should the advice not be attended to.[11]

Mindful of Prussia's support and of its growing importance in Germanic affairs, Buol supported the demand, as did Orlov once the protocols had been signed, but such a course was anathema to Britain and France. On 22 January Napoleon told Cowley that he was 'not at all disposed to comply with the wishes of the Prussian government' but he wondered if it would be possible to exclude them completely from 'any arrangements touching the general equilibrium of Europe'. To this Clarendon reluctantly agreed. He believed that by refusing to commit itself during the war Prussia had forfeited the right to participate in any further discussion of the Eastern Question but he agreed with the emperor that 'this need not prevent her adhering hereafter to the Treaty which, it might be hoped, would be the result of the pending negotiations'. Despite Buol's protests the Prussians were not permitted to send plenipotentiaries to Paris until the later stages of the conference when the revision of the Straits Convention of 1841 was discussed.[12]

The Russian acceptance of the ultimatum had been a turning-point but the war was still far from over and it would take several anxious weeks before an armistice could be signed. Although the allied armies had been prepared for the advent of peace talks ever since Sevastopol had fallen, the lack of hard news and the prevalence of rumours had made the winter months something of a limbo. In the British camp there was no shortage of warlike talk, fuelled by suggestions that the arrival of spring would see the greater part of the army removed to Asia Minor for operations against the Russians in the Caucasus. Codrington, too, had remained bullish, telling Panmure that he hoped to solve the transport problems so that his force would be ready to meet any eventuality either in the Crimea or elsewhere. Only the French seemed to be demob-happy, anxious to return home and far away from the disease and illness which were decimating their army.

The first rumours of the breakthrough arrived at the end of January. 'All say we are to have peace,' Henry Clifford wrote warily to his parents. 'I don't believe it yet, but I believe I am the only one out here who does not believe in it.' His pessimism seemed to be confirmed when, on the following day, 29 January, the Russians opened up a huge barrage from their artillery positions to the north but it was a last flourish. With slow inevitability both sides began winding down their operations and on 28 February the telegraph brought news from Paris that, at last, an armistice had been signed. Tensions evaporated and the following day senior officers from all sides met at the Traktir Bridge to agree terms for a ceasefire. It was all something of an anticlimax, made more unreal by Codrington's last-minute order, four days earlier, to introduce press censorship in the British camp. As the *Illustrated London News* noted, 'His order elicited much ridicule in consequence of its not being issued until all active operations were concluded.' That being said, Codrington set a precedent for other commanders to use in their dealings with correspondents in the wars of the future. Never again would a writer be allowed the freedom of movement and comment enjoyed by William Howard Russell.

While the politicians and diplomats started talking in Paris the soldiers in the Crimea found themselves idle and unoccupied and it was not until news arrived of the signing of the peace treaty on 2 April 1856 that they could finally relax. Ceremonial parades were held by the Russians and the allies and senior officers on both sides vied with their former enemies to provide the most lavish entertainment, Codrington telling Panmure that he had sat down to a lavish banquet given by the new Russian commander-in-chief, General Lüders, which included caviar, roast beef and two huge sturgeon. (By then Michael Gorchakov had left the Crimea in January to replace Paskevich.)

The men were also allowed to fraternise and the Russian soldiers were pleased to be able to purchase much-needed luxuries at the British shops at Balaklava. Much to their surprise, they found that they got on well together, the Russians marvelling at the supplies available to their former foes and the British and French expressing respect for the colourful Cossack troopers and imposing Imperial Guardsmen. However, the relaxed atmosphere soon caused local difficulties. La Marmora complained to Codrington that British missionaries were attempting to convert his men to Protestantism and in the British camp there was a rash of fighting, fuelled by drink, with several men being executed for murder. Relations between the British and French had also deteriorated, mainly due to an outbreak of triumphalism by the latter. In his last letter home Clifford, who generally liked the French, found that the wartime alliance was becoming increasingly shaky and that for many of his men, it was a case of business as usual:

I am glad we are not likely to be much longer with the French, for they do not see our improvements in soldiering with pleasure and cannot hide their bitter feelings towards us. With them there is a sort of over-bearing manner which our Officers will not stand, and on our part we are jealous of their good fortune in the Siege and are anxious to have a second try at it and see what we can do now we are more experienced. I heard lots of our fellows say yesterday, 'How I wish those b . . . y French would just come out with their sixty thousand men and fight us' and all that sort of thing.[13]

Their wish was not to be granted. Although the alliance between the two countries would never be an easy one, marked as it was by suspicion and antipathy, the Crimea was the first of three great European wars in which British and French soldiers would fight alongside each other.

By the end of April the allies started leaving the Crimea, at Codrington's suggestion the Sardinians going first, both to save them further expense (and exposure to the missionaries) and because they had been 'so true and so quiet in their assistance'. They were followed by the French, now sorely depleted, some regiments returning to France, others to Algiers. Then it was the turn of the British and each returning regiment was greeted with great scenes of enthusiasm as they marched through their garrison or depot towns after coming ashore at the Channel ports. All were met by Queen Victoria who felt that in some small measure she should thank them personally for their loyal services. And to remind herself of those sacrifices she commissioned from the artist Joseph Noël Paton a copy of his painting *Home* which had been shown at the Royal Academy the year before. It showed the figure of a bearded Scottish soldier, his head bandaged and his sleeve empty, returning home to his weeping wife. At his knees his young wife embraces him; the whole scene is sentimental yet realistic for it embraces not just the glory of war – he wears a Crimean Medal – but also its sacrifice.

But not all the men would go back to Britain. Some units went to India and five line infantry regiments were sent to Canada to reinforce the North American garrison as a timely reminder to the politicians in Washington. The mercenaries in the British Foreign Legion were also dispersed. Most returned from whence they had come but the men of the British German Legion were offered free transport to sail to South Africa 'as military settlers in the Cape of Good Hope and British Kaffraria' to support the local security services 'to resist the attacks of the enemy or to aid the civil power'. The majority took up the offer and many of them eventually settled in the neighbouring Orange Free State.[14]

It took until July to get all the troops out of the Crimea. Pélissier and his staff pulled out on 5 July and Codrington and his staff followed a week later on board HMS *Algiers*. In time-honoured fashion the Union flag was lowered, reveille was sounded and, not for the last time in the country's history, British troops were leaving a foreign shore, uncertain whether all their courage and sacrifices had been worth the effort.

3

Peacetime in Paris

France was determined on peace; and whatever Palmerston in
his jaunty mood may say, we could not have made war alone,
for we would have had all of Europe against us at once, and
the United States would soon have followed in their train.
The Earl of Clarendon to Lord Granville, 12 March 1856

In the lull before the conference, or Congress as the French
chose to call the proceedings in Paris, each country selected its
plenipotentiaries. Britain would be represented by Clarendon and
Cowley, France by Walewski and Bourqueny, Russia by Orlov
and Brunnov, Austria by Buol and Hübner, Turkey by Aali Pasha
and Mehemed Djemil Bey, and Sardinia by Count Cavour and
the Marquis de Villamarina. Each team had its own strengths and
weaknesses and, as had been the case in Vienna the previous year,
each would find itself having to listen to differing instructions from
their governments at home. Clarendon and Cowley were united by
distrust of any French politician other than the emperor and by a
determination to stand firm against Russia. Orlov was anxious to
protect Russia from humiliating terms and thought to do that by
attempting to drive a wedge between Britain and France. As for
Buol, although he received a standing ovation on his arrival in Paris,
his role became less significant as the conference proceeded.

The leading personality by far was Clarendon. He might not have
been a Castlereagh but he was certainly his own man. Not only did he
enjoy the confidence of the French emperor but he was respected by
Orlov whom he had first met while a young diplomat in St Petersburg.

An aristocrat who was on personal terms with many of Europe's Royal houses, Clarendon possessed a charm of manner and a finesse which put the other negotiators at ease and which placed him and Cowley in a superior position throughout the negotiations. However, beneath the social allure there lurked a steely determination to get Britain's way, whatever the cost, and to brush aside the wishes of others. Sincere in his dealings he might have been, but this did not mean that he was prepared to surrender ground: ten days into the conference he was able to tell Palmerston that 'he had never on any occasion or on any point yielded anything'.[1]

In this respect he was given able support by the British prime minister. Palmerston involved himself in all of the proceedings and proved to be as much an architect of the treaty as any of the representatives in Paris. In fact, so closely did Palmerston follow the proceedings that he sent daily despatches, frequently reinforced by telegrams, giving precise instructions to the British plenipotentiaries. Many were violently anti-Russian in tone and this proclivity helped to reinforce Orlov's belief that Palmerston had not changed since the days of Don Pacifico when British interests were best served by the despatch of a gunboat.

Here the Russian minister was mistaken. Because Palmerston could often be all bluster while Clarendon retained a polish which fascinated his colleagues it would be convenient to characterise the British prime minister as an avenging angel. In fact both men were united in their determination to protect British interests and from their correspondence a vivid picture emerges of the events in Paris. The letters also reveal much about their authors: Palmerston showed a grasp of the diplomatic technicalities which belies his reputation as a bully, while Clarendon demonstrated that he could be as much of a scold as the next man. For example, as the congress proceeded he was soon to change his tune about Napoleon. As the French emperor wavered in his support for his ally and allowed himself to be swayed by the Russians, Clarendon began to lose all his respect for him. At the time he kept his feelings to himself but later he admitted to Stratford that he found Napoleon to be 'ignorant and indolent', a man 'so weak that he might just as well be dishonest'.[2]

Clarendon arrived in Paris on 16 February and immediately plunged himself into a series of courtesy meetings with the emperor, Walewski and Brunnov. These were supposed to prepare the ground for the preliminary meetings which began on 21 February but Clarendon lost little time in reminding his colleagues that Britain would not agree to peace unless all their conditions were met and that, if they were not, preparations were already in hand 'to prosecute the war with vigour'. The following day saw the arrival of Orlov. The Russian delegation's instructions were quite simple: to save their country from mortification and through Walewski to work on the emperor. As for the British conditions, Orlov had been ordered by Nesselrode to concede the proposal for the Aaland islands, provided that they were the subject of a separate treaty, and to oppose whatever he could of their other demands. Although in his seventies, Orlov proved to be a tough and durable negotiator – he had once saved Nicholas I by felling a would-be assassin with his fist – and Clarendon was right to accord him respect. When the two men met for the first time on 25 February Clarendon reported that they 'met as old friends', the atmosphere being cordial enough for the Russian minister to reveal his astonishment that the allies had not taken Sevastopol after the Battle of the Alma:

> Throughout the conversation which lasted upward of an hour the tone of Count Orloff [sic] was moderate and becoming – he expressed no fear and made no boast – he said his object was to put an end to the war and he should regret sincerely if his mission were to fail as he was prepared to make such concessions as were not inconsistent with the dignity of Russia, but the impression left upon my mind was that Count Orloff will be unbending with respect to various points upon which it will be the duty of Lord Cowley and myself to insist and that the successful issue of the negotiations will mainly depend upon the amount of support we shall receive from our colleagues.[3]

It was a shrewd summary of the events which were to follow. Russia did prove to be obdurate on some points, namely the secession of the Bessarabian territory, and France was less forceful in Britain's support than Clarendon might have wished. The scene had already been set in the meeting with Brunnov on 18 February when the Russian ambassador argued that Russia should receive something in return for Kars, to which Clarendon responded that it was not negotiable as the whole point of the war had been the necessity of preserving the integrity of the Ottoman Empire. These territorial squabbles were destined to shape the first session of the congress which opened officially on 25 February 1856 at one o'clock in the afternoon in the impressive surroundings of the Quai d'Orsay. It settled the terms of the armistice which would last until 31 March and Clarendon noted with prim approval that Walewski had passed muster as a chairman. At the same time he told Palmerston that Brunnov 'means to be very troublesome' and in that respect his early suspicions about the Russians were not far off the mark.

At the second session the following day Orlov set out Russia's stall by agreeing, in a separate treaty, to leave Bomarsund unfortified on condition that the Bessarabian territorial demands be dropped in exchange for Kars. This was the first crisis of the congress and it was only settled by British firmness and a belated decision to compromise over the exact boundaries of the Bessarabian territory – as Napoleon told Clarendon on 28 February, the terms of Point One of the Austrian ultimatum were 'not a matter to justify the renewal of the war'. Clarendon had become uncomfortably aware of the strength of French opposition to the war and during his private audiences with the emperor he soon found himself sympathising with the general mood. At home in London Palmerston might preach resolution but in Paris Clarendon was beginning to see that, on the matter of Bessarabia, the allies might have to give ground:

> The state of things which I predicted to Your Lordship [Palmerston] has arrived. If we continue to demand that which Russia is now certain to refuse we shall stand alone in the Conference, and the Emperor's manners last night left me in no doubt that there were in his mind mingled feelings of surprise, regret and vexation, at what he thinks is our exigency, but which he will soon consider to be our obstinacy.[4]

Obviously something had to give and it was Kars which produced the solution. While Clarendon insisted that it should not be a bargaining counter, Orlov felt differently and he used its capture by Muraviev to good advantage. The deal was never specifically stated in any congress document but before the decisive seventh session on 10 March it had been agreed that Russia would return Kars without compensation and that in return there would be a reduction of the territorial demands in Bessarabia. The mouth of the Danube would be ceded but two-thirds of the land specified in the Austrian ultimatum were allowed to remain in Russian hands. On balance, this was a victory for the allies as the question of Kars had been settled in their favour and despite yielding territory to the Russians, the strategically important mouth of the Danube had been retained. Clarendon was well pleased with the outcome, writing that evening that Orlov had been 'straightforward and gentlemanlike' while Brunnov had acted 'like a low attorney' whom Orlov treated 'like his footman'.

The second territorial question involved the unification of Wallachia and Moldavia into the single state of Romania. This was a project close to Napoleon's heart. Not only did he believe it to be a buffer to future Russian territorial expansion, but he also had hopes that this mainly Latin state would be friendly to France. However, he was opposed by the Austrians and the Turks who feared that any awakening of national sentiment would upset regional stability in the Balkans. Even if the new state remained under Ottoman suzerainty its creation would encourage other nationalities to seek their independence or to combine against Ottoman rule. With Britain's support – Clarendon reiterated his argument that the war had been fought to maintain the integrity of the Ottoman Empire – this view prevailed and it was agreed that Moldavia and Wallachia, together with Serbia, should remain under Ottoman suzerainty while their privileges would be guaranteed by the signatories to the treaty. The two principalities were allowed to have independent national administrations, and within three years these assemblies were united under a common ruler, Colonel Alexander Cuza.

The next crisis arrived with the discussion of the Third Point, the question of the neutralisation of the Black Sea and the size of the ships to be allowed to remain there. Although the subject was discussed amicably enough at the fourth session on 4 March it quickly degenerated into a struggle over the size of police boats and what constituted naval arsenals and shipyards. Technically, this was a matter for Russia and Turkey to decide but much more was at stake. Russian pride was involved; the Black Sea was regarded as their territorial waters and any attempt to impose naval sanctions was considered an insult to the country's integrity. With tacit French support, Orlov fought a successful rearguard action to preserve the shipyards at Kershon and Nikolayev, the main bases, respectively, at the mouths of the Dnieper and Bug rivers, but he did not get everything his own way. The Sea of Azov, too, was excluded from the neutralisation of the Black Sea but, even so, the decision to exclude a Russian naval fleet from the Black Sea under Article XI of the treaty was a painful defeat for Orlov. Clarendon certainly thought so. Following the decisive meeting on 10 March he told Palmerston: 'We have made great progress today and peace may almost be looked upon as a fait accompli.'[5]

As the conference proceeded many of the most crucial decisions were being taken outside the formal sessions and here Napoleon proved to be a catalyst, talking late into the night at the Tuileries with each of the plenipotentiaries, sometimes in private, at other times ostentatiously making sure that the delegates saw who was receiving his patronage. 'In the midst of a crowded Assembly,' reported Clarendon at the end of the first day's session, 'I can have no doubt that he [Napoleon] wished publicly [to show] his feeling in favour of the English alliance . . . it has not been without its effect on the Russian plenipotentiaries.'[6] Gratified though Clarendon was to be so favoured, Napoleon was also talking to Orlov who fully repaid Nesselrode's instructions to flatter the emperor into taking a pro-Russian stance.

One fruit of the Russian plenipotentary's hard work was the French withdrawal of support for Britain's more extreme demands for Russia's Caucasus provinces, namely the granting of independence to Georgia and Circassia. So terrified was Buol that Russia would withdraw from the Congress if the demand was made, that he had raised the issue during the first preliminary meetings in an attempt to draw Clarendon into the open. The initiative worked as the British plenipotentiaries were unable to give a precise account of their aims and, shorn of any support from the French, the issue was quietly dropped. A disgruntled Clarendon was forced to tell an equally disappointed Stratford that without Napoleon's unqualified support it was pointless pressing ahead with the British demands. It proved to be a first and last triumph for Buol. As Clarendon noted with approval, following a meeting with Napoleon on 23 March, the plenipotentiaries had succeeded in freezing the Austrians out of the proceedings:

> The Austrian alliance which a few months ago was so ardently desired, and to secure which Her Majesty's Government were urged to accept inadmissible conditions, is now viewed with comparative indifference. The Emperor spoke with detestation of Austrian policy and in slighting tones of the Emperor of Austria, but on the other hand, there is an evident tendency on the part of the Emperor towards Russia — a dislike to

offend and great desire to be agreeable to the Emperor of
Russia.[7]

By that time the proceedings were drawing to a close. In all there
were twenty-four official sessions and innumerable private discussions
behind closed doors; the final Treaty of Paris resulted in 34 articles, with
three annexes, and its main provisions seemed to justify the terms of the
original Austrian ultimatum. ★ The integrity of the Ottoman Empire
was recognised, Russia returned Kars in exchange for concessions in
Bessarabia and agreed to the neutralisation of the Black Sea. She also
agreed to relinquish claims to the Danubian principalities and finally
dropped the right to act as guardian to the Christians resident in the
Ottoman Empire. However, the congress failed to integrate the Sultan's
promised reform programme into the final treaty. The only reference
to the Hatti-i-Humayan, which had been decreed on 18 February (and
which is discussed in the next chapter), appeared in article IX and it was
limited to a recognition of the Sultan's promises.

However, within a year of the treaty being signed, the efforts of
all the participants in the war seemed to be mocked on Good Friday
when fighting broke out amongst pilgrims and priests in Bethlehem's
Church of the Holy Sepulchre during the annual miracle of light from
heaven service. According to those present it was as bad as anything
witnessed by Robert Curzon and others before the war.

Following the signature of the treaty on 30 March 1856 – at the
last minute the British objected to a ceremony on a Sunday but
were forced to yield – each side claimed a victory of sorts. As the
guns roared out from Les Invalides at two o'clock in the afternoon
Napoleon was well satisfied with events, his pleasure having been
increased by the birth of a son. If he had not put a stamp on the
Congress by redrawing the map of Europe, he had at least retrieved
French respect and dignity. His dealings with Orlov paved the way
for rapprochement with Russia and within a decade Alexander II
would visit Paris. True, Napoleon had not been able to do anything

---

★ Peace had not broken out everywhere. Technically, the English port of
Berwick-on-Tweed on the Border with Scotland was still at war with Russia.
The declaration of war in February 1854 had been made in the name of Queen
Victoria of Great Britain, Ireland, Berwick-on-Tweed and the British Dominions.
By the time the Treaty of Paris was signed, Berwick-on-Tweed had been legally
incorporated into England and its name was omitted from the final document.

for Poland, and a pro-French Romania would not come into being for another six years, but he had manufactured a triumphant conclusion to a war which had become a drain on his country's resources.

Britain, too, felt that the peace treaty was not dishonourable – Palmerston was rewarded with the Order of the Garter – but if any country had a right to feel aggrieved it was Sardinia, the loyal 'Sardines' who had fought so uncomplainingly alongside their British allies. That was the feeling uppermost in Clarendon's mind when he wrote his final despatch on 17 April following the closing meeting of the plenipotentiaries who had stayed on in Paris to discuss broader issues, including the revision of maritime law regarding neutral countries:

> A conciliatory spirit has been maintained throughout our dis-
> cussions and although questions calculated to excite irritation
> have not infrequently arisen, they have been dealt with in calm
> and becoming tones. The Plenipotentiaries have separated in
> the most friendly terms with each other, well satisfied with the
> result of their labours and hopeful that the good understanding
> established between their respective governments may secure a
> long continuance of Peace.
>
> The only exception to the general feeling of satisfaction is on
> the part of the Sardinian-Piedmontese who lament that no measure
> should have been taken to remedy the evils under which Italy has
> so long laboured and who distrust, more perhaps than they are
> quite justified in doing, the policy and intentions of Austria.[8]

In fact Clarendon had done his best for King Victor Emmanuel's nation by stating publicly that he regretted Austria's influence in Italy but without overt French support there was little he could do to redress the situation. The next day he left Paris and was destined to remain in office for another two years until Palmerston was replaced by Lord Derby's government in 1858. Cowley lasted longer, remaining in Paris until 1867 by which time he was suspected by other members of the diplomatic community of being 'more French than he ought to be'. For their labours at the Congress both men were granted elevations in the peerage, but both declined the Queen's offer, Clarendon because he thought it would exclude his eldest son from future employment and Cowley because he could not afford the additional costs which would be incurred.

One more boil remained to be lanced: Britain's quarrel with the

United States. With terrier-like determination Marcy had pursued the issue of the guilt of Crampton and his consuls, offering as evidence the findings of the trial against Hertz. With equal firmness, and backed by Crampton's denials, Clarendon had rejected the complaints as fabrication. For Charles Rowcroft in Cincinnati, one of the consuls most blamed by Marcy for his role in encouraging recruiting agents, and who did most to dig up evidence to rebut the charges, the issue was quite simple. It had long since stopped being a question which concerned the sovereign rights of the United States: by the end of 1855 it had become an internal political problem. President Pierce was due to fight for re-nomination and he was anxious to show a firm hand. In other words, argued Rowcroft, the government was using the row 'to drive the differences up to the verge of a war, with the hope of stirring up the jealousies and passions of the masses so as to get their votes for a war party'.[9]

There was some truth to his allegation. As President, Pierce had proved to be a non-entity who failed to confront the slavery issue, and who alienated northern Democrats with his support of the Kansas-Nebraska Act of 1854. Throughout his presidency the United States had been in turmoil, economic crisis was on the horizon, the Republican party was about to become a political force and, in foreign affairs, there had been several illegal privately funded attempts to expand US territorial holdings in central America. It would not have been unnatural had Pierce attempted to divert public attention from his disastrous presidency by drumming up a crisis with Britain. Crampton was inclined to agree with that interpretation, which had the support of sections of the New York press, but, of course, he had a vested interest in ensuring that his role in the recruiting scandal was never fully exposed.

The crunch came on 28 December 1855 when Marcy sent a long and detailed letter to Buchanan, for communication to Clarendon, arguing the existence of a 'a very wide difference of opinion between this Government and that of Great Britain, in regard to the principles of law involved in the pending discussion, and a still wider difference, if possible, as to the material facts of the case'. It was a lawyer's letter, discursive and rambling, yet carefully phrased, and it contained a complete history of the bumbling attempts to raise recruits in the United States, as the facts had emerged in discussion with Crampton and, critically, from the trial of the British agents. It also contained a number of verbose quotations from international jurists stating that the enlistment of foreign nationals against the will of the host country was a serious crime. All this was related in lengthy detail but, according to Marcy, the most heinous part of the story was the subterfuge and deceit practised by Crampton and his colleagues. As for Clarendon, there was pained amazement that a politician of a friendly nation should try to cover up all the details in an attempt to present British behaviour in an acceptable light:

> I am quite certain that Lord Clarendon is not aware of the serious importance which the United States attaches to the question under discussion; otherwise he would not have so harshly characterised the conduct of the United States' officers on whom the duty to suppress recruiting for the British service was devolved; nor would he have so freely arraigned the motives of this Government for requiring some satisfaction for what it regards as a grave national wrong.[10]

The letter ended with the demand for Crampton's recall and it was finally discussed on 29 January when Buchanan was summoned to the Foreign Office. By that time, however, Clarendon's attention was fully taken up with the peace negotiations in Paris and he greeted Buchanan with scant courtesy. The details would have to await further scrutiny, he explained; meanwhile he contented himself with the observation that 'Mr Crampton had never been engaged in violating [our] neutrality laws and he considered his simple declaration to that effect far more worthy of credit than the conference of such a man as Hertz'. According to Buchanan the meeting was 'icy' and it ended on a sharp note as he expressed his own disappointment at Britain's behaviour:

> I then observed that if the same things had been done in England which had been done in the United States, they would probably realise the reason why we were so sensitive on the subject.[11]

However, Clarendon was not to be moved and Buchanan left with the impression that even after the complaint had been considered Britain would refuse to recall Crampton and the consuls. Four days later he wrote again to Marcy reporting a 'belligerent feeling' in the country about the United States and expressing his opinion that the peace with Russia was so unpopular that a crisis with the United States could provide a way out of the negotiations in Paris. Already articles had started appearing in the press calling for the main cities

on the eastern seaboard to be attacked and for regiments of black
soldiers to be raised in the West Indies for the purpose of exciting
rebellion in the southern states. However far-fetched those ideas
were, Buchanan was acutely aware of the fact that a breakdown in
diplomatic relations raised tensions so that 'the occurrence of any
untoward event may produce hostilities'.

Fortunately for Buchanan he was excused the indignity of being
recalled in retaliation for the threats made to Crampton. On 17
March he requested his passports and, amid many protestations of
goodwill, returned to the United States to pick up his political career.
He was replaced by a former vice-president, George Dallas, whose
unenviable task it was to maintain his country's dignity while building
a satisfactory relationship with the British government. Following
further protestations by Crampton the British refused to recall him
and, furthermore, Palmerston wanted to end the matter by expelling
the newly arrived Dallas. While this proposal smacked more of the
Palmerston of old it was sensibly disregarded by his cabinet colleagues.
As the Duke of Argyll noted in his memoirs there was a knack in
knowing how to handle the prickly prime minister:

> His first impulse was always to move fleets and to threaten our
> opponents, sometimes on trivial occasions, on the details of
> which he had not fully informed himself by careful reading.
> Then, on finding his proposals combated, he was candid in
> listening and in inquiring and if he found the objections reason-
> able, he could give way to them with the most perfect good
> humour. This was a great quality in a man so impulsive and so
> strong-headed as he was, and so prone to violent action. It made
> him a much less dangerous man than he was supposed to be. But
> I made it an all-important matter that he should have colleagues
> who understood him and were not afraid of him.[12]

Those qualities were badly need by his colleagues in the days that
followed. No sooner had Dallas arrived than there was news of a fresh
privateering expedition in central America. Led by William Walker,
a failed journalist, it seized Nicaragua and declared the whole of the
Mosquito coast to be in the possession of the United States. As this
infringed British rights Palmerston demanded the despatch of a battle
fleet to begin a blockade – a move which would certainly have resulted
in war with the United States. However, as Argyll noted, an injection

of common sense in the shape of Clarendon's advice to negotiate, ended the crisis. Ships were sent but there was no blockade and, by way of compromise, Pierce's administration refused to support Walker's initiative.

However, the president was not prepared to back down over Crampton. On 28 May he handed him his passports, thereby breaking off diplomatic relations with him, and Crampton was forced to return to Britain. While this was an insult, and one which Palmerston did not want to leave unchallenged, the government decided to do nothing. Crampton returned home to a knighthood and ended his career with further appointments in Hanover, St Petersburg and Madrid, retiring in 1869 after more than forty years in the diplomatic service. To the end of his life he protested his innocence in the recruiting crisis which had brought Britain and the United States so close to the brink of war.

By that time, too, a sense of normality had returned to Britain's dealings with Russia. Diplomatic relations were resumed in May when Brunnov returned to London to a post which he was to hold until 1874. The British embassy in St Petersburg reopened later that summer and was soon hard at work helping to re-establish the trading links which had been interrupted by the blockade of the Baltic. Alexander II was keen to mend fences with France and the two emperors were soon on good terms. The détente with France continued throughout the 1860s as France and Russia attempted to show a united front in the face of Prussia's steady rise to power as the main force of German unification.

It was that movement which finally gave Russia the opportunity to retrieve its honour. When the attention of the European powers was taken up with the war between Prussia and France in the late summer of 1870, Alexander abrogated the Treaty of Paris as far as the neutrality of the Black Sea was concerned. His move created a fuss but little else: in March 1871, with the Convention of London, Russia's sovereign rights in the Black Sea were restored although Turkey maintained the right to call up naval assistance if her treaty rights were infringed.

Seven years later, peace was threatened in the area and a repeat of the war in the Crimea seemed possible when Russia and Turkey found themselves at cross purposes. Once again, the Eastern Question was to blame. At Paris the problems of the Balkans had never been addressed; they remained under Ottoman rule and despite exhortations by Britain (most notably by Stratford during his tenure at Constantinople) the Porte had been loath to introduce reforms and the result had been a succession of local revolts. At first the British government, now led by Disraeli, had been minded to support the Sultan when his forces put down a serious revolt in the provinces of Bosnia and Herzegovina in the summer of 1875. This was, after all, British policy and Disraeli refused to listen to promptings by Russia, Germany and Austria that the Great Powers should intervene. 'They have begun to treat England as if we were Montenegro or Monaco,' he complained to Brunnov, still Russia's ambassador in London.

But for once Disraeli had misjudged the public mood. Within a year the *Daily News* had begun publishing accounts of the fighting in the Balkans and the descriptions of the outrages caused widespread indignation. Gladstone, the opposition leader, delivered his famous opinion in his pamphlet *The Bulgarian Horrors and the Question of the East* which called for the Turks to carry out of Europe their 'Zaptiehs and their Mudirs, their Bimbashis and their Yuzbachis, their Kaimakams and their Pashas, one and all, bag and baggage'. It was a splendidly splenetic document – the Liberal leader claimed that the soil of the Balkans was 'soaked and reeking with blood' – but Disraeli chose to play it down. When the question was debated in the House of Commons he retorted that while there had been atrocities, Turks 'seldom resort to torture but generally terminate their connection with culprits in a more expeditious manner'.

Disraeli's refusal to treat the crisis seriously could not last. In an attempt to resolve the issue in January 1877 a conference was held in Constantinople at which the new Sultan Abdulhamid II showed little interest in renewing his predecessor's pledges to introduce reforms. When the talks broke down in April Russia went to war with Turkey and by December its army was threatening Constantinople. That changed everything. For a few giddy months the past seemed to repeat itself as a wave of violent patriotism swept through the country. Forgetting the evidence of Gladstone's pamphlet the people of Britain now flocked to support gallant Turkey against the Russian bear and the war fever was strong as anything which Timothy Gowing had experienced in 1854. By Christmas there was even a new music-hall song which introduced jingoism to the language: 'We don't want to fight, but by jingo if we do/We've got the ships, we've got the men, we've got the money too!'

And in scenes which Lyons and Dundas would have recognised – except that all the ships were iron-clad, steam-powered and lower in the water – Vice-Admiral Sir George Hornby's Mediterranean fleet steamed into the Dardanelles in February 1878. At the same time the Royal Navy began preparations at Spithead to assemble a powerful fleet of ironclads and coastal assault ships to move into the Baltic and to carry out the plans laid in 1856 for the assault of Kronstadt. Knowledge of those preparations was the decisive factor for Russia knew that her navy would be incapable of defending the Gulf of Finland but, even so, Hornby's ships were obliged to remain in the Black Sea for the rest of the summer.

The reason for their presence was the unequal Treaty of San Stefano which ended the fighting between Russia and Turkey. Agreed in March 1878 it allowed Russia to have full control over the Balkans, a situation which was anathema to the European powers as it would bring the Mediterranean into Alexander's sphere of influence. This time, though, there would be no war. Remembering the lessons of two decades ago Britain's new foreign secretary, Lord Salisbury, called a conference in Berlin in the summer of 1878 with Bismarck acting as honest broker. Under its terms Austria occupied Bosnia and Herzegovina; the independence of Serbia, Montenegro and Romania was recognised; Russia was awarded Bessarabia and Bulgaria was largely returned to the Sultan.

In that it prevented a repeat of the Crimean War, it was a diplomatic triumph – Disraeli called it 'peace with honour' – but it did lay down all manner of problems which would re-emerge thirty-six years later to plunge Europe into an even worse conflict. At the time of the Congress of Berlin, however, there was universal relief and a feeling, in Britain at least, that no one wanted a repetition of the experience of the Crimean War.

4

The New World Order

The curtain is dropped, the tears dried up – and to supper with
what appetite we may!

*Lieutenant-Colonel Anthony Sterling, letter home,
on leaving the Crimea, 8 May 1856*

Within a year of the abandonment of the campaign in the
Crimea British soldiers were again in action in the east, first
in November to force the Shah Nasr-ud-din of Persia to abandon
his claims to Herat, a fortress on the Afghan-Persian border, and
then in May 1857 to quell a revolt by Indian soldiers which broke
out at Meerut in the North-Western Provinces and which spread
quickly to other garrisons. The first confrontation was exacerbated by
Persia's desire to enter into a treaty of alliance with the United States
to secure commercial rights in the region. Palmerston considered
Washington's initiative to be 'impudent intermeddling' but he knew,
too, that it was preferable to any intervention by Russia. During the
Crimean War Nesselrode had worked hard to draw Persia into a secret
alliance, offering them territorial gains in return for military assistance
but, alerted to the danger by Seymour, Clarendon had managed to
persuade the Shah to remain neutral.

Although the Foreign Office entertained doubts about the United
States's reaction to the use of British troops in Persia, the threat to
India's security had to over-ride any such qualms. An expeditionary
force landed at Bushire on the Persian Gulf in November and the
Persian troops withdrew from Herat after a short and relatively
bloodless campaign. Most of the troops were drawn from the East
India Company's army and their presence, small though it was, was

sufficient to reimpose the Pax Britannica in that unruly part of the world. It was to be the last time that they would be in action under the Company's colours: within a year everything would be changed by the mutiny which shook the British in India out of their imperial complacency.

As the revolt spread along the Ganges in May 1857 and shocking stories were published in the British press describing the rapes and the murders of innocent British women and children Palmerston was forced to act decisively. He needed the revolt to be crushed but he could not afford another military setback so soon after the events in the Crimea. With public opinion demanding the extermination of the miscreants – 'when every gibbet is red with blood; when every bayonet creaks beneath its ghastly burden; when the ground in front of every cannon is strewn with rags, and flesh, and shattered bone – then talk of mercy' was the considered verdict of a speaker at a debate in the Cambridge Union – the generals in India could not be seen to be doing nothing. To the British at home, the majority of whom knew nothing about India but avidly read overheated newspaper tales describing rape and destruction, Pandora's box had been opened and Christian civilisation was under threat. However, in this case there was to be no repetition of the Crimean blunders for the very good reason that the numbers involved, despite being inflated by the authorities, were much smaller. It also helped that there was only a handful of correspondents watching events in the Ganges valley and that by the time experienced men like Russell arrived, the revolt was as good as over.

Only half of the Bengal Army mutinied and, with many sepoys remaining loyal, the revolt was eventually put down. Amongst the Crimean veterans who took part in the campaign were Colin Campbell, sent to India to take command of the army, and Hugh Rose whose Central Indian Field Force crushed the insurrection in the south, including two brilliantly led operations to recapture the fortresses of Jhansi and Gwalior. Both men received due reward. Although thought to be too coarse and awkward to command in the Crimea, Campbell received his desserts in India where he did not have to deal with touchy allies. He was ennobled as Lord Clyde and promoted field-marshal while the equally thorny Rose became Lord Strathnairn in 1866 as commander-in-chief of the Indian army. But their successes in the mutiny proved a mixed blessing. They persuaded an uncritical press to draw exaggerated comparisons between the blunders of the Crimea and the over-blown 'victories' in India. As far as most of the British public were concerned, though, the slate had been wiped clean.

It was time, too, for Britain to withdraw from further adventures in a Europe which was no longer held in check by the Concert of 1815. With that consensus broken Napoleon III was free to concentrate on his dream of redrawing the map of Europe along national lines and within the next twenty years the continent was to experience four major wars involving the main continental powers. The first took place when France went to war on Sardinia's behalf against Austria to initiate the process which would lead to the unification of Italy. Following victories at Magenta and Solferino in 1859, both of which caused a huge number of casualties, Austria ceded Lombardy while France was awarded Savoy and Nice. Although remaining suspicious of French involvement in Italy, Britain stayed out of the war and successive governments came to believe that, in a troubled world, diplomacy could achieve more than powder and shot. Clarendon admitted as much in 1866 when he said that as far as Europe was concerned Britain was 'willing to do anything for the maintenance of peace except committing ourselves to a policy of action'.[1]

It was never an easy policy to maintain as Napoleon had emerged from the Crimean War intent on making his presence felt in the world and, all too often, his muscle-flexing impinged on British interests. In 1859, having been thwarted by Stratford in Constantinople, the French engineer Ferdinand de Lesseps finally succeeded in gaining consent for the construction of the Suez canal. The agent was the emperor who made a direct appeal to the new Khedive of Egypt behind Britain's back; permission was granted and work was begun. Palmerston was appalled – he believed it was a French plot to threaten India with the Mediterranean fleet – but such was France's potency in Europe that there was nothing Britain could do. The Middle East also provided fresh tensions a year later when France sent forces to Syria to protect the Maronite Christians following the massacre in Damascus of three thousand of their number by Muslim Druse tribesmen. At Britain's request an international convention was called to solve the crisis but the French peace-keeping forces remained in the country for a year, by which time France had been able to establish a new sphere of influence at the expense of Britain's traditional friendship with the Druse.

However, British fears about French expansionism were balanced by a contemptuous belief that Napoleon would never dare to force a quarrel with his former allies. 'I do not believe the Emperor to have any fixed policy at all,' wrote Cowley from Paris in 1862. 'He has certain ideas and desires floating in his mind which turn up as circumstances seem favourable.'[2] There was some truth to the jibe. Despite the country's re-emergence as a world power France was becoming increasingly isolated and Napoleon's foreign policy came to be governed by an inconsistency and presumption which infuriated his neighbours. Like the British government he under-rated Prussia and failed to understand the significance of its growing strength in the decade following the Crimean War. That lack of comprehension was eventually to prove his undoing.

The man responsible was Count Otto von Bismarck, a former ambassador to St Petersburg, who came to power as minister-president of Prussia in 1862. His foreign policy was simple: to create a sphere of influence for Prussia in north and central Germany and within four years he had accomplished that aim by annexing Hanover, Schleswig, Holstein, Hesse-Kassel, Nassau and Frankfurt. Helped by Austria's weakness and isolation from her former Russian allies Prussia became the dominant force not just in German but also in European politics, first defeating Denmark in 1864 to gain Schleswig and then overcoming Franz Josef's army two years later to expel Austria from the German Confederation. Following her humiliation in northern Italy Austria was excluded from German affairs and the Hapsburg empire was left with waning authority in Europe. Throughout his attempts to end the Crimean War Buol had hoped that neutral Austria, the honest broker, would be rewarded with a central position in the new European order, yet of all the participants in the Treaty of Paris she gained least and lost most.

Bismarck's triumph was made complete in the late summer of 1870 when he engineered a war against France by playing on German fears about French designs on the Rhine. In the mistaken belief that the south German states and Austria-Hungary would join him to curb Prussia's growing dominance, Napoleon III declared war on Prussia on 19 July only to see his army humiliated in a campaign which lasted a mere six weeks. Amongst the defeated generals were two veterans of the Crimea – MacMahon and Bazaine – and Napoleon himself faced the indignity of capture along with 100,000 of his troops at Sedan. It was the end of the line, too, for his time in office. The Third Republic was declared in Paris on 4 September 1870 and although the war continued into the following year, there was to be no way back for the French army. Paris fell on 28 January and Bismarck took full advantage of his army's success. At the ensuing Treaty of Frankfurt Prussia imposed draconian terms: France was forced to cede Alsace and most of Lorraine to Prussia which had already used the opportunity presented by the victory to proclaim the creation of the German Empire in the Hall of Mirrors at Versailles. Having been treated with scant courtesy at the Congress of Paris fifteen years earlier it was sweet revenge for the Prussians. By the same token the defeat and humiliation provided bitter medicine for the French who spent the next four decades smarting under the insult to their national pride.

The other victor, the Ottoman Empire, discovered itself more or less in the *status quo ante bellum*. It had ceded some territory but it had succeeded in keeping European interference in its domestic and religious affairs at arm's length. Although the question of protecting the Christian population had been accepted by the terms of the treaty, the signatories agreed that any future intercession on their behalf could only be made with the acquiescence of the Porte. For the Turks this was an important concession for they were under intense pressure from the allies to include domestic reforms as part of the peace settlement. That this demand had been met owed everything to Stratford who was determined to crown his career by urging the Turks to continue the reforms begun in 1839 and 1844. As a carrot he linked it to the protection of Christians: if the Porte gave way on the subject they would remove from the Russians a major grievance, indeed, one of the pretexts for starting the war in the first place.

This was a major achievement for the British ambassador. Throughout the war he had never lost sight of the need to keep urging the Porte to accept the need for reform and in February 1855, at a time when the war was still far from being won, he reminded the Sultan that Britain was not prepared to make sacrifices if her allies remained in such a pitifully backward state. At the same time he welcomed the Sultan's decision to show him the draft of new laws 'directed against venality and peculation'. Having commented on them he reported his findings in a lengthy letter to Clarendon. More than any other of his despatches from Constantinople, this points the way to the hard line he would adopt in the dying months of the war:

I have never ceased to recommend the prompt completion, promulgation and enforcement of all those reforms, which have been so frequently promised by the Sultan and his Ministers. The language, which I have held as well to His Majesty as to the leading Members of his Government may be summed up, essentially in very few words. Your present administrative system, I have said, is only leading you to destruction. It is antisocial; that of self, opposed to public interests. You cannot revert to the period of energetic fanaticism. That fire, in a national sense, has burnt itself out. You must open the sources of prosperity and strength, and they are to be found in a system of administration which secures justice to all, removes inequality of civil rights, encourages knowledge and industry, protects property, develops wealth, and extends the means of defence. You must also take measures to bring your revenue, unpillaged, into the coffers of state, to welcome science, capital and enterprise, from whatever quarters they come, and, above all, you must lay the axe without reserve or compromise to the roots of that corruption which spreads its poison throughout the empire, and casts a fatal shade on every germ of vegetation and every principle of life.[3]

It was an uncompromising message, but not for Stratford the feline approach. His long experience of Turkish affairs gave him an authority and a standing which even his great French rival Thouvenel would find difficult to counter: the Sultan and his officials might have resented Stratford's imperious interference but they had little option but to pay heed to his warnings. That was the significance of the message he passed on to Clarendon, ending his despatch with the hope that his exhortations might 'prove the beginning of serious reform'. It is against the background of that despatch that his last wartime efforts in Constantinople should be judged.

Following the fall of Sevastopol and the quickening moves for a peace settlement Stratford had been instructed by the Foreign Office to reapply pressure on the Porte to protect the rights of Christians. He was joined in his efforts by Thouvenel who played a fitful role, balancing his support with underhand attempts to gain additional concessions for his own country, and by the Austrian Internuncio Count Prokesh-Osten whom Stratford thought 'of no small importance' but whom Clarendon detested as 'a thoroughly loose fish . . . mendacious and unprincipled'.[4] In fact Stratford's assessment was the more reliable as, soon after his arrival on 18 December, Prokesh-Osten warned Fuad and Aali that they had no option but to bow to western wishes on the question of reform.

Before the talks began Stratford was told by Clarendon that he had to be less forceful in his dealings with the Porte and to do his utmost to lose the impression that 'every wish or intimation of any other [British] ambassador would be instantly obeyed':

> Three several times the present Turkish Government have asked that you be recalled. They did full justice of course to your eminent talents and goodwill towards Turkey, but declared they could no longer get on with you as you required that your influence should be so paramount and notorious that you were lowered in the eyes of the people, and that you would not allow the Sultan to corrégner with you (that was Aali's expression).[5]

From the frequently waspish correspondence between the two men it is difficult to know how much Clarendon was venting his own frustrations about Stratford when he claimed that he had evidence from Constantinople of a 'dogged and disagreeable determination to resist your wishes and advice', but it is true that the Turkish regime was becoming increasingly unhappy with the Great Elchi. This makes his final achievement all the more remarkable. At the first formal meeting on 9 January 1856 Stratford insisted that, while Ottoman ascendancy was paramount, the Christians needed their own privileges and that this was best applied through government reform. Unless that happened, he insisted, there would remain a 'general belief, whether shown by assertion or by admission, that the present course of Ottoman administration is really defective in action and so liable to abusive influences in every department as to require a searching and comprehensive reform.'[6]

For a few days it looked as if the Turkish ministers would stonewall but when the news arrived in mid-January of Russia's decision to accept the Austrian terms the Porte was left with no option but to settle an agreement in advance of the Paris peace talks. On 18 February the Sultan issued a firman, the Hatti-i-Humayun, which guaranteed the rights and privileges of Christians *ab antiquo* and ensured the provision of a programme of administrative, judicial and economic reforms. There was even a clause, at Stratford's insistence, abolishing executions for apostasy. With the announcement of the firman Stratford regained some of his authority in Constantinople and even Thouvenel was forced to admit that the agreement owed everything to the Great Elchi's skill and powers of persuasion. A few months later the French ambassador was forced to concede further ground when, following a picturesque ceremony in which the Sultan was awarded the Order of the Garter, Reschid Ali, Stratford's great ally, was reinstalled as Grand Vizier. As Thouvenel saw it, in a single day Stratford had made a Knight of the Garter and a Grand Vizier. It was the Great Elchi's last flourish. Following the fall of Palmerston's government in 1858 he offered his resignation and it was accepted by the new prime minister, Lord Derby.

Stratford was to live to see the retrogression of the promises contained in the Hatti-i-Haumayun and the empire's decline into extravagance and misrule during the reign of Abd-el-Aziz but, before his death in 1880, he was to feel vindicated in his actions. Two years earlier Constantinople had almost fallen to a Russian army and the resulting peace negotiations had begun the process that would lead to the eventual disintegration of the Ottoman Empire. 'Unless the Sultan's firman be carried into full effect the regeneration of this Empire is a dream and its independence a word,' he had warned in 1856.[7] In that sense at least Turkey took very little from the Crimean War other than a blind unwillingness to accept the need for reform.

Russia won nothing from the war, other than minor concessions, but by the same token her losses were not immediately terminal. While the tsar had been humiliated by losing command of the Black Sea, the truth was that his country had no money to rebuild Sevastopol or to construct a modern fleet and would not be able to do so for another quarter of a century. Russian prestige had been damaged but this was nothing compared to the country's growing financial problems. The war had demonstrated only too clearly Russia's economic weakness when pitted against modern western countries and Alexander realised that he had to introduce a rapid programme of economic and social reforms. The decision was not without benefit to the allies: Russia quickly became the largest borrowing country in Europe as London and Paris vied with one another to take advantage of the new money-market.

The tsar also realised that he could no longer rely on serf labour if Russia were to embrace new technological industries. Although his father had recognised that serfdom was 'the indubitable evil of

Russian life', and despite the fact that outbreaks of peasant violence
had been increasing in the years before the outbreak of hostilities in
the Crimea, the problem had been subjected to little more than *laissez
faire* tampering. Alexander changed all that in 1861, four years before
slavery was abolished in the United States. More than anything else,
perhaps, that liberation was one of the happier results of the war for its
discontinuance was a direct result of the quickening pace of economic
reforms in post-war Russia.

'We cannot deceive ourselves any longer,' the Grand Duke
Constantine told the tsar, 'we are both weaker and poorer than the
first-class powers.' Having had that industrial backwardness exposed
by the war Russia set about reforming itself with the result that by
1914 its industrial production was the fifth largest in the world. The
changes also encouraged social reforms, most notably in education and
the judiciary; but the eventual outcome was to alter Russia beyond
recognition as the abolition of serfdom gave impetus to the beginnings
and growth of Marxism in the last two decades of the century. By then
internal terrorism had become increasingly prevalent and Alexander II
became one of its victims when he was assassinated in March 1881 by
a member of the revolutionary People's Will party.

For some time after the war Alexander had pursued a policy of
détente with the United States and partly as a result of the friendship
sustained during the war the purchase of Alaska was concluded in
1867 at a cost of $7.2 million. The deal was facilitated by his younger
brother the Grand Duke Constantine who had mooted the possibility
shortly after the war had come to an end. In fact, he was not the first
Russian to suggest the sale of the province. As early as October 1853
the consul in San Francisco, Peter Kostrominov, had entered into
secret negotiations with the directors of the Russia-America Trading
Company to sell Russian-America, as Alaska was known, to the US
government. Although Marcy knew about the discussions he refused
to become involved because he feared that a British attack on the
Russian holdings would drag the United States into the fighting. As
Russia's military and naval shortcomings had been exposed during the
war, the case for keeping Alaska made no sense to Constantine who
argued that the United States would soon be the dominant country in
the north American continent. Better to sell it at a profit, he argued,
than to have it seized at a later date.

Although the United States would soon be plunged into the
civil war which Napoleon III had foreseen, it would emerge a

stronger nation from the experience. Slavery was abolished as a result of the Union's victory and the country became one nation with authority vested in the federal government in Washington. While reconciliation would take time and there were to be many setbacks for the black population in the southern states, most of which were not properly settled until a century later, the country itself was to change dramatically. Mark Twain called it 'the Gilded Age', a time when American industrialists had the Midas touch. By 1890 there were 166,703 miles of railroad, Thomas Edison had produced a workable and cheap telephone, the telegraph, invented by Samuel Morse in 1844, drew the country ever closer together and entrepreneurs like Andrew Carnegie and John D. Rockefeller began to exploit the wealth produced by oil and steel. Within half a century the United States had transformed itself from an agricultural nation to become the world's leading industrial power, fully justifying Soulé's comment in 1854 that it was 'a country of real importance'.

That growing pre-eminence made good relations with Britain difficult to sustain. While the wartime row over recruiting had been quietly forgotten, the trans-Atlantic connection was never particularly friendly. During the civil war Britain declared itself neutral but this seemingly innocuous decision caused great offence in the north as it meant that Britain recognised the Confederacy as a legal belligerent. In Washington there were fears too (not all of them groundless) that Britain might even favour the southern states. In November 1861 those concerns materialised when a British streamer, the *Trent*, was found to be carrying two Confederate ministers on a mission to London. When it was stopped by a US warship in the Atlantic and the ministers impressed, there was considerable jubilation in the north that the British bulldog's tail had been given a good twisting, and serve it right.

However, the applause led to second thoughts when Palmerston's government responded angrily to the insult to the British flag. A despatch was sent to Washington demanding the release of the diplomats, the Royal Navy strengthened its North Atlantic squadron and additional troops were sent to Canada. If the British press had governed policy, war with the United States would have followed, such was the strength of their anti-American attitude, but neither government wanted confrontation and wiser counsels prevailed. After a decent interval the two Confederates were released, President Abraham Lincoln having told his more anglophobe colleagues that the country could only fight one war at a time. Considering that the Union army had hardly by then covered itself with glory in the field it was something of an understatement.

Like the recruiting row, the *Trent* affair was a tiff, albeit a serious one, in a love-hate relationship which lasted throughout the century. Britain's unwillingness to declare for the Union during the civil war left an irritation which was not quickly cured and other altercations continued to cause trouble. There were disputes over fishing rights in Canadian waters and over seal hunting in the Bering Sea, and in 1895 war again seemed possible over Britain's failure to agree the frontier between British Guiana and Venezuela. To the US government this seemed to be an infringement of the Monroe Doctrine and President Grover Cleveland sent a 'twenty-inch gun note' to London. Young Winston Churchill was returning from Cuba at the time and he remembered looking soberly at the ships in the English Channel and wondering which one would take his regiment to Canada.

Once again, after a good deal of bickering, the matter was allowed to drop. At the same time Britain was involved in an increasingly bitter quarrel with the Boers in South Africa and the United States, too, was about to become preoccupied with imperial adventuring. Three years later, in 1898 following an uprising in Cuba, it was at war with Spain and after a short land campaign on the island and a successful naval engagement off Manila, Spain sued for peace. At the treaty which ended the war, signed in Paris in December that same year, Cuba became independent and the United States received the Philippines, Puerto Rico and Guam, a move aligning her to the European imperial powers which had also, in Kipling's words, taken up the white man's burden.

During the Spanish-American war, alone of the European countries, Britain stood behind the United States and that moral support helped to heal old wounds by drawing the two countries together. By then, in the forty-two years which had passed since the Paris peace treaty brought hostilities to an end in the Baltic and Black Seas, Britain had stayed clear of any involvement in European politics. True, successive governments were fully prepared, as Disraeli expressed the policy in 1866, 'to interfere as in the old days, when the necessity of her position requires it', but there would never be any question of going to war in support of any European policy.

In its place there was a pre-occupation with empire and constant debate about what should be done with Britain's colonial holdings.

The revolt in India in 1857 had also concentrated minds and caused much heart-searching about the need to impose British discipline and British standards upon the black, brown and yellow peoples. Under Disraeli, prime minister in a short-lived Tory administration in 1868 and again between 1874 and 1880, there was a widely held conception of Britain's world power being linked to the Indian empire and the importance of maintaining the connections between the two. This meant following the Palmerstonian line of supporting the Ottoman Empire and resisting Russian expansionism towards India, a policy which was well understood, but it also led to a flurry of small imperial wars in Afghanistan which troubled the liberal conscience.

Increasingly, Britain's unofficial empire, based largely on trade and local influence, was becoming regularised and brought under direct control. What it needed was logic but the edifice itself was such a motley collection of different races and religions, the countries having been acquired in piecemeal fashion, that it was difficult to think of governing it in a cohesive way. None the less, the puzzle of colonial rule was to engage politicians and political thinkers for the remaining two decades of the century as, almost absent-mindedly, a world empire took shape. With regard to Europe, as long as Britain's strategic interests were not threatened, it could be handled through diplomacy and without the threat of armed intervention, just as Clarendon had promised. Little Englanderism also played a part and after the Crimea most people regarded the fate of Moldavia or wherever – barbarous and unknown places at the end of Europe – as being insignificant to their daily lives.

In any case, in 1856 Russia had been beaten decisively and its military power revealed as a sham; in the short term the threat to India had been neutralised and in the longer term the Royal Navy still controlled the Mediterranean. In that those limited strategic requirements had been met, for Britain at least, the outcome of the Crimean War was far more satisfactory than anyone in the country could have dared to hope at its outset.

5

Learning the Lessons the Hard Way

I admit that the stamp of European authority is pretty good
evidence of the sterling value of a military dogma; but in the
absence of new rules from such quarters, let us rather do without
any than follow the old ones which will lead us astray.

Captain James St Clair Morton, US Army,
Memoirs on American Fortification, *1859*

Once the war was over and the Crimea had been evacuated,
attempts were made to count the cost, not just in financial
outlay but also in human terms. Efforts were also made to learn
from the experience although these were fairly desultory and the
sweeping reforms which might have been expected often failed to
materialise. Since most of the casualties were due to illness and disease
– only one out of ten of the British total of 19,584 had died in action
(the figure excludes those who died in the Baltic and at Varna) – the
results of the two commissions into sanitary and nursing conditions did
produce some change. The first Hospital Commission had reported
in February 1855 and its findings had introduced important reforms
at Scutari. The second Sanitary Commission, headed by Dr John
Sutherland, also produced quick results by insisting on immediate
improvements to the conditions endured by the troops in Balaklava.
The death rate fell rapidly once the narrow harbour had been cleared
of corpses and filth, and a strict regime had been instituted for the
troops' hygiene.

As a result of the exposure of the army's shortcomings in the Crimea
there was a flurry of interest in the conditions endured by the ordinary

soldier and for a brief period he became a very important person indeed. A Royal Sanitary Commission was appointed in 1857 under the chairmanship of Sidney Herbert to investigate the conditions of army barracks and hospitals and its findings merely underlined the nation's low opinion of its armed forces. The mortality rate amongst soldiers was double that of the civilian population, with the home-based army losing 20.8 per cent of its strength each year to illness or disease. The Commission placed the blame for this on insanitary conditions, poor diet and 'enervating mental and bodily effects produced by ennui'. Their recommendations led to a steady improvement in the soldier's lot; a programme was instituted to improve ventilation, sanitary conditions and waste disposal in British barracks and steps were taken to provide soldiers with better leisure facilities in an attempt to cut down on the scourge of drunkenness. Two years later parliament voted £726,841 for the improvements but reform proved to be a slow and expensive process and it was to take until 1861 before the Commission on Barracks and Hospitals could report that forty-five barracks had proper lavatories in place of the usual cesspit.

But at least the reforms in sanitation and medical services were bearing some fruit, which is more than can be said for the results of the Tulloch and McNeill Commission into the army's administration in the Crimea. Inevitably, perhaps, the Report of the Commission of Inquiry into the Supplies of the British Army in the Crimea censured the inept Commissariat Department which had proved incapable of meeting the heavy demands of the expeditionary force. Not only were its officers found to be unimaginative, poorly trained and generally querulous but the Commissary-General, James Filder, had proved to be incapable of running so large and complicated an operation. More than anything else the revelation of patent absurdities still had the power to shock. To take one instance, how had it been possible for Filder to refuse the supply of fuel for fires because it was only issued in home garrisons? The answer lay in the regulations and the Commissariat Department's strict adherence to them but by keeping to the book soldiers were allowed to freeze in the winter uplands and Filder stoutly ignored all of Raglan's pleas to give his men fuel for much-needed fires. All of this was well enough known to the politicians. Panmure and Palmerston had complained loudly about Filder's shortcomings, the latter calling him 'narrow-minded, prejudiced, opposed to every new resource and improved practice, wedded to routine, and refusing every improved arrangement', but it had been to no avail and the elderly administrator did not resign until the summer of 1855.

However, some of the sting was taken out of the report by the timing of its publication. When it appeared early in 1856 the problems in the army's supply departments had been solved to such an extent that the British contingent could have mounted another campaign in the Crimea had the need arisen. With the horror stories of the first winter fading into memory and with the much advertised improvements there was less urgency for reform and Tulloch's and McNeill's report appeared to hit the wrong note. Although its language is a model of restraint, compared at least to the majority of the published descriptions written by newspaper correspondents and serving officers, the report's authors did name names and amongst those singled out for criticism were five of Raglan's staff officers, including Airey and Estcourt.

At the time of its composition a great deal had been expected of the investigation into the much-reviled Commissariat but when the results were published the army immediately closed ranks to protect itself against criticism. The named officers demanded an inquiry and as a result a General Board was convened at the Royal Hospital, Chelsea, under the presidency of General Sir Alexander Woodford. It proved to be a time-consuming and mainly farcical process. McNeill refused to attend – he did not agree with the criticisms – with the result that Tulloch, a colonel, was forced to cross-question the plaintiffs, all senior to him in rank, alone and unaided. Eventually the task became too much for him; he fell ill and the Board was left to soldier on as best it could. Its findings came as no surprise; the army was exonerated as the supply problems it faced in the Crimea were found to have arisen from Treasury restrictions and the lack of land transport. In other words, the problems facing Raglan's expeditionary force were already present before it left for its area of operations in the Black Sea and could not be blamed on individual officers. As a result of that evidence the Land Transport Corps was kept in being as the Military Train. The Board also produced the best defence of the army in Airey's dignified opening statement.

Although he continued to serve the army loyally as a senior staff officer and became Lord Airey in 1876, those who knew him well, including Wolseley who was in a good position to judge, said that his spirit had been broken by the accusations. And yet that unwarranted persecution also gave him a strong sense of compassion and understanding.

In 1875, while serving as Adjutant-General, he risked opprobrium by giving evidence in favour of Colonel Valentine Baker who had been accused of assaulting a young woman, Miss Dickinson, on a train between Working and Esher. Despite his high-ranking support and that of the commander of the Aldershot garrison, Lieutenant-General Sir Thomas Steele (Raglan's military secretary in the Crimea), Colonel Baker was sentenced to twelve months imprisonment, fined £500 and dismissed the service. Apparently Airey was much moved by Baker's stance, voiced by his defence counsel, that he 'preferred to take himself the ruin of his own character, the forfeiture of his own commission in the Army, the loss of his social status, and all that would make life worth having, to cast even a doubt on the lady's veracity in the witness box'. Baker later saw distinguished service in the Ottoman army and died in 1887 with the rank of lieutenant-general. Whilst serving in Egypt his teenage daughter Hermione enjoyed an understanding with a British officer called Major Horatio Herbert Kitchener but her early death in 1885 extinguished her family's fond hope of an engagement to marry the ambitious young military engineer.

Airey died in 1881; Steele in 1890 and in their later years they were to witness the many fitful changes which took place in the British Army. A Staff College came into being at Camberley to provide further intensive education for promising officers, the Crimean experience having exposed the weakness of reliance on regimental soldiering alone. Recruitment problems were eased with the introduction of short-service enlistment, the number of years being reduced from twenty-one to six (later seven) years with the colours. There were also administrative reforms, with the secretary of state for war becoming responsible for supply and finance while the commander-in-chief concentrated on the army's military tasks. There was also a new medal for gallantry, the Victoria Cross. Instituted by Royal Warrant on 29 January 1856 and manufactured from the metal of captured Russian guns to a design by Prince Albert, it was open to both services and all ranks and was awarded to those who had 'performed some signal act of valour or devotion to their country'. Of the 111 Crimean recipients, one of whom was Henry Clifford, 62 were presented personally by the queen at a special parade held in Hyde Park in June 1856.

Given the conservatism prevalent in the British Army many of the reforms took time to take root. Following the success of the Minié a similar rifle, the Enfield, was introduced in all line infantry regiments but the army's red coats would not be replaced by khaki until the 1880s when campaigning in Egypt and Sudan made ceremonial dress inappropriate for operational service. As for the purchase of officers' commissions, another relic which was much criticised during the war, it was not abolished until 1871, *Punch* observing in a 'Notice to Gallant but Stupid Young Gentlemen' that they could only continue to purchase their commissions 'up to the 31st day of October. After that you will be driven to the cruel necessity of deserving them.'

By then the pace of change within the British Army was also being driven by the experience of other wars for, as the American General Ulysses S. Grant noted, warfare was becoming increasingly progressive. Military observers from the United States led by Major Delafield had travelled to the Crimea where they had inspected the British and the Russian lines (in company with Danish officers) but not the French positions, Pélissier having decided that their findings might breach security. On their return to Washington they brought with them a weight of evidence which they were able to put to good use in planning reforms for the army of the United States at a time when the nation was becoming aware of its industrial potential. Some of those lessons would be put to good use in the American Civil War which broke out in 1861.

While the fighting in the Crimea was not entirely a product of advanced industrial technology, it did usher in several changes which were developed further during the north American conflict. Amongst the most important of these were field hospitals, the electric telegraph and improved semaphore signalling. In Peto and Brassey's Balaklava railway the Americans saw how railroads could be used to transfer wounded and move supplies and they took note of the advances being made in military aviation with the development of the gas-filled observation balloon. Civil war armies were the first to use railways to transport men and supplies – Sherman's advance from Chattanooga to Atlanta was facilitated by the Military Railroad Construction Corps – and the Union army was the first in the world to appoint specialist signalling officers.

Delafield's commission also reported on the influence of the Minié rifles used to such good effect by the British and French infantrymen but although they conceded that the new weapon had range, velocity and accuracy, only one member of the commission, Major George McClellan, noted its impact during the fighting on the Inkerman plateau. Its use made the old black powder muskets obsolete and gave the

British and French infantrymen a tactical advantage, but McClellan's fellow observers chose to focus on the siege and countersiege operations at Sevastopol in which the new rifle's employment was confined to sniping. In this respect they were also influenced by the findings of Antoine Henri Jomini, an energetic French staff officer whose study of the Crimean War rejected the idea that the new weapons would change the traditional massed frontal assault and close-quarter combat with the bayonet, the much vaunted *arme terrible*. His findings seemed to be reinforced by the magnitude of the French victories at Magenta and Solferino during the war to liberate northern Italy in 1859.

Instead of examining how the new weapons might affect battlefield tactics, the Americans concentrated on Todleben's field fortifications, much admired as a tactical defence system which did not require the construction of heavily entrenched positions. McClellan noted that they 'proved that temporary works in the hands of a skilful garrison are susceptible of a longer defense than was generally supposed' and this thinking inclined the US army to believe that entrenched defence could form the basis of its tactical system. In that sense the allies' experience at Sevastopol pointed the way to the siege of Vicksburg (1863) in which the Confederate defenders were able to repel frontal infantry assaults and in so doing force Grant's army to institute a formal siege. Frontal attacks also dominated the early battles, with disastrous results for the Union army at Bull Run when inexperienced troops broke and fled in the face of disciplined rifle power.

By the end of the fighting in 1865 the conflict in the United States had also brought change to the art of warfare. The north's superior manpower and its industrial base proved that the weight of well-organised men, reserves and materiel could be decisive; Sherman's introduction of 'total war' in his 'March through Georgia' destroyed civilian morale and the will to continue the war and, as happens in any conflict, technological changes were more rapid than they might have been in peace time. Rifled artillery and the field telegraph came into their own on the battlefield, and at sea the Confederate Navy's submersible boat *H.L. Hunley* sank the Yankee sloop *Housatonic* in 1864, the first time a surface warship was sunk by a submarine. Another factor which pointed to future wars came from the soldiers' experience of battle. With Springfield and Enfield rifles capable of killing the enemy at greater range than the old muskets, soldiers had to learn to take cover in trenches, massed infantry assaults were no longer acceptable and gradually the column gave way to more flexible formations. That, too, was new to warfare.

Given the impact it had, not just in the United States but also in the wider world, the American Civil War was much studied by the European powers – although, as with the Crimean War, the lessons were not always understood. Books about it are legion and the official US records alone run to 154 volumes. It has been described as the first of the modern wars, in that it produced a mighty volume of histories, personal recollections, newspaper reports, photographs, letters, diaries, and fiction, but the forerunner was the war in the Crimea which spawned a huge number of books, many of them written during the conflict or within a year or two of its conclusion.

From private to general, the soldiers wrote down their memories or published letters and diaries, sometimes writing with a passion or literary skill that surprised the Victorian reading public; it was a catharsis which was to have no equal until the First World War. Young Timothy Gowing, the parson's son who served in the Royal Fusiliers, wrote down his memories in *A Voice from the Ranks*, a lively and colourful account of the mixture of heroism (often unsung) and horror which coloured the conflict. Although he did not spare his audience a vividly realised picture of that terrible first winter and noted with approval *Punch*'s observation that the British troops were 'lions led by donkeys', he ended his account with the patriotic thought, 'Where is the Briton that would not do or die to uphold our glorious old flag?' There was a similar dichotomy in the letters of Henry Clifford, another of the war's better eyewitnesses from the front line. His account was not published until 1956, long after his death in 1883, but Clifford then emerged as one of the first writers to understand the silent nobility of the common soldier – not a saint but an ordinary man raised to a kind of greatness by the experience of adversity. His sketches, too, provide a graphic portrayal of what it was actually like to live through the shock of battle and its terrible aftermath of broken bodies. As General Sir Bernard Paget noted when the volume was published (one hundred years after the war ended), many of the scenes would not have looked out of place had they been produced in 1917 during the 3rd Battle of Ypres, or Passchendaele.

Inevitably, because it soon came to be the best remembered incident of the war (for the British at least), the Charge of Light Brigade was a favourite subject. Inevitably, too, due to the rancour that surrounded it, the battle was fought over again in print, not always to the pleasure of the main protagonists. When Somerset Calthorpe produced *Letters from Headquarters* in December 1856 his account of war contained five criticisms of Cardigan's behaviour, the most serious being that he refused to support Scarlett's Heavy Brigade and that he was unable to rally his own brigade once it had reached the Russian guns at the culmination of its own charge. Cardigan was outraged – Calthorpe's account was not only damaging, he claimed, but in places inaccurate – and he demanded that the author, still a serving officer, face a court-martial 'for scandalous and disgraceful conduct'. This was refused but following the intervention of his relative Lord Burghersh, Calthorpe agreed to make a number of emendations in the book's third edition.

There the matter might have rested but Cardigan could not let go and in 1863, following several unsuccessful attempts to put a stop to Calthorpe's military career, the Light Brigade's erstwhile commander eventually succeeded in bringing the case to court. Although the trial ended in Cardigan's favour, in that the judges agreed that Calthorpe had made serious errors and that Cardigan's reputation had been impugned, the case was dismissed, seven years being considered to be too long a period in which to bring criminal proceedings. The Light Brigade's commander also went to extraordinary lengths to convince A.W. Kinglake that he should vindicate him in his history of the war. Over fifty letters were written to the historian denying the 'shameful, vindictive and slanderous accusations' which had been made against him and demanding that he set the record straight.[1]

By then, thanks mainly to Tennyson's eulogy, the charge had passed into folk memory and several accounts, written by ordinary troopers, had been met with acclaim. Albert Mitchell's *Recollections of One of the Light Brigade* (1862) stands comparison with Gowing, while William Pennington's *Sea, Camp and Stage* (1906) covered not only his life as a soldier, including his suitably modest account of the charge, but also memories of his subsequent career as a Shakespearean actor with the Sadler's Wells company.

At the time of the Calthorpe trial public interest in the Crimean War had been reawakened by the publication of the first of the eight volumes of Kinglake's *The Invasion of the Crimea*. This was based almost entirely on the papers of Lord Raglan which his widow had passed on to Kinglake in 1856 once the war was over. As Kinglake told the Edinburgh publisher John Blackwood in September 1862, it included 'not only all secret despatches, but also the whole of his private correspondence with ministers, with ambassadors, with generals, with reigning monarchs, with all the public characters who were brought into relations with him during the war'. For any writer it was a fascinating archive but for a writer who had lived through the war and who had seen the fighting at first hand it was an opportunity to produce the definitive history of the war:

> Now in the army and among public men there is a belief that grave injustices was done [*sic*] at the time to this country, and to some of our officers and other public servants, including Lord Raglan himself, and it is imagined – I don't say rightly or wrongly – that I am the person who, with the materials above spoken of, is to redress all the wrongs and throw new light on the war.[2]

What was more, he added, his aunt was prepared to come up to Scotland to persuade Blackwood should he be in any doubt that the book was worth publishing. In fact the publisher needed little persuasion. Not only was John Blackwood one of the most able publishers of his day, the friend and editor of writers as different as Anthony Trollope and R.D. Blackmore, but he had just lost one of his protégés and needed to strengthen his list. Shortly before Kinglake had contacted him, Blackwood had seen George Eliot take her latest novel *Romola* to the *Cornhill Magazine* for the substantial sum of £10,000: having been published by the House of Blackwood since the publication of *Scenes of Clerical Life* (1857) she plainly felt that her literary talent deserved higher reward. That change of tack, due to 'pecuniary considerations', as her position was described so delicately, undoubtedly influenced Blackwood's decision to proceed with the substantial eight volumes of Kinglake's history.

It was worth the gamble even though Blackwood was forced to concede that the work had to be as substantial as the author wanted it to be. From being a planned two-volume history it doubled twice; the final volume appeared in 1887, the patient Blackwood having agreed that 'a book cannot be estimated like a web of cloth'. Each set of manuscripts arrived in a mahogany box which once belonged to Raglan and the book sold well, being produced in several editions until the end of the century. But its critical reception was divided. Many thought that Kinglake had been too fair to Raglan, by then discredited as a leader, and Kinglake's dislike of the French was considered to be an unnecessary bias in a book which claimed to be a standard work. None the less, it is a remarkable account, combining as it does an elegant literary style with Kinglake's eye-witness observations – to refresh his memory for the fifth volume, in 1868 he walked the battlefield of Inkerman in the company of Todleben. Despite Kinglake's thoroughness, though, later generations tended to be less tolerant of his efforts: in his magisterial *History of the British Army* Sir John Fortescue dismissed the eight volumes as being 'insufferably wordy, prolix and ill-arranged – journalism, not history.'[3]

A similar fate befell William Howard Russell, at least as far as his reputation as a historian is concerned. Although he wrote two instant accounts of the campaign on his return – *The Complete History of the Crimean War* (1856) and *The British Expedition to the Crimea* (1858) – neither stood the test of the time. In contrast to Kinglake he was criticised for being too hard on Raglan and later critics scorned his fondness for using clichés such as 'the pride and splendour of war' to describe the charge of the Light Brigade. However, those shortcomings cannot detract from his achievement. Derided by Prince Albert as 'that miserable scribbler' and generally loathed by Raglan and his staff, he stuck to his task and was not afraid to reveal the many 'unpleasantnesses' he witnessed in the British camp during the first winter in the Crimea.

He returned home to a hero's welcome and to a lucrative lecture tour; and *The Times* added to the gloss by cancelling all his advance expense claims. The first of the war correspondents, Russell was to add to his deserved reputation by covering the Indian Mutiny and the American Civil War, and later in life he wrote despatches from the Austro-Prussian, Franco-Prussian and Zulu wars.

As the century progressed into its second half and the Victorians began to regard their empire as a great mission, publishers discovered that the reading public had an insatiable appetite for matters military, not just accounts of warfare but even analyses of defence questions. When Kinglake went to Blackwood he was accepted into the publisher's 'military staff' which included Laurence Oliphant who had covered the fighting in Circassia for *The Times* and Edward Hamley, author of *The Campaign of Sebastopol*, who later became professor of military history at the army's Staff College and whose *Operations of War* became a standard military text on its publication in 1867.

The other protagonists in the war also produced their versions of what happened. Bazancourt proved himself to be as prolific and as opinionated as Kinglake. Although fiercely partisan – after all, his commission to cover the war came from Napoleon III – his two volumes, *Cinq mois devant Sébastopol* (1855) and *L'expédition jusqu'à La Prise de Sébastopol* are good accounts of the tensions within French headquarters and they provide a readable, if one-sided view of the operations in the Crimea. Unlike their British counterparts all of the leading French commanders published their letters and diaries, Bosquet being a particularly astute observer of the war itself and events at headquarters. Canrobert also took the opportunity to set the record straight, or at least to provide his own version of events by dictating parts of a biography which was published together with his letters at the century's end. There are also a number of good first-hand accounts, the best being Joseph Cler's *Reminiscences of an Officer of Zouaves* but because France was soon engaged in another continental land war, against Austria in 1859, the fighting in the Crimea never captured the public's imagination in the way that it did in Britain.

Being the defeated party, Russia's historical literature from the war is dominated by recrimination amongst the leading military commanders. Full of claim and counter-claim, it makes unedifying reading, the principal commanders being more concerned to put their efforts into a good light than with any attempt to produce acceptable eye-witness accounts. Freed from the censorship which had prevailed during the war, editors made full use of the material available to them and, joyously putting the laws of libel to one side, published the descriptions of battle, however scurrilous or mendacious they might be. Kiriakov's account of his own heroism at the Alma has been described as completely fictitious from start to finish.

Surprisingly perhaps, there is no quality fiction from the war apart from Tolstoy's luminous *Sevastopol Sketches* which were published as the fighting took place and were subject, therefore, to official censorship. It has been argued, too, Tolstoy's experiences at Silistria and inside Sevastopol gave him the raw material for the battle scenes in *War and Peace*, realistic descriptions which could not have been written by anyone without military experience. Neither, *pace* Tennyson, did the war produce much poetry that goes beyond simple patriotic sentiment. But in its day and continuing long after it had passed into memory, the war in the Crimea exerted a fascination and produced a literature that far outstripped its importance at the time. For the British at least it remained an obsession principally because, for the first time, the public was brought face to face with the plight of ordinary soldiers and, having been exposed to the suffering, they showed that they cared. That they did was due entirely to the efforts of the writers who produced such eloquent and realistic accounts about what was unfolding in front of their eyes. In that respect at least the Crimean War may be counted as the first of the literary wars.

For the soldiers and sailors who took part in the battles, the war's shadow proved to be long and lasting. Although few of the senior commanders would see further action – showing self-control and a healthy realism Codrington twice refused the rank of field-marshal because the Crimean War was his only experience of active service – the war was to spawn several field-marshals including Colin Campbell, the Duke of Cambridge (appointed the army's commander-in-chief in 1856), Lord Lucan and two junior officers who had seen service in the trenches before Sevastopol, Wolseley and Wood, the latter having transferred from the Royal Navy to the army. Both men were deeply committed to the reforms which swept through the War Office in the 1860s and 1870s, much to the consternation of the conservative Cambridge, and both became well-known as soldiers and administrators. Both, too, were to be involved in the operations to save another Crimean War veteran – Charles George Gordon, a charismatic engineering officer who was murdered in Khartoum by Islamic fanatics in 1885, an incident which was to turn him into one of the many icons of the Victorian empire.

Unfortunately, for all that the Crimean War and, to an equal extent, the American Civil War were subjected to minute research and analysis, and although many younger soldiers learned greatly from the experience of the fighting, the military realities were not always fully comprehended. For the next fifty years only the Anglo-Egyptian campaign in the Sudan, fought between 1885 and 1898, was to provide British generals with command on the scale enjoyed by Raglan but as it was against lightly-armed native opposition it could hardly be counted as modern warfare. It would take the humiliating experiences of the Boer War in South Africa to demonstrate to the British Army that it still had much to learn.

Fortunately, the educational process had been improved by 1914 when another British expeditionary force was deployed in continental Europe, almost sixty years to the month after Raglan had taken his army to Eupatoria. Its mobilisation and movement to France were smooth and professional, it was well equipped, its men were disciplined and well trained and its senior commanders were experienced and highly motivated. Small, well organised and prepared, it was by far the best army which Britain had ever despatched on overseas service: it was not its fault that it quickly became bogged down in static trench warfare which required the raising of a huge volunteer army to crack the tactical stranglehold. For the first time in history the opposing armies had sufficient manpower and firepower to batten down one another along a front hundreds of miles long. There was no room for flanking manoeuvres or movement of any kind. This was to be a war of entrenchment, artillery barrage and offensives in which superior force would win the day.

In that respect the Crimean War is Janus-like. It was rooted in the black-powder art of warfare, its tactics were little different from those employed in the Napoleonic Wars, the fronts were small and manageable and senior commanders fought in the same claustrophobic front lines as their men, just as Wellington and his generals had done. And yet, with its technological innovations and the changing pace of warfare, it also foreshadowed the trenches and high velocity weapons of the First World War. Seen in that unforgiving light it is a punctuation mark which emerged almost halfway between the victory at Waterloo of 1815, which gave Europe forty years of peace, and the fighting in Flanders in 1914 which plunged Europe into a century of almost continuous warfare and confrontation between the great powers.

Epilogue

1914

There is a dry wind blowing through the East, and the parched grasses wait the spark.

John Buchan, Greenmantle, 1916

In the summer of 1914 the events of the Crimean War were as distant from the minds of most of the people of Europe as were the battles of the Napoleonic wars or the dynastic wars of the eighteenth century. Most of the men who had served in the Crimea itself or in the Baltic area of operations were dead or very old indeed and only a tiny handful of British officers could be found wearing the blue and yellow ribbon of the Crimean War Medal or the reversed gold and deep azure of the Baltic Medal. It was simply part of history, remembered for the courage of the soldiers and sailors and for the dreadful blunders which had been the downfall of so many of them. And in that time, generations of young men had grown to manhood without having to fight on the European mainland, a lengthy period of grace without equivalent in recent times. True, there had been the short sharp war of 1870–1 when Prussia had humbled France; squabbles in the Balkans had also overheated into war but in the last two decades of the century Europe was a relatively quiet place.

It was prosperous and productive, too. Advances in technology, the fruits of the industrial revolution, had produced new and increasingly cheaper consumer goods and the means of transporting them to new markets. At sea the age of sail was passing into memory as faster and bigger steamships began to rule the oceans, while on land the inexorable march of the railway system helped to shrink distances on the continent. Even Russia, so backward sixty years earlier, had managed to acquire 30,000 miles of railroad, albeit using a broader gauge than was found elsewhere in Europe. The telegraph, too, had made the world a smaller place: the first transatlantic cable had been laid in 1858 and by 1900, following the inventions of Alexander Graham Bell, Emile Berliner and Thomas Edison, the United States, Britain and most of the leading European countries had extensive telephone systems under full or partial government control.

The sense of self-confidence was matched by the buoyant financial markets. The United States had emerged as the largest economy in the world, accounting for one-third of the global industrial output, but its strength was also bolstered by gold-based investment from Europe to the tune of £350 million a year. Much of it passed through the City of London, making its bankers and financiers part of an international cartel, so linked and mutually dependent were the world's markets. In that atmosphere of co-operation, in which money circulated freely, the idea of war was abhorrent. In 1910, in his influential book *The Great Illusion* the economist Norman Angell contended that the triumph of international credit had destroyed for ever the need for the great nations to go to war: 'How can modern life, with its overpowering proportion of industrial activities and its infinitesimal proportion of military, keep alive the instincts associated with war as against those developed by peace?'

Many other links bound the world together. International bodies had been created to codify the laws of trade, communication, transport and ideas. Tourism had encouraged the middle classes to take their holidays in other countries whose pleasures were extolled by *Baedeker's Guides*, the bible of the moneyed tourist. Whether it was to the canals of Venice, the French Riviera or the German spa towns, people came together from all over Europe, provided of course that they had the money to pay for the adventure, and there was a general sense that the treasures of other countries had become communal properties. In E.M. Forster's *A Room with a View* long-established residents of the Florentine *pension* told new arrivals what to see, how to stop the electric trams, how to get rid of the beggars, how much to give for a vellum blotter, how much the place would grow upon them. 'Prato! They must go to Prato. That place is too sweetly squalid for words.'

And yet, despite the coherence of those financial and cultural relationships, there were disturbing undercurrents. Although there had been well-meant attempts to limit arms production and to revise the rules and customs of warfare there was no means of diplomatic arbitration: in place of the Concert of Europe which had given the continent half a century of peace there was a series of alliances which provided a balance of power of sorts to keep the rivalries in check. Austria-Hungary was linked to the new state of Germany and to Italy in a Triple Alliance; France marched with Russia and had an attachment to Britain through the Entente Cordiale. While the system was supposed to prevent war by making it unprofitable or self-defeating there was no shortage of potential flashpoints.

France's defeat at the hands of Prussia in 1871 and the forfeiture of all of Alsace and much of Lorraine still rankled. In the Place de la Concorde in Paris the statue of Strasbourg was covered in black crepe and surrounded by mourning garlands in perpetual grieving, and patriots like Léon Gambetta (who raised the flag of the Third Republic) told the people of France that they should never forget the dishonour. For her part Germany hankered after even more territory: nationalists flattered Kaiser Wilhelm II by telling him that his empire should stretch eastwards to embrace Russia's Polish provinces and the Baltic states. After that, why not the world or, at least, new colonies in the undeveloped colonies? Russia, too, had ambitions, especially in the Balkans where Tsar Nicholas II saw himself as the protector of the Slav races and the champion of Serbia, the most powerful of the Balkan states. Inevitably that created tension with Austria-Hungary, since 1867 a dual monarchy, which viewed with ever-growing suspicion the burgeoning Slav nationalism in the Balkans.

As for Britain, it had emerged from one of its periodic states of splendid isolation and was much alarmed by Germany's growing naval power. In 1900 Germany had enacted its Second Naval law to create a battle fleet which could rival the Royal Navy. With its naked territorial ambitions, not just in eastern Europe but also in Africa and the Pacific where the other great European powers had developed colonial empires, Germany was a threat to world stability and Britain was right to treat it with a great deal of suspicion. In 1905 and 1911 Germany had already manufactured crises with France over the extension of French influence in Morocco, both of which had been solved by arbitration. Even so the crises had convinced the warmongers that a European war was inevitable. 'It is false that in Germany the nation is peaceful but the government bellicose,' wrote the French ambassador Jules Cambon. 'The exact opposite is true.'

However, it was the Balkans which provided the lighted fuse. Just as Tsar Nicholas I had prophesied in 1853, the collapse of the Ottoman Empire, the 'sick man of Europe', had left the Eastern Question unanswered and in its unsolved state it continued to be a threat to European stability. The principal villain was Serbia which had been independent of Ottoman rule since 1878 and it had used the intervening period to extend its power and authority as a focus for Slav nationalist aspirations. Following the confused fighting in the Balkan Wars of 1912 and 1913, when Serbia first defeated the Ottoman forces and then those of its ally Bulgaria, it had received most of the province of Macedonia while the southern Dobrudja was ceded to Romania. But that was not enough: the Serbs still wanted access to the Adriatic, a move which would be hostile not just to neighbouring Italy but, more importantly, to Austria-Hungary. Not only was Vienna alarmed by the doubling in size of Serbia but it feared that its growing authority in the Balkans would encourage Slavs elsewhere to rise against the rule of the Austro-Hungarian empire.

Their fears were not groundless. Following years of bloody warfare against the Ottoman Empire the Serbs had emerged as a bellicose and backward state, quick to take offence and slow to forgive. Its history had been marked by ferocious battles in which Serbs had fought against their natural enemies and, when honour was threatened, amongst their own kind. In 1903 a group of Serb officers had shocked the rest of the world by first killing their king and queen and then throwing the bodies into the street below before hacking them to pieces. The Slav nationalists within the Hapsburg empire were no different and had created a number of secret organisations to work against what they regarded as Hapsburg oppression. If necessary, they had vowed to use violence as the final solution.

An opportunity for revenge came in the summer of 1914 when the Austro-Hungarian army held its manoeuvres in Bosnia, an Ottoman province which had been annexed by Austria-Hungary in 1908 and which contained a sizeable Slav population. With unthinking reck-lessness the army's Inspector-General, the Archduke Franz Ferdinand, concluded the military exercises on 28 June with an official visit to Sarajevo, the regional capital. This was not just the third last day of the month but a date dear to the Serb cause: Vidovdan, or St Vitus's Day, the anniversary of the great Battle of Kosovo, fought in 1389 between Serb and Ottoman forces. Although it resulted in victory for the Ottomans it remains a holy day, the date from which Serb nationalists began their long battle against Ottoman oppression. Six centuries later, though, the Turks had been replaced by the Hapsburgs as oppressors and tension in Sarajevo was high. Here was a chance for the fanatics to rewrite history; death threats had been made and the local administration had no reason to discount them.

What followed was predictable. Franz Ferdinand and his wife were assassinated by a Slav terrorist, though an Austrian citizen, called Gavrilo Princip. Subsequent investigation found that his five-man terrorist group had been given substantial assistance by the Serb armed forces and this was reinforced when they made a full confession on 2 July. It will probably never be known if they acted with the complicity of the Serb government or if they were under orders from Serb military intelligence but the evidence and the confession gave Austria-Hungary a pretext for revenge. Had they then acted decisively, and launched an immediate military operation to punish Serbia, they would not have raised the temperature in Europe sufficiently for the other powers to intervene; but, fatally, Count Berthold, the Austro-Hungarian foreign minister, hesitated.

First he set about ensuring the support of Germany and only then did he consider military action. Then it was felt necessary to send an ultimatum to Belgrade but this was not despatched until 23 July, almost a month after the assassination had taken place. None the less, it made draconian demands, the most serious being an insistence that Austro-Hungarian officials should take part in the arrest and punishment of Princip's aiders and abettors. Had Austria-Hungary acted unilaterally and declared war on Serbia the quarrel would have remained a local one, confined to the two countries, and there would have been no flashpoint and no outside involvement. But as the Serb ministers deliberated and prepared to surrender the points to their great rivals they heard from St Petersburg that Nicholas II had put his army on a war footing by announcing a 'Period Preliminary to War'.

That changed everything. With Russian support the Serbs could take on Austria-Hungary. They agreed to most of the demands but not to the clause which allowed Austria-Hungary to interfere in their domestic legal affairs and that dusty reply was despatched to Vienna on 25 July. The next day Serb forces mobilised and Russia began recalling its reservists. It was not quite war by timetable but Europe was now sliding inexorably towards Armageddon. On 28 July Austria-Hungary finally declared war on Serbia, two days later the Russians began a general mobilisation, the news of which prompted

Germany to declare war on her the next day. On 3 August Germany presented France with a declaration of war and delivered an ultimatum to Belgium demanding the use of its territory for military operations. That settled Britain's position. Not only was she linked to France through the Entente but by treaty she was bound to defend Belgium's territorial integrity. Signed in 1839, the treaty was largely the work of Sir George Hamilton Seymour, the British ambassador who had overseen his country's interests in St Petersburg when Britain had last drifted into a European war. On 4 August an ultimatum was sent to Berlin demanding the cancellation of military operations against Belgium. No answer was returned and at midnight Britain found itself at war with Germany.

The resulting war lasted four years and cost almost nine million lives. It also revived memories of the fighting in the Crimea sixty years earlier. Not only did the warfare in France and Flanders soon become a stalemate, with trench systems and artillery barrages which would have been familiar, albeit on a grander scale, to anyone who had observed the operations outside Sevastopol, but many of the place-names brought echoes of the earlier conflict. In October, in one of the first naval actions of the war, two German warships, the *Goeben* and the *Breslau*, flying the Turkish flag, bombarded Odessa and then Sevastopol, setting fire to petrol storage tanks and destroying granaries. At the time of the action, almost a Sinope in reverse, the German naval commander Admiral Wilhelm Souchon said that he had 'thrown the Turks into the powder keg' and he was not far wrong. Following Turkey's entry into the war on Germany's side Russian troops crossed Turkey's eastern border on 3 November and three days later Britain declared war on the Ottoman Empire. Echoing the sentiments voiced by Aberdeen in 1853, Margaret Asquith, wife of the British prime minister, wrote in her diary that night: 'I loathe the Turk and really hoped that he will be wiped out of Europe.'

It was to be easier said than done. Although a British-Indian force was despatched to the head of the Persian Gulf to protect the oilfields at Abadan the war against the Turks was to be no walkover. Early in 1915 the British and French war planners believed that they could achieve an easy victory by forcing the Dardanelles with a powerful naval force which would break through the Narrows into the Sea of Marmara, destroy the Turkish defences, and then proceed to bombard Constantinople. Hopes were high that the Turks would surrender and that the allies would then be in a position to impose conditions which would not only take them out of the war but would also result in the dismemberment of the Ottoman Empire. The attack would also relieve pressure on the Russians who were facing a powerful Ottoman force in the Caucasus. In a secret concordat signed with Russia on 20 March it was agreed that, in return for giving Britain hegemony in Mesopotamia, and France in Syria and the Lebanon, Russia would be given mastery of Constantinople and the Straits. It seemed to escape the negotiators' attention that Britain and France had gone to war with Russia in 1854 with the sole intention of avoiding that eventuality.

Troops were also made available to storm the Gallipoli peninsula once the naval attack had reduced the Turkish defences and it was hoped that, if successful, the operation would encourage Bulgaria and Greece to throw in their lot with the allies. However, everything depended on the battleships and when the attack began on 18 March the joint British-French squadron found that they had as fruitless a task as their predecessors enjoyed when attacking Sevastopol sixty years earlier. In addition to receiving direct hits from the Turkish artillery some foundered on the mines which the Turks had sown in great quantities at the entrance to the Narrows. Amongst the ships damaged were *Agamemnon*, successor to Lyons's flagship in the Black Sea, and *Charlemagne* whose namesake had so impressed the Sultan when it sailed through the Dardanelles in 1853. The failure led to a belated decision to land ground forces composed of British, Australian, New Zealand and French troops.

The operation proved to be as improvised as anything attempted by Raglan and Saint-Arnaud when they reconnoitred the Crimean coast-line between Eupatoria and Sevastopol. There was inadequate intelligence about Turkish dispositions and manpower and the decisions for landing were based on the same guesswork which took Raglan to the beaches at Eupatoria. The commanders even lacked detailed maps of the areas which were about to be attacked. In short it was a recipe for the disaster which followed hard on the heels of the first landings on 25 April. The allies failed to move out of their beach-heads and the fighting in Gallipoli quickly became bogged down in bloody trench warfare. By the time that the allies abandoned the peninsula early the following year they had lost 265,000 casualties, the Turks 300,000.

Gallipoli was not the last echo from the Crimea. In the summer Romania entered the war only to be defeated along the Danube and in the Dobrudja by General August von Mackensen's Bulgarian

Danube Army Group. By the end of the year Bucharest had fallen and Romanian resistance was confined to a rump of 350,000 troops which managed to retreat back into Moldavia where they enjoyed the protection of their Russian ally. More was to follow. Following the collapse of tsarist authority in the spring of 1917 the Germans took advantage of the turmoil to sweep into the Baltic provinces. Unable to broker a satisfactory peace with the new revolutionary government German troops invaded the Ukraine and at the beginning of May the following year General Groener's forces took one day to capture the port and fortress of Sevastopol. From the Baltic to the Black Sea the war was over.

It was, though, a short-lived triumph: within six months the war had run its course and another peace congress was summoned in Paris, to be held at the palace of Versailles. For the participants the proceedings brought little reward. Germany, the country which sprang into life in the years after the Crimean War, was humiliated by the demands of the treaty which ended the conflict. Russia was plunged into a civil war which produced the triumph of a communist dictatorship and long years of repression. For the Austro-Hungarian empire it was also the end of the line; it disintegrated completely and Vienna would never again play any role in deciding European affairs. The war also solved the Eastern Question by destroying Ottoman power once and for all: by 1923 the Sultanate had been abolished and Turkey had become a republic under the leadership of Mustafa Kemal whose soldiers had defied the allied invasion of Gallipoli eight years earlier.

France suffered in ways that Britain never did: her casualties were greater and much of the war had been fought over her land. It was not be wondered that, having fought the Germans twice in forty years, they were unforgiving and insisted that Germany pay for all the death and destruction.

Of the great powers, apart from the United States which became the world's strongest power, Britain emerged with a relatively light bill. Although the country was in debt to the United States and had to rebuild its merchant fleet, there had been no fighting on home territory, the casualties were fewer in comparison to those of France or Germany and the war had introduced technical innovations which helped to modernise British industry. On the battlefield its army had also been victorious, having defeated the Germans in a series of hard-won victories in 1918. It was not the fault of the soldiers that at Versailles the politicians made a compromise peace which was too weak to destroy German militarism and not strong enough to break nationalist resolve to overturn its conditions.

Versailles in 1919 was as unsatisfactory as Paris had been in 1856. It was born of compromise – like Russia, Germany had not been completely defeated in the field – and as the conference progressed it led to further concessions. By fudging territorial issues it also paved the way for future conflicts. Forced to surrender territory and to disarm, Germany felt aggrieved and remained bitter at heart for the next two decades. When another world war broke out twenty years later it was simply a continuation of the one which had preceded it. Versailles also sowed other unwelcome seeds. Serbia became Yugoslavia in 1929, but Yugoslavia lacked true homogeneity and by the end of the century the Balkans had plunged once more into anarchy and factionalism. Indeed it is one of the ironies of European history that the century is ending with outside powers intervening in the Balkan wars and making demands of the Serbs which would not be unfamiliar to the Hapsburg government of 1914.

By then, there had been two other European conflicts: the Second World War, fought between 1939 and 1945, which finally crushed German nationalism; then the Cold War which lasted until the collapse of communism in Russia in 1991. Costly in national resources and lives, the confrontation between the United States and the Soviet Union and their various allies lasted almost half a century and during that time a fragile peace was only preserved by a precarious balance of power based on the possession of weapons of mass destruction. It also continued the process of bringing Russia to its knees which had begun in the Crimea and continued with the First and Second World Wars. Only when the people of Russia rejected communism, followed in quick succession by its rout in the satellite countries of the Warsaw Pact, could Europe finally put war behind it. From Waterloo in 1815, through the Crimea in 1856 and the western and eastern fronts of 1918 and 1945 Europe has come a long way. Instead of endless warfare followed by a succession of treaties which failed to solve the underlying problems, Europe is gradually being locked together by economic, financial and cultural bonds which would have astonished Castlereagh or Metternich, far less Clarendon or Orlov. There is nothing guaranteed about the new order but, following two centuries of mayhem from the Baltic to the Black Sea and the Mediterranean, and from the Urals to the Atlantic, war between the great nations of Europe might just have become the stuff of history books.

Bibliography

Primary Sources

Public Record Office, Kew
ADM1
FO 5: Papers of the Washington Embassy
FO 7: Papers of the Vienna Embassy
FO 27: Papers of the Paris Embassy
FO 65: Papers of the St Petersburg Embassy
FO 78: Papers of the Constantinople Embassy
FO 352: Stratford de Redcliffe Papers
FO 362: Granville Papers
FO 519: Cowley Papers
FO 634: Blockade of Russian Ports
PC 6: Privy Council Records
PRO 30/12/18 Ellenborough Papers
PRO 32/22/12: Russell Papers
PRO 30/46: Eyre Papers
WO 3: Commander-in-Chief's out-letters
WO 4: Secretary at War's out-letters
WO 6: Secretary of State for War's out-letters
WO 14: Scutari Depot Minute Books
WO 28: Headquarters Records of the Crimea
WO 31: Commander-in-Chief's memoranda papers
WO 33: Miscellaneous Papers 1853–1930
WO 60: Commissariat Accounts
WO 62: Commissariat letter books
WO 93: Army Supplies Enquiry

Bodleian Library, Oxford
Clarendon Deposit

British Library, London
Aberdeen Papers
Broughton Papers
Palmerston Letterbooks
Strathnairn Papers (Henry Rose)

National Army Museum, London
Codrington Papers
Raglan Papers

National Library of Scotland, Edinburgh
Brown Papers
Blackwood Papers

Royal Archives, Windsor
RA A24–25, 639–43: Papers of Queen Victoria and Prince Albert

Scottish Record Office, Edinburgh
Dalhousie Muniment (Panmure Papers)
Archive du Ministère des Affaires Étrangères, Paris
Archive Diplomatique Français. Correspondence Politique, Russie

National Archives and Records Administration
Archive of the Department of State, Washington
Diplomatic Despatches from US Ministers; to Britain vol. 66; France
    vol. 36; Russia vol. 16

Official Publications

London
1854–5: Report from the Select Committee on the Army before
    Sebastopol, ix, I, II, III
1854–5: Report upon the State of the hospitals of the British Army
    in the Crimea and Scutari, xxxiii, I
1854–5: Order in Council, Regulating the Establishment of the Civil
    Departments, xxxii, 677
1854–5: Copies of Correspondence relating to the state of the Harbour
    of Balaclava, xxxiv, 107
1856: Reports from the Commission of Inquiry into the Supplies of
    the British Army in the Crimea, xx, 1
1856: Report of the Board of General Officers appointed to inquire
    into Statements contained in the Reports of Sir John McNeill and
    Colonel Tulloch, xxi, 1

1857: Return of casualties in the Crimea (Sess. 1), ix, 7

1857: Report to the Ministry of War of the proceedings of the Sanitary Commission despatched to the Seat of War in the East, 1855–6 (Sess. 1), lx, 241

Paris

Recueils des traités de la Porte Ottomane, avec les puissances étranges, 11 vols 1864–1911

St Petersburg

Recueil des traités et conventions conclus par la Russie avec les puissances étranges, 15 vols, 1874–1906

Vienna

Österreichische Akten zur Geschichte des Krimkrieges. 1-er Serie

Die Protokolle des Österreichischen Ministerrates 1848–1867, Österreichischer Bundesverlag für Unterrichte, Wissenschaft und Kunst, 1-er Serie

Washington

Report. US Senate, 34th Congress, 1857. Special Session. Exec. Doc. no. 1

Report on the Art of War in Europe, 1854, 1855 and 1856. Military Commission to the Theater of War in Europe. Senate Exec. Doc. no. 59. 36th Congress, 1st Session. 1860

Newspapers and Periodicals

American Historical Review
Blackwood's Magazine
British Army Review
English Historical Review
Historical Journal
History
Illustrated London News
Journal of the Society for Army Historical Research
Journal of Modern History
Morning Post
Naval and Military Gazette

Nineteenth Century
Punch
RUSI Journal
The Scotsman
Slavic Review
The Times
United Service Gazette
United Service Magazine
Victorian Studies
The War Correspondent

Secondary Sources

(i) Historical Studies

Adkin, Mark, *The Charge: The Real Reason Why the Light Brigade was Lost* (London, 1996)

Anderson, Olive, *A Liberal State at War: English Politics and Economics during the Crimean War* (London, 1967)

Bapst, Germain, Le Marechal Canrobert: *Souvenirs d'un Siècle*, vols. 1–VI (Paris, 1909–1913)

Barnett, Correlli, *Britain and Her Army* (London, 1970)

Baumgart, Winfried, *The Peace of Paris 1856: Studies in War, Diplomacy and Peacemaking*, trs. Ann Pottinger Saab (Santa Barbara and Oxford, 1981)

Bonner-Smith, D. and Dewar, A. C., *The Russian War 1854: Baltic and Black Sea Correspondence* (London, 1943)

Chamberlain, M.E., *Lord Aberdeen: A Political Biography* (London, 1983)

Chandler, David, and Beckett, Ian (eds), *The Oxford History of the British Army* (Oxford, 1994)

Clowes, William Laird, *The Royal Navy: A History*, vol. VI (London, 1901)

Compton, Piers, *Colonel's Lady and Camp Follower: The Story of Women in the Crimea* (London, 1970)

Conacher, J.B., *The Aberdeen Coalition* (London, 1968)
Britain and the Crimea (London, 1987)

Cunningham, Allan, *Anglo-Ottoman Encounters in the Age of Revolution* (London, 1993);

——*Eastern Questions in the 19th Century* (London, 1993)

Curtiss, J.S., *The Russian Army under Nicholas I, 1825–1855* (Durham NC, 1965)

Russia's Crimean War (Durham NC, 1979)

David, Saul, *The Homicidal Earl: The Life of Lord Cardigan* (London, 1997)

Dowty, Alan, *The Limits of American Isolation: The United States and the Crimean War* (New York, 1971)

Douglas, Sir George, *The Panmure Papers*, 2 vols. (London, 1908)

Ettinger, Amos, *The Mission to Spain of Pierre Soulé: A Study in the Cuban Diplomacy of United States* (London, 1932)

ffrench Blake, R.L.V., *The Crimean War* (London, 1971)

Fortescue, The Hon J.W., *A History of the British Army*, vol. XIII (London, 1930)

Goldfrank, David M., *The Origins of the Crimean War* (London, 1994)

Gooch, Brison D., *The New Bonapartist Generals in the Crimean War* (The Hague, 1959)

Gouttman, Alain, *La Guerre de Crimée* (Paris, 1996)

Greenhill, Basil and Giffard, Ann, *The British Assault on Finland* (London, 1988)

Grunwald, Constantin, *Tsar Nicholas I*, trs. Brigit

Guedalla, Philip, *The Two Marshals* (London, 1943)

Hagerman, Edward, *The American Civil War and the Origins of Modern Warfare* (Bloomington & Indianapolis, 1988)

Hibbert, Christopher, *The Destruction of Lord Raglan* (London, 1961)

Hoppen, K. Theodore, *The Mid-Victorian Generation 1846–1886, New Oxford History of England*, vol. III (Oxford, 1998)

Ingle, Harold, *Nesselrode and the Russian Rapprochement with Britain 1836–1844* (Berkeley, 1976)

James, Lawrence, *Crimea: The War with Russia from Contemporary Photographs* (Thame, 1981)

Kerr, Paul et al, *The Crimean War* (London, 1997)

Kinglake, A.W., *The Invasion of the Crimea*, 8 vols. (Edinburgh, 1863–87)

Krasinski, W.S., *Russia and Europe: The Possible Consequences of the Present War* (Edinburgh, 1854)

Lambert, Andrew, *The Crimean War: British Grand Strategy 1855–1856* (Manchester, 1990)

Laughton, John Knox, *Memoirs of the Life and Correspondence of Henry Reeve*, vol. I (London, 1898)

Lavrin, Janko, Russia, *Slavdom and the Western World* (London, 1969)

Lincoln, W. Bruce, *Nicholas I* (London, 1978)

McMunn, Sir George, *The Crimea in Perspective* (London, 1935)

Mosse, W.E., *The Rise and Fall of the Crimean System 1855–1871* (London, 1963)

Moyse-Bartlett, Hubert, *Louis Edward Nolan and his Influence on the British Cavalry* (London, 1971)

Palmer, Alan, *The Banner of Battle* (London, 1987)

Puryear, V.J., *England, Russia and the Straits Question* (Berkeley, 1931)

Rich, Norman, *Why the Crimean War?* (Hanover, 1989)

Ridley, Jaspar, *Palmerston* (London, 1970)

Saab, Ann Pottinger, *The Origins of the Crimean Alliance* (Charlottesville, 1977)

Schroeder, Paul, *Austria, Great Britain and the Crimean War* (New York, 1972)

Seaton, Albert, *The Crimean War: A Russian Chronicle* (London, 1977)

Smith, E.F.M., *The Life of Stratford Canning* (London, 1933)

Spiers, Edward, *The Army and Society 1815–1914* (London, 1980)

Strachan, Hew, *From Waterloo to Balaclava: Tactics, Technology and the British Army* (London, 1985)

Sweetman, John, *Raglan: From the Peninsula to the Crimea* (London, 1993)

Tarle, E.V., *Krymskaia Voina* (Moscow, 1950)

Temperley, Harold, *England and the Near East* (London, 1936)
    Foundations of British Foreign Policy (London, 1938)

Weintraub, Stanley, *Disraeli* (London, 1993)
    Albert (London, 1997)

Wellesley, F.A. (ed.), *The Paris Embassy during the Second Empire* (London, 1928)

Woodham-Smith, Cecil, *The Reason Why* (London, 1957)
    Florence Nightingale (London, 1964)
    Queen Victoria (London, 1972)

(ii) Personal Accounts

Adye, John, *A Review of the Crimean War to the Winter of 1854–1855* (London, 1860)

Anglesey, Marquess of (ed.), *Little Hodge* (London, 1971)

Anstruther Thomor, John, *Eighty Years' Reminiscences*, vol. 1 (London, 1904)

Argyll, George Douglas, 8th Duke of, *Autobiography and Memoirs*, vol. II (London, 1906)

Bazancourt, C.L., *Cinq mois devant Sebastopol: L'Expedition de Crimée jusqu' à la pris de Sebastopol*, trs. Gould, 2 vols. (London, 1856)

Bentley, Nicholas, *Russell's Despatches from the Crimea* (London, 1970)

Bonham-Carter, Victor (ed.), *Surgeon in the Crimea: The Experiences of George Lawson, recorded in letters to his family* (London, 1968)

Bosquet, P.F.J., *Lettres du Maréchal Bosquet à sa Mere*, 4 vols. (Pau, 1877–79)

Lettres du Maréchal Bosquet à ses Amis, 2 vols. (Pau, 1879)

Lettres du Maréchal Bosquet 1830–1858 (Paris, 1894)

Buzzard, Surgeon Thomas, *With the Turkish Army in the Crimea and Asia Minor* (London, 1915)

Calthorpe, Somerset, *Letters from Headquarters, by an Officer on the Staff,* (London, 1856)

Campbell, Colin Frederick, *Letters from Camp to His Relatives during the Siege of Sevastopol* (London, 1894)

Cardigan, Earl of, *Eight Months on Active Service* (London, 1855)

Christian, R.F., ed., *Tolstoy's Diaries* (London, 1984)

Tolstoy's Letters, vol. 1 (London, 1978)

Clifford, Henry, *Henry Clifford VC: His Letters and Sketches from the Crimea*, ed. C. Fitzherbert (London, 1956)

Don, William, *A Scot on Board the Duke of Wellington* (Brechin, 1894)

Duberly, Mrs, *Journal Kept during the Crimean War* (London, 1855)

Farquharson, Robert Stuart, *Reminiscences of Crimean Campaigning and Russian Imprisonment* (Glasgow, 1882)

Franks, Sergeant-Major Henry, *Leaves from a Soldier's Notebook* (privately printed, 1904)

Gernsheim, Helmut and Alison (eds.), *Roger Fenton: Photographer of the Crimea* (London, 1954)

Goldie, Sue M., *I have done my duty: Florence Nightingale in the Crimean War 1854–56* (Manchester, 1987)

Gowing, Timothy, *A Soldier's Story, or a Voice from the Ranks* (Nottingham, 1883); quoted from Kenneth Fenwick (ed.), *Voice from the Ranks* (London, 1954)

Hamley, E. Bruce: *The Story of the Campaign of Sebastopol* (Edinburgh, 1855)

Hodasevich, Captain R. (Captain Chodasiewicz), *A Voice from within the Walls of Sebastopol* (London, 1856)

Hughes, Rev R.E., *Two Summer Cruises with the Baltic Fleet* (London, 1855)

Lake, H.A., *Narrative of the Defence of Kars* (London, 1857)

Loy Smith, George, *A Victorian RSM* (London, 1987)

MacMullen, J.M., *Camp and Barrack Room, or The British Army as it is, by a late Staff-Sergeant of the 13th Light Infantry* (London, 1846)

Maxwell, Sir Herbert (ed.), *The Life and Letters of George William Frederick, 4th Earl of Clarendon*, 2 vols. (London, 1913)

Mitchell, Albert, *Recollections of One of the Light Brigade* (Canterbury, 1885)

Otway, Sir Arthur (ed.), *Autobiography and Journals of Admiral Lord Clarence Paget* (London, 1896)

Paget, Lord George, *The Light Cavalry Brigade in the Crimea* (London, 1881)

Rathbone, Philip H., *A Week in the Crimea*, (Liverpool, 1855)

Russell, William Howard, *The British Expedition to the Crimea* (London, 1858)

The Great War with Russia (London, 1895)

Sandwith, Humphrey, *A Narrative of the Siege of Kars* (London, 1856)

Slade, Adolphus, *Turkey and the Crimean War* (London, 1867)

Sterling, Anthony, *The Highland Brigade in the Crimea* (London, 1895)

Todleben, E.I., *Défense de Sebastopol*, 2 vols. (St Petersburg, 1863–1874)

Tolstoy, Leo, *Tales of Army Life*, trs. Louise and Aylmer Maude (London, 1932)

Windham, C.A., *Crimean Diary and Letters* (London, 1897)

Wolseley, Field Marshal Viscount, *The Story of a Soldier's Life*, vol. I (London, 1903)

Wood, H. Evelyn, *The Crimea in 1854 and 1894* (London, 1895)

Notes and References

Part I

Prologue

1. Weintraub, *Disraeli*, p.306
2. Lavrin, p.60

1 A Churchwardens' Quarrel

1. Kinglake, I p.53
2. Ibid., p.43
3. Robert Curzon, *Visits to Monasteries in the Levant* (London, 1849), p.197
4. Martens XII, p.309
5. Seymour to Russell, 13 January 1853, FO65/424/17
6. Nesselrode to Brunnov, 2 January 1853, BM AddMSS 43144
7. Seymour to Russell, 9 January 1853, FO 65/424/9
8. Seymour to Clarendon, 23 November 1853, FO/65/432
9. Seymour to Russell, 22 January 1853, FO 65/424/25
10. Lincoln, p.335
11. Seymour to Malmesbury, 4 December 1852, FO 65/423
12. Seymour to Russell, 11 January 1853, FO 65/424/13
13. Ibid.
14. Ibid.
15. Seymour to Russell, 22 January 1853, FO 65/424/24
16. Seymour to Russell, 31 January 1853, FO 65/424/43
17. Seymour to Clarendon, 24 March 1853, FO 65/425/132
18. Seymour to Russell, 21 February 1853, FO 65/424/87
19. Seymour to Russell, 21 February 1853, FO 65/424/88
20. Kinglake, I p.190

2 Menshikov's Mission

1. Saab, p.27
2. Seymour to Clarendon, 18 October 1853, FO 65/431
3. Seymour to Russell, 10 February 1853, FO 65/424/69
4. Rose to Clarendon, 17 March 1853, FO 78/930/76
5. Ibid.
6. Rose to Clarendon, 3 March 1853, FO 78/930/69
7. Rose to Clarendon, 5 March 1853, FO 78/930/71
8. Ibid.
9. Rose to Clarendon, 6 March 1853, FO 78/930/73
10. Rose to Clarendon, 11 March 1853, FO 78/930/93
11. Rose to Clarendon, 6 March 1853, op.cit.
12. Rose to Clarendon, 7 March 1853, FO 78/930/75
13. Seymour to Clarendon, 29 March 1853, FO 65/424/151
14. Rose to Clarendon, 25 March 1853, FO 78/930/119
15. Rose to Clarendon, 17 March 1853, FO 78/930/100
16. *The Times*, 18 May 1852
17. Clarendon to Stratford, 18 April 1853 FO 352/36
18. Saab, p.39
19. Seymour to Clarendon, 31 May 1853, FO65/427/262

3 Getting into Deep Waters

1. Seymour to Clarendon, 31 May 1853, FO 65/427/263
2. Ibid.
3. Ibid.
4. Ibid.
5. Ibid.
6. Clarendon to Aberdeen, 9 June 1853, Pte Clar MSS
7. Seymour to Clarendon, 7 June 1853, FO 65/427/270
8. Seymour to Clarendon, 10 June 1853, FO 65/427/282
9. Seymour to Clarendon, 16 June 1853, FO 65/427/292
10. Rose to Russell, 10 March 1853, FO/78/87
11. Kinglake, I, p.182
12. Wellesley, p.29
13. Private note, undated, FO/353/37A/2
14. Stratford to Clarendon, 22 May 1853 FO/78/932/57
15. Temperley, p.344
14. Laughton, I, p.301
15. Ibid., p.297
16. Palmerston to Clarendon, 28 June 1853, Pte Clar MSS
17. Stratford to Clarendon, 22 May 1853, FO78/932/57

4 The Thousand and One Notes

1. Seymour to Clarendon, 28 June 1853, FO/65/427/326
2. Clarendon to Stratford, 24 July 1853, FO 352/36
3. Rich, p.67
4. Saab, p.39
5. J.L. Herkless, 'Stratford, the Cabinet and the Outbreak of the Crimean War', *Historical Journal*, xviii, 3, 1975
6. Seymour to Clarendon, 5 August 1853, FO65/429/404
7. Seymour to Clarendon, 12 August 1853, FO65/429/425
8. Stratford to Clarendon, 14 August 1853, FO78/957/220
9. Seymour to Clarendon, 8 September 1853, FO/65/430/468
10. Cowley to Clarendon, 29 August 1853, FO/146/489
11. Wellesley, p.29
12. Maxwell, II, p.20
13. Ibid., pp.25–6
14. Seymour to Clarendon, FO65/430/496
15. Rich, pp.84–5
16. Cowley to Clarendon, 5 October 1853, FO27/975
17. Graham to Aberdeen, 9 October 1853, Add MSS, 43191

5 Phoney War

1. Seymour to Clarendon, 4 October 1853, FO65/431
2. Seymour to Clarendon, 6 October 1853, FO 65/431
3. Seymour to Clarendon, 11 October 1853, FO 65/431
4. MS Clar., Dep. C3, 473–481
5. Stratford to Clarendon, 5 October 1853, FO 78/939
6. Lincoln, p.346
7. Seymour to Clarendon, 14 October 1853, FO 65/431
8. Stratford to Clarendon, 21 October 1853, FO 78/939
9. Stratford to Clarendon, 22 October 1853, FO 78/939
10. Cowley to Clarendon, 24 October 1853, FO 27/975
11. Cowley to Clarendon, 3 November 1853, FO 27/976
12. Ibid.
13. Buchanan to Clarendon, 12 November 1853, US State Department Despatches, Britain, vol. 59
14. Seymour to Clarendon, 12 December 1853, FO65/433
15. Seymour to Clarendon, 16 November 1853, FO 65/432
16. Seymour to Clarendon, 5 December 1853, FO 65/433
17. Seymour to Clarendon, 26 November 1853, FO 65/432
18. Ridley, p.418

6 The Affair at Sinope

1. Lincoln, pp.344–5. 'According to regulations, at the beginning of 1853

Russian arsenals were authorised to contain 1,014,959 infantry muskets, 71,038 dragoon muskets, 69,199 carbines, 37,318 rifles and 43,248 pistols. In fact there 532,835 infantry muskets (a shortage of 482,124); 20,849 dragoon muskets (a shortage of 50,189); 21,167 carbines (a shortage of 48,032); 6198 rifles (a shortage of 31,120); and 7704 pistols (a shortage of 35,544). In all, Russian arsenals contained 647,000 fewer weapons than were authorised by regulations.'

2. Seymour to Clarendon, 12 December 1853, FO65/433
3. Slade, p.148
4. Stratford to Clarendon, 4 December 1853, FO78/941
5. Cowley to Clarendon, 12 December 1853, FO27/977
6. Seymour to Clarendon, 26 December 1853, FO65/433
7. Seymour to Clarendon, 31 December 1853, FO/65/433
8. *Daily News*, 7 January 1854
9. Weintraub, *Albert*, p.294
10. Stratford to Clarendon, 17 December 1853, FO78/941
11. Seymour to Clarendon, 2 January 1854, FO65/443
12. Maxwell, II, p.37
13. Clarendon to Stratford, 7 January 19854, FO352/37A/1
14. Seymour to Clarendon, 16 February 1854, FO65/445/165

7 Drifting towards War

1. MacMullen, p.23
2. Clifford, p.269
3. Peter Burroughs, 'An Unreformed Army?', in Chandler and Beckett, p.164
4. Wolseley, p.236
5. Bapst, p.264
6. Seymour to Clarendon, 9 January 1854, FO65/443
7. Connacher, *The Aberdeen Coalition*, p.256
8. Wellesley, p.35
9. Sweetman, pp.168–9
10. Ibid., p.170
11. Gooch, p.57
12. Clarendon to Stratford, 18 September 1854, FO352/37A/1
13. Maxwell, II, p.40

8 'Our Beautiful Guards'

1. Fox Mason, p.28
2. Seymour to Clarendon, 10 February 1854, FO65/445/138
3. Franks, p.29
4. Gowing, pp.3–4
5. Seymour to Clarendon, 6 February 1854, FO65/445/126
6. Greenhill and Giffard, p.115
7. Louis Fagan, *The Reform Club* (London, 1887), pp.93–103

8. Greenhill and Giffard, p.107
9. Panmure to Codrington, 9 June 1856, WO6/74
10. Sweetman, p.172
11. Raglan's letter of appointment, 5 April 1854, WO A Papers 14/55

9 Uneasy Partners

1. *The Letters of Private Wheeler*, edited by B.H. Liddell Hart (London, 1951) pp.49–50
2. Gooch, pp.81–2
3. Cowley to Clarendon 19 January 1854 FO27/1005/59
4. Ibid.
5. Cowley to Clarendon 4 January 1854 FO27/1005/10
6. Sweetman, p.184
7. Bentley, p.48
8. Franks, p.40
9. Duberly, p.19
10. Sterling, pp.2–4
11. Stratford to Clarendon, FO/78/979/48
12. Stratford to Clarendon, 29 June 1854, FO/352/37A/3
13. Greenhill and Giffard, p.120
14. Stratford to Clarendon, 29 June 1854, FO352/37A/3
15. Clarendon to Stratford, 13 July 1854, FO352/37A/1
16. Hibbert, p.23
17. Newcastle to Raglan, 23 June 1854, WO6/69/102
18. Seaton, p.47
19. Tolstoy, *Letters*, pp.39–42
20. Kerr, p.19

10 Opening Shots

1. Bonner-Smith pp.46–7
2. Otway, p.38
3. Lambert, p.163
4. Otway, p.42
5. Bonner-Smith, pp.52–3
6. Greenhill and Giffard, p.146
7. Napier to Admiralty, 7 July 1854, ADM1/5624
8. Bonner-Smith, p.81
9. Napier to Hall, 29 June, ADM1/5624
10. Greenhill and Giffard, p.276
11. Richard Holmes, *Firing Line* (London, 1985), p.126
12. Napier to Admiralty, 19 August 1854, ADM1/5625
13. Hughes, p.56
14. Newcastle to Jones, 14 July 1854, WO6/69

15. Napier to Admiralty, 13 September 1854, ADM1/5625/725
16. Cowley to Clarendon, telegraphic despatch, 15 October 1854, FO27/1024/1245
17. Napier to Admiralty, 10 October 1854, ADM1/5625/723

11 Varna Interlude

1. Duberly, pp.31–2
2. Franks, p.38
3. Palmer, p.56
4. Clarendon to Stratford, 12 August 1854, FO352/37A/1
5. Bentley, p.48
6. Stratford to Clarendon, 6 July 1854, FO352/37A/3
7. Adkins, p.49
8. Anstruther Thomson, I, p.165
9. Duberly, p.47
10. *The Times*, 2 August 1854
11. Beatson to Raglan, 21 August 1854, FO352/40/1
12. Stratford to Clarendon, 5 November 1854, FO78/1005/646
13. Sterling, p.23
14. Clarendon to Stratford, 18 July 1854, FO352/37A/1
15. Bentley, p.56
16. *The Builder*, 1861, pp.421–2
17. Adkin, p.50
18. Bentley, pp.56–7
19. Clarendon to Stratford, 23 September 1854, FO352/37A/1
20. Clarendon to Stratford, 18 December 1854, ibid.
21. Newcastle to Raglan, 8 June 1854, WO6/69/80
22. Sweetman, p.197
23. Bentley, pp.54–5
24. Hodge, p.23

12 Hurrah for the Crimea!

1. Newcastle to Raglan, 10 April 1854, WO6/74/1
2. Newcastle to Raglan, 29 June 1854, WO6/74/5
3. Franks, p.62
4. Sweetman, p.211
5. Moyse-Bartlett, p.141
6. Clarendon to Stratford, 23 August 1854, FO352/37A/1
7. Copy of letter, Dundas to Graham, 9 September 1854, FO/352/38/3
8. Clarendon to Stratford, 22 July 1854, FO/352/37A/3
9. Stratford to Clarendon, 27 August 1854, ibid.
10. Sterling, p.36
11. Seaton, p.60

12. Sterling, p.37

Part II

1 Advance to Contact

1. Loy Smith, p.96
2. Duberly, p.80
3. Hibbert, pp.33–4
4. John D.C. Bennett, 'Medical Services in the Crimea – A Defence', *RUSI Journal*, August 1994, vol. 139, no 4, pp.47–50
5. Hodasevich, p.18
6. Seaton, p.60
7. Clarendon to Stratford, 27 September 1854, FO352/37A/1
8. Cowley to Clarendon, 29 September 1854, FO27/1023/1172
9. Loy Smith, p.98
10. Hodasevich, p.40
11. Paget, p.18.
12. Compton, p.76
13. Loy Smith, p.99
14. Powell, p.14
15. Nolan to Stratford, 21 July 1854, FO352/39/1
16. Hodasevich, pp. 55–6

2 The Alma: The Infantry will advance

1. Kerr, p.43
2. Gowing, p.16
3. Cler, p.116
4. Gowing, p.16
5. Kinglake, II, p.213
6. Seaton, p.82
7. Ibid., p.92
8. Sterling, p.47
9. Calthorpe, I, p.170
10. Bentley, p.89
11. Ibid., p.85

3 Missed Opportunities

1. Stratford to Clarendon, 23 September 1854, FO78/1002/531; Clarendon to Stratford, 9 October 1854, FO352/37A/1
2. Newcastle to Raglan, 10 October 1854, WO6/69/224

3. Cowley to Clarendon, 9 October 1854, FO27/1023/1226
4. Seaton, p.102
5. Stratford to Clarendon, 25 September 1854, FO325/37A/3
6. Stratford to Raglan, 26 October 1854, FO352/38/2
7. Mitchell, p.55
8. David, p.269
9. Hodasevich, p.83
10. Seaton, p.96
11. David, p.269
12. Mitchell, p.55
13. Sweetman, p.227
14. Stratford to Raglan, 26 October 1854, op.cit.
15. Clarendon to Stratford, 13 October 1854, FO352/37A/1
16. Sweetman, p.228
17. Clifford, p.63
18. Clarendon to Stratford, 13 October 1854, op.cit.
19. Gooch, p.116
20. Hodasevich, p.101
21. Clifford, p.52
22. Stratford to Clarendon, 30 October 1854, FO78/1004/637

4 Ladies with Lamps

1. Clarendon to Stratford, 22 December 1854, Stratford Papers, FO352/37A/1
2. Woodham Smith, *Florence Nightingale*, pp.137–9
3. Clarendon to Stratford, 19 October 1854, Stratford Papers, FO352/37A/1
4. Stratford to Clarendon, 26 September 1854, FO78/1002/543
5. Stratford to Clarendon, 25 October 1854, FO78/1003/613
6. Duberly, p.164
7. Cowley to Clarendon, 22 October 1854, FO27/1024/1268
8. Goldie, p.37
9. Woodham Smith, *Florence Nightingale*, p.157
10. Stratford to Clarendon, 20 November 1854, FO78/1005/693
11. Stratford to Menzies, 24 October 1854; Menzies to Stratford, 26 October 1854, FO78/1005/643
12. Hoppen, p.181
13. Conacher, *Britain and the Crimea*, p.18
14. Goldie, p.63; for a different interpretation of Nightingale's work, see Hugh Small, *Florence Nightingale, Avenging Angel* (London, 1998) who argues that Nightingale did little to improve the hygienic conditions at the Scutari Hospital and on her return to Britain was much mortified by the discovery that 5000 soldiers died under her care during the winter of 1854–5.

15. Stratford to Clarendon, 5 December 1854, FO352/38/2
16. Newcastle to Lord William Paulet, 16 January 1855, WO6/70/208
17. Newcastle to Raglan, 12 December 1854, WO6/70/173
18. Kerr, p.90
19. Newcastle to Raglan, 23 November 1854, WO6/70/155; Newcastle to Raglan, 6 December 1854, WO6/70/166; Stratford to Paulet, 1 February 1855, FO78/1072/80
20. The full story of Renkioi can be found in Bennett, *RUSI Journal*, op.cit.
21. Newcastle to Raglan, 6 January 1855, WO6/70/202
22. Assistant-Surgeon Arthur Henry Taylor, 'Letters from the Crimea', *RUSI Journal*, August 1994, vol. 139, no. 4
23. The full story of the Russian Sisters of Mercy can be found in J.S. Curtiss, 'Russian Sisters of Mercy in the Crimea', *Slavic Review*, no. 25, 1966
24. Slade, p.331

5 Balaklava: A Cavalryman's Battle

1. Stratford to Clarendon, 15 October 1854, FO78/1002/594
2. Hodasevich, p.89 and p.178
3. Maude, p.106
4. Calthorpe, I, p.267
5. Paget, p.62
6. Bentley, p.123
7. Franks, p.70
8. Adkin, pp.105–6
9. Woodham Smith, *The Reason Why*, p.232
10. Seaton, p.149
11. Albert Seaton, *The Horsemen of the Steppes* (London: 1985), p.154
12. Stratford to Clarendon, 28 October 1855, FO78/1004/622
13. Copy of letter from Balaklava, author unknown, Stratford to Clarendon 31 October 1854, FO78/1004/639

6 Inkerman: An Infantryman's Battle

1. Sterling, pp. 66–7
2. Cowley to Clarendon, 4 October 1854 FO27/1023/1207
3. Seaton, p.178
4. Hamley, pp.106–7
5. Gowing, p.47
6. Hibbert, p.175
7. Seaton, p.172
8. Hamley, p.109
9. The clearest and most concise account of the battle is to be found in ffrench Blake, pp.87–101

10. Seaton, p.176
11. Clifford, p.94
12. Newcastle to Raglan, 27 November 1854, WO6/70/2208
13. Clarendon to Stratford, 13 November 1854, FO352/37A/1
14. Stratford to Clarendon, 25 November 1854, FO78/1006/707

7 Arrival of General Winter

1. Taylor, p.53
2. Sterling, p.82
3. Colquhoun to Stratford, 24 December 1854, FO78/1070/27; Stratford to Clarendon, 24 November 1854, FO78/1005/682
4. Newcastle to Raglan, 18 November 1854, WO6/70/151
5. Rose to Clarendon 1 February 1855, FO78/1128/2; Kerr, p.102
6. Clifford, p.103
7. Duberly, pp.144–5
8. Palmer, p.163
9. Royal Archives, Queen Victoria's Journal, 22 February 1855
10. Raglan to Stratford, 22 January 1855, FO78/1072/88
11. War Office memorandum, 9 February 1855, WO43/972/243; Stratford to Raglan, 3 February 1855, FO78/1072/86
12. Newcastle to Raglan, 6 January 1855, WO6/70/202
13. Newcastle to Paulet, 5 January 1855, WO6/70/no.1
14. Newcastle to Raglan, 2 February 1855, WO6/70/224
15. Clifford, p.155
16. Windham, p.98
17. Sterling, p.98
18. Newcastle to Raglan, 12 January 1855

8 Muddle in Washington, Progress in Vienna

1. Clarendon to Russell, 27 September 1854, PRO30/22/11
2. Westmorland to Clarendon, 15 November 1854, FO7/437/430
3. Westmorland to Clarendon, 13 September 1854 FO7/436/348
4. Westmorland to Clarendon, 2 October 1854, FO7/436/366
5. Westmorland to Clarendon, 4 October 1854, FO7/436/375
6. Cowley to Clarendon, 9 October 1854, FO27/1024/1228
7. Mason to Drouyn de Lhuys, 27 October 1854, US State Department, Despatches, France, vol. 36
8. Crampton to Clarendon, 23 October 1854, FO5/599/253
9. Cowley to Clarendon, 3 November 1854, FO27/1025/1321
10. Ettinger, pp.390–412
11. Washington, 1854, no.233, April 10/22
12. Buchanan to Marcy, 31 October 1854, US State Department Despatches, Britain, vol. 66

13. Cowley to Clarendon, 28 October 1854, FO27/1003/1294
13. Clarendon to Cowley, 31 October 1854, FO27/1003/1062
14. Cowley to Clarendon, 4 December 1854, FO27/1027/1459
15. Buchanan to Marcy, 15 December 1854, op.cit.
16. Rich, p.145
17. Cowley to Clarendon, 6 February 1855, FO27/1063/137
19. Stratford to Russell, 26 February 1855, FO352/41A
20. Clifford, p.144

9 'Pam' enters the Fray

1. Walpole, II, p.214
2. Panmure to Raglan, 12 February 1855 WO33/1/95/1
3. Hibbert, p.255
4. Stratford to Lyons, 9 December 1854, FO352/38/2
5. *Panmure Papers*, I, pp.150–171
6. *See* Gooch, chapters 10 and 11
7. Cowley to Clarendon, 28 February 1855, FO27/1064/230
8. Russell to Palmerston, 22 February 1855, PRO30/22/
9. Seaton, p.187
10. Stratford to Clarendon, 19 February 1855, FO78/1073/122
11. Grunwald, p.286
12. Palmerston to Russell, 28 March 1855 PRO30/22/
13. Raschid Pasha to Stratford 24 May 1855, FO352/41c/9
14. Conacher, *Britain and the Crimea*, pp.30–5
15. Russell to Clarendon, 1 April 1855 PRO30/22/
16. Hamley, p.191

10 Spring Stalemate

1. Stratford to Clarendon, 4 February 1855, FO78/1072/93
2. Stratford to Clarendon, 8 February 1855, ibid.
3. Gernsheim, p.87
4. Rathbone, pp. 61–62
5. Stratford to Clarendon, 19 March 1855, FO78/1075/210
6. Stratford to Raschid Pasha, 22 February 1855, FO352/41b/5
7. Stratford to Clarendon, 7 February 1855, ibid.
8. Cowley to Clarendon, 2 March 1855, FO27/1064/245; Rose to Clarendon, 31 March 1855, FO78/1128/38
9. Royal Archives, Queen Victoria's Journal, 16 April 1855
10. Cowley to Clarendon, 15 February 1855, FO27/1063/172; Clarendon to Cowley, 4 May 1855, FO315171/396
11. Cowley to Clarendon, 3 May 1855, FO27/1067/514
12. Ridley, p.446
13. Rose to Clarendon, 2 February 1855, FO78/1128/12

14. Panmure to Raglan, 26 March 1855, WO6/74
15. Panmure to Raglan, 31 March 1855, ibid.
16. Sterling, p.133
17. Gowing, p.79
18. Rathbone, p.66

11 Todleben's Triumph

1. Panmure to Raglan, 4 May 1855, WO6/74
2. Sweetman, pp.296–7
3. Hamley, chapter 20
4. Rose to Clarendon, 10 July 1855, FO78/1129/73
5. Hodasevich, p.158
6. Maude, p.134
7. Taylor, op.cit.
8. Clifford, pp.194–5
9. Cowley to Clarendon, 24 January 1855, FO27/1062/65
10. Le Marchant to War Office, 10 April 1855, WO43/972/305
11. Crampton to Clarendon, 12 February 1855, AHR, XLI (1936), p.495
12. Buchanan to Marcy, 6 July 1855, US State Department Despatches, Britain, vol. 66
13. Panmure to Raglan, 26 March 1855, WO6/74
14. Grunwald, p.76
15. Lyons to Admiralty, 6 May 1855, FO352/41A/2
16. Rose to Clarendon, 9–13 May 1855, FO78/1128/54–6
17. Gooch, pp.196–206
18. Rose to Clarendon, 2 June 1855, FO78/1129/62
19. Todleben, II, p.352

12 Spring Cruise, Summer Success

1. Seymour to Marcy, 5 July 1855, US State Department Despatches, Russia, vol. 16
2. Seymour to Marcy, 13 April 1854, ibid; Marcy to Seymour, 1 October 1853, William L. Marcy Papers
3. Gooch, pp.208–9
4. The Times, 3 April 1855
5. Greenhill and Giffard, p.321
6. Dundas to the Admiralty, 4 June 1855, ADM1/5626/56
7. Seymour to Marcy, 19 July 1855, op. cit.
8. Greenhill and Giffard, p.313
9. Dundas to the Admiralty, 13 August 1855, ADM1/5626/105
10. Don, p.46
11. Marcy to Crampton, 5 September 1855; Crampton to Clarendon, 10 September 1855, FO5/623/185

12. Clarendon to Marcy, 27 September 1855, US State Department Despatches, Britain, vol. 66
13. Crampton to Marcy, 13 October 1855, copied to Clarendon, FO5/623/217
14. Crampton to Clarendon, 11 December 1855, FO5/623/265
15. Clarendon to Buchanan, 16 November 1855, US State Department Despatches, Britain, vol. 66
16. Buchanan to Marcy, 31 October 1855, ibid.

13 Trench Warfare: Massacre in the Redoubts

1. Clifford, pp.220–1
2. Rose to Clarendon, 10 June 1855, FO78/1129/65
3. Gooch, p.217
4. Lieutenant-Captain Pyotr Lesli, quoted in Kerr, p.134
5. Sweetman, p.313
6. Wood, pp.320–8
7. Hamley, p.260
8. Rose to Clarendon, 23 June 1855, FO78/1129/71
9. Wolseley, p.170
10. Clifford, p.228
11. Sweetman, p.321
12. Panmure to British Headquarters, Crimea, 30 June 1855, WO6/71/4

14 Sevastopol falls

1. Sterling, p.200
2. *Panmure Papers*, I, pp.320–321
3. Ibid., pp.256–257
4. Panmure to Raglan, 4 June 1855, WO6/71/156
5. Hamley, p.149
6. Hoppen, p.180
7. Seaton, p.196
8. Panmure to Simpson, 14 July 1855, WO6/71/25
9. Rose to Clarendon, 18 August 1855, FO78/1129/81
10. *The Times*, 20 August 1855
11. Seaton, p.209
12. Sterling, p.209
13. Sterling, quoted with approval in a letter home, 7 September 1855, pp.209–12
14. Taylor, op.cit.

15 The Forgotten War: Kars and Erzerum

1. Sandwith, p.45

2. *The Times*, 7 August 1854
3. Sandwith, p.64
4. Williams to Stratford, Report on the Army at Kars, September–October 1854, FO78/1005/677
5. Stratford to Ali Pasha, 29 November 1854, FO78/1005/714
6. Stratford to Clarendon, 5 December 1854, FO78/1005/195
7. Stratford to Clarendon, 28 December 1854, FO78/1005/782
8. Sandwith, p.77
9. Stratford to Clarendon, 29 March 1855, FO78/1075/243; Stratford to Clarendon, 21 January FO78/1071/49
10. Stratford to Clarendon, 17 January 1855 FO78/1071/43; Stratford to Clarendon, 22 January 1855, FO78/1071/56
11. Translation of communication from Ali Pasha, included in Stratford's despatch to Clarendon, 29 January 1855, FO78/1071/75
12. Sandwith, p.100
13. Stratford to Ali Pasha, 17 February 1855, FO78/1073/122
14. Lake, p.100
15. Ibid., p.118
16. Brant to Stratford, 3 September 1855, FO78/1115
17. Lake, p.201
18. Williams to Brant, 19 November 1855, FO78/1133
19. Gooch, p.234; Cowley to Clarendon, 31 August 1855, FO27/1075/1149
20. Lake, p.242
21. Sandwith, p.174
22. Williams to Clarendon, 29 November 1855, FO78/1133

16 A Second Winter

1. Rose to Clarendon, 17 September 1855, FO78/1129/90
2. Rose to Clarendon, 23 September 1855, FO78/1129/91
3. Ridley, p.448
4. Baumgart, p.58
5. Cowley to Clarendon, 19 September 1855, FO27/1076/1242
6. Panmure to Simpson, 15 September 1855, WO6/71/150
7. *Panmure Papers*, I, pp.389–90
8. Panmure to Simpson, 1 September 1855, WO6/71/123; Panmure to Codrington, 7 December 1855 and 17 January 1855, WO6/72
9. Copy of Pélissier's despatch in Cowley to Clarendon, 26 October 1855, FO27/1078
10. Stratford to Clarendon, 20 August 1855, FO78/1085/621
11. Stratford to Clarendon, 3 September 1855, FO78/1086/656
12. Stratford to Clarendon, 10 September 1855, FO/78/1086/674 and 675
13. Stratford to Clarendon, 16 October 1855, FO78/1088/832
14. Sterling p.230

Part III

1 Peace Feelers

1. Buchanan to Marcy, 31 October 1855, US State Department Despatches, Britain, vol 66
2. Cowley to Clarendon, 19 November 1855, FO27/1079/1510
3. Conacher, *Britain and the Crimea*, p.144
4. Henry Temperley, 'The Treaty of Paris of 1856 and its Execution', Part I, *The Journal of Modern History*, vol IV (1932), pp. 390–1
5. Rich, p.171
6. Cowley to Clarendon, 22 November 1855, FO27/1079/1522
7. Ibid.
8. Mosse, p.20
9. Cowley to Clarendon 28 December 1855, FO271081/1682; Cowley to Clarendon, 27 January 1856, FO27/1122/144
10. Clarendon to Seymour, 24 January 1856, FO7/474/47

2 Tying up some loose ends

1. Cowley to Clarendon, 12 January 1856, FO27/1121/73
2. Seymour to Clarendon, 12 January 1856, FO7/480/29
3. Seymour to Clarendon, 16 January 1856, FO7/480/44
4. Seymour to Clarendon, 8 January 1856, FO7/480/16
5. Clarendon to Seymour, 15 January 1856, MS Clar C135/78–83
6. Seymour to Clarendon, 23 January 1856, FO7/480/63
7. Seymour to Clarendon, 22 January 1856, FO7/480/52
8. Cowley to Clarendon, 29 January 1856, FO27/1122/1649.
9. Cowley to Clarendon, draft, 17 January 1856, FO27/1164/89
10. Cowley to Clarendon, 6 January 1856, FO27/1121/35
11. Seymour to Clarendon, 9 January 1856, FO7/480/21
12. Cowley to Clarendon, 23 January 1856, FO27/1122/126
13. Clifford, p.282
14. Conditions for the Formation of a Military Settlement in British South Africa, WO43/972/338

3 Peacetime in Paris

1. Clarendon to Palmerston, 29 February 1856, FO27/1164/23
2. Clarendon to Stratford, 19 December 1856, FO353/44A
3. Clarendon to Palmerston, 25 February 1856, FO27/1164/12
4. Clarendon to Palmerston, 3 March 1856, FO27/1164/29
5. Clarendon to Palmerston, 10 March 1856, FO271168/52
6. Clarendon to Palmerston, 25 February 1856, FO27/1164/15

7. Clarendon to Palmerston, 24 March 1856, FO27/1165/72
8. Clarendon to Palmerston, 17 April 1856, FO27/1165/115
9. Crampton to Clarendon, 19 November 1855, FO5/624/249
10. Marcy to Buchanan, 28 December 1855, FO7/641/255
11. Buchanan to Marcy, 1 February 1856, US State Department Despatches, Britain, vol. 66
12. Argyll, II, p.47

4 The New World Order

1. Hoppen, p.235
2. Wellesley, p.237
3. Stratford to Clarendon, 19 February 1855, FO78/1074/122
4. Clarendon to Stratford, 31 December 1855, FO/352/42
5. Clarendon to Stratford, 4 January 1856, FO352/44
6. Stratford to Clarendon, 9 January 1856, FO78/1170/29
7. Stratford to Clarendon, 18 April 1856, FO78/1177/460

5 Learning the Lessons the Hard Way

1. The letters came to light in 1998 in the museum of the Lancashire Fusiliers, Bury, Lancashire
2. F.D. Tredrey, *The House of Blackwood 1804–1854* (Edinburgh and London, 1954), pp.123–4
3. Fortescue XIII, p.233

Index